# ASHTON AND REID
## ON
# CLUB LAW

# ASHTON AND REID
# ON
# CLUB LAW

**David Ashton** MA (Oxon) FCIArb

*of Gray's Inn*

*Barrister • Chartered arbitrator •*

*Accredited mediator*

**and**

**Paul W Reid** MA (Cantab)

*of the Inner Temple*

*Barrister • Recorder of the Crown Court*

**JORDANS**

2005

Published by
Jordan Publishing Limited
21 St Thomas Street
Bristol BS1 6JS

British Library Cataloguing-in-Publication Data

A catalogue record for this book is available from the British Library.

ISBN 0 85308 849 7

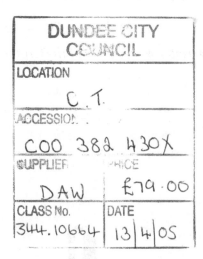

Typeset by The Partnership Publishing Solutions Ltd www.the-pps.co.uk
Printed and bound in Great Britain by Antony Rowe Ltd, Chippenham, Wilts

# FOREWORD

An up-to-date and comprehensive book on Club Law is long overdue. We have waited a long time, but the wait has been worthwhile.

The concept of the club is founded in the 17th century when like-minded persons came together in coffee houses for political and social ends. In the next century 'gentlemen's clubs' emerged, notably White's (probably the earliest) and The Garrick (of which I am a proud member). Sports clubs were not far behind, the Jockey Club, MCC and the Royal and Ancient immediately spring to mind. They became a peculiarly English institution with a distinctive ethos of 'clubability'. The members jealously and zealously regarded the association as 'their' club run by and for the members with an unincorporated structure and in an informal yet democratic manner. The concept worked so well that it attracted the attention of others who recognised the merits and advantages of a club and who were inspired to adopt the formula as a means of creating institutions with far wider purposes and pursuits. Hence the emergence of a whole spectrum of clubs, associations and societies which include, for example, working men's clubs, British Legion clubs, gaming clubs, societies devoted to hobbies and even fan clubs. In all, a total running into tens of thousands. A later development was the creation of a more complex creature, incorporated clubs registered under the Industrial and Provident Societies Act or the Companies Act.

It is immediately apparent that the authors have undertaken a monumental task to produce in one volume the law and practice relating to the whole spectrum. A glance at the list of statutes and statutory instruments alone reveals the complexity of the subject and the dedication required to tackle the subject. But we need not worry.

How fortunate that the publishers chose to entrust the task into such safe hands. David Ashton in 1964 re-wrote the book on Club Law published by the Working Men's Club and Institute Union and in the course of many years in practice he has acted for or advised numerous clubs, ranging from top football clubs to the local angling club. For 17 years he was counsel to the Kennel Club. Paul Reid has developed a particular expertise in Club Law, having been for the last 15 years Standing Counsel to the National Golf Clubs' Advisory Association, in the course of which he has written over a thousand opinions for golf clubs on all aspects of law and practice.

The end result is one of the most impressive works of its type that I have ever encountered. It describes and explains the law and practice in an exemplary manner. The hallmark of this book is its lucidity, practicality and readability. Every club secretary of every club of every description must acquire a copy, keep it to hand and be ready to refer committees, officers and members to its contents. It would be remiss of lawyers in this field to be without it.

*The Rt Hon Sir Philip Otton*
*20 Essex Street*
*London WC2R 3AL*

*February 2005*

# PREFACE

The gestation period of this book has been longer than anticipated because, although we knew at the outset that Club Law was a subject of considerable breadth and diversity, it soon became clear that if the book was to be of any real value to legal practitioners, clubs generally and club secretaries in particular, we had to broach all those topics normally associated with an active club. Our task was not made easier by the variety of forms which a club can take; especially interesting is the commonly-met unincorporated members' club: 'that anomalous group of human beings' which as a club is something more than the aggregate of its members, yet is not a legal person, and yet again has been given a fiscal personality for tax purposes and a criminal personality for statutory offences.

We have been very fortunate in the number and skill of our colleagues at 13 King's Bench Walk and elsewhere who have assisted us by reading, improving and correcting various chapters or sections of the book which we had written. At 13 KBW they were Sinclair Cramsie, Gabriel Buttimore, Arthur Blake, Clare Harrington and Charles Pimlott; elsewhere they were E. James Wyllie, Philip Jones, Charlotte Jones and Michael Shaw, the Secretary of the National Golf Clubs' Advisory Association. We pay particular tribute to Peter Thompson QC, a former member of our chambers, who read the whole of the first and the final draft of the book and who made many helpful suggestions and gave much-valued guidance on the text.

The reader will observe that in order to make the text more readable we have called into existence the wholly fictitious town of Basset, being the county town of Bassetshire. This town and county have been peopled with characters taken from the famous song of Widdecombe Fair.

Club Law is a neat generic term for the area of law and practice which is covered by this book, but we should make it clear that the scope of the book includes all clubs, societies and associations of whatever form or nature. For the sake of simplicity we have used the word 'club' in the text, as far as possible, as including the whole spectrum of clubs, societies and associations.

We have endeavoured to state the law as at 31 December 2004 except in paragraphs 9-01 and 9-77 where we have cited the various regulations appertaining to the Licensing Act 2003 and which were published on 20 January 2005.

*David Ashton*
*Paul W Reid*
*13 King's Bench Walk*
*Temple*
*EC4Y 7EN*

*February 2005*

# CONTENTS

# TABLE OF CASES

# TABLE OF STATUTES

Those paragraph numbers in **bold** type indicate where the Act is set out in part or in full.

# TABLE OF STATUTORY INSTRUMENTS

Those paragraph numbers in **bold** type indicate where a Statutory Instrument is set out in part or in full.

# LAW REPORT ABBREVIATIONS

| | |
|---|---|
| A & E: | Adolphus & Ellis' Reports (1834–40) |
| AC: | Law Reports, Appeal Cases in the House of Lords (1865 to date) |
| ACSR: | Australian Corporations and Securities Reports (Australia) (1989 to date) |
| All ER: | All England Reports (1936 to date) |
| Atk: | Atkyn's Chancery Reports 1736–55 |
| B & Ald: | Bernewall & Adolphus' Kings Bench Reports (1830-34) |
| BCC: | British Company Law Cases (1983 to date) |
| BCLC: | Butterworth Company Law Cases (1983 to date) |
| Bos & P: | Bosanquet & Puller's Common Pleas Reports (1796–1804) |
| B & S: | Best and Smith's Queen's Bench Reports (1861–65) |
| BTC: | British Tax Cases |
| Car & P: | Carrington & Payne's Nisi Prius Reports (1823–41) |
| CB: | Common Bench Reports by Manning, Granger & Scott (1845-46) |
| CB(NS): | Common Bench Reports by Manning, Granger & Scott (New Series) (1856–65) |
| CCLR: | Consumer Credit Law Reports |
| Ch: | Law Reports, Chancery Division (1891 to date) |
| Ch App: | Law Reports, Chancery Appeal cases (1865–75) |
| Ch Div: | Law Reports, Chancery Division (1876–90) |
| CL: | Common Law Reports (1853–55) |
| CLY: | Current Law Yearbook (1947 to date) |
| CMLR: | Common Market Law Reports |

| | |
|---|---|
| COD: | Crown Office Digest (1988–2000) |
| Cr App Rep: | Criminal Appeal Reports (1908 to date) |
| Crim LR: | Criminal Law Reports (1954 to date) |
| De GM & G: | De Gex Macnaghten & Gordon's Bankruptcy Reports (1851–57) |
| E & B: | Ellis & Blackburn's Queen's Bench Reports (1852–58) |
| EG: | Estates Gazette (1858 to date) |
| EGLR: | Estates Gazette Law Reports (1985 to date) |
| EHRR: | European Human Rights Reports (1979 to date) |
| F & F: | Foster & Finlayson's Nisi Prius reports (1858–67) |
| H & C: | Hurlestone and Coltman's Exchequer Reports (1862–66) |
| HL Cas: | Clark's House of Lords Cases (1847–66) |
| ICR: | Law Reports, Industrial Cases Reports (1975 to date) |
| Independent: | The Independent newspaper (1986 to date) |
| IR: | Irish Reports (1894 to date) |
| IRLR: | Industrial Relations Law Reports (1972 to date) |
| JP: | Justice of the Peace (Weekly Notes of Cases) (1887 to date) |
| KB (QB): | Law Reports, Queen's Bench Division (1890 to 1901 and 1952 to date), King's Bench (1901–52) |
| LGR: | Knight's Local Government Reports (1903 to date) |
| LG Rev: | Local Government Review (1971 to date) |
| LJ Ex: | Law Journal Reports, Exchequer cases (New Series) (1831–75) |
| LJMC: | Law Journal Reports, Magistrates' Cases, New Series (1831–96) |
| LJ QB: | Law Journal Reports (new series), Queen's Bench cases (1837–1946) |
| Lloyd's Rep: | Lloyd's List Law Reports (1951 to date) |
| LR Eq: | Law Reports, Equity cases (1865–75) |
| LR Ex: | Law Reports, Exchequer cases (1865–75) |
| LR Ir: | Law Reports (Ireland) (1878–93) |
| LRQB: | Law Reports Queen's Bench (1865–75) |
| LT: | Law Times Reports (1859 to 1947) |
| M & G: | Manning & Granger's Common Pleas Reports (1840–45) |
| M & W: | Meeson & Welsby Exchequer Reports (1836–47) |
| NSW LR: | New South Wales Law Reports (1880–1900 and 1971 to date) (Australia) |
| NZLR: | New Zealand Law Reports (1883 to date) (New Zealand) |

| | |
|---|---|
| P & CR: | Planning and Compensation Reports (1949 to date) |
| Price: | Price's Exchequer Reports (1814–24) |
| QBD: | Law Reports, Queen's Bench Division (1875–90) |
| R: | Rettie's Session Cases, 4th series (1878–98) |
| RA: | Rating Appeals (1962 to date) |
| RPC: | Reports of Patent, Design and Trade Mark Cases (1884 to date) |
| RTR: | Road Traffic Reports (1970 to date) |
| RVR: | Rating & Valuation Reporter (1965 to date) |
| SA: | South Africa Law Reports (1947 to date) (South Africa) |
| SC: | Session Cases (Scotland) |
| Sim (NS): | Simon's Vice-Chancellor's Reports, New Series (1850–52) |
| SLT: | Scots Law Times (1893 to date) (Scotland) |
| Sol Jo: | Solicitors' Journal (1857 to date) |
| Stark: | Starkie's Nisi Prius Reports (1814–22) |
| STC: | Simon's Tax Cases (1973 to date) |
| Times: | The Times newspaper (1785 to date) |
| Times LR: | The Times newspaper reports published separately from the newspaper (1990 to date) |
| TC: | Reports of Tax Cases (1875 to date) |
| TLR: | Times Law Reports (1884–1952) |
| WLR: | Weekly Law Reports (1953 to date) |
| WN: | Weekly Notes (1862–1952) |
| WR: | Weekly Reporter (1853–1906) |

# DEFINITION OF A CLUB

**CLUB** *klub, n* a heavy tapering stick, knobbly or thick at one end, used to strike with; a cudgel; a bat used in certain games; an instrument for playing golf; a playing card with black trefoil pips; a combination, bunch; a clique, set; an association of persons for social, political, athletic or other ends; an association of persons who possess premises or facilities which all members may use; a clubhouse, or the premises occupied by a club; a nightclub. – *vt* to beat with a club; to use a heavy object as a club; to throw into confusion(*military*); to gather into a bunch; to combine. – *vi* (*esp* with *together*) to join together for some common end; to share in a common expense; to visit nightclubs. – *adj* **clubbable** or **clubable** sociable – *n* **clubbability** or **clubability**. – **club class** a class of seat on an aircraft between tourist class and first class; **club-face** the face of a golf club; **club-foot** a deformed foot; **club-haul** (*nautical*) to tack, *esp* in an emergency; **club-head** the head of a golf club; **clubhouse** a house for the accommodation of a club; **clubland** the area around St James's in London, where many of the old-established clubs are; **club-law** government by violence; **club-line** (*printing*) a short line at the end of a paragraph; **clubman** a member of a club or clubs; a frequenter of clubs; a man-about-town; **club moss** any primitive mosslike plant of the order Lycopodiales; **clubroom** the room in which a club meets; **clubroot** a fungal disease which attacks the roots of plants of the genus Cruciferae; **club sandwich** a sandwich of three slices of bread or toast, containing two fillings – **in the club** (*slang*) pregnant; **join the club** (*colloquial*) we are all in the same position; me too; **on the club** (*slang*) certified unfit to work. [Old Norse and Swedish *klubba*; same root as **clump**].

*Taken from the* Chambers Dictionary *1998*

# PART 1

## The formation and dissolution of a club

# Chapter 1

## THE FORMATION OF A CLUB

## 1.  THE DEFINITION OF A CLUB

**1-01**   As may be seen from the definitions of a club set out on the preceding page xxxiv, the word 'club' has multifarious uses in the English language. Club law, not to be confused with club-law, is a concept generally recognised in English law and it is the aim of this book to elucidate the law and practice which govern this branch of the law[1]. The definition of a club for the purposes of club law needs explanation. Everyone has experience of or has heard about clubs. They come in all shapes and sizes: Arsenal Football Club, the Kennel Club, the Royal Automobile Club, the Garrick Club, the Acol Bridge Club, St Ediths Working Men's Club, the Sevenoaks Vine Cricket Club and so on. Clubs' terminology to describe themselves is equally variegated: a club may, for example, be called also an association, a centre, a circle, a federation, a fellowship, a fraternity, a fund, a guild, an institute, an institution, a society or a union[2]. The Chambers Dictionary refers to 'an association of persons for social, political, athletic or other ends; an association of persons who possess premises or facilities which all members may use'. But for the purposes of club law, however, this definition needs qualification. To be recognised as a club at law we consider that it must fulfil all of the following criteria:

---

[1]     See Megarry V-C's comment in *In re GKN Bolts & Nuts Ltd Sports and Social Club* [1982] 1 WLR 774 at 776, 'As is common in club cases, there are many obscurities and uncertainties, and some difficulty in the law.'

[2]     A trade union is an unincorporated members' club where the members are bound together by a contract of membership but trade unions are so specially regulated by statute as to form a separate class of their own, and are outside the scope of this book.  A trade union has quasi-corporate status and is prohibited from registering as a company under the Companies Act 1985 or under the Friendly Societies Act 1974 or under the Industrial and Provident Societies Act 1965: s. 10 of the Trade Union and Labour Relations (Consolidation) Act 1992.

(1) it must comprise two or more persons who are voluntarily bound together for a common purpose[3];
(2) it must exist for a lawful purpose other than simply for the purposes of trade[4];
(3) it must not be of a temporary nature[5];
(4) it must have a constitution or a set of rules which fairly regulates the conduct of its members towards each other[6];
(5) there must be a defined process for the admission of members[7];
(6) it must possess what can best be described as collegiality, that is, the process of making decisions and agreeing on actions shared by all the members[8].

## 2.    HISTORICAL INTRODUCTION

**1-02**    The origin of clubs in the sense that we are using the word can be traced back in England to the mid seventeenth century. The first coffee-house in London was introduced from Oxford in 1652 by a person known simply as Jacob the Jew, and the coffee-house rapidly took root; by 1663 there were over 80 coffee-houses in the City of London. These establishments were used by coteries in need of a regular meeting place; one such place, in nearby Westminster, was Miles's coffee-house which was the venue of the Rota Club founded for political debate. In the mid 1650s there met in Oxford a group of scientific virtuosi who instituted an organised club (each member paying a weekly shilling towards its expenses) which later in 1662 coalesced into the Royal Society for Improving Natural Knowledge. On 26 July 1660 Samuel Pepys recorded in his diary, 'we went to Wood's at the Pell Mell (our old house for clubbing) and there spent till ten at night'.

---

[3]     *Conservative Central Office v Burrell* [1982] 1 WLR 522 CA at 525.
[4]     *Kowloon Stock Exchange v Commissioner of Inland Revenue* [1985] 1 WLR 133 PC at 139 (where the court held that the Stock Exchange was a not a club because it existed to aid the profit-making activities of its members); *Wise v Perpetual Trustee Co.* [1903] AC 139 PC at 149; *Flemying v Hector* [1836] 2 M & W 172; *Stafford Borough Council v Elkenford Ltd* [1977] 1 WLR 324, CA.
[5]     See, for example, Licensing Act 1902, s. 24(1); Shop Clubs Act 1902, s. 2(b); Gaming Act 1968, s. 11(2), s. 40(4)(c), sch. 3 para 7(1).
[6]     Burrell's case op. cit. at 525.
[7]     Burrell's case op. cit. at 525.
[8]     *Val de Lobo (Turismo) Limitada v Chandler*, unreported 2 October 1997 per HH Judge Peter Crawford QC sitting as a High Court Judge. An outward and visible sign of this is the election (not appointment) of a managing committee to look after the affairs of the club on behalf of all the members.

**1-03**   The eighteenth century saw a big increase in drinking and social clubs, which commonly met on a weekly basis at a tavern to eat or sing or debate, a well-known example being the Kit-Kat Club of notable Whigs who used to meet at the Flask Tavern in Hampstead, but many humbler clubs existed as well. At the same time, on a more intellectual level, in 1764 was founded in London the Literary Club, among whose members were Sir Joshua Reynolds the artist, Edward Gibbon the historian, Dr Johnson of dictionary fame, Oliver Goldsmith the playwright, David Garrick the actor, and Adam Smith the economist. In 1836 and 1837 Charles Dickens published his famous novel called *The Posthumous Papers of the Pickwick Club* which dealt with certain members' various adventures around England[9]. In the nineteenth century, too, there grew up 'the gentleman's club' which was so characteristic of Victorian society and which earns a mention in the Chambers Dictionary under 'clubland' ('the area around St James's in London, where many of the old-established clubs are'). Although White's Club, the earliest, was founded in 1736 as a direct descendant of White's chocolate-house, most of these clubs such as the Athenaeum, the Travellers and the Reform, were founded in the nineteenth century and were housed in grand edifices. The club had come of age. Since then there has been a proliferation of clubs of every description and they can now be numbered in their thousands[10]. There are, for example, British Legion clubs, constitutional clubs, fan clubs, hobbies clubs, hunting clubs, rotary clubs, senior citizens' clubs, sports clubs, village clubs and working men's clubs. Up and down the country they exist, practically no town in England or Wales without its fair share of clubs, involving a very large segment of the population.

## 3.   CLASSIFICATION OF CLUBS

**1-04**   For the purposes of this book clubs may be classified as either members' clubs or as proprietary clubs. Members' clubs as a classification has various sub-divisions:
(1) unincorporated clubs[11];
(2) working men's clubs registered under the Friendly Societies Acts[12];

---

[9]   The members in question were Mr Pickwick himself and Messrs Tupman, Snodgrass and Winkle, who were obliged to report to the rest of the membership.

[10]   There are, for instance, about 23,500 members' clubs holding a registration certificate under the Licensing Act 1964 according to the Department for Culture, Media and Sport (January 2005), an increase of 500 from the previous year.

[11]   This category includes unincorporated institutions established under the Literary and Scientific Institutions Act 1854: see further **1-46** below.

[12]   The current Acts are the Friendly Societies Acts 1974 and 1992, together with the Friendly and Industrial and Provident Societies Act 1968.

(3) clubs registered under the Industrial and Provident Societies Acts (which from here on we shall call 'IPSA clubs')[13];

(4) shop clubs registered under the Shop Clubs Act 1902;

(5) incorporated clubs registered under the Companies Acts.

**1-05** Some types of club, such as an investment club, where the primary purpose of the club is the acquisition of gain for its members, do not come within the scope of this book[14]. Other organisations calling themselves clubs are not clubs at all: see further **1-42** below.

## 4.    THE DECISION TO FORM A CLUB

**1-06**  In the paragraphs below are set out the different characteristics of each mode of club and what steps one needs to take to bring about the formation of any given mode of club.  The choice is an important one to get right since it will have legal and financial consequences. Accordingly, what follows is an outline of the essential differences between the various types of club.

## 5.    FORMATION OF MEMBERS' CLUBS

### 1-07   Unincorporated members' clubs

By far the most common type of club is the unincorporated members' club. Its undoubted popularity is because it is the easiest, cheapest and the most informal way of forming a club. Added to which is the twofold advantage, admittedly shared by all members' clubs, (1) the use of the concept of the trust whereby trustee members can hold and manage the club property and assets on behalf of all the members and (2) the favourable treatment which such clubs have received over the last century under the Licensing Acts[15]. Many historic clubs such as Marylebone Cricket Club ('MCC') continue to this day to be unincorporated members' clubs, despite the fact that in the case of MCC it comprises some 18,000 members, was the governing body in the cricket world for over two centuries and owns valuable property

---

[13]      The current Acts are the Industrial and Provident Societies Act 1965, the Friendly and Industrial and Provident Societies Act 1968, the Industrial and Provident Societies Act 1975, the Industrial and Provident Societies Act 1978 and the Industrial and Provident Societies Act 2002, which together may be cited as the Industrial and Provident Societies Acts 1965 to 2002.

[14]      Investment clubs are best regarded as a form of partnership.

[15]      The first Act which brought clubs within its purview was the Licensing Act 1902.

in the shape of the Lords Cricket Ground. Another example is the Royal and Ancient Golf Club of St Andrews, which for well over a century was the governing body of the whole sport. So too the Jockey Club, founded in 1752 and still the governing body in the world of horse racing, was an unincorporated members' club until it received a royal charter in 1970. Such an organisational structure would not be tolerated unless it worked in practice.

**1-08**   An unincorporated association is a 'creature of contract'[16]. An unincorporated members' club comes within this category. The club itself is not a legal entity[17]. An unincorporated club comprises its members for the time being[18] and such a club has been described as 'the most anomalous group of human beings that is known to the law'[19]. In *Leahy v Attorney General for New South Wales* [1959] AC 457 PC Viscount Simmonds referred to 'the artificial and anomalous conception of an unincorporated society which, though it is not a separate entity in law, is yet for many purposes regarded as a continuing entity and, however inaccurately, as something other than an aggregate of its members'[20]. The contract in question is that which exists between the members themselves. The terms on which they contract with one another are the rules of the club[21]. The consideration for such a contract is the member's subscription to the club[22]. But it has also been said that membership of a club is not merely a contract since membership often gives the member valuable proprietary and social rights[23].

**1-09**   In essence an unincorporated members' club is a club for members run by the members with no outside control. This in turn ensures privacy for the club's affairs as well as flexibility. On joining the club the member acquires both rights and liabilities as between himself and the other members. The contractual rights are easily discernible because they comprise what are compendiously called the

---

[16]    *Conservative Central Office v Burrell* [1982] 1 WLR 522 CA at 527.

[17]    *Steele v Gourley and Davis* [1886] 3 TLR 118 at 119; *John v Rees* [1970] Ch 345 at 398D (Megarry J).

[18]    *Gaiman v National Association for Mental Health* [1971] Ch 317 at 335E.

[19]    *Feeny and Shannon v MacManus* [1937] IR 23 at 32.

[20]    A good illustration of the point that Viscount Simmonds was making is the treatment of an unincorporated club as having a fiscal personality in the law of taxation: see **17-02** below.

[21]    *In re Sick and Funeral Society of St John's Sunday School, Golcar* [1973] 1 Ch 51 (Megarry J).

[22]    The *Golcar* case, supra, at 59H, save as between the founder members when the consideration would be the mutual promises to join the club when formed.

[23]    *John v Rees* [1970] Ch 345 at 397G; *Rigby v Connol* [1880] 14 Ch D 482 CA; *Lee v Showmen's Guild of Great Britain* [1952] 2 QB 329 at 341–342 (Denning LJ).

privileges of membership. The property rights are much less easily defined, and are discussed below[24].

**1-10** It is generally well known, and one of its attractions, that in an unincorporated member's club the liability of the individual member is limited to his entrance fee (if any) and his subscription. In *Wise v Perpetual Trustee Company* [1903] AC 139 PC at 149 Lord Lindley put the matter thus:

> Clubs are associations of a peculiar nature. They are societies the members of which are perpetually changing. They are not partnerships; they are not associations for gain; and the feature which distinguishes them from other societies is that no member as such becomes liable to pay to the funds of the society or to anyone else any money beyond the subscriptions required by the rules of the club to be paid so long as he remains a member. It is upon this fundamental condition, not usually expressed but understood by everyone, that clubs are formed; and this distinguishing feature has often been judicially recognised.

**1-11** On the other hand, the responsibility for transactions and activities carried on by the club rests normally with the managing committee. It is they to whom creditors or injured persons will look for payment of the club's debts or compensation for injuries suffered on club premises[25]. This may have severe financial consequences for the members of the club who are also members of the committee[26] and may be seen as a serious disadvantage of an unincorporated club.

**1-12** Surprising as it may seem, there is no authority as to what counts as the moment of birth of an unincorporated members' club. It has been said, 'In the case of a member's club the usual procedure will be for those wishing to establish the club to hold a meeting at which a resolution will be passed embodying the decision to bring the club into being'[27]. However, this statement needs qualification. If there were no rules or only draft rules at the date of the resolution, it may be asked how the club could be in existence without there being rules agreed between all the founder members, or at least the basic rules so agreed. It is likely that the court would have to be satisfied that there was a valid and enforceable contract between the founder members before it made a finding that the club existed. Thus a resolution to establish a club with rules to be formulated later will be an inchoate contract and will have no legal significance. The question is not simply

---

24      See **8-02** below.
25      See **12-04**(2) below (as to contract) and **12-18**(3) (as to tort).
26      See **12-05** and **12-47** below as to protecting the committee.
27      *Daly's Club Law* (7th edn, 1979) p 10.

an academic one. In the unreported case of *Hanuman v Guyanese Association for Racial Unity and Democracy* [1996][28] the plaintiff unsuccessfully sued the officers of an unincorporated members' club for disbursements paid by him for the benefit of the association in setting up the association. The county court judge found as a fact[29] that the association did not come into being until all the expenditure had been made so that he held there was no contractual basis on which the association itself or its officers could be liable, and the Court of Appeal refused leave to appeal against that decision. Therefore it may be surmised that until all the criteria set out in paragraph **1-01** are satisfied, it cannot be safely assumed that an unincorporated members' club has been established.

## 1-13   Registered clubs: introduction

In the nineteenth and early twentieth centuries Parliament intervened to a limited and perhaps haphazard extent by permitting certain registered clubs. An early form of registered society was the unincorporated friendly society[30] and in 1875 Parliament authorised a new species of society called a working men's club to be registered under the Friendly Societies Act 1875[31]. The consequence of registration was to formalise the constitution of the club and make it subject to the control of the Registrar of Friendly Societies. Meanwhile, Parliament had permitted certain members' clubs to be registered under the Industrial and Provident Societies Act 1852[32]. This registration also formalised the constitution of the club and made it subject to the control of the Registrar of Friendly Societies, but with one big difference: on registration the club acquired corporate status so that the club itself was now a legal person, which was a very significant step towards protecting the committee members of the club from liability. It should be added here that there are common features in the two extant statutory codes and in particular they prescribe a common system of accounting for clubs registered under either the Friendly Societies Act or the Industrial and Provident Societies Act[33].

---

[28]    Reference LTA/96/5434/G: before Aldous and Phillips LJJ on 13 June 1996.
[29]    What facts the judge relied on to come to this conclusion do not appear from the Court of Appeal judgments.
[30]    The first Friendly Society Act was passed in 1793. It was predicated on the idea of members coming together for the purpose of an insurance business based on thrift and self-help.
[31]    A working men's club is not a friendly society as such since it does not fall within the statutory definition of a friendly society: see s. 7(1)(a) of the Friendly Societies Act 1974.
[32]    Hitherto such clubs had been registered under the Friendly Societies Act.
[33]    See the Friendly and Industrial and Provident Societies Act 1968.

**1-14**  In 1992 the Friendly Societies Commission was set up to supplement the office of the Chief Registrar of Friendly Societies[34]. However, by the Financial Services and Markets Act 2000 the Treasury was empowered to transfer to itself or to the Financial Services Authority (1) the functions of the Friendly Societies Commission[35], (2) the functions of the Chief and Assistant Registrar of Friendly Societies[36] and (3) the functions concerning the registration of industrial and provident societies[37]. These transfers all took place in 2001 with the result that the Treasury has, in the main, the powers of making regulations and orders, while the Financial Services Authority has taken over the other functions and is now the regulating authority for working men's clubs and IPSA clubs[38].

**1-15**  Meanwhile, back in 1902, Parliament had intervened to protect members of shop clubs (otherwise known as thrift funds) from compulsory membership at the instance of their employer. Shop clubs under the Shop Clubs Act 1902 (now repealed by the Wages Act 1986)[39] have only ever played a minor part in the history of clubs.

**1-16**  In 2003 the Financial Services Authority published figures showing that there were then 11,867 registered clubs, which was 51 fewer clubs than the previous year. However, there were 226 new IPSA clubs (which included 27 societies set up as 'benefit of the community' societies by supporters of individual football clubs).

**1-17     Incorporated friendly societies**

In 1992[40] Parliament created a new form of friendly society, namely, an *incorporated* friendly society, with the intention that the Friendly Societies Act 1974, whilst not repealed, would become obsolete[41]. We have not dealt separately with these societies in this book because, like trade unions, they are of such a specialised nature that they fall outside its scope. They undoubtedly have some characteristics of a club in that they have a membership governed by rules[42] and by

---

[34]     S. 1 of the Act of 1992.
[35]     S. 334 of the Financial Services and Markets Act 2000.
[36]     Ibid. s. 335.
[37]     Ibid. s. 338.
[38]     Financial Services and Markets Act 2000 (Mutual Societies) Order 2001 (SI 2001/ 2617).
[39]     A *voluntary* shop club can still be formed: see **1-29** below.
[40]     See the Friendly Societies Act 1992.
[41]     See the annotations to this Act by Ian Swinney, LLB in Current Law Statutes 1992 vol 3 page 40–6.
[42]     Friendly Societies Act 1992, Sch. 5, para 5.

section 10 of the Act of 1992 they can include social activities which are not inconsistent with their other permitted activities. But their main activities are business activities[43] and it is doubtful whether they satisfy criterion no.2 (existing for purposes other than trade) or criterion no.6 (the need for collegiality)[44]. It is interesting to see, however, that by section 65(4) of the Licensing Act 2003 incorporated friendly societies can apply for a club premises certificate, but this is only because section 65(5) has deeming provisions in their favour, which suggests that without them the incorporated friendly society would not be a qualifying club.

## 1-18    Working men's clubs

The Friendly Societies Act 1875 defined working men's clubs as 'societies for purposes of social intercourse, mutual helpfulness, mental and moral improvement, and rational recreation'[45]. The Friendly Societies Act 1974 was the main consolidating Act relating to friendly societies until the passing of the Friendly Societies Act 1992. By this last-mentioned Act no further registration of working men's clubs may take place under the Act of 1974[46], but clubs already registered are permitted still to function under the aegis of the Act of 1974[47].

**1-19**   The advantages of registration under the Friendly Societies Act are that it provides a structured and orderly framework for the club to carry on its activities[48]. The club must have rules binding on its members[49], it must keep proper books of account[50], and it may invest its funds[51] or make loans to its members[52] or make charitable donations for the benefit of its members[53]. Although the club will remain a

---

[43]    See Friendly Societies Act 1992, Sch. 2: class A is insurance business; class B is general business; and class C is business not falling within A or B.

[44]    Ian Swinney LLB in his annotations referred to in footnote 41 above says that, unlike the early societies which regarded playing a social role as an essential part of their function, modern friendly societies are formed to take advantage of tax-exempt status and are really to be regarded as insurance companies, albeit of a special type.

[45]    Friendly Societies Act 1875, s. 8(4).

[46]    Section 93(1) of the Act of 1992. S. 7(1)(b)–(f) of the Act of 1974 identifies the five non-friendly societies which may remain under the aegis of the Act of 1974. Of these five, benevolent societies and old people's homes societies, as well as working men's clubs, may be truly classified as unincorporated member's clubs.

[47]    See Friendly Societies Act 1992, s. 93(2).

[48]    See Friendly Societies Act 1974, s. 7(2). Sch. 2 specifies the mandatory contents of the rules: see APPENDIX 6.

[49]    S. 22 of the Act of 1974.

[50]    Ibid. s. 29.

[51]    Ibid. s. 46.

[52]    Ibid. s. 48.

[53]    Ibid. s. 52.

voluntary unincorporated members' club, registration under the Act means that the club's property vests in one or more trustees of the club[54] and legal proceedings concerning its property will be in the name of the club[55]. Registration also means that the club automatically has provisions governing the resolution of disputes[56] and what happens in the event of dissolution[57].

**1-20**    Owing to the eventual demise of the Act of 1974, Parliament has encouraged clubs registered under the Friendly Societies Acts to convert to societies under the Industrial and Provident Societies Act 1965: section 84A of the Act of 1974[58]. There was already power under section 84 of this Act[59] to convert into a company under the Companies Acts.

## 1-21    IPSA clubs

The main purpose of the original Industrial and Provident Societies Act 1852 was to provide a method of incorporation for societies carrying on an industry, business or trade (hence the word 'Industrial') in order to make provision for the future needs of members (hence the word 'Provident'). The focus of the original legislation was on the working class. An example in practice is the case of *Trebanog Working Men's Club and Institute Limited v Macdonald* [1940] 1 KB 576 CA where the club was registered under the Industrial and Provident Societies Acts 1893 to 1913 and where the object of the club was stated in its rules as being 'to carry on the business of club proprietors, by providing for the use of its members, and for such associates…as are admitted to honorary membership, the means of social intercourse, mutual helpfulness, mental and moral improvement, rational recreation, and the other advantages of a club'. Because of the attraction of incorporation the focus was widened under the subsequent Industrial and Provident Societies Acts to include all classes of persons (involving, for instance, some golf or tennis clubs[60]) yet the old and rather antiquated title has remained. Despite incorporation, IPSA clubs remain in essence members' clubs[61].

---

[54]    Friendly Societies Act 1974, ss. 54 and 58. See further **5-15** below.
[55]    Ibid. s. 56. See further **18-09** and **18-21** below.
[56]    Ibid. ss. 77 and 79.
[57]    Ibid. ss. 93 and 94.
[58]    Inserted by Schedule 16 of the Act of 1992.
[59]    Replaced by s. 91 of the Act of 1992.
[60]    See *Addiscombe Garden Estates Ltd v Crabbe* [1958] 1 QB 513 CA (tennis club).
[61]    *Trebanog Working Men's Club and Institute Ltd v MacDonald* [1940] 1 KB 576; see Josling and Alexander, *The Law of Clubs* (6th edn, 1987) p 190.

**1-22** The Acts of 1965 to 2002 are now the governing legislation. As for new registrations, a club may be registered under the Act of 1965 for the purpose of carrying on any industry, business or trade if either the club is a bona fide co-operative society[62] or if the club is conducted for the benefit of the community and there are special reasons why the club should be registered under the Act of 1965 rather than as a company under the Companies Act 1985[63]. Membership is by ownership of at least one share[64]; the shares may be of any denomination and the overall number need not be limited but generally speaking no person may have a total shareholding of more than £10,000[65].

**1-23** The advantages of registration under the Act of 1965 are (1) that upon registration the club becomes a body corporate by its registered name, with perpetual succession and a common seal, the members having limited liability as under the Companies Acts[66] and (2) that upon registration all the property of the club will vest in the club itself[67]. Registration also has the advantages of providing a structured and orderly framework for the club to carry on its activities. The club must have rules binding on its members[68], it must make annual returns to the regulating authority[69], it must display its latest balance sheet at its registered office[70], and it may make advances to its members[71] or invest its funds[72]. Registration also means that the club automatically has provisions governing the resolution of disputes[73] and what happens in the event of dissolution[74].

**1-24** The disadvantages of registration under the Act of 1965 are the loss of club's control of its own affairs, the inflexibility of its rules and the loss of privacy appertaining to its affairs.

---

[62] S. 1(2)(a) of the Act of 1965. This does not include a society whose object is to make a profit mainly by paying interest on money invested with the society: ibid. s. 3.

[63] Ibid. s. 1(2)(b).

[64] S. 6(1) of the Industrial and Provident Societies Act 1965 as amended by s. 1(1) of the Act of 1975.

[65] Industrial and Provident Societies Act (Increase in Shareholding Limit) Order 1981 (SI 1981/395).

[66] Industrial and Provident Societies Act 1965, s. 3.

[67] Ibid. s. 3.

[68] Ibid. s. 14. Schedule 1 to the said Act specifies the contents of the rules: see APPENDIX 4.

[69] Ibid. s. 39. The regulating authority with effect from 2001 is the Financial Services Authority.

[70] S. 40 of the Act of 1965.

[71] Ibid. s. 21.

[72] Ibid. s. 31.

[73] Ibid. s. 60.

[74] Ibid. s. 55.

**1-25**   To form a club, application is made to the Financial Services Authority who will provide the necessary paperwork[75]. A fee is payable. The application must be made by at least seven persons wanting to register a new club[76]. The word 'Limited' must be the last word of the name of the club, unless the Authority is satisfied that the club's objects are wholly charitable or benevolent[77]. If the club is a charity, it does not need to register with the Charity Commission[78].

## 1-26   Credit unions

These are self-help associations, run on mutual lines, in which members agree to pool part of their savings to provide themselves with a source of low-cost credit. Although popular in many parts of the world they have never flourished in Great Britain to any great extent[79]. They are now regulated by the Credit Unions Act 1979 and credit unions may be registered under the Industrial and Provident Societies 1965. Therefore they may be regarded as a species of an IPSA club, and so are not dealt with separately in this book, although it is right to add that the Act of 1979 does contain provisions which apply solely to credit unions, such as a minimum membership of at least 21[80] and a maximum membership of 5,000[81].

## 1-27   Shop clubs

A shop club or thrift fund is a club whereby a workman or employee connected with a workshop, factory, dock, shop or warehouse on the one hand and the employer on the other hand both make contributions to a savings club. In Victorian times employers often made the joining of such a club compulsory for the workman and the Shop Clubs Act 1902 was passed to regulate the situation. In future the employee could only be *compelled* to join such a club if (a) it was registered and certified under the Friendly Societies Act and (b) three-quarters of the work force desired the establishment of such a club[82]. An unregistered

---

[75]     Information and a form may be obtained from the Financial Services Authority's website, *www.fsa.gov.uk*.

[76]     Industrial and Provident Societies Act 1965, s. 1(1)(b).

[77]     Ibid. s. 5.

[78]     The club will be an exempt charity within the meaning of the Charities Act 1993: s. 3, sch. 2.

[79]     Their numbers are declining: 531 credit unions were registered in England and Wales in 2003, a decrease of 16 from the previous year.

[80]     Credit Unions Act 1979, s. 6(1).

[81]     Ibid. s. 6(2).

[82]     Shop Clubs Act 1902, s. 2.

shop club, however, was and is permissible provided that membership thereof is *voluntary*[83]. Because of the development of trade union law and the advent of national insurance contributions few clubs have taken advantage of the statutory provisions and, indeed, the Act of 1902 was wholly repealed by the Wages Act 1986.

**1-28**   All shop clubs are unincorporated members' clubs. The schedule to the Shops Act 1902 governs the rules of the *registered* shop club and makes provision for such matters as the conditions under which a member becomes entitled to benefits[84], the manner of altering the rules[85], the investment of funds and the keeping of accounts[86], the dissolution of the club[87] and the calling for an investigation into the club's affairs[88].

**1-29**   Since 1986 any *voluntary* new shop club (or similar) would no doubt be formed by the employer, with suitable rules, and the club would be treated like any other unincorporated members' club.

## 1-30   Incorporated members' clubs

Incorporation of a club under the Companies Act has been available since 1855[89]. At law such a club is a very different creature from an unincorporated members' club. The club itself will be a legal person distinct from the members themselves[90]. It does not, however, alter the relationship of the members amongst themselves. This will be the same as obtains in an unincorporated club, that is to say, the contractual relationship will be governed by the rules of the club. In earlier days the rules were set out in the articles of association or more commonly in the bye-laws. Nowadays most clubs have a special article of association which stipulates that there shall be a separate rule book which governs the activities of the club.  This is an important distinction because the rule book will be a *contractual* document whereas the articles set forth in the 1985 Tables A and C emanate

---

[83]   See *Balchin v Lord Ebury* [1903] 48 Sol Jo 83.
[84]   Schedule to the Shop Clubs Act 1902, para ii: see **APPENDIX 2**.
[85]   Ibid. para iii.
[86]   Ibid. para v.
[87]   Ibid. para xi.
[88]   Ibid. para xii.
[89]   The current Act is the Companies Act 1985 (as amended).  Limited liability under a company was first introduced in 1855 and there have been codifying or consolidating Acts in 1862, 1908, 1929, and 1948.
[90]   *Saloman v Saloman & Co Ltd* [1897] AC 22. The articles are a form of statutory contract between the company and the members: *Globalink Telecommunications Ltd v Wilmbury Ltd* [2003 1 BCLC 145 at 154e.

from a *statutory* instrument[91]. If there is any conflict between the articles and the rules, the articles will prevail, having statutory force. As with an unincorporated club, the rules must be read in the context of the objects clause, in this instance being the memorandum of association[92].

**1-31**   Incorporation with limited liability under the Companies Act 1985 takes one of two forms: either as a company limited by shares or a company limited by guarantee.

**1-32**   A company limited by shares normally has working capital created by the issue of shares. Members invest their capital into the company by purchasing the shares in the expectation that a dividend will be paid in respect of those shares. Therefore these companies are usually formed with the idea of trade or profit in mind. The memorandum of association of the company must state that the liability of its members is limited[93].

**1-33**   It is important to ensure that after incorporation provision is made for all the members of the club to become members of the company. This is because if there is a holding of the shares by non-members of the club, the club will cease to be a members' club but will become a proprietary club with the company as the proprietor[94]. Accordingly the articles of association need to make special provision for the holding of one share each by all the members of the club and by no one else and on cessation of membership for the transfer of the share either to a new member or to the club itself. Another area of difficulty, if shares of the company are held by non-members of the club, is the granting of a registration certificate for the supply of intoxicating liquor in that such a club will not be able to comply with the requirements of Schedule 7 of the Licensing Act 1964, nor will it be granted a club premises certificate under the Licensing Act 2003 in that it will be unable to fulfil the conditions set out in sections 62 to 64 of the 2003 Act.

---

[91]     Companies (Tables A to F) Regulations 1985 (SI 1985/805).

[92]     See generally *Inland Revenue Commissioners v Eccentric Club Ltd* [1924] 1 KB 390.

[93]     Companies Act 1985, s. 2(3).

[94]     This is implicit from the judgment of Lord Evershed MR in *Automobile Proprietary Limited v Brown* [1955] 2 All E R 214, CA (concerning the Royal Automobile Club) where he refers to *Challoner v Robinson* [1908] 1 Ch 49 CA and *Inland Revenue Commissioners v Eccentric Club Limited* [1924] 1 KB 390, CA.

**1-34**   A company limited by guarantee is not allowed to have any share capital[95]. Accordingly, there is no question of any dividend being paid by the company to the members. Instead of buying shares the members of the company give a guarantee. The amount of the guarantee must be stated in the memorandum of association and the memorandum must state that the liability of the members is limited. The amount of the guarantee is entirely a matter for the members of the company: it may be £1 or £10,000. It goes without saying that the larger the guarantee the more likely it is that traders will do business with the company, but many members feel that a substantial guarantee breaches the cardinal rule of a members' club that liability should be limited to the member's entrance fee and subscription.

**1-35**   Where a club is incorporated as a company limited by guarantee, the members of the company will be the members of the club. Any change in the membership can be automatically reflected in the identity of the guarantors, so that there should never be any disparity between the membership of the company and the membership of the club. A company limited by guarantee may be entitled to charitable grants or awards from public funds[96], whereas a company limited by shares would not be so entitled. As a generalisation the statutory obligations under the Companies Act 1985 are less onerous, and therefore cause less expense, than with a company limited by shares. A member's rights and liabilities under a company limited by guarantee are basically the same as under a company limited by shares (save as to the right to receive a dividend) and the same régime will apply to a director's duties.

**1-36**   The perceived advantages of an incorporated club are:
(1) it protects the managing committee from liability in respect of the club's transactions and activities which result in a claim being made against the club: it is the club itself that will bear the responsibility;
(2) it relieves the committee member from being personally involved in any litigation concerning the club: the claim or defence will be in the name of the club;
(3) ownership of the club's property will reside in the club itself as opposed to the trustee members or ordinary members of the club[97];

---

[95]   It was previously allowed but since 22.12.80 no further guarantee companies can be registered having a share capital: Companies Act 1980, s. 1(2).
[96]   Where, for example, there is a ban on distribution of profits.
[97]   As to trustees holding the club's property, see **5-15**, **8-06** and **8-20** below.

(4) because 'perpetual succession' is a consequence of separate legal personality, it enables gifts and bequests to be made to the club more easily, especially if the gift or bequest is intended to be for the benefit of future members as well as present members[98];

(5) borrowing is easier because companies can create 'floating charges' over their assets which means a creditor can secure a loan made to the company without hindering the use of the assets in the meantime.

**1-37**  One of the disadvantages of incorporation is that the club will be subject to the whole regimen of statutory control exercised through the courts. Further disadvantages are the costs and the hassle of complying with statutory obligations on an on-going basis, for example, the filing of annual accounts at Companies House[99] or the notification of a change of company director[100]. This compliance requires both expenditure and diligence: for example, the omission of the club secretary to send to the registrar of companies in the prescribed form notification of a change of director could result in the prosecution of the company and its officers and their being fined, with a daily default fine for continued contravention[101].

**1-38**  A company limited by guarantee, however, has a greater simplicity in its corporate structure than a company limited by shares. Unless special articles of association are adopted, the articles set out in Table A will apply to a company limited by shares[102]. In a company limited by guarantee, the articles of association must be in accordance with Table C or as 'near to that form as circumstances permit'[103]. For example, for a company limited by guarantee, Article 3 of Table C states: *'No person shall be admitted a member of the company unless he is approved by the directors'*, and Article 4 of Table C states: *'A member may at any time withdraw from the company by giving at least 7 clear days' notice to the company. Membership shall not be transferable and shall cease on death'*. No such provisions are to be found in Table A and the principles governing admission to and withdrawal (or expulsion) from membership of a company limited by shares are found in a

---

[98]    See **8-17** below.
[99]    Companies Act 1985, s. 365.
[100]   Ibid. s. 288(2).
[101]   Ibid. s. 288(4)
[102]   Ibid. s. 8(1)(2); Companies (Tables A to F) Regulations 1985 (SI 1985/805).
[103]   Ibid. s. 8(4); and the said regulations. See *Gaiman v National Association of Mental Health* [1971] 1 Ch 317 (where the draftsman of the articles in a company limited by guarantee had inserted an extra provision concerning the resignation of members which was upheld by the court). See **7-04** below for a further reference to this case.

combination of the articles of association, the Companies Acts, the common law applicable to companies and any shareholders' agreement.

**1-39**   To form a company, any two or more persons associated for a lawful purpose may, by subscribing their names to a memorandum of association and complying with the requirements of the Companies Act 1985 in respect of registration, form an incorporated company[104]. It is also common to purchase an 'off the shelf' company, where all the formalities have already been carried out, and to make suitable changes to the company name and its memorandum and articles of association. It is usual to employ a solicitor to make the necessary arrangements.

## 6.    CHOOSING THE ESSENTIAL STRUCTURE

**1-40**   The crucial question whether the club should be an unincorporated members' club, an industrial and provident society or an incorporated members' club has no simple, straightforward answer. The most one can say is that if ease of operation is the deciding factor, the unincorporated members' club is a well-tried and successful formula; if peace of mind is the deciding factor, a members' club registered under the Companies Act or the Industrial and Provident Societies Act may be the answer; and if incorporation is decided upon, the better vehicle for a member's club is a company limited by guarantee rather than one limited by shares[105]. A question which is often asked is whether an unincorporated club should become incorporated[106]. There is undoubtedly a trend towards this, especially in relation to large-scale clubs. However, if the club is in a healthy financial state and there is no need or intention to mortgage property or borrow monies, it is considered that the statutory control and obligations referred to in **1-37** will usually outweigh the benefits of incorporation. There may also be some tax implications in changing from an unincorporated status to an incorporated one[107].

---

[104]    Companies Act 1985, s. 1.

[105]    Or possibly a 'community interest company' as envisaged in the Companies (Audit, Investigations and Community Enterprise) Bill presently before Parliament.

[106]    Conversion into a company from an unincorporated members' club is no formality but a matter of substance: *Gaiman v National Association for Mental Health* [1971] Ch 317 at 335E (Megarry J).  For one thing the directors of the company will have duties towards the company itself, not merely duties to the other members as in an unincorporated club.

[107]    See **17-14** below.

**1-41**   In line with the trend referred to above, there has been some active encouragement from the government to persuade IPSA clubs to convert to, or amalgamate with, or transfer their engagements to a company. In pursuit of this encouragement there was passed the Industrial and Provident Societies Act 2002 which (a) made it easier than hitherto to convert into a company[108] and (b) enables the Treasury through secondary legislation to assimilate certain parts of IPSA law to company law[109]. So perhaps in reality the choice lies between an unincorporated members' club and an incorporated members' club.

# 7.   FORMATION OF PROPRIETARY CLUBS

**1-42**   It is important to distinguish a true proprietary club from a club which is referred to by a business man in his trading or business activities. In commerce the word 'club' is commonly used when a trader wants to target a particular segment of the public in order to offer persons favourable trading terms or to make a promotional offer. For example, Tesco plc, which operates a chain of grocery superstores, runs what it calls its Clubcard scheme; you apply to join its club by written application and once admitted the member obtains trading benefits from the club by way of discounted prices, etc. Likewise, many book clubs, clothing clubs, and holiday clubs owned by proprietors do not qualify as true clubs because they would not satisfy the criteria set out in paragraph **1-01** above, in particular the second criterion (not existing simply for profit) and the sixth criterion (possessing collegiality). The distinction turns on the degree of control, both financial and physical, which the proprietor chooses to exercise over the members of the club, and in some cases the dividing line between a true proprietary club and a marketing device can be a fine one. As an example of a true proprietary club, one can take the Groucho Club in London, which is a social club with many members coming from the media world. The club is owned by a proprietor who provides all the facilities and controls all the finances but there are proper club rules and, importantly, there is a membership committee comprising members of the club (plus one representative of the proprietor) which vets all applications for membership and which alone makes the decision whether to accept or reject the application. A proprietor may protect the name of his club by a passing-off action[110].

---

[108]   Industrial and Provident Societies Act 2002, s. 1.
[109]   Ibid. s. 2.
[110]   *Ad-Lib Club Ltd v Granville* [1971] 2 All ER 300.

**1-43**   Nevertheless, a proprietary club is a very different legal concept from a members' club because the club will be owned by an outside person or company and the normal purpose of the club is for the proprietor to make a profit out of it[111]. To draw the distinction between members' clubs and proprietary clubs, the former are often referred to as *private* members' clubs[112]. The proprietor will own or provide the club premises, the furniture and the stock and will make them available to club members on such terms as he thinks fit[113]. The payment for the entitlement to use the facilities provided is the member's subscription[114]. When the period of the subscription expires the proprietor's obligations cease unless, and the exception needs emphasising, by consent of both parties the subscription is renewed. The relationship is solely one of contract between the proprietor on the one hand and the individual member on the other hand. There is no direct contractual relationship between the members themselves. The relationship between the member and his fellow-members will be a social one. The club, however, will not be eligible for a club registration certificate or for a club premises certificate for licensing purposes. Nor is there any question of the members having any property rights in the club property[115].

**1-44**   The liability for any debt or any transaction of the club will remain with the proprietor and so it will be he who will sue or be sued, not the members, in respect of club purchases or the conduct of its affairs. This position still applies where the proprietor has given the management of the club wholly or partly to a committee of members.

**1-45**   A proprietary club will come about either because a group of persons wish to form a members' club but do not have the money, ability or inclination to own or run a club so that they entrust the task to a person or company to do it for them, or because a proprietor sees an opportunity in the market place for a members' club with facilities which he is able to provide.

---

[111]   *Inland Revenue Commissioners v Eccentric Club Ltd* [1924] 1 KB 390 CA at 421 (Warrington LJ).
[112]   See, for example, *John v Matthews* [1970] 2 QB 443 DC at 447 E (Lord Parker CJ).
[113]   *Bowyer v Percy Supper Club Ltd* [1893] 2 QB 154 DC.
[114]   Ibid.
[115]   *Baird v Wells* [1890] 44 Ch D 661 at 676 (Stirling J).

# 8.   FORMATION OF CLUBS AFFECTED BY STATUTORY PROVISIONS

## 1-46   Literary and scientific institutions

Many of the learned societies and institutions of this country were incorporated by royal charter, whilst others have been incorporated under the Companies Acts. The majority, however, are not incorporated and count as unincorporated members' clubs. Whether incorporated or not, the provisions of the Literary and Scientific Institutions Act 1854 applies to every institution[116] 'for the time being established for the promotion of science, literature, the fine arts, for adult instruction, the diffusion of useful knowledge, the foundation or maintenance of libraries or reading rooms for general use among the members or open to the public, of public museums and galleries of paintings and other works of art, collections of natural history, mechanical and philosophical inventions, instruments, or designs'[117]. The Act deals with the nature, constitution, property, internal regulation and dissolution of the institution, and also with legal proceedings by or against the institution, and accords privileges and powers to the institution not normally enjoyed by private clubs and institutions[118].

## 1-47   Other clubs

More often than not clubs have specialised activities. Many of these clubs are regulated or part-regulated by statute, sometimes in order to control or restrict the club's activities and sometimes to the club's advantage or in order to help the club function efficiently. Set out in **Appendix 11** is a list of some of the more common specialist clubs, indicating in broad terms which statutes are applicable to their activities. A number of these clubs have a governing or central organisation to which the clubs belong and to whom the club can often turn in the event of a problem arising.

---

[116]    Except the Royal Institution. Certain other institutions, such as the British Museum and the National Gallery, are governed by specific acts of Parliament and therefore fall outside the ambit of the Act of 1854.

[117]    S. 33 of the Act of 1854. The Act of 1854 applies to institutions established before this Act. An early example of such an institution was the Russell Literary and Scientific Institution, founded in 1808 to provide a library and lectures on literary and scientific subjects for its members (*In re Russell Institution, Figgins v Baghino* [1898] 2 Ch D 72). Ss. 18 to 33 of the Act appear in APPENDIX 1.

[118]    *In re Russell Institution, Figgins v Baghino* [1898] 2 Ch D 72.

# 9.   UMBRELLA ORGANISATIONS

**1-48**   There are several organisations in the United Kingdom which have a large number of clubs under their jurisdiction. Perhaps the best known is the Football Association. Under its aegis are 43 County Football Associations to which the astonishing number of 37,500 football clubs are affiliated, involving about a million players. Other examples are Rotary International in Great Britain and Ireland which has over 1,800 clubs within this territory and some 59,000 club members, and the English Golf Union ('EGU') which has some 1,910 clubs belonging to its organisation and some 740,000 members. Sometimes the umbrella organisation like Rotary insists on all the clubs having a standard set of rules, others like EGU have clubs with as many different sets of rules as there are clubs. But all these clubs are genuine members' clubs and the same general principles of club law will be applicable to them as in the case of a single, free-standing members' club. A problem which can occur, however, is when a member of one club affiliated to an umbrella organisation is permitted entry as of right into another club as an associate; care has to be taken in relation to the rules of the host club and in connection with the Licensing Acts[119].

# 10.   CHARITABLE STATUS OF CLUB

**1-49**   There may be occasions when it is suitable or advisable for a club or intended club to apply for charitable status[120]. To be a charity at law, a trust or institution must be established for purposes which are exclusively charitable. Charitable purposes may be classified into four principal divisions derived from the Statute of Charitable Uses enacted in 1601 under Elizabeth I. They are: (1) the relief of poverty, (2) the advancement of education, (3) the advancement of religion, and (4) other purposes beneficial to the community not falling under the preceding heads. Falling under the last head is the provision of facilities for recreation or other leisure-time occupation, if the facilities are provided in the interests of social welfare[121]. The advantages of charitable status are financial in that there are tax incentives to make donations to charities; a charity enjoys exemption from direct taxes such as corporation tax; and a charity enjoys mandatory rating relief

---

[119]   Discussed at **9-36** below.
[120]   For the topic of charities generally, see 5(2) *Halsbury's Laws of England* (4th edn, 2001 reissue).
[121]   Recreational Charities Act 1958. It applies in particular to the provision of facilities at village halls, community centres and women's institutes.

in respect of premises which it occupies[122]. On the other hand, such a club will be subject to the jurisdiction of the Crown and to the supervision of the Charity Commission.

**1-50**   There can be no denying that a statutory definition of what constitutes a charitable organisation would be a desirable improvement in this unclear branch of the law. To this end the government intends to pass a new Charities Act. The Charities Bill is about to receive the Royal Assent. The bill stipulates that a charitable purpose is one which is for the public benefit and which includes one of the following purposes: (1) the prevention or relief of poverty; (2) the advancement of education; (3) the advancement of religion; (4) the advancement of health; (5) the advancement of citizenship or community development; (6) the advancement of the arts, heritage or science; (7) the advancement of amateur sport; (8) the advancement of human rights, conflict resolution or reconciliation; (9) the advancement of environmental protection and improvement; (10) the relief of those in need by reason of youth, age, ill-health, disability, financial hardship or other disadvantage; and (11) the advancement of animal welfare.

**1-51**   The Charity Commission, in consultation with the government, made it known in 2002 that it will now recognize the following activities as being for charitable purposes[123]:
(1) the promotion of community participation in healthy recreation by the provision of facilities for the playing of a particular sport;
(2) the advancement of physical education of young people not undergoing formal education.

### 1-52   Community amateur sports clubs

At the same time the Government recognised the important role that sports clubs played in promoting social and community inclusiveness and, in particular, promoting good health through regular exercise. But this contribution was not acknowledged by the tax system. It is an historical fact that the sports club sector has suffered from a lack of cash and a lack of adequate facilities, despite the many volunteers involved within the sector. Worse still, there has been a decline in participation of healthy sports which has added to the problems of local sports clubs. The government therefore introduced a package of tax reliefs to support community amateur sports clubs ('CASC')[124].

---

[122]   See *Halsbury's Laws of England* op. cit. paras 371 to 382.
[123]   See Coulson, *Questions and Answers on Club Law* (2nd edn, 2002) p 27.

Despite not being registered as charities, such clubs will be eligible for many of the same tax reliefs on income or on donations as are normally given to charities.

**1-53** But there are distinctions to be noted. To qualify as a charity the club must promote community participation in healthy recreation by providing facilities for playing particular sports, and the club needs to register with the Charity Commission. To qualify as a community amateur sports club the club must as its main purpose provide facilities for, and promote participation in, one or more eligible sports, and the club needs to register with the Inland Revenue. In other words, in a charity the sports facilities are a means to an end, namely, the encouragement of the community to participate in healthy sports, whereas in a CASC the sport is the end in itself. In Appendix 16 there is a table which compares the tax position of sports clubs in general with the advantages and disadvantages of being a sports charity or a CASC. It should be pointed out, however, that any club is bound to lose some of its autonomy if it becomes accountable to the Charity Commission or the Inland Revenue. A problem also arises because the entrance to membership is intended to be non-selective as befits a charitable or community-based club[125]. This might well mean that the club could not insist on the applicant being proposed and seconded by existing members of the club. The club would no doubt retain the ability to limit the number of members[126] and to impose age limits for applicants[127]. Presumably the club would retain the right to make entry conditional upon the candidate demonstrating his sports ability if there were too many applicants for the available places[128], but if there were available places this right might be in jeopardy were the applicant to say he was willing to learn the sport in question; indeed, a case could be made out that a non-selective process should be operated on a first-come-first-served basis. So it remains to be seen how this admission process will work in practice. As they say, tax advantages usually come with strings attached. On the other hand, we assume that, whatever loss of autonomy is involved, the club would still be eligible for a club premises certificate under the Licensing Act 2003[129], as we cannot imagine that it was Parliament's intention to deprive the club of this facility when it was widening its parameters of membership.

---

[124] Finance Act 2002, s. 58, Sch. 18.
[125] Para 1(a) of Sch. 18 refers to the club being 'open to the whole community'.
[126] See **4-02** below.
[127] See **4-16** below.
[128] See **4-17** below.
[129] For alcohol licensing, see CHAPTER 9 below.

# Chapter 2

## THE CLUB'S CONSTITUTION OR RULES

### 1.   THE PRIMACY OF CLUB RULES

**2-01**   The club's set of rules is the bedrock of club law. A well-drawn set of rules[1] is crucial to the well-being and proper functioning of any club, no matter into what category the club falls. Rules should cater for all the exigencies which the club is likely to be confronted with. If a problem arises in a club, the first reaction of the committee or the members should be, 'What do the rules say about it?'[2] This does not mean to say that all sets of rules need to be complicated or minutely detailed. The extent of the rules depends on the extent of the club's activities. As a general proposition, rules should deal with matters of substance, not matters of procedure. Matters of detail or procedure can often be best dealt with in bye-laws or regulations if the need arises. It goes without saying that the rules should be expressed in clear and simple language, which does not need the training of a lawyer to expound what is the true meaning of any given rule[3]. Rules (and bye-laws) should always be dated so the members know when a particular rule or amendment came into force.

---

[1]      It is possible to have a set of enforceable *oral* rules but a club with such rules would be a very small coterie of like-minded persons. An interesting, literary, mid-twentieth-century example was the Inklings, a club consisting of C S Lewis (*The Chronicles of Narnia*), J R R Tolkien (*The Lord of the Rings*), Nevill Coghill (modern verse translator of Chaucer's *The Canterbury Tales*) and Charles Williams of the Oxford University Press, who used to meet in CS Lewis' rooms at Magdalen College, Oxford and in the Eagle and Child public house in Oxford.

[2]      As long ago as 1836 in the case of *Flemyng v Hector* [1836] 2 M & W 172 (concerning the Westminster Reform Club) the courts were emphasising the importance of the club rules (Parke B at 184–185).

[3]      See Megarry J's comment in the *Re Sick and Funeral Society of St John's Sunday School, Golcar* case [1973] Ch 51 at 61F: 'I have already observed that the rules are not well drafted, and I do not intend to explore all the difficulties discussed in argument'.

**2-02** A paradigm example of the need for well-drawn rules is the case of *Royal Society for the Prevention of Cruelty to Animals v Attorney-General and others* [2002] 1 WLR 448. The Society went to court to obtain guidance on whether its membership policy and associated membership scheme were constitutional. The Society was founded in 1824 as an unincorporated association but was incorporated by a private Act of Parliament in 1932. The rules governing its members were made in 1932 and amended or altered in 1964, 1976, 1979, 1983, 1991 and 1997. Their confused state drove Mr Justice Lightman to conclude his judgment by saying:

> At the same time consideration should be given whether and how the rules should be amended generally so that they no longer represent a patchwork of amendments over the years with the inevitable construction difficulties to which such a patchwork gives rise and whether the society should adopt in their place a set of rules which are clear and consistent and enable it to function effectively.

## 2.    CONTENTS OF THE RULES

**2-03** At the most basic level, the rules should make provision[4] for:
(1)    the name of the club;
(2)    the object and purposes of the club[5];
(3)    the election or admission of members[6];
(4)    the payment of subscriptions[7];
(5)    the resignation of members[8];
(6)    the suspension and expulsion of members[9];
(7)    the management of club affairs[10];
(8)    general meetings of the members[11];
(9)    the alteration of the rules[12];
(10)  the dissolution of the club[13].

**2-04** For a complex organisation which, say, has a national identity and branches and perhaps a disciplinary role as well, the rules will

---

[4]     Since 1902 clubs registered under the Licensing Acts must have rules covering items (1) to (9) inclusive. There will be no such requirement under the Licensing Act 2003.
[5]     See **2-08** below.
[6]     See **4-01** below.
[7]     See **4-36** below.
[8]     See **7-02** below.
[9]     See **7-09** below
[10]    See CHAPTER 5 below.
[11]    See CHAPTER 6 below.
[12]    See **2-25** below.
[13]    See CHAPTER 3 below.

need to be a lot more comprehensive and make provision accordingly.
For example, the index to the constitution or rules of such a club might
read as follows:

*General*
(1)   Name of the club
(2)   Object and purposes of the club
(3)   Charitable status [if any][14]
(4)   Powers [if, say, it has a royal charter]
(5)   Patron[15]
(6)   President[16]
(7)   Vice-Presidents[17]
(8)   Trustees[18]

*Membership[19]*
(1)   Categories of member
(2)   Qualification for membership
(3)   Election of candidates
(4)   Privileges of membership
(5)   Entrance fee
(6)   Subscriptions
(7)   Resignation
(8)   Suspension & expulsion
(9)   Disciplinary proceedings
(10)  Restrictions on members

*Management[20]*
(1)   Management of the club's affairs
(2)   Composition of the Council [the ruling body]
(3)   Meetings of the Council
(4)   Board of Management [the managing committee]
(5)   Committees
(6)   Secretary General
(7)   Branches
(8)   Notice to members

---

[14]   See **1-49** above.
[15]   See **5-03** below.
[16]   See **5-05** below.
[17]   See **5-05** below.
[18]   See **5-15** below.
[19]   See CHAPTER **4** below.
[20]   See CHAPTER **5** below.

*Meetings*[21]
(1)   Annual General Meeting
(2)   Special meetings
(3)   Procedure at general meetings

*Financial provisions*
(1)   Power to borrow[22]
(2)   Accounts
(3)   Auditor[23]
(4)   Investment manager

*Miscellaneous*
(1)   Amendment of the rules[24]
(2)   Amendment of the bye-laws[25]
(3)   Arbitration[26]
(4)   Interpretation of the rules[27]

*Dissolution*[28]
(1)   Resolution to dissolve the club
(2)   Assets on dissolution.

**2-05**   In deciding how detailed the rules should be or what special rules ought to be included, the members or their committee should think ahead as to what problems might arise in any particular area of the club's activity. For example, the players in a football club might find themselves outnumbered by the social members of the club. The social members are welcome because they generate cash at the club. But what if a developer offers to buy the club's playing field? The players are all against the offer but the social members are all in favour of it. The solution adopted by some sports clubs is to have a rule that states if any motion, which is put to the members at a general meeting, is prejudicial to the interests of the playing members, the non-playing members shall not be entitled to vote on it. The authors do not necessarily recommend any such rule but it demonstrates the need for foresight when compiling the rules. If the rule is not there when it is needed, it may be too late to insert it as an amendment[29].

---

21    See **CHAPTER 6** below.
22    See **5-37** below.
23    See **5-14** below
24    See **2-25** below.
25    See **5-26** below.
26    See **5-48** and **18-30** below.
27    See **2-23** below.
28    See **CHAPTER 3** below.

**2-06** All clubs start out with the big advantage that candidates or applicants for membership must perforce join the club on its terms, not on their terms. If a candidate were to approach a club secretary and say, 'I would like to apply for membership of your club but I don't like your rule that says members must wear red jackets in the clubhouse on Saturdays', the secretary would no doubt respond, 'In that case, don't bother to apply'. It is only once the member has joined the club that he is in a position to get the rule altered and of course he may find the great majority of the members are in favour of the red jacket rule.

**2-07** A members' club incorporated under the Companies Act will usually set out the rules of the club in its articles of association or in its bye-laws. A club registered under the Friendly Societies Acts must include the club rules which are set out in Schedule 2 of the Act of 1974[30]. A club registered under the Industrial and Provident Societies Acts must include the club rules which are set out in Schedule 1 of the Act of 1965[31]. A shop club registered under the Friendly Societies Act must include the rules which are set out in the Schedule to the Shop Clubs Act 1902[32].

## 3.   STATEMENT OF THE OBJECTS OF THE CLUB

### 2-08   Unincorporated members' clubs

A club's objects clause should be stated in a suitably wide form to cover all the activities it may wish to pursue. This ensures that the club's funds and assets are expended in a proper manner. But the stated objects should be fairly reflected in the name of the club[33]. Because circumstances change over the years and the club's activities may take a new direction or have a new emphasis, a provision can be inserted in the objects clause which states that no one object is to predominate

---

[29]    See *In re West Sussex Constabulary's Widows, Children and Benevolent (1930) Fund Trusts* [1971] Ch 1 at 9E.
[30]    Schedule 2 appears in APPENDIX 6.
[31]    Schedule 1 appears in APPENDIX 4.
[32]    The schedule appears in APPENDIX 2. The Act of 1902 was repealed by the Wages Act 1986, but this did not affect clubs already registered.
[33]    See **2-14** below for an example of too great a divergence in an incorporated club. Although not unlawful, it would be very odd if an unincorporated members' club called itself the Basset Rugby Football Club when it in fact played association football. This misleading name might give rise to an actionable misrepresentation. Yet the Basset Football Club could legitimately say that its name was appropriate to the playing of rugby football, association football or even American football.

over another or the wording of the objects clause can be such that no one object prevails over another object[34].

**2-09**    If the club's object was stated to be the provision of facilities for the playing of golf, would it matter if the club started spending its funds on the provision of facilities for the playing of squash? The answer is that it would matter, because the expenditure would have been unauthorised; the club's auditor might take exception to it and the committee who spent the money might be vulnerable to reimburse the club, unless *all* the members ratified the expenditure or unless the objects clause was amended with retrospective effect[35] to include the playing of squash[36]. Presumably in most cases the members would be aware of the expenditure on squash facilities and would be consenting to their committee spending the club's money in this way, so that no problem would arise in fact, but it is plainly not good practice to have the objects clause and the club expenditure out of kilter.

## 2-10   Working men's clubs

A working men's club registered under the Friendly Societies Act must state in its rules the *whole* of the objects for which the club is established and the purposes for which the club's funds are to be applicable[37].

**2-11**    It should be noted that it is not competent for a club registered under the Friendly Societies Act to convert itself into a company with objects more extensive or widely differing from the objects specified in the club rules, although once converted it can exercise such powers of altering or enlarging its objects set out in its memorandum of association as the Companies Acts permit[38].

## 2-12   IPSA clubs

A club registered under the Industrial and Provident Societies Act must state in its rules what its objects are[39]. Its position is analogous

---

[34]     See **2-31** below for an example of the advantage of a suitably wide objects clause.
[35]     As to retrospective alteration of the rules, see **2-27** below.
[36]     See *Baker v Jones* [1954] 1 WLR 1005 (where the payments made by British Amateur Weightlifters' Association to solicitors to defend libel actions brought against some of its members were held illegal because there was no power in the rules to use the funds in this manner).
[37]     Para 3(1) of Schedule 2 of the Act of 1974.
[38]     *Blythe v Birtley* [1910] 1 Ch 228, CA.
[39]     Paragraph 2 of Schedule 1 of the Act of 1965.

to that of a company and there is no requirement to state in the rules the whole of the objects for which the club is established, as obtains in the case of clubs registered under the Friendly Societies Act. Thus the objects clause of a club can be drawn in a suitably wide form. For example, in *Cyclists' Touring Club v Hopkinson* [1910] 1 Ch 179, where the club was registered under section 23 of the Companies Act 1867 as an association not for profit, Mr Justice Swinfen Eady stated:

> In my opinion, the payment to a retired servant of the club by way of an annuity, or by way of pension, or by way of gratuity, is within the powers of the club as being a payment in furtherance of the best objects of the club. The fact that the payment is made by way of gratuity and not under any legal liability does not make it a payment outside the objects of the club.

## 2-13 Shop clubs

A club registered under the Shop Clubs Act 1902 must state in its rules the *whole* of the objects for which the club is established.

## 2-14 Incorporated members' clubs

The objects of the company will be set out in the memorandum of association and the company has the capacity only to enter into contracts authorised by the objects clause. Thus any contract outside the scope of this clause is *ultra vires* of the company and is void, even if the whole body of shareholders were to assent to it[40] (unlike an unincorporated club where unanimous ratification of unauthorised expenditure is possible: see **2-09** above). The moral of the story is that the objects clause should be drawn in a suitably wide form[41], but not so wide as to be divorced from the name of the club. In the unreported case of *Re Claremont Liberal Club Limited* [1910][42] registered under the Companies (Consolidation) Act 1908, the club applied in September 1910 to Mr Justice Swinfen Eady for sanction to extend its activities 'to work mines, promote companies, underwrite shares, and sell coal and coke'. The judge refused permission on the ground that in order to carry out these activities the club would first have to change its name to a general purposes company. There is, however, little restriction on the choice of name. The Secretary of State has the power to reject a name if he is of the opinion that it would constitute a criminal offence

---

[40]     *York Corporation v Henry Leetham & Sons Ltd* [1924] 1 Ch 557 at 573.
[41]     See *Cyclists' Touring Club v Hopkinson* [1910] 1 Ch 179 cited in **2-12** above.
[42]     Cited by B T Hall in his book on Club Law published in August 1915 by the Working Men's Club & Institute Union Limited.

or is offensive[43]. This presumably would include names thought to be obscene or blasphemous or defamatory[44].

**2-15** Certain guarantee companies and other private companies are entitled to omit the word 'Limited' from their name if the objects of the company are the promotion of commerce, art, science, education, religion, charity or any profession, provided that it requires its profits (if any) to be applied in promoting its objects; no dividend is paid to its members; and on winding up it assets are transferred to another body with similar objects rather than distributed to the members[45].

## 2-16 Proprietary clubs

The objects clause will be drafted by the proprietor and insofar as the assets and funds of the club belong to the proprietor the objects clause is of less significance than in a members' club. Nevertheless, a proprietary club should concisely state what are the objects of the club so that the members are aware of the sort of club they are applying to join.

## 4. BINDING NATURE OF THE RULES

### 2-17 Unincorporated members' clubs

The club rules are impliedly binding on each member as a matter of contract law[46]. It is, however, a wise precaution to state in every set of rules that on joining the club the member expressly agrees to be bound by the rules as may be made from time to time, and for the new member to be provided with a copy of the rules[47]. The importance

---

[43] S. 26 of the Companies Act 1985.
[44] See *Gore-Browne on Companies* (50th edn, 2004) para 6[2]. It is a nice point whether Sir Francis Dashwood Bt would have been permitted to register his company as the Hell Fire Club Limited; its memorandum of association would have made interesting reading.
[45] S. 30 of the Companies Act 1985.
[46] See *In re Sick and Funeral Society of St John's Sunday School, Golcar* [1973] Ch 51 at 60E.
[47] This is not essential as may be seen from *Raggett v Musgrave* [1827] 2 Car & P 556 (where the rules were accessible but not posted in the clubhouse or sent to the members, yet were still held to be binding on the members). And see *John v Rees* [1970] 1 Ch 345 at 388F (where Megarry J said, 'In the case of a club, if nobody can produce any evidence of a final resolution to adopt a particular set of rules, but on inquiry the officers would produce that set as being the rules upon which it is habitual for the club to act, then I do not think the member would be entitled to reject those rules merely because no resolution could be proved').

of express rules is underlined by the fact that further rules, however desirable, will not be implied into club rules unless either they are necessary to give business efficacy to the contract of membership or because the implied term represents the obvious, but unexpressed, intention of the parties[48]. As will be seen, such rules as those dealing with expulsion of members[49] or amendment of the rules[50] will not be implied into the rules in the absence of express rules to this effect.

**2-18** It is common for clubs to make it a rule that the elected candidate shall not be entitled to the privileges of membership until he has paid the entrance fee (if any) and his first subscription. In this event the election constitutes an offer of membership so that on notification of his election the candidate can reject the offer and decline membership because the contract is only complete when he had paid the entrance fee and the first subscription[51]. If there is no such rule the candidate's application is the offer and the acceptance is the notification of election.

## 2-19 Registered clubs

By section 22(1)(b) of the Friendly Societies Act 1974 and by section 14(1) of the Industrial and Provident Societies Act 1965 it is provided that the rules of clubs registered under these Acts are binding on the members. Under section 21 of the former Act and section 15(1) of the latter Act the club is obliged to provide a copy of the rules for a small fee to the member on demand.

**2-20** The Shop Clubs Act 1902 is silent on the point but it is considered that the members are all impliedly bound by the rules of their particular club, especially as the Act mandatorily requires each registered shop club to provide for certain fixed rules.

## 2-21 Incorporated members' clubs

Although the articles of association and any bye-laws govern the internal affairs of the company, which means that all members of the company (the club members) are bound by them, most clubs nowadays have a specific article of association which states that there shall be a separate rule book which governs the activities of the club.

---

[48] See *Chitty on Contracts* (29th edn, 2004) para 13-004.
[49] See **7-09** below.
[50] See **2-25** below.
[51] *Re New University Club (Duty on Estate)* [1887] 18 QBD 720 at 727.

As a result the members will find themselves bound by the rules as a matter of contract law[52].

## 2-22  Proprietary clubs

The proprietor will set out the club rules as part of the contract between himself and the individual club member and these rules will bind the member as a matter of contract law.

# 5.    INTERPRETATION OF THE RULES

**2-23**  As to the manner in which club rules should be approached, in 1881 in *Dawkins v Antrobus*[53] Jessel MR said that the ordinary rules of construction were to apply as with any other contract. However, a hundred years later in 1982 the courts saw club rules in a different light. In *re GKN Nuts & Bolts Ltd Sports and Social Club*[54] Megarry V-C said:

> In [club] cases the court usually has to take a broad sword to the problems, and eschew an unduly meticulous examination of the rules and resolutions. I am not, of course, saying these should be ignored; but usually there is a considerable degree of informality in the conduct of the affairs of such clubs, and I think that the courts have to be ready to allow general concepts of reasonableness, fairness and common sense to be given more than their usual weight when confronted by claims to the contrary which appear to be based on any strict interpretation and rigid application of the letter of the rules. In other words, allowance must be made for some play in the joints[55].

But a word of caution has to be added. In the same case the Vice Chancellor emphasised the need for 'scrupulous observance of the rules' when it came to changing the property rights of members[56]. The same scrupulous observance of the rules will be required when it comes to a question of suspension or expulsion of the member[57].

**2-24**  It is in order for a club rule to state that if there is any dispute about the meaning or interpretation of a rule, the dispute shall be put

---

[52]     See **1-30** above.
[53]     [1881] 17 Ch D 615 at 621.
[54]     [1982] 1 WLR 774 at 776.
[55]     The speech of Lord Hoffman in *Mannai Investments v Eagle Star Assurance Co Ltd* [1997] 2 WLR 945 at 966 provides helpful guidance as to the modern approach of interpretation.
[56]     At 783.
[57]     See **7-12** below.

to the committee for a ruling thereon. What the rule cannot go on to say is that the committee's decision is final with no recourse to the courts because this ouster of the court's jurisdiction is contrary to public policy and void[58].

# 6.   ALTERATION OF THE RULES

## 2-25   Unincorporated members' clubs

It is of cardinal importance that the rules contain an express provision whereby the members are empowered to alter the club's rules by way of amendment, addition or revocation because when a member joins the club he does so on the terms of a contract set out in the rules at that point in time and such a contract cannot be subsequently varied without the consent of all the members[59]. No power to alter the rules will be implied into the contract. In *Harrington v Sendall* [1903] 1 Ch 921 a member of the Oxford and Cambridge University Club, an unincorporated members' club, agreed to be bound by 'the following rules and regulations'. The club wished to raise its subscription rule from 8 guineas to 9 guineas and Mr Harrington as a member objected. The court rejected the club's argument that as a social club it could not carry on at all unless there was an implied power to alter the rules as the necessities of the club might demand. The court also rejected the club's argument that Mr Harrington had acquiesced in the rule change because he had never objected to other rule changes in the past. The case provides several object lessons: first, by a slight alteration in the language of the rules Mr Harrington would have been bound by amendments of the rules, for example, the rules could easily have said that the member was bound by 'the rules and regulations as may be made from time to time'. Secondly, it is unwise to stipulate the amount of the subscription in the rule itself instead of adopting some general phrase, for example, 'such amount as may be determined by the members in a general meeting'. Thirdly, acquiescence may be difficult to prove.

**2-26**   On this last point, however, there may be occasions when

---

[58]      *Lee v Showmen's Guild of Great Britain* [1952] 2 QB 329 CA at 342 (Denning LJ); *Baker v Jones* [1954] 1 WLR 1005 at 1010.
[59]      See *Dawkins v Antrobus* [1881] 17 Ch D 615 CA at 621 (Jessel MR)]; *Harrington v Sendall* [1903] 1 Ch 921 at 927 (Joyce J); and *re Tobacco Trade Benevolent Association* [1958] 3 All ER 353 where Harman J stated at 355B, 'This body [an unincorporated charity] started with no power to alter its rules, and such a body cannot alter its rules by its own motion except possibly by the concurrence of *every* member of the body' (emphasis added).

acquiescence may be inferred from a lack of opposition or objection to the new rule. In *Abbatt v Treasury Solicitor* [1969] 1 WLR 1575 CA, the unincorporated British Legion Club in 1954 affiliated to a different umbrella organisation[60], changed its name to the Old Castle Club, adopted a new set of rules, registered under the Friendly Societies Act 1896 and conveyed its property to new trustees. In 1960 the club sold part of its land and the purchasers raised a query as to title. Here the Court of Appeal held on the facts that although the rules of the old club contained no express power to amend or alter them the members as a body had acquiesced in the rule changes, so that the new club was the same as the old one but 'dressed in different clothes'. In the course of his judgment Lord Denning MR stated[61]:

> It is true that the old rules contained no express power to amend or alter them. But I should have thought it was implied that the members could, on notice, by a simple majority in general meeting, amend or alter the rules. In any event, however, if at such a meeting a majority purport to amend or alter the rules, and the others take no objection to it, but instead by their conduct acquiesce in the change, then those rules become binding on all.'

It may be doubted, however, that Lord Denning's first proposition as to the implied power of amendment accurately sets out the law in the light of clear authority contrary to this proposition[62].

**2-27** *Retrospective amendment*  Whether the rules can be altered retrospectively can pose a problem. In *Dawkins v Antrobus* [1881] 17 Ch D 615 CA Colonel Dawkins, a member of the Travellers Club, an unincorporated members' club, put a pamphlet about General Stephenson, another member of the club and a serving officer, in a wrapper endorsed on the outside 'Dishonourable conduct of Colonel (now Lieutenant-General) Stephenson' and sent it by post to his official address at the Horse Guards. For that conduct he was expelled from the club under an expulsion rule which existed at the time of the alleged misconduct but not when he had joined the club and the court held that Colonel Dawkins was bound by the inserted rule. Lord Justice Brett stated[63] that an expulsion rule could have no retrospective effect and this proposition is readily understandable in the context of that case. But whether all retrospective alterations are invalid is a different matter. It is considered that in principle there is nothing

---

[60]    From the British Legion to the Working Men's Club & Institute Union Limited.

[61]    At 1583D.

[62]    See the cases cited in footnote 59 above. In the *Tobacco Trade* case at 355C Mr Justice Harman in 1958 declined to infer acquiescence of a purported alteration which had taken place in 1871 and not objected to since that date.

[63]    At 632.

objectionable in a retrospective rule provided that it is made by the members acting *bona fide* in the interests of the club as a whole. There is a presumption in statute law that legislation is not retrospective or retroactive, especially in relation to vested rights and obligations[64], and a similar presumption should be made in club rules so that the occasions on which a retrospective rule would be appropriate are few and far between[65].

**2-28** *Fundamental alteration* The question arises whether a rule is so important or fundamental to the objects or nature of the club that it may not be subsequently altered without dissolving the club. The answer depends on the reaction of the members to such a rule change. There are three possible scenarios:

(1) *all* members agree to the change. There is no difficulty here as a new contract of membership will have been created;

(2) the dissenting member or members all resign[66]. This leaves the remaining membership  free to operate under the rule change;

(3) the club may have to be dissolved.  Suppose the Basset Dining Club was restricted to 25 male members whose raison d'être was the enjoyment of convivial small dinners with cigars and brandy. If there was a rule change whereby the membership was open to women or the membership limit was increased to 100, the only workable or fair solution might well be to dissolve the club.

**2-29** What amounts to a fundamental rule change is a question of fact in each case. So the example given in **2-28**(3) above might not in every circumstance amount to a fundamental change. Increasing the membership of the Basset Hockey Club from 25 to 100 or the enlargement of the membership to include women players as well as men players would be unlikely to be accepted by the court as a fundamental change. In *Morgan v Driscoll* [1922] 38 TLR 251, the plaintiff was a priest who was a member of an unincorporated association known as the Secular Catholic Clergy Common Fund. Under its rules of 1861 an incapacitated member had an absolute right to an allowance from the fund. In 1918, under a rule permitting amendment, the association amended its rules to make the allowance discretionary. Mr Justice Sargent upheld the amendment as valid on the ground that it 'did not go to the foundation of the association and was not incompatible with the fundamental object of the association' which was to give financial aid to incapacitated clergymen. In *Doyle*

---

[64]    See *Wilson v First County Trust (No.2)* [2003] 3 WLR 568 HL, especially the speech of Lord Rodger of Earlsferry at 618.

[65]    See the hypothetical example given in **2-09** above.

[66]    As to the resigning member's unexpired subscription, see **4-39** below.

*v White City Stadium* [1935] 1 KB 110 CA at 121 Lord Hanworth MR concurred with this proposition and gave as an example of incompatibility an alteration of the rules whereby a society connected with boxing turned itself into a society for conducting horse-racing.

**2-30** The next question which arises is whether a duly passed alteration to a fundamental rule actually binds those members who objected to it. The answer here is in the negative if it can be reasonably considered that the parties would not have contemplated any such alteration when the member joined the club. In *Hole v Garnsey* [1930] AC 472, the case concerned the liquidation of a society registered under the Industrial and Provident Societies Act 1893 and called the Wilts and Somerset Farmers Limited. The object of the society was to dispose of agricultural and dairy produce produced by its members. The rules contained a power of amendment (Rule 64) and a duly passed amendment required the members to take additional shares. The House of Lords held that the amended rule was not effective against members who had not assented to it. Lord Tomlin in his speech stated[67]:

> Does a power enabling a majority[68] to amend the rules justify as against a dissenting member any alteration whatever, where, as here, neither by the statute[69] nor by the rules themselves is any one rule expressed to be more fundamental and unalterable than any other?

> The answer in my judgement must be in the negative. In construing such a power as this, it must, I think, be confined to such amendments as can be reasonably considered to have been within the contemplation of the parties when the contract was made, having regard to the nature and circumstances of the contract. I do not base this conclusion upon any narrow construction of the word 'amend' in Rule 64, but upon a broad general principle applicable to all such powers.

> If no such principle existed I see no reason why a dairy society in Wiltshire should not by the means of the exercise of [an amending] power find itself converted into a boot manufacturing society in Leicester with an obligation on the members to contribute funds to the new enterprise.

**2-31** But against this principle it should be remembered that, as Lord Sumner remarked in the case of *Hole v Garnsey*[70], the courts have gone far to support the autonomy of social clubs and their power to affect members by rules and regulations, passed regularly and in good faith.

---

[67]     At 500.
[68]     In this instance a three-fourths majority.
[69]     In this instance the Industrial and Provident Societies Act 1893.
[70]     At p 491.

A striking example of this is the case of *Thelluson v Viscount Valentia* [1907] 2 Ch 1 CA. The Hurlingham Club was formed in 1868 with a power to amend the rules. Rule 2 read: 'The club is instituted for the purpose of providing a ground for pigeon-shooting, polo, and other sports'. From inception pigeon-shooting was carried on at the club, prizes being given and competitions arranged by the committee. Polo and other sports had been carried on for a shorter period. The membership itself was divided into shooting and non-shooting members. In 1905 the majority of members duly passed a resolution discontinuing the sport of pigeon-shooting at the club, and a minority of members brought an action against the committee for a declaration that the resolution was null and void. The action failed because no particular sport was fundamental to the existence of the club, it being successfully argued by the club that its fundamental purpose was the association of its members.

**2-32** But can a person remain a member of a club if he had in no way accepted a rule change which fundamentally altered the terms of his contract of membership? Let us take Lord Hanworth's example of a boxing club which by a duly passed amendment of the rules turned itself into a horse-racing society. Leaving aside the question of dissolution,[71] we consider that the answer lies in the member's election. He can either elect to resign or he can elect to remain a member[72]. If he chooses the latter course, he will have irrevocably acquiesced in the rule change, which will thus become binding on him. Payment of his next subscription would be conclusive evidence of his election to remain a member. What a member cannot do is to remain a member and simply assert that he was not bound by the fundamental rule change which he disagreed with.

**2-33** Subject to the fundamental-alteration point referred to in **2-28** above, once a rule has been validly amended or acquiesced in, it is binding on all the members, old and new, whether or not they voted against the amendment or took no part in the voting[73]. The fact that a duly passed alteration of the rules has not come to the member's attention or that he had received no actual notice of the alteration does not affect the validity of the rule[74].

---

71      See **2-28** above.
72      *Farnworth Finance Facilities v Attryde* [1970] 1 WLR 1053 CA at 1059D (Lord Denning MR).
73      See *Burke v Amalgamated Society of Dyers* [1906] 2 KB 583 per Lawrence LJ at 591.
74      See *Doyle v White City Stadium* [1935] 1 KB 110 CA at 122 and 134. However, giving proper notice of the general meeting, at which the rule alteration is to be considered, is essential: see **6-08** below.

**2-34** *Amendment procedure*    It is good practice to state in the power to amend that any resolution to amend the rules shall either be the subject of a special meeting called specifically for that purpose or, if raised at the annual general meeting, notice in writing of the proposed resolution is to be given by the member at least 14 days prior to the holding of the AGM. It is to be noted that a rule which stipulates that an annual general meeting is to be held 'for general purposes' does not encompass a power to alter or amend the rules of the club[75]. It is also good practice to state in the power to amend that the resolution to amend the rules shall be carried by substantially more than a simple majority of the members present and entitled to vote at the meeting, say by a three-quarters or two-thirds majority[76]. If there is no such stipulation in the rules, it is considered that the resolution will be capable of being passed on a simple majority[77], and this is perceived to be unsuitable because the rules should not be altered lightly and a substantial majority demonstrates that the amendment commands proper support in the club.

**2-35**    Since 1902[78] any club which supplies intoxicating liquor to its members or their guests has been required to register under the Licensing Acts and in each case the club has had to state the mode of altering its rules, so that the power to amend the rules is now a commonplace feature of club rules. Nevertheless, since 1961 the Licensing Acts have given statutory power to clubs to amend their rules in certain respects where no express power existed before[79]. There is no such requirement under the Licensing Act 2003.

## 2-36    Literary and scientific institutions

In institutions established under the Literary and Scientific Institutions Act 1854[80] the members have a statutory right to alter, extend or abridge their rules in relation to the purpose or purposes for which the institution was established[81] but if two-fifths of the members consider the alteration injurious to the institution, they may apply

---

[75]      See *Harrington v Sendall* [1903] 1 Ch 921 at 926.
[76]      For example, s. 4(2) of the Credit Unions Act 1979 stipulates that the rules of a credit union may not be amended except by a resolution passed by not less than two-thirds of the members present at a special meeting.
[77]      This point is not free from doubt: see **6-30** below.
[78]      See s. 24 of the Licensing Act 1902.
[79]      See para 4 of Sch. 8 of the Licensing Act 1961, now superseded by s. 191 of the Licensing Act 1964.
[80]      See **1-46** for the categories of institution to which this Act applies.
[81]      S. 27 of the Act of 1854.

within three months of the alteration being made to the Department of Trade and Industry which has power to conduct an inquiry and prevent the alteration if it considers it to be injurious to the institution[82]. This statutory provision would appear to override any contrary provision contained in the club's rules.

## 2-37  Registered clubs

Clubs which are registered under one of the three Acts are required by the relevant statute to make provision in their rules for the manner of 'making, altering or rescinding of rules'[83]. No amendment of the rules will be valid until it has been registered with the Financial Services Authority[84]. Any alteration of the rules, however, must not be incompatible with the fundamental objects of the club.

## 2-38  Incorporated members' clubs

The company has the ability to alter or delete any of its articles of association at any time by special resolution[85] and the company cannot deprive itself of this power by a statement to this effect in the articles[86]. If the club rules are set out in the articles one way of making the rules less susceptible to alteration is to ensure that the objects clause in the memorandum of association is carefully, even tightly, drawn. As with the articles, the memorandum may be altered by special resolution[87] but, unlike the articles, there is a built-in procedure for objecting to these alterations by making an application to the court[88]. Any alteration of the articles must be compatible with the objects expressed in the memorandum. Thus in *Re Cyclists' Touring Club* [1907] 1 Ch

---

[82]     S. 28 of the Act of 1854.

[83]     Friendly Societies Act 1974, Sch. 2, para 4; Industrial and Provident Societies Act 1965, Sch. 1, para 5; and Shop Clubs Act 1902, Sch. para iii.

[84]     S. 10(1) of the Industrial and Provident Societies Act 1965; s. 12(3) of the Friendly and Industrial and Provident Societies Act 1968; and s. 18(1) of the Friendly Societies Act 1974. Under the first-mentioned Act a member has to give his prior consent in writing if the rules are amended to require him to take or subscribe for further shares: s. 14(2).

[85]     Companies Act 1985, s. 9.

[86]     *Walker v London Tramways Co* [1879] 12 Ch D 705.

[87]     Companies Act 1985, s. 4 (as substituted by the Companies Act 1989, s. 110(2)).

[88]     Companies Act 1985, ss. 5, 6. It should be noted that under the White Paper 2002 (Modernising Company Law, Cm 5553) it is proposed that new companies will not have a memorandum of association but will be under a duty to give similar information to Registrar of Companies. This information would be alterable by special resolution but would allow companies to entrench specific provisions by imposing a higher hurdle than a 75% majority, the entrenching provision itself only being alterable by unanimous member agreement.

269 the club was registered under section 23 of the Companies Act 1867 as an association not for profit and its object was to promote, assist and protect cyclists. A majority of the members resolved to change the name of the club to The Touring Club and to include among the persons to be assisted all tourists, including motorists. The court held that the proposed alteration was not possible since one of the stated objects of the club was to protect cyclists against motorists.

**2-39**   If, as is now usual, the club's rules were set out in a separate rule book pursuant to one of the articles, a question might arise as to what would happen if the rule book contained no power to alter the rules. It is submitted that the right answer would be for the company to issue a new set of rules pursuant to the power contained in the articles, this time making sure that the rules did contain an express power to alter the club rules.

## 2-40   Proprietary clubs

If a proprietor is running a members' club, it is important for him to insert in the club's rules a well-expressed power to amend the rules because this avoids any argument as to precisely what powers of amendment the club and he respectively have at their disposal. The scope of the amending rule depends on the level of control he has chosen to exercise over the club. Many proprietors retain the sole right to amend the rules. A proprietor is entitled to and usually does offer membership on an annual basis so that on renewal he has the opportunity of amending the rules more to his liking since any contract he makes will be with each individual member, who is free to choose whether to accept or reject the offer of a new contract. It is considered, however, that the proprietor could not have different rules for members of the same class since this would not be consistent with the fourth criterion (the need for fair rules) and the sixth criterion (the need for collegiality) referred to in 1-01 above.

# Chapter 3

## DISSOLUTION OF A CLUB

### 1.  INTRODUCTION

**3-01**  It is a matter of concern that many clubs do not have adequate rules when it comes to dissolution of the club; especially is this so in unincorporated members' clubs. One does not need to look far for the reason, however. The rules are drafted at the beginning of the club's life when dissolution is not on the agenda. Nobody has thoughts of dissolution and the topic is often dismissed as irrelevant. But the fact of the matter is that proper provision in the rules dealing with dissolution is both practical and sensible and will avoid a potentially acrimonious or disastrous end to the club's life.

**3-02**  At the outset the rule makers need to ask themselves not only what problems they might envisage on the forced demise of the club on the grounds, say, of lack of money or lack of members but what outcome they would desire if the club was dissolved when fully solvent and was in possession or ownership of valuable property or assets. Express rules dealing with the event of dissolution is a far better solution than letting the general law of the land provide the answer in the absence of express rules. For example, in the case of *Abbatt v Treasury Solicitor* [1969] 1 WLR 561 and 1575 CA, already referred to in **2-26** above, the trustees of the new club contracted in 1960 to sell part of the land 'inherited' from the old club in 1954 for the sum of £300. The purchaser raised a query as to title. Who owned this land? It had belonged to the members of the old club but that club no longer existed. Did the members of the new club own it? No, said the judge, it belonged to the members of the old club who were members at the date of dissolution in 1954. Yes, said the appeal court, overruling the judge. The case involved four separate parties, namely, the trustees of the new club, the trustees of the old club, a representative of the members of the old club and the treasury solicitor, and outings in three different courts[1]. One of the options open to the court was to hold that the Crown owned the land as *bona vacantia*[2], so that no member either of the old club or the new club owned the land, this being a worst-case scenario. The case vividly demonstrates the need for a proper rule on dissolution in every set of club rules[3].

## 2.    DISSOLUTION OF MEMBERS' CLUBS

### 3-03   Unincorporated members' clubs

In the ordinary way the members of the club will need to pass a resolution to dissolve the club. It is common to stipulate in the rules that a resolution to dissolve the club may be passed, and only passed, at a general meeting specially convened to consider the resolution to dissolve and that a two-thirds or three-fourths majority of those present at the meeting and entitled to vote will be required before the resolution is carried. It is also usual practice to require a specified number of members to sign the requisition for this special meeting, and sometimes this is put at a higher figure than required for a requisition to consider business other than the dissolution of the club. If the club has a registration certificate, however, the rules must fix a number of requisitionists which does not exceed 30 nor more than one-fifth of the total number of members entitled to attend and vote at a general meeting (whichever is the less)[4]. There will be no such restriction on numbers under the Licensing Act 2003.

**3-04**   In *Re William Denby & Sons Ltd Sickness and Benevolent Fund* [1973] 1 WLR 973 was a case concerning an unregistered friendly society but what was said in that case would equally apply to an unincorporated members' club. Mr Justice Brightman said there were four situations where the society could be regarded as dissolved so as to render the unspent assets distributable in some direction[5]. They were:

---

[1]      I.e. proceedings in the Andover County Court, the High Court of Justice and the Court of Appeal.
[2]      See the headnote at 1575F. *In re Trusts of the Brighton Cycling and Angling Club* (1953) *The Times*, 29 April CA: the assets of a club which had ceased to exist were declared *bona vacantia* (i.e. ownerless goods) to which the Crown was entitled.
[3]      Another good example of the need for dissolution rules is the case of *In re Sick and Funeral Society of St John's Sunday School, Golcar* [1973] 1 Ch 51.
[4]      Licensing Act 1964, Sch. 7, para 2(3).
[5]      For ownership rights of a member and distribution on dissolution, see CHAPTER **8** below.

(1) the occurrence of an event upon the happening of which the rules prescribe dissolution[6];
(2) where all the members agree;
(3) where the court orders dissolution in the exercise of its inherent jurisdiction[7];
(4) where the substratum upon which the society was founded has gone[8].

**3-05** Mere, or even a long period of, inactivity on the part of the members of the club does not mean that the club is defunct or dissolved[9]. But inactivity coupled with other circumstances may demonstrate that all concerned regard the club as having ceased to have any purpose or function, and so no longer existing. Short inactivity coupled with strong circumstances or long inactivity coupled with weaker circumstances may equally suffice to draw the inference of non-existence. In all cases the question is whether, putting all the facts together, they carry sufficient conviction that the club is at an end and not merely dormant[10].

**3-06** It is becoming increasingly common for the rules to state that in the event of a dissolution of the club the surplus assets (that is, the assets remaining after all the club's debts and liabilities have been met) should not be distributed to the members, which otherwise would be their entitlement[11], but will be transferred or given to some club or other organisation having the same or similar objects as the dissolving club. This is a very effective remedy against carpet-bagging members who simply wish to dissolve the club for mercenary reasons[12],

---

[6]     *In re Printers and Transferrers Amalgamated Trades Protection Society* [1899] 2 Ch 184.
[7]     *In re Lead Co's Workman's Fund Society* [1904] 2 Ch 196; *Blake v Smither* [1906] 22 TLR 698; *Re Witney Town Football and Social Club* [1994] 2 BCLC 487 at 491f. The court here means the High Court of Justice as the county courts, being created by statute, have no inherent jurisdiction.
[8]     *In re Customs & Excise Officers' Mutual Guarantee Fund* [1917] 2Ch 18 (guarantee fund otiose because officers' fidelity bonds no longer required); *Feeny and Shannon v MacManus* [1937] IR 23 (dining club's premises destroyed in the Irish uprising of 1916); *In re St Andrews Allotments Association* [1969] 1 WLR 229 (sale of the land containing the allotments). Cf. *Re Stamford Working Men's Club* (1952) *The Times,* 24 October and (1953) *The Times,* 29 April CA.
[9]     *In re GKN Bolts & Nuts Ltd Sports and Social Club* [1982] 1 WLR 774 at 779G.
[10]    Ibid. at 780G.
[11]    See **8-03** below.
[12]    This became a particular concern of many golf clubs in the 1980s, at a time when there was a considerable increase in the value of club land and premises, as a result of which many clubs adopted a *cy-près* type of clause. The cy-*près* doctrine in the law of charities obtains where the charitable trust is impossible or impracticable to carry out and the court applies the charitable property as nearly as possible resembling the original trust: *Snell's Equity* (31st edn, 2004) at para 21-29.

although it has to be said that no rule can be entrenched immutably[13].
Further, any lottery funding by the National Lottery is now contingent
on the club having a *cy-près* type of dissolution clause in its rules.

### 3-07  Literary and scientific institutions

The dissolution of this type of club is governed by section 29 of the
Literary and Scientific Institutions Act 1854 and is carried out by a
resolution of three-fifths of its membership. In the event of any dispute
on dissolution concerning the adjustment of its affairs, the matter
must be referred to the local county court for the dispute to be resolved.

### 3-08  Working men's clubs

The dissolution of this type of club is governed by section 93 of the
Friendly Societies Act 1974 and can be carried out in one of the
following ways:
(1) upon the happening of any event declared by the rules to be the
    determination of the club (or branch);
(2) by the consent of three-quarters of the members of the club (or
    branch) testified by their signatures to the instrument of
    dissolution[14] and, in the case of a branch, with the consent of the
    central body of that branch or in accordance with the rules of that
    central body;
(3) by an award of dissolution made by the Financial Services
    Authority under section 95 after its investigation of the affairs of
    the club.

**3-09**   In addition, the Financial Services Authority can apply to the
court under section 87 of the Act of 1974 for a compulsory winding-
up order of the club if it receives a report on the affairs of the club
from an inspector appointed by him and it appears to him it is in the
interests of the members of the club or of the public that the club
should be wound up.

---

[13]      Registering the club as a charity would entrench the *cy-près* rule, but this may not be
a viable or desirable option.
[14]      The instrument has to comply with the provisions of s. 94 of the Act of 1974.

## 3-10   IPSA clubs

The dissolution of this type of club is governed by sections 55 (as amended[15]) and 56 of the Industrial and Provident Societies Act 1965 and can be carried out in one of the following ways:

(1)  in the same manner as a company registered under the Companies Acts: see **3-13** below;

(2)  by the consent of not less than three-fourths of the members of the club testified by their signatures to the instrument of dissolution[16];

(3)  by an order of the court on a petition presented to the court by the Financial Services Authority on the ground that the club is not a bona fide co-operative society and/or being conducted for the benefit of the community, and that it would be in the interests of investors or depositors or any other person that the club should be wound up.

It is considered, by analogy with company law, that a creditor or member of the club can also petition for the winding up of the club[17].

**3-11**   In addition, the Financial Services Authority has power to cancel the registration of the club on various grounds under section 16 of the Act of 1965, the most important ones of which are, in relation to clubs, where the membership has fallen below seven members and where the club has ceased to exist[18].

## 3-12   Shop clubs

By paragraph xi of the Schedule to the Shop Clubs Act 1902 the rules of a shop club must contain a dissolution rule which states that there can be a voluntary dissolution of the club by consent of not less than five-sixths in value of the persons contributing to the funds of the club[19] and of every person for the time being entitled to benefit from the funds of the club (unless their claims be first satisfied or adequately provided

---

[15]    By the Insolvency Act 1986, s. 439 (2), Sch.14: the words 'Insolvency Act 1986' were substituted for the words 'Companies Act 1948'.

[16]    The instrument has to comply with the provisions of s. 58 of the Act of 1965.

[17]    See *In re Surrey Garden Village Trust Ltd* [1965] 1 WLR 974 (where certain members unsuccessfully petitioned for the winding up of an industrial and provident society; the petition was dismissed, not on the ground that the members had no standing to bring the petition, but on the ground that the petition was opposed by a considerable number of other members and was oppressive and an abuse of process).

[18]    As to whether a club has ceased to exist, see **3-05** above.

[19]    This would include the employer as contributor.

for). The court will also have inherent jurisdiction to dissolve the club[20].

## 3-13   Incorporated members' clubs

The dissolution of such a club is carried into effect by winding up the company. A winding up is either voluntary or compulsory.

**3-14** *Voluntary*   There are two species of voluntary winding up, namely, members' voluntary and creditors' voluntary. In either case the members in general meeting must pass a resolution for voluntary winding up[21]. A members' voluntary winding up can only occur if the club is solvent, and this involves a statutory declaration of solvency that the directors have made a full enquiry into the company's affairs and have formed the opinion that the company will be able to pay its debts in full together with interest[22]. A creditors' voluntary winding up comes about because the directors are unable to make the declaration of solvency[23].

**3-15** *Compulsory*   The court has jurisdiction to wind up a company compulsorily on the seven grounds set out in section 122 of the Insolvency Act 1986 but the two grounds which are most likely to affect a club are:
(1) the company is unable to pay its debts[24];
(2) the court is of the opinion that it is just and equitable that the company should be wound up[25].

An application for a compulsory winding-up order is by a petition presented to the court by the company or its directors or by a creditor or, in more limited circumstances, by a contributory (a member of the company)[26].

---

[20]     See **3-04**(3) above.
[21]     Insolvency Act 1986, s. 85(1).
[22]     Ibid. s. 89(1).
[23]     Ibid. s. 90.
[24]     Ibid. s. 122(1)(f). The definition of inability to pay debts is set out in s. 123: either the club cannot pay its debts as they fall due or the value of the club's assets is less than its liabilities (including contingent and prospective liabilities).
[25]     Ibid. s. 122(1)(g).
[26]     Ibid. s. 124.

## 3. DISSOLUTION OF PROPRIETARY CLUBS

**3-16** It is not strictly necessary for the rules of a proprietary club to deal with the question of dissolution of the club because of the nature of the contractual relationship between the proprietor and the club member. On the expiry of the period of the subscription, which no doubt will be the same date for all the members, the proprietor can simply say that he has decided to close down the club and the member will have no say in the matter. If the proprietor dissolves the club before the expiry of the period of the subscription, the individual member will have a claim in damages against the proprietor for the unexpired period of the subscription and for the loss of amenities during this period[27], unless the rules expressly cater for this contingency. On the other hand, it is considered good practice for a proprietor to state in the club rules the situation as to dissolution of the club since this avoids argument if or when dissolution occurs.

## 4. MEMBERS' LIABILITY ON DISSOLUTION

### 3-17 Unincorporated members' clubs

The member's liability, unless the rules otherwise provide, will be limited to the payment of his entrance fee (if any) and to his subscriptions[28]. As far as contracts entered into by the club are concerned, the member's liability will depend on the general law of agency[29].

### 3-18 Working men's clubs

Although the Friendly Societies Act 1974 is silent on the point, it is considered that on dissolution the member's liability will be restricted to his subscriptions and that, as far as contracts entered into by the club are concerned, his liability will depend on the general law of agency[30]. It is to be noted, however, that under section 87(3) of the said Act the Financial Services Authority can direct the members or

---

[27]  *Re Curzon Syndicate Ltd* [1920] 149 LT Jo. 232. See **4-38** below for a further discussion of this case.

[28]  *Wise v Perpetual Trustee Co* [1903] AC 139 PC at 149: see **1-10** above.

[29]  See further **12-03** below.

[30]  See 19(1) *Halsbury's Laws of England* (4th edn, 1995 re-issue) para 198. See further **12-03** below.

officers of the club to pay some or all of the expenses of the inspector's report referred to in paragraph 3-09 above.

### 3-19   IPSA clubs

By section 57 of the Act of 1965, where the club is wound up as if it were a company, the liability of a past or present member to contribute to the payment of the club's debts and liabilities or the expenses of winding up shall be as follows:

(1) a person who ceased to be a member not less than one year before the beginning of the winding up is not liable to contribute anything[31];

(2) a person is not liable to contribute anything in respect of a debt or liability after he ceased to be a member;

(3) a non-member (i.e. a past member) is not liable to contribute anything unless it appears to the court that the contributions of the existing members are insufficient to satisfy the just demands on the club;

(4) no contribution shall be required from any person exceeding the amount (if any) unpaid on shares in respect of which he is liable as a past or present member;

(5) where a withdrawable share has been withdrawn, a person is taken to have ceased to be a member in respect of that share as from the date of the notice or application for withdrawal.

### 3-20   Shop clubs

The schedule to the Act of 1902 is silent on this point and we consider that, unless the rules otherwise provide, the liability of any member will be limited to his contribution to the funds of the club and, generally speaking, the member will be in the same position as a member of an unincorporated club.

### 3-21   Incorporated members' clubs

The memorandum of association of the company, whether limited by shares or guarantee, must state that the liability of its members is limited[32].

---

[31]     The liability of a member does not cease on his death so that his estate will take over his liability: see *In re United Service Share Purchase Society Ltd* [1909] 2 Ch 526.
[32]     Companies Act 1985, s. 2(3).

**3-22**   Where the company is limited by shares, the members of the company are not personally entitled to the benefits of, or liable for the burdens arising from, the trading of the company. Their rights are confined to receiving from the company their share of the profits or, after a winding up, of the surplus assets and their liabilities are confined to the amounts due from them to the company in respect of unpaid shares[33]. Creditors therefore know that they cannot look to the whole property of the individual members to pay them but are restricted to the property of the company[34]. Section 74 of the Insolvency Act 1986 regulates the member's liability on the winding up of the company[35]. The maximum liability of present and past members is limited to the amount unpaid on the shares[36].

**3-23**   Where the company is limited by guarantee, the memorandum of association must state, not only that the member's liability is limited, but also that each member 'undertakes to contribute to the assets of the company if it should be wound up while he is a member, or within one year after he ceases to be a member, for payment of debts and liabilities of the company contracted before he ceases to be a member'[37]. The limit of liability is the amount of the guarantee[38]. Past guarantors are only liable if the current guarantees do not meet the company's debts[39].

## 3-24   Proprietary clubs

The proprietor is solely responsible for the club's debts. The member of the club will have no liability to the club's creditors unless by a quite separate contract made between him and the creditor he expressly assumes liability, for instance, by giving a guarantee in respect of the club's indebtedness to the club's bankers.

---

[33]   *Gore-Browne on Companies* (50th edn, 2004) para 7[1].
[34]   Ibid. para 7[1].
[35]   The members are obliged to 'contribute' to the company's assets, hence the members are known as contributories.
[36]   Insolvency Act 1986, s. 74(2)–(d).
[37]   Companies Act 1985, s. 2(3) and (4).
[38]   See **1-34** above.
[39]   Insolvency Act 1986, s. 74(2)(a)–(c).

# 5.    IMPACT OF INSOLVENCY LEGISLATION

### 3-25    Unincorporated members' clubs

The Insolvency Act 1986 raises issues in relation to the affairs of an unincorporated members' club which need to be addressed. Sections 220 and 221 of the Insolvency Act 1986 empower the court to wind up compulsorily an 'unregistered company' which includes 'any association'.  Under this régime the association can only be wound up if it is dissolved or has ceased to carry on business, or is unable to pay its debts, or the court is of the opinion that it would be just and equitable to wind up the association. The question arises whether an unincorporated members' club is caught by these provisions. If it is, section 226 makes any contributory (i.e. the club member) liable to pay or contribute to the payment of any debt or liability of the club, the very antithesis of limited liability and of course way beyond the member's entrance fee and annual subscriptions. Under previous but similar legislation the courts have held that an unincorporated members' club cannot be wound up as an unregistered company because the reference to the 'principal place of business' of the unregistered company demonstrated that the winding-up régime had no applicability to any association which was not engaged in trade or commerce and which was not conducted for gain[40] .

**3-26**    An attempt by the creditors was made in *Re Witney Town Football Club and Social Club* [1994] BCLC 487 to wind up the club under section 221 on the ground that it was unable to pay its debts. This was a club of *professional* footballers founded in 1885 and it owned property of considerable value. It owed debts of about £30,000 to five creditors. Rule 2 of its rules stated: 'The club shall exist solely for the purpose of professional Association Football. The club will also provide various social amenities for its members'. The members numbered some 500 whose liability under the rules was restricted to their subscriptions. Rule 17 of its rules stated that 'upon dissolution of the club, all net assets shall be devoted to Association Football and not distributed between the members'. On appeal from the dismissal of the winding up petition, Mr Justice Morritt held that whether or not a club was 'an association' within the meaning of section 220 depended on the true construction of the rules rather than the size and activity of the club[41] . He decided that its rules were within the

---

[40]     *Re St James Club* [1852] 2 De GM & G 383; *Re Bristol Athenaeum* [1890] 43 Ch D 236; *Re Russell Institution* [1898] 2 Ch 72 at 79.
[41]     So that the fact the footballers were professional was of no consequence.

category of a normal club and as such the club was outside the detailed statutory winding up provisions. The judge added the comment that the club could still be wound up by the High Court under its inherent jurisdiction[42]. This is of course quite a different matter from being wound up under the provisions of the Insolvency Act 1986 where a liquidator would be appointed, one of whose duties would be to receive proofs of debt from unsecured creditors.

## 3-27   Working men's clubs and shop clubs

Their position is the same as an unincorporated club.

## 3-28   IPSA clubs

It would seem by the insertion of the reference to the Insolvency Act 1986 in section 55(a) of the Industrial and Provident Societies Act 1965 that the legislature was contemplating that if the club was wound up under section 55 it would be subject to the statutory insolvency régime, subject to the modification that any reference to the Registrar of Companies in the Insolvency Act 1986 shall mean the Financial Services Authority[43]. However, since IPSA clubs do not have directors, but officers only, it is plain that those parts of the Insolvency Act 1986 dealing with the liability of directors cannot apply to IPSA clubs. It is to be noted, however, that the misfeasance and the fraudulent trading (but not the wrongful trading) referred to in the next paragraph can be committed by an officer of the 'company' (i.e. the club) or by a person taking part in the management of the 'company'. This potential liability would thus not affect the ordinary club member.

## 3-29   Incorporated members' clubs

Leaving aside the limited liability of the members of the company (i.e. the ordinary members of the club), which is dealt with in 3-21 to 3-23 above, the position of the club member as a company director

---

[42]      At p 491. The county court cannot wind up a club because it has no inherent jurisdiction. And see *In re William Denby & Sons Ltd Sick and Benevolent Fund* [1971] 1 WLR 973 at **3-04** above.

[43]      S. 55(a)(i) of the Industrial and Provident Societies Act 1965. In fact the Insolvency Act 1986 makes no reference to the Registrar of Companies. The Companies Acts 1948 and 1985 do refer to such a registrar and Parliament must have overlooked this point when substituting the Insolvency Act 1986 for the Companies Act 1948 in s. 55(a). What Parliament was (sensibly) trying to do was to swap the Registrar of Friendly Societies for the Registrar of Companies. In any event, the Financial Services Authority has now taken over the functions of the Registrar of Friendly Societies.

should be borne in mind. In the course of winding up a company certain provisions of the Insolvency Act 1986 impose personal liability on a director where misfeasance[44] or fraudulent trading[45] or wrongful trading[46] can be established. Further, there is also the question of disqualifying a director under section 6 of the Company Directors Disqualification Act 1986 if in an insolvent liquidation he is found to be 'unfit' to be a director[47]. Unfitness here can mean incompetence if (a) the director caused the company to trade whilst insolvent *and* (b) there was no reasonable prospect of meeting creditors' claims[48]. Although in clubs a miscreant director and others who are caught by these provisions will be a shareholder or member of the company, it is their management, or lack of it, which gives rise to liability, not their membership of the company. Thus the ordinary club member will fall outside the ambit of all these provisions.

### 3-30   Voidable preference

Where the club is incorporated and is insolvent or approaching insolvency, a point to take into consideration is the question of payment of outstanding monies to creditors, say the repayment of loans made to the club. Suppose that 10 people have each lent £1,000 to the club; nothing is said about the date of repayment, so that the loans are repayable on demand. One lender now demands the return of his loan. Can the club do this lawfully without notifying the other lenders or obtaining their consent? The answer is in the affirmative as a matter of contract law. But the moment an incorporated members' club is insolvent or approaching insolvency, the matter can take on a new dimension. By section 239 of the Insolvency Act 1986 if the club were to give a preference to a creditor which puts him into a better financial position than he otherwise would have been in the event of an insolvent liquidation, the court has power to order the creditor to repay monies to the club[49]. Such a preference must take place within a period of six months ending with the onset of insolvency (i.e. the date of the presentation of the petition for an administration order or the date of the commencement of winding up)[50]. There is, however,

---

[44]    Insolvency Act 1986, s. 212.
[45]    Ibid. s. 213.
[46]    Ibid. s. 214. In this instance the remedy only applies to *insolvent* liquidations.
[47]    For criminal liability and disqualification, see **15-19** below.
[48]    *Secretary of State for Trade and Industry v Creegan* [2002] 1 BCLC 99 CA. In other words, merely trading insolvently is not enough on its own.
[49]    Insolvency Act 1986, s. 241(d).
[50]    Ibid. s. 240(1)(b) and 3(b).

the complicating factor that a preference cannot be impugned unless there was a desire by the club to improve the creditor's position in an insolvent liquidation[51], not simply a desire to confer a benefit on the creditor[52]. Accordingly, assuming the club's financial position was a parlous one, for it to repay one creditor in full without the consent of, or at least without informing, the other creditors might lead to serious repercussions for the club and/or its directors.

## 3-31 Administration order

There should also be mentioned the possibility of an administration order being made under the Insolvency Act 1986. This process was devised in 1986 to help companies facing insolvency by giving them an opportunity to obtain an administration order with a view to entering into a voluntary arrangement with its creditors or, alternatively, to allow a more advantageous realisation of assets than would be effected on a winding up. It is therefore a half-way house on the road to liquidation. It is interesting to see that this process is available to 'unregistered companies', which would include an unincorporated association[53].

## 3-32 Proprietary clubs

If the proprietor is a company, the provisions of the Insolvency Act 1986, which are referred to in paragraph 3-29 above, will apply to the directors of this company, not to the club's officers. The liquidator of the proprietor company, however, will be under a statutory duty to get in, realise and distribute the company's assets to the company's creditors[54], so that the members of the club might find themselves with a new proprietor not to their liking, or with no club at all if the liquidator were to sell the club premises with vacant possession. Any claim for damages against the company in respect of the unexpired portion of the subscription period will form the subject matter of a proof of debt lodged by the member as an unsecured creditor.

---

[51]  Insolvency Act 1986, s. 239(5).
[52]  *Re M C Bacon* [1991] Ch 127.
[53]  *In re Salvage Association* [2004] 1 WLR 174 at 179C (Blackburne J) (where the general committee of the association, unregistered but incorporated by royal charter, successfully petitioned the court for an administration order).
[54]  Insolvency Act 1986, s. 143(1).

**3-33** If the proprietor is an individual person and he becomes bankrupt, his assets will, generally speaking, automatically vest in his trustee in bankruptcy[55] who, like the liquidator, will take steps to realise any asset for the benefit of the bankrupt's creditors[56], with the same possible results as are mentioned in **3-32** above.

---

[55]  Insolvency Act 1986, s. 306.
[56]  Ibid. s. 324(1).

# PART 2

# Internal relationships: the club and its members

# Chapter 4

## ADMISSION TO MEMBERSHIP

## 1.   FORMAL PROCESS

**4-01**   A formal process of admitting members into a club is what distinguishes a club from an amorphous group of people who happen to come together for a particular occasion or event. The occasion or event may recur many times with the same people coming together but their gathering can in no wise be described as a club[1]. The process of admission could in theory be very simple. The relevant club rules could provide that the club was open to all those who supported its objects and that upon the payment of a specified sum the applicant for admission would be admitted into the club[2]. In practice a club, of whatever nature, will want to ensure as far as possible that its members are congenial to one another so that a process of selection is introduced. Thus one commonly talks about the *election* of members to a club rather than admission of members. This ability to reject those persons who are, or apparently are, unsuitable or unacceptable to join the club is an important factor in sustaining a club over a long period of time[3]. But the ability to reject is no longer an unfettered right because, as is discussed below[4], Parliament has already intervened, and may do so again, in an attempt to ensure that people are not unfairly excluded from societies or activities which they would like

---

[1]   *Stafford Borough Council v Elkenford Ltd* [1977] 1 WLR 324 CA.
[2]   See e.g. *Woodford v Smith* [1970] 1 WLR 806 (where the printed application form was entitled 'Membership Form' and stated, 'I consent to my name being included in the list of members of the Fulham and Hammersmith Ratepayers' and Residents' Association, and I undertake to pay an annual subscription of £...' ).
[3]   *Nagle v Feilden* [1966] 2 WLR 1027 CA where Lord Denning at 1032 said, 'If a man applies to join a social club and is black-balled, he has no cause of action: because the members have made no contract with him. They can do as they like'
[4]   See **4-18** below.

to join or participate in, but are unable to do so because of the discrimination exercised against them.

**4-02**  It is the normal practice in the vast majority of members' clubs for the ordinary members to be elected and, where the club holds a registration certificate, it is compulsory[5]. This can be either done by the members in general meeting or, since that is often an unwieldy procedure, more commonly done by the committee which has been elected by the members. Whichever way is chosen, the procedure should appear in the rules. There is nothing improper in a club placing a maximum number on the members it will admit to the club or laying down criteria which the candidate must fulfil, subject to exceptions under legislation appertaining to race relations[6] and, potentially, sex discrimination[7] and disability discrimination[8]. It is usual for the club to require a candidate to be proposed and seconded by members of the club but there is no requirement at law that this should be the case; the rules may permit the candidate simply to apply to the club secretary who will refer the matter to the committee or the members, as the case may be, for their decision.

**4-03**  In a proprietary club it is common for the proprietor to make the decision whether to admit the applicant without there being any election by the members. Sometimes, however, the proprietor establishes a membership committee to deal with applications for membership, in which case he might retain a power of veto in respect of any particular application or he might insist on some representation on the committee[9].

## 2.   CATEGORIES OF MEMBERSHIP

**4-04**  The majority of clubs have more than one category of member and it is important to clarify in the rules what are the rights and obligations of each category of member.

---

[5]      Licensing Act 1964, Sch. 7, para 3(1). The Licensing Act 2003, however, does not talk in terms of election but of admission: s. 62(2).

[6]      See **4-19** below.

[7]      See **4-22** below.

[8]      See **4-24** below.

[9]      See the example given in **1-42** above.

## 4-05 Ordinary members

In every club this class of member will form the vast majority of the membership since it is these members who in the ordinary course of events pay the entrance fee (if any) and the annual subscription which keeps the club afloat financially. They are often referred to in the rules as full members[10].

**4-06** It is customary for ordinary members to be annual members in the sense that their subscription is renewable on a yearly basis, but there are occasions when ordinary membership is offered for a longer term than one year. If a club wished to raise a certain sum of cash straightaway, it could offer a five-year membership whereby the member paid his five years' subscriptions forthwith at a discounted rate. There is no legal requirement that all categories of member shall be at the same subscription or for the same period of time.

**4-07** On occasion disputes arise as to whether or not somebody is a member of a club[11]. This should not present any problem in practice. The member's application is normally done on a written form provided by the club or done by written communication from the club secretary. It is commonplace, however, for these documents to be lost or misplaced. This does not matter because the best evidence of continuing membership is the demand for, and the payment of, the annual subscription. With regard to IPSA clubs, the member will be issued with a certificate recording the number of shares held and if the club is a company limited by shares, the member will be issued with a share certificate of one share (usually a £1 ordinary share). The certificate will demonstrate to the outside world that he is either a member of the registered IPSA club or the incorporated company, as the case may be, and thereby a member of the club. If the club is a company limited by guarantee, no such documentation will arise. With regard to proprietary clubs, the proprietor will be wise to issue a club membership card both on admission to the club and on renewal of the annual subscription. In the absence of such a document, the member can rely on the demand for and payment of his subscription as evidence of his continuing membership.

---

[10]  See *In Re GKN Nuts & Bolts Ltd Sports and Social Club* [1982] 1 WLR 774 at 784B.
[11]  See e.g. *Woodford v Smith* [1970] 1 WLR 806.

## 4-08   Life members

Life membership is, as its name indicates, for the member's lifetime.
It is offered on the same financial basis as the five-year membership
referred to in paragraph 4-06 above. The life member will pay all his
subscriptions in one go, discounted for the fact that the club is receiving
a large part of the money in advance of the dates it would otherwise
have become due. Life members invariably enjoy the full privileges of
membership, save that no further subscriptions will become due from
the member. Life membership does not render the member immune
from being suspended or expelled from the club, though no doubt due
consideration would be given to the fact of life membership in dealing
with the matter. A life member, like all other members, is entitled to
resign from the club. A life member who resigned or was expelled
would not be entitled to claim back any proportionate part of his life
membership fee because the whole sum was paid on an earlier date
as the consideration for being granted life membership. Care must be
taken in the drafting of the rule relating to the club's ability to offer
life membership. No further annual subscription may be demanded,
but it may be that the club would wish to reserve the right to require
all members, including life members, to pay a levy at some time in
the future to cover an unexpected item of expenditure. If so, the rules
would have to make express provision for such demand being made
of life members.

## 4-09   Honorary members

Honorary membership is usually offered to a member or non-member
of the club as a reward for past services or assistance to the club or
who by reason of his distinction or position or experience in the field
of activity in which the club operates will be an ornament to the club
or will be able to assist the club in some material way. It is common
practice for the honorary numbers to be elected by the managing
committee and their number restricted in the rules. These members
do not pay any entrance fee or subscription. They enjoy the privileges
of membership save that almost invariably they have no voting rights
at general meetings and are ineligible for election to any office within
the club. Their position should be clearly stated in the rules. Some clubs
have a category of honorary life members[12] where the member is
excused from any further subscription but is still able to participate
fully in the activities of the club.

---

[12]     Some clubs award a vice-presidency to a meritorious member instead of an
honorary life membership.

## 4-10   Junior members

It is common, especially in sporting or recreational clubs, for there to be a junior section or family section where the members are aged under 18 years. The position with regard to junior members should be carefully spelt out in the rules[13]. The following are important points to bear in mind:

(1) a minor, that is, a person under 18, is not liable for any contract save contracts for necessaries[14] so that technically the junior member will not be liable for his subscription. Because of this it is essential that the parent or sponsor of the junior member countersigns the application form for membership in the capacity of contracting party;

(2) there is no defence of minority when it comes to the law of tort[15]. If, however, a junior member through negligence or wilfulness causes damage to club property or injury to someone on club property, he will be unlikely to have the financial resources to pay compensation. Therefore, on the same application form, it is a wise move to make the parent or sponsor expressly agree to make good any damage or injury caused by the junior member. The consideration for such agreement will be the granting of junior membership;

(3) a junior member should take no part in the running of the club and therefore the rules should spell out precisely what privileges or restrictions shall apply to junior membership;

(4) it is considered good practice for a junior member on attaining his majority to apply to become an ordinary (or full) member of the club in accordance with the established procedure set out in the rules.

## 4-11   Associate members

This phrase is used in different senses:

(1) it is a form of membership which comes with fewer privileges than ordinary (or full) membership. In a few large or important clubs,

---

[13]    An example of a junior membership rule is contained in **APPENDIX 15**.

[14]    *Chitty on Contract* (29th edn, 2004) para 8-004. Necessaries are such things as relate to the person of the minor e.g. necessary food, drink, clothing, lodging and medicine. Under s. 3 of the Minors' Contracts Act 1987 the court has power to require the minor to transfer any property he has acquired under an unenforceable contract if it is just and equitable to make him do so.

the applicant may have to start his membership at this level and then progress to full membership;

(2) it is a form of reciprocal membership where the members of another club are admitted to the host club on a temporary basis because, say, the other club is shut for refurbishment or where, say, a cricket club offers associate membership for the summer months to its neighbouring football club which shuts for these summer months;

(3) it is a form of membership used by umbrella organisations where the rules of the umbrella organisation and the rules of the host club permit entry into the host club of members of other affiliated clubs, albeit with restricted privileges. Here the associate will often pay the umbrella organisation a fee in order to exercise his rights as an associate member[16];

(4) it is a term of art used by section 67 of the Licensing Act 2003. In this context a person is an associate member of a club if in accordance with the rules of that club he is admitted to its premises as being a member of another club and the other club is a recognised club, that is to say, it is a club which satisfies conditions 1 to 3 of the general conditions set out in section 62 of the Act[17].

In the light of the various uses of the phrase, 'associate member', it is important that the rules are explicit and clear on this topic. It should be added that often these members are simply referred to as associates.

## 4-12   Temporary members

There is nothing to prevent a club from having a category of temporary members but it is a category which needs to be handled with care. The club members need to be satisfied that such a category will be of benefit to the club. The category must form only an insignificant proportion of the overall membership, otherwise the club may cease to be a genuine members' club, and will jeopardize the club's registration certificate, if it has one[18]. It is a good practice for the rules

---

[15]     *Clerk and Lindsell on Torts* (18th edn, 2000) paras 4-55 to 4-59.

[16]     See by way of example the case of *Dockers' Labour Club and Institute Ltd v Race Relations Board* [1976] AC 285 in **4-20** below.

[17]     See **9-22** below for these conditions and **9-36** below for a discussion of associate members under the Licensing Act 2003.

[18]     Licensing Act 1964, Sch. 7, para 3(2). There is no equivalent provision in the Licensing Act 2003 but a surfeit of temporary members will make it very difficult for a club to comply with the condition that it must be a club established and conducted in good faith as a club: s. 62(4) of this Act.

to state that any temporary member shall be admitted only on the authority of, say, two members of the managing committee and that the temporary membership will only last for a limited period, say, 14 days. The rule can limit temporary membership to a particular occasion. Suppose the Basset Chess Club held an annual chess tournament in Basset which lasted for four days and attracted Grandmasters and many chess devotees; the rules or bye-laws could cater specifically for the admission of persons attending this event as temporary members for the week in which the tournament was held. The admission of temporary members is subject to the two-day rule[19]. It should be added that if temporary members are admitted, they are entitled to enjoy all the facilities of the club, so that it would be wrong to exclude them from, say, participating in a club raffle or from a particular bar.

### 4-13 Affiliates

This term has been in the past and still is used as a synonym for a member of a society or an associate[20]. This is a recipe for confusion in club law. In this context it is best used as denoting a connection between the club and/or its members and another, larger group of clubs, all of which have a common interest or aims, and which does not necessarily involve the affiliates in any paying membership of the larger group. An example of affiliation used in this context is set out in Appendix 13 in the rules of the Bassetshire Hockey Umpires Association. See also footnote 155 in CHAPTER 11 for another example of affiliation in club law.

## 3. RESTRICTIONS ON RIGHT TO REJECT APPLICATIONS FOR MEMBERSHIP

**4-14** By its very nature a club discriminates in its admission procedure. As described in **4-01** above, the members of a club admit to membership those whom they find congenial by reason of mutual interests, sporting ability, adherence to a political persuasion or whatever. There is nothing to prevent the members of a club excluding applicants for membership for reasons which to an outside observer may seem completely unreasonable, but what they cannot do is exclude for reasons which Parliament has declared to be unlawful.

---

[19] Licensing Act 1964, s. 41(1)(a); Licensing Act 2003, s. 62(2).
[20] See the Oxford Shorter English Dictionary.

Almost without exception social and sporting clubs require a proposer and a seconder; some insist on the applicant providing support from several members. Such requirements are unexceptional and, as has been noted in **2-06** above, an applicant cannot object to the criteria for selection before he has been elected. The introduction of the Community Amateur Sports Club ('CASC')[21] has complicated the issue in that a club which applies to register as a CASC, or to receive lottery funding, must make its application procedure open to the whole community, unless it has good reason to believe that the person in question would be disruptive or prejudicial to the good conduct of the club[22].

## 4-15   Lawful discrimination

There is no single test which one can apply to distinguish lawful discrimination from unlawful discrimination. It is possible only to proceed by way of examples.

## 4-16   Age limits

At present (2004) there is nothing to prevent a club discriminating against an applicant for membership on the grounds of age, or to impose restrictions on membership on the same grounds. But one point needs to be borne in mind. There has been issued a government consultation document entitled 'Equality and Diversity: Age Matters'[23] concerning the Government's intention to introduce legislation outlawing discrimination on the grounds of age in the context of employment, pursuant to European Council Directive 2000/78/EC. There is no immediate (2004) timetable for legislation, nor any plans to extend these proposals beyond the law relating to employment.

## 4-17   Lack of sports ability

It probably goes without saying that a sports club is entitled to insist on a minimum standard of ability before considering an application for membership. An applicant for playing membership of MCC cricket club is no doubt required to display a considerable standard of skill if he is to stand any chance of his application being accepted. Most

---

[21]     See **1-52** above.
[22]     This statement is taken from information provided by the Inland Revenue in 2004 on its website, *www.inlandrevenue.gov.uk/casc*.
[23]     Prepared by the Department of Trade and Industry and dated 2 July 2003.

private golf clubs, too, require an applicant for full membership either to have a recognised handicap or to be able to demonstrate a good knowledge of and ability in the game. On the other hand, a village cricket or soccer club may well not make such demands, on the basis that a place in a team can always be found for an enthusiast.

## 4-18 Unlawful discrimination

This falls into three categories: discrimination on the grounds of race, sex and disability. The relevant legislation is the Race Relations Act 1976, the Sex Discrimination Act 1975 and the Disability Discrimination Act 1995. In short, private members' clubs are exempt, so far as membership is concerned, from the provisions of the last two Acts, but not of the first one. The reason for this exemption is that such clubs do not supply goods, facilities or services to the public or to a section of the public, as will be seen below.

## 4-19 Racial discrimination

This form of discrimination was the earliest to be tackled by legislation, the first Race Relations Act being in 1965, followed by the Act of 1968 and culminating in the Act of 1976. This last-mentioned Act for the first time brought clubs into its ambit where the club comprised 25 or more members[24]. It is unlawful for a club to discriminate against a person on racial grounds when considering his application for membership or by refusing or deliberately omitting to accept his application for membership[25].

**4-20** The reason for extending the scope of the Act in 1976 was two House of Lords' decisions, namely, *Charter v Race Relations Board* [1973] AC 868 and *Dockers' Labour Club and Institute Limited v Race Relations Board* [1976] AC 285[26]. In the former case the application of a Mr Shah, an Indian, to join the East Ham Conservative Association, was rejected on the grounds of his colour. At that time it was unlawful for a person, who provides (whether or not for payment) facilities for entertainment, recreation or refreshment to the public (or to a section of the public), to discriminate against a person by refusing or deliberately omitting to provide him or her with such facilities on racial grounds[27], and this is still the case. The House of Lords, however, held

---

24    Race Relations Act 1976, s. 25(1)(a).
25    Ibid. ss. 1 and 25.
26    The case was decided on 16 October 1974.
27    Race Relations Act 1968, s. 2, now Race Relations Act 1976, s. 20.

that the Act did not apply to a club where people met on private premises and where the rules of the club genuinely provided for nomination and personal selection of its members; in other words, the club was not providing such facilities to the public or a section of the public. In the latter case, a Mr Sherrington who was coloured belonged to the Meadow Street Labour Club in Preston. In that town was another club, the Dockers' Labour Club, which operated a colour bar. Both clubs were members of the Working Men's Club and Institute Union, an umbrella organisation. Mr Sherrington, having paid his associate's fee, was entitled to enter the Dockers' Labour Club as an associate, but was requested to leave the club because of the colour bar. The House of Lords held once again that the Dockers' Labour Club fell within the private sphere and thus the Race Relations Act did not apply to its activities. (These two cases are still applicable when it comes to the question of sex and disability discrimination in clubs).

**4-21** The Act of 1976 provides an exemption where the main object of the club is to enable the benefits of club membership to be enjoyed by persons of a particular racial group which is defined otherwise than by colour[28]. This is a curious exemption. The London Welsh Rugby Club, for example, could lawfully restrict its members to Welsh persons only so long as the club was not excluding *black* Welshman. Bizarre though it may seem, the club would appear to have the right to exclude Welsh Jews or Welsh gypsies.

## 4-22 Sex discrimination

Discrimination on the grounds of sex is brought within the ambit of the Sex Discrimination Act 1975, whether it is discrimination against men[29] or against women[30], or against those who have undergone or who are undergoing or intend to undergo 'gender reassignment'[31]. It is unlawful for a person, who provides (whether or not for payment) facilities for entertainment or recreation or refreshment to the public or to a section of the public, to discriminate against a man or woman by refusing or deliberately omitting to provide him or her with such facilities on the grounds of their sex, or to provide such facilities on terms less favourable than would have applied to persons of the opposite sex[32]. Because of the *Charter* and the *Dockers' Labour Club*

---

[28]     Race Relations Act 1976, s. 26.
[29]     Sex Discrimination Act 1975, s. 2.
[30]     Ibid. s. 1.
[31]     Ibid. s. 2A, inserted by Sex Discrimination (Gender Reassignment) Regulations 1999 (SI 1999/1102), and see Gender Recognition Act 2004, s. 9.
[32]     Sex Discrimination Act 1975, s. 29.

cases it is lawful for private members' clubs to operate sexual discrimination when it comes to admitting the opposite sex as members of the club. It should be noted, however, that this exemption may well not be long lived[33]. One existing anti-sex discrimination rule does apply; this is where a club holds a registration certificate under the Licensing Act 1964 and the club comprises both sexes: here all members must have equal voting rights at general meetings[34].

**4-23** A problem arises, or will arise, where a club has different sections for men and women, which is a common occurrence in sporting circles. There is nothing discriminatory if each section is capped at the same number, say 250 for each section. The sex discrimination comes about when one section outnumbers the other section, say there is a fixed limit of 300 for men and a fixed limit of 200 for women. The defect of this latter arrangement is that were a man and a woman to apply to join the same club at the same time, they might find themselves achieving membership at different times, or the one being admitted and the other being refused, simply on the grounds of their sex. Once admitted into membership, however, arrangements can be made, based on the fact of the different sexes, which are not unfairly discriminatory in their nature, for example, sports competitions solely for men or solely for women[35].

## 4-24 Disability discrimination

Similar provisions apply to disability discrimination as apply to sex discrimination in that the wording of the Disability Discrimination Act 1995 follows the wording of the Sex Discrimination Act 1975. The Act of 1995 applies where a person has a physical or mental impairment of such a character that it has a substantial and long-term adverse effect on his ability to carry out normal day-to-day activities[36]. It is unlawful for a person, who provides (whether or not for payment) facilities for entertainment or recreation or refreshment to the public or to a section of the public, to discriminate against a man or woman by refusing or deliberately omitting to provide him or her with such facilities on the grounds of their disability[37]. Once again, because of

---

[33]    See **4-25** below. See also **9-25** below for another form of sexual discrimination.
[34]    Licensing Act 1964, sch. 7, para 2(4). As noted in **9-25** below, this has not been carried forward into the Licensing Act 2003.
[35]    See Sex Discrimination Act 1975, s. 44. This also applies to persons of 'acquired gender': see Gender Recognition Act 2004, s. 19.
[36]    Disability Discrimination Act 1995, s. 1. Schedule 1 of the act elaborates on the definition of disabled person.
[37]    Ibid. s. 19.

the *Charter* and the *Dockers' Labour Club* cases it is lawful for private members' clubs to practise discrimination against disabled persons when it comes to admitting them to membership of the club. It should be noted, however, that this exemption may well not be long lived[38].

## 4-25   Existing exemptions

It is considered that the current (2004) exemptions applicable to private members' clubs under the sex and disability legislation will inevitably be removed in due course, although the progress of the amending legislation has been very slow. The Sex Discrimination (Clubs and Other Private Associations) Bill is presently making its way through Parliament, and it is highly likely that there will be a new Disability Discrimination Bill in the near future dealing with clubs. As with racial discrimination, both bills will bring within their ambit clubs of twenty-five or more members. This means that clubs would be wise to take steps now to alter their rules to remove discriminatory provisions. It has long been recognised that it is unlawful to discriminate on the grounds of race, and fortunately cases where clubs have been taken to court for alleged racial discrimination are rare. It has to be recognised too that discrimination on the grounds of sex or disability is equally unacceptable.

## 4-26   Remedies

With regard to racial discrimination, individuals have the right to take their complaint to a designated county court[39] where they can obtain the remedies of injunction, declaration and (unlimited) damages[40]. The Commission for Racial Equality can also issue a non-discrimination notice[41] and may apply for an injunction where there is persistent discrimination[42]. With regard to sex discrimination in relation to the provision of goods, facilities, or services or in relation to premises, individuals have the right to take their complaint to the county court[43] where the sanction against the offending party includes the granting of an injunction and a declaration[44] and the award of (unlimited) damages[45]. The Equal Opportunities Board can also issue a non-

---

[38]  See **4-25** below.
[39]  Race Relations Act 1976, s. 57.
[40]  Ibid. s. 57(2).
[41]  Ibid. s. 58.
[42]  Ibid. s. 62.
[43]  Sex Discrimination Act 1975, s. 66.
[44]  Ibid. s. 62(2).
[45]  Ibid. s. 66(2).

discrimination notice[46] and may apply for an injunction where there is persistent discrimination[47]. With regard to disability discrimination, individuals have the right to take their complaint to the county court[48] where they can obtain the remedies of injunction, declaration and (unlimited) damages[49], including compensation for injury to feelings[50]. The Disability Rights Commission has no power of investigation of complaints or power of enforcement, but instead has advisory powers[51].

## 4. GUESTS AND VISITORS

**4-27** If there is no supply or sale of alcohol involved in the club's activities, the topic of members' guests or of visitors to the club's premises or its meetings, does not need to be addressed in the rules or bye-laws. The difference between a guest and a visitor in this context is that a guest will be an invitee of the member whereas a visitor will be a member of the public. It will be a matter for the discretion of the committee or the members to decide if or when they will admit guests or visitors to participate in the club's activities and on what terms admission will be permitted. If the club feels more comfortable in regulating the entry of such persons, there is nothing untoward in making bye-laws to cover the situation and/or insisting that any guest or visitor coming into the club has to sign the visitors' book. If the club has a registration certificate under the Licensing Act 1964, visitors (i.e. who are not guests of the members) may be admitted to the club premises under section 49 if the rules permit visitors and certain conditions are complied with: these conditions are set out in paragraph A12-7 of Appendix 12. The visitor provisions of section 49 are not repeated in the Licensing Act 2003. This last Act only refers to associate members and the guests of associate members: for further discussion see **9-35** to **9-37** below.

---

[46]     Sex Discrimination Act 1975, s. 67.
[47]     Ibid. s. 71.
[48]     Disability Discrimination Act 1995, s. 25(3).
[49]     Ibid. s. 25(5).
[50]     Ibid. s. 25(2).
[51]     Ibid. s. 28.

## 5.    DATA PROTECTION ACT 1998

**4-28**  This Act regulates the processing of information about individuals held by the data controller[52] (in a club normally the secretary). The Act was passed to give effect to European Council Directive 95/46/EC which had been issued as a response to the greater ease with which data could be processed and exchanged as a result of advances in information technology. The primary objective of the Act is to protect an individual's right to privacy and to protect the accuracy of his personal data held by others in a computerised form or in a similarly organised manual filing system[53]. Data here means information recorded in a form in which it can be processed by computer or other automatic equipment or processed by manual records held in a 'relevant filing system'[54]. Secondly, data means information about a living individual who can be identified from the data, and includes any expression of opinion about the individual and any indication of the intentions of the data controller or any other person in respect of that individual[55] (for example, the committee's appraisal of the honesty of the club treasurer, or the club's intention to ask a member to resign his membership on the grounds of his unpopularity). Personal data may be processed fairly and lawfully if the data subject has given his consent[56]. Sensitive personal data may be processed fairly and lawfully if the data subject has given his *explicit* consent[57]. Sensitive personal data means information as to the

---

[52]    A data controller is a person who (either alone or jointly or in common with other persons) makes decisions with regard to specific personal data. This will include decisions as to the purposes for which and the way in which those personal data are processed. A person is a data controller with regard to specific personal data if processing has not yet occurred but he intends that it will.  Thus, if a person collects personal data via a tear-off portion of a document, which he then intends to place in a computer base, he is a data controller: see s. 1(1) of the Act of 1998 and the annotations of Andrew Charlesworth LLB in Current Law Statutes 1998 vol 1 page 29–11.

[53]    *Durant v Financial Services Authority* [2003] (unreported) EWCA Civ 1746 (Auld, Mummery and Buxton LJJ) at para 4 of the judgments which were given on 8 December 1903; see also *Campbell v MGN Ltd* [2003] 2 WLR 80 CA at para 73 of the judgment of the court (overruled in the House of Lords but not on this point). Lord Phillips of Worth Matravers MR at 100 described the Act as 'a cumbersome and inelegant piece of legislation' whilst the trial judge (Morland J) had described the path to his conclusion as weaving his way through a thicket (ibid. at 100). The invasion of privacy engages Article 8 of the European Convention for the Protection of Human Rights.

[54]    Data Protection Act 1998, s. (1).

[55]    Ibid. s. 1. Mere mention of the data subject in a document does not necessarily amount to personal data; it has to be information that affects his privacy, whether in his personal or family life, business or professional capacity (per Auld LJ at para 28 of his judgment in *Durant's* case).

[56]    Ibid. Sch. 2, para 1.

[57]    Ibid. Sch. 3, para 1.

racial or ethnic origin of the data subject, his political opinions, his religious beliefs, his physical or mental health, his sexual life, the commission of any offence by him, and his membership of a trade union[58].

**4-29** Schedule 2 to the Act sets out six grounds for the lawful processing of personal data and Schedule 3 to the Act sets out nine grounds for the lawful processing of sensitive personal data. The grounds are too complex to set out here but it is worth pointing out that one of the grounds for processing personal data, apart from consent, is that the processing is necessary for the purposes of legitimate interests pursued by the data controller or the club to whom the data has been disclosed[59]. Likewise, one of the grounds for processing sensitive data, apart from consent, is that the processing is carried out in the course of the club's legitimate activities, provided the club is not established or conducted for gain and it exists for political, philosophical, religious or trade-union purposes and further provided that the sensitive personal data is not disclosed to a third party without the data subject's consent[60]. The data subject can request the information which is held about him provided he makes the request in writing and pays a fee not exceeding the prescribed maximum, currently (2004) £2.00[61].

### 4-30 Data protection principles

The eight principles are set out in Part I of Schedule 2 to the Act. They may be summarised as follows:

All personal data must:
(1) be fairly and lawfully processed;
(2) be processed for a specified and lawful purpose;
(3) be adequate, relevant and not excessive;
(4) be accurate and, where necessary, kept up to date;
(5) not be kept for longer than necessary;
(6) be processed in accordance with the rights of the individual;
(7) be kept secure;
(8) not be transferred to a country outside the European Economic Area unless that country ensures an adequate level of protection for such data.

---

[58]    Data Protection Act 1998, s. 2.
[59]    Ibid. Sch. 2, para 6(1).
[60]    Ibid. Sch. 3, para 4.
[61]    Ibid. s. (1)(2), and Data Protection (Subject Access) (Fees and Miscellaneous Provisions) Regulations 2000 (SI 2000/191) (amended by SI 2001/3223).

## 4-31　Data in a manual filing system

An important point to note concerns the accessibility of manual data held in a 'relevant filing system'. In the unreported case of *Durant v Financial Services Authority* [2003][62] Lord Justice Auld had this to say about the Act in relation to manual records[63]:

> It is plain ... that Parliament intended to apply the Act to manual records only if they are of sufficient sophistication to provide the same or similar ready accessibility as a computerised filing system. That requires a filing system so referenced or indexed that it enables the data controller's employee responsible to identify at the outset of his search with reasonable certainty and speed the file or files in which the specific data relating to the person requesting the information is located and to locate the relevant information about him within the file or files, without having to do a manual search. To leave it to the searcher to leaf through files, possibly at great length and cost, and fruitlessly, to see whether it or they contain information relating to the person requesting information and whether that information is data within the Act ... cannot have been intended by Parliament.

This judicial pronouncement has the curious effect of seemingly encouraging a club to keep personal data on a casual and haphazard basis as a way of avoiding the Act but this would only be of assistance to a disorganised club. A properly run club probably now needs to computerise its records and thus most clubs will have to face the fact that the Act will apply to them.

## 4-32　Consent

We consider that details of members' names and addresses may be kept by the club on its computer or in an organised manual file in any event without infringing the provisions of the Act in that by joining a club the member impliedly consents to his fellow members knowing who he is and where he lives[64]. We consider that the club can go one step further and say that in joining the club the member impliedly consents to the club's processing information which enables the club to contact the member other than by using the postal service, e.g. by telephone, fax or e-mail. Other personal information will be more difficult to process or store without express consent, such as the age of the member or his occupation[65]. The most effective way of obtaining

---

[62]　[2003] EWCA Civ 1746.
[63]　At para 48 of his judgment.
[64]　See *R(Robertson) v Wakefield Metropolitan District Council* [2002] QB 1052 (Maurice Kay J) paras 29 to 34 of the judgment.
[65]　[2002] 2 WLR 889 at paras 29 to 34.

consent under the Act is to include an expression of consent in the application form which the member signs when he applies to join the club and, in the case of existing members, to include an expression of consent in the form accompanying the demand for payment of the member's annual subscription. A suitable form of words might be: 'In making this application I explicitly consent to the Basset Social Club obtaining, recording and holding my personal data (including sensitive data) solely for club purposes either on its computer or in an organised manual filing system. This information may include my full name and address and, where applicable, my telephone and fax numbers and my e-mail address. I consent to the club disclosing to other members my full name and address. This disclosure may also include my telephone and fax numbers and my e-mail address, unless I have ticked all or part of the box below'. The wording for the existing member should start, 'By renewing my subscription, I explicitly consent (etc)'. The box needs to be so worded that it gives the applicant or the member the opportunity to permit partial disclosure only of the means of contact to other members.

### 4-33 Notification to the Commissioner

Provided the club is processing and storing personal data for its own purposes and will not be divulging any personal data to outside third parties, there will be no need for the data controller to notify the Information Commissioner[66]. Thus it is thought that the great majority of small clubs will be exempt from notification. Nevertheless, the Commissioner has power to enforce the Data Protection Principles against those who are exempt from notification[67]. This is done by way of an enforcement notice[68]. If the data controller is under a duty to notify, he must pay the notification fee[69], currently (2004) the sum of £35.00[70].

---

[66] See ss. 16 to 20 of the Data Protection Act 1998, ss. 16–20 for the requirement of notification.

[67] Ibid. s. 40(1). See also the annotation by Andrew Charlesworth LLB in Current Law Statutes 1998 vol 1 page 29–25.

[68] Ibid. s. 40(1).

[69] Ibid. s. 18(6).

[70] Data Protection (Notification and Notification Fees) Regulations 2000 (SI 2000/188).

**4-34   Exemptions**

Part IV of the Act provides for exemptions to certain parts of the Act. Areas of activity where exemptions are granted include:
(1) national security[71];
(2) crime and taxation[72];
(3) health, education and social work[73];
(4) regulatory activity[74] e.g. data processed by the Director of Fair Trading in the course of his statutory functions;
(5) journalism, literature and art[75];
(6) research, history and statistics[76].


# 6.   PRIVILEGES OF MEMBERSHIP

**4-35**   Apart from being common practice not to allow a member any privileges until he has paid the entrance fee and his first subscription, in two cases there is a compulsory requirement for privileges to be deferred. Where the club is the holder of a registration certificate under the Licensing Act 1964, by Schedule 7 of the Act the club rules must state that there is to be an interval of at least two days between nomination and admission to the privileges of membership[77], and in the case of a person becoming a member without prior nomination or application[78], there must be a like interval between becoming a member and being admitted to the privileges of membership. Likewise, under the Licensing Act 2003 the club rules must state that a person may not be admitted to membership or, as a candidate for membership be admitted to any of the privileges of membership, without an interval of at least two days between his nomination or application for membership and his admission to such privileges[79]. The phrase, 'at least two days', means that it covers a period of four days (see **6-12** below), so that an application for membership received on Monday morning will mean that the candidate or member cannot

---

71      Data Protection Act 1998, s. 28.
72      Ibid. s. 29.
73      Ibid. s. 30.
74      Ibid. s. 31.
75      Ibid. s. 32.
76      Ibid. s. 33.
77      Licensing Act 1964, s. 4(1). This includes temporary members.
78      Presumably the intention of Parliament was to prevent the licensing laws being circumvented by the instant grant of membership of a club. But the authors have yet to come across a bona fide club where a candidate or applicant could acquire instant full membership without prior nomination or application.
79      Licensing Act 2003, s. 62(2). This includes temporary members.

take advantage of the privileges until Thursday morning at the earliest.

## 7.   ENTRANCE FEE AND SUBSCRIPTIONS

**4-36**   Insofar as the management of clubs is in the hands of the committee, the ordinary member has little, if any, say in the day-to-day running of the club. One means of democratic control is the fixing of the entrance fee (if there is one) and the fixing of the annual subscription by the members in general meeting, usually at the Annual General Meeting[80]. The usual course is for the committee to put forward the amounts of the proposed subscription for the various categories of member for the coming year. If, for example, there is a sharp rise in the subscription rates, the committee will be obliged to account to the members at the meeting for their stewardship over the past year which has necessitated the raising of the subscriptions, and this is an exercise to be welcomed. In some large clubs, especially if they contain an element of overseas membership, the members are content to let the committee decide on the annual rates of subscription. There is, however, nothing untoward in giving the committee the power (or a temporary power) to raise annual subscriptions by some agreed inflation factor or to increase the subscriptions by a limited amount, say not exceeding 5% of the previous year's subscriptions.

**4-37**   It is not uncommon for clubs to allow members to pay their subscriptions by instalments[81]. It is conceivable that the provisions of the Consumer Credit Act 1974 might come into play if the payment is to be made by more than four instalments or if the member is charged interest on the principal sum outstanding. This would involve the club in obtaining a consumer credit licence. Rather than risk the local trading standards officer making a fuss on this point, the problem is best avoided by making sure the transaction is an exempt one under the Act.

**4-38**   Problems are sometimes encountered where the club has been dissolved and recently joined members have complained that they are entitled to a refund in whole or in part of the entrance fee in addition

---

[80]   In some old-established clubs one will occasionally find that the members do not pay a subscription as such but a levy is made on the members at the end of the club's financial year to cover the expenses incurred over the previous year. The levy can therefore be treated as a kind of subscription, the first year's expenses being met out of the entrance fees.

[81]   Arrears of subscriptions are dealt with in **7-05** below.

to the unexpired portion of the subscription. We consider that no part of this fee is refundable as it comprised the consideration for the ability to join the club in the first place and is in no wise carried forward into the period of membership. But the point may not be free from doubt. In *Re Curzon Syndicate Ltd* [1920] LT Jo 232 (Lawrence J) one of the plaintiffs successfully claimed back her entrance fee in the liquidation when the proprietary club closed down. But special circumstances may have applied here. In 1917 Mrs H, who was the governing director of the company which owned the club and who was personally the lessor of the club premises, posted in the clubhouse a notice, in reply to a rumour that the club was going to close down, stating that the club would be carried on permanently. On 25 March 1919 Mrs H obtained judgment against the company for arrears of rent and on the same day closed the club, with the notice still being in place. The law report does not indicate the date when the plaintiff paid her entrance fee or the date when she became a member, nor the basis of recovery of the entrance fee. The judge may have come to the conclusion that with the notice still in place for all the members to see, there was an implied term in the contract of membership that the club would not shut down save on reasonable notice. That being so, the company was in breach of the implied term by instant closure, and accordingly the entrance fee was recoverable as an item of wasted expenditure.

**4-39**    Another problem which might occur is if a member resigned because the other members had passed by the requisite majority a fundamental rule change with which he disagreed (see **2-28** to **2-32** above). Suppose the member had paid his annual subscription a few days before the rule change and he now elects to resign his membership. Can he claim back the unexpired portion of his subscription from the club or its members? This raises a point of some difficulty. Unfair as it may seem, we do not consider such recovery is possible, save in a proprietary club. In a members' club the will of the majority of the members is paramount. As against the dissenting member the majority could argue that they were not in breach of any term of the contract of membership since the rules gave the members an unfettered power to alter the rules, which power had been democratically and procedurally exercised in a bona fide manner. This would mean that if the dissenting member wished to resign, that was his undoubted right but such right was exercised of his own volition. And this argument is likely to succeed in court. Nonetheless we have no doubt that the correct solution to this problem is for the club to make an ex gratia refund of the subscription or the relevant portion of it. In a proprietary club, however, we consider that there would be an implied term in the contract of membership made between the proprietor and the member that no fundamental change to the rules, which adversely affected the position of the members, would take place during the period of the annual subscription. This implied term is necessary to give business efficacy to the contract and is not unfair on the proprietor since at the end of such period he can alter the rules to suit himself, and this might entail a fundamental rule change not to the liking of the members. If a member does not wish to renew his subscription on these new terms, that is a matter for him, and the contractual relationship between the proprietor and the member will simply cease.

# Chapter 5

## CONTROL OF THE CLUB'S AFFAIRS

### 1.   INTRODUCTION

**5-01**   In the absence of any rule to the contrary all ordinary (i.e. full) members of a club would have an equal say in the management of an unincorporated members' club. This form of Athenian democracy is impractical although occasionally found. When the Pre-Raphaelite Brotherhood was founded in 1848 by six artists and a sculptor, this was in effect a club which ran on such lines[1]. But in practice a club of any size or longevity cannot function without delegation of the members' powers of management to officers of the club and to a managing committee[2]. This is true, whatever the legal nature of the members' club. As far as proprietary clubs are concerned, it is common for the proprietor to establish a committee to act as an intermediary between him and the members since this set-up works to the mutual advantage of the proprietor and the members, although as a matter of contract law no such committee is necessary.

### 2.   OFFICERS OF THE CLUB

**5-02**   Officers of a club fall into two categories; they are either honorary posts or managerial posts. Since the functions of most honorary officers are generally well known it is unusual to specify in

---

[1]     Its unity of purpose, overtly demonstrated by its logo 'PRB', lasted until about 1853 when they all went their own separate ways.

[2]     Other names are also used such as the executive committee. In many clubs it will simply be called the committee. The Licensing Act 1964 refers to an *elective* committee. Although this is a correct use of the adjective, most club members would normally refer to an *elected* committee (in contrast to an appointed one).

the rules precisely what duties their post entails but if any unusual or specific duties are required of them this should be expressly spelt out. On the other hand, with managerial officers it is good practice to state in the rules or the bye-laws, as and when necessary, what duties the post entails.

## 5-03   Patron

The first two definitions of 'patron' in the Chambers Dictionary[3] are given as '[1] a protector; [2] a person, group or organization, etc which gives support, encouragement and often financial aid'. A patron of a club therefore tends to fall into one of two categories; (1) he or she is a person of high rank or eminence who formally supports the objects of the club and acts as its 'protector'[4] but is not a member of the club because this might otherwise impose duties and obligations on the patron which are unacceptable to him or her; or (2) they are a group of members in the club who give the necessary support and encouragement to other members of the club.

**5-04**   The formal patron commonly holds the post at pleasure. The appointment is usually in the hands of the managing committee and is or should be an uncontroversial appointment. In many clubs, however, a formal patron is considered an unnecessary or inappropriate embellishment and the group of members who comprise the patrons will be the president and vice-presidents. It is not uncommon for the rules to state 'The club shall be under the patronage of one President and as many Vice-Presidents as the Committee shall determine'.  Unlike a formal patron, these patrons will have achieved their office of president or vice-president by an election process.

## 5-05   Presidents

The presidency of a club is usually an honorary post, unlike the chairmanship of the club, which involves managerial functions. In many clubs the president performs an ambassadorial role, having previously given yeoman service to the club over a period of time. It is the president who will 'preside' at important functions such as the annual general meeting or at the annual dinner. At the AGM the

---

3        Published 1998.
4        In classical Roman times a patron was a patrician who gave legal protection to a client in return for services.

president will normally open the proceedings and then hand over to the chairman to deal with the formal part of the meeting. If the president is to be given any managerial duties, these should be specified in the rules[5]. It is usual for a president to be supported by one or more vice-presidents. The vice-presidents themselves are usually elected to their office for the same reason as the president. They are a useful addition to a club because they form a pool of candidates for the presidency when the need arises and they can deputise for the president when he is absent.

**5-06** The office of vice-presidency is likewise usually an honorary one. Unlike presidents, however, vice-presidents often take part in the running of a club so that, for example, the chairman of the club might well be a vice-president as well. We consider that combining the honorary office of president with the managerial office of chairman is incompatible and should not be countenanced.

## 5-07 Chairman (or Chair)

One has to draw a distinction here between the chairman[6] of the club and the chairman of the managing committee. Almost invariably they are one and the same person. The chairman of a club is one part of a triumvirate that often ensures that the club operates in an efficient way with the least fuss and bother, the other two members being the secretary and the treasurer. That this triumvirate commonly exists is because the managing committee, into whose hands the control of the club's affairs has been placed, is usually a much larger body which may well meet on a regular but infrequent basis. The chairman's main roles are, as his title suggests, the chairmanship of the members in general meeting and the chairmanship of the managing committee. The chairman is the senior and most influential member of the club who takes part in the running of the club and it is not uncommon for the secretary or treasurer (or employees of the club) to consult him about a club matter and, if possible, obtain a decision on the matter. There is nothing untoward about this procedure provided that any decision of substance taken by the chairman is reported to the committee at its next meeting and the chairman's decision is ratified by the committee[7].

---

[5]    For example, the President of the Chartered Institute of Arbitrators, despite his ambassadorial role, is still required to make appointments of arbitrators.

[6]    Unlike all the other officers, the word 'chairman' has a masculine connotation and some clubs feel happier with the description 'Chair'. If this description is adopted, the word will often carry a capital 'C' to distinguish the person from the item of furniture.

[7]    See *R v Brent Health Authority, ex parte James* [1985] QB 869 at 878.

## 5-08   Secretary

This is the officer who generally speaking will be in charge of the day-to-day running of the club. In many clubs he will be the honorary secretary. This may sound confusing as he does not hold an honorary office. The word 'honorary' in his title means that he receives no remuneration for performing his duties. The secretary has various important administrative tasks: they are to maintain an up-to-date list of members and their addresses and their contact numbers; to collect subscriptions; to deal with club correspondence; to organize and attend general meetings of the club and prepare the minutes thereof; to liaise between the committee and the sub-committees; and to prepare a report on the club's activities since the last AGM and to circulate the same amongst the membership.

**5-09**   If the secretary is a paid official, he will have a contract of employment in which his duties will be spelt out in the usual way[8]. In many clubs, especially golf clubs, a paid secretary is the most prominent figure of authority in the club[9]. Although he reports to the managing committee, in practice much of the day-to-day running of the club will be in his hands. A paid secretary should never be a member of the club because of possible conflicts of interest between his obligations to his employer (the club) and his obligations to his fellow members.

## 5-10   Treasurer

This is an important officer who should keep and maintain the accounts of the club in good order. In particular, he is responsible for preparing the accounts for the members at the annual general meeting; this will involve at the minimum a balance sheet and a profit and loss account detailing the income and expenditure over the past year. The treasurer will be answerable to the managing committee during the year leading up to the annual general meeting. In almost all clubs the treasurer will be an unpaid officer and thus will be the Honorary Treasurer, and for the sake of outward propriety a lot of treasurers are insistent that they are referred to by their proper title.

**5-11**   In many clubs there needs to be liaison between the Secretary and the Treasurer to ensure that financial matters are properly

---

[8]    See CHAPTER **14** below for the topic of employment.
[9]    Because (a) he is always there; (b) he is not transitory like an elected officer; and (c) he is the person to whom correspondence and complaints are addressed.

handled. The treasurer will be under a duty to bank without delay in the club's name all monies received from the secretary. It is the treasurer's task to see that club monies are spent solely for club purposes but it is usually the secretary's duty to organize that payments are made on time, such as the renewal of insurance premiums or the payment of value added tax. However, by section 108 (as amended)[10] of the Taxes Management Act 1970 the treasurer or the person acting as treasurer is the officer responsible for the payment of corporation tax by the club[11].

## 3.    ELECTION OF OFFICERS

**5-12**  The president and vice-presidents are elected officers. Sometimes their tenure is annual, sometimes it is for a longer period but, unlike a formal patron, it is not good practice to grant these presidencies for an unlimited duration[12]. As to the mode of election, practice varies; sometimes it is solely in the hands of the committee, sometimes it is solely in the hands of the members in general meeting and sometimes it is in the hands of the members but only on the recommendation of the committee, so that if the recommendation is rejected the members cannot proceed to elect their own candidate but must await a fresh recommendation from the committee. As for the chairman, in many clubs he is elected by the managing committee from one of its own number immediately after the annual general meeting. In other clubs the nomination for chairman is open to the whole membership and is part of the election of the officers and committee at the annual general meeting. It is important for the rules to be clear on this point. The hon. secretary and the hon. treasurer are usually elected officers but sometimes the rules stipulate that they are to be appointed by the committee from amongst its own number. For the election of members of the committee, see **5-17** below.

### 5-13  Voting

A democratic voting system will almost inevitably be a complex affair if it is based on the premise that any person elected to an office should have at least 50 per cent of the votes cast. It is of course a relatively simple matter if there are only two candidates because one of them

---

[10]    See Finance Act 1993, Sch. 14, para 7 and Companies Consolidation (Consequential Provisions) Act 1985, Sch. 2.

[11]    For the topic of taxation see CHAPTER **17** below.

[12]    There are some very old established clubs where the President holds office for life.

will normally get more than 50 per cent of the votes. The only difficulty here lies in what happens if there is a tie. The usual solution to this problem is to adopt the solution provided in parliamentary elections, that is, to decide the election by lot[13]. A contest between two candidates is necessarily run on the basis of 'first past the post'. The real difficulties arise when the 'first past the post' voting system is adopted and the contest is between three or more candidates. 'First past the post' often means (as in our national politics) that a candidate with a minority of votes is elected: a case of the tail wagging the dog. Despite its obvious deficiencies, we consider that for the vast majority of clubs 'first past the post' will be a satisfactory voting system because of its uncomplicated nature and the swiftness of the result[14].

## 4.   AUDITOR

**5-14**   If an unincorporated club is of any substance, it is common to appoint an auditor (usually an honorary auditor) to examine and officially verify the accounts of the club. The rules of a working men's club must make provision for an auditor[15]; so too must the rules of an IPSA club[16], although there is now a power for clubs registered under the Friendly Societies Act or the Industrial and Provident Societies Act to opt out of an audit if certain conditions are met[17]. All companies must appoint an auditor[18], although there is an exemption for very small companies[19]. The auditor has an independent role to play and is not an officer of the club.

## 5.   TRUSTEES

**5-15**   Where the club is unincorporated and holds assets and property, it is customary for trustees to be appointed according to the

---

[13]      See Representation of the People Act 1983, sched.1, para 49. In *Fryer v Harris* (1955) *The Times*, 30 July where the votes were equally divided, the returning officer spun a coin to decide the election.

[14]      Another reason for using 'first past the post' is the dearth of candidates in many club elections. Far from having a surfeit of candidates, many clubs have difficulty in persuading members to become officers of the club. Any club interested in using a voting system other than 'first past the post' should contact the Electoral Reform Society in London.

[15]      Friendly Societies Act 1974, Sch. 2, para 6.

[16]      Industrial and Provident Societies Act 1965, Sch. 1, para 10.

[17]      Deregulation (Industrial and Provident Societies) Order 1996 (SI 1996/1738).

[18]      Companies Act 1985, s. 385(2).

[19]      Ibid. ss. 249A and 249B; Companies Act 1985 (Accounts of Small and Medium-sized Enterprises and Audit Exemption)(Amendment) Regulations 2004 (SI 2004/16).

rules and for the assets and property to be vested in trustees on trust for the whole membership. Where the club owns or leases land, this is a mandatory requirement because property cannot be conveyed to or registered at the Land Registry in the name of a non-existent person. The trustees will invariably be full members of the club. In the case of a working men's club, there must be one or more trustees appointed by a resolution of a majority of members at a general meeting or in such other manner as the rules provide[20]. The appointment must be notified to the Financial Services Authority[21]. In the case of an unincorporated literary or scientific institution, it is usual for assets and property to be vested in trustees but if none are appointed in respect of personal property, 'the money, securities for money, goods, chattels and personal effects' shall be vested in the governing body of the institution[22]. Trustees are often appointed where the club is incorporated under the Companies Acts or registered under the Industrial and Provident Societies Act 1965 but technically this is not necessary because the club is a legal person and can hold assets and property in its own right. The question of trusteeship is further discussed in **8-06** below.

## 6. MANAGING COMMITTEE

**5-16**   For the efficient management of the club it is this committee which has delegated to it the control and management of all the affairs of the club. It is therefore important that the rules specify the composition, the powers and duties of this committee. In some cases it is mandatory for the club to have a managing committee: all registered members' clubs require this body[23] and, where the club is the holder of a registration certificate, by paragraph 1 of Schedule 7 to the Licensing Act 1964 the affairs of the club must be vested in such a committee.

### 5-17   Election

The election of the committee is necessarily set out in the rules. If the club holds a registration certificate, paragraph 4 of Schedule 7 to the Licensing Act 1964 contains mandatory stipulations about the tenure

---

[20]      Friendly Societies Act 1974, s. 24(1), (2) (as substituted by the Friendly Societies Act 1992).
[21]      Ibid. s. 24(3), (4).
[22]      Literary and Scientific Institutions Act 1854, s. 20.
[23]      Friendly Societies Act 1974, Sch. 2, para 5; Industrial and Provident Societies Act 1965, Sch. 1, para 6; Shop Clubs Act 1902, Schedule, para iv.

and election of the managing committee. Even with the demise of this Act and the non-appearance of such stipulations in the Licensing Act 2003, we consider that paragraph 4 embodies the best practice and should be followed in any event. As to *tenure*, this may be for not less than one year but not more than five years. As to *election*, this must be held annually, and if all the elected members do not go out of office in every year, there must be fixed rules for determining those who are to retire. All the members of the club, who are entitled to vote at the election and are of not less than two years' standing, must be capable of being elected, subject to any provision for nomination and any provision prohibiting or restricting re-election. A rule whereby say a third shall retire each year can assist the continuity of management. It is usual to permit committee members to put themselves forward for re-election on the expiry of their term of office, subject sometimes to a maximum number of consecutive years which the member may serve in his elected capacity. It is also good practice to ensure, either through the members' decision in general meeting or in the rules, that the committee meets on a regular basis so that a weather eye is kept on the activities of the club.

## 5-18   Exercise of powers

It is axiomatic that the powers of the club should be exercised for the benefit of the club as a whole and not for some section or faction thereof[24], and this is supported by the Licensing Acts 1964 and 2003 because in each case the statute requires the club to be established and conducted in good faith as a club[25]. It is also important to realise that members are delegating their powers of control to the *whole* committee and not to the individual members thereof[26]. Consequently it is essential that the rules state that the powers of the committee may be exercised by a quorate number of the committee, otherwise any decisions of committee must be taken by the whole committee. Subject to any express rule to the contrary, the committee will be empowered to determine its own procedures as to how it will operate[27]. Pursuant to this power a committee can appoint a sub-committee or a working party; or delegate a task to a particular officer of the club; or co-opt a member of the club on to the committee to give added expertise; or fill a casual vacancy on the committee for the remainder of the term

---

[24]    *Woodford v Smith* [1970] 1 WLR 806 at 816E; *Lambert v Addison* [1882] 46 LT 20 at 25.

[25]    S. 41(2)(a) of the Act of 1964 and s. 62(4) of the Act of 2003.

[26]    *Brown v Andrew* [1849] 18 LJ Ex 153; *R. v Liverpool City Council ex p Professional Association of Teachers* (1984) *The Times,* 22 March.

[27]    *Cassell v Inglis* [1916] 2 Ch 211 at 231.

of a committee member (say when this member resigns from the club)[28], although a lot of clubs may prefer to see such powers specified in the rules. Whenever the committee adopts any of these procedures which involve sub-delegation, it is crucial that it requires the persons delegated to report their activities to the committee for approval and ratification, since ultimately the club's affairs are the responsibility of the committee and it is they who are answerable to the members.

**5-19** The committee should be astute in spotting potential conflicts of interest. The committee may decide that the roof of the clubhouse needs substantial repair and a building contractor who is a committee member volunteers to carry out the work for a reasonable price. The conflict arises because it is in the club's best interest to get the job well done for as low a price as possible and in the building contractor's best interest to ensure his 'reasonable price' is as profitable as possible. Any conflict should be dealt with by the committee either by having a policy of not dealing contractually with any club member or by making sure that all conflicts of interest are properly disclosed and that any decision on the subject matter of the conflict excludes the member when it is taken.

**5-20** When the committee's (or the members') conduct has come under the scrutiny of the courts, the courts themselves have been at pains to point out that they do not sit in judgment on this conduct[29]. In club cases, provided the committee has the exclusive competence to make the decision in question, the courts will not look to see whether any decision was right or reasonable; it will suffice if the impugned decision was in accordance with the club rules and was done honestly and not in excess of jurisdiction[30]. Lord Justice Brett in *Dawkins v Antrobus* [1881] 17 Ch D 615 CA at 630 robustly put it as follows:

> The only question is, whether [the decision] was done bona fide. Now, it is true that an element, in considering whether a matter has been done in good faith, is the question whether what has been done is really beyond all reason. If that were so it would be evidence of want of good faith; but even where that [unreasonableness] exists, it is not a necessary conclusion that there has been a want of good faith, for, even after having come to the conclusion that a decision was wholly unreasonable, one might be convinced ... that nevertheless there was no malice – that what was done was done in good faith. Therefore the mere proof that it was contrary to reason is no sufficient ground for interference of the Court.

---

[28]     For clubs which hold a registration certificate there is statutory power to fill a casual vacancy: Licensing Act 1964, Sch. 7, para 4(5).

[29]     See *Dawkins v Antrobus* [1881] 17 Ch D 615 CA at 630 (Brett LJ); *Young v Imperial Ladies Club Ltd* [1920] 2 KB 523 CA at 535 (Scrutton LJ).

[30]     *Lee v Showmen's Guild of Great Britain* [1952] 2 QB 329 CA at 350–351 (Romer LJ).

We are here talking about the committee's decisions on social rights and social duties; different considerations apply when, for example, the committee sits in judgment on the members of a trade or profession[31].

### 5-21   Vote of no confidence

On occasion there may come a time when the members have lost confidence in their committee to run the club acceptably or properly. This situation needs careful handling if the committee take the view that, despite what the members generally may think, their stewardship of the club's affairs is beneficial to the club. It must be remembered that the committee would have been elected for a finite period and so are entitled to stay in office until the next election. The easy answer therefore is to vote the committee out of office at the next election.

**5-22**   But the situation might be such that the members feel that they have to take action prior to the next election. The procedure would be for the members to requisition a special meeting in order to pass a vote of no confidence in the committee and a resolution calling upon the committee to resign forthwith. It is here that the members may encounter choppy waters. What happens if the secretary or the committee refuse or simply fail to call the duly requisitioned meeting? The answer is that the requisitionists themselves can convene the meeting[32]. But what happens if the committee then blithely ignore the vote of no confidence and the call to resign which, say, had been overwhelmingly passed at the meeting? The answer is for the members to treat the committee's refusal to act upon these resolutions as a ground for expulsion from the club. This in turn might produce another procedural hurdle caused by the fact that it is usually the committee who exercises the power of expulsion. However, the committee would not be able to exercise the power on this occasion since they would be the accused and the first rule of natural justice is that no-one can act as a judge in his own case[33]. In any event the committee is ultimately answerable to the general body of members, so in these particular circumstances we consider that the power of expulsion would reside in the members generally who would thus be entitled to convene a special meeting to deal with what would undoubtedly be a critical situation in the club.

---

[31]    See **16-07** below.
[32]    See **6-07** below.
[33]    See **7-15** below.

**5-23** *Registered clubs* It should be noted that under the legislation cited in footnote 23 above all registered clubs must make provision in their rules for the removal of the committee as well as rules for appointing it.

## 5-24 Literary and scientific institutions

Under the Literary and Scientific Institutions Act 1854, if no governing body is constituted on the establishment of the institution, the members themselves shall have the power to create their own governing body[34].

## 7. SUB-COMMITTEES

**5-25** It is possible for a club to have as many co-equal committees as it wants. But in practice it has been found be more satisfactory and efficient to have one main committee (the managing committee) with as many sub-committees as may be necessary, which are answerable to the managing committee[35]. This sub-delegation of power, whilst very useful, should be expressly authorised by the rules and should be carefully supervised by the managing committee. The rules should state that all sub-committees shall conduct their business in accordance with directions from the managing committee and that they shall periodically report their proceedings to the managing committee for approval and ratification. If decisions made by the sub-committee, for example, those of a disciplinary sub-committee, are to have binding force on the members of the club, it is essential that the rules should spell out this power, emphasising that the decision is being made on behalf of the managing committee[36]. It is usual for the rules to provide that members of all sub-committees shall retire automatically on the date on which the annual general meeting is held but to make them eligible for re-appointment by the managing committee immediately after the meeting if it sees fit to do so. The point of automatic retirement

---

[34]    Literary and Scientific Institutions Act 1854, s. 32.

[35]    Para 4(4) of Sch. 7 of the Licensing Act 1964 states that a sub-committee shall be treated as an elective committee if its members are appointed by the managing committee and not less than two-thirds are members of the managing committee.

[36]    If the disciplinary sub-committee exercises power over non-members of the club by virtue, say, of some contract (e.g. as the Kennel Club does) or of some royal charter (e.g. as the Jockey Club does), it is important that its rules and procedures scrupulously avoid any unfairness or apparent bias, and this may mean giving autonomy to the sub-committee, which autonomy it would not normally have: see para 95 of Lord Hope's speech in *Porter v Magill* [2002] 2 AC 357 at 491 for the need for an unbiased judge at common law.

is that it gives the committee, whose composition may have substantially changed as a result of elections at the annual general meeting, the opportunity of re-constituting any sub-committee to assist it in the business of running the club.

## 8.   BYE-LAWS

**5-26**   Bye-laws are a form of subordinate legislation. In club law they exist for the purpose of governing the details or minutiae of internal management and administration of a club where it is unnecessary to burden the main rules with such matters. In the case of a members' club no term will be implied that the committee or the members in general meeting shall have power to make bye-laws, unless (which is unlikely to occur in practice) *all* the members have consented to this course[37]. Therefore there must be express power in the rules to make bye-laws. An exception is an institution established under the Literary and Scientific Institutions Act 1854 which gives the governing body statutory power to make bye-laws 'for the better governance of the institution, its members or officers and for the furtherance of its purpose and object'[38]. It is usual to leave the making of bye-laws to the managing committee; this has the advantage that they may be amended or altered as the circumstances require by the committee itself rather than by the more cumbersome procedure of amendment by the members in general meeting. The enabling rule should state for what purpose or purposes the bye-laws may be made. Bye-laws must be consistent with the main rules, nor should they contain matters of principle which usurp the function of the main rules. Nor must they be unduly oppressive of any minority of the club[39]. In order to ensure that bye-laws are sufficiently brought to the attention of the members, it is good practice to exhibit them on a notice board in the club premises.

**5-27**   It is a common practice for clubs to impose a modest or reasonable fine if the member is either in substantial breach of the bye-laws or is a persistent offender in a small way[40]. Although in the ordinary course of events dealing with a breach of the bye-laws is a

---

[37]    The exception is based on the premise that, if all consent, the members' contract with each other will have been lawfully varied.

[38]    Literary and Scientific Institutions Act 1854, s. 24.

[39]    *Merrifield Ziegler & Co v Liverpool Cotton Association* [1911] 105 LT 97 at 104.

[40]    Under s. 24 of the Act of 1854 a literary or scientific institution may impose a reasonable pecuniary penalty for breach of its bye-laws provided that three-fifths of its members have confirmed this power at a special meeting.

much less serious matter than dealing with expulsion or suspension, which can terminate or curtail the member's privileges of membership, nevertheless the rules of natural justice as set out in **7-15** below must be followed, albeit in a less formal way than with the expulsion or suspension process. Nor do we consider that a system of review or appeal is a necessary or desirable adjunct of giving the committee power to impose a modest or reasonable fine for breach of the bye-laws.

## 9.    CONTROL BY DIRECTORS IN AN INCORPORATED MEMBERS' CLUB

**5-28**    All incorporated clubs must have directors[41] who will manage the business of the company[42]. It is a curious fact that the Companies Acts have never defined directors. Section 741(1) of the Companies Act 1985 states that a director includes 'any person occupying the position of director by whatever name called'. It is generally accepted that a director is a person who manages the affairs of the company for the benefit of himself and the shareholders or members of the company[43]. Most directors will be *de jure* directors, that is, properly appointed in accordance with the law and the company's articles. A few directors may be *de facto* directors, that is, directors who claim to act and purport to act as directors but whose appointment is invalid for some reason or other[44]. An even fewer number may be *shadow* directors, that is, persons in accordance with whose directions or instructions the directors of the company are accustomed to act[45].

**5-29**    Most incorporated clubs will also have a managing committee, some or all of whom will be directors of the company. Where the membership of the committee does not coincide with the board of directors a potential problem can arise. Assume there are 12 members of the committee but only four are directors. Will the eight committee members who are not directors be counted as directors? The answer is, alas, not a simple one. For certain provisions, e.g. insolvency of the company[46] or disqualification of directors[47], the answer might be in

---

[41]    Companies Act 1985, s. 282.

[42]    See article 70 of Table A: Companies (Tables A to F) Regulations 1985 (SI 1985/805).

[43]    *Re Forest of Dean Coalmining Co* [1879] 10 Ch D 451 at 453 per Jessel MR.

[44]    *In re Hydrodam (Corby) Ltd* [1994] 2 BCLC 180 at 183 (Millett J).

[45]    Insolvency Act 1986, s. 251; *Secretary of State for Trade and Industry v Deverell* [2000] 2 WLR 907 CA.

[46]    *Re Hydrodam (Corby) Ltd* [1994] 2 BCLC 180 (wrongful trading under Insolvency Act 1986, s. 214).

[47]    *Re Lo-Line Electric Motors Ltd* [1988] BCLC 698 at 707 (Browne-Wilkinson V-C).

the affirmative but it would all depend on the role which the non-director committee member actually played in the club's affairs. But except in the realm of insolvency of the club, the non-director committee member is very unlikely to be faced with personal liability of any sort arising under company law legislation[48].

**5-30**   A director by virtue of his office owes, broadly speaking, two categories of duty towards the company itself: (1) fiduciary duties (that is, duties of good faith and honesty) and (2) duties of skill and care[49]. These duties are owed to the company, not to individual members of the club[50]. In *In re Barings plc (No.5)* [1999] 1 BCCL 433 at 489 Mr Justice Jonathan Parker gave a helpful overview of what was expected of a director:

> (i) Directors have, both collectively and individually, a continuing duty to acquire and maintain a sufficient knowledge and understanding of the company's business to enable them properly to discharge their duties as directors. (ii) Whilst directors are entitled (subject to the articles of association of the company) to delegate particular functions to those below them in the management chain, and to trust their competence and integrity to a reasonable extent, the exercise of the power of delegation does not absolve a director from the duty to supervise the discharge of the delegated functions [which importantly includes a duty to monitor delegates in the performance of their delegated functions] [51]. (iii) No rule of universal application can be formulated as to the duty referred to in (ii) above. The extent of the duty, and the question whether it has been discharged, must depend on the facts of each particular case, including the director's role in the management of the company.

**5-31**   Directors are responsible for keeping proper accounting records which disclose with reasonable accuracy at any time the financial position of the company[52]. In respect of each financial year the directors must lay before the company in general meeting copies of the accounts for the year[53], which must include the company's profit and loss account, its balance sheet and the directors' report[54]. This report must contain 'a fair review' of the development of the business of the company during the financial year[55]. Directors are also

---

[48]   For civil liability to non-members or third parties, see CHAPTER **12** below.
[49]   See generally, *Gore-Browne on Companies* (50th edn, 2004) Part V.
[50]   *Percival v Wright* [1902] 2 Ch 421.
[51]   The words in square brackets were inserted by the Court of Appeal in *Hollins v Russell* [2003] 1 WLR 2487 at 2540 (para 196).
[52]   Companies Act 1985, ss. 221 and 222 as replaced by the Companies Act 1989, s. 2.
[53]   Companies Act 1985, s. 241(1).
[54]   Ibid. s. 239.
[55]   Ibid. s. 235 and Sch. 7.

responsible for safeguarding the assets of the company[56] and hence for taking reasonable steps for the prevention and detection of fraud[57]. On the other hand, directors may properly delegate their functions to a club official if they are justified in trusting the official to perform his duties competently and honestly[58] or, it is submitted, to a managing committee if the articles or the club rules permit this[59].

**5-32**   Occasions will sometimes arise where the director's duties to the company may conflict with his or her duties to the members as a whole. Take the case of an obstreperous employee whom the members resolve in general meeting should be dismissed forthwith. Against this resolution a director must remember that under section 309 of the Companies Act 1985 he is under a duty to have regard to the interests of the company's employees. In addition, the employee will no doubt have contractual and statutory rights in connection with his employment, and these rights must be honoured. The director's duty to the company will weigh equally with his duty to the members[60]. If the director were to fail in his duty, the company could look to him for redress.

**5-33**   Can a committee member who is a director maintain that he or she is a *non-executive* director and therefore has less onerous duties to the company than an executive director? Take the instance of the Duchess of Abercorn in *Young v Imperial Ladies Club Limited* [1920] 1 KB 523 CA[61], who was excused by Lady Samuel, the chair of the executive committee, from attending any committee meeting because she was too busy elsewhere to attend such meetings. Suppose the duchess had been a director of the company as well as a committee member. And suppose on the same ground she was excused attendance at board meetings. Could the duchess have used this reason for non-performance of her duties as director? The answer is probably in the negative as the courts today have much eroded the distinction between executive and non-executive directors[62]. Club members who become directors are well advised to assume that

---

[56]    *Selangor United Rubber Estates Ltd v Craddock (No.3)* [1968] 1 WLR 1555 at 1575.

[57]    In *In re Kingston Cotton Mill Company (No.2)* [1896] 2 Ch 279, CA, Lopes LJ said at 288 of a company auditor: 'He is a watch-dog, not a bloodhound'. A similar remark could be made of a company director. It has elsewhere been remarked that a company director has 'a duty of curiosity'.

[58]    *Re City Equitable Fire Insurance Co Ltd* [1925] Ch 407 at 429.

[59]    See *Land Credit & Co of Ireland v Lord Fermoy* [1870] 5 Ch App 763 (a lawful delegation by the board of directors to a committee of directors pursuant to the articles).

[60]    *Gaiman v National Association* [1971] Ch 317 at 335F.

[61]    See **7-12** below for a discussion of this case.

[62]    See *Gore-Browne on Companies* (50th edn, 2004) para 15[14].

abdication of responsibilities is no longer acceptable in the courts[63].

## 10.   CONTROL BY PROPRIETOR IN A PROPRIETARY CLUB

**5-34**   The proprietor has full control. If he makes provision for a committee, he will spell out what powers of management he is delegating to the committee, including the expenditure of the proprietor's money.

## 11.   CASH BASIS OF A MEMBERS' CLUB

**5-35**   As we have seen[64], when a member agrees to join a members' club, he is agreeing to pay the entrance fee (if any) and the annual subscription but nothing more. Therefore it follows that absent any agreement (either within or without the rules) a member does not authorise his fellow members to pledge his credit in any club transaction[65]. It is for this reason that a members' club should operate on a cash basis. In *Todd v Emly* [1841] 7 M & W 427 at 434 Mr Baron Parke said[66]:

> The evidence shews that a fund was subscribed, which fund was to be administered by a committee. The committee can only be supposed to have agreed to do that which the subscribers to the club had power to do themselves to do, that is, to administer the fund as far as it went. They were not expected to deal on credit, except for such articles as it might be immediately necessary for them to have dealt with on credit. The making [of] purchases of what was necessary would be only what they ought to do according to the trust reposed in them, and these must be taken to be purchases for ready money, unless distinct evidence was given that they were authorised to enter into contracts on the part of the general body for the common purpose, and to deal on credit, so as to make one the agent of the other. It might be different, perhaps, in the case of hiring the servants of the establishment, where there must necessarily be credit for certain period, because you cannot pay wages down[67] but as to butcher's meat, wine, furniture, and almost anything else, those may be ready money transactions.

---

[63]      Several common law jurisdictions support this proposition: see e.g. *Howard v Herrigal* [1991] (2) SA 660 at 678 (South Africa). On 17 October 2003 Langley J in the High Court of Justice in London refused to strike out a claim for £3.3bn made by Equitable Life Assurance against its non-executive directors for failure to carry out their duties properly in connection with the honouring of costly guaranteed annuity policies which led to the near-collapse of the company.

[64]      See **1-10** above.

[65]      *Flemyng v Hector* [1836] 2 M & W 172  (Parke B at 184 and Alderson B at 187).

[66]      The case is further discussed at **12-04**(2)(a) below.

[67]      I.e. in advance.

The club should therefore not operate a system of deficit budgeting. In any given year the expenditure should be forecast as accurately as possible and the annual subscription fixed accordingly (taking into account of course other sources of income such as investments and fund-raising activities). Since it is the committee member in an unincorporated members' club (unlike his counterpart in a registered or incorporated members' club) who is vulnerable to creditors' claims[68], it is the duty of the committee member to keep a vigilant eye on expenditure to ensure that it will be met from existing club funds, or from authorised borrowing such as a bank loan or overdraft, or from an authorised levy on the members. If there is a surplus of income in any year which earns interest, tax will be payable on such interest[69].

## 5-36 Drawing cheques

No officer of a club has an inherent right to sign cheques on behalf of the club. It is part of the committee's function to authorise those officers of the club who may sign cheques drawn on the club's account, unless the rules or bye-laws deal with this point. It is a wise precaution to stipulate that all cheques must be signed by two officers of the club.

# 12. POWER TO BORROW MONIES

## 5-37 Unincorporated members' clubs

These clubs have no inherent or implied power to borrow monies; this is a concomitant of the club being run on a cash basis. Thus either the rules must contain an express power to borrow monies or *all* the members of the club must consent to the borrowing in question. If there is an express power to borrow in the rules, it is good practice to put some ceiling on the amount which may be borrowed without the consent of the members being first obtained in general meeting.

## 5-38 Literary and scientific institutions

These institutions have no implied power to borrow for purposes which fall outside the activities described in section 33 of the Literary and Scientific Institutions Act 1854. In *Re Badger, Mansell v Viscount Cobham* [1905] 1 Ch 568 the Stourbridge Institute was established for

---

[68]  For third party liability, see CHAPTER 12.
[69]  For taxation, see CHAPTER 17.

the promotion of literature, science and art. It was managed by a council. At its premises was a much used billiard room and the majority of the council resolved either to build a new room (its preferred option) or to repair the old room, but either course required the borrowing of money. There was no express power in the rules to borrow money. Mr Justice Buckley held that there was no implied power to borrow money to build a new billiard room since this was outside the purposes contemplated by the Act. He held, however, that under section 19 of the Act the council could call upon the trustees of the property to repair the existing room, in which case the trustees would have a charge on the property for moneys so expended and would be entitled to reimburse themselves if necessary by raising a mortgage on the institute's premises[70].

## 5-39   Registered clubs

None of these clubs has any inherent or implied right to borrow monies. A shop club, it is envisaged, would not at any stage need to borrow monies. On the other hand, it is considered that there would be nothing improper in a working men's club or a club registered under the Industrial and Provident Societies Act borrowing monies if there was an express power in the rules authorising such borrowing in order to carry out the objects or purposes of the club.

## 5-40   Incorporated members' clubs

In the absence of an express provision in the memorandum, a power to borrow will not be implied 'unless it be properly incident to the course and conduct of the business for its proper purposes'[71]. Thus, generally speaking, any trading or commercial company will have an implied power to borrow monies so long as borrowing is not prohibited by the memorandum[72]. Insofar as clubs do not exist simply for trade purposes (see the second criterion referred to in 1-01 above), it is considered that an incorporated members' club will not have any implied power to borrow monies, necessitating an express power. If the memorandum were silent on the point, the question arises whether the members of the company at a general meeting could pass a special resolution to permit, say, a specific item of borrowing to carry out some lawful transaction. The answer is in the negative because such borrowing would be *ultra vires* of the company; the company would

---

[70]    See also *Re Cleveland Literary and Philosophical Society's Land* [1931] 2 Ch 247.
[71]    *Blackburn Building Society v Cunliffe, Brooks & Co* [1882] 22 Ch D 61 at 70.
[72]    *Gore-Browne on Companies* (50th edn, 2004) para 28[2].

first have to alter its memorandum to include a power of borrowing. Such a resolution would not become valid even if *all* the members assented, thus differentiating it from an unincorporated members' club. If the company has power to borrow, it will also have the power to give security[73]. Any restriction on borrowing or security can be contained in the articles. It is usually limited to a specified amount at any given time without the need for the prior consent of the members, or sometimes is limited to a multiple of the issued share capital and reserves, and sometimes is limited to the amount of the company's net assets.

It is also worth pointing out that in order to obtain a company loan a bank will sometimes require a director of that company to give a personal guarantee in respect of the loan, which immediately negates the principle of limited liability.

### 5-41 Proprietary clubs

Any borrowing of money will be the proprietor's concern.

## 13. CLAIMS BY MEMBERS AGAINST THE CLUB

### 5-42 Unincorporated members' clubs

In the ordinary course of events the managing committee will owe no duty in contract or in tort to the member that he will be safe in using the club premises because no member assumes such a responsibility towards his fellow members as an incidence of membership. An unlikely exception would be if the rules contained an express rule to the contrary. Whatever may be the legal position, it is clear that members of the committee and those members entrusted by the committee to carry out tasks on its behalf need protection from financial liability: this is discussed in **12-05, 12-47** and **12-48** below.

**5-43** As to contract, in *Shore v Ministry of Works* [1950] 2 All ER 228 CA the case (despite its name) concerned the Corsham Community Centre, an unincorporated members' club. The plaintiff-member was injured by a brick dislodged from the clubhouse roof whilst attending an entertainment at the club and she sued the committee for damages for breach of an implied warranty of her contract of membership that

---

[73]    *Re Patent File Co* [1870] 6 Ch App 83.

the premises were safe for the purposes for which she was admitted as a member of the club. Her action failed at first instance and on appeal because the court held that the contract contained no such implied warranty.

**5-44**   As to tort, the committee's lack of liability is because the club has no legal personality of its own so that if the member were to sue his own club (or any members as representing the club) for breach of a duty of care he would in effect be suing himself. Thus in *Robertson v Ridley* [1989] 1 WLR 872 the plaintiff was a member of the Sale and Ashton-on-Mersey Conservative Club, which was an unincorporated members' club. He was riding his motorcycle on the driveway which led away from the club but failed to see a pothole, with the result that he fell off and was injured. He brought an action against the chairman and secretary of the club for damages for breach of the common duty of care under section 2(2) of the Occupiers' Liability Act 1957 and lost both at first instance and on appeal. The decision has been criticised[74] and later cases have attempted to water down its impact by suggesting that there is no blanket immunity for members of a club against claims by another member of the club[75].

**5-45**   In *Prole v Allen* [1950] 1 All ER 476[76] a member sued the committee and the club steward in negligence for injuries suffered when at night he fell down some unlighted steps on the club premises. The steward had switched off the light prior to the accident. The claim failed against the committee but succeeded against the steward because of the responsibility vested in him by all the members. Mr Justice Pritchard put the matter thus:

> He was appointed by all the members, operating through the committee, and, in my judgment, he thereupon became the agent of each member to do reasonably carefully all those things which he was appointed to do, and in that way he came to owe a duty to each of the members to take reasonable care to carry out his duties without negligence.

---

[74]   See *Clerk & Lindsell on Torts*, (18th edn, 2000) para 4-93.

[75]   *Owen v Northampton Borough Council* [1992] 156 LG Rev 23, CA. And see *Grice v Stourport Tennis, Hockey and Squash Club* [1997] CLY para 3859 CA (where Beldam LJ stated that the plaintiff, who was a member of the club, should be permitted to amend his pleadings to claim damages for personal injury against the trustees of the unincorporated club, its chairman of the ground and premises committee and the club steward since the law did not prevent one member suing those other members who undertook a responsibility which gave rise to liability). This case too has been criticised by Clerk and Lindsell op.cit. para 10–11.

[76]   In *Robertson v Ridley* the members of the Court of Appeal disagreed as to the correctness of the decision in *Prole v Allen*.

**5-46** In *Jones v Northampton Borough Council* [1990] Times LR 387 CA the plaintiff, a member of the Shepherd Social Club (an unincorporated members' club), sued the council and Mr Owen, who was another member and the chairman of the club, for an injury suffered when playing indoor football. Mr Owen had hired the pitch for a competition and was warned by the council that because of a leak in the roof the pitch contained a pool of water and that he would be entitled to cancel the hiring. Mr Owen chose to go ahead with the competition and the plaintiff was injured when an opponent slipped in the water and heavily collided with him. Mr Owen relied on the two cases cited in **5-44** and **5-45** above but was found guilty of negligence. Ralph Gibson LJ had this to say[77]:

> The [two] cases relied on by [Mr Owen] were no more than examples of the rule that the mere fact of common ownership of a club, even coupled with membership of a committee on the part of a defendant, did not by itself give rise to a duty of care.
>
> ...
>
> No doubt the nature of the relationship between members of a club would [often][78] be such that it would be impossible to find that one member had undertaken any responsibility to inspect, or to enquire, or to consider whether circumstances would or might give rise to a risk of injury.
>
> But there might be circumstances in which a member [or officer of the club or a member of the committee[79]] acquired knowledge both of the actual danger and of the fact that, if a warning was not given, the members on whose behalf he had undertaken to perform a task would be exposed to a risk of injury. In such circumstances it was open to the court to find that a duty of care existed [to the injured member] and was broken.

There then ensued the case of *Owen v Northampton Borough Council* [1992] 156 LG Rev 23 CA which concerned the apportionment of liability for Mr Jones' injury as between Mr Owen and the council. In his judgment Lord Justice Purchas stated[80]:

> The membership of a club, apart from wholly exceptional circumstances not relevant to this appeal, cannot have the effect of excluding ordinary liability in tort of the Donoghue v Stevenson[81] type once a duty to take care as between neighbours is established.

---

[77]   At 388.
[78]   The lord justice added this word in the later case of *Owen v Northampton Borough Council* [1992] 156 LG Rev 23 CA.
[79]   See p 388.
[80]   At 31.
[81]   [1932] AC 562. 'Neighbour' is used in a technical sense: see **12-23** below.

**5-47  Other clubs**

A working men's club is in the same position as an unincorporated member's club. Clubs registered under the Industrial and Provident Societies Act and incorporated members' clubs are different because here the club is a legal person and the member can sue his own club for damages. A claim can be brought against the owner of a proprietary club, whether the owner be a limited company or an individual person.

# 14.  DEALING WITH INTERNAL DISPUTES

**5-48  Introduction**

Many clubs are anxious that if a dispute arises between two members or between a member and his club or the managing committee, it should be dealt with privately within the four walls of the club rather than being publicly trailed in the local county court or some other court. As a result, in some clubs there is an internal complaints procedure which must be used before recourse is made to the courts. As to the requirement for natural justice in operating internal procedures, see **7-15** below. On the other hand, the club may wish to prevent the matter going to court at all. This is usually achieved by the insertion of an arbitration clause in the rules[82]. What happens, however, if the aggrieved member ignores the arbitration clause because he wants, say, the publicity of a court case and issues a claim form against the club? The answer is for the club to seek a stay of the court proceedings under section 9 of the Arbitration Act 1996. Such a stay is mandatory unless the arbitration agreement is null and void, inoperative or incapable of being performed. A further point to note is that an individual may waive his right of access to the courts under Article 6(1) of the European Convention on Human Rights[83] by entering into a contract in which he agrees to submit disputes to arbitration[84].

---

[82]    It is also a well-known fact that appealing the arbitrator's award or recourse to the courts is made intentionally difficult under the Arbitration Act 1996. For the topic of alternative dispute resolution see **18-29** below.

[83]    The Human Rights Act 1998 incorporated this convention into UK domestic law.

[84]    *Deweer v Belgium* [1979–1980] EHRR 439 at para 49.

## 5-49 Unincorporated members' clubs

The rules must specifically deal with this point since a contractual term to exclude recourse to the courts in the event of a dispute will be void on public policy grounds[85] unless accompanied by the provision of arbitration. If the rules are silent on the point, no term will be implied into them that the complaint or dispute must be dealt with internally.

## 5-50 Working men's clubs

Dispute settlement is a mandatory matter for the rules[86]. The Friendly Societies Act 1992 put in place substituted provisions as to how disputes are to be resolved[87]. Disputes shall be resolved by arbitration in the manner directed by the rules and, without derogating from this right to go to arbitration, the club may establish internal procedures for the resolution of complaints or the parties may consent to a reference to an adjudicator for investigation and settlement of the complaint.

## 5-51 IPSA clubs

Unlike the Friendly Societies Acts, the Industrial and Provident Societies Act 1965 does not make dispute settlement a mandatory matter for the rules. Instead, the Act regulates the position as follows: if the rules give directions as to the manner in which disputes are to be decided, this procedure must be adopted, unless the parties to the dispute by consent refer the matter to the county court[88]. Whichever procedure is adopted, any decision on the dispute shall be binding and conclusive on all parties without appeal and shall not be removable into any court of law or restrainable by injunction[89]. If the rules direct that the dispute shall be heard by justices in a magistrates' court, the parties to the dispute may by consent refer the matter to

---

[85]     *Lee v Showmen's Guild of Great Britain* [1952] 2 QB 329 CA at 342 (Denning LJ); *Baker v Jones* [1954] 1 WLR 1005 at 1010.

[86]     Ss. 7(2) of the Friendly Societies Act 1974 and Part I (9) of Sch. 2 thereof.

[87]     Ss. 80 and 81 of the Friendly Societies Act 1992 replacing ss. 76–80 of the Act of 1974.

[88]     S. 60(1)(2) of the Act of 1965 as amended by s. 83 of the Friendly Societies Act 1992.

[89]     Ibid. s. 60(3). Parliamentary draftsmanship has gone awry here. In 1965 the original version of s. 60 gave as an alternative to arbitration a determination of the dispute by the Chief Registrar of Friendly Societies. In 1992, in substituting the county court for the Chief Registrar, Parliament overlooked the prohibition that the decision was not to be removable to any court of law. The prohibition would still apply to decisions made via an internal procedure.

the county court[90]. If the rules are silent on the question of dispute settlement, or if no decision on the dispute is made within 40 days after application for a reference under the rules, any party to the dispute may apply to the county court or to a magistrates' court for a determination of the dispute[91].

## 5-52  Shop clubs

Dispute settlement is a mandatory matter for the rules[92]. No other statutory provision applies. The procedure laid down by the rules must be followed, although presumably it would be in order for the parties to the dispute mutually to consent to some other mode of dispute resolution.

## 5-53  Incorporated members' clubs

The situation is the same as for an unincorporated club: see **5-49** above. Any provision for resolution of the dispute by some internal procedure or by arbitration must appear in the club rules or in the articles or bye-laws.

## 5-54  Proprietary clubs

It is for the proprietor to frame a suitable rule dealing with disputes between him and the members. One would have thought that any sound proprietor would prefer the confidentiality of arbitration to the glare of court proceedings.

---

[90]    S. 60(5) of the Act of 1965.
[91]    Ibid. s. 60(6).
[92]    Shop Clubs Act 1902 Sch. para viii.

# Chapter 6

# MEETINGS

## 1. INTRODUCTION

**6-01**  The holding of meetings of club members is an essential part of club life. It is therefore important that the holding of these meetings is adequately dealt with within the rules and that meetings are properly convened, constituted and conducted when they take place. What follows is applicable to all clubs, save that there are statutory provisions relating to incorporated members' clubs[1].

## 2. ANNUAL GENERAL MEETING

**6-02**  Nowadays it is almost unheard of for the rules of a members' club not to make provision for the holding of an annual general meeting. It is a mandatory requirement if the club holds a registration certificate[2] and, although this requirement has not been carried through to the Licensing Act 2003, we consider that an absence of any procedure whereby an AGM is held would probably offend against the sixth criterion (the need for collegiality) referred to in **1-01** above. Its importance lies in the fact that it provides the opportunity for the members to receive reports about the club activities during the preceding year and to discuss the way forward for the coming year. The main items of business of an AGM are: receiving reports from the secretary and the treasurer; receiving and, if thought fit, approving the club's accounts for the preceding financial year; electing the officers of the club; fixing the subscriptions; and

---

[1]    See **6-37** below.
[2]    Licensing Act 1964, Sch. 7, para 2(1).

transacting the general business of the club. The date of the AGM is often fixed in the rules by specifying an actual date (or sometimes the month) which must not be passed in each year without an AGM having been held. Commonly, too, the rules stipulate that an interval of more than 15 months must not elapse between successive AGMs, and this is a mandatory requirement if the club holds a registration certificate[3].

**6-03**  The item 'any other business' (often abbreviated to 'AOB') needs clarification. Its proper use at an AGM is to deal with points arising out of the *general* business of the club, that is, what has gone before in the other items on the agenda. Some rules draw a distinction between general and special business[4] by defining all business as special save those items regularly appearing on the AGM agenda, in order that the AOB item at the AGM cannot be abused. The AOB item at the AGM cannot be used to pass a specific proposal or to raise important matters unconnected with the general business of the club. On the other hand, the AOB item is a proper opportunity for members to put questions or observations to officers of the club. The dividing line between the proper use and the improper use of the AOB item is a fine one, and it ultimately falls to the chairman of the meeting to decide where to draw the line.

**6-04**  Some rules dealing with important matters such as the amendment of the rules or the dissolution of the club state that such matters may only be dealt with 'at a meeting called for the purpose'. Can such matters be raised at an AGM? The answer is in the negative because an AGM is convened to conduct the general business of the club, which does not include special business such as amendment of the rules or dissolution of the club[5]. The doubt can easily be avoided by stating in the rule, 'at a *special* meeting called for the purpose', if this is the wish of the members. However, it is common practice nowadays, in order to save time and money, for amendments to the rules, especially non-contentious ones, to be permitted at the AGM provided proper notice is given to the members. In this event, the item on the agenda will be marked 'Special business'[6].

---

3    Licensing Act 1964, Sch. 7, para 2(1).
4    Special business is not be confused with special resolutions, a term of art used in company law.
5    *Harington v Sendall* [1903] 1 Ch 921 at 926.
6    See the example given in Appendix 15.

## 3.   SPECIAL MEETINGS

**6-05**   These are meetings of the club members which deal with special business, that is to say, meetings which are called for a particular and stated purpose (or purposes) and which, generally speaking, cannot be dealt with at an AGM. Their correct legal name is a special general meeting or, in company law, an extraordinary general meeting (or EGM)[7]. It is important that the rules deal with such meetings, although it is considered that where the rules are silent on the subject it is an inherent right of club members to meet together, so that the ability to hold a special meeting would be implied into the rules[8]. The only business that can be transacted at a special meeting is that business for which the meeting was called.  There will therefore be no AOB item at the end of the agenda.

**6-06**   Special meetings are convened by order of the managing committee or on the requisition of the members. The rules should stipulate the actual number of members required for a valid requisition. If a club has a registration certificate, the rules must specify a number not exceeding 30 or more than one-fifth of the total membership (whichever is the less)[9]. This provision is not repeated in the Licensing Act 2003 but nevertheless it is considered a good working rule for all clubs. Membership here means ordinary members. If a club has fewer than 150 members, the specified number would necessarily be less than 30; for a club with 100 members a requisition by 20 members would suffice. The question arises whether a requisition can be made orally as well as in writing. Many rules talk in terms of a requisition *signed* by a specified number which presupposes a written document. A requisition is a formal demand and it may be doubted whether an oral demand would be valid[10].

**6-07**   The question arises as to what happens if the committee (or the directors of an incorporated club) fail or refuse to convene a duly requisitioned meeting. In incorporated clubs this difficulty is surmounted by section 368 of the Companies Act 1985 giving the

---

[7]      Regulation 36 of Table A Articles of association: SI 1985/805. Clubs commonly refer to their special meetings as EGMs.

[8]      In this event it would be for the committee to lay down the requisite procedural rules for convening and holding the special meeting: see the judge's remarks quoted in **6-08** below.

[9]      Licensing Act 1964, Sch. 7, para 2(3).

[10]      In the Chambers Dictionary (1998) the first definition of 'requisition' refers to a formal demand; the second definition refers to military supply; and the third definition is 'the *written* order for the supply of materials' (emphasis added).

power to the requisionists themselves to convene the meeting[11]. In an unincorporated members' club holding a registration certificate the rules must contain a provision that the members entitled to attend and vote at a general meeting shall have the ability to summon a general meeting[12]. With regard to other unincorporated members' clubs, in order to get over this problem, some rules expressly state that if the secretary fails to convene a meeting which has been properly requisitioned, the requisitionists themselves shall be entitled to convene the meeting. In the absence of an express rule we consider that the requisitionists themselves would have an implied right to convene the meeting, otherwise it would render nugatory their right to requisition such a meeting.

## 4.    NOTICE OF MEETINGS

**6-08**   It is axiomatic that in order to attend a general meeting and participate therein each member entitled to vote[13] at such a meeting must receive a notice which tells him (1) the date, (2) the time, (3) the place and (4) the nature of the business to be discussed or transacted. The rules should specify what length of notice a member will receive in respect of any type of meeting, an exception being committee meetings where at the end of one meeting the committee very often decides the date of the next meeting there and then; this new date must, however, be circulated to those committee members who did not attend the original meeting. In *Labouchere v Earl of Wharncliffe* [1879] 13 Ch D 346 the plaintiff was a member of the Beefsteak Club, who had an altercation with another club member and then wrote a letter and articles about it in a magazine called Truth. A general meeting was called by the committee to consider the expulsion of the plaintiff and the resolution to expel him was carried. The rules required a fortnight's notice of the meeting. In the member's action against the club Sir George Jessel MR had this to say about the time and manner of giving notice of meetings[14]:

> In the present instance a meeting of the committee was held on the night of the 31st October, and concluded on the morning of the 1st November. That meeting decided to proceed in a very proper way, both by posting a notice in the coffee-room of the club and by sending a circular to each of the members. So far as I am aware there is no common law [precept] for clubs

---

[11]     See **6-39** below.
[12]     Licensing Act 1964, Sch. 7, para 2(3).
[13]     So that members without votes, such as honorary or junior members, need not be notified.
[14]     At 352.

as to the mode in which notices should be issued; and where no [club] rule prescribes a mode, it is within the general functions of a committee of a club to say how notices should be given on each particular occasion.

Some matters connected with a club concern only those who habitually use it; and in connection with these matters, the posting of a notice in the coffee-room or the library is a very sensible plan to follow. But more important matters sometimes [arise] – matters relating, perhaps, to some organic change – matters connected with the general mode of conducting the club – matters connected with the conduct of a particular member; and in such cases it is only right to give notice by circular to those who do not habitually or daily use the club that these matters are coming on for consideration, in order that they may attend and take part in the discussion. When the latter course was adopted, the committee were bound to give a fortnight's notice. In this case the notice was for 14th November. If it was posted on 1st November, that would not be a fortnight's notice, and it was posted on the 1st November.

The judge therefore held that, as the meeting was irregularly called, the committee had no power to expel Mr Labouchere[15]. Thus there is a general rule that notices for meetings must be given timeously for there to be a valid meeting.

**6-09**  There is a second and equally important general rule which is that an omission to give due notice of a meeting to even one member of a body, who is entitled to attend and who is not beyond summonable distance, renders invalid the meeting and any decision thereat[16]. Although in the trilogy of cases cited in footnote 16 all the judges refer to the decision being *void*, it is probably more accurate to describe it as *voidable* since an invalid decision may in some circumstances be acquiesced in[17] or ratified[18] or the omission may be excusable[19]. An important exception relates to incorporated clubs in that by Article 39 of Table A[20] the accidental omission to give notice of a meeting to, or the non-receipt of notice of a meeting by, any person entitled to receive notice shall not invalidate the proceedings of that meeting.

---

[15]    At 354.
[16]    *Smyth v Darley* [1849] 2 HL Cas 789 at 803 (Lord Campbell LC) (concerning the election of an officer, namely, the county treasurer of the city of Dublin); *Young v Imperial Ladies Club Ltd* [1920] 2 KB 523 CA at 536 (Scrutton LJ) (concerning the expulsion of a member of a club); and *John v Rees* [1970] Ch 345 at 402B (Megarry J) (concerning the suspension of a local Labour Party).
[17]    *Abbatt v Treasury Solicitor* [1969] 1 WLR 1575 CA at 1583E.
[18]    *In re Sick and Funeral Society of St John's Sunday School, Golcar* [1973] 1 Ch 51 at 57E (Megarry J).
[19]    *Young v Imperial Ladies Club Ltd supra* at 536.
[20]    Companies (Tables A to F) Regulations 1985 (SI 1985/805).

**6-10**   If the general rules referred to in **6-08** and **6-09** above were to apply in their full rigour, this could be very inimical to organising valid meetings. One has to remember that at common law a notice is not served merely by putting it in the post[21]; it has to be received – after all, the purpose of a notice is to notify[22]. But in contract law a 'posting rule' grew up, based on commercial convenience, whereby if the acceptance of an offer was permissible by post, the acceptance was put into effect when the letter was posted[23]. But this posting rule is not considered to be of general application. A convenient way out of the difficulty is for the rules to permit the sending of notices by post and to include an express deeming provision, such as 'A notice shall be deemed to have been effected at a time at which the letter would be delivered in the ordinary course of post'[24]. With such a rule it will be essential for the secretary to keep a post book to show when the notice was sent out. If electronic means of communicating the notice are intended to be used, the rules should make specific provision for this. It should be borne in mind, however, that court documents may be served by fax, but not by e-mail, because this latter form of communication is not yet considered reliable enough (e.g. problems caused by viruses or by the interception of third parties or the fact that the document can be altered by the recipient)[25]. Although a member might well have a legitimate grievance if he did not receive, or received late, a posted or other notice of an important meeting, we consider that any request for the meeting to be reconvened should be refused if (1) the meeting was otherwise quorate and (2) the managing committee is satisfied that neither the aggrieved member's attendance at the meeting nor his vote thereat would have affected the outcome of the decision taken or the resolution passed[26]. Upon refusal the member's remedy would be to seek a court declaration that the meeting was invalid, an expensive and fruitless exercise if on

---

[21]     *Beanby Estates Ltd v Egg Stores (Stamford Hill) Ltd* [2003] 1 WLR 2064 (Neuberger J) at 2075C.

[22]     *Blunden v Frogmore Investments Ltd* [2002] 2 EGLR 29 CA at 32.

[23]     *Henthorn v Fraser* [1892] 2 Ch 27 at 33.

[24]     For documents served pursuant to statute, s. 7 of the Interpretation Act 1978 imports a deeming provision as to service if the document was sent by post (*C A Webber Ltd v Railtrack plc* [2004] 1 WLR 320 CA) or if served pursuant to court rules such as CPR rule 6.7 (*Anderton v Clwyd County Council (No.2)* [2002] 1 WLR 3174 CA). Both cases held that the deeming provision complied with human rights legislation.

[25]     See *R v Minors* [1989] 1 WLR 441 CA at 443 (Steyn J). But see CPR Practice Direction 5B which authorised for a limited period a pilot scheme in the Walsall County Court for communication by e-mail, and see also CPR Practice Direction 6, para 3.3 which permits service by e-mail.

[26]     If more than one member is complaining about breaches of the two general rules, the committee must of course consider the cumulative effect of the absence of such members from the meeting.

reconvening the meeting the same result occurs.

**6-11** Despite what is said in the last paragraph, the cost of sending a notice by postage is so disproportionately high in relation to sending one by e-mail or exhibiting the same on the club's web-site that every club should contemplate whether its rules should make provision for electronic means of communication as well as by post. It can be argued in favour of electronic communication that not only is it cheaper than postage but it is also swifter and absolves the secretary from a tedious administrative chore in preparing and sending out letters. The rules, however, need to cater for persons who do not have access to e-mail, either by choice or for some other reason; otherwise the club will be impliedly stipulating that only those persons with a computer will be eligible for membership, and this must be wrong in principle.

**6-12** The computation of time has given rise to many disputes in the law[27]. Suffice it to say that the general rule is that where the expression, '14 days' notice', is used the day of service is excluded[28], so the judge in *Labouchere's* case was correct in saying the notice was one day short. The rule applies too if the fixed period of time is described as 'from' such-and-such a date[29]. It is otherwise if the fixed period of time is described as 'beginning with' such-and-such a date; here the first day is included[30]. If the notice prescribed is one of '14 clear days' or 'not less than 14 days', or 'at least 14 days', the last day has to be subtracted as well as the day of service when computing the period[31], thus covering a period of 16 days. If the rules are silent on the question of notice, reasonable notice must be given.

**6-13** If a meeting is adjourned for any reason, a fresh notice of the adjourned date does not have to be sent out to those members who did not attend the original meeting[32]. Those attending the meeting should be told by the chairman of the adjourned date. If the meeting is adjourned without a date being fixed for its resumption or if the adjournment is for 14 days or more, it is good practice to send notice of the adjourned meeting to all members. In this regard the company law practice should be followed[33].

---

[27] See the notes to CPR rule 2.8 in the White Book Civil Procedure 2004.

[28] *Zoan v Rouamba* [2000] 1 WLR 1509 CA at para 23 of the judgment of the court, citing *Young v Higgon* [1840] 6 M & W 49.

[29] Ibid. at para 23, citing *Goldsmiths' Co v West Metropolitan Railway Co* [1904] 1 KB 1.

[30] Ibid. at para 24, citing *Hare v Gocher* [1962] 2 QB 641.

[31] *R v Turner* [1910] 1 KB 346, CA at 359-360.

[32] *Scadding v Lorant* [1851] 3 HL Cas 418 at 446.

[33] See **6-40** under Notice of meetings.

## 5.  AGENDA

**6-14**   The agenda for a general meeting is normally prepared by the secretary. A specimen agenda for an AGM may be found at Appendix 15. Formal motions which are proposed to be put to the meeting should be set out in full; this is especially important if the agenda is for a special meeting called for a particular purpose. It is improper to depart from the order in which the items are set down in the agenda unless a majority of the meeting agrees to the contrary[34]. The agenda for a committee meeting is sometimes prepared by the secretary, at other times by the committee chairman. It is good practice to try to keep the committee agenda running in the same order from meeting to meeting. It is important for a committee agenda to have an item 'Matters Arising', that is to say, arising out of the minutes of the last meeting.

## 6.  CHAIR OF MEETINGS

**6-15**   The chair of the club by virtue of his office is the correct person to chair general meetings of club members. What sometimes confuses the members is who is to chair the meeting in the absence of the chair. In incorporated clubs this should pose no problem because regulations 42 and 43 of the articles of association prescribed by Tables A and C[35]: lay down a set procedure as to who should chair the meeting[36]. In all other clubs one first has to look in the rules or bye-laws as to what, if anything, is said about the chairmanship of meetings. If the rules and bye-laws are silent and the chair is absent from the meeting, the first task of the meeting will be to elect a chair from those persons present at the meeting.  Commonly it is the secretary who deals with this situation; he should seek the nomination of a senior and respected member who he thinks will control the meeting properly. This person does not necessarily have to be an officer of the club or a member of the committee. Once elected as chair of the meeting, that person does not automatically cease to be the chair if perchance the designated chair were later to arrive at the meeting. This would depend on how far the meeting had progressed; in its early stages he might well stand down.

---

[34]     *John v Rees* [1970] Ch 345 at 378.

[35]     Companies Act 1985, s. 8; Companies (Tables A to F) Regulations 1985 (SI 1985/805).

[36]     Articles 36 to 63 inclusive of Table A appear in APPENDIX 9.

## 6-16   Chair's duties

The duties cast upon a chair of a meeting are not only important but must be properly exercised to ensure a well-conducted meeting, remembering Mr Justice Megarry's dictum that, 'Above all, [the chair's] duty is to act not as dictator but as a servant of the members of the body, according to law'[37]. The chair's duties may be summarised as follows:

(1) to check that the meeting has been properly convened;

(2) to ensure that a quorum of members is present;

(3) to welcome such guests or visitors as are permitted at the meeting;

(4) to adjourn the meeting to a larger meeting place if the chosen place is too small to accommodate the members present (if one is available)[38] or to adjourn the meeting to a later date at a different venue or, if necessary, to abandon the meeting[39];

(5) to keep order and, if possible, to restore order if disorder breaks out and, in the latter event, to adjourn the meeting either for a short time or generally if his efforts to restore order are in vain[40];

(6) to remain impartial throughout the meeting, and to stand down if he has a personal interest in the outcome of any motion;

(7) to rule on a point of order[41];

(8) not to alter the order of the agenda unless a majority of the meeting agrees to this course[42];

(9) not to introduce a motion of his own which is not on the agenda[43];

(10)  to see that speakers address the chair[44] and that questions are asked through the chair;

(11)  to deal with amendments to motions in the correct order[45];

(12)  to ask the secretary, or he himself, to read out the precise motion

---

[37]   *John v Rees* [1970] 1 Ch 345 at 377E.

[38]   In *Byng v London Life Association Ltd* [1989] 1 All ER 560 CA the court held at 565d that for a meeting to be validly constituted it is not necessary for all members to be physically present in the same room provided that proper audio/visual aids are used to enable the members in any overflow room to participate in the meeting.

[39]   Ibid. at 569c; *Mulholland v St Peter's, Roydon, Parochial Church Council* [1969] 1 WLR 1842 at 1848E.

[40]   The duty to keep order was described by Megarry J as the first duty of a chairman in *John v Rees* [1970] 1 Ch 345 at 382D. In the same case is a detailed discussion of the chairman's power of adjournment in the event of disorder and how it should be exercised (at 379B onwards). If a chairman validly adjourns a meeting and leaves the chair, no-one else can replace the chairman and continue with the meeting.

[41]   *Re Indian Zoedone Co* [1884] 26 Ch D 70 at 77.

[42]   *John v Rees* [1970] 1 Ch 345 at 378A.

[43]   Ibid. at 377C.

[44]   He should curtail long speeches and prevent second speeches if others want to speak. If the chairman is speaking, or he rises to speak, he will take precedence over other speakers.

[45]   See **6-17** below.

which is being put to the meeting to be voted on;

(13)   to oversee that voting procedures are conducted properly;

(14)   to appoint tellers or scrutineers for the counting of votes;

(15)   to declare the result of any vote on a motion.


## 7.    AMENDMENTS TO MOTIONS

**6-17**   Meetings consider motions. If the members at the meeting are 'moved' to vote in favour of a motion, the approved motion becomes a resolution whereby the members are 'resolved' to act in accordance with the motion. Experience shows that, unless properly handled, amendments to motions can cause havoc at a meeting. Sometimes the chairman is forewarned because the original motion and the proposed amendments are all set out in the agenda. The chairman does not have to take the amendments in the chronological order in which they were set down in the agenda; he should take them in the most logical order and he can prepare his thoughts on this before the meeting. Members, however, are entitled to propose amendments from the floor during the debate so long as they are within the scope of the motion of which notice was originally given[46]. Any amendment should be precisely formulated and not a simple contradiction or disagreement with the original motion because that is done by voting against the motion. It is far better if any such proposed amendment is reduced to writing but provided its effect is made reasonably clear it may be submitted orally to the meeting[47]. If the proposed amendment is of an acceptable nature, it is customary for the chairman to ask for a seconder[48]. If found, the proposer, but not the seconder, should be allowed to speak in support of the amendment. The amendment is then discussed and the chairman, not the proposer, should sum up the situation if necessary. The amendment is then put to the vote, and if successful the amended motion now becomes the motion before the meeting and can itself be the subject of amendment. If unsuccessful, the original motion continues to be discussed.

We would add that in putting forward the proposed amendment to the meeting for the members to decide whether to accept or reject it, we consider that this item can be decided on a simple majority[49]. If

---

[46]    *Torbock v Lord Westbury* [1902] 2 Ch 871 at 874.

[47]    *Henderson v Bank of Australasia* [1890] 45 Ch D 330 CA.

[48]    There is no legal requirement that a seconder is necessary but the absence of a seconder goes to the chairman's discretion whether to accept the amendment: *Young v Sherman* [2001] 40 ACSR 12 (NSW Supreme Ct).

[49]    Unless, which is unlikely, the rules stipulate to the contrary.

the proposed amendment is accepted, then any substantive decision of the meeting thereafter must be on such majority as the resolution requires, for example, a three-fourths majority on a motion to alter the rules.

## 8.   MEMBERS' RESOLUTIONS

**6-18**   A question which arises is whether a resolution passed by the members in general meeting is binding on the managing committee, bearing in mind that the committee will normally have control of all the club's affairs. Could the committee ignore the resolution? The answer depends on whether the resolution was intended by the members to be a binding decision on the whole membership or whether the resolution is to be construed as a recommendation to the committee, which could be ignored if the committee thinks fit. A resolution to amend the rules or to dissolve the club would plainly fall within the first category; a resolution that the club should buy a new television set for the clubhouse would equally plainly fall within the latter category. Many other resolutions would not produce a self-evident answer; each resolution would need to be analysed in order to categorise it correctly.

**6-19**   A clear example of when the committee would be entitled to ignore the resolution is where the club has a registration certificate, and the purchase and supply of intoxicating liquor is vested in the committee under the rules[50]. Here a resolution passed by the members, say, to change the brewer who supplied the club could be treated by the committee as a recommendation only, even if the resolution had been carried by a handsome majority of the members. In an appropriate case, the members' remedy would be either to requisition a special meeting to pass a vote of no confidence in the committee[51] or to vote the committee out of office at the next AGM elections.

## 9.   QUORUM

**6-20**   A quorum is the number of persons who must be present at a general or committee meeting to constitute a valid meeting. It is crucial for the proper running of a club that a rule (or bye-law) deals with

---

[50]      Licensing Act 1964, s. 41(2)(c). The members may themselves manage the purchase and supply of intoxicating liquor in general meeting instead of the committee (ibid. s. 41(2)(c)), but except in a very small club this would not be a wise move.
[51]      See further **5-21** above.

this point. In relation to general meetings of an unincorporated members' club and in the absence of such a rule, potentially all members would have to attend for a valid meeting to take place. In the Australian case of *Ball v Palsall* [1987] 10 NSW LR 700 Mr Justice Young had this to say, after reviewing the English authorities[52]:

> Where the constitution of an unincorporated association makes no provision for a quorum for meetings of the association, in theory the business of that association can only be transacted when all the members are present; however, by consensual compact between the members some lesser number can be a quorum and in determining that lesser number, the activities of the members after the consensual compact was made are relevant.

Evidence from the officers of a club that an unwritten rule as to quorum had been habitually used in the past could prove sufficient to justify a quorum less than the whole membership[53].

**6-21**   In relation to committee meetings and in the absence of a quorum rule, the quorum for a committee will be the entire committee because the delegation of powers is not to the individual members of the committee but to the committee as a whole[54]. Such a quorum would be hopelessly impracticable.

On the other hand, it is good practice to avoid too small a number for a quorum for a general meeting of the members since this will prevent a clique from running the club[55]. This is an important point for incorporated clubs to consider because of regulation 40 of Table A lays down that two persons shall form a quorum at a general meeting. In companies limited by shares this can be overcome by a special article and in a company limited by guarantee it can be overridden by specifying a different quorum in the articles, bearing in mind that Table A only has to be followed 'as near to that form as circumstances admit'[56].

**6-22**   One must draw a distinction between a quorum required to requisition a meeting and, once convened, the quorum required for a valid meeting to take place. The two quorums do not have to be the same number. If a club has a registration certificate, the quorum

---

[52]   At 703B.
[53]   See *John v Rees* [1970] Ch 345 at 388F (Megarry J).
[54]   *Brown v Andrew* [1849] 18 LJ QB 153; *R v Liverpool City Council ex p Professional Association of Teachers* (1984) *The Times*, 22 March.
[55]   At common law the minimum number for a quorum is two: *R v Secretary of State for the Environment ex p Hillingdon* [1986] 1 WLR 192.
[56]   Companies Act 1985, s. 8(4).

required for a valid requisition of a general meeting must not exceed 30 or be more than one-fifth of the total number of members entitled to attend meetings and vote thereat (whichever is less)[57] and this is regarded as a good working rule for all clubs[58]. If a club has 300 members, one-fifth is 60, but the requisition only requires 30 signatures. However, it is perfectly in order for the rules to stipulate that the quorum for the meeting itself shall be a higher number, say 50 or 60. A question which also arises is whether a meeting has to be quorate at all times or only at the beginning of the meeting. Suppose several members left during the course of a meeting, and their leaving made the quorum insufficient. Could the meeting validly continue? The answer is in the negative because what is required is that the meeting must be quorate both at the beginning of the meeting when the chairman declares the meeting open, and when any decision is made during the meeting[59]. However, a member who left the meeting deliberately so as to remove the quorum cannot rely on the lack of quorum in challenging decisions made after his departure[60]. An apparent exception is the case of *Re Hartley Baird Ltd* [1955] Ch 143 which concerned a company meeting. Mr Justice Wynn-Parry held that since the articles expressly stipulated for a quorum to be present at the *beginning* of the meeting, there was no requirement for a continuing quorum throughout the meeting. Two members at least must be present throughout the meeting, otherwise the proceedings would not constitute a meeting[61].

**6-23** If there is no quorum at the scheduled start of a meeting, in unincorporated members' clubs, it is customary to allow a short period of grace, say 30 minutes, to see if the required quorum can be established by latecomers. This is sometimes expressed in the rules or bye-laws but even if they are silent it is considered that it would be in the chairman's power to adjourn the start of the meeting for a short while for the benefit of those members who are present and who may have travelled a considerable distance to attend the meeting or have given up their leisure time to do so[62]. In incorporated members' clubs, regulation 41 of the 1985 Table A permits a period of grace of up to a half an hour if no quorum is present at the appointed time.

---

57    Licensing Act 1964, Sch. 7, para 2(3).
58    Even though this rule has not been carried through to the Licensing Act 2003.
59    *Henderson v James Louttit and Co Ltd* [1894] 21 R (Ct of Sess) 674 at 676. And see reg. 41 of the 1985 Table A articles of association (at **APPENDIX 9**).
60    *Ball v Pearsall* [1987] 10 NSW LR 700 at 705B.
61    *Sharp v Dawes* [1876] 2 QBD 26 CA  at 29; *Re London Flats, Carbon* [1969] 1 WLR 711.
62    See *John v Rees* [1970] 1 Ch 345 at 383A.

## 10.  VOTING

**6-24**  There are four ways of voting which are used in club meetings[63]:
(1) by acclamation;
(2) by a show of hands;
(3) by poll;
(4) by ballot.

### 6-25  Acclamation

Sometimes it is not necessary to put a motion to a formal vote since the chairman of the meeting will have sensed that mood of the meeting does not require this step[64].

### 6-26  Show of hands

This is usually the first method of voting at a meeting. If the meeting is large it is sensible to appoint scrutineers to help count the votes. The chairman can order a recount if necessary[65]. The chairman is entitled to vote along with the other members[66]. Indeed, it is common to give the chairman an additional or casting vote in the rules[67] unless the club has a registration certificate when this is not allowed in general meetings[68].

### 6-27  Poll

A chairman may proceed to voting by poll without there first being a show of hands[69]. A poll openly records the number of votes, either by an individual voting slip or by signing a voting list, and is a more accurate way of establishing the true vote. A member who is dissatisfied with the vote by show of hands can demand a poll as of right, unless there is a rule to the contrary[70]. Once a valid request for

---

63      A fifth way is voting by division (a method long used by Parliament but seldom if ever used by clubs).
64      *Re The Citizens Theatre Ltd* [1946] SC 14 at 18. This voting is sometimes recorded in the minutes as 'Nem. Con.' This is shorthand for 'Nemine contradicente' i.e. with no one dissenting. This is not the same thing as a unanimous decision in favour.
65      *Hickman v Kent [or] Romney Marsh Sheepbreeders Associations* [1920] 36 TLR 528 at 533.
66      *Nell v Longbottom* [1894] 1 QB 767 at 771.
67      There is no common law right to a casting vote: *Nell v Longbottom* supra at 771.
68      Licensing Act 1964, Sch 7, para 2(4).
69      *R v Rector of Birmingham* [1837] 7 A & E 254.
70      *Re Wimbledon Local Board* [1882] 8 QBD 459 CA.

a poll has been made, the result of any vote by a show of hands ceases to have effect[71]. A poll has to be taken of all the members entitled to vote[72]. This raises the question whether the poll is restricted to those attending the meeting or whether it means all the members of the club, which would normally necessitate the adjournment of the meeting. The answer is that the decision should be left to those attending the meeting. In *R v Rector of St Mary, Lambeth* [1838] 8 A & E 356 all the ratepayers of a large parish were entitled to vote in the election of the churchwardens and a meeting was duly convened. The election was conducted on a show of hands, and after the result several ratepayers demanded a poll of the whole parish, but the majority of the ratepayers at the meeting decided that it should be restricted to those present, and this decision was upheld by the Court of Exchequer Chamber. The court quoted an extract from Prideaux's *Directions to Churchwardens* (10th edn, 1835), which neatly summarises why absent members cannot complain if they do not attend meetings: '[if persons properly qualified are duly assembled] at the time and place appointed, the present include the absent, and the major part of the present include all the rest. For those who absent themselves after [due] notice given, do it voluntarily, and therefore devolve their vote upon those who are present'.

## 6-28   Ballot

It is common for officers of a club to be elected by secret ballot at the annual general meeting, if the office is contested. The secretary should prepare the ballot papers before the meeting with the names of the candidates arranged in alphabetical order. The chairman usually lets each candidate introduce himself and say a few words in support of his candidature. The vote is taken by each member marking with a cross his choice of candidate. The vote is then counted by the secretary or the scrutineers if appointed.

## 6-29   Voting by proxy

There is at common law no right to appoint proxies[73]. There must therefore be an express rule permitting this mode of voting[74]. On a

---

[71]    *R v Cooper* [1870] LR 5 QB 457.
[72]    *R v Rector of St Mary, Lambeth* [1838] 8 A & E 356.
[73]    *Harben v Phillips* [1883] 23 Ch D 14; *Woodford v Smith* [1970] 1 WLR 806 at 810D.
[74]    For incorporated members' clubs Regulation 59 of the 1985 Table A gives a right to a proxy vote on a poll. Forms of proxy are set out in Regulations 60 and 61. For these regulations see APPENDIX 9.

show of hands, each member has one vote only even though he may be acting as proxy for several members[75]. This is because it is a counting of hands; nothing more. If the voter is unhappy with the outcome, he can demand a poll as of right and then *all* the proxy votes are taken into account[76]. Where a poll is demanded after a show of hands, the club should consider whether the poll should be conducted by postal voting rather than by proxy voting, as experience shows that postal voting elicits a better response[77]. The rules, however, would have to cater specifically for postal voting. Two examples of a proxy form may be seen in **Appendix 9**.

## 6-30   Voting majority

This is another area where the rules need to make clear what majority is required for any resolution of the members to be binding on the membership as a whole. It has long been established that where the duties which are imposed on a corporation are of a public nature, the will of the corporation may be expressed by a simple majority of the members, so that the act of the majority becomes the act of the corporation[78]. But this rule does not appear to apply to private duties where a unanimous decision of the body is required[79]. However, Lord Denning MR in *Abbatt v Treasury Solicitor* [1969] 1 WLR 1575 at 1583D expressed the view that, absent an express rule in an unincorporated members' club, the members had an implied power to amend their rules by a simple majority, and by implication to make any other decision by this majority. Doubt has already been expressed as to the existence of the implied power of amendment[80] but this does not mean that the Master of the Rolls was wrong on the voting majority point[81].

**6-31**   In *Knowles v Zoological Society of London* [1959] 1 WLR 823 CA the society had over 7,000 fellows (members). In 1958 at a general meeting to confirm the adoption of new bye-laws 1,788 fellows voted

[75]   *Ernest v Loma Gold Mines Limited* [1896] 2 Ch 572 at 579 (Chitty J).
[76]   Ibid. at 579–580.
[77]   *Shackleton on Meetings* (9th edn, 1997) para 7-23.
[78]   *Attorney General v Davy* [1741] 2 Atk 212; *Grindley v Barker* [1798] 1 Bos & P 229 at 236.
[79]   *Harington v Sendall* [1903] 1 Ch 921 (unincorporated members' club); *Perrott & Perrott Ltd v Stephenson* [1934] 1 Ch 171 (company).
[80]   See **2-26** above.
[81]   *Warburton on Unincorporated Associations* (2nd edn, 1992) p 28 supports the view that if the rules are silent as to the majority required to pass a resolution, a simple majority will be sufficient.

in favour whilst 1,227 voted against, 18 abstained and one vote was disallowed and the motion was passed by a simple majority at the meeting. The rules required confirmation by 'a majority of fellows entitled to vote'. Did this mean all the fellows of the society or only those present at the meeting? The Court of Appeal held the latter, but it is wiser if the rule states, 'a majority of members *present at the meeting and* entitled to vote'. The case also draws attention to the need, on this form of wording, to count abstentions and wasted votes. Although members tend to think that by abstaining or wasting their vote they are remaining neutral, they are in fact assisting the opposition to the motion because their presence at the meeting will be taken into account in calculating the required majority. Similarly, abstainers would count towards the majority if the rule simply stated, 'a majority of the members present at the meeting'[82]. It would only be otherwise if the rule stated, 'a majority of those members present *and voting* at the meeting'. In this last event the number of abstainers would not be included in the calculation of the majority. Which form of wording should be used is a matter of preference for the individual club.

**6-32**   Under paragraph 4 of schedule 7 of the Licensing Act 1964 all members must have equal voting rights at general meetings. Because of this it is unlawful to give the chairman of the meeting a casting vote in addition to his ordinary vote. In order to give special weight to the chairman's vote, some clubs give the chairman a casting vote only at general meetings. Schedule 7 is being repealed by the Licensing Act 2003, so that when this Act comes fully into force it will proper once again to give the chairman of the meeting an additional or casting vote, if that is what the club wishes to do.

## 11.   MINUTES

**6-33**   The concept behind the recording of minutes of a meeting is that the club has a 'fair and accurate' record of what has been decided or resolved. It thus saves argument at a later stage when recollection of the particular meeting has faded from the memory. The minutes should be as concise as the circumstances require. The minutes of general meetings of the members will normally need to be recorded in greater detail than those needed for committee meetings. The minutes should record the essential elements of the discussion and

---

[82]    See, for example, s. 4(2) of the Credit Unions Act 1979 where this form of words is stipulated.

the full text of any resolution which was passed. They should avoid comment and expressions of opinion. It is seldom helpful to record the proceedings in descriptive terms, such as *'Mr H with some heat denounced the motion as a trick contrived for the purpose of expelling Mr A'*, even if that is what he had said and the manner in which he had said it. No doubt Mr H's opposition to the motion would mean his voting against it, which will be recorded, and this will be a sufficient recognition of his disapproval of the motion.

**6-34**    There are various methods of recording minutes but they should all follow the basic pattern as set below:

*Method 1:*
Mr A attended before the committee re the charge of misconduct, namely, his rudeness to the President at the New Year's party.

Resolved: that Mr A be suspended from membership for three months. Voting for 9, against 3, abstention 1.

This method simply records, in the order in which they came before the meeting, each matter discussed and the eventual result. The next method records in addition all amendments, the names of movers and seconders, the fate of the various proposals and the ultimate result.

*Method 2:*
Mr A attended before the committee re the charge of misconduct, namely, his rudeness to the President at the New Year's party. Mr A admitted the facts and apologised for his conduct. Mr A then retired from the committee room.

Mr B moved, and Mr C seconded, that he be reprimanded by the chairman of the club.

Mr D moved as an amendment that he be expelled from the club. Mr E seconded. Voting for the amendment: for 5, against 8.

Mr F then moved a further amendment, which was seconded by Mr G, that Mr A be suspended for three months. This amendment was carried and, on being put as the substantive motion, was carried by 9 votes in favour to 3 votes against, with one abstention.

Resolved: that Mr A be suspended from membership for three months.

**6-35**    As to distribution, minutes of general meetings should be supplied to the whole membership, whereas minutes of committee meetings are generally considered confidential to the committee members[83]. Some committees maintain an Action List so that the progress of any matter can be monitored over a period of time. Another way of keeping track of a particular topic is to give it an individual number which can be carried forward from meeting to meeting. The chairman of the committee should sign the minutes of the previous meeting once the members of the committee have approved their accuracy.

## 12. COMMITTEE MEETINGS

**6-36** As mentioned in **5-18** above, the managing committee is the master of its own procedures. But the rules (or the bye-laws) should deal with ancillary matters such as the frequency of committee meetings and the number of attendees who shall form a quorum for business to be validly conducted. The chairman of the club should chair the managing committee by virtue of his office. There should be provision for an alternative chairman if the designated chairman is absent[84]. If the rules are silent on the question of who should take the chair, it is up to the members present at the committee meeting themselves to choose their own chairman[85]. It is usual for the rules to give the chairman a casting or additional vote at committee meetings. This additional vote is lawful and does not contravene the provision in paragraph 2(4) of Schedule 7 of the Licensing Act 1964 which stipulates that all members must have equal voting rights at general meetings if the club has a registration certificate, since committee meetings do not count as general meetings. Otherwise the general rules of procedure for general meetings apply equally to committee meetings, although there is much greater informality in conducting the latter.

We would add that if through indolence or neglect or for any other reason, no committee meeting was convened when plainly it should have been, we consider that any member of the committee would probably have an inherent right to convene a committee meeting on

---

[83]     In a company the directors' minute book is confidential because it contains the record of the private affairs of the company (see *Gore-Browne on Companies* (50th edn, 2004) para 11[24]), and by analogy this seems to apply to the committee's minute book. But the analogy cannot be pressed too far because in an unincorporated members' club the committee is acting on behalf of the members collectively (not on behalf of a separate entity such as a company) and the question might be asked why the members are disentitled from inspecting the committee's minute book.

[84]     This is commonly done by making provision for a vice-chairman.

[85]     This would also apply to sub-committees where, more often than not, the chairman of the club would not be part of its composition.

reasonable notice; otherwise the management and control of the club's affairs would become rudderless, to the obvious detriment of the club.

## 13.   STATUTORY REQUIREMENTS FOR INCORPORATED CLUBS

**6-37**   These clubs must comply with the provisions of the Companies Act 1985. Equally they must comply with their articles of association which invariably make special provision for the holdings of meetings, the categorisation of business and adjournment of meetings, etc. Special provisions in Table A are directed to the holding and conduct of meetings (which include notice, quorum, and voting) for companies limited by shares and Table C repeats most of these provisions for companies limited by guarantee[86]. Noted below are some of the important statutory requirements as to company meetings.

### 6-38   Annual general meeting

Every company must hold in each year a general meeting as its annual general meeting, and not more than 15 months must elapse between the date of one annual general meeting and the next[87]. Provided that a company holds its first AGM within 18 months of its incorporation, it need not hold an AGM in the year of its incorporation or in the following year[88]. It is customary to state in the articles that all business except as therein mentioned (such as considering the company accounts, receiving the directors' reports, electing directors) is deemed to be special business, which will mean that any other business will have to be transacted at an extraordinary general meeting.

### 6-39   Extraordinary general meetings

Under the articles it is usual to provide that only special business of which notice has been given can be transacted at an EGM. These meetings can be convened by the directors whenever they think proper[89] or may be requisitioned by the members themselves holding one-tenth of the paid up share capital or one-tenth of the total voting rights[90]. The directors must forthwith proceed to convene the meeting

---

[86]   Regulations 36 to 63 of Table A appear in APPENDIX 9 and Articles 1 to 8 of Table C appear in APPENDIX 10.
[87]   Companies Act 1985, s. 366.
[88]   Ibid. s. 366.
[89]   See *Gore-Browne on Companies* (50th edn, 2004) para 11[13].
[90]   Companies Act 1985, s. 368(2).

on a members' requisition[91]. If not convened within 21 days from the date when the members' requisition is deposited at the registered office of the company, the requisionists themselves can convene a meeting for a date in three months' time[92]. If the directors do convene a meeting, the meeting itself must be held within 28 days of the notice convening the meeting[93]. The court may direct that a general meeting of the company be held on such terms as it thinks fit[94].

## 6-40   Notice of meetings

Notice of a general meeting must be given to all members, who are entitled to vote at the meeting, in the manner prescribed by the articles; otherwise the company is not 'corporately assembled'[95]. For this reason it is customary to provide in the articles that the accidental omission to give notice to or the non-receipt of a notice by any person entitled to receive notice shall not invalidate the proceedings. The length of notice for the annual general meeting and for any meeting at which a special resolution is to be passed is not less than 21 days' notice in writing and in the case of any other meeting is 14 days' notice in writing[96]. As to notice of an *adjourned* meeting, it is to be noted that under Article 57 of the 1948 Table A, if the adjournment is for 30 days or more, a fresh 21-day notice of the meeting is required; otherwise it is not necessary to give any notice of the adjourned date. Under Regulation 45 of the 1985 Table A, where the meeting is adjourned for 14 days or more, seven clear days' notice must be given specifying the time and place of the adjourned meeting and the general nature of the business to be transacted; otherwise it is not necessary to give any notice of the adjourned date.

## 6-41   Minutes of meetings

Every company must cause minutes of all proceedings of general meetings, and of meetings of its directors, to be entered in books kept for the purpose[97]. It is good practice to have separate books for general and board meetings because books containing minutes of general

---

[91]     Companies Act 1985, s. 368(1).

[92]     Ibid. s. 368(4).

[93]     Ibid. s. 368(8) as inserted by the Companies Act 1989, Sch. 19, para 9.

[94]     Ibid. s. 371; see *Re British Union for the Abolition of Vivisection* [1995] 2 BCLC 1 (where the court permitted proxy voting at a future EGM because the previously held EGM had degenerated into a near riot).

[95]     *Gore-Browne on Companies* (50th edn, 2004) para 11[19].

[96]     Companies Act 1985, ss. 369 and 378(2).

[97]     Ibid. s. 382.

meetings are required to be kept at the company's registered office and are open to inspection by members[98]. As a matter of law this right of inspection does not apply to the directors' minute book which is accessible only to the directors, the company secretary and the auditors for the purpose of any audit[99]. This is understandable in the context of companies quoted on the Stock Exchange but a different practice may be acceptable in members' clubs which happen to be incorporated. It is a matter for the directors to decide but in some clubs, especially small ones where there is considerable overlap between the membership of the board of directors and the membership of the committee, the directors are more relaxed about the confidentiality of the directors' minute book on the basis that they have nothing to hide from their fellow committee members.

### 6-42   Resolutions at meetings

For certain acts of the company an ordinary resolution at a meeting will not suffice and an 'extraordinary resolution' or a 'special resolution' must be passed[100], in which event the requirements of section 378 of the Companies Act 1985 must be followed since any departure from the procedure there laid down will render the resolution void. The articles of association may prescribe what business of the company requires a special resolution, but a special resolution may also be required by law, for example, changing the name of the company[101], altering the objects stated in the memorandum[102] or altering or adding to the articles[103].

## 14.   MEETINGS OF MEMBERS IN PROPRIETARY CLUBS

**6-43**   General meetings of the members in a proprietary club are just as much an essential element as they are in a members' club. If therefore there was no provision for meetings (either for general or special business) in the club rules, it is doubtful whether the club would constitute a club at law, since the sixth criterion (the need for collegiality) referred to in **1-01** above would not be fulfilled.

---

[98]     Companies Act 1985, s. 383(1).
[99]     See *Gore-Browne on Companies* (50th edn, 2004) para 11[24].
[100]    Requiring a majority of not less than three-fourths of the members: Companies Act 1985, s. 378(1).
[101]    Ibid. s. 28.
[102]    Ibid. s. 4.
[103]    Ibid. s. 9.

# Chapter 7

## CESSATION AND CURTAILMENT
## OF MEMBERSHIP

## 1.  INTRODUCTION

**7-01**  This is a topic which has relevance to all clubs of whatever description. It is also an important topic for those members who find themselves at the wrong end of expulsion or suspension proceedings. If the managing committee do not get the procedure right or make a mess of the substantive hearing of the proceedings, the club will face the prospect of litigation being brought against it by the aggrieved party, with its attendant unpleasantness and with the risk of costs being awarded against the club. In proprietary clubs the practice varies; sometimes it is the proprietor who exercises the powers of expulsion and suspension and at other times the proprietor delegates these powers to a committee of the club.

## 2.  RESIGNATION

**7-02**  It will be recalled from **1-01** above that the first criterion of a club is the voluntary nature of the association of the members who comprise the club.  From this criterion follows the proposition that a member may at any time voluntarily retire from a club by his resignation or withdrawal from it. In *Finch v Oake* [1896] 1 Ch 409 Lord Justice Lindley put the position as follows[1]:

> What then is the position of a member who has paid his subscription of 10s 6d[2] for the current year? Can he withdraw from the association at any moment at his own pleasure, or can he withdraw only with the consent of his fellow members? In my opinion, when he has paid his

---

[1]  At 415.
[2]  This was half a guinea in imperial coinage and 52.5 pence in decimal coinage.

subscription for the year he is under no obligation whatever to his fellow members. By paying his subscription he no doubt acquires certain rights and benefits. But what is there to prevent him from retiring from the association at any moment he wishes to do so? Absolutely nothing. In my opinion no acceptance of his resignation is required, though of course he cannot get back the 10s 6d which he has paid. The other members have no power to say that he shall not retire, and there is no law that a resignation which cannot be refused must be accepted before it can take effect. If therefore a member of this association chooses, even from mere caprice, to retire from it, he can do so at any time without the consent of the other members, and in order to become a member he must be re-elected.

**7-03**   This judicial statement needs some clarification:

(1) the right to resign is inherent and is not dependent on a club rule giving permission to resign. On the other hand, we see no reason why this right should not be expressly regulated in the rules, for example, by stipulating that the resignation must be in writing or that it must be on 14 days' notice;

(2) no particular form of words is required to constitute a valid resignation. In the case of *In re Sick and Funeral Society of St John's Sunday School, Golcar* [1973] 1 Ch 51 Mr Justice Megarry had this to say[3]:

> There can be no magic in the word 'resign', nor in whether the resignation is written or oral. The essence of the matter seems to me to be whether the member has sufficiently manifested his decision to be a member no more. I cannot see why such a manifestation should not be conduct instead of by words: the only question is whether the member's decision has been adequately conveyed to the society by words or deeds ...

(3) the need for re-election is important and was re-affirmed in the *Golcar* case[4]. Could the committee waive the resignation as an act of management? We doubt whether it could since it will now be dealing with a non-member, and the members of the club might take the objection that the re-election had occurred without the proper formalities being observed, such as the need for a proposer and seconder. It would be different if an express rule governed the position[5].

---

3     *In re Sick and Funeral Society of St John's Sunday School, Golcar* [1973] 1 Ch 51 at 62C.

4     At 63A.

5     *Lambert v Addison* [1882] 46 LT 20 (where the court upheld a bye-law, which permitted former members of the club to be re-admitted on paying arrears of subscription but without the formalities of an election and without paying the entrance fee).

(4) Lord Justice Lindley was being too dogmatic in saying that a member of a club owed 'no obligation whatever' to his fellow members. We consider that club members owe to one another various obligations or duties under the contract of membership. Some obligations such as the payment of subscriptions are express; others such as the requirement to behave properly in the clubhouse are implied. The question arises whether the exercise of the undoubted right to resign could result in the member being in breach of his contract of membership. Suppose the Upper Basset Cricket Club had an outstanding opening batsman who had paid his annual subscription on 1 January. Could he without warning resign on 1 May and immediately join and play for the Lower Basset Cricket Club, their arch rivals? The answer is in the affirmative as a matter of contract law because a person makes no promise, express or implied, that he will continue as a member for the period of his paid-up subscription. The position may be different in practice because of the rules issued by the game's governing body or by the league in which the clubs are playing since such rules might prohibit the switching of clubs in this fashion.

**7-04** What is the legal effect of a request by the committee to the member that he resign his membership? In *Gaiman v National Association for Mental Health* [1971] Ch 317 the defendant association, which was a company limited by guarantee without share capital, had an article of association which read:

> Article 7   A member shall forthwith cease to be a member ... (B) if he is requested by resolution of the council[6] to resign.

There had been a recent influx of new members, all of whom were Scientologists and who fundamentally disagreed with the way the association was run. Under Article 7 the association duly requested the resignation of 302 of these members. Mr Justice Megarry held that, whilst the word 'resign' was somewhat of a euphemism, what terminated the membership was not the resignation but the request to resign. In other words, it was a *forced* resignation. The judge upheld the association's request as effectively terminating their membership. This had been done in accordance with the association's rules, which gave a right of appeal (which had been exercised), and in the honest belief that it was in the best interests of the association, but it was also done in contravention of the rules of natural justice. This case should

---

[6]    The governing body of the association.

be treated with considerable caution because the judge specifically relied on the 'generous set of statutory rules governing companies and the rights of members' as enabling him to disapply the rules of natural justice in the field of company law[7]. In the ordinary course of events we consider that a forced resignation is tantamount to expulsion and no unincorporated members' club will succeed in upholding in court an expulsion dressed up as a resignation where there has been a disregard of the rules of natural justice. That is not to say that an *invitation* to a member to resign his membership has no place in the options available to a managing committee in the event of unacceptable behaviour on the part of the member. This has long been used as a beneficial face-saving device which has prevented many a ruction at the club[8].

## 3.    LAPSED MEMBERSHIP

**7-05**   There is no implied term of the contract of membership that if a member fails to pay his subscription by the specified date, or within a reasonable time of it becoming due, his membership will lapse[9]. The club's primary remedy is to sue the member for the arrears of subscription. If the arrears are of long standing, say of at least one year or more, the club can argue that the member has repudiated his obligations under the contract of membership and it can then accept the repudiation which will discharge the contract[10]. This will have the effect of cancelling the membership but leaving the club with the ability to sue for the arrears of subscription. What is a neater solution is to have an express rule which states that in the event of a failure to pay the subscription within a specified period after it has become due the member's membership shall *automatically* lapse[11]. The rule can be made less draconian by stipulating in the rules (or in the bye-laws) that the member will receive in writing a reminder that his subscription is overdue and a warning that his membership will automatically lapse if the arrears are not paid by a certain date.

---

[7]    At 335G.

[8]    See *Fisher v Keane* [1879] 11 Ch D 353 CA; *Dawkins v Antrobus* [1881] 17 Ch D 615 CA; and *Lambert v Addison* [1882] 46 LT 20 for Victorian examples of the use of this device.

[9]    In a proprietary club arrears of subscription do not pose the same problem as in a members' club. This is because at the end of the subscription year the proprietor can simply refuse to renew the contract of membership with a defaulting member.

[10]    *In re Sick and Funeral Society of St John's Sunday School, Golcar* [1973] 1 Ch 51 at 62–63.

[11]    This will still leave the member liable for any arrears of subscription.

**7-06** It is common practice, however, to reinstate the member if he tenders the arrears and his current subscription. Is this reinstatement within the powers of the committee, considering that it is now dealing with a non-member? Does not the ex-member have to apply for re-election? Mr Justice Megarry in the *Golcar* case [1973] 1 Ch 51 at 62 said that lapse of membership could be described as 'tacit resignation'. Despite this dictum we consider that the committee would normally have power to reinstate lapsed membership on the basis that a lapse is quite different from a resignation; the former comes about through the member's non-compliance with the rules relating to the payment of subscriptions, whereas the latter is a deliberate decision taken by the member. As the innocent party the club can always waive the non-compliance but it cannot undo the member's decision which will already have taken effect. An exception might be where the notice of resignation was required to be, say, on 14 days' notice. Here we consider that it could be withdrawn by mutual consent before the expiry of the 14-day period.

## 7-07  Power to remit arrears of subscription

It might be thought that the remission of a member's annual subscription, say because he has fallen on hard times, might be considered simply as a valid act of management or as an acceptable act of kindness on the part of the committee. But the legal position is not as simple as that. It will be recalled from **1-08** above that in a members' club the consideration for the promise whereby each member agreed to be bound by the rules of the club was the payment of the annual subscription. Without consideration contracts are not enforceable unless contained in a deed[12]. So if the committee remitted on compassionate grounds the whole of the annual subscription, where is the consideration for the member's promise to be bound by the club rules for the period of that subscription? Could the excused member say, for example, that he was not bound for that period by any expulsion rule? We consider that the answer is in the negative because the consideration would probably be construed by courts in a different way. It is normally construed as a detriment to the promisee (the member), the detriment being the payment of the subscription. But consideration may consist of a benefit to the promisor (the club). In *Edmonds v Lawson* [2000] QB 501 the relationship between a pupil barrister (the promisee) and the members of her chambers (the promisor) was held to be contractual even though she paid no

---

[12]     *Chitty on Contract* (29th edn, 2004) para 3-01; *Currie v Misa* [1875] LR 10 Ex 153.

pupillage fee[13]. The requirement of consideration was satisfied because it was to the benefit of the barristers' chambers to have a pool of candidates from which to choose their members. Likewise, it can be cogently argued that it is of benefit to the club to retain an excused member, especially if he is a star player in a sports club or a committee member in a social club or simply considered a good club member whose presence in the club contributes to its well-being. Thus an excused member is still bound by club rules. Some clubs avoid this problem by giving the committee the express power to remit the whole or part of a subscription in the exercise of its discretion.

### 7-08   Literary and scientific institutions

A member who is in arrear with his subscription may be sued by the institution 'as a stranger'[14] and, moreover, in any proceedings under the Literary and Scientific Institutions Act 1854 a person who is in arrear with his subscription shall not be counted as a member or entitled to vote[15]. Presumably this means that the member cannot take any active part in the conduct of the proceedings.

## 4.   EXPULSION

**7-09**   If the rules of any members' club are silent on the topic of expulsion of a member of the club, no such power will be implied into the rules[16]. Provided there is provision to amend the rules, they would first have to be amended to give the club the necessary power to expel a member[17]. In the absence of an expulsion rule it will not be possible as an alternative to convene a special meeting of all the members to discuss and, if necessary, to act on a motion to expel a member. This is so even if every member of the club attended the meeting and voted unanimously for expulsion. The power to expel must always be expressly given in the rules.

**7-10**   The power to expel may be given to the membership as a whole but this is generally considered too cumbersome a procedure to be practical and so the power is usually devolved to the managing

---

[13]     See also *Modahl v Brithish Athletic Federation Ltd* [2002] 1 WLR 1192 CA per Latham LJ at paras 50–52 of his judgment.
[14]     Literary and Scientific Institutions Act 1854, s. 25.
[15]     Ibid. s. 31.
[16]     See *Dawkins v Antrobus* [1881] 17 Ch D 615, at 620 (Jessel MR at first instance).  See **2-27** above for the facts of this case.
[17]     Ibid. at 621.

committee. A common (and proper) rule is one which states that the club shall have power to expel a member if his conduct, whether within the club premises *or elsewhere*, is injurious to the good name of the club or is such that in the opinion of the committee it renders him unfit to be a member[18]. It is also good practice for the rules to state that pending the hearing of any case or complaint against the member the committee shall have power to exclude the member from the club premises. This is not prejudging the case; it is simply an act of good management. This power of exclusion, however, must be expressly given in the rules.

**7-11** If a member of a club has any complaint about the expulsion process or the end result of that process, his remedy is contractual, which will involve a claim for a declaration or injunction or damages, as the case may be. It is now very unlikely that he will be entitled to seek a judicial review of the club's actions since this is a public law remedy[19].

## 7-12 Compliance with rules

It is essential that the procedure laid down by the rules is strictly followed, otherwise the expulsion will be declared void. In *Young v Imperial Ladies Club Limited* [1920] 1 KB 81 and [1920] 1 KB 523 CA a notice was issued convening a special meeting of the executive committee 'to report on and discuss the matter concerning Mrs Young and Mrs L', but no notice was sent to the Duchess of Abercorn who had previously indicated that owing to other calls on her time she would not be attending committee meetings. The committee met and decided to erase Mrs Young's name from the list of members. At first instance Mr Justice Roche held that as the rules had been substantially adhered to and as there was no breach of the rules of natural justice, the omission to notify the duchess of the meeting did not invalidate the proceedings of the committee. The Court of Appeal allowed Mrs Young's appeal on the grounds (1) that the omission to summon the absent member of the committee invalidated the proceedings of that body and (2) that the notice did not state the object of the meeting with sufficient particularity.

---

[18]     [1881] 17 Ch D 615, at 616; *Fisher v Keane* [1879] 11 Ch D 353 CA at 358.
[19]     *R v Disciplinary Committee of the Jockey Club, ex p Aga Khan* [1993] 1 WLR 909 CA at 933 (Hoffman LJ); see further **16-03** below. See also *Law v National Greyhound Racing Club Ltd* [1983] 1 WLR 1302.

**7-13**   It should be noted, however, that what swayed the Court of Appeal was the insufficiency of the reason for not summoning the duchess, namely, her expressed unwillingness to attend committee meetings. There may be a valid reason for not summoning a committee member, such as his confinement to bed with a serious illness or the impossibility of his attendance at the meeting because of the distance he would have to travel[20]. However, far better would be an invariable practice to send out a notice to all committee members irrespective of whether it is known if this will result in their attendance.

**7-14**   So, too, the notice, which is given to the member summoning him before the committee, must comply strictly with the rules. A rule which provided for a notice of a certain number of days would not be complied with if it was given one day late; this non-compliance would then be fatal to any decision to expel the member[21]. If the rules are silent as to the length of notice to be given to the member for attendance on the committee, the notice must be of a reasonable length.

### 7-15   Rules of natural justice

Subject to one caveat, in dealing with any case which concerns the possible expulsion of the member, it is important that the rules of natural justice are applied to the proceedings. A power of expulsion has been described as being of a quasi-judicial nature[22]. These rules are encapsulated in three propositions[23]:

(1) the right to be heard by an unbiased tribunal[24];
(2) the right to have notice of the charges of misconduct[25]; and

---

[20]      [1920] 1 KB 523, at 536. *Contrast P (a minor) v National Association of School Masters* [2003] 2 WLR  545 HL (where a union ballot was not invalidated by the accidental omission to send ballot papers to two members entitled to vote).
[21]      *Labouchere v Earl of Wharncliffe* [1879] 13 Ch D 346. See **6-08** above for the facts of this case.
[22]      *Fisher v Keane* [1879] 11 Ch D 353 CA at 360.
[23]      *Ridge v Baldwin* [1964] AC 40 at 132 (Lord Hodson).
[24]      *Nemo judex in causa sua* (No man should be a judge in his own case). See *R v Bow Street Metropolitan Stipendiary Magistrate ex parte Pinochet Ugarte* [2000] 1 AC at 119 and 147. See also *Ellis v Hopper* [1858] 3 H & N 766 (where a dispute arose as to whether the plaintiff's horse or the defendant's mare should be declared the winner of a race. The printed programme said the stewards' decision was final. Three of the four stewards found for the plaintiff. One of these three had a pecuniary interest in the result because he had bet on the plaintiff's horse. The trial judge, Pollock CB, upheld the steward's decision. The Exchequer Chamber subsequently upheld the judge's decision on the basis that, if one disregarded the biased steward, there was still a two to one majority in the plaintiff's favour). It is doubtful whether this case would be so decided today.
[25]      *Fisher v Keane* [1879] 11 Ch D 353 CA (where the plaintiff member had been suspended from membership of the Army and Navy Club without prior notice being given to him).

(3) the right to be heard in answer to those charges[26].

Any decision which was made in proceedings which did not operate these rules of natural justice will be liable to be set aside by the court[27]. The rules apply equally to an honorary member as to an ordinary member[28]. The caveat is that if the club were an incorporated one (which entails a large number of statutory rules governing the company and the rights of members) the court might not apply the rules of natural justice if there were sufficient indications that these rules were not to apply in any given case[29].

## 7-16 Putting right errors

Sometimes things go amiss and the managing committee or the appellate tribunal realise that mistakes have been made as to procedure or there has been non-compliance with the rules, and the question arises how to cure the problem. If looked at from the point of view of the member, he will on the face of things be entitled to go to court to obtain a declaration that the decision was invalid and of no legal effect by reason of the breach of the club rules or the rules of natural justice. That being so, the appellate tribunal (or the managing committee if there is no appellate tribunal) on being satisfied that the decision was defective as alleged, can simply remit the matter to the first instance tribunal without going into the merits of the appeal. In other words, the slate is wiped clean and the expulsion process starts afresh[30].

**7-17** Different considerations arise if the defect is not in the procedure but arises in the course of the hearing on the merits, for example, the tribunal applies the wrong burden of proof or it wrongly excludes relevant evidence or it plainly draws a wrong inference from the facts. The option to remit for a fresh hearing will still exist but

---

[26]     The *audi alteram partem* rule (Hear the other side). See *R (X) v Chief Constable of West Midlands* [2004] 1 WLR 1518, paras 113 to 132 of the judgment (Wall J).

[27]     *Lee v Showmen's Guild of Great Britain* [1952] 2 QB 329 CA; *Fountaine v Chesterton* [1968] 112 Sol Jo 690 (cited in *John v Rees* [1970] Ch 345 at 398). Where the club rules expressly exclude the rules of natural justice (which would be very rare), such exclusion might well be unenforceable on the grounds of public policy: see Denning LJ in *Lee's* case at 342; contrast on this point *Russell v Duke of Norfolk* [1949] 1 All ER 109 CA (see **16-02** below).

[28]     *John v Rees* [1970] Ch 345 at 398E.

[29]     *Gaiman v National Association for Mental Health* [1971] Ch 317 at 335G (Megarry J); and see **7-04** above.

[30]     *Leary v National Union of Vehicle Builders* [1971] 1 Ch 34 at 48E (Megarry J). In the same passage the judge said that there did not need to be a formal annulment of the first decision before starting afresh.

commonly the solution will be to let the appeal go ahead and in effect have a complete re-hearing at the appellate level. This solution did not find favour with Mr Justice Megarry in *Leary v National Union of Vehicle Builders* [1971] 1 Ch 34 where he stated[31]:

> If one accepts the contention that a defect of natural justice in the trial body can be cured by the presence of natural justice in the appellate body, this has the result of depriving the member of his right of appeal from the expelling body. If the rule and the law combine to give a member the right to a fair trial and the right of appeal, why should he be told that he ought to be satisfied with an unjust trial and a fair appeal?

However, in *Calvin v Carr* [1980] AC 574 PC (which concerned the disqualification of a jockey imposed under the Rules of Racing of the Australian Jockey Club) Lord Wilberforce in the Privy Council considered that the above proposition was too broadly stated and went on to say[32]:

> First there are cases where the rules provide for a rehearing by the original body, or some fuller or enlarged form of it. The situation may be found in social clubs. It is not difficult in such cases to reach the conclusion that the first hearing is superseded by the second or, putting it in contractual terms, the parties are taken to have agreed to accept the decision of the hearing body, whether original or adjourned. ... At the other extreme are cases where, after examination of the whole hearing structure, in the context of the particular activity to which it relates (trade union membership, planning, employment, etc) the conclusion is reached that a complainant has the right to nothing less than a fair hearing both at the original and at the appeal stage.

Lord Wilberforce said there was an intermediate situation where the conclusion to be reached is that the complainant should be taken to have agreed what in the end is a fair decision, notwithstanding some initial defect. He added[33]:

> It is for the court, in the light of the agreements made, and in addition having regard to the course of the proceedings, to decide whether, at the end of the day, there has been a fair result, reached by fair methods, such as the parties should fairly be taken to have accepted when they joined the [club]. Naturally there may be instances when the defect is so flagrant, the consequences so severe, that the most perfect of appeals or rehearings will not be sufficient to produce a just result.

---

[31]    At 49D.
[32]    At 592D.
[33]    At 593C.

The subject was revisited by the Court of Appeal in *Modahl v British Athletic Federation Ltd* [2002] 1 WLR 1192 who applied the *Calvin* case in circumstances where the existence of an untainted appellate process had cured the defect in the original disciplinary committee.

## 7-18   Good faith

The decision to expel must be taken by the committee acting in good faith, that is, acting for the benefit of the club as a whole[34], and must of course come within the powers granted by the rules. Here the committee's decision to expel must be a reasonable one based on the facts before it[35]. So long as the decision was not so unreasonable as to be perverse, the court will not interfere with the committee's decision even if the court considered it was wrong[36]. On the other hand, it is highly unlikely that a court would accept as enforceable any rule which gave a power of expulsion which had retrospective effect[37]; such a rule would in any event be unacceptable to the membership at large.

## 7-19   Quorum and voting majority

It is plain that the committee must be quorate when considering the issue of expulsion but it lends more weight to any decision if the relevant meeting is attended by a large majority of the committee. It is normal practice to require that a decision to expel a member must be carried by at least a two-thirds majority of the committee present at the meeting, and very often a three-quarters majority is preferred. The same voting majority should be used for any appellate process.

---

[34]   *Tanussi v Molli* [1886] 2 TLR 731 (concerning the Italian Couriers Club).
[35]   *Dawkins v Antrobus* [1881] 17 Ch D 615 CA at 622 (where Jessel MR said that the committee must act 'with reasonable and probable cause'); *Andrews v Salmon* [1888] 4 TLR 490.
[36]   *Richardson-Gardner v Fremantle* [1870] 24 LT 81; and see *Weinberger v Inglis (No.2)* [1919] AC 606 (an extreme example of non-interference by the courts in that the sole reason for the decision of the committee of the Stock Exchange for not re-electing the plaintiff as a member in 1917 was his German birth, even though he was a naturalised British subject who had been a member of the Stock Exchange without blemish for the previous 22 years).
[37]   *Dawkins v Antrobus* [1881] 17 Ch D 615 CA; see **2-27** above for the facts of this case.

# 5.  SUSPENSION

**7-20**  Everything said about expulsion applies with equal force to suspension[38]. A power to suspend the member must be express. Further, although the powers of expulsion and suspension usually go hand-in-hand in the rules, we consider that an express power to expel would not of itself include the lesser power to suspend. It has been said that if the conduct complained of is of a serious nature it would be in order for the committee to suspend the member, even in the absence of a specific power of suspension, until a proper enquiry can be completed[39], but this is doubtful because until a member is *proved* guilty of misconduct he is entitled to assert his innocence and thus enjoy the privileges of membership, subject to an authorised act of management such as excluding the member from the clubhouse pending the hearing of the case or complaint.

## 7-21  Consequences of suspension

It is common for the rules to spell out the consequences of suspension. A suspended member loses all the privileges and rights of membership for the period of suspension (save where it is a case of partial suspension: see **7-24** below). One of the rights of membership is the opportunity to be elected an officer of the club or a member of the committee or a sub-committee. If the suspension occurs during a period of office, the member must stand down temporarily from that office. That much is clear. What is not so clear is whether a suspended member can be nominated or elected to an office or to the committee. We consider that as a matter of law this is possible because the suspended member still retains his membership. Upon election, however, the suspended member will be unable to assume office and this might be highly inconvenient for the management of the affairs of the club as well as undesirable as a matter of principle. Consequently an express rule prohibiting nomination or election of a suspended member to any office or responsible position in the club is, we think, the proper solution to this problem.

**7-22**  Because the suspended member remains a member of the club he remains liable for his subscription or for any other authorised levy on the members. Can a suspended member still visit the club as a guest of another member? Most rules are silent on this point. We consider that the answer is in the negative because as a guest he would almost

---

[38]   *John v Rees* [1970] 1 Ch 345 at 396G et seq. (Megarry J).
[39]   See *Josling & Alexander on Law of Clubs* (6th edn, 1987) at p 40.

certainly be using the club's facilities in one way or another during his visit and his suspension has taken away this privilege; thus the change of status from member to guest cannot be used as a ploy to avoid the consequences of suspension.

**7-23** Suspension should always be for a definite period, otherwise it may be tantamount to expulsion. It is common practice to limit suspension in the rules or in practice to a period not exceeding 12 months (or sometimes less) on the basis that if the member's conduct deserves suspension for a longer period than this, the correct remedy is expulsion from the club.

### 7-24 Partial suspension

It should be noted that suspension can take the form of a *partial* suspension of the member's privileges. For example, the member may have been guilty of being unacceptably drunk at the club, in which case he might be banned from purchasing alcoholic drinks at the club bar for a period of months whilst retaining the other privileges of membership. Could a similar ban on the member be imposed if he were found guilty of a drink/driving offence on his way home from the club? The answer depends on the actual circumstances of the case. If he was a member of a temperance society and the society had the usual rule that it could suspend the member for conduct which took place elsewhere than the society's premises and which was injurious to the good name of the society or rendered him unfit to be a member, we consider that a suspension based on a drink/driving offence would be upheld by the courts. If, however, he was a member of a social club, different considerations might apply. If the member had been convicted for a *second* time of a drink/driving offence we consider that a committee would be justified in banning the member from the bar on the ground that drink/driving offences are not only criminal matters but amount to seriously anti-social behaviour. Whether the committee would take the same course in relation to a *first* drink/driving offence would depend much more on the committee's discretion in these matters.

## 6. DISCIPLINARY PROCEEDINGS

**7-25** These do not form a separate category in the sense that everything which is said about expulsion and suspension applies equally to disciplinary proceedings brought by the club against one of its members. Disciplinary proceedings relate to misconduct which involves or touches upon the member's behaviour while he or she was participating in the activity for which the club was established or primarily established, and usually but not exclusively involves sporting or recreational clubs. Disciplinary powers, like expulsion and suspension powers, must be expressly granted in the club rules. Where disciplinary proceedings differ from expulsion or suspension proceedings is in the sanctions or punishments which are available to the disciplinary committee or tribunal. For example, on a complaint being proved, the Kennel Club has the power in appropriate cases to disqualify its members (and any non-member who agrees to submit to its rules) from judging at any dog show or competition. In addition, disciplinary proceedings often contain the power to fine a guilty party, a sanction not usually associated with expulsion or suspension.

## 7.    APPEALS

**7-26**   In many cases it is good practice for the rules to provide review or appellate machinery for a member who is aggrieved by a committee's decision to expel or suspend him. For example, if a member of a golf club is expelled or suspended he will lose his handicap certificate by virtue of the rules of the English Golf Union who run the handicap system. This will be a serious blow to the golf player. A review is often carried out by the committee (and is therefore suitable for an appeal against suspension) whereas an appeal may take the form of an application for the convening of a special meeting where the committee's decision will be put to the membership for approval or otherwise (and is therefore suitable for an appeal against expulsion). Another form of appeal is for the club to have its own appellate tribunal. If at all possible, the appellate tribunal should consist of different members from those who sat on the trial body but this is not essential as a matter of law[40]. Some clubs include in their rules a provision whereby the appellant member is entitled to representation, legal or otherwise: we consider this to be a good practice and indeed clubs without such a provision in their rules should normally allow, on a concessionary basis, the attendance of a representative, if this is requested. It is also common for clubs to have no review or appeal procedure written into their rules. In this event, if the rules are silent as to a right of review or appeal, we consider that the committee would be acting within its managerial powers to permit an *ad hoc* review or appeal, if the circumstances warranted it.

---

[40]    *Leary v National Union of Vehicle Builders* [1971] 1 Ch 34 at 48E (Megarry J).

## 8. REPRIMAND AND WARNING

**7-27** A reprimand of a member by the committee over his misbehaviour in the club and/or a warning that such misbehaviour must not be repeated is on a different footing from expulsion or suspension because it does not involve any loss of the privileges of membership. The committee's powers in this respect are sometimes given expressly in the rules but, if not, we consider that as part of its management of the club's affairs the committee would have an inherent right to reprimand or warn any member about the standard of his behaviour. As with bye-laws, we do not consider that a system of review or appeal is a necessary or desirable adjunct of the committee's power to reprimand or warn a member.

# Chapter 8

## OWNERSHIP OF CLUB PROPERTY

## 1.   INTRODUCTION

**8-01**   Whereas no person would in the ordinary course of events join a club merely to see what assets he could acquire as a result of his membership, it is not an uncommon feature of clubs that during its lifetime or on its demise there arise questions of the true ownership of the club's assets. This may occur because a developer makes an attractive offer to purchase the club premises, thereby resulting in a windfall profit, or the club may founder through lack of members whilst retaining an undistributed fund of money. Those in charge of running the club therefore need to understand how the law works when it comes to the ownership of assets.

## 2.   UNINCORPORATED MEMBERS' CLUBS

**8-02**   It is not always easy to discern where the legal and beneficial ownership lies in respect of assets and property held by these clubs. Let us assume that the Basset Constitutional Club has some cash in hand at the clubhouse, a current account in credit at the bank, some silverware and pictures, some furniture and stock in the clubhouse, and that the club is the freehold owner of the clubhouse. Who actually owns all this? The simple answer would appear to be the members of the club and, in the absence of any contrary indication, that would be the right answer. But this simple answer begs the question, on what legal basis is this ownership founded? It is this question which we try to answer below.

## 8-03   General propositions

We consider that the following thirteen propositions can be established:

(1) in deciding any question of ownership, one must first look at the rules to see what they say on the subject[1]. Provided they are lawful[2], express rules must be followed;

(2) the legal position is today governed solely by the law of contract[3] and not by the law of trusts or other equitable doctrine[4];

(3) if the rules are silent on the question of ownership, the club's assets belong to the existing members of the club in common beneficial ownership[5];

(4) this common ownership is neither a joint tenancy nor a tenancy in common so as to entitle the member to an immediate distributive share[6];

(5) the member's interest in the club's assets lasts only so long as his membership lasts[7]. Once his membership ceases, for whatever reason, e.g. resignation, expulsion or death, his interest ceases[8];

(6) a member's interest is not transmissible[9] nor does it pass to his estate when he dies, even though he was a member at the date of his death[10];

(7) the members of the club can vary the rules as to ownership of assets, in the same way as any other contract may be validly varied, if the members are all agreed (or, if the rules so allow, by a majority vote); and there is in the ordinary course of events no private trust or trust for charitable purposes which hinders this process[11];

---

[1]    *In re Bucks Constabulary Widows' and Orphans' Fund Friendly Society (No.2)* [1979] 1 WLR 936 at 943C (Walton J).

[2]    That is, do not contain rules which offend, say, against the principles governing alienability or perpetuity.

[3]    *Bucks Widows' Fund* [1979] 1 WLR 936 at 952A and 953A.

[4]    *In re Gillingham Bus Disaster Fund* [1958] Ch 300 at 314 (Harman J); *Tierney v Tough* [1914] 1 IR 142 (O'Connor MR).

[5]    *Murray v Johnstone* [1896] R 981 at 990 (Lord Moncrieff).

[6]    *In re Recher's Will Trusts* [1972] Ch 526 at 538C (Brightman J). See **8-08** and **8-10** below for further reference to this case.

[7]    *Murray v Johnstone* [1896] R 981 at 990.

[8]    *Bucks Widows' Fund* [1979] 1 WLR 936 at 943C–D.

[9]    *In re St James' Club* [1852] 2 De GM & G 383 at 387 (Lord St Leonards LC).

[10]    *Murray v Johnstone* [1896] R 981 at 990.

[11]    *In re Recher's Will Trusts* [1972] Ch 526 at 539C.

(8) in the absence of any words which purport to impose a trust, any funds flowing into the club, e.g. by way of subscription, fund-raising or gift, would count as an accretion to the general funds of the club[12];

(9) in the absence of any rule to the contrary, a term is implied into the contract subsisting between all the members that the club's surplus funds should on dissolution belong to the then existing members[13];

(10) the distribution on dissolution should in principle be in equal shares for all members[14], but could be on some other basis, if the rules or the facts warranted it[15];

(11) where the rules have written into them some basis of inequality among the different classes of members in relation to their contractual burdens and benefits of membership (e.g. different rates of subscription for town and country members or different rates for senior and junior members), this inequality would normally follow into the distribution of surplus funds of the club on dissolution[16];

(12) the managing committee or the club's trustees can in the course of their duties[17]:

    (a) put the club's assets at risk from creditors' claims under contracts made with the club;

    (b) cause third parties to obtain contractual or proprietary rights over the club's property e.g. by the club taking out a mortgage;

    (c) declare with the consent of the members a valid trust in respect of some or all of the club's property;

(13) if the club has become moribund, for example, because all the

---

[12]     *In re Recher's Will Trusts* [1972] Ch 526 at 539E.

[13]     *Bucks Widow's Fund* [1979] 1 WLR 936 at 952B. A *cy-près* rule is an example of a contrary rule.

[14]     *Bucks Widow's Fund* [1979] 1 WLR 936 at 952B.

[15]     *In re GKN Bolts & Nuts Ltd (Automotive Division) Birmingham Works Sports & Social Club* [1982] 1 WLR 774 (Megarry V-C) (where only the full members were held entitled to participate in the surplus funds to the exclusion of other classes of member such as the honorary members and the temporary members).

[16]     *In re the Sick and Funeral Society of St John's Sunday School, Golcar* [1973] Ch 51 (Megarry J) (where a per capita basis was applied save for child members who were to receive a half share only because their contributions to the society were payable at half the adult rate).

[17]     *Bucks Widows' Fund* [1979] 1 WLR 936 at 940A–C. See further **8-06** below for trusteeship.

members have died or are untraceable, the assets will accrue to the Crown as *bona vacantia*, that is, treated as ownerless[18].

**8-04**   If the club dwindles to one member it will cease to exist as a club[19] but we see no reason why the principles set out in propositions (1) to (12) in **8-03** above should not apply to that one member in this terminal situation.

## 8-05   Alienation of club property

Because each member has an interest in the club property there is no power, in the absence of express provision in rules, for the committee of the club or for a majority of the members to dispose of club property against the wishes of a minority, unless it can be said that the disposal was authorised by the rules of the club and was consistent with the purposes of the club. This principle is well illustrated by the Scottish appellate case of *Murray v Johnstone* [1896] R 981, which, it is submitted, would have equal application in English law. In that case a silver cup was presented to the curling clubs of Dumfriesshire and these clubs, which were unincorporated, framed rules under which the cup was to become the property of the club which won the cup twice in succession. In 1893 the Upper Annadale Club did so win and the members of that club at a subsequent general meeting resolved to present the cup to Mr Johnstone who was the club's star player. Mr Murray and four other members of the club brought an action against Mr Johnstone for the return of the cup to the club. The court granted the relief sought and Lord Moncrieff at 990 stated the law as follows:

> But the question is, had a majority [of members] the powers to do so against the wishes of a substantial minority? I am of the opinion that it was beyond the powers of a majority of the club to alienate the trophy.
>
> In the present case if they [the members] had merely resolved that the cup should be held for the club by the defender [Mr Johnstone] as long as he remained a member, the resolution might have been justified as a reasonable act of management. But what is proposed is to alienate the club's property, and this I think cannot be done by the vote of the majority.
>
> In the course of argument it was urged that [on] this view it would be illegal for a majority of the members of a club to make a present out of the club funds to a secretary on his retiring, or to an old servant, or to present a medal

---

[18]     *Bucks Widows' Fund* [1979] 1 WLR 936 at 942H and 943F; *Cunnack v Edwards* [1896] 2 Ch 679 CA; *Re Trusts of the Brighton Cycling and Angling Club* (1953) *The Times*, 29 April.
[19]     *Bucks Widows' Fund* [1979] 1 WLR 936 at 943E. A tontine society is different because here the last survivor automatically takes the benefits.

or other prize to a member. Such a question seldom, if ever arises. If the gift proposed is substantial, it is usually made or eked out by private subscription among the members. If it is trifling, nobody objects. But if objection were taken by a minority, each case would depend upon its own circumstances, and fall to be decided according as the gift was or was not fairly authorised by the constitution and purposes of the club. Here what is proposed to be done is not to buy a prize or souvenir for the defender, but to present him with a valuable trophy, which was presented to the club as a body and intended to remain its property.

## 8-06 Trusteeship

It may come as no surprise to the reader to learn that although well-established in English jurisprudence and much used for several centuries, there is as yet no agreed classification of trusts[20]. One way of looking at the situation is to put into a separate category bare (or simple) trusts and to treat all other trusts being special (or active) trusts[21]. The need for interposing a trust in an unincorporated members' club is that it would be highly inconvenient for the ownership of property to reside in all the members and, in the case of land, impossible for it to do so[22]. There is said to be a bare trust whenever the trustee holds trust property in trust for an adult beneficiary[23]. Where the club holds valuable property, it is normal for the club to have formal trustees, who will declare that they hold the club property upon trust for the members in accordance with the rules of the club[24] and as directed by the committee. Under this arrangement the club's property is vested in the trustees under a *bare* trust for the members as a whole[25]. Here the trustees' control over the trust property is minimal and the beneficiaries' (members') control is paramount. The trustees of a bare trust have no active duty to perform; they are merely the repository of the 'bare' legal title of the trust property and have at all times to comply with the directions of the beneficiaries acting through the committee[26]. And, indeed, the fact that the club property is vested in trustees on trust for the members is a quite separate matter and does not bear upon the contractual relationship as between the members themselves[27].

---

[20]  48 *Halsbury's Laws of England* (4th edn, re-issue 2000) para 524.
[21]  *Hanbury and Martin on Modern Equity* (15th edn, 1997) p 69.
[22]  Ibid. p 359.
[23]  Ibid. p 69.
[24]  *In re Bucks Constabulary Widows' and Orphans' Fund Friendly Society (No.2)* 1 WLR 936 at 939H.
[25]  Hayton and Marshall, *The Law of Trusts and Equitable Remedies* (11th edn, 2001) p 215.
[26]  Gray, *Elements of Land Law* (2nd edn, 1993) p 40.
[27]  *The Bucks Widows' Fund* [1979] 1 WLR 936 at 952B.

**8-07**   A bare trust has to be distinguished from a *special or active* trust where the trustee is charged with the performance of substantial duties in respect of the control, management and disposition of the trust property, coupled with fiduciary duties owed to the beneficiaries[28]. The trusts referred to in **8-03**(7) and **8-03**(12)(c) above would be special trusts (including charitable trusts) as opposed to bare trusts.

**8-08**   One other sort of trust needs to be mentioned and that is a *purpose* trust. A purpose trust is one where the donor or testator establishes a trust fund for a purpose rather than naming a beneficiary. Charitable trusts often come into this category, for example, a trust fund established for the relief of poverty. In *Re Recher's Will Trusts* [1972] Ch 526 a testatrix by her will dated 23 May 1957 gave a share of the residue of her estate to the London and Provincial Anti-Vivisection Society, an unincorporated association, which had ceased to exist on 1 January 1957. Mr Justice Brightman held that this would have been a valid gift to the *members* of the society but for the fact that the society had been dissolved before the date of the gift. But if the testatrix had left the money on trust to the society for the *purpose* of advancing the cause of anti-vivisection the gift would have failed since it was a non-charitable purpose and could not be construed as a gift to any person[29].

**8-09**   The principal statute relating to trusts is the Trustee Act 1925[30]. The powers conferred by this Act are in addition to the powers conferred by the instrument creating the trust[31], unless a contrary intention is shown[32]. It is usual to appoint more than one trustee[33] and the number of trustees must not exceed four[34]. The rules should contain provision as to the powers of the trustees to invest the funds of the club. This power is sometimes exercised at the trustees' own discretion (with or without a cap on the value of the transaction) and

---

[28]   Gray op. cit. p 40.

[29]   But see *In re Lipinski's Will Trusts* [1976] 1 Ch 235 (Oliver J) (where the gift was not treated as a purpose trust but as an absolute gift to the members of an unincorporated, non-charitable association with a super-added (non-binding) direction as to how the money was to be used).

[30]   Other Acts are the Variation of Trusts Act 1958; the Trustee Investments Act 1961; the Trusts of Land and Appointment of Trustees Act 1996; and the Trustee Act 2000.

[31]   *Re Rees, Lloyds Bank Ltd v Rees* [1954] Ch 202.

[32]   *Re Turner's Will Trusts, District Bank Ltd v Turner* [1937] Ch 15.

[33]   Because a sole trustee cannot give a valid receipt for the proceeds of sale of land: Trustee Act 1925, s. 14(2)(a) (as inserted by the Trusts of Land and Appointment of Trustees Act 1996).

[34]   Trustee Act 1925, s. 34(2)(a) (as amended by the Trusts of Land and Appointment of Trustees Act 1996).

sometimes on the direction of the committee. Trustees will have a *lien* over the trust property against all costs, expenses and liabilities properly incurred as trustee[34a]. It is essential, however, for the rules to make provision for the trustees to be indemnified against risk and expense out of club funds because the trustees cannot look to the members for an *indemnity* in the absence of such a rule[34b]. The rules will also deal with the trustee's tenure of office and make provision in the event of his resignation from the club or his retirement from office or his death. Very commonly the rules will contain a provision that the committee by resolution shall have the power to remove a trustee, and will contain a further provision that the committee is the nominated person under section 36 of the Trustee Act 1925 to appoint a new trustee.

## 8-10   Gifts and bequests to the club

This is a topic which demonstrates one of the potential disadvantages of an unincorporated members' club. The general principles concerning such gifts or bequests were stated by Mr Justice Brightman in the case of *re Recher's Will Trusts* [1972] Ch 526. In the course of his judgment he gave some guidance on gifts and bequests to unincorporated associations[35]:

> A trust for non-charitable purposes, as distinct from a trust for individuals, is clearly void because there is no beneficiary. It does not, however, follow that persons cannot band themselves together as an association or society, pay subscriptions and validly devote their funds in pursuit of some lawful non-charitable purpose. An obvious example is a members' social club. But it is not essential that the members should only intend to secure direct personal advantages to themselves. Or the association may be one which offers no personal benefit at all to the members, the funds of the association being applied exclusively to the pursuit of some outside purpose. Such an association of persons is bound, I would think, to have some sort of constitution; i.e. the rights and liabilities of the members will inevitably depend on some form of contract *inter se*, usually evidenced by a set of rules.

**8-11**   Later in his judgment Mr Justice Brightman explained how gifts and bequests could legitimately swell the coffers of an unincorporated association such as a members' club[36]:

---

[34a]   Trustee Act 1925, s. 30; *Re Beddoe* [1893] 1 Ch 547 at 548.
[34b]   See *Snell's Equity* (31st edn, 2005) para 7-87.
[35]   At 538E.
[36]   At 539D.

The funds of such an association may, of course, be derived not only from the subscriptions of the contracting parties but also from donations from non-contracting parties[37] and legacies from persons who have died. In the case of a donation which is not accompanied by any words which purport to impose a trust, it seems to me that the gift takes effect in favour of the existing members of the association as an accretion to the funds which are the subject-matter of the contract which such members have made *inter se*, and falls to be dealt with in precisely the same way as the funds which the members themselves have subscribed. So, in the case of a legacy. In the absence of words which purport to impose a trust, the legacy is a gift to the members beneficially, not as joint tenants or as tenants in common so as to entitle each member to an immediate distributive share, but as an accretion to the funds which are the subject-matter of the contract which the members have made *inter se*.

**8-12**   It may be gleaned from the above quotations that the trouble arises when the gift or bequest to the club is made subject to a trust. Prior to the Perpetuities and Accumulations Act 1964 there were serious legal obstacles for persons making such gifts or bequests to an unincorporated members' club. The problem was twofold[38]. First, the gift could not be an absolute gift because the club, unlike an individual or a company, had no legal personality. Secondly, if it was intended (as often happened) as a gift to present and *future* members it could not be a valid gift because the intention to benefit future members of the club necessarily required the capital to be kept intact and only the income used. This infringed the rule against perpetuities and rendered the gift void. So the Act of 1964 was passed which permitted an unincorporated members' club to treat the gift as valid until such time as it became established that the vesting must occur after the end of the perpetuity period[39] (that is, after a life plus 21 years or, alternatively, after a fixed term of 80 years). This statutory remedy has gone a long way to removing the legal obstacles referred to.

---

[37]      See *Tierney v Tough* [1914] 1 IR 142 (where the benefit society's fund was made up of contributions both from the canal company (the employer) and from the boatmen (the employees) and, on the society's dissolution, the employer's contributions were held to be absolute gifts to the society).  It is surmised that this principle would apply in a shop club case or any similar set up involving both the employer and the employee where the object of the exercise was to confer financial benefits on the employee-members.

[38]      Hayton and Marshall op. cit. 3-224.

[39]      Perpetuities and Accumulations Act 1964, s. 3.

## 3.   OTHER CLUBS

### 8-13   Literary and scientific institutions

If the institution is unincorporated, during its lifetime its assets and property will be dealt with as any other unincorporated body. If incorporated under a royal charter (as many have been), its trustees will no doubt hold the assets and property under a bare trust. If incorporated under the Companies Acts, its assets and property will be held either by trustees or by the institution itself. Upon dissolution, under section 30 of the Literary and Scientific Institutions Act 1854 any assets of the institution, which remain after the satisfaction of all its debts and liabilities, shall not be paid to or distributed among the members but shall be given to some other institution to be determined by the members at the time of the dissolution or, in default, to be determined by the judge of the county court of the district in which the principal building of the institution is situated[40]. An exception is where the institution is a joint stock company[41], in which case the surplus assets may be distributed to the members[42].

### 8-14   Working men's clubs

Being unincorporated members' clubs, their position is basically as set out above, but with some statutory provision made under the Friendly Societies Act 1974. In particular, all property belonging to a working men's club, whether acquired before or after the club was registered, shall vest in trustees of the club for the use and benefit of the club and its members[43].

### 8-15   IPSA clubs

Being incorporated means that this type of club can hold assets and property in its own name, although it is common for such assets and property to be vested in trustees for the use and benefit of the club

---

[40]      Literary and Scientific Institutions Act 1854, ss. 29, 30.
[41]      As defined in s. 683 of the Companies Act 1985. A joint stock company is one registered under one of the Joint Stock Companies Acts, a forerunner of the company limited by shares. Once this type of company is registered under the Companies Act 1985, it is deemed to be a company limited by shares (s. 683(2)).
[42]      *Re Bristol Athenaeum* [1889] 43 Ch D 236 (held to be joint stock company); *Re Russell Institution* [1898] 2 Ch 72 (held not to be a joint stock company).
[43]      Friendly Societies Act 1974, s. 54.

and its members[44]. The club's rules will give some guidance as to investment of funds and distribution of profits because these matters must be provided for in the club's rules[45].

## 8-16   Shop clubs

A voluntary shop club is in the same position as an unincorporated members' club which is dealt with above. A registered shop club will still be an unincorporated members' club but some regulation of its position is contained in the schedule to the Shop Clubs Act 1902. The club's rules must provide for the investment of funds and a valuation of its assets and liabilities must take place at least once in every five years[46].

## 8-17   Incorporated members' clubs

An incorporated club has its own legal personality distinct from its members[47]. This separate personality means that the club itself can legally own property acquired through purchase or gift.

**8-18**   A vital distinction has to be drawn between the member's contractual rights under his contract of membership and his statutory rights under the Companies Acts or the Insolvency Act 1986. In other words, we are now talking about *beneficial* ownership as opposed to *legal* ownership.

**8-19**   An incorporated club is still a members' club and the members' rights as between themselves are governed by the club rules[48]. Any express rules as to the ownership or distribution of the club's assets must be followed. The rules may provide for the company itself to hold the assets on trust for the members or the company may appoint trustees to perform this task, and this trusteeship must be acted upon as a matter of law. Where the incorporated club's position departs from the unincorporated club is in the event that the rules of the incorporated club are silent as to the beneficial ownership of the club's assets.

---

[44]   See *Addiscombe Garden Estates Ltd v Crabbe* [1958] 1 QB 513 CA for an example of an IPSA club's property being held by trustees.

[45]   Industrial and Provident Societies Act 1965, Sch. 1, paras 12 and 14.

[46]   Shop Clubs Act 1902, Sch. paras v and x.

[47]   *Saloman v Saloman & Co* [1897] AC 22.

[48]   See **1-30** above.

**8-20**   Silence in the unincorporated members' club's rules will invoke the application of the propositions set out in **8-03** above. Silence in the incorporated members' club's rules will bring into play the principles of company law. The property of a company in no sense belongs to the members of the company[49] and it carries on its own business, not that of its members[50]. In the ordinary course of events the company is not a trustee of its property for its members[51]. In the absence of any trusteeship or contractual rights by virtue of the club rules, the members will have *no* property rights in the company's assets *at all*. Their tangible rights are limited to when the company is wound up. In the absence of contractual rights under the club rules, the position will be governed by the members' statutory rights under the Companies Acts and the Insolvency Act 1986, that is to say, if there are surplus assets once the company's debts and liabilities have all been paid, they will be distributed among the members of the company according to their rights and interests in the company[52]. This may result in the same distribution as would have occurred had the club been an unincorporated one. But this legal situation should awaken those running the club to the importance of having express contractual rules dealing with the ownership of the club's assets and, in particular, the need for trustees. Provided the trust was set up when the company was fully solvent[53], a beneficiary under a bare trust of assets held by the company (or by the club's trustees) as trustee has a proprietary interest in those assets and is not relegated to the position of an unsecured creditor[54]. With a bare trust the property is ring-fenced in the event of the insolvent liquidation of the club because it would not be an asset of the company of which the liquidator could take custody and control and thus be available for distribution to the *unsecured* creditors[55]. The property would not of course be ring-fenced from a *secured* creditor such as a mortgagee or debenture holder if monies had been lent to the club on the security of the property[56].

---

[49]   *Bank voor Handel en Scheepvaart NV v Slatford* [1953] 1 QB 248.
[50]   *Gramaphone & Typewriter Co Ltd v Stanley* [1908] 2 KB 89.
[51]   *Butt v Kelsen* [1952] Ch 197 CA.
[52]   Insolvency Act 1986, ss. 107, 143(1).
[53]   This eliminates the risk of the trust being set aside under whichever statutory régime is applicable on winding up.
[54]   *Gore-Browne on Companies* (50th edn, 2004) para 59[3].
[55]   Insolvency Act 1986, s. 144(1). The cases show that the basic principle is that only those assets which are beneficially owned by the company fall to be administered and distributed in accordance with the winding-up legislation and rules: Gore-Browne op cit para 59[3].
[56]   This mirrors the position of unincorporated clubs: see **8-03**(12)(b) above.

**8-21**   As with unincorporated clubs, if the incorporated club wishes
to transfer or give its surplus assets to persons other than the members
on dissolution of the club, then provision must be made for this
eventuality in the articles or in the club rules. This is a common
occurrence in companies limited by guarantee.

## 8-22   Proprietary clubs

The proprietor is the sole owner of all the club's assets and property
with the members having no interest in the same[57].

---

[57]     *Baird v Wells* [1890] 44 Ch D 661 at 676.

# Chapter 9

## SUPPLY AND SALE OF ALCOHOL
## BY THE CLUB

## 1.   MEMBERS' CLUBS

### 9-01   Introduction

As mentioned in 1-07 above, members' clubs have long enjoyed favourable treatment when it comes to the licensing laws. From 1964 until the enactment of the Licensing Act 2003 the supply of alcohol[1] on club premises was regulated by Part 2 of the Licensing Act 1964 under a system which all are agreed worked reasonably well. This is evidenced by the fact that some 23,500 members' clubs currently (January 2005) hold registration certificates, allowing them to supply alcohol to members and guests on club premises[2]. However, the government rightly came to the conclusion that the existing licensing laws did not reflect the present day needs of society and, as a result has enacted the Act of 2003. The reform of the system will repeal 22 Acts of Parliament and involve the consequential amendment of over 60 other Acts[3]. The new Act, when in force, will radically change the basis on which clubs are regulated in the supply and sale of alcohol.

The Licensing Act 2003 was passed on 10 July 2003 but did not come into force on this date by reason of the transitional provisions which

---

[1]      The Act of 1964 referred to 'intoxicating liquor' (s. 201)(1)) whilst the Act of 2003 refers to 'alcohol'. The former expression is technically correct in that the brewing industry refers to water as 'liquor' but is rather pedantic, whilst the latter expression is shorthand for the more accurate expression 'alcoholic drinks'. The meaning of alcohol is defined in s. 191 of the Act of 2003 as 'spirits, wine, beer, cider or any other fermented, distilled or spirituous liquor' with certain exceptions such as perfume and alcohol in confectionery.
[2]      Figure issued by Department of Culture Media and Sport, 2004.
[3]      Licensing Act 2003, Schs. 6 and 7.

are set out in Schedule 8. Because of the fundamental difference in how licensing is to be regulated in the future and the complex nature of the proposed changes the conversion to the new regime will take place in two stages. On the 'first appointed day'[5] clubs may start applying for a premises licence[6] and/or for a club premises certificate[7], and these will take effect on 'the second appointed day'[8]. The first appointed day has been designated by the Secretary of State as 7 February 2005 and the second appointed day is forecast by the government as a date in or about November 2005. Just in time for the first appointed day the relevant regulations have been published; there are five statutory instruments which together form the major part of the implementation of the Licensing Act 2003 and which are necessary in order to bring into force the transitional provisions set out in Schedule 8 to the Act[9]. Application forms may be viewed and downloaded from the website of the Department of Culture, Media and Sport, namely, www.culture.gov.uk.

**9-02**    Because of the abolition of the old régime this chapter primarily deals with the new régime. A brief summary of the old régime is called for in the main text and a synopsis of the position under the Licensing Act 1964 is contained in **Appendix 12**.

## 2.    OLD RÉGIME

**9-03**    Parliament recognised that the supply of alcohol to a member in a members' club was not a sale, although the member had paid money to obtain it. The property of the club belonged to all the members in common, and what appeared to be a purchase by the member was no more than a reimbursement of club funds[10].

---

5        Licensing Act 2003, s. 197(3)(f) and Sch. 8, para 1(1).
6        Ibid. Sch. 8, para 2(2).
7        Ibid. Sch. 8, para 14(2).
8        Ibid. s. 197(3)(f) and Sch. 8 para 1(1).
9        The regulations are Licensing Act 2003 (Transitional Provisions) Order 2005 (SI 2005/40); Licensing Act 2003 (Personal Licences Regulations 2005 (SI 2005/41); Licensing Act 2003 (Premises Licenses and Club Premises Certificates) Regulations 2005 (SI 2005/42); Licensing Act 2003 (Licensing Authority's Register) (Other Information) Regulations 2005 (SI 2005/43); and Licensing Act 2003 (Hearings) Regulations 2005 (SI 2005/44).
10       *Graff v Evans* [1882] 8 QBD 373 DC; *Trebanog Working Men's Club and Institute Ltd* [1940] 1 KB 576 DC.

## 9-04 Registration certificate

Accordingly, the Licensing Act 1964 prohibited the *supply* of alcohol to club members or their guests unless the club obtained a registration certificate from the magistrates' court[11]. Originally and on first renewal granted for one year, on the second or subsequent renewal the registration certificate could be granted for up to 10 years[12]. In the absence of objection, there was only limited scope for refusing to grant or renew a certificate[13] and this factor, coupled with its validity for ten years, proved of great advantage to clubs. If a club did not qualify for a registration certificate, it could apply to the magistrates for a justices' on-licence[14], sometimes called a 'club licence'.

**9-05** With a registration certificate a club was permitted to supply alcohol to its members and their guests on club premises[15] and to members only for consumption off the club premises[16]. Further, a club was allowed to sell alcohol to non-members of the club for consumption on club premises, provided that the rules authorised such sale and the rules did not contravene the general requirement that the club was established and conducted in good faith as a club[17]. The magistrates could impose conditions on the sale to non-members[18] and, subject to certain exceptions[19], the supply of alcohol in clubs was restricted to the permitted hours generally applicable[20].

**9-06** In order to qualify for registration under the Act of 1964 a members' club had to abide by the 'two-day rule' whereby no person could be elected to membership without an interval of two days between their nomination or application for membership and their becoming a member of the club[21]. Additionally, the club's rules were required to comply with Schedule 7 to the Act of 1964. These rules, which may be found in **Appendix 3**, contained many sensible provisions and as a consequence the standard of many club rules was

---

[11]   Licensing Act 1964, ss. 39(1) and 40(1).
[12]   Ibid. s. 40(2) and (3).
[13]   Ibid. ss. 45 and 46.
[14]   Ibid. s. 55.
[15]   Ibid. s. 39(1).
[16]   Ibid. s. 39(2).
[17]   Ibid. s. 49(1) and (2).
[18]   Ibid. s. 49(3).
[19]   Such as a special hours certificate (s. 78) or an occasional licence (s. 80).
[20]   Ibid. s. 62 (as amended by the Licensing Act 1988 and the Licensing (Sunday Hours) Act 1995).
[21]   Ibid. s. 41 and Sch. 7, para 3(1). For clubs registered under the Friendly Societies Act or the Industrial and Provident Societies Act there was a similar provision contained in s. 42.

improved. For some reason the government has not seen fit to repeat this schedule in any shape or form in the Licensing Act 2003, which we regard as a pity, as most of the provisions will have relevance to clubs regulated under the new régime[22].

**9-07**   If a registration certificate or a justices' on-licence expires before the bringing into force of the Licensing Act 2003, the provisions of the Licensing Act 1964 must be complied with.

### 9-08   Other provisions affecting clubs

The restaurant certificate[23], the supper hours certificate[24], the extended hours order[25], and the special order of exemption[26] have all been swept away by the Licensing Act 2003; so too has the justices' on-licence[27]. All these provisions will remain in force, however, until the Licensing Act 2003 itself is brought fully into force.

### 9-09   Children

There was one surprising lacuna in the Licensing Act 1964. There was no statutory reason why persons under the age of 18 years could not belong to, enter or consume alcohol at a registered club, although the court might have held that the club was being conducted 'for an unlawful purpose' if under-age drinking was a regular feature of club activity and might therefore have upheld an objection to the renewal of the registration certificate[28]. In contrast, the Licensing Act 2003 has fully addressed the topic of children and under-age drinking.

## 3.   NEW RÉGIME

### 9-10   Objectives

Unlike any previous licensing legislation the Licensing Act 2003 sets out objectives, which the licensing authorities must promote when

---

[22]   Care has to be taken, for example, over the voting provisions set out in the Licensing Act 1964, Sch. 7, para 2(3) in that discrimination as regards voting may breach any discrimination legislation which is enacted: see **4-18** above.
[23]   Licensing Act 1964, ss. 68 and 69.
[24]   Ibid. s. 76.
[25]   Ibid. s. 70.
[26]   Ibid. s. 74.
[27]   Ibid. s. 1.
[28]   Ibid. s. 44(1)(d).

carrying out their functions[29]; they are as follows[30]:

(1) the prevention of crime and disorder;

(2) public safety;

(3) the prevention of public nuisance;

(4) the protection of children from harm.

In addition, the licensing authority must have regard to the following in carrying out its functions[31]:

(5) its own published statement of licensing policy[32];

(6) any guidance issued by the Secretary of State[33];

- guidance was issued on 7 July 2004 and may be viewed on the government website (www.culture.gov.uk).

**9-11**   The scheme of the Act of 2003 is to define what are licensable activities and qualifying club activities and then to apply a statutory code to each of the main categories: Part 3 deals with the premises licence; Part 4 deals with the club premises certificate; Part 5 deals with permitted temporary activity. These three categories are called 'authorisations' in the Act.  Part 6 deals with the personal licence.

## 9-12   The major reforms

The following is a summary of the major changes which will occur once the Licensing Act 2003 comes into force:

(1) All licensable activities, which cover the sale of alcohol, entertainment, some sporting activities, late night refreshment licences, theatres and cinemas, will be brought into one licence at whatever venue. Hitherto there were six licensing régimes covering these matters;

(2) the new authorisations by way of the premises licence and the club premises licence will attach to the premises to which they relate. Hitherto the justices' on-licence attached to the person (eg Peter Gurney the licensee of the Basset Arms public house) and the registration certificate attached to the entity (eg the registration certificate of the Basset Rugby Club);

---

[29]   Licensing Act 2003, s. 4(1).

[30]   Ibid. s. 4(2).

[31]   Ibid. s. 4(3).

[32]   Ibid. s. 5. This section stipulates the licensing authority's obligations on this topic. Its official title is 'licensing statement'.

[33]   Ibid. s. 182. This section places a duty on the Secretary of State to issue guidance. Its official title is 'licensing guidance'. Interestingly, s. 182(4) refers to any revision of the guidance as 'coming into force', which is rather strong language for mere guidance.

(3) the justices' on-licence will be abolished. In its place will come the premises licence;

- generally renewal will not be required: the licence will last until surrendered or revoked or lapses (if the licence specifies that it has effect for a limited period, it will last until that period expires);

(4) the registration certificate will be abolished. In its place will come the club premises certificate;

- renewal will not be required: the certificate will last until withdrawn, surrendered or revoked;
- the new certificate requires an operating schedule and a plan of the club premises;

(5) the concepts of permitted hours, extended hours and special hours will be abolished. In its place will come flexible hours to suit the individual premises;

(6) occasional licences and occasional permissions will be abolished. In their place will come temporary event notices which will permit licensable activities on a temporary basis;

(7) the sale or supply of alcohol to children will be the same for clubs as other licensed premises. Special provisions will come into force aimed at regulating the presence of children in licensed premises and the consumption of alcohol by children;

(8) licensing by magistrates will be abolished. In its place will come regulation by the new licensing authorities, which will be the local councils.

## 4.    LICENSABLE ACTIVITIES

**9-13**   The Act of 2003 sets out the four categories[34]:

(1) the sale by retail of alcohol;

(2) the supply of alcohol by or on behalf of a club to, or to the order of, a member of the club;

(3) the provision of regulated entertainment[35];

(4) the provision of late night refreshment.

---

[34]    Licensing Act 2003, s. 1(1).
[35]    See CHAPTER 10 for this topic.

## 9-14  Qualifying club activities

For the purposes of the above four categories the following are also qualifying club activities:

(1) the sale by retail of alcohol by or on behalf of a club to a guest of a member of the club for consumption on the premises where the sale takes place (i.e. a variant of **9-13**(1) above);

(2) the supply of alcohol by or on behalf of a club, or to the order of, a member of the club (i.e. a repetition of **9-13**(2) above);

(3) the provision of regulated entertainment where that provision is by or on behalf of a club for members of the club or members of the club and their guests (i.e. a variant of **9-13**(3) above)[36].

# 5.   AUTHORISATIONS

**9-15**  Authorisation is required for any licensable activity[37]. An authorisation is one of the following[38]:

(1) a premises licence;

(2) a club premises certificate;

(3) a temporary event notice.

There is nothing to prevent a club holding a premises licence and a club premises certificate at the same time[39]. The decision as to whether to hold one or other, or both, is one for the club to make in the light of its own circumstances and requirements: see **9-17** below. In addition, it is possible for the same premises to be the subject of up to 12 temporary event notices per calendar year[40]. Since most clubs at present hold a club registration certificate and will, we assume, apply for a new club premises certificate, we will deal first with that part of the Act.

## 9-16  Statutory guidance

The Secretary of State published Guidance pursuant to section 182 of the Act on 7th July 2004.[41] Paragraph 5.65 reads as follows:

---

[36]    See CHAPTER **10** for this topic.

[37]    Licensing Act 2003, s. 2. It is an offence to carry on a licensable activity otherwise than under and in accordance with an authorisation under s. 2.

[38]    Ibid. s. 2(4).

[39]    Ibid. s. 2(3).

[40]    Ibid. s. 107(4).

[41]    For the full text see www.culture.gov.uk.

The approach taken in the 2003 Act to applications for new and major variations is based on five main policy aims. These are that:

(1)    the main purpose of the licensing regime is to promote the licensing objectives;

(2)    applicants for premises licences or for major variations of such licences are expected to conduct a thorough risk assessment with regard to the licensing objectives when preparing their applications. This risk assessment will inform [the applicant of] any necessary steps to be set out in an operating schedule to promote the four licensing objectives;

(3)    operating schedules, which form part of an application, should be considered by professional experts in the areas concerned, such as the police and environmental health officers, when applications for premises licences and club premises certificates are copied to them by applicants;

(4)    local residents and businesses are free to raise relevant representations, which relate to the promotion of the licensing objectives, about the proposals contained in an application; and

(5)    the role of a licensing authority is primarily to regulate the carrying on of the licensable activity when there are differing specific interests in those activities to ensure that the licensing objectives are promoted in the wider interests of the community.

When considering applications, it is expected that licensing authorities will seek to uphold these policy aims.

Although the reference is to applications for premises licences, we consider that it is likely that the relevant authorities will have equal regard to risk assessments made by applicants for club premises certificates. It is worth noting that by the time of publication in 2005 the Fire Service will no longer perform this service free of charge.

## 9-17    Combining authorisations

The Licensing Act 2003 expressly allows persons to hold two or more authorisations at the same time[42]. The question arises whether a club should contemplate applying for a premises licence as well as a club premises certificate. The advantage of a premises licence is that it enables the club to carry on the full range of licensable activities compared with the more limited range of permissible licensable activities under the club premises certificate. The disadvantage of the premises licence is that it is subject to a stricter and more onerous system of regulation than operates under the club premises certificate and it also requires the holder of a personal licence.

**9-18**    It is not difficult to envisage that a club might have different parts of its premises covered by different authorisations. A club might

---

[42]    Licensing Act 2003, s. 2(3).

have a room or bar which is covered by a club premises certificate and have a separate functions room which is covered by a premises licence and which might be a valuable source of income. Another combination might be to have a different form of authorisation for different nights of the week in respect of the same room, say a particular room to act as a public bar on Saturday nights only under a premises licence with the other days of the week being covered by a club premises certificate. We do not think it feasible, or within the contemplation of the Act, to have a premises licence and a club premises certificate in operation for the same room or premises *at the same time*. Imagine if you had club premises supplying alcohol to members under a club premises certificate and the same premises being used at the same time for authorised regulated entertainment (without alcohol) to members of the public under a premises licence. It would be well nigh impossible to ensure that alcohol was not being sold to members of the public at a crowded bar.

**9-19**  It will no doubt be common to have a club premises certificate used in conjunction with one or more temporary event authorisations. This is because the club premises certificate may contain a restriction as to the hours of operation or a restriction as to the area of the club premises which is licensed (e.g. a certificate covering the clubhouse itself but not any part of its grounds).

## 6.    CLUB PREMISES CERTIFICATE

**9-20**  A club premises certificate will be granted in respect of premises 'occupied by, and habitually used for the purposes of, a club'[43]. This certificate has been specially designed for clubs and is likely to be the preferred option of most clubs which wish to carry on the licensable activities set out in **9-14** above. The certificate will declare that the club premises may be used for the qualifying club activities set out in the certificate[44].

### 9-21  Advantages

As one commentator has felicitously put it, 'The Government has been anxious to retain the unique character of clubs in general and to ensure that they keep their sometimes quirky nature, whilst at the same time bringing them into the new regime with sufficient regulation

---

[43]     Licensing Act 2003, s. 60(1)(a).
[44]     Ibid. s. 1(2).

to ensure that their special nature is not abused'[45]. Unlike other licensed premises, clubs to which a club premises certificate attaches enjoy the following advantages:

(1) there is no requirement for a member or employee of the club to hold a personal licence;

(2) there is no requirement to specify a designated premises supervisor in the licence;

(3) there are no police powers of immediate closure of the club premises, nor any court powers of closure of all club premises in a particular area[46];

(4) the police and authorised officers have more restricted rights of entry into the club because of the private nature of the premises[47].

## 9-22  Qualifying conditions

To qualify for a club premises certificate the club must satisfy certain conditions[48]. There are five general conditions[49], and three additional conditions[50] if a club intends to supply alcohol, which the club must satisfy in order to qualify for a club premises certificate:

*General:*

(1) under the rules of the club a person may not be admitted to membership or, as a candidate for membership be admitted to the privileges of membership, without an interval of at least two days between their nomination or application for membership and their admission as member of the club (this replicates an existing qualification for obtaining a registration certificate[51]);

(2) where the rules of the club permit persons to become members without prior nomination or application, those persons must not be admitted to the privileges of membership without an interval of at least two days between their becoming members and their admission to such privileges (this replicates an existing qualification for obtaining a registration certificate[52]);

---

[45]    Barker and Cavender, *Licensing – The New Law* (2003) para 8.1.4.
[46]    See Licensing Act 2003, ss. 160 and 161; and see **9-66** and **9-79** below.
[47]    See ibid. s. 179(7). But see the rights of entry under s.90(5) at **9-46** below and under s. 108 at **9-66** below.
[48]    Ibid. ss. 61 and 63.
[49]    Ibid. s. 62.
[50]    Ibid. s. 64.
[51]    Licensing Act 1964, s. 41(1)(a).
[52]    Ibid. s. 41(1)(b).

(3) the club is established and conducted in good faith as club (this replicates an existing qualification for obtaining a registration certificate[53]).

If the licensing authority concludes that the club does not satisfy this condition, it must give the club notice of the decision and the reasons for it[54];

(4) the club has at least 25 members (this replicates an existing qualification for obtaining a registration certificate[55]).

If the club membership falls below this number the licensing authority will serve a notice of withdrawal of the certificate[56] but the notice must state that it will not take effect for three months from the date of the notice[57], in order to give the club an opportunity to achieve the required number of members;

(5) alcohol is not supplied, or intended to be supplied, to members on the premises except by or on behalf of the club (this replicates an existing qualification for obtaining a registration certificate[58]);

*Additional:*

(6) insofar as the purchase of alcohol for and its supply by the club are not managed by the club in general meeting or by the general body of members, such purchase and supply are managed by an elected committee of members aged 18 years and over; save as to the composition of the elected committee (this replicates a existing qualification for obtaining a registration certificate[59]).

Whatever the size of the club we consider it an unwise move to allow the members generally to manage this aspect of club affairs;

(7) no arrangements have been made, or are intended to be made, for any person to receive at the expense of the club any commission, percentage or similar payment in connection with the purchase of alcohol by the club (this replicates an existing qualification for obtaining a registration certificate[60]);

(8) no arrangements have been made, or are intended to be made, for any person directly or indirectly to derive pecuniary benefit

---

[53] Licensing Act 1964, s. 41(2)(a).
[54] Licensing Act 2003, s. 63(3).
[55] Licensing Act 1964, s. 41(2)(a).
[56] Licensing Act 2003, s. 90(1).
[57] Ibid. s. 90(2).
[58] Licensing Act 1964, s. 41(2)(b).
[59] Ibid. s. 41(2)(c).
[60] Ibid. s. 41(2)(d)(i).

from the supply of alcohol to club members and their guests *except*:
(a)  any benefit accruing to the club as a whole;
(b)  any benefit which a person derives indirectly by reason of the supply giving rise or contributing to a general gain from the carrying on of the club; the exceptions mirror similar exceptions which obtain in the law relating to gaming and lotteries[61].

The person referred to in (b) is the club member who will indirectly benefit from profitable sales of alcohol at the club.

We consider that a bonus paid to the bar steward as a club employee for say increasing bar profits from the sale of alcohol to members and their guests would be caught by the prohibition contained in this condition[62].

## 9-23  IPSA clubs, etc

Industrial and provident societies, working men's clubs registered under the Friendly Societies Act and miners' welfare institutes merit a special mention[63] in the Licensing Act 2003 to ensure that they qualify as clubs within the legislation. They must, however, meet the statutory requirements concerning their constitution and management.

## 9-24  Test of good faith

The matters to be taken into account in determining whether the club is established and conducted in good faith as a club are[64]:
(1)  any arrangements restricting the club's freedom of purchase of alcohol;
(2)  any provision in the rules or any arrangement under which any of the club's income or assets may be applied other than for the benefit of the club or for charitable, benevolent or political purposes;
(3)  the arrangements for informing the membership about the club's finances;

---

[61]    See ss. 33(2) and 51A of the Gaming Act 1968 at **11-17** and **11-27** below.
[62]    See Barker and Cavender, op. cit. para 8.3.2, say that this prohibition would not prevent a bar steward from receiving 'a bonus for overall performance', if his contract so allowed, but any such bonus would have to be carefully worded and calculated to ensure compliance with this prohibition.
[63]    Licensing Act 2003, ss. 65 and 66.
[64]    Ibid. s. 63.

(4) the state of the club's books of account and records;

(5) the nature of the premises occupied by the club.

These five factors replicate the existing test of good faith when a club applies for a registration certificate[65].

**9-25** Absent, however, from the new Act is any requirement to include in the rules of the club those matters relating to meetings and voting rights which are contained in Schedule 7 to the Act of 1964. Whereas much of the content of this schedule is in fact repeated elsewhere in the Act of 2003, there is one surprising omission. There is no requirement that all club members entitled to use the club premises must be entitled to vote at general meetings, and must have equal voting rights[66]. This means that the new legislation has deleted the anti-discriminatory provisions of the Act of 1964, and clubs will now be able lawfully to adopt discriminatory voting procedures, for example, against women members, whereas hitherto this was only permissible if the club was primarily a men's club (and vice versa)[67]. It may be that the legislature was anticipating the enactment of the Sex Discrimination (Clubs and Other Private Associations) Bill, the intention of which is to remove the exemption of private members' clubs from the Sex Discrimination Act 1975[68]. This Bill, which is a private member's bill and consequently has no government support, has suffered the same fate as previous attempts to remove this exemption in that debate on it has stalled and there is at present (the end of 2004) no sign of its being resurrected.

## 9-26 Application for certificate

An application for a club premises certificate may be made by any qualifying club for 'any premises which are occupied by and habitually used for the purposes of the club'[69]. The application is made to the licensing authority in whose area the club premises are situated[70]. Regulations will require the application to be advertised in the prescribed form and in such a manner as will enable any interested

---

[65]   Licensing Act 1964, s. 41(3).

[66]   Ibid. Sch. 7, para 2(4). Certain exceptions were set out in 2(4)(a)–(c).

[67]   Very few clubs are either primarily for men or primarily for women, but women's institutes are a good example of the latter.

[68]   See **4-22** above.

[69]   Licensing Act 2003, s. 71(1).

[70]   Ibid. s. 71(2). If the premises are situated in the areas of two or more licensing authorities the licensing authority is the one in whose area the greater or greatest part of premises is situated: s. 68(3).

parties to make representations to the licensing authority[71], and notice of the application will also need to be given within the prescribed period to each responsible authority for the area in which the premises are situated, that is to say, the police, the fire authority, the environmental health authority and the planning authority[72]. The application must be accompanied by[73]:

(1) a club operating schedule;

(2) a plan of the premises to which the application relates, in the prescribed form;

(3) a copy of the rules of the club.

**9-27** Before determining the application the licensing authority must be satisfied that proper advertisement and notification has been made by the club[74]. The procedure for the determination of the application is set out in section 72. Essentially the procedure deals with (a) hearing relevant representations made by an interested party or a responsible authority concerning the application and (b) the mandatory granting of the certificate subject to conditions, if any or if appropriate.

- An 'interested party' is defined in the Act of 2003 as a person or persons living in or being involved in a business in the vicinity of the club premises, or a body representing such persons[75];
- A 'responsible authority' is defined in the Act of 2003 as any of the following whose role covers the area in which the club premises are situated: the chief office of police, the fire authority, the health and safety authority, the local planning authority, and the environmental authority[76];
- A representation will be relevant:
  (1) if it is concerned with the likely effect of the grant of the application upon the promotion of the licensing objectives[77], and
  (2) if it is made by an interested party or responsible authority within the specified time and has not been withdrawn prior to the hearing[78], and it is not considered frivolous or vexatious by the licensing authority[79].

---

[71] Licensing Act 2003, s. 71(6).
[72] Ibid. ss. 69(4) and 71(6)(b).
[73] Ibid. s. 71(4).
[74] Ibid. s. 72(1)(b).
[75] Ibid. s. 69(3).
[76] Ibid. s. 69(4). If a club premises are on a vessel, the responsible authorities are a navigation authority, the Environment Agency, and the British Waterways Board (or the Secretary of State): s. 69(4)(h).
[77] Ibid. s. 85(5)(a).
[78] Ibid. s. 85(6)(a), (b).
[79] Ibid. s. 85(6).

## 9-28  Club operating schedule

This is a crucial document and must be in the prescribed form and include a statement of the following matters[80]:

(1) the qualifying club activities to which the application relates;
(2) the times during which it is proposed that the activities are to take place;
(3) any other times during which it is proposed that the premises are to be open to members and their guests;
(4) if applicable, whether the supply of alcohol is proposed to be for consumption on the premises, or for both on and off the premises;
(5) the steps which it is proposed to take to promote the licensing objectives;
(6) such other matters as may be prescribed by the Secretary of State.

## 9-29  Plan of premises

Consideration should be given to the proper extent of the licensed premises. Premises means 'any place'[81]. It is important that the extent is not too narrow, say restricted to the clubhouse and its immediate environs such as its lawns, forecourt and terrace or balcony, when it is known that social occasions take place elsewhere, for instance, a cricket club which has a marquee on the edge of its cricket ground during a festival or a golf club which has a drinks tent on the ninth or tenth tee or mobile refreshment facilities during a competition. In addition, a problem will arise if, as is very likely, unaccompanied children[82] will be present. They are prohibited from being on premises which are exclusively or primarily used for the supply of alcohol for consumption on those premises[83] at a time when the premises are open for such consumption[84]. Consequently, if the relevant premises are too narrowly defined there is a greater likelihood of their being construed as 'primarily' for the consumption of alcohol and therefore out of bounds to unaccompanied children. On the other hand, it may be important that the extent is not too widely drawn. Simply putting the whole cricket ground or the whole golf course as the proposed licensed premises may cause the licensing authority to question the

---

[80]  Licensing Act 2003, s. 71(5).
[81]  Ibid. s. 193. It also includes a vehicle, vessel or moveable structure.
[82]  A child is defined as an individual under the age of 16 years: ibid. s. 145(2)(a). A child is unaccompanied if he is not in the company of an individual aged 18 or over: ibid. 145(2)(b).
[83]  Ibid. s. 145(4)(a).
[84]  Ibid. s. 145(1)(a), which makes it an offence for any club employee or officer or member of the club who allows the unaccompanied child to remain on the premises.

suitability of the plan or the bona fides of the club. If the plan omits an area which is later wanted to be used for the sale or supply of alcohol, the club can always fall back on a temporary event notice[85].

## 9-30   Inspection of premises

Where a club applies for a club premises certificate or applies for a variation of a certificate or an application is made for a review of the certificate, authorised persons or the police may inspect the club premises within 14 days after the making of the application, provided that 48 hours' notice is given of the intended inspection[86]. The authorised persons are defined in section 69(2) of the Act of 2003 and comprise an officer of the licensing authority, an inspector from the fire authority, a health and safety inspector, an environmental health inspector, an inspector or surveyor of ships (if a vessel is involved) and any other prescribed person[87]. The licensing authority can extend the 14-day period by up to seven days if the authorised person or the police constable had taken steps in good time to make the inspection but this had not proved possible within the time allowed[88]. In other words, the onus is very much on the inspecting authority to arrange the inspection in good time.

## 9-31   Conditions on grant

Conditions can be imposed on the certificate provided that they are consistent with the club operating schedule accompanying the application (which schedule itself has to comply with the licensing objectives)[89], or where they are required in relation to off-sales[90] or to the exhibition of films[91]. The club premises certificate can be granted with different conditions that apply to the various areas of the club premises, or to different qualifying club activities, giving the authority maximum flexibility[92].

---

[85]     See **9-58** below.
[86]     Licensing Act 2003, s. 96(1)–(4).
[87]     Ibid. s. 69(2).
[88]     Ibid. s. 96(7), (8).
[89]     Ibid. s. 72(2).
[90]     Ibid. s. 73. See further **9-39** below.
[91]     Ibid. s.74. The admission of children (i.e. those under 18) is subject to restrictions recommended by the licensing authority.
[92]     Ibid. s. 72(10).

## 9-32 Form of certificate

Although the exact form will be prescribed in regulations[93], the certificate will include:
(1) the name and registered address of the club;
(2) the address to which the certificate relates;
(3) a plan of the premises;
(4) the qualifying club activities for which the premises may be used; and
(5) any conditions to which the certificate is subject.

The certificate will be accompanied by a summary of the certificate[94].

## 9-33 Duty to keep and produce certificate and display summary[95]

If the certificate authorises a qualifying club activity then the club secretary must ensure that the certificate (or a properly certified copy) is kept at the premises to which it relates and that a nominated person is responsible for it. That person must be:
(1) the secretary, or
(2) any member of the club, or
(3) any person who works at the premises for the purposes of the club.

The licensing authority must be notified of the identity of the nominated person. The secretary commits an offence if he fails to do so without reasonable excuse[96].

The nominated person must ensure that the summary of the certificate, or a certified copy of the summary, is prominently displayed at the premises, together with a notice specifying the position the nominated person holds at the club. He commits an offence if he fails to do so without reasonable excuse[97].

## 9-34 Loss of certificate or summary

The local authority must provide a copy, upon payment of a fee, if the certificate or summary is lost, stolen, damaged or destroyed, when

---

93      Licensing Act 2003, s. 78.
94      Ibid. s. 78.
95      Ibid. s. 94.
96      Ibid. s. 94(5).
97      Ibid. s. 94(6).

satisfied that the certificate or summary has thus become unavailable and that, if lost or stolen, the matter has been reported to the police[98].

## 9-35   Guests

Members' guests are expressly allowed to purchase alcohol from the club provided that the alcohol is for consumption on the premises where the sale takes place[99]. This authorisation includes associate members of the club and the guests of the associate members[100].

## 9-36   Associate members

Under section 67 of the Act of 2003 a person is an 'associate member' for the purposes of the Act if he is admitted to the club in accordance with the rules of the club as a member of another club and that other club is a 'recognised club'.[101] With most clubs this will present no difficulties, as they will have few casual visitors who are not members of clubs with which they are directly affiliated; as, for example, where a club specifically extends an open invitation to members of another known club. It will, however, create considerable problems for golf clubs, which typically allow members of other clubs to visit, pay a green fee, and enjoy the full facilities of the club, including the bar. This raises the question of the casual visitor, not a member of a recognised club, who pays a green fee to play a round of golf and who would expect to be able to go into the bar and buy himself a drink. There is no provision for this in the new legislation. This person will, if admitted to the course, have to go elsewhere for alcoholic refreshment. Most private members' clubs will require proof of membership of another club in the form of a handicap certificate before allowing a player on the course but many, particularly 'holiday' clubs, do not; and this lacuna in the legislation could prove costly to such clubs, not only because of the loss of bar revenue but also by virtue of the fact that with an important facility unavailable to the visitor the green fee will have to be reduced. In addition, the Act applies only to England and Wales, and so it is possible to construe the definition of 'recognised club' as excluding any club outside the jurisdiction. How a club secretary is to determine whether or not a green-fee-paying player's home club fulfils the requirements of section 62 of the Act

---

[98]     Licensing Act 2003, s. 79.
[99]     Ibid. s. 1(2)(b).
[100]    Ibid. s. 67(1).
[101]    Ibid. s. 67. A recognised club is defined in s. 193 as being a club which satisfies conditions (1), (2) and (3) of the general conditions in s. 62: see **9-22** above.

(that is to say, is a 'recognised club'), which gives to that player associate-member status of the host club, is an unsolved conundrum. This is a matter of no mean importance because a secretary who allowed such a casual visitor to buy alcohol may well be committing an offence under section 136[102].

**9-37** Exactly the same difficulty arises in circumstances where a sporting club holds a major event, such as a county rugby match or a golf tournament. Here the club would expect to host a large number of people in addition to the players, such as officials, coaches, and supporters who may not be members of another club, let alone of a recognised club. They would, however, all expect to be able to use the bar. One solution would be for the club to acquire a premises licence, but this would defeat the point of the club having the advantages of a club premises certificate. Another solution would be for the club to adopt a rule whereby all those *formally* attending such an event would automatically become guests of the club committee. In this situation it would obviously be wise for the names and addresses of all these persons to be recorded by the club in order to avoid any accusation that the club was open to all-comers and, in consequence, not being conducted in good faith. There is nothing in the guidance issued by the Secretary of State which deals with this point, but it is understood from talks which interested bodies have had with government officials that section 67 is to be given a generous interpretation.

### 9-38 Hours of operation

The principal variation likely to be sought by clubs is as to opening hours. These must be specified in the Operating Schedule and can be whatever hours are required by the club, subject to the overriding provisions of the licensing objectives and in particular any objections by the police based on the crime prevention objective[103]. So clubs should examine their activities over the course of the last year or so and decide what hours are appropriate. There is no requirement that premises have to be actually open during all the hours set out in the operating schedule: if the club is empty it can be closed. So in many cases it may be appropriate to set out in the operating schedule later

---

[102]     Namely, allowing a licensable activity to be carried on otherwise than in accordance with an authorisation.
[103]     The police and other bodies have expressed concern at the prospect of 24-hour drinking under the Licensing Act 2003, especially in relation to 'binge drinking' and consequent violent behaviour. Whether this aspect of the Act will be modified as a consequence is unknown.

hours on Fridays and Saturdays – midnight, 2.00 am, or whatever the club deems appropriate – and 11.00 or 11.30 pm on other days. In determining this, it goes without saying that clubs have to be conscious of staff working hours and balance their interests against the undoubted advantage of the flexibility conferred by the availability of longer hours. Managing committees need to be aware of the need to monitor the situation regarding opening hours, and members need to be conversant with opening hours, which should be published by notice in the clubhouse and/or set out in the bye-laws. If the bar steward is authorised to close the bar before the end of published opening hours, this fact should be made known to the members in order to avoid any argument with members who insist that they can go on drinking right to the end of the published hours.

## 9-39   Off sales

A club premises certificate may not authorise the supply of alcohol for consumption off the club premises unless it also authorises the supply of alcohol to members for consumption on the premises[104]. There are three mandatory conditions which will appear on the certificate[105]:

(1) the off-supply must be made at a time when the club is open for on-supply;

(2) the off-supply must be in a sealed container;

(3) the off-supply must be made to a club member in person; it may not be made to a member's guest.

## 9-40   Change of name or address or rules of the club

Where a club holds a club premises certificate, or has made an application for such a certificate which has not yet been determined, the club secretary must inform the licensing authority within 28 days of any change of name of the club or any alteration of its rules[106]. If the club holds such a certificate and ceases to use the registered address, it must inform the licensing authority as soon as reasonably practicable[107]. Failure by the club to comply with these requirements causes the secretary to commit an offence[108].

---

[104]     Licensing Act 2003, s. 73(1).
[105]     Ibid. s. 73(2)(3).
[106]     Ibid. s. 82.
[107]     Ibid. s. 83.
[108]     Ibid. ss. 82(6) and 83(6). It should be noted that under s. 82 it is the secretary's specific duty to notify, whereas under s. 83 it is the club's specific duty to notify. It is not clear why such a distinction was made.

## 9-41 Variation of certificate

It is open to a club to apply for a variation of the club premises certificate at any time[109], subject to requirements as to the prescribed form of the application and fees[110] and as to advertisement and notification of various authorities[111]. These requirements will be set out in regulations to be published[112]. The club will also be open to inspection by the police, fire authority or environmental health department[113]. The club must send to the licensing authority its club premises certificate, or an explanation of why the certificate is not available[114]. If the licensing authority receives any relevant representations[115] a hearing must be held, unless all parties agree that this is not necessary. If no relevant representation is received, the licensing authority must grant the variation sought[116], and issue an amended certificate together with, if necessary, a new summary[117]. If relevant representations have been received and considered, the licensing authority may either modify the conditions of the certificate or reject the whole or part of the application[118]. The guiding principle, as elsewhere in the Act, is the promotion of the licensing objectives[119].

## 9-42 Review of certificate

An interested party, a responsible authority, or a member of the club may apply at any time to a licensing authority for a review of the certificate[120]. If the local authority is both the licensing authority and a responsible authority it may, in its capacity as responsible authority, apply for a review and then determine the application in its capacity as licensing authority[121]. This is an interesting statutory avoidance of the first rule of natural justice which states that no person shall be a judge in his own case, and gives rise to a situation which might provoke an application for judicial review if the application is not dealt with in a scrupulously fair manner by the licensing authority.

---

[109]   Licensing Act 2003, s. 84(1).
[110]   Ibid. s. 84(2).
[111]   Ibid. s. 84(4).
[112]   Ibid. s. 84(4).
[113]   Ibid. s. 84(4) and s. 71(6).
[114]   Ibid. s. 84(3).
[115]   See **9-27** above.
[116]   Ibid. s. 85(2).
[117]   Ibid. s.93(1).
[118]   Ibid. s. 85(3), (4).
[119]   Ibid. s. 85(3)(b).
[120]   Ibid. s. 87(1). For the definition of an interested party and a responsible authority, see **9-27** above.
[121]   Ibid. s. 89.

Regulations will provide for the giving of notice and the advertisement of the application. The licensing authority may at any time reject the application if it is satisfied that the ground for the application for review is not relevant to the licensing objectives; or if made by a party other than a responsible authority, it is frivolous or vexatious; or it is a repetition of a ground unsuccessfully relied on in an earlier application and a reasonable time interval has not elapsed since the earlier occasion[122]. If the application for review is rejected the applicant must be informed on which ground the rejection has been based and, where the ground was that the application was frivolous or vexatious, the licensing authority must give reasons for its decision[123].

If, however, the application is not rejected by the licensing authority under section 87(4) it must hold a hearing to consider the application and any relevant representations[124], whereupon it may take such prescribed steps as it considers necessary to promote the licensing objectives[125]. The steps are[126]:

(1) to modify the conditions of the certificate;
(2) to exclude a qualifying club activity from the scope of the certificate;
(3) to suspend the certificate for a period not exceeding three months[127];
(4) to withdraw the certificate.

## 9-43 Termination of certificate

A club premises certificate will remain in force until it is either surrendered, or withdrawn by the licensing authority following the failure of the club to continue as a qualifying club[128] (or after a review: see **9-42** above).

**9-44** *Surrender* Where the club decides to surrender its premises certificate it may give the licensing authority notice to that effect[129]. The notice must be accompanied by the certificate or, if not practicable, must be accompanied by a statement giving reasons for failure to

---

[122] Licensing Act 2003, s. 87(4), (5).
[123] Ibid. s. 87(6).
[124] Ibid. s. 88(2). As to 'relevant representations', see **9-27** above.
[125] Ibid. s. 88(3).
[126] Ibid. s. 88(4).
[127] During which time the certificate has no effect: s. 80(2).
[128] Ibid. s. 80(1).
[129] Ibid. s. 81(1).
[130] Ibid. s. 81(2).

produce it[130], and the certificate lapses on receipt of the notice by the licensing authority[131].

**9-45** *Withdrawal* Where it appears to the licensing authority that a club in possession of a premises certificate no longer satisfies the conditions for being a qualifying club in relation to a qualifying activity the authority must give notice to the club withdrawing the certificate insofar as it relates to that activity[132]. If the only condition not satisfied is that relating to the required minimum number of 25 members, the notice withdrawing the certificate must state that the withdrawal does not take effect until after a period of three months following the date of the notice, and that it will not take effect if at the end of that period the numbers have increased to the required minimum number[133].

### 9-46 Right of entry

If the licensing authority has reasonable grounds for believing that the club does not satisfy the conditions for being a qualified club in relation to any qualifying activity and that evidence to that effect may be obtained at the club's premises, it may apply to a justice of the peace for a warrant authorising a constable to enter the premises, if necessary by force, in order to search them for that purpose[134]. The search must be made within one month of the date of the warrant, and a person entering under the authority of a warrant may seize and remove any documents relating to the business of the club[135].

## 7. PREMISES LICENCE

**9-47** A club may make an application for a premises licence[136]. This licence will cover all the licensable activities set out in (1) to (4) in **9-13** above. Where a premises licence authorises the supply of alcohol there will be two mandatory conditions attached to this form of licence[137]:

(1) no supply of alcohol may be made when there is no designated premises supervisor in respect of the premises licence, or at a time when the designated premises supervisor does not hold a personal

---

[131]    Licensing Act 2003, s. 81(3).
[132]    Ibid. s. 90(1).
[133]    Ibid. s. 90(2).
[134]    Ibid. s. 90(5).
[135]    Ibid. s. 90(5) and (6).
[136]    Ibid. s. 16(1)(c).
[137]    Ibid. s. 19.

licence or his personal licence has been suspended; and

(2) every supply of alcohol must be made or authorised by a person who holds a personal licence.

## 9-48  Designated premises supervisor

This is the individual person for time being specified in the licence as the premises supervisor. He must hold a personal licence[138]. Supervision does not mean that the supervisor has to be present whenever alcohol is sold[139]. There are provisions to cater for the change in the identity of the supervisor[140]. A holder of a personal licence, who is the applicant for a premises licence, does not have to be the designated supervisor of the premises to which the premises licence relates but he may be so[141].

## 9-49  Application for licence

One of the persons who may apply for a premises licence is a recognised club[142]. The application may be made in respect of one or more licensable activities. It is likely that the Secretary of State will make regulations prescribing the form of the application, the manner in which it is to be made, and the information and documents that must accompany it[143] and that he will also prescribe the amount of any fee[144]. The application must be accompanied by[145]:

(1) an operating schedule;

(2) a plan (in the prescribed form) of the premises to which the application relates;

(3) if the licensable activities include the supply of alcohol, a form of consent (in the prescribed form) given by the individual whom the applicant wishes to have specified as the premises supervisor.

---

[138]     Licensing Act 2003, s. 19(3). See **9-55** below.

[139]     See Barker and Cavender on *Licensing: the New Law* (2003) para 7.12.2.

[140]     An application to vary the supervisor may include a request that the variation of supervisor may take immediate effect because e.g. he has died; in this event the variation will take effect when the application is received by the licensing authority: Licensing Act 2003,, s. 37. This replaces the old protection order which is abolished.

[141]     Ibid. s. 15(2).

[142]     Ibid. s. 16(1)(c). A recognised club is defined in s. 193 as meaning a club which satisfies conditions (1), (2) and (3) of the general conditions set out in s. 62: see **9-22** above.

[143]     Ibid. s. 54.

[144]     Ibid. s. 55.

[145]     Ibid. s. 17(3).

## 9-50 Operating schedule

This is a crucial document and must be in the prescribed form and include a statement of the following matters[146]:

(1) the licensable activities to which the application relates;

(2) the times during which it is proposed that these activities are to take place;

(3 any other time during which it is proposed that the premises are to be open to the public;

(4) where the applicant wishes the licence to have effect for a limited period, that period;

(5) where the activities include the supply of alcohol:

    (a) the prescribed information in respect of the individual whom the applicant wishes to have specified in the licence as the premises supervisor;

    (b) whether the supply is proposed to be for the consumption on the premises or off the premises or both;

(6) the steps which it is proposed to take to promote the licensing objectives;

(7) such other matters as may be prescribed.

## 9-51 Form of licence

The premises licence and the summary of a premises licence must be in the prescribed form[147]. Regulations which are made in respect of this form must provide for the following[148]:

(1) specify the name and address of the holder of the personal licence;

(2) include a plan of the licensed premises;

(3) if the licence is for a limited period, specify that period;

(4) specify the licensable activities for which the premises may be used;

(5) if the licensable activities include the supply of alcohol, specify the name and address of the individual (if any) who is the premises supervisor;

(6) specify the conditions subject to which the licence has effect.

## 9-52 Variation of licence

Where an application is made by a licence holder to vary the premises licence and the requirements as to advertisement, etc, of the

---

[146]     Licensing Act 2003, s. 17(4).

[147]     Ibid. s. 24(1).

[148]     Ibid. s. 24.

application have been complied with, and in the absence of any relevant representations, the licensing authority must grant the application[149]. Application may be made to vary the licence in order to specify a different individual as the premises supervisor[150].

### 9-53   Review of licence

A very similar set of provisions applies to the review of a premises licence as applies to a club premises certificate[151] save that the persons who can make an application for review are restricted to an interested party or a responsible authority[152].

### 9-54   Termination of licence

A premises licence has effect until it is revoked under section 52 (following an application for review), or on the expiration of any period to which the licence was expressed to be limited[153] or, in the case of a club, ceases to be a recognised club[154], or it is surrendered[155].

## 8    PERSONAL LICENCE

**9-55**   A personal licence is a licence granted by a licensing authority to an individual authorising that individual to supply, *or to authorise the supply*, of alcohol in accordance with a premises licence[156]. This supply can take place either by retail sale or by supply by or on behalf of a club to, or to the order of, a member of the club[157]. The emphasised words are important because, as stated above[158], there is no requirement in the Act of 2003 that the designated premises supervisor, who must hold a personal licence, has to be present on all occasions when alcohol is sold or supplied. A person may only hold one personal licence at any one time[159].

---

[149]   Licensing Act 2003, ss. 34 and 35. As to relevant representations see **9-27** above.
[150]   Ibid. s. 37.
[151]   See **9-42** above.
[152]   Ibid. ss. 13, 51, 52 and 53. As to an interested party or relevant authority, see **9-27** above.
[153]   Ibid. s. 26.
[154]   Ibid. s. 27(1)(e). A recognised club is defined in s. 193 as meaning a club which satisfies conditions (1, (2) and (3) of the general conditions set out in s. 62: see **9-22** above.
[155]   Ibid. s. 28.
[156]   Ibid. s. 111(1).
[157]   Ibid. s. 111(2).
[158]   At **9-48** above.
[159]   Ibid. s. 118.

## 9-56  Application for personal licence

Application is made to the relevant licensing authority[160] and the procedure for determination is set out in section 120 of the Act of 2003. The salient points to note are that the licensing authority must grant the licence if it appears to it that:

(1) the applicant is aged 18 years or over;
(2) he possesses a licensing qualification[161] or is a person of a prescribed description[162];
(3) 'no personal licence held by him has been forfeited in the period of five years ending with the day the application was made; and
(4) he has not been convicted of any relevant offence or any foreign offence[163].

## 9-57  Continuing duty

It should be noted that there is a continuing duty to notify the licensing authority of any relevant conviction or foreign conviction[164] or any change of name or address of the applicant[165]. If the holder of a personal licence is charged with a relevant offence, he must produce that licence to the court before which he appears or, if that is not practicable, he must notify the court of the existence of the personal licence, the identity of the licensing authority and the reasons why he cannot produce the licence[166]. Failure to do so is in itself an offence[167]. The court may, upon conviction of a personal licence holder for a relevant offence, order the forfeiture of the licence or its suspension for a period not exceeding six months[168], and must notify the relevant licensing authority[169].

---

[160]    Licensing Act 2003, s. 117.
[161]    Defined in ibid. s. 120(8).
[162]    'Prescribed' here means prescribed by regulations: ibid. s. 193.
[163]    Ibid. s. 120(2). For 'relevant offence' see Sch. 4 to the Act of 2003. 'Foreign offence' means an offence (other than a relevant offence) committed outside England and Wales: s.113(3).
[164]    Ibid. ss. 123 and 124.
[165]    Ibid. s. 127.
[166]    Ibid. s. 128.
[167]    Ibid. s. 128(6).
[168]    Ibid. s. 129.
[169]    Ibid. s. 131. The licence holder is under a similar duty of notification: s. 132.

## 9.     TEMPORARY EVENT NOTICE

**9-58**   The temporary event notice is the third type of authorisation for licensable activities provided for under the 2003 Act[170].

### 9-59   Service of notice

A temporary event notice must be given by an individual aged over eighteen years[171], where it is proposed to use premises[172] for one or more licensable activities within a 96-hour (four-day) period[173]. The individual thereupon becomes the premises user for the purposes of the event[174]. The temporary event notice must be given in duplicate to the relevant licensing authority not later than ten working days before the beginning of the event period[175]; must be in the prescribed form[176]; must be accompanied by the prescribed fee[177]; and must contain the following details[178]:

(1) the relevant licensable activities;
(2) the 'event period', i.e. the period (not exceeding 96 hours) during which the licensable activities will be carried on;
(3) the times of day during the event period when the licensable activities will be carried on;
(4) the maximum number of persons (which must be less than 500) which the premises user proposes will be on the premises at any one time;
(5) whether any supply of alcohol will be on or off the premises or both;
(6) such other matters as may be prescribed.

Where there is to be a supply of alcohol, the notice must make it a condition of using the premises that such supply is made by or under the authority of the premises user[179].

The licensing authority must return one of the two notices before the end of the first working day following the day on which it was

---

[170]     Licensing Act 2003, s. 2(4)(c).
[171]     Ibid. s. 100(3).
[172]     These do not necessarily have to be club premises.
[173]     Ibid. s. 100(1).
[174]     Ibid. s. 100(2).
[175]     Ibid. s. 100(7)(a). A working day is defined in s. 193 as meaning any other day than a Saturday, a Sunday, Christmas Day, Good Friday or a day which is a bank holiday under the Banking and Financial Dealings Act 1971 in England and Wales.
[176]     Ibid. s. 100(4).
[177]     Ibid. s. 100(7)(b).
[178]     Ibid. s. 100(5).
[179]     Ibid. s. 100(6).

received[180], having marked an acknowledgment of receipt in the prescribed form[181]. The premises user may withdraw the notice not later than 24 hours before the event period[182]. This may be important because a notice duly withdrawn does not count towards the 24 hour restriction mentioned in the next paragraph.

## 9-60 Limits on number of notices

A maximum of 12 temporary event notices may be served in respect of the same premises in any one calendar year[183] and the premises themselves cannot be used for more than 15 days in a calendar year for temporary event purposes[184]. An important point to remember is that if the event period straddles two calendar years the restrictions apply separately in relation to those two years, that is to say, the event is counted twice, once in the first year and once in the second year[185]. A personal licence holder may give up to 50 temporary event notices in any one year[186]; and any other person may give up to five such notices[187]. Consequently three members of a club in possession of a club premises certificate could give the maximum of 12 temporary event notices. There must, however, be at least 24 hours' interval between event periods in respect of the same premises, where the notices are given by the same premises user or by individuals who are associated. 'Associated' here means[188]:

(1) the spouse of the individual giving the notice;
(2) directly related to one another[189];
(3) living together as man and wife;
(4) the spouse of a person falling within categories (2) and (3);
(5) in business together where that business relates to one or more licensable activities;
(6) the one is the agent or employee of the other.

The Secretary of State may by order substitute different limits on the number of notices[190].

---

[180]    If the day or receipt was not a working day, the receipt must follow before the end of the second working day: s. 102(1)(b).
[181]    Licensing Act 2003, s. 102(1) and (2).
[182]    Ibid. s. 103(1).
[183]    Ibid. s. 107(4). 'Year' means calendar year: s. 107(13)(b).
[184]    Ibid. s. 107(5).
[185]    Ibid. s. 107(5).
[186]    Ibid. s. 107(2)(b).
[187]    Ibid. s. 107(3)(b).
[188]    Ibid. s. 101.
[189]    This means a child, parent, grandchild, grandparent, brother or sister: s. 107(3).
[190]    Ibid. s. 107(12).

## 9-61   Counter notice where limits exceeded

Where a licensing authority receives a temporary event notice and is satisfied that the provisions limiting the number of applications have been exceeded, it must give a counter notice in the prescribed form to the premises user[191]. This counter notice excuses the licensing authority from complying with the acknowledgment provisions referred to in **9-60** above[192], but the counter notice must be given not later than 24 hours before the beginning of the event period[193]. Where a counter notice is given, the licensing authority must send a copy of it to the chief officer (or officers) of police[194]. The counter notice overrides the provisions relating to police objections[195].

## 9-62   Police objections

The premises user must also give a copy of the notice to the relevant chief officer of police[196] not later than 10 working days before the event period[197]. If, following receipt of the notice, the chief officer of police is satisfied that allowing the premises to be used as requested in the notice would undermine the crime prevention objective, he must give an 'objection notice' to the licensing authority and the proposed premises user, not later than 48 hours after he has received the temporary event notice[198]. The licensing authority must thereupon hold a hearing to consider the objection notice, unless all are agreed that this is unnecessary[199]. If the licensing authority then considers that it is necessary for the promotion of the crime objective to do so, it may prevent the temporary event from taking place by giving the premises user a counter notice to that effect[200]. Notice of this decision must be given (with reasons) to the premises user and also to the chief officer of police[201]. The decision must be given at least 24 hours before the beginning of the event period[202].

---

[191]    Licensing Act 2003, s. 107. As to the relevant limits, see **9-60** above.
[192]    Ibid. s.102(3).
[193]    Ibid. s. 107(8).
[194]    Ibid. s. 107(11).
[195]    Ibid. ss. 105(6)(b), 106(6) and 107(9).
[196]    This means the chief officer of police for the area in which the premises are situated or, where the premises are situated in two or more police areas, the chief officer of police for each area.
[197]    Ibid. s. 104(1).
[198]    Ibid. s. 104(2).
[199]    Ibid. s. 105(2)(a).
[200]    Ibid. s. 105(2)(b).
[201]    Ibid. s. 105(3).
[202]    Ibid. s. 105(4).

**9-63** *Modification of objection notice* At any time before a hearing is held or dispensed with, the chief officer of police and the premises user may agree to modify the notice by making changes to the notice as served[203]. In this event the objection notice is treated as withdrawn[204]. A copy of the modified notice must be sent to the licensing authority by the chief officer of police[205]. If the premises are situated in more than one police area, every chief officer must consent to the modification[206].

## 9-64 Duty to keep, display and produce notice

The premises user must ensure that the notice is kept at the relevant premises in his custody or in the custody of a nominated person working at the premises[207]. He must also ensure that a copy of the (endorsed) notice is prominently displayed on these premises[208]. If he fails to comply without reasonable excuse, the premises user commits an offence[209].

## 9-65 Loss of notice

The local authority must provide a copy, upon payment of a fee, if the notice is lost, stolen, damaged or destroyed, when satisfied that the notice has thus become unavailable and that, if lost or stolen, the matter has been reported to the police[210]. The application for a replacement notice, however, must be made within one month of the event specified in the notice[211].

## 9-66 Closure of and right of entry into club premises

The magistrates' court has power to close premises covered by a temporary event notice for 24 hours in an area experiencing disorder on the application of a police officer of the rank of superintendent or above[212]. Further, a police officer of the rank of inspector or above may make a closure order of premises covered by a temporary event notice

---

203  Licensing Act 2003, s. 106(2).
204  Ibid. s. 106(3)(a).
205  Ibid. s. 106(4).
206  Ibid. s. 106(5).
207  Ibid. s. 109(3)(a).
208  Ibid. s. 109(3)(b).
209  Ibid. s. 109(4).
210  Ibid. s. 110.
211  Ibid. s. 110(2).
212  Ibid. s. 160 (1)(b) and (2).

for 24 hours if he reasonably believes that there is or will be disorder in the vicinity and closure is necessary for public safety or that a public nuisance is being caused by noise coming from the premises[213]. The police also have power to enter the premises to which a temporary event notice relates at any reasonable time to assess the likely effect of the notice on the promotion of the crime prevention objective, and it is an offence to obstruct a constable in the exercise of this power[214].

## 10.  PROPRIETARY CLUBS

**9-67**  Inevitably proprietary clubs will require a premises licence, rather than a club premises certificate, as they will not meet the conditions for qualification in sections 62 and 64 and will therefore not be qualifying clubs within the meaning of the Act.

## 11.  TRANSITIONAL PROVISIONS

**9-68**  A more accurate description of these provisions would be *conversion* provisions since they set out how existing on-licences and registration certificates will convert to premises licences and club premises certificates. These provisions are set out in Schedule 8 to the Act. Premises licences are dealt with in Part 1, club premises certificates in Part 2[215].

### 9-69  Club premises certificate

Clubs holding an existing registration certificate on the first appointed day[216] may, within six months beginning with that day, apply for the grant of a club premises certificate[217]. The application must be accompanied by the fee and the relevant documents, that is[218]:
(1) the existing club certificate, or a certified copy of it[219];
(2) a plan in the specified form of the premises to which that certificate relates;

---

[213]     Licensing Act 2003, s. 161(1)(2)(8). See also the Anti-Social Behaviour Act 2003 in **9-79** below.
[214]     Ibid. s. 108.
[215]     Part 2 of Sch. 8 appears in APPENDIX 8.
[216]     7 February 2005.
[217]     Ibid. Sch. 8, para 14(2).
[218]     Ibid. Sch. 8, para 14(5).
[219]     That is, certified by the chief executive of the licensing justices, or by a solicitor or notary public, or by 'a person of a specified description': ibid. para 14(6). We look forward to learning the identity of this curious last category.

(3) such other documents as may be specified by the Secretary of State.

A copy of the application and documentation must be given to the chief officer of police for the police area in which the premises are situated not later than 48 hours after the application is made[220]. Subject to what is said in the next paragraph, if the applicant complies with these provisions the licensing authority must grant the application[221]. Where the application is granted the licensing authority must give the applicant a notice to that effect and, more importantly, a new certificate. If the licensing authority fails to determine the application within two months beginning with the day on which it received it, it is deemed to be granted[222] and takes effect on the second appointed day[223]. Any club would be well advised to make the application early in the sixth month period following the first appointed day, as it is likely to be the case that the licensing and responsible authorities will take some time to get accustomed to the new régime and delays will occur. Then in the event of a refusal the appeal process can be commenced without delay: this applies in particular to any initial variation: see **9-74** below.

**9-70** *Police objections* If in the opinion of the chief officer of police the granting of the certificate would undermine the crime prevention objective, he must within 28 days of the receipt by him of the application give the applicant and the licensing authority a notice to that effect[224]. Where notice of objection is given, the licensing authority must hold a hearing to consider it and reject the application if it considers it necessary for the promotion of the crime prevention objective to do so[225]. The licensing authority must give the applicant a notice setting out its reasons for the rejection of the application. There is a right of appeal against a rejection[226], and the police similarly can appeal against the grant of a certificate where they have made an objection which has not been withdrawn[227].

---

[220] Licensing Act 2003, Sch. 8, para 15(1).
[221] Ibid. Sch. 8, para 16(2).
[222] Ibid. Sch. 8, para 16(4).
[223] Ibid. Sch. 8, para 18(2).
[224] Ibid. Sch. 8, para 15(2).
[225] Ibid. Sch. 8, para 16(3).
[226] This is, to the magistrates' court: ibid. s. 181.
[227] Ibid. Sch. 8, para 21.

**9-71   Premises licence**

A person holding one or more existing on-licences on the first appointed day may, within six months beginning with that day, apply for the grant of a premises licence to succeed one or more of the existing licences[228]. The application must specify[229]:
(1) the existing licensable activities under the existing licence(s);
(2) if any existing licence authorises the supply of alcohol, specified information about the person whom the applicant wishes to be the premises supervisor;
(3) such other information as may be specified by the Secretary of State.

**9-72**   The application must be accompanied by the fee and the relevant documents, that is[230]:
(1) the existing licence or, if there is more than one, each of them (or certified copies);
(2) a plan in the specified form of the premises to which the existing licence(s) relates;
(3) any children's certificate in force in respect of licensed premises (or a certified copy of any such certificate);
(4) a form of consent in the specified form, given by the individual (if any[231]) named in the   application as the person whom the applicant wishes to be the premises supervisor[232];
(5) a form of consent in the specified form, given by the applicant or the existing licence holder;
(6) such other documents as may be specified by the Secretary of State.

**9-73**   Thereafter the determination of the application proceeds in a manner similar to that set out in **9-69** above, relating to the conversion of existing registration certificates[233], and if the licensing authority fails to determine the application within two months of the day it was received, it is to be treated as having been granted[234], and will take effect on the second appointed day[235].

---

[228]   Licensing Act 2003, Sch. 8, para 14(2).
[229]   Ibid. Sch. 8, para 2(4).
[230]   Ibid. Sch. 8, para 14(5).
[231]   The words '(if any)' would appear to be superfluous in that the consent of the relevant individual is essential: Sch.8, Part 1, paras 2(4)(b), 2(6)(d).
[232]   Ibid. Sch. 8, para 2(6)(d).
[233]   See generally, ibid. Sch. 8, paras 3, 4 and 5.
[234]   Ibid. Sch. 8, para 4(4).
[235]   Ibid. Sch. 8, para 6(4): forecast as being in or about November 2005.

## 9-74 Initial variation

Hidden in Schedule 8 of the Act of 2003 is a trap for the unwary. By paragraph 14(2) the club may, within the period of six months beginning with the first appointed day, apply to the licensing authority for a club premises certificate to succeed the existing registration certificate. One of the documents which has to accompany the application is a plan (in the specified form) of the premises to which the registration certificate relates[236]. If the licensing authority fails to determine the application within two months beginning with the day on which it received it, the application is deemed to be *granted*[237]. Thus far, the matter is straightforward. It will be seen, however, from paragraph 9-29 above that careful consideration needs to be given to the extent of the licensed premises under the new régime. The club's new plan might differ very considerably from its old plan. This will count as a variation and, you might think helpfully, paragraph 19(1) of Schedule 8 permits an applicant for a club premises certificate to apply *at the same time* for a variation of the certificate to-be-granted so that the premises are licensed on the second appointed day in accordance with the new plan. Herein lies the rub. If the licensing authority fails to determine the application for variation within two months beginning with the day on which it received it the application is deemed to be *rejected*[238]. In which event the club will have to make a free-standing application for variation[239]. Presumably the intention of the legislature is to allow any existing set-up to go through unimpeded but to require any new set-up to be more carefully scrutinised by the new licensing authorities.

In the case of an application for a premises licence, there are similar provisions relating to initial variation as those which apply to club premises certificates[240].

---

[236]   Licensing Act 2003, Sch. 8, para 14(5)(b).
[237]   Ibid. Sch. 8, para 16(4).
[238]   Ibid. Sch. 8, para 19(3).
[239]   See 9-41 above.
[240]   See generally, ibid. Sch. 8, para. 7.

## 12.  APPEALS

**9-75**   The appeals procedure is set out in Schedule 5 to the Act. Part
1 of the Schedule deals with premises licences[241], Part 2 with club
premises certificates[242] and Part 3 with 'Other Appeals'[243]. Appeal is
to the magistrates' court for the petty sessions area in which the
premises concerned are situated for all cases[244], save appeals against
the decision of a licensing authority to reject an application for the
grant or renewal of a personal licence, where it is made to the
magistrates' court for the petty sessions area in which the licensing
authority's area (or any part of it) is situated[245]. In each case a notice
of appeal must be given within the period of 21 days commencing
with the day on which the appellant was notified by the relevant
licensing authority of the decision appealed against.  On appeal the
magistrates' court may:
(1) dismiss the appeal;
(2) substitute for the decision appealed against any other decision
    which could have been made by the licensing authority; or
(3) remit the case to the licensing authority to dispose of it in
    accordance with the direction of the court,

and may make such order as to costs which it thinks fit.[246]

**9-76**   Under the Act of 1964 all decisions of the magistrates' court
could be appealed to the Crown Court. This is no longer the case[247].
Under the new régime appeal is to the High Court by way of case

---

[241]     E.g. an appeal will lie for the following: rejection of applications for a premises
licence under s. 18, (Sch. 5, para 1); rejection of variation application under ss. 35 and 39
(Sch. 5, paras 1, 4 and 5); transfer under s. 44 (Sch. 5, para 6); a decision to impose
conditions under s. 18 (Sch. 5, para 2); a decision on the review under s. 52 (Sch. 5,
para 8).
[242]     E.g. an appeal will lie for the following: rejection of application for club premises
certificate under s. 72 (Sch. 5, para 10); rejection of variation application under s.85
(Sch. 5, paras 10 and 12); decision to impose conditions under s. 72, (Sch. 5, para 11) a
decision on review under s. 88 (ibid. para 13); withdrawal of certificate under s. 90 (Sch. 5,
para 14).
[243]     Temporary event notices, where the chief officer of police gives notice of objection
under s. 104(2) (Sch. 5, para 16(1)); where the licensing authority gives a counter-notice
under s. 105(3) (Sch. 5, para 16(2)); personal licences where the licensing authority has
rejected an application under ss. 120 or 121 (Sch. 5, para 17), and review of premises
licence following the making of a closure order under s.167 (Sch. 5, para 18).
[244]     Sch. 5, paras 9 and 15.
[245]     Ibid. Sch. 5, para 17(6).
[246]     Ibid. s. 181(2).
[247]     This is because under the old régime the original licensing decisions were made by
the magistrates and an appeal lay to the Crown Court, whereas under the new régime the
original licensing decisions are to be made by local councils and an appeal will lie to the
magistrates' court.

stated, save in the case of a decision of a magistrates' court relating to a closure order made on the application of a senior police officer[248]. Here the right of appeal to the Crown Court is preserved[249]; notice of appeal must again be given within 21 days beginning with the day on which the decision appealed against was made.

## 13. FEES

**9-77** The intention of the government is that the new system of licensing will be self-financing. This will inevitably mean that it will be more expensive than under the old régime, which has caused some considerable consternation in the club world. For example, a golf club will be assessed on the rateable value of the whole golf course say 120 acres, whereas the premises containing the licensed bar will form only a small fraction of the whole acreage. The premises licence and the club premises certificate will, however, not require renewal[250] although there will be a not insubstantial annual fee. The initial cost will be determined by a banding system dependent on the non-domestic rateable value of the club's premises. By the fees regulations issued on 20 January 2005[251] the fees applicable on the first appointed day (7 February 2005) will be as follows[252]:

The chargeable bands are:

| A | B | C | D | E |
|---|---|---|---|---|
| £0–4,300 | £4,301–£33,000 | £33,001–£87,000 | £87,001–£125,000 | £125,001+ |

The fees for applications are:

| | | | | |
|---|---|---|---|---|
| £100 | £190 | £315 | £450 | £635 |

With annual fees being:

| | | | | |
|---|---|---|---|---|
| £70 | £180 | £295 | £320 | £350 |

---

[248] Licensing Act 2003, Part 8. This applies only to licensed premises or those subject to a temporary event notice; a full consideration of this part of the Act is outside the scope of this book.
[249] Ibid, s. 166.
[250] See **9-43** AND **9-54** above.
[251] Licensing Act 2003 (Fees) Regulations 2005 (SI 2005/79) and Licensing Act 2003 (Transitional Conversion Fees) Regulations 2005 (SI 2005/80).
[252] These fees are considerably higher than those put forward in the government consultation document in 2004; this is because the licensing authorites protested that the proposed fees were too low to cover their costs of administering the new régime.

Other fees will be required[252]. For a number of minor applications such as notification of a change of address or alteration of the rules and for copies of documentation, the fee will be £10.50; for applications for a transfer of premises licence the fee will be £23; for a temporary event notice the fee will be £21[253].

# 14. OFFENCES

**9-78** There are numerous offences which can be committed under the new régime. They are mostly contained in Part 7 of the Act of 2003: see **Appendix 8**. The committee of any club supplying or selling alcohol will be well advised to familiarise themselves with this list of offences. The matter is further discussed in **15-02** and **15-09** below.

### 9-79 Anti-Social Behaviour Act 2003

It is worth noting that this Act has since 20 January 2004 given the police the power to close premises if a police officer not below the rank of superintendent has reasonable grounds for believing:
(1) that at any time during the relevant period the premises have been used in connection with the unlawful use, production or supply of a Class A controlled drug[254], or
(2) that the use of the premises is associated with the occurrence of disorder or serious nuisance to members of the public[255].

The superintendent can then authorise the issue of a closure notice for service by a constable at the premises in question[256]. Thereafter a constable must apply to the magistrates' court for the making of a closure order and the application must be heard within 48 hours of the service of the notice[257]. The court may adjourn the hearing for not more than 14 days to enable an interested party to make representations as to why the order should not be made[258]. These powers are distinct from the closure provisions of Part 8 of the Licensing Act 2003 which relate only to premises in respect of which there is in effect a premises licence or a temporary event notice[259].

---

[253]    Further details can be obtained from the government website, *www.culture.gov.uk*.
[254]    A temporary event notice may contain more than one temporary event and a flat fee is chargeable which is not dependent on the number of events comprising the notice.
[255]    Licensing Act 2003, s. 1(1)(a).
[256]    Ibid. s. 1(1)(b).
[257]    Ibid. s. 1(2), (5), (6).
[258]    Ibid. s. 2(1), (2)
[259]    Ibid. s. 2(6).
[260]    See ibid. ss. 160 and 161 at **9-66** above.

# Chapter 10

## ENTERTAINMENT PROVIDED BY THE CLUB

### 1. INTRODUCTION

**10-01**  Entertainments of various kinds are staged or provided by clubs, sometimes as part of a club's core activities, sometimes for the enjoyment of its members, and at other times to raise funds for the club. It is a sphere of activity which needs the club's attention because in putting on the entertainment other people's rights are often affected (we are here talking about copyright), and many entertainments are regulated by central or local government as a matter of public policy (we are here talking about the need for a licence). The topic of entertainment has been revisited by the Licensing Act 2003 so that much entertainment provided in clubs will now be regulated by this Act, even though no alcohol is being supplied at the entertainment and even though no member of the public is present at the entertainment. The question of noise nuisance should also be borne in mind[1]. What is set out below applies to all clubs of whatever type they may be.

### 2. COPYRIGHT

**10-02  What is protected**

Copyright protects original literary, dramatic, musical and artistic work; sound recordings, films, broadcasts and cable programmes; and typographical arrangements[2]. It is an economic and property right

---

[1]    See **10-27** below.
[2]    Copyright, Designs and Patents Act 1988, s. 1.

(which enables the creator to earn money) which is to be distinguished from his moral rights in the same material (which protects his reputation). The principal act is the Copyright, Designs and Patents Act 1988 as amended by the Duration of Copyright and Rights in Performances Regulations 1995[3], the Copyright and Related Rights Regulations 2003[4] and other regulations. There is a good reason why clubs need to take notice of copyright and that is because typically these days an author, composer or playwright or the recording company assign their copyright to a collecting society. It is the collecting society who will issue the licence to perform and who will collect the royalties for distribution to the author or composer etc. A collecting society with a large handful of copyrights is in a powerful position to dictate the terms of the licence, and aggrieved persons can challenge the fees charged by complaining to the Copyright Tribunal[5]. A club which puts on dramatic or musical or video entertainment without checking whether a contractual licence from the copyright owner is required will sooner or later find itself in trouble. We should add that the copyright owner has exclusive rights to make adaptations of the original work[6], so that for example editing a play or putting on an abridged version would not escape the copyright legislation.

**10-03** In many instances there will be separate copyrights to contend with. Take the playing of recorded songs in the clubhouse. The club may find that the copyright in the words of the songs belongs to one person, the songwriter; the copyright in the music belongs to another person, the composer; and the copyright in the recording itself belongs to a third person, the recording company. It was this diverse holding of the various copyrights that led to the formation of the collecting societies, and from an administrative point of view it makes the club secretary's job a lot easier to deal with a small number of bodies rather than a large collection of individual copyright owners. The main collecting societies are Performing Rights Society Limited and Phonographic Performances Limited. The downside of the situation is that the societies are usually more zealous in chasing people than would be the case with individual copyright owners.

---

[3]    SI 1995/3297.
[4]    SI 2003/2498.
[5]    Copyright Act 1956, s. 23 and Copyright, Designs and Patents Act 1988, s. 45.
[6]    Ss. 16(1)(e) and 21(1) of the Act of 1988.

## 10-04   Performance in public

This is the crux of the matter. There are various exceptions to the régime of copyright, such as fair dealing for the purposes of research or criticism or review[7]. Another important exception is that no breach of copyright takes place in domestic or quasi-domestic situations, where the recording, for example, is played amongst family members[8]. The purpose of the copyright legislation is to protect the copyright owner in those situations where the listener or viewer would normally expect to have to pay for such entertainment. Hence the importance of the concept of performance *in public.* A members' club might be forgiven for thinking that performance limited to its own members (and their guests) was not a performance in public. But the club would be wrong: the legal situation has to be looked at from the copyright owner's point of view. Would the owner regard the audience as part of *his* public? If so, the performance is 'in public', even if as between the performers and the audience each side would regard the performance as being in private. Thus in *Harms (Incorporated) Ltd v Martans Club* [1927] 1 Ch 526 the performance of music by a dance band solely to club members in a dining and dancing club was held to be in public. Likewise, in *Jennings v Stephens* [1936] 1 Ch 469 CA the performance of a play by members of a Women's Institute for their own members was held to be in public. In a similar vein, music played to employees of a factory whilst they were working constituted a performance in public[9]. In all these cases a breach of copyright was established[10].

## 10-05   'Sound recording' exception

An exception to the copyright régime is contained in section 67 of the Copyright, Designs and Patents Act 1988[11]. A sound recording is defined as '(a) a recording of sounds, from which sounds may be reproduced or (b) a recording of the whole or part of a literary, dramatic or musical work, from which sounds reproducing the work or part may be reproduced'[12]. For this exception to apply the

---

[7]   See Copyright, Designs and Patents Act 1988, Chapter III.

[8]   *Ernest Turner Electrical Instruments Ltd v Performing Right Society Ltd* [1943] Ch 167 CA per Goddard LJ at 175.

[9]   *Ernest Turner Electrical Instruments Ltd v Performing Rights Society Ltd* [1943] Ch 167 CA.

[10]   See also *Performing Rights Society v Rangers F C Supporters Club* [1975] RPC 626 and *Performing Rights Society v Hammond* [1934] Ch 121 CA.

[11]   As amended by the Copyright and Related Rights Regulations 2003 (SI 2003/2498).

[12]   Copyright, Designs and Patents Act 1988, s. 5A.

following conditions must be met:
(1) the club is not established or conducted for profit and its main objects are charitable or otherwise concerned with advancement of religion, education or social welfare;
(2) the sound recording is played by a person who is acting primarily and directly for the benefit of the club and who is not acting with a view to gain;
(3) the proceeds of any charge for admission to the place where the sound recording is heard are solely for club purposes;
(4) the proceeds of any goods or services sold by or on behalf of the club on the occasion of and in the place where the sound recording is played are applied solely for club purposes.

### 10-06   Televisions and radios

As originally enacted, section 72 of the Copyright, Designs and Patents Act 1988 contained a provision that the showing or playing of a broadcast in public did not amount to an infringement of copyright if it was not played to a paying audience. Since then the right to free public performance has been drastically cut down by amendment of the section[13]. The overall effect of the section as amended is that where a club has a television or radio playing for the benefit of the club members, the club will not only need a television-and-radio licence, but will be likely to need a licence from Performing Rights Society Limited and a further licence from Phonographic Performances Limited, unless the programme being broadcast does not include (a) any literary, dramatic or musical works which are subject to copyright or (b) any commercially released sound recordings[14].

### 10-07   Duration of copyright and remedies for breach

The copyright in any work, save sound recordings, lasts for the lifetime of the individual(s) who created the work, plus 70 years[15]. Companies may obtain the copyright by an assignment to them of the individual's rights. The copyright in sound recordings lasts simply for 50 years from first release[16]. The remedies for breach of copyright are damages, an injunction to prevent further breach, an account of profits made

---

[13]     As a result of the Rental and Related Rights Directive (SI 1992/100) and Information Society Directive (SI 2003/29).

[14]     See *Copinger and Skone James on Copyright* (15th edn, 2004) para 9-200.

[15]     Copyright, Designs and Patents Act 1988, s. 12 as substituted by the Duration of Copyright and Rights in Performances Regulations 1995 (SI 1995/3297).

[16]     Ibid. s. 13A as amended by the regulations referred to in the previous footnote.

as a result of the breach and delivery up of the offending material[17].

**10-08**  Aside from copyright, it is a criminal offence to make a record or film of any dramatic or musical work without the written consent of the performers, except for private and domestic use[18]. This prohibition covers the sale, letting or performance in public of any such record or film[19].

## 3.  PUBLISHING BOOKS

**10-09**  The publisher of any printed book within the United Kingdom is obliged by statute to send a copy to the British Library Board within one month of publication and to certain other libraries on their request for a copy[20]. A book is widely defined: it includes any book, pamphlet or magazine, and any map, plan, chart or table[21]. By and large, club literature will not be subject to this obligation because the material is not 'published', that is to say, copies of the work are not issued to the public. However, it would be different if a club were to publish a history of the club which was available for sale in the local shops or if the club were to publish a booklet on the aims of the club or the facilities which it offered and made this booklet available generally.  In these circumstances we consider that the statutory obligation would arise.

## 4.  REGULATED ENTERTAINMENT

### 10-10  Introduction

This is another area which will be radically altered by the Licensing Act 2003, which is forecast to come fully into force probably in late 2005. The present system of licensed entertainment will be replaced by a system of regulated entertainment. This chapter will therefore deal primarily with the new system but will retain in the main text a brief outline of the present system until its replacement by the provisions of the Licensing Act 2003.

---

17   Copyright, Designs and Patents Act 1988, ss. 96 and 97.
18   Performers Protection Acts 1958 to 1972: see now Copyright, Designs and Patents Act 1988.
19   Ibidem.
20   Legal Deposit Libraries Act 2003, s. 1.
21   Ibid. s. 1(3).

## 5.    OLD RÉGIME

### 10-11    General propositions

Insofar as clubs are concerned, two basic propositions apply where entertainment is provided by clubs:

(1) *Private entertainment*  Where a club's entertainment, whether it be musical, dramatic, sporting or whatever, involves live performers in front of an audience comprising solely of club members and their guests, no entertainments licence of any sort is needed by the club[22];

(2) *Public entertainment*  Where a club's entertainment involves music or dancing or entertainment of a like kind in any place in England or Wales to members of the public, an entertainments licence must be obtained from the district council or, in London, from the relevant Borough Council or from the Common Council of the City of London.

**10-12**    The test therefore is whether the entertainment is open to the public in general (if so, it is public) or whether it is restricted to a specific class of persons (if so, it is private)[23]. It makes no difference to the outcome whether the entertainment is free or involves an entrance fee. A good illustration of the test in practice is given by the case of *Panama (Piccadilly) Ltd v Newberry* [1962] 1 WLR 610 DC. The Panama Club staged a dancing, singing and music show on its premises in London. The reception clerk would ask members of the public who came into the club if they would like to see the show and if they replied yes, he would say, 'It will cost you 25 shillings which is membership to the club and the first show is free.' The persons would fill up and sign an application form which, although it had space for a proposer and seconder, none was asked for, and on payment of 25 shillings the clerk gave them a slip of paper which indicated that they were guests of the club committee for liquor licensing purposes, and they were thereupon allowed entry into the show. The club was convicted of keeping the premises for dancing, singing and music without an entertainments licence from the London County Council. The club argued that once a person had signed an application form he ceased to be a member of the public, but the Divisional Court held that the

---

[22]     *Severn View Social Club v Chepstow Justices* [1968] 1 WLR 1512. Some sporting contests such as boxing, judo and wrestling contests do require a licence: see e.g. the Local Government (Miscellaneous Provisions) Act 1982, s. 1, Sch. 12, para 2.
[23]     *Boughey v Rowbotham* [1886] 4 H and C 711; *Cawley v Frost* [1976] Cr App Rep 20.

reality of the situation was that any member of the public could go into the club, pay his 25 shillings and see the show, so that he still remained a member of the public despite his signing the application form; and the court upheld the conviction.

## 10-13  Plays

If a play is to be performed in a public place, for example, the local theatre, or is to be performed on private premises which the public, or a section of it, is permitted to attend, the club must obtain a theatre licence from the local authority[24]. If the play is a musical or a ballet, no further licence for music and dancing is necessary[25]. Plays may be performed on Sundays[26]. Whilst censorship by the Lord Chamberlain was abolished a long time ago, it is still a criminal offence to present or direct a play which is obscene[27] or which is likely to provoke a breach of the peace[28] or likely to incite racial hatred[29].

## 10-14  Films

If a film or video entertainment is to be shown publicly, the club must obtain a cinema licence from the local authority[30]. A video game counts as a 'cinematograph exhibition' and requires a cinema licence[31]. Clubs may hold private cinema or video shows without a licence unless promoted for private gain or unless children are involved[32]. Film shows may take place on Sundays[33]. It is a criminal offence to show a film which is obscene[34].

**10-15**  The Video Recordings Acts 1984 and 1993 require many video recordings in the English language to be classified and labelled according to their suitability for viewing by stated age-groups and the

---

[24]  Theatres Act 1968, ss. 12 to 14 (to be repealed).
[25]  Ibid. s. 12(2) (to be repealed).
[26]  Sunday Theatres Act 1972, s. 1 (to be repealed). The ability to perform on Sundays is subsumed into the Licensing Act 2003.
[27]  Theatres Act 1968, s. 2 (to remain in force). See *DPP v Whyte* [1972] AC 849 (corrupting the already corrupted still amounts to an offence under the Obscene Publications Act 1959).
[28]  Ibid. s. 6 (to remain in force).
[29]  Public Order Act 1986, s. 20 (to remain in force).
[30]  Cinemas Act 1985, s. 24 (to be repealed).
[31]  *British Amusement Catering Trades Association v Westminster City Council* [1987] 1 WLR 977 CA.
[32]  Cinemas Act 1985, ss. 5, 6 (to be repealed).
[33]  Sunday Cinemas Act 1972, s. 1 (to remain in force).
[34]  Obscene Publications Act 1959, ss. 1, 2 (to remain in force).

Act regulates their supply in the course of any business. 'Business' here includes any activity carried on by a club[35]. If the video recording has been registered with the Department of Trade and Industry for cinema release, the provisions of the Act of 1984 do not apply[36].

## 10-16  Control over private premises

Local authorities are empowered to adopt the Private Places of Entertainment (Licensing) Act 1967[37] if they want to do so. The purpose of the Act is to enable local authorities to have control over music and dancing or similar entertainments which are not public but which nevertheless are promoted for private gain.

## 6.  NEW RÉGIME

### 10-17  Regulation and authorisation

The whole system of the licensing of entertainment has been simplified and, insofar as clubs are concerned, the provision of entertainment on club premises will now be regulated by the Licensing Act 2003, whether or not alcohol is being sold or supplied to those attending the entertainment. The distinction between private and public entertainment is abolished. Section 1(1)(c) of the Act stipulates that the provision of regulated entertainment is a licensable activity and section 1(2)(c) makes the provision of such entertainment by the club to its members and guests a qualifying club activity for a club premises certificate. Section 2 requires licensable activities to be authorised. Schedule 1 to the Act contains the detailed provisions which will apply to regulated entertainment.

**10-18**  The reform of the system will either repeal or significantly amend 15 Acts of Parliament, including the Private Places of Entertainment Act 1967, the Theatres Act 1968, the Cinemas Act 1985 and various local government acts[38].

---

[35]    Video Recordings Act 1984, s. 21(1) (to remain in force).
[36]    See ibid. s. 9(2)(a) (to remain in force).
[37]    The whole Act is to be repealed.
[38]    Licensing Act 2003, Schs. 6 and 7.

## 10-19  Definition of regulated entertainment

The following forms of entertainment fall within the definition of regulated entertainment:

(1) a performance of a play[39];
- this means a performance of any dramatic piece, where the whole or a major proportion of it involves the playing of a role by one or more persons, who are actually present, by way of speech, singing or action (including improvisation)[40];
- a rehearsal counts as a performance[41];
- the Minister stated in the House of Commons on 1 April 2003 that poetry readings and performances by stand-up comedians (which do not involve music) will not count as regulated entertainment[42];

(2) an exhibition of a film[43];
- this means any exhibition of moving pictures[44];

(3) an indoor sporting event[45];
- this means any sporting event which takes place inside a building where the spectators are accommodated wholly inside that building[46];
- a sporting event means any contest, exhibition or display of any sport[47];
- sport includes any game in which physical skill is the predominant factor or any form of physical recreation which is also engaged in for the purposes of competition or display[48];
- a building means any roofed structure (other than a structure with a roof which may be open or closed) and includes a vehicle, vessel or moveable structure[49];

(4) a boxing or wrestling entertainment[50];
- this means any contest, exhibition or display of boxing or wrestling[51];

---

[39] Licensing Act 2003, Sch. 1, para 2(1)(a).
[40] Ibid. Sch. 1, para 14(1).
[41] Ibid. Sch. 1, para 14(2).
[42] Hansard, HC Standing Committee D, col 62 (a statement probably covered by the rule in *Pepper v Hart* [1993] AC 593).
[43] Ibid. Sch. 1, para 2(1)(b).
[44] Ibid. Sch. 1, para 15.
[45] Ibid. Sch. 1, para 2(1)(c).
[46] Ibid. Sch. 1, para 16(1).
[47] Ibid. Sch. 1, para 16(2).
[48] Ibid. Sch. 1, para 16(2).
[49] Ibid. Sch. 1, para 16(2).
[50] Ibid. Sch. 1, para 2(1)(d).
[51] Ibid. Sch. 1, para 17.

(5) a performance of live music[52];
- for the purposes of this and the next category music includes vocal or instrumental music or any combination of the two[53];

(6) any playing of recorded music[54];

(7) a performance of dance[55];

(8) entertainment of a similar description to that falling within categories (5), (6) and (7)[56].

## 10-20 Entertainment facilities

Regulated entertainment includes the provision of entertainment facilities which enable persons to take part in the entertainment, where the entertainment is either the making of music, or dancing, or entertainment of a similar description[57].

**10-21** The Secretary of State has the power (by order) to amend both the descriptions of regulated entertainment and entertainment facilities[58].

## 10-22 Exemptions

Various exemptions from regulation are permitted under the new régime. They are set out in Schedule 1 to the Act of 2003. Insofar as clubs are concerned, the relevant exemptions are as follows:

(1) incidental music[59];
- the provision of entertainment consisting of the performance of live music or the playing of recorded music is not regulated to the extent it is incidental to some activity which itself is neither a regulated entertainment nor the provision of entertainment facilities;
- the Act does not define the word 'incidental' which is no doubt used in its meaning of 'accompanying in a subordinate capacity'. An example would be a piano being played in the background in a club or restaurant;

---

52      Licensing Act 2003, Sch. 1, para 2(1)(e).
53      Ibid. Sch. 1, para 18.⁵⁴   Ibid. Sch. 1 para 2(1)(f).
55      Ibid. Sch. 1, para 2(1)(g).
56      Ibid. Sch. 1, para 2(1)(h).
57      Ibid. Sch. 1, paras 1(1)(b), 3(2) and 18. This would include karaoke.
58      Ibid. Sch. 1, para 4.
59      Ibid. Sch. 1, para 7.

(2) television and radio[60];

- the normal use of a television and a radio is not regulated under the new Act (their use is already regulated by other statutes);

(3) garden fêtes;

- the provision of any entertainment or entertainment facilities at a garden fête or similar function or event is not regulated unless it is promoted with a view to applying the whole or part of its proceeds for the purposes of private gain[61];
- private gain in this context has the same meaning as set out in section 22 of the Lotteries and Amusements Act 1976 (for which see **11-41**(2) below)[62];
- the use of the word 'garden' would suggest that only outdoor functions or events can take the benefit of this exemption;

(4) morris dancing[63];

- morris dancing (or similar) is not regulated where it is performed with unamplified, live music nor where facilities are provided to enable persons to take part in such dancing;

(5) moving vehicles[64];

- the provision of entertainment or entertainment facilities on a moving vehicle is not regulated. This exemption is no doubt to cater for street carnivals and the like.

**10.23** The above exemptions will only apply where there is no sale or supply of alcohol when the entertainment or the entertainment facilities are being provided. If alcohol is available, then the appropriate authorisation will be needed, that is to say, a premises licence or a club premises certificate or a notice of a temporary event.

## 10-24 Dancing and live music in small premises

A postscript was added at the last minute to the Licensing Bill in order to deal with the exception of the 'two-in-a-bar' rule whereby under section 182 of the Licensing Act 1964 exemption was granted from the need to obtain a music and dance licence in respect of public entertainment by way of music and singing only which is provided solely by the reproduction of recorded sound, or by not more than

---

60    Ibid. Sch. 1, para 8.
61    Ibid. Sch. 1, para 10(1),(2).
62    Ibid. Sch. 1, para 10(3).
63    Ibid. Sch. 1, para 11.
64    Ibid. Sch. 1, para 12.

two live performers, or by a combination of both. Section 177 of the Licensing Act 2003 gives a reprieve to the 'two-in-a-bar' rule. Put simply, certain premises are free to provide (a) unamplified, live[65] music or[66] (b) facilities for enabling persons to take part in such music, between 8 am and midnight without interference from the licensing authority (i.e. without conditions being imposed), provided that no other form of regulated entertainment is taking place at the same time and provided the following criteria are fulfilled:

(1) the premises have a premises licence or a club premises certificate;
(2) the licence or certificate allows for both the supply of alcohol and music entertainment;
(3) the supply of alcohol on the premises is primarily for consumption on those premises;
(4) the premises are limited to a permitted capacity of 200[67].

### 10-25   Procedures relating to authorisation, etc.

Since there will be now one unified system of licensing which will apply to both the sale and supply of alcohol and the provision of regulated entertainment and entertainment facilities, the reader is referred to CHAPTER 9 which deals with (a) a club's ability and entitlement to obtain the necessary authorisation, (b) the various procedures which a club must follow to apply for, vary, or transfer the club premises certificate or premises licence, and (c) the circumstances whereby any authorisation is revoked or withdrawn or otherwise comes to an end.

### 10-26   Statutory guidance

As with the licensing of alcohol, the Secretary of State is under a duty to issue guidance as regards regulated entertainment[68] and the licensing authority must publish its own statement of licensing policy as regards regulated entertainment[69].

---

[65]    The live performers are not restricted to two in number.
[66]    Licensing Act 2003, s. 177(4)(a). The word 'or' means in this context 'and/or'.
[67]    Permitted capacity means the number of persons stipulated in a fire certificate issued under the Fire Precautions Act 1971 or the number recommended by the local fire authority: Licensing Act 2003, s. 177(8).
[68]    Ibid. s. 182. Its official title is 'licensing guidance'.
[69]    Ibid. s. 5. It official title is 'licensing statement'.

## 7.   NOISE NUISANCE

**10-27**   This is a recurrent problem in modern society on a crowded island[70]. The Environmental Protection Act 1990 allows the local authority to take action against individuals or companies who create a nuisance through pollution of some kind, and noise nuisance is one variety of pollution[71]. If a complaint is made to the local authority, the environmental health officer is bound to investigate the complaint, and will try to resolve the matter amicably. If the noise nuisance persists the local authority will issue a formal abatement notice which, if not complied with, may result in a prosecution under the Act[72]. An unfortunate situation can arise where a newcomer moves into a property close to the club and then complains about loud music, whereas the previous owner had never made any complaint about the club's dances or playing of music despite having lived in the property for many years. The answer is that the newcomer has the right to complain if on an objective basis the music amounts to noise nuisance. It is no answer at law to say that the club was there first or that the newcomer voluntarily came to the nuisance and so must accept the situation as he finds it[73], although these facts may carry weight with the local authority in deciding what action to take under the Act.

The club should also be aware of the provisions of the Anti-Social Behaviour Act 2003: see **9-79** above.

---

[70]     See *Kennaway v Thompson* [1980] 3 All ER 329 CA at 333*e–f*. See also **12-26** below for examples of two cases involving noise nuisance.
[71]     See Environmental Protection Act 1990, s. 79(1)(g). Noise is now labelled as a statutory nuisance.
[72]     Ibid. s. 80. If a club's premises were to be construed as business premises, the maximum fine is £20,000: s. 80(6).
[73]     *Sturges v Bridgman* [1879] 11 Ch D 852.

# Chapter 11

# GAMING AND LOTTERIES RUN BY CLUBS

## 1.  INTRODUCTION

**11-01**  Gambling is probably an inherent human trait and is now tolerated by British governments rather than prohibited: the present scheme of governmental regulation is a compromise between toleration and prohibition[1]. This compromise suits the government because of the excise duties levied upon gaming and lotteries and it suits clubs because it provides a source of income for the club as well as pleasurable activity for the participants. Regulation is now principally contained in the Betting, Gaming and Lotteries Act 1963 and more especially in the Gaming Act 1968, together with the Lotteries and Amusements Act 1976[2]. Of pivotal importance is the Gaming Board for Great Britain because one of its statutory duties is to keep under review the extent, character and location of gaming facilities in Great Britain[3].

---

[1]     The rigour of the earlier law is demonstrated by *R v Ashton* [1852] 1 E & B 286 (a successful appeal against conviction concerning the playing of dominoes without stakes in a public house under the gaming acts then in force which rendered all games of chance unlawful except games of pure skill). The playing of dominoes and cribbage for modest stakes is now permitted on premises licensed for the retail sale of liquor: Gaming  Act 1968, s. 6.

[2]     Certain sections of the Gaming Act 1968 and the Lotteries and Amusements Act 1976, which are likely to affect clubs, are set out in **APPENDICES 5** and **7** respectively.

[3]     Gaming Act 1968, s. 10(3). Great Britain comprises England, Wales and Scotland.

## 2.    GAMING

### 11-02    Games of chance

The definition of gaming means the playing of a game of chance for winnings in money or money's worth, whether or not the player is at risk of losing money[4]. A game of equal chance is where all the players have an equally favourable chance of winning the game (such as bingo) whereas in a game of unequal chance the bank has the advantage over the other players (such as roulette)[5]. A game of chance includes a game of chance and skill combined[6], such as bridge, whist or poker. Games of skill such as chess or draughts are outside this definition.

**11-03**    We deal with the régime in *descending* order of strictness. This is because the Act of 1968 starts from the premise that bankers' games and games of unequal chance shall not take place *at all* [7] unless the game played is of a kind specified in regulations made by the Home Secretary[8]. The regulatory régime is divided up as follows:
(1)  no playing of restricted games of chance unless the club is *licensed* under Part II of the Gaming Act 1968;
(2)  no playing of certain restricted games of chance unless the club is *registered* under the said Part II;
(3)  the *unrestricted* playing of games of equal chance.

## 3.    LICENSED CLUBS

### 11-04    Need for a licence under Part II

The following games are currently specified as being permissible: roulette, the dice game sometimes known as craps, the various versions of baccarat (including chemin de fer, punto banco and its modified

---

[4]      Gaming Act 1968, s. 52 (1); c.f. *McCollom v Wrightson* [1968] 2 AC 522 (no offence of gaming at common law where, at a hotel, there was free bingo with no stake hazarded and with free prizes).
[5]      If the position of banker can be won or lost, or the position of banker circulates amongst the players, one can convert a game of unequal chance into a game of equal chance. But this fact makes no difference to the statutory régime which, with one exception, prohibits banker's games save on licensed premises.
[6]      Ibid. s. 52(1).
[7]      Apart from domestic occasions in a private dwelling or in a hall of residence or similar establishment: ibid. s. 2.
[8]      Ibid. s. 13.

version punto 2000), blackjack (or pontoon or vingt-et-un), casino stud poker, and super pan 9[9]. Such games may not take place except in a club which is licensed[10] and no person shall participate in the gaming unless he is a member of the club specified in the licence, physically present on the club premises when the gaming takes place and eligible to take part in the gaming[11], or he is a bona fide guest of such a member[12]. The club will be a proper club and no person can take part in the gaming held there unless he was admitted as a member pursuant to a written application made by him in person on the club premises and 24 hours have elapsed since his application for membership[13], or unless after becoming a member he has given notice in writing in person on the club premises to the licence holder (or his authorised agent) that he intends to take part in gaming at the club and 24 hours have elapsed since giving the notice[14].

## 11-05   Who can apply for a licence

If an individual, the applicant must be over 21 years of age, currently resident in Great Britain and had been so for a period of six months immediately preceding the date of the application[15]. If a corporate body, its incorporation must have taken place in Great Britain[16]. The applicant must be a person whom the Gaming Board considers to be of good character, reputation and financial standing who will in all respects properly conduct the gaming at the club premises[17]. In practice, a gaming licence is normally obtained by commercial, proprietary gaming clubs, not by the generality of members' clubs who will be content to apply, if at all, for registration under Part II of the Act of 1968. Licensed clubs will also include commercial bingo clubs which are dealt with separately under the gaming legislation, even though bingo is not a restricted game, it being a game of equal chance. These clubs are invariably proprietary clubs and their position is set out in **11-56** below.

---

[9]    Gaming Clubs (Bankers' Games) Regulations 1994 (SI 1994/2899).
[10]   Gaming Act 1968, s. 11(1).
[11]   Ibid. ss. 12(1)(a), (2)(a).
[12]   Ibid. s. 12(2)(b).
[13]   Ibid. s. 12(3)(a).
[14]   Ibid. s. 12(3)(b).
[15]   Ibid. Sch. 2, para 4(4)(a), (b).
[16]   Ibid. Sch. 2, para 4(4)(c).
[17]   Ibid. Sch. 2, para 4(5), (6).

## 11-06   Procedure for applying

The licensing procedure is set out in Schedule 2 to the Gaming Act 1968 which deals with the grant, renewal, cancellation and transfer of gaming licences. The provisions of Schedule 2 are complex: the application is made to a committee of justices for the petty sessions area in which the club is situated[18]; a certificate of consent must have been obtained from the Gaming Board prior to the application[19]; and there is an appeal procedure to the Crown Court by the club in the event of an application being refused[20] or by the Gaming Board in the event of the application being granted[21]. Commonly the major issue before the committee is the local demand for the gaming facilities in question because if the committee is not satisfied on this score it is likely to dismiss the application[22]. A licence will only be granted in permitted areas, namely, county boroughs having a population of 125,000 or more and in some 13 specified smaller towns or areas[23]. There are powers of cancellation of the licence[24] and a power to transfer the licence[25].

## 11-07   Duration and renewal of licence

Both the original licence[26] and the renewed licence last for one year[27].

## 11-08   Fees and duty payable

The current (2004) fees are £29,640 for the grant of a gaming licence, £8,150 for its renewal, and £7,855 for its transfer[28]. Gaming duty is payable under the Gaming Duty Regulations 1997[29].

---

[18]     Gaming Act 1968, Sch. 2, para 1 and Betting, Gaming and Lotteries Act 1963, Sch. 1, para 1.
[19]     Gaming Act 1968, Sch. 2, paras 3, 4.
[20]     Ibid. Sch. 2, paras 29, 30.
[21]     Ibid. Sch. 2, paras 31, 32.
[22]     See ibid. Sch. 2, paras 18, 19. See *R v Manchester Crown Court, ex p Cambos Enterprises Ltd* [1973] 117 Sol Jo 222.
[23]     Gaming Clubs (Permitted Areas) Regulations 1971 (SI 1971/1538) as amended by SI 1974/595. This particular restriction does not apply to licences which limit gaming to bingo, bridge or whist.
[24]     Gaming Act 1968, Sch. 2, para 36.
[25]     Ibid. Sch. 2, paras 55–58.
[26]     Ibid. Sch. 2, para 52(1)(a).
[27]     Ibid. Sch. 2, para 52(1)(b).
[28]     Ibid. s. 48(3) as amended by the Gaming Act (Variation of Fees)(England and Wales Order 2003 Sch. 2, art 2 (SI 2003/508). The fees are substantially reduced if the licensing authority imposes restrictions under the Gaming Act 1968, Sch. 2, para 25.
[29]     SI 1997/2196 as amended by SI 2000/2408.

# 4. REGISTERED CLUBS

## 11-09 Need for registration under Part II

If a club wishes to include the playing of the restricted games of pontoon or chemin de fer as part of its facilities at the club or if it wishes to make a charge for admission in excess of that permitted by section 40 of the Gaming Act 1968, which is currently (2004) £15 per player per day for bridge and/or whist and 60 pence in any other case[30], then the club must apply for registration under Part II of the Act[31]. The procedure for registration is substantially less complex and cheaper than the procedure for a licence.

- It should be pointed out that game of pontoon which is permitted does not include blackjack or any other form of pontoon whose rules do not provide for the right to hold the bank to pass amongst the players in certain events arising in the course of play[32].

## 11-10 Who can apply for a registration certificate

A bona fide members' club which is not of a temporary nature and which has not less than 25 members may apply[33]. It has been commented that the registration system is meant for those genuine members' clubs which wish to provide gaming merely as a subsidiary activity and that the object of the registration is to check the club's credentials; and to impose conditions sufficient, but no more, to prevent the club from being captured or exploited by commercial interests[34]. This is borne out by the fact that the only substantive ground for a refusal to register on the first registration, once the club has established its bona fides, is that the principal purpose for which the club is established or conducted is gaming (unless, as an exception, the gaming in question is exclusively the playing of bridge and/or whist)[35].

---

[30]    See further **11-16** and **11-18** below.
[31]    Gaming Act 1968, s. 11(2).
[32]    Gaming Act (Registration under Part II) Regulations 1969 (SI 1969/550) as amended by SI 1973/355 and SI 1976/1902.
[33]    Gaming Act 1968, Sch. 3 para 7(1).
[34]    *Underhill's Licensing Guide* (12th edn, 1995) para 4.32.
[35]    Gaming Act 1968, Sch. 3, para 7(2). On renewal the committee has wider powers of refusal: paras 9, 10.

## 11-11   Procedure for applying

The registration procedure is set out in Schedule 3 to the Gaming Act 1968 which deals with the grant, renewal and cancellation of registration certificates. Applications may be made at any time of the year to a committee of justices for the petty sessions area in which the club is situated, and the committee shall sit in the months of January, April, July and October (and may sit on additional days) to hear the application[36]. The application must be made in the prescribed form[37]. Not later than seven days after making the application the applicant must send copies to the appropriate officer of police and the appropriate collector of excise duty[38]. Not later than 14 days after making the application the applicant must give notice of the application by advertising it in a newspaper circulating in the petty sessions area[39] and the notice must contain the name of the club, the location of the relevant premises, and a statement that any person who desires to object to the registration of the club should send to the clerk to the justices by a specified date (not being earlier than 14 days after publication of the advertisement) two copies of a brief statement of his objection[40]. Care should taken over the wording of the advertisement in that the inclusion of additional or unauthorised material will render the advertisement invalid[41], apart from some 'trifling typographical error' not the fault of the applicant[42]. A copy of the newspaper advertisement must be sent to the clerk to the justices not later than seven days after its publication[43]. There is a right of appeal to the Crown Court by the club in the event of an application being refused or against the imposition of restrictions on the grant or renewal of registration[44], or by the Gaming Board in the event of the application being granted or renewed[45].

---

[36]     Gaming Act 1968, Sch. 3, para 2 and Sch. 2 paras 1 and 2A, and the Betting, Gaming and Lotteries Act 1963, Sch. 1, para 1. Para 2A was added by the Betting, Gaming and Lotteries (Amendment) Act 1984.
[37]     Gaming Act (Registration under Part II) Regulations 1969 (SI 1969/550 as amended by SI 1973/355 and 1976/1902.
[38]     Gaming Act 1968, Sch. 3 para 3.
[39]     Ibid. Sch. 3, para 3 and Sch. 2, para 6(1).
[40]     Ibid. Sch. 3, para 3 and Sch. 2, para 6(2) as amended by the Gaming Amendment Act 1990.
[41]     *R. v Leicester Gaming Licensing Committee, ex p. Shine* [1971] 1 WLR 1216 DC (a case concerning the grant of a gaming licence) but applicable to registration too by virtue of the said Sch. 3, para 3.
[42]     *R. v Dacorum Gaming Licensing Committee, ex p EMI Cinemas and Leisure Ltd* [1971] 3 All ER 666 DC (gaming licence).
[43]     Gaming Act 1968, Sch. 3, para 3 and Sch. 2, para 7(1).
[44]     Ibid. Sch. 3, para 12.
[45]     Ibid. Sch. 3, para 13.

## 11-12 Duration and renewal of registration

The original registration certificate lasts one year[46], as does a renewed certificate[47], save that an application for renewal may request a renewal for a number of years not exceeding ten, which may be granted in the justices' discretion[48]. An application to the clerk to the justices to cancel the registration may be made at any time by any person[49], including the Gaming Board[50]. The grounds on which a renewal may be refused or on which a cancellation may be sought are set out in paragraph 9 of Schedule 3 to the Act of 1968 and include a conviction for an offence under the Gaming Act 1968, disturbance or disorder at the club, the dishonest conduct of gaming, unlawful use of the club premises and the continuing non-payment of gaming duty. There is a right of appeal to the Crown Court against cancellation[51].

## 11-13 Fees and duty payable

No club shall be registered in the first place or have its registration certificate renewed except on payment of fees payable under section 48(3) of the Gaming Act 1968[52]. The current (2004) fees are £235 for registration of a club and £120 for its renewal[53]. Gaming duty is payable under the Gaming Duty Regulations 1997[54].

## 11-14 The conduct of gaming

Possessing a registration certificate does not absolve the club from various restrictions and conditions set out in the Gaming Act 1968, which are as follows:

(1) no person shall participate in the gaming unless he is a member of the club and there has been an interval of at least 48 hours between the time when he applied or was nominated for membership of the club and the time when he begins to take part

---

46    Gaming Act 1968, Sch. 3, para 19(1)(a).
47    Ibid. Sch. 3, para 20(2).
48    Ibid. Sch. 3, para 20(1).
49    Ibid. Sch. 3, para 14 and sched 2, para 36(1).
50    Ibid. Sch. 3, para 16(1).
51    Ibid. Sch. 3, para 16(2).
52    Ibid. Sch.3, para 23.
53    Gaming Act (Variation of Fees) Order 2001 (SI 2001/726).
54    SI 1997/2196 as amended by SI 2000/2408 and Gaming Duty (Amendment)
Regulations 2003 (SI 2003/2247).

in the gaming[55], or he is a bona fide guest of such a member[56];

- this means that the club itself cannot participate as player or act as banker[57];

(2) a player must be physically present in the club when the gaming takes place[58];

(3) if restricted games are played, they must be ones which are permitted[59];

(4) the charge for taking part does not exceed £2 per day per person[60]:

- for this purpose a day runs from midday on one day to midday on the next[61],
- this charge is in addition to any charge lawfully made under section 40[62] and is therefore of advantage to clubs where games other than bridge or whist are to be played;

(5) the club's charges for taking part in the gaming must be displayed on the club premises and have been notified to the justices not less than 14 days before they come into effect[63];

(6) no person under the age of 18 years shall be present in the room whilst gaming is taking place[64].

# 5.   UNRESTRICTED GAMING

## 11-15   Part I of the Gaming Act 1968

Subject to certain qualifications, games of equal chance are permitted under this part of the Act in members' clubs without any licence or registration certificate being required. Such games would include backgammon, bingo, brag (the variant where there is no bank and the players bet against each other), bridge, cribbage, dominoes, poker and whist. Such clubs are not affected by section 5 of the Act (which

---

55      Gaming Act 1968, s. 12(6)(a).
56      Ibid. s. 12(6)(b). And see *Mackby v Ladup Ltd* [1975] 139 JP Jo 121 DC (a case concerning the Hertford Gaming Club where the court laid down the criteria for deciding whether a guest was bona fide).
57      In *Rogers v.Cowley* [1962] 1 WLR 770 DC, Winn J at 777 thought that those who hold the bank are players because of the definition of player in s. 28 of the Betting and Gaming Act 1960 (a definition repeated in s. 55 of the Betting, Gaming and Lotteries Act 1963).
58      Gaming Act 1968, s. 12(4), (7).
59      Ibid. s. 13. See **11-09** above for the permitted games.
60      Reg 3(1) of the Gaming Act (Registration under Part II) Regulations 1969 (SI 1969/550) as amended by SI 1975/1902.
61      Ibid. reg 3(2).
62      See **11-16** below.
63      Gaming Act 1968, s. 14(2).
64      Ibid. s. 17.

prohibits gaming in public places) or by section 6 of the Act (which applies to licensed premises selling intoxicating liquor). The qualifications are:

(1) the club must not make any charge for taking part in the gaming. Entrance fees and subscriptions do not count as a charge for this purpose[65]. The prohibition is subject to permissible charges under section 40 of the Act;

(2) the club must not make any levy on stakes or winnings[66], that is to say, all stake money must be returned to the players as winnings or a cash prize;

(3) the gaming must not take place on premises to which the public has access[67].

## 11-16 Permissible charges for play in clubs

Section 40 of the Gaming Act 1968 provides a valuable relaxation of qualification (1) above because it enables the club without any formality to play games of equal chance on club premises, whilst at the same time permitting the club to make a charge for the right to take part in the gaming. The club, however, must not be of a temporary nature and must have 25 or more members[68]. The charges must not exceed those specified in an order made by the Home Secretary[69] which currently (2004) are as follows: in the case of gaming which consists exclusively of playing bridge and/or whist and which takes place on a day on which the club premises are not used for any other gaming (save for gaming machines[70]), the sum specified is £15 per person per day; for any other case the sum specified is 60 pence per person per day[71]. The charges are in addition to any stakes hazarded in the gaming[72].

## 11-17 Exempt entertainments with gaming

A valuable exception to the regulatory régime is also provided by section 41 of the Gaming Act 1968. This section allows games of equal chance to be played at members' clubs as an entertainment promoted otherwise than for the purposes of private gain (these are known as

---

[65] Gaming Act 1968, s. 3(3).
[66] Ibid. s. 4.
[67] Ibid. s. 5.
[68] Ibid. s. 40(4).
[69] Ibid. s. 40(2).
[70] See **11-22** below.
[71] Ibid. s. 40(2) and Gaming (Small Charges) Order 2000 (SI 2000/2802).
[72] Gaming Act 1968, s. 40(3)(a).

exempt entertainments). In *Payne v Bradley* [1962] AC 343 the receipt by a workingmen's club of the proceeds of bingo sessions organised by the club to meet its general expenses of maintaining the club was held to be a private gain to the club and its members and therefore illegal under the then Betting and Gaming Act 1960. The decision in this case, however, was reversed by section 51A of the Gaming Act 1968[73]. This section permits the proceeds of gaming at an exempt entertainment to be applied to any purpose calculated to benefit the club as a whole and the fact that the application results in benefit to an individual member shall not be treated as private gain. Section 51A applies to clubs which are established and conducted wholly for non-commercial purposes, or wholly or mainly for the purpose of participation in or support of athletic sports or athletic games.

- Hire or maintenance charges in respect of gaming equipment at an exempt entertainment shall not be treated as the application of the proceeds for the purpose of private gain unless the charges are based wholly or partly by reference to the extent to which the equipment is used at the entertainment[74].

**11-18** Currently (2004) the club must not charge each player more than £4 (whether by way of entrance fee or stake or otherwise) in respect of all games played at the entertainment[75]. The total value of all the prizes and awards must not exceed £400[76]. The whole of the proceeds, after deducting the prizes and awards and the reasonable cost of providing the facilities, must be applied for purposes other than for private gain[77]. If two or more entertainments are promoted on the same premises by the same persons on the same day, this counts as one entertainment[78]. The corollary of this situation is that where there is a series of entertainments not held on the same premises or by the same persons or on the same day, they are to be treated as separate entertainments, thereby impliedly sanctioning a further payment from the players[79]. If the series of entertainments culminates in a final entertainment, and if each of the players at the final entertainment has taken part in another entertainment held on a previous day, the total value of the prizes and awards in respect of the final

---

[73]　　Section inserted by the Lotteries and Amusements Act 1976, s. 25 and Sch. 4, para 5.
[74]　　Gaming Act 1968, s. 51A(3).
[75]　　Ibid. s. 41(3); Gaming Act (Variation of Monetary Limits) (No.2) Order 2000 (SI 2000/2803).
[76]　　Ibid. s. 41(4); and see the said Order.
[77]　　Ibid. s. 41(5), (6).
[78]　　Ibid. s. 41(7).
[79]　　Ibid. s. 41(8)(a).

entertainment can (2004) be increased to but not exceed £700[80].

## 6.  BINGO PLAYED AS A GAME

### 11-19   Members' clubs

Even though section 20 of the Gaming Act 1968 makes special provision for bingo clubs, the Act nowhere defines what bingo is. It is a game played between a number (often a large number) of players. Each player is given a card with a series of numbers on it. The person in charge draws out a bag or a special box (the tombola) a random number, or the number may be selected mechanically. The number is called out or displayed and if it corresponds to a number on the card, the player crosses out the number. The first person to cross out all or certain of the numbers on his card makes known his completion and wins a prize. The game is generally now called bingo but is also known by the names of housey-housey, lotto or tombola[81]. Depending on how the game is played, bingo may constitute a lottery as opposed to a game and therefore be unlawful unless it comes into one of the permitted categories of lottery[82]. It is lawful if played under Part II of the Gaming Act 1968 as 'cash' bingo or gaming for prizes, or played as an amusement with prizes under the Lotteries and Amusements Act 1976 as 'prize' bingo.

**11-20**   Bingo is a game of equal chance and therefore what is said in paragraph **11-15** above applies to the playing of this game on club premises. Bingo may also be played at an 'exempt entertainment' either as a small lottery (see **11-41** below) or as an 'amusement with prizes' (see **11-42** below). It should also be noted that members' clubs have been fully exempt from bingo duty since 1992[83].

**11-21**   Mention should be made of the use of 'snowball' prizes. If the club utilises any part of the stake money to fund these prizes, it will be illegal because stake money hazarded by one group of players is being retained by the club as possible winnings by a later group of

---

[80]   Gaming Act 1968, ss. 8(b) and 9; and see the Gaming Act (Variation of Monetary Limits) (No.2) Order 2000 (SI 2000/2803).
[81]   See *Payne v Bradley* [1962] AC 343 at 354.
[82]   *DPP v Armstrong* [1965] AC 1262 (postal bingo was held to be an unlawful lottery on the facts of this case); *DPP v Regional Pool Promotions Ltd* [1963] 2 WLR 209 DC (where bingo played by the six million members of the Spastics League Club was held to be an unlawful lottery because there was no active participation by any of the members).
[83]   Finance (No.2) Act 1992, s. 7.

players and this contravenes the rule that the chances in the game must be equally favourable to all players[84]. The solution to the problem is for the club to create out of its own funds or out of the entrance charge a special 'snowball' prize. In this event the prize will not be derived from previously staked money and will be lawful. Additionally, if bingo is played as a game at an entertainment not held for private gain (see **11-17** above) it is in order for the club to retain some of the stake money for general club funds.

## 7.    GAMING MACHINES

### 11-22   Introduction

Gaming machines[85] are another useful source of income for clubs but there is strict control over their use by virtue of Part III of the Gaming Act 1968. A gaming machine is one which is constructed or adapted for the playing of a game of chance by means of the machine and which has a slot or other aperture for the insertion of money or tokens[86]. In most cases an excise duty, known as amusement machine licence duty, is payable is respect of their use[87]. There are restrictions on whom may sell or supply machines to the club or maintain them[88]. We deal below with the various types of machine in *ascending* order of control.

## 8.    PLAY-AGAIN MACHINES

**11-23**   These are slot machines which do not pay out prizes but merely afford the winner the opportunity to play again free or to return to him coins or tokens not exceeding the value of his stake. There is no maximum charge for one play but manufacturers of machines will conventionally set them to operate for 20 or 30 pence. Pinball and

---

[84]     Gaming Act 1968, s. 2(1)(b).
[85]     Colloquially known as fruit machines. In their earlier form they had a lever at the side of the machine which had to be pulled to operate it; hence their colloquial name of one-armed bandits.
[86]     Ibid. s. 26(1). Some machine games depend on skill alone and are not subject to any control. An example is the mechanical football game which has two, or sometimes four, players at the controls, a game which at one time appeared in a great many French cafés.
[87]     Betting and Gaming Duties Act 1981, ss. 21–26, Sch. 4, as amended by the Finance Act 1995, s. 1, Sch. 3.
[88]     Gaming Act 1968, s. 27, Sch. 6. The persons in question must hold a certificate from the Gaming Board.

video-game machines come into this category[89].

## 11-24 The control

By section 52(5) of the Gaming Act 1968 this does not count as gaming and so any number of these machines may be played on club premises without restriction or control and they are not subject to any duty.

## 9. AMUSEMENT MACHINES

**11-25** These are slot machines which are governed by sections 33 and 34 of the Gaming Act 1968. The maximum charge (2004) for one play is 30 pence[90]. Here the player is usually afforded the opportunity to play again free and, in addition, may receive (2004) *one* of the following benefits for successful play[91]:

(1) a money prize not exceeding £5 or a token exchangeable only for this sum of money;

(2) a non-monetary prize or prizes whose value does not exceed £8 or a token exchangeable only for these prizes;

(3) a money prize not exceeding £5 together with a non-monetary prize which does not exceed £8 less the amount of the money prize, or a token exchangeable only for such combination of prizes[92];

(4) one or more tokens which can be used for further play and, insofar as they are not used, can be exchanged for non-monetary prizes at the appropriate rate.

## 11-26 The control

In order to make available these machines on club premises, the club must hold a licence or a registration certificate issued under Part II of the Gaming Act 1968 (see **11-10** above); or a permit issued under Schedule 9 of the Act pursuant to section 34 (see **11-28** below)[93]. There is no limit to the number of machines save where they are authorised under a permit; here the local authority will specify the maximum

---

89    Betting and Gaming Duties Act 1981, s. 23(3) as amended.
90    Gaming Act 1968, s. 34(2); Gaming Act (Variation of Monetary Limits) (No.2) Order 1997 (SI 1997/2079).
91    Gaming Act 1968, s. 34(3).
92    The references to £5 were substituted by the Gaming Act (Variation of Monetary Limits) (No.2) Order 1997 (SI 1997/2079) and the references to £8 were substituted by the Gaming Act (Variation of Monetary Limits) (No.2) Order 1995 (SI 1995/2288).
93    Gaming Act 1968, s. 35(a).

number. Only certain persons may remove money from a gaming machine (apart from money delivered as winnings): an officer of the club, a member of the club or a person employed by the club in connection with the club premises[94], for example, a bar steward. It is a wise move for the managing committee to authorise in writing the person who has the task of removing money from the machine. The Secretary of State has power to make regulations as to the keeping of records and accounts relating to the machine[95] but to date (2004) has not done so.

## 11-27 Exempt entertainments with amusement machines

An exception to this control is contained in section 33 of the Act. If the club has no licence or registration certificate, amusement machines may be used at an entertainment of the following kind where it takes place elsewhere than on licensed or registered club premises: bazaars, sales of work, fêtes, dinners, dances, sporting and athletic events and other entertainments of a similar character, whether limited to one day or extending over two or more days[96]. To rely on this exception three stipulations are laid down:

(1) the whole proceeds of the entertainment, after deducting the expenses thereof, must be devoted to purposes other than private gain[97];
(2) the opportunity to play a gaming machine or to take part in other authorised gaming or lotteries at the entertainment must not be the only, or only substantial, inducement to attend the entertainment[98];
(3) the club must comply with any regulations under which the Secretary of State may impose restrictions in addition to those specified in (1) and (2) above[99]. To date (2004) no regulations have been made.

## 11-28 The Part III permit for amusement machines

Applications for a permit are set out in Schedule 9 of the Gaming Act 1968. The procedure is relatively straightforward and cheap. It is made

---

[94]   Gaming Act 1968, s. 36.
[95]   Ibid. s. 37.
[96]   Ibid. s. 33(1).
[97]   Ibid. s. 33(2) as substituted by the Lotteries Act 1975, s. 20 and Sch. 4, para 6. As to private gain see the Gaming Act 1968, s. 51A at **11-17** above.
[98]   Ibid. s. 33 (2A) as substituted by the Lotteries Act 1975.
[99]   Ibid. s. 33(5).

by the person who is the occupier of the club premises[100]. The application is made to the local authority in whose area the club premises are situated, save where the club has a club licence rather than a registration certificate under the Licensing Act 1964[101], in which case the application is made to the licensing justices[102]. The grant of the permit is within the discretion of the local authority[103]. The local authority will pass a resolution on the grant or renewal of the permit imposing a condition which limits the number of permitted machines[104]. The local authority shall not refuse a permit without giving the applicant an opportunity of being heard on the matter[105]. Renewal shall not be refused unless the club has refused to allow inspection of its premises, or conditions of the grant have been broken, or because of the unacceptable manner in which the machines have been used at the club[106]. There is a right of appeal to the Crown Court against the refusal to grant or renew a permit or against the imposition of a condition[107].

- In an unincorporated members' club the question as to whom occupies the club premises may cause some difficulty (see **12-30** below). Despite this, we suggest it will be in order for a club to apply in its own name as the occupier without any further elaboration.

## 11-29  Conditions of permit

Where the local authority grants a permit in respect of club premises the following conditions shall automatically apply[108]:
(1) if admission to the club premises is restricted to those over 18 years of age, no person under this age is admitted therein;
(2) if admission to the club premises is open to all ages:
   (a)  the location of the machine is separated from the remainder

---

[100]  Gaming Act 1968, Sch. 9 para 5(b).
[101]  See para A12-2 of **APPENDIX 12** for the club licence (to be abolished under the Licensing Act 2003). In future all applications will be made to the local council.
[102]  Gaming Act 1968, Sch. 9, para 1.
[103]  Ibid. Sch. 9 para 8(1)(a). But see *Aitken v Motherwell and Wishaw Licensing Court* [1971] SLT 25 (Sheriff's Court) (where it was held that the licensing court had no power under the Gaming Act to make a 'blanket' or 'policy' decision but must use its discretion afresh in every case; no doubt a correct decision on the law but a decidedly odd decision on the facts of the case).
[104]  Ibid. Sch. 9, para 2(c).
[105]  Ibid. Sch. 9, para 6.
[106]  Ibid. Sch. 9, para 8(1)(b)(ii) and (iii).
[107]  Ibid. Sch. 9, paras 11–14.
[108]  Ibid. Sch. 9, para 10B, added by the Deregulation (Gaming Machines and Betting Office Facilities) Order 1996 (SI 1996/1359).

of the premises by a physical barrier which is effective to prevent access except by an entrance designed for this purpose;

(b) only persons over 18 shall be admitted to this location;

(c) the said access is supervised;

(d) the whole location is able to be observed;

(e) that at the entrance to and inside the location are prominently displayed notices which indicate that the area is prohibited to those under 18.

By a curious oversight the conditions do not stipulate by whom the access is to be supervised or by whom the location is to be observed. We suggest that some responsible person (or persons) in the club is designated for this task; he or she might be an officer or a member of the club or a club employee.

## 11-30   Duration and renewal of permit

A permit is initially granted for three years[109] and may be renewed for a similar period or longer as the local authority shall allow[110]. The permit may also be cancelled by the court if the holder of the permit is convicted of an offence under section 38 of the Gaming Act 1968[111].

## 11-31   Fees and duty payable

No permit shall be granted or renewed except on payment of fees payable under section 48(3) of the Gaming Act 1968[112]. The current (2004) fee is £32 for the grant or renewal of a permit[113]. Gaming machine licence duty is payable under the Betting and Gaming Duties Act 1981 as amended[114]. If the licence is granted in respect of premises it is called an amusement machine licence, and if granted in respect of a machine rather than premises it is called a special amusement machine licence. There are special provisions if the amusement machine is a small-prize machine (a machine that does not pay out more than £10 in a single game)[115]. No duty is payable in respect of gaming machines at an exempt entertainment[116].

---

[109]    Gaming Act 1968, Sch. 9, para 18(1)(a).
[110]    Ibid. Sch. 9, para 8(1)(b).
[111]    Ibid. s. 39(2).
[112]    Ibid. Sch. 9, para 21.
[113]    Gaming Act (Variation of Fees) (No.2) Order 1991 (SI 1991/2177).
[114]    Amended by various Finance Acts, especially the Finance Act 1995.
[115]    Gaming Act 1968, s. 22(2).
[116]    Betting and Gaming Act 1981, s. 21(1) and Sch. 4, Part I, as amended.

# 10. JACKPOT MACHINES

**11-32**  These are slot machines governed by section 31 of the Gaming Act 1968. They are colloquially known as jackpot machines. The current (2004) maximum charge for one play is 50 pence[117]. Any benefit from successful play must be coins delivered by the machine[118]. The current (2004) maximum prize is regulated as follows: in the case of a registered club the sum is £250; in the case of a machine on bingo club premises the sum is £500; and in the case of a licensed club it is £1,000[119]. Every machine must display thereon the following information[120]:

(1) the value of the prize (or, if there are different prizes, the value of each prize) which can be won by playing the game once;

(2) if there are special circumstances in which the prize or prizes cannot be won, stating what those circumstances are;

(3) the percentage, or minimum percentage, of the takings which the machine is designed to pay out.

## 11-33  The control

In order to make available these machines on club premises, the club must hold a licence or registration certificate issued under Part II (see **11-04** and **11-09** above) or a registration certificate under Part III (see **11-35** below) of the Gaming Act 1968. The maximum number of such machines which may be available for gaming is three in the case of a registered club; or four in the case of bingo club premises; or six in the case of a licensed club[121]. A licensed club may apply on the grant or renewal of a licence for a direction that it be allowed to have more than the prescribed number of jackpot machines and, if granted, the authority will specify the maximum number[122]. Where jackpot machines are available at the club, members of the public must not have access to the club premises[123]. Only certain persons may remove money from a gaming machine (apart from money delivered as winnings): an officer of the club, a member of the club or a person

---

[117]    Gaming Act 1968, s. 31(3); the Gaming Act (Variation of Monetary Limits) (No.2) 1998 (SI 1998/2152).

[118]    Gaming Act 1968, s. 31(4).

[119]    Gaming Machines (Maximum Prizes) Regulations 1998 (SI 1998/2150).

[120]    Ibid. s. 31(7). The Secretary of State may prescribe by regulation how the information is to be displayed but to date (2004) he has not done so.

[121]    Ibid. s. 31(2), as substituted by the Deregulation (Gaming Machines and Betting Office Facilities) Order 1996 (SI 1996/1359).

[122]    Ibid. s. 32.

[123]    Ibid. s. 31(8).

employed by the club in connection with the club premises[124], for example, a bar steward. It is a wise move for the managing committee to authorise in writing the person who has the task of removing money from the machine. The Secretary of State has power to make regulations as to the keeping of records and accounts relating to the machine[125] but to date (2004) has not done so.

## 11-34  Exempt entertainments with jackpot machines

The exception, which applies to amusement machines under section 33 of the Act (see **11-27** above), equally applies to jackpot machines.

## 11-35  Registration under Part III for jackpot machines

A bona fide members' club which is not of a temporary nature and which has not less than 25 members may apply[126]. Registration will not be given (or renewed) to a club where it appears to the justices that the club premises are frequented wholly or mainly by persons under the age of 18 years[127].

**11-36**  The registration procedure is set out in Schedule 7 to the Gaming Act 1968 which deals with the grant, renewal and cancellation of registration certificates. Applications may be made at any time of the year to the clerk to the justices for the petty sessions area in which the club is situated[128]. The application shall specify the name, objects and address of the club and the premises that the club proposes to be registered[129] and a copy of the application must be sent to the appropriate officer of police within seven days of making the application[130].

## 11-37  Duration and renewal of registration

Both the original registration certificate[131] and the renewed certificate[132] last for five years.

---

124    Gaming Act 1968, s. 36.
125    Ibid. s. 37.
126    Ibid. Sch. 7, para 8.
127    Ibid. Sch. 7, para 7.
128    Ibid. Sch. 7, paras 1 and 3(1).
129    Ibid. Sch. 7, para 3(2).
130    Ibid. Sch. 7, para 3(3).
131    Ibid. Sch. 7, para 22(a).
132    Ibid. Sch. 7, para 22(b).

## 11-38 Fees and duty payable

The current (2004) fees are £115 for registration of a club and £70 for its renewal[133]. Gaming machine licence duty is payable under the Betting and Gaming Duties Act 1981 as amended. No duty is payable in respect of gaming machines at an exempt entertainment[134].

# 11. LOTTERIES

## 11-39 Definition and illegality

It is important to understand what is meant by a lottery because section 1 of the Lotteries and Amusements Act 1976 states that *all* lotteries are unlawful save (a) those which constitute gaming, (b) those permitted under the Act, and (c) the National Lottery[135]. Yet no definition of lottery is to be found in the Act. A lottery has been described as a scheme for distributing prizes by lot or chance[136]. If any merit or skill is involved in determining the distribution of prizes, this is not a lottery[137]. Thus in *News of the World v Friend* [1973] 1 WLR 248 the House of Lords held that a 'spot the ball' competition in a newspaper was not unlawful as a lottery because of the skill required to put the ball in its most logical position, not necessarily its historic position. Likewise, a competition to guess the number of sweets in a jar or the weight of a cake is not a lottery. Again, neither forecasting the result of football matches for the purpose of football pools[138] nor a competition to forecast the first four horses in a race[139] is a lottery. On the other hand, it may be safely assumed that any normal club raffle[140] (where one or more articles are distributed by lot) or a sweepstake (where participators' stakes are pooled and numbers, horses, etc are assigned by lot and prize(s) awarded accordingly on the outcome of an event) will be a lottery[141].

---

[133] Gaming Act (Variation of Fees) Order 2000 (SI 2000/1212) and the Gaming Act (Variation of Fees) (England, Wales and Scotland) Order 2002 (SI 2002/642).
[134] Betting and Gaming Act 1881, s. 21(1) and Sch. 4, Part I, as amended.
[135] The National Lottery exception was added by the National Lottery Etc Act 1993.
[136] *Taylor v Smetten* [1883] LR 11 QBD 207.
[137] *DPP v Bradfute and Associates Ltd* [1967] 2 QB 291 at 295G (Lord Parker LCJ).
[138] *Moore v Elphick* [1945] 2 All ER 155.
[139] *Stoddart v Sagar* [1895] 2 QB 474
[140] Raffles and sweepstakes are best dealt with as amusements with prizes: see **11-42** below.
[141] *R. v Hobbs* [1898] 2 QB 647.

**11-40   Lawful exceptions**

Under the Act of 1976 there are four exceptions which concern
clubs where a lottery may be conducted lawfully:
(1) small lotteries incidental to exempt entertainments;
(2) lotteries as amusements with prizes at exempt entertainments.
(3) private lotteries;
(4) societies' lotteries.

No lottery duty is payable in respect of any lottery except the National
Lottery[142].

## 12.   SMALL LOTTERY AT EXEMPT ENTERTAINMENT

**11-41**   This is dealt with under section 3 of the Lotteries and
Amusements Act 1976. An exempt entertainment has the same
meaning as in the Gaming Act 1968, namely, it means a bazaar, sale
of work, fête, dinner, dance, sporting or athletic event or other
entertainment of a similar character, whether limited to one day or
extending over two or more days[143]. To be lawful the club's lottery
must satisfy the following conditions[144]:

(1) the lottery must be 'incidental to', that is, subordinate to, the main
     entertainment and persons attending the entertainment must not
     have been induced to do so on the basis of the lottery taking place;

(2) the whole proceeds of the entertainment (including the proceeds
     of the lottery) must be devoted to purposes other than private gain:
     (a) private gain is defined negatively: any purpose for which the
          club is established and conducted either wholly for non-com-
          mercial purposes or wholly or mainly for the purpose of par-
          ticipation in or support of athletic sports or athletic games,
          and which is calculated to benefit the club as a whole is *not* a
          purpose of private gain; and, further, it does not become a
          purpose of private gain merely because in carrying out the
          purpose this results in a benefit to an individual member[145];
     (b) from the whole proceeds the club is permitted to deduct the
          following expenses: those of the entertainment (but not those
          of the lottery); those incurred in printing the lottery tickets;

---

142   Introduced by the Finance Act 1993.
143   Lotteries and Amusements Act 1976, s. 3(1).
144   Ibid. ss. 3(2) and 3(3).
145   Ibid. s. 22.

and those incurred in purchasing lottery prizes not exceeding the sum of £250[146];

(3) there shall be no money prizes;

(4) tickets or chances may only be sold or issued on the premises where the entertainment takes place, and the result must be declared during the progress of the entertainment.

## 13. AMUSEMENT WITH PRIZES AT EXEMPT ENTERTAINMENT

**11-42** This is dealt with under sections 15 and 16 of the Lotteries and Amusements Act 1976, the former with non-commercial entertainments and the latter with commercial ones. Members' clubs will fall under section 15 only. This category overlaps with the small lotteries referred to in **11-41** above but is of wider ambit. The expression 'amusement with prizes' is nowhere defined in the Act and would seem to cover a multitude of pastimes and activities which give amusement and which offer prizes. Section 15 applies to any amusement with prizes 'which constitutes a lottery or gaming or both'[147], but expressly excludes from its ambit any gaming on licensed or registered premises. If the amusement constitutes a lottery it shall not be an unlawful lottery within section 1 of the Act of 1976[148]. Whether or not the amusement constitutes a lottery, the following conditions must be observed under section 15:

(1) the facilities for winning prizes at amusements or other facilities at the entertainment for participating in lotteries or gaming must not be the only, or only substantial, inducement to attend the entertainment[149];

(2) the whole proceeds of the entertainment, after deducting the expenses of the entertainment, must be devoted to purposes other than private gain[150].

    (a) Hire or maintenance charges in respect of lottery or gaming equipment or in respect of a gaming machine at an exempt entertainment shall not be treated as the application of the proceeds for the purpose of private gain unless the charges

---

[146]    The limit was increased from £50 by the Exempt Entertainments (Variation of Monetary Limit) Order 1993 (SI 1993/3222).
[147]    Lotteries and Amusements Act 1976, s. 15(1).
[148]    Ibid. s. 15(2).
[149]    Ibid. s. 15(4)(b).
[150]    Ibid. s. 15(4)(a). As to private gain, see **11-41**(2) above.

are based wholly or partly by reference to the extent to which the equipment is used at the entertainment[151].

(b) Because section 15 refers to *gaming* as well as lotteries, a curious anomaly arises in that a club could hire gaming equipment for a restricted game such as roulette for say a dinner dance at a local hotel (but not on the club premises[152]) provided the hiring was for a set fee from an authorised supplier holding a certificate under section 27 of the Gaming Act 1968.

**11-43**   The provisions of sections 3 and 15 of the Lotteries and Amusements Act 1976 might have to be reconciled on occasion. Could a club hold a dinner dance at a local hotel and promote a lottery with the price of participation being included in a numbered entrance ticket? The club says that the lottery in question is a permissible amusement with prizes and, as is usual, distributes the tickets before the entertainment takes place. Suppose the police were to say that it was also a small lottery at an exempt entertainment which required that the sale or issue of tickets to participants shall only take place on the premises where the entertainment itself is taking place? It might therefore be the case that the earliest point in time at which the tickets could lawfully be handed over to those attending the dinner dance was at the door of the premises as and when they arrived for the function.

## 14.   PRIVATE LOTTERY

**11-44**   This is dealt with under section 4 of the Lotteries and Amusements Act 1976. A private lottery includes one which is promoted in Great Britain for members of one society established and conducted for purposes not connected with gaming, betting or lotteries[153]. To be lawful the club's lottery must satisfy the following conditions[154]:

(1) the lottery is authorised in writing by the governing body of the club;

(2) the sale of tickets or chances must be confined to (a) club members and (b) to any other persons physically present on the club

---

[151]    Lotteries and Amusements Act 1976, s. 15(5).

[152]    The playing of restricted games on club premises is not permitted without a licence or registration even where the occasion is an exempt entertainment: ibid. s. 41(1)(b).

[153]    Ibid. s. 4(1).

[154]    Ibid. s. 4(1A)(b), s. 4(1B)(b), s. 4(3)(a)-(f). Subsections (1A) and (1B) were inserted by the National Lottery Etc Act 1993.

premises[155];

(3) the whole proceeds, after deducting only expenses incurred for printing and stationery, shall be devoted to the provision of prizes and/or to club purposes;

(4) there shall be no written notice or advertisement of the lottery other than a notice exhibited on club premises, or such announcement or advertisement (if any) as appears on the ticket itself;

(5) the price of every ticket or chance shall be the same, and the price of every ticket shall be stated on the ticket;

(6) every ticket shall state on its face the following information:
   (a) the name and address of each promoter,
   (b) the persons to whom the sale of tickets is restricted,
   (c) no prize won in the lottery shall be paid or delivered except to the person to whom the winning ticket was sold, and
   (d) no prize will be paid or delivered except as stated on the ticket;

(7) no ticket is to be issued and no chance is to be allotted save on the full price being paid;

(8) no money from the sale of the ticket or the chance is to be returned to the purchaser under any circumstances;

(9) no lottery tickets shall be sent through the post.

## 15. SOCIETY'S LOTTERY

**11-45** A society's lottery includes one that is promoted in Great Britain by a club which is established and conducted wholly or mainly for participation in or support of athletic sports or games or cultural activities, or for purposes which are neither purposes for private gain nor purposes of a commercial undertaking[156]. This is a very different animal from a private lottery because of the ability to sell tickets to members of the public. The prizes too will be much larger and, correspondingly, there is much stricter control.

• Any of the said purposes for which the club is established and conducted and which is calculated to benefit the club as a whole is not a purpose of private gain merely because in carrying out the purpose this results in a benefit to an individual member[157].

**11-46** To be lawful the club's lottery must satisfy the following

---

[155] For this purpose, each local or affiliated branch or section of a club shall be regarded as a separate and distinct club: ibid. s. 4(2).
[156] Lotteries and Amusements Act 1976, s. 5(1), (3)(a).
[157] Ibid. s. 5(2).

conditions:

(1) the club itself must be registered with the local authority or the Gaming Board[158] (see **11-47** and **11-48** below);

(2) the lottery is promoted in accordance with a scheme approved by the club[159];

(3) the promoter of the lottery shall be a member of the club authorised in writing by the club to act as promoter[160];

(4) every lottery ticket must state the name and address of the promoter and the date of the lottery[161];

(5) no ticket or chance shall be sold for more than £1[162];

(6) the price of every ticket or chance shall be the same, and the price of every ticket distributed or sold shall be stated on the ticket[163];

(7) no person shall participate in the lottery except after payment in full of the price of the ticket or chance[164];

(8) no money from the sale of the ticket or chance is to be returned to the purchaser under any circumstances[165];

(9) no payment other than the price of the ticket or chance shall be required of a person as a condition of participating in the lottery[166];

(10) no prize shall exceed in amount or value the sum of £25,000 or 10 per cent of the total value of the tickets or chances sold in the lottery (whichever is the greater)[167];

(11) the total value of tickets or chances sold in any one lottery shall not exceed the sum of £2,000,000[168];

(12) the total value of tickets or chances sold in all such lotteries held in any one calendar year and promoted on behalf of the same club shall not exceed £10,000,000[169];

(13) the amount of the proceeds of a club's lottery put aside for the provision of prizes shall not exceed 55 per cent of the whole proceeds of the lottery[170];

(14) the amount spent on expenses of the lottery (exclusive of prizes)

---

[158]    Lotteries and Amusements Act 1976, s. 5(3)(b).
[159]    Ibid. s. 5(3)(c).
[160]    Ibid. s. 11(1)(a).
[161]    Ibid. s. 11(1)(b).
[162]    Ibid. s. 11(2).
[163]    Ibid. s. 11(3).
[164]    Ibid. s. 11(4).
[165]    Ibid. s. 11(4).
[166]    Ibid. s. 11(4A) inserted by the National Lottery Etc Act 1993.
[167]    Ibid. s. 11(5) as substituted by the said Act of 1993.
[168]    Ibid. s. 11(6) as amended by the Lotteries (Variation of Monetary Limits) Order 2002 (SI 2002/1410).
[169]    Ibid. s. 11(7)(8)(9) as amended by the Lotteries (Variation of Monetary Limits) Order 2002 (SI 2002/1410).
[170]    Ibid. s. 11(11) as amended by the Lotteries (Variation of Monetary Limits) Order 1997 (SI 1997/43).

shall be the lesser of the following sums: on the one hand the expenses actually incurred and on the other hand 35 per cent of the whole proceeds of the lottery where they do not exceed £20,000; 15 per cent where the whole proceeds exceed £20,000; or such larger percentage not exceeding 35 per cent which the Gaming Board authorises where the whole proceeds exceed £20,000[171];

(15)  the club must comply with regulations made by the Secretary of State under section 12 of the Act of 1976. Under the current (2004) regulations of 1993 the club must ensure compliance with the following[172]:

(a)  no ticket or chance shall be sold by or to a person under the age of 16;

(b)  no ticket or chance shall be sold to a person in any street[173];

(c)  every ticket or chance shall be sold by means of a machine;

(d)  every ticket must state the name of the registration authority with which the club is registered;

(e)  no ticket shall be supplied to the club which enables a ticket to be identified as a winning ticket before it is sold;

(f)  no prize shall be offered on the basis that the winning thereof depends upon the purchase of more than one ticket or chance, except this is permissible if the price of the two or more tickets or chances does not exceed £1.

## 11-47  Local authority registration

Registration is with the local authority if the total value of the tickets sold or to be sold £20,000 or less[174], and the application procedure is set out in Schedule 1 to the Lotteries and Amusements Act 1976. The local authority is under a duty to register the club if the application is duly made and the appropriate fee is paid. There is, however, a power to refuse registration or to revoke it because of a previous refusal or revocation by the Gaming Board, and there are other powers of refusal or revocation which shall not be exercised unless the club has been given the opportunity of being heard on the matter. There is a right of appeal to the Crown Court where registration is refused or revoked.

---

[171]    Lotteries and Amusements Act 1976, s. 11(12) as amended by the Lotteries (Variation of Monetary Limits) Order 1997 (SI 1997/43).
[172]    The Lotteries Regulations 1993 (SI 1993/3223).
[173]    Save that a sale by a person in a kiosk to a person in the street is permissible: reg. 4(2).
[174]    Lotteries and Amusements Act 1976, s. 5(3)(b), (3A)(a). Sub-s (3A) was inserted by the National Lottery Etc Act 1993.

- *Fees payable*  The current (2004) fees are £35 on registration and £17.50 on renewal on 1 January in each year.
- *Returns*  The promoter of the lottery must make a return to the local authority within three months of the date of the lottery. The return must contain the required particulars, and must be certified by two other members of the club who are over 21 and who were appointed in writing as certifiers by the governing body of the club. The return will be preserved by the local authority for at least 18 months and any member of the public may inspect it during office hours free of charge.

**11-48   Gaming Board registration**

Registration is with the Gaming Board if the total value of the tickets sold or to be sold in a particular lottery exceeds £20,000, or if the total value of tickets sold or to be sold in any calendar year by the club in respect of this and other lotteries exceeds £250,000[175], and the application procedure is set out in Schedule 1A of the Act. Registration here is a more comprehensive version of the application made to the local authority. In particular, under Part II of Schedule 1A the Gaming Board may require information from the club or it may inspect and take copies of documents belonging to the club. Where lottery tickets sold in any one calendar year exceed £100,000, accounts in respect of the lottery or lotteries, which have been prepared by an eligible auditor, must be sent to the Board. There are powers of refusal and revocation of the registration and a right of appeal to the Crown Court in the event of a refusal or revocation.

- *Fees payable*  The current (2004) fees are £4,810 on registration and £188 on renewal[176]. The registration is renewal at three-yearly intervals commencing on 1 January.
- *Returns*  The club must make a return to the Gaming Board within three months of the date of the lottery in such form, and containing such information, as the Board may direct. The return will be preserved for at least 18 months and any member of the public may inspect it during office hours on payment of a prescribed fee.

---

[175]     Lotteries and Amusements Act 1976, ss. 5(3)(b) and 5(3B),(3C), 3(E) and (3F).
Sub-s (3B), (3C), (3E) and (3F) were inserted by the said Act of 1993.
[176]     Lotteries (Gaming Board Fees) Order 2004 (SI 2004/532).

# 16. SALE OF CHANCES

**11-49** The reference to the sale of chances in the rules governing small lotteries, private lotteries and societies' lotteries shows that the conduct of these lotteries does not necessarily depend on the issue or distribution of tickets but can be done orally or by an exchange of correspondence, although the sale of tickets is the normal method of conducting lotteries because it provides an instant and contemporaneous record of the participants. It is not uncommon, however, in private lotteries, which are designed to enhance the club's funds, that there are no non-members of the club who are participants; here the members may be approached by telephone or e-mail at their home address concerning their willingness to take part in the lottery and the members can orally respond by agreeing to purchase a chance (or chances) for a set amount. The committee (or usually a delegated person) then brings into existence the necessary paperwork, the club member pays for his chance and at this point numbers are allotted to each chance preparatory to the draw taking place.

## 11-50  Winning tickets

What should a club do if the purchaser of a winning ticket either is not present when the draw takes place or he is there but overlooks the fact that he is holding a winning ticket? A distinction has to be made here between a private lottery and a society's lottery. Under section 4 of the Act of 1976 all tickets sold in a private lottery must state that the prize will *only* be given to the purchaser(s) of the winning ticket(s). Thus the club must find the winner but what if this proves impossible? There appears to be no ready solution and in these circumstances we consider that it will not be improper for the prize to go back to the club. Although occasionally done, the unclaimed prize should not be the subject of a re-draw with a different winner. The answer to this problem is to keep a proper record of the participants. No such problem arises with a society's lottery under section 5 of the Act of 1976 because there is no equivalent restriction as laid down in section 4 and therefore no contravention of the law occurs if an unclaimed prize is not distributed. The problem, however, should be avoided once again by keeping a proper record of all participants in the lottery.

On the question of winning tickets, is a club entitled to make it an express condition of say a raffle that the winner must be present at the clubhouse when the draw takes place? The answer is in the affirmative if the raffle (which is a lottery) can be properly categorised as an amusement with prizes at an exempt entertainment and the condition in question is made known to the participants beforehand. In these circumstances if the purchaser of the winning ticket is not present at the draw, it will be legitimate forthwith to make a re-draw.

Further, is it permissible to make the draw of prizes in the reverse order, that is to say, you start with the lowest prize and finish with the main prize? This practice is occasionally adopted to make the draw more exciting by leading up to the climax of the main prize. It has the disadvantage, however, that *unless the first winning ticket is put back into the draw* the purchaser of that ticket is denied the opportunity of winning the main prize and therefore he has not had an equal chance with other participants of winning the lottery. This is a formidable argument against the reverse-order practice and it can only be justified, if at all, by making it an express term of the lottery to which the participants have consented.

Another point that requires consideration is the nature of prizes where the winning ticket is sold to a young member or a young guest at say a club raffle. Suppose one of the prizes was a box of cigars or a bottle of whisky: could this lawfully be won by a child? We believe not[177], and that the answer is to offer the winner a substitute prize of equal value.

## 17.   BETTING

**11-51**   It is well to remember that section 1 of the Betting, Gaming and Lotteries Act 1963 creates two offences of which clubs should take note:
(1) no person shall use any premises, or cause or knowingly permit any premises to be used, as a place where persons resorting thereto may effect pool betting transactions;
   - a pool betting transaction may be defined as the collective stakes of a number of people who combine in a betting arrangement[178];

---

[177]   The sale or supply of tobacco is prohibited to someone under 16 years: Children and Young Persons Act 1933, s. 7(1) as amended; and the supply of alcohol by a member or officer of the club is prohibited to a person under 18; Licensing Act 2003, s. 151(4), (5)(b).
[178]   A technical definition may be found in s. 10 of the Betting and Gaming Duties Act 1981.

(2) no person shall use, or cause or knowingly permit any other person to use, any premises for the purpose of putting into effect any other betting transactions by that person or, as the case may be, by that person in conjunction with other persons on those premises.

**11-52** These offences arise because there are strict rules stipulating that betting transactions are to take place in licensed betting offices only by persons holding a bookmaker's permit[179]. The most that can occur lawfully on club premises are the writing out of personal betting slips for subsequent visits to a licensed betting office, or the transfer of a completed slip to a personal friend for taking to the licensed betting office, or the telephoning of bets to a bookmaker on an open-telephone line of account. Many managing committees discourage or forbid any such activity within club premises. One activity not frowned upon, however, is the holding of race nights in the club: this is acceptable because, not only does it benefit club funds, but it is run on strictly controlled lines as gaming at an exempt entertainment under section 41 of the Gaming Act 1968 (see **11-17** above)[180].

## 18.   PROPRIETARY CLUBS

### 11-53   General applicability of betting, gaming and lottery law

What has been said above has general application to all clubs of whatever nature. A licensed gaming club will invariably be a proprietary club (see **11-05** above). One area, which is dealt with below, is in the playing of bingo on a commercial scale rather than on a domestic scale, and this is also the province of proprietary clubs.

### 11-54   Commercial bingo clubs

The government has never had any quarrel with the playing of bingo and on occasion has even given it a helping hand. By section 20 of the Gaming Act 1968 a club can obtain a licence under Schedule 2 of the Act which is limited to the playing of bingo only. In order to make the game more attractive, that is, the ability to offer larger prizes, section 20 permitted bingo to be played simultaneously on different

---

[179]   Betting, Gaming and Lotteries Act 1963, ss. 2, 9.
[180]   See also *Stoddart v Sagar* [1895] 2 QB 474 (competition to forecast the first four horses in a race held not to constitute a lottery).

bingo club premises[181]; this was known as 'linked bingo'. The Gaming (Bingo) Act 1985 extended this idea to 'multiple bingo' by taking advantage of the instantaneous monitoring of the progress of the game by computer technology. This enables many more than the two to four clubs normally participating in linked bingo. The Act also allowed larger cash prizes, initially in 1985 not exceeding £50,000, and currently (2004) increased to £2 million[182]. The Bingo Act 1992 allowed a bingo club *either* to advertise locally its existence and location and to invite applications for membership *or* to indicate what prizes can be won at the club, but not to advertise both at the same time; and the club may advertise the prizes of multiple bingo in the national newspapers and on television but not elsewhere.

### 11-55 Membership, hours of playing and charges

As with all licensed gaming clubs, there needs to be a 24-hour interval between an application for membership of the club and the commencement of play[183], but there is no requirement to make the application on the club premises[184]. Persons under 18 years may be present at bingo games but are not allowed to play[185]. Bingo may be played between the hours of 10 in the morning and eleven in the evening save for Saturday when the evening hours are extended to midnight and for Sunday when the opening time is restricted to two in the afternoon[186]. The current (2004) charge for admission to the premises must not exceed £20 in respect of an individual person and the charge must not exceed £10 for each chance in playing a game of bingo[187]. Three games of multiple bingo may be played on any bingo club premises in any period of 24 hours beginning at midnight and the period allowed for the playing of any game of multiple bingo is 30 minutes[188].

---

[181]    Thereby giving birth to a perfect legal fiction, namely, that the Act was to have effect as if the different premises were the same premises: s. 20(2).

[182]    Gaming (Bingo) Act (Variation of Monetary Limit) Order 2002 (SI 2002/1909).

[183]    Gaming Act 1968, s. 20(5).

[184]    Ibid. s. 20(5)(a).

[185]    Ibid. s. 20(6).

[186]    Gaming Clubs (Hours and Charges) Regulations 1984 (SI 1984/248) as amended by SI 1988/1027, SI 2000/899 and 2000/1879 and as further amended by the Gaming Clubs (Charges) (Amendment) Regulations 2002 (SI 2002/1902).

[187]    Gaming Clubs (Hours and Charges) Regulations 1984 (amended as indicated in the last footnote).

[188]    Gaming Clubs (Multiple Bingo) Regulations 1986 (SI 1986/834).

## 11-56  Fees and duty payable

The current (2004) fees are £3,915 for the grant of a bingo licence, £1,495 for its renewal and £1,595 for its transfer. A current (2004) fee of £167,000 is payable to the Gaming Board for a certificate of approval as an organiser of multiple bingo issued under the Gaming (Bingo) Act 1985; the certificate is renewable at three-yearly intervals at a current (2004) fee of £160,000[189]. Bingo duty is payable under section 17 of the Betting and Gaming Act 1981 (as amended) and in accordance with Part II of Schedule 3 to the Act and the Bingo Duty Regulations 1988[190].

## 11-57  Commercial casino clubs

Another form of proprietary gaming club may arise as a result of the Gambling Bill presently (2004) before Parliament where the government is proposing to allow some 24 super-casinos in the UK.

---

[189]   Gaming (Bingo) Act (Fees) Order 1986 (SI 1986/833) as amended by the Gaming Act (Variation of Fees) (England, Wales and Scotland) Order 2002 (SI 2002/642).
[190]   SI 1988/333.

Part 3

---

# External relationships: the club and third parties

# Chapter 12

## CLUB'S CIVIL LIABILITY TO THIRD PARTIES

## 1.  CONTRACT

### 12-01  Introduction

Whatever its nature and whatever its size, during the course of its lifetime a club will be involved in contractual relationships of many sorts, either as purchaser of goods and services or as the provider for payment of services and facilities. It is therefore crucial for those persons in charge of the club's affairs that they are aware of their rights and obligations when entering into a contract. What follows below is the legal situation looked at from the point of view of liability rather than entitlement. Two points need emphasising. First is the importance of the law of agency, especially in the realm of unincorporated members' clubs. The second is the desirability of recording agreements which have been made. It is common practice for people to enter into an agreement by telephone or by word of mouth since this is the way of the world and we have no quarrel with this procedure. But a note or letter, by post, fax or e-mail, which is sent straight afterwards and which *confirms* the agreement, will often prevent a dispute arising later on.

## 2.  UNINCORPORATED MEMBERS' CLUBS

### 12-02  General propositions

There are three general propositions to remember when considering the club's or the individual member's contractual liability to a third

party[1]:
(1) the club is not a legal person[2];
(2) the member's liability is normally limited to his entrance fee (if any) and his subscription[3];
(3) whether the member can be held personally liable for contracts purporting to have been made on behalf of the club depends on the law of agency[4].

## 12-03 Agency

The general rule of the law of agency is that the contract of the agent is the contract of the principal[5], so that the agent has power to bind and entitle his principal whilst he himself drops out of the transaction, incurring neither rights nor liabilities[6]. With an unincorporated members' club this immediately begs the question, who is the principal if the club is not a legal person?

**12-04**  Let us assume that a member or the committee has purported to act as agent for the club when making a contract. The answer to the question is that if a person makes a contract on behalf of a non-legal person he may be held to have contracted in a *personal* capacity[7]. So in each case it is important to identify the real principal behind the contract and to see what authority that person had to act in the way in which he or she did. In resolving the question, the following nine propositions should be borne in mind:

(1) No member of the club is liable for the debts of the club save to the extent that he has authorised an officer of the club (say the secretary) or an official of the club (say the bar steward) or some other members (say the managing committee) to pledge his personal credit[8].

    (a) Authority comes in three categories: express, implied or ostensible. Express authority (also called actual authority) is where the principal gives the agent by means of spoken words or in writing the ability to act on his behalf. Implied authority

---

1    The converse situation, namely, pursuing the club's contractual entitlement in contract, is discussed at **18-03** below.

2    *Conservative Central Office v Burrell* [1982] 1 WLR 522 CA at 527.

3    *Wise v Perpetual Trustee Co* [1903] AC 139.

4    *Maritime Stores Ltd v H P Marshall & Co Ltd* [1963] 1 Lloyd's Rep 602 at 608.

5    *Chitty on Contract* (28th edn, 2004) para 32-082.

6    *Chitty* op.cit. para 32-001.

7    *Bradley Egg Farm v Clifford* [1943] 2 All ER 378 CA at 386F (Scott LJ).

8    *Steele v Gourley and Davis* [1887] 3 TLR 772 CA; *Wise v Perpetual Trustee Co* [1903] AC 139 PC; *re St James Club* [1852] de GM & G 383 at 390 (Lord St Leonards LC).

(sometimes called usual authority) is where the agent is put into a position which normally carries with it the ability to act in certain matters of behalf of the principal. Ostensible authority (also called apparent authority) is where the principal[9] holds out the agent as having the requisite authority to act on his behalf when in fact the agent had no such authority, or had limited authority only, which was unknown to the other party.

(b) Proving the necessary agency is all-important in establishing liability against the principal. Take the case of *Wood v Finch* [1861] 2 F & F 447, where a member and a trustee-member of a coal-club, which was formed on the principle of buying coal wholesale on a cash basis out of members' paid-up subscriptions, were held not liable to the plaintiff-coal merchant for the price of goods ordered by the club secretary on credit terms. Contrast it with the case of *Cockerell v Aucompte* [1857] 2 CB(NS) 440, another case concerning a coal-club, where the committee authorised the secretary to buy coal but did not furnish him with any funds to pay for it. Here the court held that the committee authorised the purchases on credit and, because the secretary was its servant or agent, his credit was *their* credit and the committee members were held liable to the coal merchant.

(2) The members of the managing committee, being in control of the club's affairs, are in the ordinary course of events personally liable for all contracts made (or acquiesced in[10]) by them on behalf of the club, because they will be held to be the principals[11]. In this event the committee members will be liable to the full extent of the contract, not merely to the full extent of the club's funds[12].

---

[9] It is important to note that it is not sufficient for the agent to represent the extent of his authority; the holding out must be done by the principal: *Att-Gen. for Ceylon v Silva* [1953] AC 461 PC at 479.

[10] *Stansfield v Ridout* [1889] 5 TLR 656 (where the committee of the Beaconsfield Conservative Club in Battersea authorised the secretary to purchase beer from the plaintiff brewer; the action was brought against 4 members of the club, only one of whom was a member of the committee but all of whom had signed cheques for various goods ordered by the secretary; and all were held liable to the plaintiff); *Steele v Gourley and Davis* [1886] 3 TLR 772 CA at 773 (Lord Esher MR). See also *Rowntrees of London (Builders) Ltd v Screenwriters Club Ltd* [1953] 162 EG 352 CA (where it was held that if the committee members want to displace the ordinary inference that the secretary or the steward orders goods on behalf of the club, as opposed to ordering them for their own personal use, evidence must be called by them to rebut the inference).

[11] *Glenester v Hunter* [1831] 5 Car & P 62 at 65 (Tindal CJ); *Steele v Gourley and Davis* [1886] 3 TLR 772 at 773; *Bradley Egg Farms Ltd v Clifford* [1943] 2 All ER 378 at 386.

[12] *Pink v Scudamore* [1831] 5 Car & P 71.

(a)  This proposition leads to a point of considerable practical
     significance. It will be recalled that the committee must act
     unanimously unless (which is the norm) it is expressly
     authorised to act by a majority[13]. The question which arises
     is whether a committee member, who opposes or dissents
     from a decision of the majority, say, to enter into a contract
     with a particular third party, is liable to that third party if the
     committee defaults on its obligations under the contract. At
     first sight the answer would appear to be in the negative. In
     *Todd v Emly* [1841] 7 M & W 427 a wine merchant sued two
     committee members of the Alliance Club for the price of goods
     ordered by the steward. The plaintiff won at first instance but
     the appeal court, the Exchequer Chamber, ordered a re-trial.
     The plaintiff won the second trial but again the Exchequer
     Chamber ordered a re-trial: [1841] 8 M & W 505[14]. Neither
     defendant had ordered the wine nor been present at any
     committee meeting when authority to place an order was
     given to the steward. On the second appeal Mr Baron
     Alderson stated in his judgment at 510:

> In order to make the case out, and to establish the liability of the
> committee generally, the jury should be satisfied that what was
> done was not only within the knowledge of the committee generally
> but that it was in the particular knowledge of the two defendants.

The same judge in the course of argument had stated at 508:

> It might be that the majority only gave authority, and that the
> defendants dissented from it. If so, I should think they only were
> liable who voted for it.

The sting in the tail lies in what the court had said in its earlier
judgments. Mr Baron Alderson stated at 435 as follows:

> … here the committee were authorised only to deal, as a body, for
> ready money. But at the same time, if any of the members of the
> committee choose not to contract for ready money, those members
> of the committee who have so contracted are liable upon their own
> contract, and the members who have not concurred in it are not
> liable, *unless that be the common purpose for which the committee
> was appointed.* (emphasis added).

The 'common purpose' point was emphasised in the same
appeal at 434 by Mr Baron Parke:

---

13   See **5-18** above.
14   Sadly history does not relate what happened on the third trial.

> Then we come to the other, which is the main point of the case, and upon which it may be urged, that where parties enter into one common purpose of acting together, each of them has authority to bind the others to the extent of attaining that common purpose. But the defect of the plaintiff's case is, that there is no common purpose shewn, of dealing on credit for such articles as supplied in this case[15].

The 'common purpose' exception is likely in practice to mean that the dissenting member of the committee may well find himself potentially liable on a contract which he had not agreed nor approved of and, depending on the nature or size of the contract, this state of affairs might involve his resignation from the committee.

(b) Another question which arises under this proposition is whether a new member of the committee can be held liable in respect of authorised contracts made before his election. On the face of things, the answer is in the negative because the principals are fixed at the date when the contract was made and there is no such procedure as 'rolling substitutes' (unless the other party were to agree to this, which would technically be known as novation). However, there are two points to be made: first, we consider that the new member may by his conduct on the committee be estopped from denying that he was a principal under the contract. Take the example of the committee placing an order for building works in January; the new committee member is then elected in July; and in October as such member he votes in favour of a resolution to sue the builder for defective workmanship; in these circumstances he is at risk of being treated as a principal by his adoption of the contract[16]. Secondly, it follows that a member who resigns from the committee is still liable on those contracts which the committee had earlier entered into on behalf of the club when he was on the committee[17].

(3) The managing committee of the club has no implied authority to pledge the credit of the members generally, for example, when ordering goods to be supplied[18] or work to be done[19] or when

---

[15]  See also the judge's remarks in the same case quoted in **5-35** above.

[16]  See in this context the discussion on estoppel in *Chitty on Contracts*, op. cit. para 37-052.

[17]  *Parr v Bradbury* [1885] 1 TLR 285 and 525 CA (continuing liability of a member under a debenture entered into before cessation of membership).

[18]  See *Todd v Emly* [1841] 7 M & W 427 at 434 (Parke B's judgment is quoted at **5-35** above); *Hawke v Cole* [1890] 62 LT 658.

[19]  *Fleming v Hector* [1836] 2 M & W 172.

borrowing monies on debentures[20]. Consequent upon this lack of implied authority, if the committee is authorised to make a contract on behalf of all the members, that authority is restricted to the existing funds of the club[21]. A long established exception to this rule is the employment of staff where by the nature of things the services are purchased on credit[22]. Another exception is where the club has no funds and thus any contract made by the committee would to the members' knowledge involve the pledging of their credit:

(a)  In *Pilot v Craze and Evans* [1888] 4 TLR 453 the stewards of a jubilee fête formed part of a committee to provide public entertainments in honour of Queen Victoria's Golden Jubilee, and two of the stewards were sued and held liable for the rent of tents and flags hired on credit by the manager for a sports day. The court found that the manager had actual and implied authority from the stewards to do all acts necessary for the sports day, the committee as a whole being well aware there were no available funds upon which to draw.

(4) The committee or the members as a body may clothe the agent with ostensible authority by holding him out as having proper authority to make a contract on behalf of the members which pledges their credit[23]. Here each case has to be decided on its own facts leading sometimes to seemingly bizarre results:

(a)  In the case of *Steele v Gourley and Davis* [1886] 3 TLR 118, 669 and 772 (where the proprietary Empire Club became an unincorporated members' club called the New Empire Club) the butcher succeeded in recovering the price of meat supplied to the new unincorporated club but in the later case of *Overton v Hewett* [1886] 3 TLR 246, the fishmonger failed to recover the price of fish and poultry supplied to the new unincorporated club, the difference being that in the first case the defendant committee members had by their conduct authorised the steward to purchase the goods whereas in the second case the plaintiff could not point to any such conduct on the part of the committee members.

(b)  In the case of *Harper v Granville Smith* [1891] 7 TLR 284,

---

[20]    *Re St James Club* [1852] De GM & G 383 at 390.
[21]    *Cockerell v Aucompte* [1857] 2 CB(NS) 440.
[22]    See *Todd v Emly* cited in **footnote 19** above.
[23]    *Barnett and Scott v Wood* [1888] 4 TLR 278 CA at 279 (Lord Esher MR) (where a jeweller was suing the committee of a football club for the price of prizes sold and delivered to the club).

(where the proprietary Salisbury Club became an unincorporated members' club called the New Salisbury Club) the wine merchant succeeded in recovering payment for champagne supplied to the new unincorporated club but a year later in the case of *Draper v Earl Manvers* [1892] 9 TLR 73 the milkman failed to recover the price of milk delivered to the new club, the difference being that in the first case the members of the committee were aware of the transaction when the order was placed whereas in the second case the committee had under the rules delegated its purchasing function to a sub-committee and took no part in ordering the milk.

(5) The rules of the club may *expressly* authorise the committee to make contracts on behalf of the members[24]. In this event the whole membership will be liable as co-principals on any authorised contract. The usual rule which vests the control of all the club's affairs in a managing committee would not by itself give to the committee the requisite express authority[25]; this is because the committee must be taken to know of and assent to the general proposition that an unincorporated members' club is run on a cash basis (see 5-35 above).

(6) The club member[26] or the committee member[27] may assume personal liability with regard to any contract made with the club by 'previous concurrence or subsequent approbation'[28], either individually or collectively, say, at a special meeting of the members, but this is much less likely to occur at the present time, as far as club members are concerned, because of the emergence of the now entrenched rule that the members are prima facie only liable for club debts up to the limit of their entrance fee and subscriptions[29].

(7) The club member or the committee member may assume personal liability by ratifying an *unauthorised* contract made by an agent

---

[24]     A rule found in some early Victorian clubs but an unwise one and seldom if ever found in modern times.

[25]     *Flemyng v Hector* [1838] 2 M & W 172 at 185 (Parke B).

[26]     *Delauney v Strickland* [1818] 2 Stark 416 (Abbott LCJ).

[27]     *Earl of Mountcashell v Barber* [1853] 14 CB 53.

[28]     *Delauney v Strickland* [1818] cited above. And see *Lee v Bissett* [1856] 4 WR 233 (where a solicitor-member of the Naval and Military Club successfully sued certain members of the club in their personal capacity for his fees for work done on behalf of the club, the members in question being those who had subscribed £60 each to carry on the club, which was in financial straits, thereby enabling the club to employ the solicitor).

[29]     *Wise v Perpetual Trustee Co* [1903] AC 139 PC.

of the club[30]. This is more likely to involve their personal liability because the circumstances of the unauthorised transaction will inevitably be brought to the specific attention of the ratifying party, otherwise there will be no ratification. The ratifying party will then become personally liable[31]. A form of ratification is where the goods are ordered by the club's agent without authority but are used by the club members. Mere use of the goods without knowledge of the unauthorised contract does not amount to ratification. But once the members know about the true situation and acquiesce in it, they will have ratified the transaction in question and, further, it is likely that in respect of future transactions of the same description involving the same supplier and agent, the committee or the members will be taken as having held out that particular agent as being authorised to transact business on their behalf.

(8) A member who has authority to enter into a contract on behalf of the club should never sign the contract in his name alone even if he has made it clear to the other contracting party that he is an agent only, because he could be held personally liable as well as the managing committee[32]. When acting for the club, a member should always sign his own name on a document followed by the words of agency and then the principal's name; for example, 'Tom Pearce for and on behalf of the Basset Pony Club'.

(9) If a member purports to make a contract on behalf of the club when he has no authority of any sort to make the contract, he will be liable in damages to the other party for breach of warranty of authority[33]. On the other hand, if the other party is aware that the member has no such authority, he will not be liable if the club rejects the contract[34].

---

[30] *Jones v Hope* [1880] 3 TLR 247 (note) CA at 249 (Cotton LJ) (concerning the liability of the officers an unincorporated volunteer corps to a wine merchant for goods supplied).

[31] Ibid. at 249.

[32] *Brandt (H O) Co v H N Morris & Co Ltd* [1917] 2 KB 784 at 793 ('when a man signs a contract in his own name he is prima facie a contracting party and liable, and there must be something very strong on the face of the document to shew that liability does not attach to him').

[33] *Collen v Wright* [1857] 7 E & B 30, affirmed on appeal [1857] 8 E & B 647 (a prime example of judicial law making: see Cockburn CJ's dissenting judgment at 658). The correct measure of damages flowing from this breach of warranty can raise a 'troublesome issue': *Habton Farms v Nimmo* [2003] 3 WLR 633 CA (where the Court of Appeal was divided on the issue of damages).

[34] *Jones v Hope* [1880] 3 TLR 247 (note) at 248; *Overton v Hewett* [1886] 3 TLR 246.

## 12-05   Protecting the committee

It may be seen from paragraph **12-04**(2) above that the members of the managing committee are vulnerable to being held personally liable to the club's creditors and proper consideration should be given as to how these members may best be protected. In fact, there are various ways of doing this:

(1) *Express exclusion or restriction of liability*   Exclusion or restriction of liability by contract is permissible. The committee can try to limit the liability of the committee members by persuading the other party to the contract to permit an express clause in the contract whereby the committee was only liable to the extent of the club's funds. This might mean that the committee would have to divulge precisely what those funds were and the members as a whole might not look too kindly on such disclosure. Alternatively, the committee can by an express clause seek to exclude or restrict liability generally or to set a maximum limit on the amount of its liability. This may not be acceptable to the other party and in any event may be affected by the provisions of the Unfair Contract Terms Act 1977. Were the other party to contract on the club's 'written standard terms of business', any exclusion or restriction of liability on the club's part must satisfy the requirement of reasonableness[35].

(2) *Raising subscriptions*   Faced with a shortfall in funds wherewith to carry out the club's activities or to embark on a particular project, it is not only perfectly in order to call a special meeting to raise subscriptions generally or to have a one-off rise in the subscription or to make a levy on the members, but such a remedy is a classic way of overcoming a shortfall[36].

(3) *Lien*   If the committee has incurred personal liability by reason of entering into some authorised contract for the benefit of the club the committee will have a lien on the club property to the extent of their liability. The Irish case of *Minnit v Lord Talbot de Malahide* [1876] LR 1 Ir 143 is instructive on this point. The members of the Irish Farmers' Agricultural Club in general meeting authorised the committee to borrow £1,000 for building works to the club premises and for the provision of fittings and furniture. The committee raised the money on the security of guarantees given by certain members of the committee. This course of action was

---

[35]   Unfair Contract Terms Act 1977, s. 3.
[36]   *Flemyng v Hector* [1836] 2 M & W 172 at 183 (Lord Abinger CB).

approved by the members in general meeting. The work was carried out and the fittings and furniture were provided. The work and goods were not fully paid for out of club funds and the club failed, whereupon the guarantees were called upon and honoured. The club property was sold and the committee members were held entitled to reimbursement out of the proceeds of sale by virtue of their lien[37].

(4) *Indemnity*   Although it is considered unwise to give the members of the managing committee a blanket indemnity in the rules for any expenditure which they may incur in that capacity, there is nothing untoward or unusual in a more restricted rule which states that the members of the committee, the officers of the club, and the officials of the club shall be indemnified by the club out of club funds against any legal claims made against them in connection with the proper discharge of their duties.

(5) *Insurance*   Although this aspect may assume greater significance when it comes to tortious claims[38], proper consideration should also be given to the obtaining of insurance in relation to the contractual activities of the committee. A paradigm example would be the case of *Bradley Egg Farm Limited v Clifford* [1943] 2 All ER 378 where the defendants were the executive council of an unincorporated association called the Lancashire Utility Poultry Society. The Society entered into a contract with the plaintiff to carry out tests on its poultry. Its employee negligently caused damage to the poultry when carrying out the tests and the plaintiff successfully sued the members of the council for substantial damages. Failure to carry insurance in these circumstances would be foolish.

(6) *Contribution*   Where a member of the committee has paid out monies in respect of an authorised contract, he is entitled to a contribution from his fellow members of the committee[39], but he will have no right to an indemnity from the members of the club[40] (in the absence of an express rule conferring an indemnity).

---

[37]      In fact the proceeds of sale were insufficient and the committee members obtained a court order ([1881] LR 7 Ir 407) that they were entitled to an indemnity from the members as to the outstanding balance. This order would not be made today because of the definitive ruling in *Wise v Perpetual Trustee Co* [1903] AC 139, PC that the member's liability is in the ordinary course of events restricted to his entrance fee and subscriptions.

[38]      See **12-17** below.

[39]      *Earl of Mountcashell v Barber* [1853] 14 CB 53 at 69.

[40]      *Wise v Perpetual Trustee Co* [1903] AC 139 PC at 149.

# 3. LITERARY AND SCIENTIFIC INSTITUTIONS

## 12-06 Protecting the trustees

The trustees of such an institution who, reason of their being the legal owner of the institution's building or premises, are liable for any payment of rates, tax, charges, costs and expenses, shall be indemnified by the governing body of the institution. In default of such indemnity trustees are entitled to hold the building or premises as a security for their reimbursement and, to achieve this, may sell or mortgage the property[41].

# 4. WORKING MEN'S CLUBS AND SHOP CLUBS

**12-07** These clubs are not legal persons and so the principles set out in **12-02** to **12-04** above are equally applicable to them. These clubs, however, must have trustees in whom the club's property is vested as legal owners[42]. It is important that there are rules to indemnify the trustees against risk and expense out of club funds[43].

# 5. IPSA CLUBS

**12-08** These clubs are legal persons and to this extent their position is akin to that of incorporated clubs when it comes to liability in contract to third parties. The members of the club will have no personal liability. On the other hand, these clubs have no directors but officers and a committee instead[44], so none of the statutory régime applicable to company directors is of relevance to these clubs. However, the ordinary principles of agency set out in **12-04**(1) above are applicable when one is asked to consider the liability of the club itself. One important point needs to be mentioned. There is no equivalent of section 36C of the Companies Act 1985 which is applicable to IPSA clubs (as to which section, see **12-15** below). This means that, as with unincorporated clubs[45], a person purporting to deal contractually with

---

[41]    Literary and Scientific Institutions Act 1854, s. 19. See also the trustees' power to mortgage the institution's property in connection with their borrowing of monies at **5-38** above.

[42]    See **5-15** and **8-14** above.

[43]    See further **8-09** above.

[44]    'Officer' is defined as any treasurer, secretary, member of the committee, manager or servant other than a servant appointed by the committee and excludes an auditor: Industrial and Provident Societies Act 1968, s. 74, Sch. 1.

[45]    See **1-12** above.

a club *before* its incorporation, will have no remedy for goods supplied or services rendered, unless he can establish some collateral contract with a person connected with the club[46].

## 6.   INCORPORATED MEMBERS' CLUBS

**12-09**   The club itself is a legal person so that on the face of things contractual entitlement and contractual liability rests with the club itself and not with the members. The ordinary member will normally have no contractual liability in respect of the club's activities or purchases etc because the principal will be the company itself; indeed, the memorandum of association of the company is obliged to state, 'The liability of the members is limited', whether the company is limited by shares or by guarantee[47].

### 12-10   Director's liability

The club member who is a director of the company needs to understand his position in law as far as the extent of his personal liability is concerned. The difficulty lies in the fact that although a company has its own separate legal personality it has no ability to think or act for itself, so it can only act by resolution of its members in general meeting or by its agents[48]. And so the law of contract has applied adapted rules of agency whereby the company can be contractually bound[49]. There are, however, various restrictions on a company to act in a contractual capacity which are generally gathered together under the rubric of 'ultra vires'[50]. Broadly speaking, the categories of restrictions which an incorporated club needs to consider are as follows:

---

[46]      *Shanklin Pier Ltd v Detel Products Ltd* [1951] 2 KB 854. It is conceivable that in certain circumstances a claim may lie in unjust enrichment: see *Chitty on Contract* (29th edn, 2004) para 29-016.

[47]      This clause will appear as the fourth clause in the memorandum of association: Tables B and C as set out in the schedule to the Companies (Tables A to F) Regulations 1985 (SI 1985/805).

[48]      *Ferguson v Wilson* [1866] 2 Ch App 77 at 89.

[49]      See *Gore-Browne on Companies* (50th edn, 2004) para 7[17] and chapter 8.

[50]      I.e. beyond its powers. In *Rolled Steel Products (Holdings) Ltd v British Steel Corporation* [1985] 2 WLR 908 CA Slade and Browne-Wilkinson LJJ at 938 and 953 lamented the fact that *ultra vires* had a double meaning: first, acts beyond the *capacity* of a company (category no.1 in **12-10**) and, secondly, acts not beyond the capacity of the company but simply beyond the *authority* of either the board of directors or a majority of the shareholders or members of the company (categories nos.2, 3 and 4 in **12-10**). A useful summary of the legal position of ultra vires acts is set out by Slade LJ in his judgment at 946E to 947C.

(1) those contained in the memorandum of the company;
(2) those contained in the articles of the company;
(3) those contained in resolutions passed under the articles;
(4) the fiduciary duties of directors, e.g. acting bona fide for the benefit of the company, which may restrict the *authority* of the board by restricting the *actions* of the individual director;
(5) the normal rules of agency.

**12-11**  So where a director member has purported to make a contract on behalf of the club, the breach of a restriction in category (1) will render the transaction void and thus render the member liable for breach of warranty of authority[51]. A breach of the restrictions in categories (2), (3) and (4) will render the transactions voidable only, because they may be ratified by the board of directors or by the shareholders or members of the company[52], which will exonerate the director member from personal liability but, if not ratified, will leave him vulnerable to an action for breach of warranty of authority. As to category (5), save in very small clubs, transactions are frequently decided upon not by the board of directors but instead by individual directors or by officers of the club or by employees of the company. Where the other party knows or is put on enquiry that the director, officer or employee has no authority, the transaction will be voidable at the instance of the company[53]; if ratified, the director, officer or employee will be exonerated from liability; if not ratified, the other party will have no recourse against any of them personally[54]. Where the other party does not know of the lack of authority, the company will be bound by the transaction if its agent appears to have acted within his ostensible authority[55]; in this event the director, officer or employee will not be exposed to any personal liability because his agency will have been authorised. If, however, that person is not covered by any category of authority[56], he will be vulnerable to an action for breach of warranty of authority.

**12-12**  Members who are directors should also be aware of the four situations where the director may become personally liable for the debts of the company or to contribute to the company's assets[57]. They

---

[51]    *Collen v Wright* [1857] 7 E & B 301, affirmed [1857] 8 E & B 647.
[52]    See *Gore-Browne on Companies* (50th edn, 2004) para 8[1].
[53]    *Russo-Chinese Bank v Li Yau Sam* [1910] AC 174; see Gore-Browne, op cit para 8[21].
[54]    *Jones v Hope* [1880] 3 TLR 247n; *Overton v Hewett* [1886] 3 TLR 246.
[55]    *Freeman and Lockyer v Buckhurst Park Properties (Mangal) Ltd* [1964] 2 QB 480, CA; see Gore-Browne, op cit para 3.1.
[56]    See para **12-04**(1)(a) above as to the categories of authority.
[57]    See **3-29** above.

are: a director being made liable for misfeasance or breach of fiduciary or other duty[58]; being made liable for fraudulent trading[59]; being made liable for wrongful trading[60]; or acting whilst disqualified as a director[61]. Liability for wrongful trading only arises in the context of an insolvent winding up[62]. In addition, the director may be personally liable under section 349(4) of the Companies Act 1985: see **12-14** below.

## 12-13　Protecting the director

There are various ways in which a director may be relieved from liability which would otherwise fall on him for breach of duty:

(1) *Ratification by ordinary resolution*　Some breaches of duty can be overlooked through the director's conduct being disclosed to the members in general meeting and ratified by the passing of an ordinary resolution. It is not always easy to draw the line as to what is ratifiable in this manner. Examples of ratifiable conduct are failing to disclose an interest in a contract to which the company is a party[63]; obtaining a secret profit in circumstances where there was no misappropriation or misapplication of company property[64]; and breach of the duties of skill and care[65]. On the other hand, breaches involving a failure of honesty of the director's part[66], or involving a fraud on or oppression of the minority of shareholders[67] are not capable of being excused by this route.

(2) *Ratification by the consent of all members*　The approval of the director's conduct by every member of the company, either before or after the breach of duty, will relieve the director in all cases from

---

[58]　　Insolvency Act 1986, s. 212.

[59]　　Ibid. s. 213.

[60]　　Ibid. s. 214.

[61]　　Company Directors Disqualification Act 1986, s. 15.

[62]　　Insolvency Act 1986, s. 214(2).

[63]　　*North-West Transportation Co v Beatty* [1902] AC 83.

[64]　　*Regal (Hastings) Ltd v Gulliver* [1967] 2 AC 134 (Note) at 150A (case decided in 1941).

[65]　　*Pavlides v Jensen* [1956] Ch 565 at 576. See *Globalink Telecommunications Ltd v Wilmbury Ltd* [2003] 1 BCLC 145 (where the company's articles indemnified directors out of company assets against losses or liabilities as director, but the court emphasised the need for a specific contract as between the company and the director, evidence of which was absent in this case). Contrast the director's position with the member's position: see **1-30** above.

[66]　　*Mason v Harris* [1879] 11 Ch D 97, CA.

[67]　　*Cook v Deeks* [1916] 1 AC 554 PC.

liability provided that the breach is not *ultra vires* the company and does not involve a fraud on its creditors[68].

(3) *Provision in the articles* Articles 78 and 84(2)(a) of the 1948 Table A and regulations 85 and 94(a) of the 1985 Table A (which a great many companies adopted and adopt as the model form of articles of association and which have statutory force) contain provisions that appear to modify and even in part, exclude the duties of directors. Yet section 310(1) of the Companies Act 1985 makes void any provision, whether in the articles or elsewhere, exempting any officer of the company from, or indemnifying him against, any liability which by virtue of any rule of law would otherwise attach to him in respect of any negligence, default or breach of duty or breach of trust of which he may be guilty in relation to the company. This circle has not yet been squared satisfactorily[69]. But at least section 310(3) of the Companies Act 1985[70] now makes clear that a company may lawfully purchase and maintain for any officer or auditor insurance against the liabilities set out in section 310(1). This insurance is well worth taking out.

(4) *Release by the court* Under section 727(1) of the Companies Act 1985 a director may be relieved from liability in certain defined circumstances. What the director has to prove is (1) that he acted honestly, (2) that he acted reasonably, and (3) that he ought fairly to be excused from liability. The third element involves the discretion of the court being exercised in the director's favour[71]. Any relief granted will be on such terms as the court thinks fit.

## 12-14 Failure to mention the company's name

Members who are directors should be aware of section 349(4) of the Companies Act 1985 which states:

> If an officer of a company or a person on its behalf sign or authorises to be signed on behalf of the company any bill of exchange, promissory note, endorsement, cheque or order for money or goods in which the company's name is not mentioned as required by subsection (1), he is liable to a fine; and he is further personally liable to the holder of the bill of exchange,

---

[68]     *Gore-Browne on Companies* (50th edn, 2004) para 17[3].
[69]     An attempt at reconciling the section with Table A was made in *Motivex Ltd v Bulfield* [1986] 2 BCC 99/403 (Vinelot J).
[70]     As substituted by s. 137 of the Companies Act 1989.
[71]     *Re J Franklin & Son Ltd* [1937] 4 All ER 43 in relation to an earlier enactment in identical terms.

promissory note, cheque or order for money or goods for the amount of it (unless it is duly paid by the company).

The requirement of subsection (1) is that the company's name must be mentioned in legible characters in all those documents which are referred to in the quoted subsection (4). It is therefore the duty of the club generally and the club secretary in particular to make sure that these documents comply with the statutory requirement.

## 12-15  Protecting third parties

In 1989 Parliament reformulated sections 35 and 36 into the Companies Act 1985, so as to guarantee the efficacy of transactions in favour of those persons dealing with the company in good faith (thus in effect abolishing the doctrine of *ultra vires* as far as third parties are concerned). The following propositions may be stated:

(1) the validity of an act done by a company shall not be called into question on the ground of lack of capacity by reason of anything in the company's memorandum[72];

(2) if a person deals with the company in good faith, the power of the board of directors to bind the company, or authorise others to do so, shall be deemed to be free of any limitation under the company's constitution[73];

(3) there is no duty to enquire as to the capacity or authority of directors[74];

(4) a contract which purports to be made by or on behalf of a company at a time when the company has not been formed, has effect (subject to any agreement to the contrary) as one made with the person purporting to act for the company or as its agent for it, and he is personally liable on the contract accordingly[75];

  • In *Phonogram Ltd v Lane* [1982] QB 938 the court held that the person purporting to act for the company is liable personally, even though all parties were aware at the relevant time that no company was then in existence.

But it should be noted that the reverse is not true: the company will not be able to bring an action against the person dealing with the club

---

72      Companies Act 1985, s. 35(1) as substituted by the Companies Act 1989.
73      Ibid. s. 35A(1). This had already appeared in the old s. 35(1) in compliance with s. 9(1) of the European Communities Act 1972.
74      Ibid. s. 35B. This had already appeared in the old s. 35(2) in compliance with s. 9(1) of the European Communities Act 1972.
75      Ibid. s. 36C. This had already appeared in the old s. 36(4) in compliance with s. 9(2) of the European Communities Act 1972.

if the transaction is *ultra vires* of the company[76].

## 7. PROPRIETARY CLUBS

**12-16** Here any contract touching or concerning the club will be the liability of the proprietor insofar as third parties are involved, such as suppliers of goods to the club. An individual member of the club might, however, become personally liable if by some independent contract he became liable to the third party, such as signing a guarantee in favour of the proprietor's creditor, but nothing less than an independent contract will suffice to make the club member liable for the contractual affairs of the proprietor.

## 8. TORTS

### 12-17 Introduction

A tort is a civil wrong (not arising in contract) in respect of which an action for damages or compensation lies. A club's liability in tort may arise either through the activities of its members or by virtue of its occupation or ownership of club premises. We are here dealing with situations where the club activities impinge on the well-being of third parties who are not members of the club. Any managing committee will or should know, often because of complaints, whether the activities of its members or the state of repair of the club property carry the risk of adversely affecting other people's well-being or enjoyment of life. As with agency in the law of contract, so here the doctrine of vicarious liability is an important factor which committees need to understand.

## 9. UNINCORPORATED MEMBERS' CLUBS

### 12-18 General propositions

There are three general propositions to remember when considering a member's tortious liability to third parties[77]:

---

[76]  *Bell Houses Ltd v City Wall Properties Ltd* [1966] 1 QB 207.
[77]  The converse situation, namely, pursuing the club's remedy in tort, is discussed at **18-03** below.

(1) the club is not a legal person[78];
(2) the member, if he is the actual tortfeasor, will potentially be personally liable to the injured or aggrieved party[79];
(3) the managing committee, as the managers and controllers of the club's affairs, will potentially be vicariously liable for the acts or omissions of those persons (whether employees or members of the club) who were acting in the course of their employment or acting in a manner authorised by the committee, and the members of the committee may thus become personally liable for the tort[80].

## 12-19   Vicarious liability[81]

A person is liable not only for the torts committed by himself but also for those which he has authorised or ratified[82]. Authorisation or ratification is not the same thing as vicarious liability, which has different parameters. In *Lister v Hesley Hall Ltd* [2002] 1 AC 215 Lord Millett at 243D said: 'Vicarious liability is a species of strict liability. It is not premised on any culpable act or omission on the part of the employer; an employer who is not personally at fault is made legally answerable for the fault of the employee'. The two most important classes of person for whose torts the managing committee may be vicariously liable are employees and independent contractors. As a generalisation, there is substantially less vicarious liability in relation to independent contractors as compared with employees, so it is important to ascertain into which category a person falls who is retained or employed by the club.

## 12-20   Club's liability for torts of employee

The exact nature of the relationship that exists between the members of the club and its employees is unclear. It is probably true to say that no contractual relationship exists because of the members' monetary liability being restricted to their entrance fees and subscriptions[83]. The

---

[78]     *Conservative Central Office v Burrell* [1982] 1 WLR 522 CA at 527. Any judgment obtained against such a club will be set aside: *London Association for the Protection of Trade v Greenlands Ltd* [1916] 2 AC 15 at 20.
[79]     *Baker v Jones* [1954] 1 WLR 1005 at 1011 (this includes authorising the tortious act).
[80]     *Jones v Northampton Borough Council* [1990] Times LR 387 CA at 388.
[81]     For the topic of vicarious liability generally, see *Clerk and Lindsell on Torts*, (18th edn, 2000) chap 5.
[82]     *Ellis v Sheffield Gas Consumer's Co* [1853] 2 E & B 767.
[83]     See Clerk and Lindsell op cit. para 5-19. But see *Campbell v Thompson and Shill* [1953] 2 WLR 656 discussed at **14-03** below.

position is almost certainly different in relation to the managing committee since they are in control of the club's affairs. However, being in control of the club's affairs is not the same thing as being in control of a person's work, which is one of the indicia that a person is an employee rather than an independent contractor[84]. The modern approach of the courts is to adopt a 'multiple' test where all aspects of the relationship are assessed before coming to the conclusion that a person is an employee[85]. In *Mattis v Pollock (trading as Flamingos Nightclub)* [2003] 1 WLR 2158 (where a club owner was held liable for the violent acts of assault of his doorman) the Court of Appeal stated that the established test for vicarious liability required a broad approach, namely, was the employee's action so closely connected with what the employer authorised or expected of him in the performance of his employment that it would be fair and just to hold the employer vicariously liable for the damage sustained as a result of the employee's act?

## 12-21 Club's liability for torts of independent contractor

The general rule is that if a person employs an independent contractor to do work on his behalf, the employer is not responsible for any tort committed by the contractor or by the contractor's employees in the course of the execution of the work[86]. There are exceptions: if the law imposes a strict or absolute duty on the employer, the duty is said to be non-delegable and the employer will be liable for the torts committed by his independent contractor. Examples are statutory duties[87] or common law duties such as the duty to prevent the escape of fire[88]. (The common law categories of non-delegable duties are said to be not yet closed[89]). Another exception is where the employer engages an independent contractor to do work which is inherently dangerous or which involves a special risk of damage. Here the

---

[84]    *Mersey Docks and Harbour Board v Coggins and Griffith (London) Ltd* [1947] AC 1 at 17 (Lord Porter).

[85]    *Ready Mixed Concrete (South East) v Minister of Pensions and National Insurance* [1968] 2 QB 497 at 516; *Market Investigations Ltd v Minister of Social Security* [1969] 2 QB 173 at 185 where Cooke J posed a rule-of-thumb guide: 'Is the worker in business on his own account?' If he is, he will not be an employee.

[86]    *D & F Estates Ltd v Church Commissioners for England* [1989] AC 177 at 208E (Lord Bridge).

[87]    *Gray v Pullen* [1864] 5 B & S 970 (defendant had statutory power to lay drains and a duty to reinstate the road after the drains were laid; the independent contractors negligently reinstated the road, for which the defendant was held liable).

[88]    *Balfour v Barty-King* [1957] 1 QB 496.

[89]    See *Clerk and Lindsell on Torts*, op cit para 5-52.

employer is under an absolute duty to take care and will be liable for the negligence of his contractor[90].

**12-22**   A further exception is where the defendant employs an independent contractor but is in breach of a *personal* duty to take care towards others. The case of *Brown v Lewis* [1892] 12 TLR 455 provides an interesting illustration of a committee's liability. The committee of the Blackburn Rovers Football Club had the power and duty to provide a spectators' stand. It needed repairing and the committee employed a workman to repair it. The stand was negligently repaired and collapsed, injuring the plaintiff. Although the law report is silent on the point, it would appear that the workman was an independent contractor. The committee was held liable, not because of the negligently carried out work, but because the committee had negligently chosen an incompetent person to carry out the work. This is therefore not a case of vicarious liability but a situation where the committee was held liable for breach of a personal duty of care to a third party[91].

## 12-23   Negligence and nuisance

The torts which are most likely to be of concern to a club are negligence and nuisance. Negligence is the tort of widest application because it is based on conduct rather than the protection of a particular interest such as a right of way. As was said by Lord Macmillan in the celebrated case of *Donoghue v Stevenson* [1932] AC 562 (the snail-in-the-bottle-of-ginger-beer case) at 619 'the categories of negligence are never closed'. In the same case Lord Atkin at 580 made an oft-repeated statement of principle which is still applicable today:

> The rule that you are to love your neighbour becomes in law, you must not injure your neighbour; and the lawyer's question, who is my neighbour? receives a restricted reply. You must take reasonable care to avoid acts or omissions which you can reasonably foresee would be likely to injure your neighbour.

---

[90]    *Honeywill & Stein Ltd v Larkin Bros Ltd* [1934] 1 KB 191 (negligence: dangerous flash photography used by contractor); *Matania v National Provincial Bank Ltd* [1936] 2 All ER 633 CA (nuisance: escape of dust and noise caused by building contractor carrying out structural alterations).

[91]    See also *Pinn v Rew* [1916] 32 TLR 451 (defendant farmer held personally liable for injury caused to a person on the highway by one of his animals being driven to his farm where he employed only one drover as an independent contractor when the situation called for more than one drover) and *M'Laughlin v Pryor* [1842] 4 M & G 48 (concerning the defendant's hire of a carriage and horse driven by two postillions as independent contractors; defendant held personally liable for injury to driver of a gig because he had interfered with the postillions' manner of carrying out their work).

To this principle, which involves the concepts of proximity and foreseeability, is now added a caveat that the court also has to be satisfied that the imposition of a duty of care must be fair, just and reasonable[92].

**12-24** On the other hand, the tort of nuisance is based on the interference by one occupier with the right in or enjoyment of land occupied by someone else. Two points can be clearly made: first, there must be an *escape* from the defendant's land to the claimant's land and, secondly, it is a tort directed to the protection of interests in land so that a claim for personal injuries falls outside the scope of this tort[93]. The escape in question may be noise[94] or unpleasant smells[95], or may simply be the causing of crowds to collect on your own land so that they spill over on to neighbouring land[96]. It is said to be a tort of strict liability but the exact boundary between nuisance and negligence is now blurred because the modern tendency is to assimilate the two torts[97].

**12-25** *Examples* The situation is best understood through the medium of examples:

(a) An intriguing case, from a legal point of view, is *Miller v Jackson* [1977] QB 966. The Lintz Cricket Club in County Durham had been established about 1905. In about 1972 some new houses were lawfully built whose gardens abutted the cricket field. Cricket balls were hit into the gardens by batsmen. The club installed a high fence and then a higher fence but still eight or nine balls a year landed in the gardens or on the houses themselves. Mrs Miller sued the club in negligence and nuisance and at first instance obtained an injunction to prevent cricket being played and damages as compensation. On appeal one judge, Lord Denning MR, held that there was negligence sounding in damages but that the established

---

[92]    *Caparo Industries plc v Dickman* [1990] 2 AC 605 at 617.
[93]    *Transco plc v Stockport Metropolitan Borough Council* [2003] 3 WLR 1467 at 1473 (Lord Bingham).
[94]    *Soltau v De Held* [1851] 2 Sim (NS) 133 (ringing of church bells); *Hawley v Steele* [1877] 6 Ch D 521 (use of common land for rifle practice and firing); *Newman v Real Estate Debenture Corp* [1940] 1 All ER 131 (banging of shop and lift doors); *Dunton v Dover* [1978] 76 LGR 87 (playground noise).
[95]    *Adams v Ursell* [1913] 1 Ch 269 (fried fish shop).
[96]    *Walker v Brewster* [1867] LR 5 Eq 25 (crowds caused by the holding of fêtes in a neighbouring property); *Lyons, Son & Co v Gulliver* [1914] 1 Ch 631 CA (theatre crowds obstructing highway access to plaintiff's nearby trading premises).
[97]    *British Road Services Ltd v Slater* [1964] 1 WLR 498 at 504 (Lord Parker CJ); *Goldman v Hargrave* [1967] 1 AC 645 at 657 (Lord Wilberforce). A recent example of this trend is the case of *Delaware Mansions Ltd v Westminster City Council* [2001] 1 AC 321: see **12-35** below.

playing of cricket on this particular ground did not constitute a nuisance and he said that no injunction should be granted because an injunction was not an available remedy in negligence; another judge, Lane LJ, held that there was both negligence and nuisance sounding in damages and that the injunction should continue; and the third judge, Cumming-Bruce LJ, held that there was negligence and nuisance sounding in damages but that no injunction should be granted as a matter of discretion. So Mrs Miller got £400 and the injunction was discharged. An interesting point is that Mrs Miller came to the nuisance but this did not disqualify her from complaining about the club's activities[98], although this fact could be taken into account when it came to the question of remedy[99].

(b) The above case should be contrasted with *Bolton v Stone* [1950] 1 KB 201 CA and [1951] AC 850 where Miss Stone had been hit and injured by a cricket ball driven out of the Cheetham Cricket Club ground in Manchester while standing in the road outside her house. The evidence was that balls had been hit out of the ground some six times in 30 years. Miss Bolton sued the club members, it being an unincorporated club, in nuisance and negligence. The risk of harm was foreseeable but the chances were very small and so the club argued that it was reasonable to ignore the risk. Miss Bolton won in the Court of Appeal on the basis that all the members of the club were liable in negligence as occupiers of the ground in failing to prevent balls being hit out the ground. The House of Lords allowed the appeal on the quite different basis that the committee of the club was not negligent in failing to take precautions to prevent such an accident.

Neither case, therefore, gives clear guidance on a matter of practical importance to many clubs.

### 12-26

(a) In *Castle v St Augustine's Links Ltd* [1922] 38 TLR 615 the plaintiff-motorist's eye was seriously injured by a golf ball driven on to the highway from an adjoining golf links (which was a common occurrence) and he recovered damages in nuisance against the golf club.

(b) In *Hilder v Associated Portland Cement Manufacturers Ltd* [1961] 1 WLR 1434 the defendant owned and occupied some grassland

---

98    *Sturges v Bridgman* [1879] 11 Ch D 852.
99    *Kennaway v Thompson* [1980] 3 All ER 329 CA at 333d.

by its factory and allowed local children to play there. The boundary of this land was a low brick wall. Adjoining the land was a busy highway. A child kicked a ball over the wall which caused a rider to fall off his motorcycle and be killed. The defendant was held liable in negligence to the motorcyclist's widow.

(c) In the New Zealand case of *Evans v Waitemata District Pony Club* [1972] NZLR 773 all the club members were held liable in negligence for injuries caused to some paying spectators. The club had failed to provide a suitable number of convenient tethering places for the horses, and when two horses became frightened they broke free from their tether and started galloping wildly around the paddock.

(d) In *Kennaway v Thompson* [1980] 3 All ER 329 all the members of the Cotswold Motor Boat Racing Club were held liable in nuisance to a lakeside house owner in respect of their powerful and noisy racing boats on Whelford Lake.

(e) In *Tetley v Chitty* [1986] 1 All ER 663 the all the members of the Medway Kart Club were held liable in nuisance for causing excessive noise to local residents from go-kart racing on Temple Marsh in Rochester, and the Medway Borough Council was held equally liable in nuisance because as landlord it had persisted in permitting the go-kart racing despite being warned about the noise nuisance.

(f) On the other hand, in *Blake v Galloway* [2004] 1 WLR 2844 CA the defendant was held not liable in negligence for the claimant's serious eye injury caused by the throwing of a piece of tree bark during good-natured and high-spirited horseplay[100]. This was because of the tacit understanding that the claimant impliedly consented to a risk of a blow to any part of his body, provided the object was thrown 'without [gross] negligence and without intent to cause injury'[101]. In other words, there is still a duty of care in horseplay but to found liability the claimant has to prove 'recklessness or a very high degree of carelessness'[102].

---

[100] A friendly snowball fight would come into this category.
[101] At para 24 of the judgment of Dyson LJ.
[102] Ibid. para 16 of the judgment of Dyson LJ.

## 12-27   Access to club and nuisance

It may be the case that the club has a right of way which is used as a means of access to the club. If the right is created by grant, the class of persons who are entitled to use it may be expressly defined or limited in the terms of the deed; but a grant of this nature must be construed, not strictly, but in accordance with the intention of the parties. Thus in *Baxendale v North Lambeth Liberal and Radical Club* [1902] 2 Ch 427 the court held that the right of way granted to the club was exercisable by all persons lawfully going to and from the club, which included the members of the club, the associate members, tradespeople and employees of the club, and that this user was reasonable. If there is an excessive use of the right of way, however, it may become an actionable nuisance.

## 12-28   Occupiers' liability

At common law an occupier's liability was based on the tort of negligence. In 1957 the Occupiers' Liability Act was passed whereby a 'common duty of care' was substituted for the common law rules. Section 2 of the Act states:

(1)  An occupier of premises owes the same duty, the 'common duty of care', to all his visitors, except insofar as he is free to and does extend, restrict, modify or exclude his duty to any visitors by agreement or otherwise.
(2)  The common duty of care is a duty to take such care to see that the visitor will be reasonably safe in using the premises for the purposes for which he is invited or permitted by the occupier to be there.

**12-29**   *Who is an occupier*   The Act does not define an occupier and so the pre-1957 rules govern this point. It includes owner-occupiers[103] and lessees[104] and other persons provided they have sufficient control over the premises to ensure their safety and to appreciate that a failure of their part to use care may result in injury to a person coming on them[105]. If the club were to hire out its premises for a particular occasion to a third party it is considered that it would still remain the occupier for the purposes of the Act although, in the absence of an express term in the hiring, the club does not warrant the premises are suitable for the purpose for which they are hired[106]. Conversely, it is

---

[103]    See *Clerk and Lindsell on Torts* (18th edn, 2000) para 10-08.
[104]    *Wheat v E Lacon & Co Ltd* [1966] AC 552 per Lord Denning at 577 to 579 but it excludes the landlord even if he has undertaken the obligation to repair. The landlord, however, may have duties under the Defective Premises Act 1972: see **12-34** below.
[105]    See *Wheats'* case at 579A.
[106]    *Wheeler v Trustees of St Mary's Hall, Chislehurst* (1989) *The Times,* 10 October.

considered that the club in the ordinary course of events would not become the occupier of premises which it hired from someone else for its own club activities.

**12-30** An unincorporated members' club cannot be held liable as occupier because it is not a legal person[107]. If the club premises are vested in trustees, it is they who will be treated as occupiers and will be the defendants to any action[108]. The managing committee does not owe a duty of care to visitors on club premises[109]. The members as a whole may be considered the occupiers[110], but this must be on the basis that each member as an individual owed a duty of care to visitors, and this is very unlikely in fact. But what happens in the case of a club with no trustees but which occupies premises? The logical conclusion, if the above statements are correct, is that there will be no occupier for the purposes of the Act. As this is an absurdity, it is considered that the courts will strive to attach liability to someone, and since some person or persons must in fact have the responsibility of keeping the club premises in good repair, those persons may well be held to have a personal duty of care to visitors[111].

**12-31** *Who is a visitor* The duty of care is owed to visitors but the Occupiers' Liability Act 1957 does not define a visitor and so the pre-1957 rules govern this point too. Visitors are those who would have been treated as invitees or licensees at common law. Permission to enter the club premises may be express or implied. Permission to enter may be given by an employee of the occupier but what if the employee had no authority to give permission to enter or, worse still, gave permission contrary to his instructions? The answer lies in the application of the rules relating to vicarious liability[112]. One curious point should be noted. An independent contractor (eg a building contractor) may be an occupier of club premises as well as the club itself[113]. Suppose the building contractor against the club's instructions invites a person on to the premises who is then injured. Is that person

---

[107]    *Verrall v Hackney Borough Council* [1983] QB 445 CA at 461 G (May LJ).
[108]    *Clerk and Lindsell on Torts* (18th edn, 2000) para 10-11.
[109]    See *Robertson v Ridley* [1989] 1 WLR 872 CA (where the plaintiff-member was suing his own club) discussed at **5-44** above.
[110]    *Grice v Stourport Tennis, Hockey and Squash Club* [1997] 9 CL 592 CA (where the plaintiff-member was suing his own club). Clerk and Lindsell, op. cit. at para 10-11 casts serious doubt on the correctness of this decision.
[111]    See *Prole v Allen* [1950] 1 All ER 476 (where the plaintiff-member was suing his own club) discussed at **5-45** above.
[112]    See para **12-19** above.
[113]    *Wheat v E Lacon & Co Ltd* [1966] AC 552; *AMF International Ltd v Magnet Bowling Ltd* [1968] 1 WLR 1028 at 1052B.

a visitor or trespasser? The answer is that he will be a trespasser *vis-à-vis* the club but a visitor *vis-à-vis* the contractor and liability will be decided accordingly[114].

**12-32** Whether a visitor remains a lawful visitor on club premises for the entirety of his stay can raise nice points of argument. A licence to enter is often a restricted one, that is, limited to those parts which it may be reasonably supposed the visitor will go. A visitor who strays into other parts of the club, say the kitchen, and is injured there may find himself without remedy[115], although an involuntary or accidental straying will not convert a lawful visitor into a trespasser[116]. Further, a visit to a club would normally include an invitation to use the lavatory and a visitor remains a lawful visitor if he strays whilst making a reasonable search for it[117]. A licence to enter can always be revoked, but a visitor does not become a trespasser until he has had a reasonable time in which to leave[118].

**12-33** *Trespassers* At common law a trespasser on to other people's property did so at his own risk[119]. But trespassers are not all malevolent and a rambler or a child might innocently wander on to someone's land and injure himself. So in 1984 the Occupiers' Liability Act was passed whereby a limited statutory duty of care replaced the common law rules. An occupier owes a duty of care to trespassers if is aware of any danger on his property or has reasonable grounds to believe it exists; and he knows or has reasonable grounds to believe that trespassers may be in the vicinity of the danger; and it poses a risk against which he may reasonably be expected to offer some protection[120].

---

[114]  *Ferguson v Welsh* [1987] 1 WLR 1553.
[115]  *Lee v Luper* [1936] 3 All ER 817; *Mason v Langford* [1888] 4 TLR 407.
[116]  *Braithwaite v South Durham Steel Co* [1958] 1 WLR 986.
[117]  *Gould v McAuliffe* [1941] 2 All ER 527.
[118]  *Robson v Hallett* [1967] 2 QB 939. And see *Stone v Taffe* [1974] 1 WLR 1575 CA.
[119]  *Robert Adie & Sons (Colleries) Ltd v Dumbrek* [1929] AC 358 (defendant had no liability to trespassing child killed by unguarded machinery). But see *British Railways Board v Herrington* [1972] AC 877 (where the House of Lords held that landowners did in fact owe a limited duty of care to trespassers).
[120]  S. 1(3) of the Act. See the trio of trespassing swimmers' cases: *Ratcliff v McConnell* [1999] 1 WLR 670; *Donoghue v Folkestone Properties Ltd* [2003] QB 1008 CA; and *Tomlinson v Congleton Borough Council* [2003] 3 WLR 705 HL.

## 12-34  Landlord's liability

A landlord is not an occupier and had no liability at common law for any defect in the property which he had leased to a tenant[121]. Here again Parliament stepped in and in 1972 passed the Defective Premises Act which provides a statutory remedy against the landlord in certain cases. Section 3 abolished the common law rule by virtue of which vendors and lessors of land were held immune from liability for negligence in building or other work carried out on the land before the sale or letting. And section 4 imposes a duty of care on a landlord for defects in the state of the premises which he has let and where he has an obligation or right to remedy such defects. The duty is to take such care as is reasonable in all the circumstances to see that the tenant and all those who might be affected by the defect are reasonably safe from personal injury or damage to their property. This duty arises when the landlord is put on notice that the defect exists[122].

## 12-35  Land and buildings adjoining highways

An occupier of land and buildings which adjoin or are close to a highway has an obligation not to use his land, or to allow his land or buildings to get into such a condition, as to amount to a nuisance[123]. Thus in *Tarry v Ashton* [1876] 1 QBD 314 the occupier of a building was held liable in nuisance when the lamp attached to the building and overhanging the pavement fell down and injured a passer-by. A tree on the occupier's land is not a nuisance merely because its branches overhang the  highway[124], but if the overhanging branches hinder or obstruct the reasonable use of the highway, this will be a nuisance[125]. The club may also be liable in nuisance for damage caused to neighbouring property by the encroaching roots of its tree; the principle here 'can be summed up in the proposition that, where there is a continuing nuisance of which the defendant knew or ought to have known, reasonable remedial expenditure may be recovered by the owner who has had to incur it' [126].

---

[121]   *Cavalier v Pope* [1906] AC 428.
[122]   Defective Premises Act 1972, s. 4(2).
[123]   E.g. see the cases of *Bolton, Castle* and *Hilder* cited in **12-25** and **12-26** above.
[124]   *Noble v Harrison* [1926] KB 332.
[125]   *Hale v Hants and Dorset Motor Services* [1947] 2 All ER 628.
[126]   *Delaware Mansion Ltd v Westminster City Council* [2002] 1 AC 321 at 335E (Lord Cooke of Thorndon).

## 12-36   Injuries at sport

Many clubs are sporting clubs whose activities include the playing of physically competitive sports such as rugby football. These activities should command the special attention of managing committees (and of course the attention of the governing bodies of the sports in question). The sports rules will be framed so as to minimise the element of danger and the risk of physical injury. In *Vowles v Evans* [2003] 1 WLR 1607 CA the claimant was an amateur rugby player with the Llanharan Rugby Football Club; he was playing in a match as hooker when the scrum collapsed, causing him serious injuries which rendered him paraplegic[127]. He sued the referee, the Welsh Rugby Union (who conceded they were vicariously liable for the referee whom they had appointed) and the chairman and secretary of his club. The referee and the Union were found guilty of negligence, but not the club. The Court of Appeal, upholding the judge, approved[128] the general statement of law put forward by Gleeson CJ in an Australian case also involving rugby football, *Agar v Hyde* [2000] 201 CLR 552, as follows:

> After all, opposing players can already sue each other for intentionally and negligently inflicted injuries[129]; they can sue the referee for negligent failure to enforce the rules; and the sports administrator that dons the mantle of an occupier assumes well established duties of care towards players, spectators and (in the case of golf clubs) neighbours. A duty of care is not negated merely because participation in the sport is voluntary.

**12-37**   In *Smoldon v Whitworth* [1997] PIQR 133, another case of an injured hooker, the Court of Appeal explained the nature of the referee's duty to the players; Lord Bingham of Cornhill CJ stated at 138:

> The level of care required is that which is appropriate in all the circumstances, and the circumstances are of crucial importance. Full account must be taken of the factual context in which a referee exercises his functions, and he could not be properly held liable for errors of judgment, oversights or lapses of which any referee might be guilty in the context of a fast-moving and vigorous contest. The threshold of liability is a high one. It will not be easily crossed.

The important message of the above cases is that clubs should make

---

[127]   His primary complaint against the referee was his failure to insist on non-contestable scrummages on finding that there was no specialist prop forward to replace an injured prop forward.

[128]   At 1615B.

[129]   See *Condon v Basi* [1985] 1 WLR 866 CA.

sure that referees and umpires who control their games and matches are properly trained, graded and appointed, and also properly insured in respect of their activities.

## 12-38   Safety of spectators

Apart from the question of the occupiers' liability[130] and the question of the safety of players[131], there is the allied question of spectators' safety which should command the attention of managing committees. One starts off with the proposition that spectators who come to watch sports or competitions will appreciate that watching may involve a risk that they may be injured. Although it may not be possible to eradicate every element of danger, spectators are entitled to assume that the club in permitting spectators has given proper thought to their safety. In *Hall v Brooklands Auto Racing Club* [1933] 1 KB 205 CA the spectator-plaintiff was injured when two cars, travelling at some 100mph, nudged one another and caused one vehicle to somersault and fall into the spectators' enclosure. There was nothing wrong with the track or the barriers and no accident like it had happened in the 23 years of the existence of the defendant club owner. The plaintiff lost his action in negligence against the club. Likewise, in *Wooldridge v Sumner* [1963] 2 QB 43 CA the spectator-plaintiff lost his action in negligence against the horseman of experience and skill in respect of injuries suffered when his galloping horse deviated from the course and knocked down the plaintiff[132]. In that case Sellers LJ said:

> But provided the competition or game is being performed within the rules and the requirement of the sport and by a person of adequate skill and competence the spectator does not expect his safety to be regarded by a participant.

That principle was expressed by Diplock LJ in the same case as follows:

> A person attending a game or competition takes the risk of any damage caused to him by any act of a participant done in the course of and for the purpose of the game or competition notwithstanding that such act may involve an error of judgment or a lapse of skill, unless the participant's conduct is such as to evince a reckless disregard of the spectator's safety[133].

---

[130]    See **12-28** above.
[131]    See **12-36** above.
[132]    The plaintiff had also unsuccessfully sued the British Horse Society under the Occupier's Liability Act 1957.
[133]    See also *Wilks v Cheltenham Homeguard Motor Cycle and Light Car Club* [1971] 1 WLR 668 CA (where the spectator-plaintiff unsuccessfully sued a motorcyclist for negligently injuring him during a motorcycle scramble when the motorcyclist inexplicably left the course and went into the spectators).

Here perhaps the important message for the club is that it should instil into its membership a desire to win, but not to win at all costs, and club rules should be framed to cater for unacceptable behaviour in a game or competition. Obtaining insurance to guard against the risk of injury to spectators is also sensible; the risk of injury may be small but the potential damages may be great and the smallness of the risk will no doubt be reflected in the amount of the insurance premium.

## 12-39  Exclusion of liability

It will be recalled from paragraph **12-28** above that an occupier can exclude or restrict his liability to his visitors 'by agreement or otherwise'. A suitably worded disclaimer of liability in an appropriate place or document, whereby the occupier gives explicit warning of a danger, may suffice in discharging the occupier's duty of care[134]. Exclusion of liability by contract is permissible but may be subject to the restrictions set out in the Unfair Contract Terms Act 1977. Business occupiers are prohibited from excluding or restricting their liability for death or personal injury[135] and can only exclude or restrict their liability for damage to a visitor's property if the contract or the notice satisfies the requirement of reasonableness[136]. Residential or private occupiers are exempt from these provisions, save where the visitor contracts on the club's 'written standard terms of business'; here any exclusion or restriction of liability must satisfy the requirement of reasonableness[137]. Whether a club is a business occupier may not always be an easy question to answer. The Act does not define what is a business. In *Addiscombe Garden Estates v Crabbe* [1958] 1 QB 513[138] the Shirley Park Lawn Tennis Club Limited was registered under the Industrial and Provident Societies Act 1893 and its objects were to carry on the business of a lawn tennis club. The plaintiff purported to give a written licence to Mr Crabbe and the other trustees of the club to use its tennis courts and clubhouse. The Court of Appeal, upholding the judge, held that the trustees on behalf of the club had

---

[134]     *White v Blackmore* [1972] 2 QB 651 CA at 670 (Buckley LJ) and 674 (Roskill LJ) (where the widow of a spectator killed at a jalopy car racing circuit, by reason of the defective arrangement of ropes fencing off the track, lost her action because of a notice absolving the organisers from liability for personal injury, fatal or otherwise, 'howsoever caused to spectators'). Lord Denning MR at 659 delivered a powerful dissenting judgment.

[135]     Unfair Contract Terms Act 1977, s. 2(1).

[136]     Ibid. s. 2(2).

[137]     Ibid. s. 3.

[138]     The reader might wonder why the trustees were sued and not the club itself which was a body corporate. Presumably this was because the plaintiff was relying on a documentary licence made with the four individual trustees, and not with the club itself.

in reality been granted a tenancy agreement and that it was a *business* tenancy protected by Part II of the Landlord and Tenant Act 1954. The club was no doubt a private members' club and it seems unlikely that the legislature was intending to include such a club as a business occupier within the meaning of the Unfair Contract Terms Act 1977 but the point is not beyond argument.

## 12-40  Contributory negligence

Where a club is found to be in breach of a duty of care, the fact that the claimant's own negligence contributed to the damage in question will result in an apportionment of damages according to the fault on either side[139]. In other words, the claimant will have failed to take reasonable care for his own safety and thus contributed to his own damage[140]. This doctrine will apply to all cases in the tort of negligence but it is an undecided question whether it applies in the tort of nuisance[141]. The point is not merely of academic interest. There has been more than one instance of a person erecting say a greenhouse near to the boundary of a sports or golf club in the knowledge that balls do or might escape on to his land and thereby damage his greenhouse but he has gone ahead anyway and built it. Coming to the nuisance is no defence to the nuisance[142] but *knowingly* coming to it may eventually persuade a court to construe the provisions of the Law Reform (Contributory Negligence) Act 1945 so as to include within its ambit any tort except where there was intentional wrongdoing[143].

## 12-41  Dishonesty and fraud

The question sometimes arises whether the club is liable for the dishonest or fraudulent acts of its employees. Suppose an employee goes into the club's changing room and steals a member's valuable

---

[139]    Section 1(1) of the Law Reform (Contributory Negligence) Act 1945.
[140]    *Nance v British Columbia Railway* [1951] AC 601 PC at 611 (Lord Simon).
[141]    See *Clerk and Lindsell on Torts* (18th edn, 2000) para 3-30.
[142]    *Sturges v Bridgman* [1979] 11 Ch D 852.
[143]    See *Miller v Jackson* [1977] QB 966 where Lane LJ said at 986, 'It does not seem just that a long established activity, in itself innocuous, should be brought to an end because someone else chooses to build a house nearby and so turn an innocent pastime into an actionable nuisance'. As to intentional wrongdoing, see *Standard Chartered Bank v Pakistan National Shipping Corporation (Nos. 2 and 4)* [2003] 1 AC 959 at para 18 of Lord Hoffman's opinion (no defence of contributory negligence available where a director was held personally liable for a fraudulent misrepresentation which he had made on behalf of the company).

watch. Is the club liable to make good the loss? As a general rule an employer is not liable for his employee's dishonest conduct unless the wrongful act was committed in the course of employment. But, it might be asked, how can theft ever be within the scope of anyone's employment? The answer at law lies in whether the goods have been entrusted to the employee for safe keeping: if yes, the theft was committed in the course of employment[144]; if no, the employee was acting outside his employment and the employer has no liability. Thus in the example of the stolen watch, if it had been the changing room attendant who stole the watch, the club would be liable to the owner, but if say it had been an opportunistic club chef it would escape liability. It should be pointed out that the employer's liability for the misconduct of his employee does not depend on showing that the employer in some way benefited from the dishonesty or fraud; the employer may be liable if the employee intended solely to benefit himself[145].

## 12-42   Defamation

The tort of defamation consists of libel and slander; in broad terms the distinction between the two is that libel is defamation in permanent form (e.g. written words) whereas slander is in transitory form (eg spoken words)[146]. A defamatory statement is one which is untrue and likely to disparage in a substantial way a third person; in other words, it is the tort which protects one's reputation and good name. It is an area of the law whose complexities and absurdities have often been criticised[147], although recent attempts have been made to rationalise and simplify it[148]. What amounts to a defamatory statement is hard to pin down. Generally speaking, if the words complained of cause a person to be hated or despised or ridiculed or cause others to shun or avoid him or to lower him in the estimation of other, right-thinking persons, they can be said to be actionable statements. But times change and whereas in 1846 it was held defamatory of a person to publish a statement that he had been blackballed on seeking admission to a

---

[144]     *Morris v C W Martin & Sons Ltd* [1966] 1 QB 716 (dry cleaning employers held liable for theft of a fur coat entrusted to the employee for cleaning); *Nahhas v Pier House (Cheyne Walk) Management* (1984) *The Times*, 10 February (company held liable for thefts committed by its porter when he burgled a flat in the block using keys entrusted to his custody).

[145]     *Lloyd v Grace, Smith & Co* [1912] AC 716.

[146]     *Gatley on Libel and Slander* (10th edn, 2004) para 1.3.

[147]     E.g. *Morrell v International Publishing Co* [1989] 3 All ER 733 per May LJ at 734.

[148]     E.g. *Lucas-Box v News Group Ltd* [1986] 1 WLR 147 CA; and the Defamation Act 1996.

club[149], such a statement might not be considered defamatory today[150]. And in another old case, *Robinson v Jermyn* [1814] 1 Price 11 it was held that it was not necessarily defamatory for the proprietors of the Cassino Club in Southwold to post a notice in the club in that the two plaintiffs had been excluded from a particular room in the club, 'not being persons that the proprietors or the annual subscribers think it proper to associate with'. The court said that the notice did not mean that these persons were unfit for general society (which was the substance of the plaintiffs' allegation) but only unfit as members of that club.

**12-43**   What would happen if the club's secretary had circulated a written notice to the local newspapers that wrongly stated that the claimant in a libel action had been expelled from membership of the club for misconduct[151]? In essence, a defence will lie if the defendant justifies the statement (that is, he agrees it is or may be defamatory but asserts that it is true and therefore not libellous); or the defendant can make a plea of 'fair comment' (that is, he agrees the statement is or may be defamatory but the words complained of are fair comment on a matter of public interest); or the defendant can make a plea of privilege (that is, he agrees that the statement is or may be defamatory but he asserts that he had a legitimate interest or duty in publishing the statement and the person to whom it was communicated had a corresponding interest or duty to receive it). Unless it is covered by 'absolute' privilege, the privilege referred to is 'qualified' because it can be destroyed by malice (that is, knowingly abusing the privileged occasion). All these defences are highly technical. Also should be noted the offer to make amends introduced by the Defamation Act 1996 which came into effect on 28 February 2000 and which may now be pleaded by way of defence[152].

**12-44**   The committee should beware of posting contentious notices in the clubhouse, say that A or B or C are defaulters in the payment of their subscriptions. This may well be a hostage to fortune since one or more of the non-payers may take umbrage and cause a row in the club or they may assert the notice is a defamatory and libellous statement. Notice of default is best sent direct to the home of the member in question so that there is no question of publication to third parties. It is not unknown too for a mischievous or an aggrieved

---

[149]   *O'Brien v Clement* [1846] 16 M & W 159.
[150]   *Gatley on Libel and Slander* op cit para 2.19.
[151]   As happened in *Birne v National Sporting League* (1957) *The Times*, 12 April.
[152]   Defamation Act 1996, ss. 2–4 and CPR PD53 paras 3.1 to 3.3.

member to put up on a club notice board a derogatory statement, say, about a fellow member with whom he has fallen out or whom he thinks is carrying on an improper relationship with his wife. Let us assume the notice is both defamatory and libellous. Is the club or the committee in any way liable to the member who has been defamed? The answer is set out below in the next two paragraphs.

**12-45**  An action for libel will not lie against an unincorporated members' club in its collective name since it does not constitute a legal person whereby it can publish or authorise the publication of a libel[153]. (For the same reason such a club cannot bring a libel action against somebody[154].) The persons who will be liable are those who authorised or directed its publication[155]. In *Birne v National Sporting League* (1957) *The Times*, 12 April the plaintiff-bookmaker had been expelled from the league but wrongfully so. The secretary of the league published the fact of expulsion. The judge found the secretary had acted with malice on a privileged occasion and the committee and the proprietor of the league were held liable to the plaintiff because they had given the secretary a free hand and the principals were liable for the malice of their agent. On the other hand, in *Longdon-Griffiths v Smith* [1951] 1 KB 295 the four trustees of the National Deposit Friendly Society published on a privileged occasion a report which was defamatory of the plaintiff, who was the society's general secretary. One of the trustees was actuated by malice. This did not destroy the privilege of the other three trustees. The case of *Egger v Viscount Chelmsford* [1965] 1 QB 248 CA involved the Kennel Club, which is an unincorporated members' club. The secretary of the club's show regulations committee published a letter defamatory of the plaintiff. Here five members of the committee were held to have been actuated by malice but not the remaining four members whose defence of qualified privilege succeeded[156]. In addition, the secretary who wrote the letter was not guilty of malice and this was an independent defence since an innocent agent is not liable for the malice of his principal.

**12-46**  Suppose, however, the committee had no idea that the derogatory statement referred to in **12-44** above had been put on the club notice board but it then becomes aware of it. Up to the time of its knowledge of the statement, the committee will have the defence

---

153     *London Association v Greenlands* [1916] AC 15.
154     *Electrical [etc] Union v Times Newspapers Ltd* [1980] 1 WLR 98.
155     *Mercantile Marine v Toms* [1916] 2 KB 243 CA at 246–247.
156     It is important to realise that the four innocent committee members were not tortfeasors at all; the privilege attaches to the individual publisher, not to the publication.

of innocent dissemination[157]. But is the committee liable if it does nothing about it and lets it remain on the club notice board? The answer is that once the committee has become aware of the statement, it will have a reasonable opportunity to check its contents before deciding whether to remove the statement[158]. If the committee then decide to let it stay, and it subsequently turns out to be libellous, the committee will have been guilty of authorising its publication, and therefore liable to the defamed member[159]. The immediate removal of the statement is plainly the safest course.

## 12-47   Protecting the committee

The answer lies in insuring the committee against tortious liability. The insurance  should include cover for the consequences of the fraudulent or dishonest conduct of the club members or its employees, where such consequences are visited upon the club itself and the club as a whole has played no part in the fraudulent or dishonest conduct.

## 12-48   Protecting the member

There are occasions when it will be proper to spend club funds on insurance premiums to obtain insurance cover in order to protect the member against tortious liability. A clear example relates to the activities of members who are referees and umpires in sports clubs[160]. It would be a financial calamity for the member if as a rugby referee he was held liable in negligence in relation to a collapsed scrum which resulted in paraplegic injury to the hooker[161] and he then faced the prospect of paying the damages out of his own monies. Indeed, we consider that the committee might be in dereliction of its duties in managing the club's affairs if it failed to consider the insuring of its members against claims for negligence, especially if it was common knowledge that the members' activities, though lawful, entailed a risk of injury to persons or damage to property.

---

[157]   Now to be found in s. 1 of the Defamation Act 1996.
[158]   See *Gatley on Libel and Slander* (10th edn, 2004) para 6.25.
[159]   *Godfrey v Demon Internet Ltd* [2001] QB 201.
[160]   See **Appendix 13** for a set of rules which gives an express power to the committee to insure the activities of its members.
[161]   See *Vowles v Evans* [2003] 1 WLR 1607 CA cited in **12-36** above.

# 10.  COMPLIANCE WITH DISABILITY LEGISLATION

### 12-49   Temporary admission of members of the public

If the club is providing goods, facilities or services to the public or a section of the public, the sex and disability discrimination legislation will apply when it comes to the admission of members of the public into the club. An example would be a golf club: suppose two competent golfers, who both belonged to a recognised golf club and who were visiting the neighbourhood, arrived at the clubhouse at the same time and sought to play there as associates, as permitted by the club rules. The visitors would be green-fee-paying members of the public. One was a man, the other was a woman. In these circumstances it would be unlawful for the club to permit the admission of the man but not the woman simply because she was a woman. Now suppose that the male visitor was disabled and could not carry his clubs around the golf course except by a motorised buggy. In the absence of any reasons related to personal safety the disabled player has to be allowed to use his buggy[162]. Similarly, guests of members (i.e. those who have been invited in accordance with club rules) are a section of the public; thus a member's guest who used a wheelchair and who was unable to obtain access to the club's dining room, and was thereby deprived of the society of his host at this particular location, would have a legitimate complaint under the Act.

**12-50**   On 1 October 2004 the provisions of Part 3 of the Disability Discrimination Act 1995 came into force. This deals with discrimination other than in employment. This means, in simple terms, that clubs which provide (whether or not for payment) facilities for entertainment, recreation or refreshment to the public (or to a section of the public) will have to be more 'user-friendly' towards disabled people. The duty is as follows: where the club has a practice, policy or procedure which makes it impossible or unreasonably difficult for disabled persons to make use of such facilities which the club provides, or is prepared to provide, to members of the public, it is the club's duty to take reasonable steps to change its practice, policy or procedure to ensure that disabled persons can use the facilities[163]. The Act goes on to explain[164] that where a physical feature (for example, one arising from the design or construction of a building or the approach or access

---

[162]     See **4-11**(4) footnote 17 below.
[163]     Disability Discrimination Act 1995, s. 21(1).
[164]     Ibid. s. 21(2).

to premises) makes it impossible or unreasonably difficult for disabled persons to make use of such facilities, it is the club's duty to take reasonable steps :

(1) to remove the feature;
(2) to alter it so that it no longer has that effect;
(3) to provide a reasonable means of avoiding the feature; or
(4) to provide a reasonable alternative method of making the facility in question available to disabled persons.

**12-51**  This duty is tempered by other provisions of the Act which state that the club as the provider of facilities is not obliged, in making adjustments, to take any steps which would fundamentally alter the nature of the facilities it provides or the nature of its business[165], or which would cause it to incur expenditure exceeding the prescribed maximum[166], which will be calculated according to various criteria and contained in regulations[167]. Quite how this will work in practice remains to be seen. In addition, any discriminatory conduct may be justified on various grounds such as the danger to health and safety (including that of the disabled person)[168], the incapacity of the disabled person to give an informed consent to (reasonable) discrimination[169], and the preservation of the facilities for other, non-disabled occupiers in another part of the same building[170].

## 11.  WORKING MEN'S CLUBS

**12-52**  The member's liability in tort is the same as applies to an unincorporated members' club.

## 12.  IPSA CLUBS

**12-53**  The member's liability in tort is akin to that of an incorporated members' club save that IPSA clubs have no directors, only officers and members.

---

[165]    Disability Discrimination Act 1995, s. 21(6). See also the Disability Discrimination (Services and Premises) Regulations 1996 (SI 1996/1836) and 1999 (SI 1999/1191); and the Disability Discrimination (Providers of Services) (Adjustment of Premises) Regulations 2001 (SI 2001/3253).
[166]    Ibid. s. 21(7).
[167]    Ibid. s. 21(8). No regulations have as yet (2004) been drafted.
[168]    Ibid. s. 24(3)(a). For example, the justification might be wet weather precluding the use of buggies or wheeled trolleys since they might damage the golf course. Another example of justification might be that the layout of the golf course was such that it was physically impossible to provide safe pathways for the use of buggies or trolleys.
[169]    Ibid. s. 24(3)(b).
[170]    Ibid. s. 24(3)(c) and (d). This justification only applies to 'small premises' as defined in s. 23(4) and (5).

## 13.   INCORPORATED MEMBERS' CLUBS

**12-54**   Of the three propositions set out in paragraph **12-18** above, the first one does not apply and, as regards the third one, it needs to be reformulated as follows:

> 'the club, being a legal person, will potentially be vicariously liable for the acts or omissions of those persons (whether employees or members of the club) who were acting in the course of their employment or acting in a manner authorised by the club'.

In all other respects the principles set out in **12-18** to **12-46** above, which apply to determine the tortious liability of unincorporated clubs, apply equally well to incorporated ones, save that the legal personality of an incorporated club makes a substantial difference in defamation cases: see **12-56** below.

### 12-55   The director's liability

In normal situations it is the club which will be liable for any tort committed and the director will have no liability[171] but there are exceptions. The director will be personally liable (as well as the company) if he makes a fraudulent misrepresentation on behalf of the company: *Standard Chartered Bank v Pakistan National Shipping Corporation (Nos. 2 and 4)* [2003] 1 AC 959. And if a director exercises control other than through the board of directors, he may become a joint tortfeasor with the company: *MCA Records Inc v Charly Records Ltd* [2003] 1 BCLC 93 CA (director successfully personally sued for procuring breaches of copyright by his company).

### 12-56   Defamation

In *Electrical, Electronic, Telecommunication and Plumbing Union v Times Newspapers Ltd* [1980] 3 WLR 98 Mr Justice O'Connor at 101 put the legal position succinctly in respect of a corporate body suing for libel:

> So you have got to [have legal] personality which is capable of being defamed before a plaintiff can bring an action for libel. Of an individual there is no difficulty; so too a corporate body. That is an extensive term which is just as well to have in mind. Corporate bodies are of a very much wider variety than most people think. The obvious example with which we are all familiar is a limited company, but there are a wide variety of corporate bodies which have been set up by charter, by special Act of

---

[171]   *Williams v Natural Life Health Foods Ltd* [1998] 1 WLR 830 HL.

Parliament, by letters patent and so forth, and they all have corporate existence; and again, the law is clear, that a corporate body has a personality which can be defamed and it can bring an action in its own name for the libel on itself.

By the same reasoning an incorporated club can be sued for any libel which it has published or authorised to be published.

## 14.  PROPRIETARY CLUBS

**12-57**   Apart from the individual member who is the actual tortfeasor and liable as such (see proposition no.2 in **12-18** above), it is the proprietor who shoulders the burden of vicarious liability, not the members or the committee in a proprietary club. It would also appear that, unlike in an unincorporated members' club[172], the proprietor does warrant to the member that his club premises are safe to use because the proprietor will have admitted the member for reward[173].

---

[172]   See **5-43** above.
[173]   *Shore v Ministry of Works* [1950] 2 All ER 228 at 232E (Jenkins LJ).

# Chapter 13

## LANDLORD AND TENANT RELATIONSHIPS

## 1.  INTRODUCTION

**13-01**  Members' clubs are sometimes the owner of valuable freehold property, commonly their clubhouse and perhaps some surrounding land. Some clubs may have the opportunity to lease some part of their premises or property to a third party to produce income, on some occasions to a residential user, on other occasions to a business user. Other clubs may lease their club premises from a freeholder or from a landlord who himself has a superior landlord. Some clubs may want to house employees whose accommodation goes with the job; these clubs need to know the difference between a tenancy and a licence, or what sort of tenancy agreement will best suit the club. Because of its activities it will be seen that a club needs to know about business tenancies. A lease will contain 'the usual covenants' if the lease is silent on the point, and other covenants too, and the club needs to know what they mean or entail. Over the centuries the common law has evolved many rules regulating the landlord and tenant relationship, such as the remedy of forfeiture, but Parliament throughout the twentieth century brought in more and more statutory codes regulating residential tenancies both in the public and the private sector, and regulating business tenancies. These codes usually had the aim of restricting the landlord's right to terminate a tenancy. It has been remarked in relation to residential tenancies that, 'There is no doubt that the present situation is unnecessarily complicated and is overdue for reform'[1]. If in doubt as to its legal position, it is strongly recommended that a club should seek legal advice when dealing with club property in order to safeguard its assets and to understand fully its legal position.

---

[1]    *Blackstone's Civil Practice* 2004, chap 85, para 85.1.

## 2.    LEASES

**13-02**    There are possible only two legal estates in land, freehold and leasehold estates. In legal language the former is called 'a fee simple absolute in possession' and is the greater estate and the latter is called 'a term of years absolute' and is the lesser estate[2]. In reality the freehold estate gives absolute ownership of land[3] whereas the leasehold estate creates an interest in land for a fixed period of maximum duration. A term of years is normally called a lease or a tenancy (which terms are interchangeable). It does not matter whether the period is fixed and therefore self-determining, or periodic and therefore capable of renewal. There is no doubt that the lease plays an important part in both the social and economic affairs of the country; hence the frequency of the business tenancy, the residential lease and agricultural holdings.

**13-03**    With certain exceptions[4] the lease must be contained in a formal document[5]. It is the essence of a lease that the tenant should be given exclusive possession of the property[6], which differentiates it from a licence, although the dividing line between the two is sometimes a fine one[7]. A lease creates not only an estate in land (i.e. is binding against all the world) but is also a contract between the landlord and the tenant[8], for example, the tenant's covenant (promise) to pay rent or the landlord's covenant to carry out structural repairs.

**13-04**    As to formalities, an unincorporated members' club cannot hold property in its own name[9]. This means that trustees must be appointed to hold property, both freehold and leasehold, belonging to the club. A literary and scientific institution and a working men's club must hold all its property in trustees' names[10]. An IPSA club and an incorporated members' club can hold property in its own name

---

[2]    Law of Property Act 1925, s. 1.

[3]    In passing should be mentioned Part 1 of the Commonhold and Leasehold Reform Act 2002 which was implemented by regulations on 27 September 2004. The main feature of commonhold is that it provides a vehicle for freehold ownership of buildings or land where there are common parts held by a commonhold association (ie the entity which owns the freehold of the common land).

[4]    The most important exception is a lease for a term not exceeding three years (Law of Property Act 1925, ss. 52(2)(d), 54(2)).

[5]    *Crago v Julian* [1992] 1 WLR 372 CA at 376C (Nicholls V-C).

[6]    *Street v Mountford* [1985] AC 809.

[7]    See **13-39** below.

[8]    *City of London Corporation v Fell* [1994] 1 AC 458.

[9]    See **5-15** above.

[10]    Literary and Scientific Institutions Act 1854, s. 19; Friendly Societies Act [1974], s. 54.

because they are legal persons, but it is common for it to be held in the name of specially appointed trustees.

## 3.    RESIDENTIAL TENANCIES

**13-05**    In the private sector there are two statutory codes, one under the Rent Act 1977 and the other under the Housing Act 1988 as amended by the Housing Act 1996, the main difference being the high level of security granted to the tenant under the former code and the much lower level of security which is possible under the latter code.

## 4.    RENT ACT 1977

**13-06**    This Act will generally only apply to tenancies created before 15 January 1989. In view of this, it is likely that a club will be concerned only with the residential situation under the Housing Acts 1988 to 1996 and in particular with the form of tenancy called the assured shorthold tenancy. We can therefore limit our discussion to saying that under the Rent Act 1997 the tenant, once any contractual tenancy has been determined, has a personal *protected* status which means that the landlord can only recover possession via a court procedure by proving by one or more of the permitted statutory grounds for obtaining possession and  then in relation to some of the grounds persuading the court that it is reasonable to make the order for possession.

## 5.    HOUSING ACTS 1988–1996

**13-07**    The Housing Act 1988 created assured tenancies and assured shorthold tenancies, the latter having much less security than the former. Originally the only way of creating the latter was by serving a valid section 20 notice (which set out important information for the tenant) *before* the agreement was entered into. In the absence of a valid notice the tenancy defaulted to an assured tenancy. The Act of 1988 was amended because so many landlords and their agents got the documentation wrong, which meant there was an ever increasing number of occupiers with a high degree of security. Since 28 February 1997 the default tenancy has been an assured shorthold tenancy (usually referred to by its abbreviated name of shorthold tenancy) which cannot be determined before the expiry of six months (save under a section 8 ground) but which otherwise gives no security of tenure and which requires no formality, and hence this type of tenancy has become very popular with landlords.

**13-08** It is important to realise that the shorthold tenancy works the other way round than hitherto: a tenancy will automatically be a shorthold tenancy unless the landlord serves a notice in the prescribed form on the tenant either before or during the course of the tenancy that he is granting an assured tenancy[11]. The difference between the two is considerable in practice: under the assured tenancy the landlord can only obtain possession by proving one of the grounds under schedule 2 of the Housing Act 1988, whereas additionally under the shorthold tenancy the landlord can obtain possession simply by showing (a) that the tenancy has come to an end and (b) that the tenant has been given proper notice requiring possession.

## 13-09   Terms of the tenancy

By and large the parties are free to enter into an assured tenancy on whatever terms they agree. However, to qualify as an assured tenant, the tenant must be an individual[12] and he must occupy the dwelling as his only or principal home[13]. The tenancy itself may be for a fixed term or a periodic tenancy. In addition, there are statutorily implied terms that the tenant will give the landlord access to the dwelling-house to enable him to execute repairs thereat[14] and that he will not without the consent of the landlord assign the tenancy or sub-let or part with possession of the whole or any part of the dwelling[15]. Most importantly, section 11 of the Housing Act 1985 (which applies to leases of dwelling houses for a term of less than seven years) imposes general repairing obligations on the landlord. In brief, the landlord must keep in repair the structure and exterior of the dwelling-house and keep in repair and proper working order the installations for the supply of water, gas, electricity and sanitation at the property. It is not possible to contract out of these statutory provisions.

**13-10** If the fixed term expires and the tenant is still in occupation the tenancy now becomes a periodic assured tenancy. If the tenancy

---

[11]     Housing Act 1988, Sch.2A, para 1.
[12]     Ibid. s. 1(1)(a). If it is a joint tenancy, each tenant must be an individual.
[13]     A stricter test than under s. 2 of the Rent Act 1977 (where the tenant has merely to occupy the dwelling-house as his residence).
[14]     Housing Act, s. 16.
[15]     Ibid. s. 15. The refusal of consent may be unreasonable (see s.15(2)) because there is no corresponding restriction as in business tenancies that the consent must not be unreasonably withheld (Landlord and Tenant Act 1927, s. 19).

is a periodic one in the first place and the landlord serves a notice to quit it, this will be of no legal effect and the periodic tenancy continues on its original terms.

**13-11** Because shorthold tenancies are created much more informally, there is now an obligation on the landlord to provide a written statement of certain essential terms of this form of tenancy which have not been evidenced in writing, as follows:
(1) the date on which the tenancy began;
(2) the amount of rent payable and the dates on which it is payable;
(3) any term providing for the review of rent;
(4) in the case of a fixed-term tenancy, the length of that term[16].

## 13-12 Security of tenure: assured tenancy

Under an assured tenancy (as opposed to a shorthold tenancy) the only method by which a landlord can obtain possession, other than by the tenant voluntarily leaving, is by establishing one or more of the statutory grounds. In essence the relevant grounds, as far as clubs are concerned, are as follows:

*Mandatory grounds:* holiday lettings out of season[17]; student lettings during vacations[18]; the landlord's intention to demolish, reconstruct or carry out substantial works in respect of the whole or part of the dwelling-house[19]; inherited periodic tenancy[20]; serious rent arrears[21].

*Discretionary grounds:* the availability of suitable alternative accommodation[22]; some rent arrears[23]; persistent rent arrears[24]; breach of tenant's obligation under the tenancy other than arrears of rent[25]; deterioration of the premises through acts of waste or through the neglect or default of the tenant[26]; causing a nuisance or annoyance to adjoining occupiers or using the premises for immoral or illegal purposes[27]; ill-treatment of the furniture provided by the

---

[16]    Housing Act 1988, s. 20A inserted by the Housing Act 1996.
[17]    Ground 3.
[18]    Ground 4.
[19]    Ground 6.
[20]    Ground 7. See further **13-15** below.
[21]    Ground 8.
[22]    Ground 9.
[23]    Ground 10.
[24]    Ground 11. This ground would apply where there was no actual arrears but the tenant was persistently late in paying his rent on the due date.
[25]    Ground 12.
[26]    Ground 13.
[27]    Ground 14.

landlord[28]; recovery of possession against a former employee where the premises were let to him in consequence of that employment[29]; tenancy induced by false statement of the tenant[30].

Discretionary grounds means that the landlord must additionally satisfy the court that it is reasonable to make an order for possession. It should be noted too that during the currency of a fixed term, it is only open to the landlord to seek possession on one or more of the statutory grounds *which involve the tenant's default* and where there is a term of the tenancy which allows the landlord to re-enter or put an early end to the tenancy of breach of covenant[31]. Once the fixed term has expired or in the case where the tenancy has always been periodic, then any of the statutory grounds may be relied upon.

### 13-13  Security of tenure: shorthold tenancy[32]

To qualify as a tenant under a shorthold tenancy, the tenant must first of all qualify as an assured tenant (see **13-09** above), that is to say, the tenant must be an individual[33] and he must occupy the dwelling as his only or principal home[34]. A shorthold tenancy can now be for a fixed term of less than six months[35] or paradoxically for a term (greatly) exceeding six months[36] or it may be a periodic tenancy. Because the shorthold tenancy is a species of assured tenancy, it is open to the landlord to seek possession on the statutory grounds in the same way as for assured tenants. This is likely only to be of relevance where the landlord wishes to obtain possession prior to the expiry of an initial fixed term or where he wants to obtain possession within the first six months of the grant of a shorthold tenancy.

**13-14**  With effect from 28 February 1997 the landlord will be granting a six-month tenancy in that he will not be able recover possession before the expiry of that period (unless he has statutory grounds: see **13-12** above). *This six-month period is the extent of the*

---

28    Ground 15.

29    Ground 16.

30    Ground 17.

31    Housing Act 1988, s. 7(6).

32    The text is dealing with tenancies created after 28 February 1997. Somewhat different rules apply for tenancies created before 28 February 1997.

33    Ibid. s. 1(1)(a). If it is a joint tenancy, each tenant must be an individual.

34    A stricter test than under s. 2 of the Rent Act 1977 (where the tenant has merely to occupy the dwelling-house as his residence).

35    Hitherto a protected shorthold tenancy had to be for six months certain (Housing Act 1988, s. 20(2)).

36    Although in practice this would very rarely happen.

*tenant's security.* The time starts running from the grant of the original tenancy, even if the tenancy has been extended by the landlord[37]. Additionally and most importantly, the landlord can obtain possession without establishing fault simply by giving at least two months' notice in accordance with section 21 of the Housing Act 1988; this notice can be given so as to expire at the end of the six-month period referred to.

## 13-15   Succession

There is a limited right to succession under an assured tenancy. Only the tenant's spouse is capable of succeeding to the tenancy and only one succession is permitted[38]. If the deceased tenant was already a successor, there will no further right of succession[39]. It should be noted here that both a fixed-term and a periodic assured tenancy form part of the deceased tenant's estate and can therefore be passed to a third party under a will or under the rules of intestacy. This new tenant, however, may be unknown to the landlord and an undesirable tenant, to boot: hence the need for the mandatory ground for possession under Ground 10.

## 13-16   Excluded tenancies

For various policy reasons the Housing Act 1988 excludes from protection certain categories of tenancy, the relevant ones being, as far as clubs are concerned, as follows:
* High rent accommodation where the rent payable exceeds £25,000 per year[40]; very low rent accommodation where the rent payable is less than £1,000 per year in London or £250 per year elsewhere[41]; land exceeding 2 acres in extent let together with a dwelling-house[42]; lettings to students[43]; holiday lettings[44]; agricultural holdings[45]; and business tenancies[46].

---

[37]     Housing Act 1988, s. 21(5) as inserted by Housing Act 1996, s. 99.
[38]     Housing Act 1988, s.17.  A common law husband or wife counts as a spouse (s.17(4)).  And see *Ghaidan v Godin-Mendoza* [2003] Ch 380, CA.
[39]     Ibid. s. 17(3).
[40]     Ibid. Sch. 1, para 2.
[41]     Ibid. Sch. 1, para 3 to 3C.
[42]     Ibid. Sch. 1, para 6.
[43]     Ibid. Sch. 1, para 8.
[44]     Ibid. Sch. 1, para 9.
[45]     Ibid. Sch. 1, para 7.
[46]     Ibid. Sch. 1, para 4.

## 13-17   Recovery of possession

There are only two ways of recovering possession:
(1) the tenant leaves voluntarily;
(2) the landlord obtains a court order for possession.

**13-18**   As regards (full) assured tenancies, the landlord can only recover possession by establishing one or more of the statutory grounds for possession as set out in **13-12** above. In all cases he should first serve a notice complying with section 8 of the Housing Act 1988 specifying the ground(s) of possession relied upon[47].

As mentioned above, a fixed term assured tenancy can only be brought to an end *prior to its expiry* where there is provision in the agreement permitting the landlord to re-enter for the breach complained of. In all other cases the section 8 route is available. Once the section 8 notice has been served and the time specified in the notice has expired, the landlord may then commence possession proceedings, and he then has to satisfy the court that he can establish one of the statutory grounds for possession, either mandatory or discretionary. In the event of a mandatory ground the order for possession will follow as a matter of course[48], and in the event of a discretionary ground the court will only make an order for possession if it is reasonable to do so[49].

**13-19**   As regards shorthold tenancies, the landlord may follow the section 8 notice route in the same way and in the same circumstances as for an assured tenancy. Additionally, he can simply give at least two months' notice in accordance with section 21.

If it was a *fixed-term* tenancy, the court will make an order for possession where:
(1) the term has expired, and no further tenancy is in existence except a statutory periodic shorthold tenancy following on from the expiry date[50]; and
(2) the tenant has been given not less than two months' notice in writing that possession of the dwelling-house is required by the landlord[51]; and

---

47    Standard forms are available from various legal stationers and can be obtained on-line at *www.oyez.co.uk.*
48    Housing Act 1988, s. 7(3).
49    Ibid. s. 7(4).
50    Ibid. s. 21(1)(a).
51    Ibid. s. 21(1)(b) as amended by the Housing Act 1996, s. 98.

(3) the order for possession will not take effect earlier than six months after the beginning of the tenancy (or the beginning of the original tenancy if the order sought relates to a replacement tenancy)[52].

**13-20**   If the tenancy was a *periodic* one, the court will make an order for possession where:
(1) the tenant has been given not less than two months' notice in writing specifying a date upon which possession is required[53]; and
(2) the date specified must be the last day of a period of the tenancy, and must be no earlier than the earliest date on which the tenancy could have been brought to an end by a notice to quit, had a notice to quit been served on the same day as the said notice[54]. (This is a trap for the unwary and a landlord should always add after the date given in the notice words to the following effect: '[date] or at the end of the period of your tenancy which ends next after the expiration of two months from the service upon you of this notice'); and
(3) the order for possession will not take effect earlier than six months after the beginning of the tenancy (or the beginning of the original tenancy if the order sought relates to a replacement tenancy)[55].

## 6.   BUSINESS TENANCIES

### 13-21   Introduction

The reason why members' clubs need to know about business tenancies is that the protection given by Part II of the Landlord and Tenant Act 1954 applies to the occupation of a tenant of premises for 'the purposes of business'[56], and 'business' is defined as not only including a trade, profession or employment but 'any activity carried on by a body or persons, whether corporate or incorporate'[57]. Thus where the trustees of an IPSA club took a tenancy of some tennis courts and a clubhouse, the activity of a tennis club was held to be a business purpose within the Act[58]. It is therefore surmised that virtually all those members' clubs which have a leasehold interest of their premises will have protection under Part II of the Landlord and

---

52      Housing Act 1988. s. 21(5) as inserted by the Housing Act 1996, s. 99.
53      Ibid. s. 21(4)(a).
54      Ibid. s. 21(4)(b).
55      Ibid. s. 21(5) as inserted by the Housing Act 1996, s. 99.
56      Landlord and Tenant Act 1954, s. 23(1).
57      Ibid. s. 23(2).
58      *Addiscombe Garden Estates Ltd v Crabbe* [1958] 1QB 513 CA.

Tenant Act 1954[59].

## 13-22   Occupation of premises

The club must occupy the premises in question by virtue of a tenancy, which can be either a fixed-term tenancy or a periodic one. A sub-tenancy is sufficient but not a tenancy at will[60] nor a licence[61]. The word 'premises' in the Act is not defined but has been construed broadly: it includes a building or part of a building or simply land with no building on it. Thus in *Bracey v Read* [1963] Ch 88 a tenancy of land without buildings, namely, some gallops on the Lambourn Downs used for training racehorses, was held to be a protected business tenancy[62]. Where the club property is held by trustees on trust for the members, the carrying on of the business by the beneficiaries (the members) is treated as equivalent to occupation by or the carrying on of business by the tenant[63].

## 13-23   Security of tenure

The security of tenure is achieved by the automatic continuation of the tenancy under section 24 of the Act of 1954 and the tenant's right to apply for a new tenancy. The tenancy will not come to an end unless it is terminated in one of the ways set out in the Act. This means that the business tenancy will continue after the expiry of a fixed-term tenancy and after the service of a landlord's notice to quit in respect of a periodic tenancy. The statutory methods of terminating a tenancy under the Act of 1954 are:

(1) by the landlord giving notice to terminate under section 25;
(2) by the tenant making an application for a new tenancy under section 26;
(3) by the tenant giving notice to terminate the tenancy under section 27.

---

[59]     There are limits, however: see *Hillil Property v Narraine Pharmacy* [1980] 39 P & CR 67 (occupying premises to dump waste and rubbish not a protected activity); compare *Groveside Properties Ltd v Westminster Medical School* [1983] 267 EG 593 (where a tenancy of a flat for medical students was held to be not merely for residential purposes but to foster a collegiate spirit, thus counting as an activity for business purposes).

[60]     *Wheeler v Mercer* [1957] AC 416.

[61]     *National Car Parks Ltd v Trinity Development Co* [2002] 2 P & CR 253.

[62]     On the other hand, agricultural tenancies are excluded from Part II of the Act of 1954: s.43(1)(a).

[63]     Landlord and Tenant Act 1954, s. 41(1).

### 13-24  Section 25 notice

The 'competent' landlord[64] must serve the notice in the prescribed form[65]. It must be served not more than 12 months nor less than 6 months before the date of termination specified in the notice[66]. The notice must:

(1) specify the date at which the tenancy is to come to an end[67];
(2) require the tenant within two months after the giving of the notice to notify the landlord in writing whether or not, at the date of termination, he will be willing to give up possession of the premises[68];
(3) state whether the landlord would oppose the tenant's application for a new tenancy and, if so, on what grounds[69];
(4) with effect from 1 June 2004 and where the landlord does not oppose the grant of a new tenancy, the terms proposed for the new tenancy[70].

**13-25**   If there is a break clause in the tenancy, the club may find that the landlord will serve two notices, a section 25 notice and a break clause notice, each terminating the tenancy. It might be asked why one combined notice would not be sufficient. The answer is this: if the notice complies with the Act but does not fulfil the provisions of the break clause it will be of no effect and the tenancy will continue on a contractual basis, and the landlord will have to wait until the next break clause or until the tenancy expires; on the other hand, if the notice fulfils the provisions of the break clause but does not comply with the Act, the contractual tenancy will be brought to an end but will be automatically continued under section 24 of the Act until the landlord serves a valid section 25 notice.

**13-26**   The tenant's notification that he is not willing to give up possession does not have to be in any prescribed form, as long as the

---

[64]    Negotiation for a new tenancy will not be meaningful if, say, the immediate landlord is a leaseholder for a term which is only a few days longer than the tenant's interest, so the Act of 1954 provides a mechanism for identifying the one landlord with whom the tenant should deal and who is called the competent landlord (s.44(1)).

[65]    See Form 1 in the Landlord and Tenant Act 1954, Part II (Notices Regulations 1983 (SI 1983/133 as amended by SI 1989/1548), Sch. 2.

[66]    Landlord and Tenant Act 1954, s. 25(2).

[67]    Ibid. s. 25(1).

[68]    Ibid. s. 25(5).

[69]    Ibid. s. 25(6). For the grounds of opposition see **13-27** below.

[70]    Ibid. s. 25(8) as inserted by Arts. 2 and 4 of the Regulatory Reform (Business Tenancies) (England and Wales) Order 2003 (SI 2003/3096). This presumably means realistic proposals: see *Mount Cook v Rosen* [2003] 1 EGLR 75 (where 'proposal' under the Leasehold Reform Housing & Urban Development Act 1993 was held to mean a realistic proposal which could be justified by expert valuation evidence).

he makes clear his unwillingness[71]. The two-month time limit may be waived by the landlord[72]. Once he has given a valid notice of unwillingness, the tenant may then apply to the court for a new tenancy[73]. Such application must be made not less than two months nor more than four months after the service of the landlord's section 25 notice[74]. If no application is made, the tenancy will come to an end on the termination date specified in the section 25 notice.

## 13-27  Grounds of opposition

Section 30(1) of the Act of 1954 provides seven grounds of opposition upon which the landlord can rely in opposing the application for a new tenancy:

Ground (a): the tenant's failure to comply with repairing obligations;

Ground (b): the tenant's persistent delay in paying rent;

Ground (c): the tenant's substantial breach of other obligations or his misuse or mismanagement of the premises;

Ground (d): suitable alternative accommodation is available;

Ground (e): the landlord requires the whole property for subsequent letting (this rarely arises in practice);

Ground (f): the landlord intends to demolish or reconstruct the premises (a common ground);

Ground (g): the landlord intends to occupy the premises himself either for business purposes or as his residence.

Under grounds (a), (b) and (c) the court has a discretion whether to grant or refuse a new tenancy. There is no discretion if the landlord establishes his opposition under grounds (d), (e), (f) and (g): no new tenancy will be granted. Ground (g) is not available to the landlord unless the landlord has owned his interest in the property for at least five years prior to the termination of the tenancy. Under grounds (d),

---

71      See e.g. *Mehmet v Dawson* [1983] 270 EG 139 (where a letter expressing willingness to purchase the freehold was held insufficient) c.f. *Lewington v Trustees for the Protection of Ancient Buildings* [1983] 45 P & CR 336.

72      *Kammins Ballrooms Co Ltd v Zenith Investments* (Torquay) Ltd [1971] AC 850.

73      Landlord and Tenant Act 1954, ss. 24 and 29.

74      Ibid. s. 29(3).

(e) and (f) the landlord may be able to satisfy the court that he can make good the ground of opposition at a date not later than one year after the date of termination specified in the section 25 notice and, if so, the court will make a declaration to this effect, and no new tenancy will be granted[75].

## 13-28 Compensation for quitting premises

Grounds of opposition (e), (f) and (g) are based not on the default of the tenant but on the needs of the landlord, so that if the ground of opposition is made out the tenant will be entitled to compensation[76]. Furthermore, by section 37A of the Landlord and Tenant Act 1954[76a] the tenant will be entitled to compensation where possession of the premises has been obtained by the landlord by misrepresentation or concealment of material facts. The court may order the landlord to pay the tenant such sum as appears sufficient by way of compensation for damage or loss sustained by the tenant as the result of quitting the holding. This new form of compensation applies across the board to all grounds of opposition[76b]. It is important to note, however, that in order to receive compensation the tenant has to be in occupation at the expiry of the notice[77].

## 13-29 Terms of the new tenancy

These terms will be decided by the court if the parties cannot agree. They will include what property will be included the new tenancy[77a], its duration[78], the rent[79] and other terms[80]. Between the service of a section 25 notice and the granting of a new tenancy there may be a considerable time interval and the existing rent will continue to be paid. If this rent was low the tenant had everything to gain by delay, so that since 1969 by section 24A of the Act of 1954[81] the landlord has been able to apply to the court for an interim rent to be determined

---

[75]     Landlord and Tenant Act 1954, s. 31(2).

[76]     Ibid. s. 37.

[76a]    Inserted by Arts. 2 and 20 of the Regulatory Reform Order cited in footnote 70 above.

[76b]    Ibid. s. 37(1) as amended by Arts. 2 and 19 of the said Regulatory Reform Order.

[77]     *Sight and Sound Education Ltd v Books etc Ltd* [1999] 3 EGLR 45.

[77a]    Ibid. s. 32(1)

[78]     Ibid. s. 33.

[79]     Ibid. s. 34(1).

[80]     Ibid. s. 35; e.g. including a break clause (*Leslie and Godwin Investments Ltd v Prudential Assurance Co Ltd* [1987] 2 EGLR 2) or excluding an option to purchase (*Kirkwood v Johnson* [1979] 38 P &CR 392).

[81]     Added by the Law of Property Act 1969.

which is reasonable for the tenant to pay. On the other hand, if the existing rent is higher than rents currently being obtained it is the landlord who gains by delay, so that with effect from 1 June 2004 the tenant can now apply to the court for a reasonable interim rent to be determined[81a].

**13-30** It should be noted that with effect from 1 June 2004 the landlord as well as the tenant can apply for a new tenancy and, conversely, that the landlord can apply for an order from the court that there no new tenancy be granted[81b]. This means that the landlord's ground or grounds of opposition will be used as a springboard for an order for possession against the tenant. The landlord's application may be made as soon as he has served his section 25 notice[81c].

## 13-31   Section 26 notice

Generally speaking a tenant may take the initiative and serve a notice under section 26 of the Act of 1954 requesting a new tenancy. The effect of a section 26 notice is to terminate the tenant's current tenancy immediately before the date specified in the request for the beginning of the new tenancy[82]. The notice must be in the prescribed form and must be served on the competent landlord[83]. The timescale applicable to a section 26 request is very similar to the timetable applicable to a section 25 notice. Generally speaking, however, it may be unwise to serve a section 26 notice because, until it is known whether the landlord wishes to terminate the existing tenancy, it will not be in the interests of the tenant to request a new one; the existing tenancy will continue in any event under section 24 and very often will be on terms more favourable than those of a new tenancy.

## 13-32   Section 27 notice

The tenant may not wish to apply for a new tenancy, in which case he may serve a notice on the landlord under section 27 of the Act of 1954. This provision only applies to fixed-term tenancies. The tenant must give notice in writing to the *immediate* landlord not later than three months before the date on which the tenancy would come to

---

[81a]   Ibid. s. 24A(1) as substituted by Arts 1 and 18 of Regulatory Reform Order cited in footnote 70.

[81b]   Ibid. s. 29(2) as substituted by Arts 2 and 5 of the said Regulatory Reform Order.

[81c]   Ibid. s. 29(2).

[82]   Landlord and Tenant Act 1954, s. 26(5).

[83]   See **13-24** above.

an end by effluxion of time[84]. Once the notice is given, section 24 will not apply and the tenancy will come to an end on its contractual date. If the contractual date has passed, so that the tenancy is being continued under section 24, the tenant can still give a section 27 notice; three months' notice in writing must be given to the immediate landlord and the notice must expire on a quarter day[85].

## 13.33   Relief from forfeiture

Many leases contain an express right of re-entry or forfeiture in the event of specified events, such as the tenant's breach of covenant or the bankruptcy of the tenant. The right to forfeit is not enforceable by action or otherwise unless and until the landlord serves on the tenant a notice[86]:

(1) specifying the event or breach complained of;
(2) if capable of remedy, requiring the tenant to remedy the breach;
(3) requiring the tenant to pay compensation for the breach.

The breach can be waived, for example, if, in a forfeiture concerning non-payment of rent, the landlord brings an action for arrears of rent[87]. Unless there are exceptional circumstances, relief from forfeiture in the case of failure to pay rent will be granted if the tenant pays the arrears of rent plus costs. In other cases, the tenant has the right to apply to the court for relief where it may grant or refuse relief on such terms as it thinks fit[88], such as making an order for payment of compensation or granting an injunction to restrain future beaches.

## 13-34   Contracting out of the Act of 1954

Originally any attempt by the landlord to contract out of the provisions of Part II of the Act of 1954 was rendered void[89], but in 1969 the Act was amended to permit the court on the joint application of the parties to authorise the business tenancy to exclude the security provisions of the Act[90]. The application, however, had to precede the grant of the tenancy[91]. From 1 June 2004 it will no longer be necessary to apply to the court for authorisation. The new procedure for

---

[84]   Ibid. s. 27(1).
[85]   Ibid. s. 27(2).
[86]   Law of Property Act 1925, s. 146.
[87]   *Dendy v Nicholl* [1858] 4 CB(NS) 376.
[88]   Law of Property Act 1925, s.146(2).
[89]   Landlord and Tenant Act 1954, s. 38(1).
[90]   By adding a new s. 38(4).
[91]   *Essexcrest Ltd v Evenlex Ltd* [1988] 1 EGLR 69.

contracting out requires the landlord to give a notice in writing to the tenant, urging the tenant to obtain independent legal advice before accepting a tenancy with no security provisions, and the tenant has to sign a declaration that this warning has been given[92].

## 7.   COVENANTS IN LEASES

### 13-35   Usual covenants

The following covenants are 'usual' in a lease or tenancy[93].

On the part of the landlord:
- a covenant for quiet enjoyment of the leased property.

On the part of the tenant:
- A covenant to pay rent
- A covenant to pay tenant's rates and taxes
- A covenant to keep the premises in repair and deliver them up in repair at the end of the term
- A covenant to permit the landlord to enter and view the state of repair (if the landlord has undertaken any obligation to repair)
- A condition of re-entry for non-payment of rent  (but not for breach of any other covenant).

### 13-36   Common covenants

There are commonly inserted into leases, with the concurrence of both parties, covenants against assignment, covenants against the carrying on of certain trades or activities, and provisos for forfeiture for breaches of any covenant, whether for payment of rent or otherwise. In the case of *Ranken v Hunt* [1894] 38 Sol Jo 290 DC the Hoddlesden Working Men's Club's lease contained a covenant that its premises should not be used for 'sale of wine malt liquor or spirituous liquors'. The club rules provided for the purchase of such liquors and its distribution at fixed prices amongst the members, the profits being applied to the general purposes of the club. The court held that this was not a sale within the meaning of the covenant. It should be noted that a covenant not to assign, sub-let or part with possession may be

---

[92]     If the declaration is made less than 14 clear days before the tenancy commences, the declaration must be in the form of a statutory declaration made before another solicitor retained for the sole purpose of administering the oath.
[93]     *Hampshire v Wickens* [1878] 7 Ch D 555.

an absolute undertaking or a qualified one. It is qualified where the prohibition is not to do these things without the landlord's consent. In this event, the covenant is subject to the proviso that the consent will not be unreasonably withheld[94].

## 8.   LICENCES

### 13-37   Introduction

The basic distinction between a lease (or tenancy) and a licence is that under the former the tenant has exclusive possession of premises against all others whereas under the latter he has no such possession[95], that is to say, the landlord retains a degree of control over the occupied premises. Broadly speaking, there are two situations where a club will come across a licence, the first being when it itself is a licensee of another person and the other is when it acts as employer. An example of the first category is where a cricket club is the freehold owner of the club premises and the surrounding cricket field which it uses during the summer months but allows another club in the winter months, say a hockey club, to occupy the premises with all its facilities under a licence. An example of the second category is where a cricket club employs a groundsman to look after its pitches and grounds and provides on-site accommodation for the employee.

### 13-38   Club as licensee

What will be involved is a contractual licence, a form of contract enforceable by both the licensor and the licensee[96], and in many ways will not differ much from a tenancy agreement. The big difference is the lack of security, especially at the end of the licence. In order to continue at the same premises the club will of necessity have to re-negotiate a new licence on the best terms that it can obtain. It is also important for a club to ensure that it obtains a contractual licence because of the licensor's power at common law to revoke a *bare* licence at any time[97]. What the club should aim for is 'a licence coupled with

---

[94]      Landlord and Tenant Act 1927, s. 19(1). And see *Design Progression Ltd v. Thurloe Properties Ltd* [2005] 1 WLR 1 (exemplary damages awarded to tenant in respect of landlord's breach of its statutory duty in relation to consent).
[95]      *Street v Mountford* [1985] AC 809.
[96]      *Verrall v Great Yarmouth Council* [1980] 3 WLR 258 CA ; *Tanner v Tanner* [1975] 1 WLR 1346 CA.
[97]      *Thompson v.Park* [1944 KB 408 CA. *Wood v Leadbitter* [1845] 13 M & W 838.

an equity', that is to say, where the court will imply a negative
contractual term in restraint of revocation before the expiry of the
contractual period of the licence; and the courts today are much more
willing to imply such a term than hitherto[98]. It is easier, however, to
imply the term where the licence comprises a specific period of time[99].
A contractual licence held by the club will be held sometimes in the
name of trustees and at other times in the name of the club[100].

## 13-39   Club as licensor

Since the advent of the commonly used shorthold tenancy in 1997,
the need for landlords to think of devices to avoid the much greater
security of tenure enjoyed by protected tenants under the Rent Act
and by assured tenants under the Housing Act has to a large extent
evaporated. The device usually relied on was the licence which gives
no security of tenure and where the landlord can obtain a court order
for possession without having to rely on any statutory ground or
without giving any reason. Many of these so-called licences were
exposed in the courts as a sham[101]. However, there is still a legitimate
call for the use a licence where the accommodation goes with the job,
a classic example being the caretaker of premises. If the club employee
is genuinely required to occupy the premises for the better
performance of his or her duties, the club is entitled to give that person
a licence only of residential accommodation. The employee will
become a service occupier or service licensee, even where exclusive
possession of the accommodation has been given to the employee[102].
Although the label which the parties put on the transaction is not
definitive[103], it is still important to use the right terminology when
granting a licence, and words like 'the payment of rent' should be
avoided when granting a licence[104].

---

[98]      *Chandler v Kerley* [1978] 1 WLR 693 CA per Lord Scarman at 697 ('where the parties
have contracted for a licence, equity today will provide an equitable remedy to protect the
legal right').
[99]      See *National Provincial Bank Ltd v Hastings Car Mart Ltd* [1964] Ch 665 CA at 686
(Lord Denning).
[100]     See **5-15** and **13-04** above.
[101]     See e.g. *Antoniades v Villiers* [1990] 1 AC 417.
[102]     *Norris v Checksfield* [1991] 1 WLR 1241.
[103]     *Crancour v Da Silvaesa* [1986] 1 EGLR 81 CA.
[104]     See *Addiscombe Garden Estates Ltd v Crabbe* [1958] 1 QB 513 CA (where the plaintiff
purported to give the defendant trustees of the club a licence but its language and terms
were construed by the court as creating the relationship of landlord and tenant).

## 13-40 Protection from eviction

At common law when a tenancy or licence comes to an end the landlord or licensor is entitled to re-enter and take possession of the premises. However, some residential occupiers, and in particular licensees, had no statutory protection once the contractual period had come to an end. Parliament therefore passed the Protection from Eviction Act 1977 whereby if a residential tenancy or licence has come to an end and the occupier continues to reside in the premises, it will be a criminal offence to deprive the occupier of possession save through a court order[105] or to unlawfully harass him[106]. The fact that criminal proceedings are taken under the Act will not prejudice the right of the occupier to seek a civil remedy against the landlord or licensor, such as damages for a breach of the covenant for quiet enjoyment[107].

It should also be noted that, in addition to damages at common law, a residential tenant may be able to claim damages for unlawful eviction under sections 27 and 28 of the Housing Act 1988.

## 9. PROPRIETARY CLUBS

13-41 Whether the proprietor is the freehold or leasehold owner of the club premises, the club will be either the licensee of the proprietor if it is a separate entity or the proprietor himself will be in occupation of the premises. In either event there will be no question of the club having protection under Part II of the Landlord and Tenant Act 1954 nor will the club have any landlord and tenant relationship with the proprietor's employees.

---

[105]    Protection from Eviction Act 1977, s. 1(2).
[106]    Ibid. ss. 1(3) and 3A.
[107]    Ibid. s. 1(5).

# Chapter 14

## EMPLOYMENT OF THIRD PARTIES

## 1. INTRODUCTION

**14-01** Clubs are frequently employers of staff. This employment brings in its wake a whole raft of statutory law and regulation. The potential liability of employing a significant number of staff is such that it has led one writer[1] to advocate that this factor alone should make an unincorporated members' club give careful thought to some form of corporate status as a protection from liability. We do not dissent from the proposition that such a club should give careful thought to this topic, but instead our emphasis would be that the employment of staff requires the managing committee to pay close attention to employment law if the club is to avoid its potential exposure to liability. The Department for Education and Employment and the Department of Trade and Industry produce a large number of free explanatory leaflets which deal with specific areas of employment law (e.g. unfair dismissal or redundancy payments) which are helpful to lawyers and non-lawyers alike to understand the position. The following paragraphs are intended to give an outline of the main areas of employment law which clubs of whatever type are likely to encounter when employing staff[2].

## 2. WHAT IS EMPLOYMENT

**14-02** This point has already been touched upon when considering the club's liability for torts[3]. The distinction here is between a contract

---

[1]   *Warburton on Unincorporated Associations* (2nd edn, 1992) p 92.
[2]   See Harvey on Industrial Relations and Employment Law for detailed guidance.
[3]   See **12-20** to **12-21** above.

*of* service (or a contract of employment in modern parlance) under which an employee will work and a contract *for* services under which an independent contractor (or self-employed person) will provide services to the employer. There is no one simple test for discerning the difference between an employee and a self-employed person. The label which the parties themselves gives to the relationship is not decisive; one has to look at the reality of the situation and all the terms of the contract will be looked at objectively in order to arrive at the right answer[4]. The following are generally considered to be essential to a contract of employment:

(1) an obligation on the employee to provide work personally[5];
(2) a mutuality of obligation (usually an obligation on the part of the employer to make work available and a corresponding obligation on the employee to carry out the work)[6];
(3) a right by the employer to exercise a degree of control over the way in which the work is carried out[7].

**14-03**　If these minimum requirements are met, other factors, such as stipulations as to hours of work, whether holiday pay is paid, who provides the tools and equipment, who bears the loss and how the contract is terminated, are looked at to see whether the contract can properly be characterised as one of employment[8]. By way of an example, a professional at a golf club may well satisfy the essential requirements of a contract of employment but the unusually relaxed terms under which golf professionals tend to work might mean that he could not be properly characterised as an employee. The distinction is significant because the more important statutory rights do not apply to a contract for services.

## 3.　WHO IS THE EMPLOYER

**14-04**　In the case of incorporated clubs and those registered under the Industrial and Provident Societies Act 1965 the question poses no problem because the club has a separate existence from its members. This problem arises in the case of unincorporated clubs which have no legal personality. In the ordinary course of events the managing committee would be the employer as it is they who control the affairs

---

4　　*Carmichael v. National Power plc* [1999] 1 WLR 2042, HL at 2049C (Lord Hoffman).
5　　*Express & Echo Publications Ltd v. Tanton* [1999] IRLR 367 cf. *Macfarlane v. Glasgow C.C.* [2001] IRLR 7.
6　　*Carmichael v. National Power* above.
7　　*Ready Mixed Concrete v. Minister of Pensions and National Insurance* [1968] 2 QB 497.
8　　*Hall v. Lorimer* [1994] ICR 218.

of the club[9]. But this may not be the complete answer. In *Campbell v Thompson and Shill* [1953] 2 WLR 656, the plaintiff was employed as a cleaner at the City Livery Club, an unincorporated club, which had some 2,500 members. She fell and injured herself on the club's premises whilst at work and brought an action for damages for negligence and breach of duty against Mr Thompson as honorary secretary and Mr Shill as chairman of the house committee. The judge allowed these two persons to represent the whole body of club members. In the course of his judgment Mr Justice Pilcher stated[10]:

> I am well satisfied in the present instance that all the members of the City Livery Club have both as the employer of the plaintiff and the technical occupier of the club premises the same common interest in resisting the plaintiff's claim.

This is an interesting case because it is to be assumed that the plaintiff had been informally engaged as a cleaner by Mr Thompson or Mr Shill without any consultation with the members before the engagement or without any ratification by the members after the engagement in that this would have been a run-of-the-mill engagement not requiring either prior authorisation or ratification from the members, yet the judge drew the conclusion that the whole membership of 2,500 was her employer[11]. We would be surprised if the case were successfully to withstand the scrutiny of the Court of Appeal today.

## 4. CONTRACT OF EMPLOYMENT

**14-05** Notwithstanding the weight of statutory intervention the contract of employment remains the basis of the relationship between the employer and the employee. Although a contract of employment may be either written or oral or partly both, it is better practice for the employer to provide the employee with a contract in writing. The written contract should identify such parts of the staff handbook or other document as to which the employer wishes to give contractual effect.

**14-06** The employer must in any event give the employee a written statement of particulars of certain terms of his contract not later than two months after the beginning of the employment[12]. There is an

---

[9] See paragraph **5-16** above.
[10] At 451.
[11] See also *Prole v Allen* [1950] 1 All ER (discussed at **5-45** above) where the club steward was held by the judge to have been appointed by all the members.
[12] Employment Rights Act 1996, s. 1(1).

obviously sound reason for this requirement. When disputes arise or
are referred to an employment tribunal, it is essential that each side
knows what its rights and obligations are and many a time the first
area of dispute is what was agreed between the parties. The following
statutory particulars must be set down[13]:

(1) the names of the employer and the employee;
(2) the date when the employment began;
(3) the date on which the employee's *continuous* employment began[14];
(4) the scale or rate of remuneration, or the method of calculating the
    remuneration;
(5) the interval at which remuneration is: paid (e.g. weekly, monthly);
(6) the terms and conditions relating to hours of work;
(7) any terms relating to:
    (a) holidays
    (b) sick pay
    (c) pensions;
(8) the length of notice the employee is obliged to give and entitled to
    receive to terminate the contract of employment;
(9) the job title or a brief description of the employee's work;
(10) where the employment is not intended to be permanent, the
     period for which it is expected to continue or, if it is for a fixed
     term, the date when it is to end;
(11) either the place of work or, where the employee is required or
     permitted to work at various places, an indication of those places
     and the employer's address;
(12) any collective agreements which directly affect the terms and
     conditions of the employment;
(13) where the employee is required to work outside the UK for more
     than a month, certain further particulars like the currency of
     remuneration;
(14) any disciplinary rules applicable to the employee (or referring
     to some accessible document containing these rules);
(15) the identity of the person:
     (a) to whom the employee can apply if he is dissatisfied with any
         disciplinary decision or any decision to dismiss him;
     (b) to whom the employee can apply for the purpose of seeking
         redress of any grievance relating to his employment and the
         manner in which such application should be made (or

---

[13]    Employment Rights Act 1996, s. 1(3), (4) and (5).
[14]    As to continuous employment, see **14-09** below.

referring to some accessible document containing the procedure)[15].

**14-07** It is not compulsory for the contract of employment to set forth the terms and conditions relating to *all* the above items. What is required is *notice* of any terms agreed. If the contract does not include any particular item, e.g. no contractual pension is provided, the statement should say so[16]. It also has to be understood that the statutory written statement is not the contract of employment itself nor conclusive evidence of it[17], but in many cases the employer and employee will be content to treat this statement as evidence of a binding contract of employment. Likewise a written contract can itself be relied upon as the statement of particulars so long as it includes all the necessary statutory information.

## 14-08 Implied terms

In addition to the terms expressly agreed between the parties, there are terms which may be implied into the contract of employment on the grounds either that they reflect the obvious (albeit unexpressed) intention of the parties; or that they are necessary to give business efficacy to the contract; or that they reflect the usual (i.e. 'reasonable, certain and notorious'), custom and practice of the particular employer; or that they are implied by virtue of a specific statutory provision. Examples of terms commonly implied into contracts of employment are:

(1) on the part of the employee, that he will carry out his duties with due diligence and care; that he will obey lawful and reasonable orders; that he will serve his employer with fidelity and in good faith; and that he will not disclose confidential information[18];

(2) on the part of the employer, that he will not without reasonable and proper cause conduct himself in a manner calculated or likely to destroy or seriously damage the relationship of trust and confidence which exists between employer and employee[19];

---

[15]     As to items (1) to (13), see the Employment Rights Act 1996, s. 1(3), (4) and (5). As to items (14) and (15) see s. 3 of this Act (as amended by s. 35 of the Employment Act 2002). Items (14) and (15) do not apply to procedures relating to health and safety: Employment Rights Act 1996, s. 3(2). The Employment Act 2002, s. 36 abolished the exemption whereby an employer with fewer than 20 employees did not need to inform employees of disciplinary procedures.

[16]     Employment Rights Acts 1996, s. 2(1).

[17]     *Robertson v British Gas Corporation* [1983] ICR 351 CA.

[18]     *Chitty on Contracts* (29th edn, 2004) paras 39-055 to 39-073.

[19]     *Malik v Bank of Credit and Commerce International SA* [1998] AC 20.

A term will not be implied if to do so would contradict an express term of the contract.

## 5.  CONTINUOUS EMPLOYMENT

**14–09**  This is a concept which is important for many of the statutory employment rights, such as the right to claim a redundancy payment or compensation for unfair dismissal, which are conferred only on those employees who have accrued sufficient continuous employment. There are technical rules (outside the scope of this work) as to what does and does not count as continuous employment. Broadly speaking any week during the whole or part of which the employee's relationship was governed by a contract of employment counts towards continuous employment[20]. Periods of part-time employment, irrespective of the number of hours worked per week, still count in the computation of continuous employment. Continuity will not be broken by periods of maternity leave, sickness absence, or absence due to a temporary cessation of work[21].

**14-10**  Continuity is preserved if an employee is transferred to an 'associated employer', e.g. a subsidiary or sister company of the previous employer[22], or if the transfer is the result of a 'transfer of undertaking', e.g. on the purchase of the previous employer's business[23]. Likewise, the death of an employer does not break continuity nor does a change in partners, personal representatives or trustees[24]. In an unincorporated club the employee would in the ordinary course of events be employed by the committee and it is considered that a change in the composition of the committee through say death of a member or through the election of different members to serve thereon does not break continuity. What would happen if the *entire* committee was replaced at one particular election? Is this a new employer? We consider it would make no difference; the employer would still be 'the committee', whatever its composition.

---

[20]     Employment Rights Act 1996, s. 212(1).
[21]     Even if there is no contract of employment in existence during these periods: ibid s.212(3).
[22]     Ibid. s.218(6).
[23]     Ibid. s.218(2).
[24]     Ibid. s. 218(4) and (5).

## 6.  PAY

**14-11**  The question of pay is primarily governed by the terms of the contract of employment, the particulars of which must form part of the statutory written particulars[25]. Some important payment rights, however, are regulated by statute and these rights are discussed below.

### 14-12  Minimum wage

At the present time (2004) the minimum wage for those over 21 years is £4.85 per hour and for those aged between 18 and 21 years is £4.10 per hour. There is currently no statutory minimum wage for those under 18 years[26]. The employer must maintain records of hours worked and payments made. The employee may request inspection of these records and ask for a copy of them[27].

### 14-13  Holiday pay

An employee has a statutory right to take four weeks' paid annual leave[28]. There is no continuous employment requirement to qualify for this right. The employee is entitled to be paid for any period of leave at the rate of one week's pay for each week of leave. If the contractual holiday rights are more generous than the statutory rights, the contractual rights will apply. Bank Holidays should count as paid holiday days[29]. An employer cannot contract out of the holiday pay provisions[30].

### 14-14  Sick pay

If there is no sick pay entitlement under the contract of employment the employee may be entitled to statutory sick pay. Generally speaking, the entitlement is 28 weeks. In order to qualify for statutory sick pay the employee must have four or more consecutive days of sickness during which he is too ill to work; he must notify his employer of his

---

[25]     See **14-06** above.
[26]     A curious omission in that one would have thought that youngsters would need greater protection from exploitation, not less.
[27]     See the National Minimum Wage Act 1998 and the National Minimum Wage Regulations 1999 (SI 1999/584) as amended.
[28]     Regulation 13(1) of the Working Time Regulations 1998 (SI 1998/1833).
[29]     *Tucker v British Leyland Motor Corporation Ltd* [1978] IRLR 493 at 496.
[30]     Regulation 35 of the Working Time Regulations 1998 (1998/1833).

absence; and he must supply evidence of his incapacity to work[31].

**14-15**  Certain categories of employee are excluded from the entitlement to statutory sick pay. They include the following:
(1)  those over 65 years on the first day of sickness;
(2)  those whose employment is of not more than three months' duration;
(3)  those whose average weekly earnings is less than the weekly lower earnings limit for paying national insurance contributions, presently (2004) £77 per week;
(4)  those who are pregnant and go off sick during the maternity pay period;
(5)  those who have already used up their 28-week entitlement in the three-year period[32],

**14-16**  The amount of statutory sick pay is currently (2004) £66.15 per week. If an employer refuses to pay statutory sick pay the employee can ask for written reasons for that decision[33]. The employee can then appeal to the Inland Revenue who will consider whether he is so entitled[34].

## 14-17  Deductions

Deductions may be made from wages either because it is required by statute (e.g. an attachment of earnings order); or it is permitted by the terms of the contract of employment; or the employee has given his prior written consent to the deduction[35]. If the deduction is made pursuant to a term of the contract of employment, that term must have been shown to the employee (or, if not in writing, its effect notified in writing) before the deduction is made[36]. Wages in this context include any bonus, commission, holiday pay, statutory sick pay and statutory maternity pay[37]. Excluded from the definition of wages are, for example, payments in respect of expenses incurred by the employee in carrying out his job; payments by way of pension; and

---

[31]    See ss. 151 and 152 of the Social Security Contributions and Benefits Act 1992; s.14 of the Social Security Administration Act 1992; and reg. 7 of the Statutory Sick Pay (General) Regulations 1982 (SI 1982/894) as amended.
[32]    Sch. 11 to the Social Security Contributions and Benefits Act 1992 as amended; s.18(2) of the Social Security Act 1985; and the Statutory Sick Pay (General) Regulations 1982 as amended.
[33]    s.14(3) of the Social Security Administration 1992.
[34]    Statutory Sick Pay and Statutory Maternity Pay (Decisions) Regulations 1999 (SI 1999/776).
[35]    Employment Rights Act 1996, ss. 13(1), 15(1).
[36]    See ibid. ss. 14 and 15.
[37]    Ibid. s. 27(1).

redundancy payments[38]. The employee's remedy for wrongful deductions is to make a complaint to the employment tribunal within three months of the deduction being made[39].

## 14-18 PAYE and NIC

For income tax purposes the wages of employees count as 'the emoluments of employment' and are chargeable to tax under Schedule E of the Income and Corporation Taxes Act 1988. PAYE (Pay as You Earn) is a form of tax collection imposed on the employer and applies to all employees who are subject to tax under Schedule E. Under this Act the PAYE system also collects NIC (National Insurance Contributions) from both the employer and employee[40].

# 7. MATERNITY LEAVE

**14-19** Female employees have a statutory entitlement to maternity leave[41] and maternity pay. If their contract of employment also includes a contractual entitlement to maternity leave and maternity pay then they can chose whichever scheme is more favourable. The statutory scheme is both detailed and oddly complex. Its main provisions are set out below.

## 14-20 Compulsory maternity leave

An employer must not allow an employee to work for at least two weeks commencing with the day on which childbirth occurs[42].

## 14-21 Ordinary maternity leave

An employee is entitled to ordinary maternity leave ('OML') of 26 weeks. Her OML starts on the earliest of the following dates:
(1) the date notified by the employee as the date on which she intends her period of OML to commence (which must be no earlier than

---

[38]     Employment Rights Act 1996, s. 27(2).
[39]     Ibid. s. 23. There is a discretionary power to extend this time limit if the tribunal is satisfied that it was not reasonably practicable to present the claim within the three-month period: s. 23(4).
[40]     Income and Corporation Taxes Act 1988, ss. 203, 203A and 204. NIC are in effect a form of taxation.
[41]     Employment Rights Act 1996, ss. 71 to 75.
[42]     Ibid. s. 72.

the beginning of the 11th week before the expected week of childbirth ('EWCh');

(2) the first day on which the employee is absent from work wholly or partly because of pregnancy or childbirth after the beginning of the fourth week before EWCh; or

(3) the day after the day on which childbirth occurs[43].

An employee's entitlement to OML is conditional upon her giving her employer proper notice of her OML[44]. Having received such notice, the employer must confirm when the employee's OML (or, if applicable, her additional maternity leave) is due to end. The employee must give 28 days notice if she intends to return early[45].

**14-22** At the end of her OML an employee is entitled to return to her previous job unless during her OML she has been made redundant. She is entitled to return on terms and conditions no less favourable than those that she would have enjoyed had she not been absent e.g. with the benefit of any pay rises awarded during her absence[46].

## 14-23 Additional maternity leave

An employee, who has been continuously employed by her employer for not less than 26 weeks at the beginning of the 14th week before her EWC, is entitled to an additional maternity leave ('AML') of 26 weeks commencing at the end of her OML[47]. At the end of her AML, unless she has been made redundant, she is entitled to return to her previous job or, if that is not reasonably practicable, to another job which is both suitable and appropriate[48].

## 14-24 Maternity pay

In order to qualify for statutory maternity pay the employee must have been continuously employed by her employer for at least 26 weeks ending with the week immediately preceding the 14th week before her expected week of confinement ('EWCo'). In addition, her normal

---

[43]   Maternity and Parental Leave Regulations 1999 (SI 1999/3312), reg. 6 as amended.
[44]   Ibid. reg.4.
[45]   Ibid. reg.11(1).
[46]   Ibid. reg.18A.
[47]   Ibid. regs. 5 to 7.
[48]   Ibid. reg. 18A.

weekly earnings for the period of 8 weeks ending with the week immediately preceding the 14th week before EWCo must not be less than the lower limit for the payment of national insurance contributions; and she must have become pregnant and reached, or have been confined before reaching, the start of the 11th week before EWCo[49].

**14-25** The employee is entitled to statutory maternity pay for each week of the maternity-pay period, that is to say, for 26 weeks commencing when the employee, having given proper notice, stops work. This start may not be earlier than the 11th week before EWCo nor later than the week immediately following the week of confinement[50]. This means that the employee, if she wishes, can continue to work until the date of confinement and not lose her entitlement to statutory maternity pay. The notice in question is 28 days[51]. The employee must provide a maternity certificate signed by a doctor or midwife as evidence of her pregnancy and of the expected date of confinement[52]. The amount of statutory maternity pay is currently (2004) as follows: for the first six weeks of the maternity-pay period it is nine-tenths of the employee's normal weekly earnings for the period of eight weeks immediately preceding the 14th week before EWCo[53]. Thereafter it is a payment of £100 per week or 90% of the woman's normal earnings, whichever is the lesser sum.

## 8. PATERNITY LEAVE

**14-26** In order to qualify the employee must have been continuously employed for at least 26 weeks ending with the 15th week before the expected week of confinement ('EWCo'). The employee must be either the child's father and have, or expect to have, responsibility for the child's upbringing; or be married to or be the partner of the child's mother and have the main responsibility for the upbringing of the child. The employee is entitled to two weeks paid leave for each child. The pay is currently (2004) the lower of £102.80 or 90% the employee's average weekly earnings. The leave may be taken during the period of 56 days commencing with the child's birth or the first day of EWCo.

---

[49]     Social Security Contributions and Benefits Act 1992, s. 164(1), (2).
[50]     Ibid. s. 165, as amended by SI 1994/1230 reg. 3 and by SI 1986/1960 reg. 2 (itself amended by SI 1994/1347 reg.2); Employment Act 2002, s. 18.
[51]     Employment Act 2002, s. 20.
[52]     Social Security Administration Act 1992, s. 15.
[53]     Social Security Contributions and Benefits Act 1992, s. 166 as amended by SI 1994/1367 reg. 6.

As with maternity leave, the employee's entitlement is conditional upon him giving the proper notice. At the end of his leave the employee is entitled to return to the same job (or, if that is not reasonably practicable, to another job which is suitable and appropriate) on the same terms and conditions as if he had not taken leave. An employer cannot contract out of the obligation to provide paternity leave and pay[54].

## 9.   PARENTAL LEAVE

**14-27**   An employee who has been continuously employed for a year and has or expects to have responsibility for a child is entitled to 13 weeks unpaid parental leave for each child (18 weeks if the child is disabled). This leave should ordinarily be taken before the child's fifth birthday[55].

## 10.   TIME OFF WORK

**14-28**   Employees have additional rights to take time off work in a variety of situations including:
(1) time off with pay for the purpose of trade union official duties; or for ante-natal appointments; or to enable an employee under notice of redundancy to look for alternative employment[56];
(2) time off without pay for the purpose of trade union activities and representation; or for public duties (e.g. sitting as a magistrate)[57].

## 11.   RIGHT NOT TO SUFFER DETRIMENT

**14-29**   An employee's primary statutory rights e.g. to maternity leave, paternity leave, etc are in most cases reinforced by a corresponding secondary right not to be subjected to a detriment for exercising the primary right[58]. In addition, there are particular activities which do not involve the exercise of a statutory right but which Parliament has

---

[54]     See the Paternity and Adoption Leave Regulations 2002 (SI 2002/2788).
[55]     See the Maternity and Parental Leave Regulations 1999, regs. 13–20 as amended.
[56]     Trade Union and Labour Relations (Consolidation) Act 1992, s. 168; Employment Relations Act 1999, ss. 52, 55.
[57]     Trade Union and Labour Relations Act 1992, s. 170; Employment Relations Act 1999, s. 50.
[58]     E.g. Maternity and Parental Leave Regulations 1999, reg. 19; Paternity and Adoption Leave Regulations 2002, reg. 28.

chosen to protect by a right not to be subjected to a detriment for carrying out the activity: see **14-30** to **14-32** below. An employee who has been unlawfully subjected to a detriment at work can present a complaint to the Employment Tribunal if he does so within three months beginning with the date on which the detriment occurred or within such further period as the tribunal considers reasonable if it was not reasonably practicable for the complaint to be presented within the three month period. The tribunal will declare the claim to be well founded and may award such compensation as it considers just and equitable in all the circumstances.

## 14-30 Trade union activities

It is unlawful for an employer to subject his employee to a detriment for membership of, or for taking part in the activities of, a trade union[59]. It should be noted that the purpose of a particular course of action by the employer is determined by the object which the employer desires to achieve rather than the consequences of that course of action.

## 14-31 Health and safety activities

An employee has a right not to suffer detriment on grounds connected with health and safety[60]. This protection applies particularly to employees who are carrying out health and safety duties assigned to them; or who are health and safety representatives; or who in the absence of a health and safety representative bring health and safety issues to the attention of their employers and are subjected to a detriment as a result.

## 14-32 'Whistleblowing'

An employee has the right not to suffer detriment because he has made a public interest disclosure. These provisions apply to employees who make protected disclosures of qualifying information[61]. 'Qualifying information' is information which in the reasonable belief of the employee tends to show that there has been or is likely to be a crime; a breach of other legal obligation; a miscarriage of justice; a danger to health and safety; or damage to the environment; or to show

---

[59]     Trade Union and Labour Relations Act 1992, s. 146.
[60]     Employment Rights Act 1996, s. 44.
[61]     Ibid. s. 43A and 43B.

that one of the above matters has been or is likely to be deliberately concealed[62]. The disclosure of this information to an employer in good faith is 'protected'. Disclosure in good faith to certain prescribed persons e.g. the Inland Revenue and the Health and Safety Executive is 'protected' if the employee reasonably believes that the information is relevant to the prescribed person and that it is true. Disclosure in good faith to other third parties is 'protected' if the employee reasonably believes that the information is true; the disclosure is not made for personal gain; the disclosure is reasonable; and there has been prior disclosure to the employer. Disclosure to third parties without prior disclosure to the employer is 'protected' only in more limited circumstances[63].

# 12. PART-TIME AND FIXED TERM EMPLOYEES

### 14-33    Part-time employees

Part-time workers have the right not to be treated less favourably than comparable full-time workers whether as regards the terms of their contract or by being subjected to a detriment. In determining whether a part-time worker has been treated less favourably, where appropriate a pro rata principle is applied (e.g. in relation to pay and other benefits). If the employee establishes less favourable treatment then the burden moves to the employer to justify it on objective grounds. This protection is particularly relevant to employees' contractual benefits such as membership of a bonus scheme or an occupational pension scheme. Employers should be careful not to exclude part-time workers from membership of such schemes unless there are proper reasons for doing so[64].

### 14-34    Fixed-term employees

Fixed-term employees are employed under a contract which is due to terminate on the expiry of a specific term, on the completion of a particular task or on the occurrence or non-occurrence of a specific event other than normal retirement age. As with part-time workers, fixed-term employees have the right not to be treated less favourably than comparable permanent employees whether as regards the terms

---

[62]    Ibid. s. 43B.
[63]    Ibid. ss. 43C to 43H.
[64]    See the Part-Time Workers (Prevention of Less Favourable Treatment) Regulations 2000 (SI 2000/1551).

of their employment or by being subjected to a detriment. In determining whether a fixed-term employee has been treated less favourably, where appropriate a pro rata principle is applied. If the employee establishes less favourable treatment then the burden moves to the employer to justify it on objective grounds. Treatment can be justified on the grounds that the terms of the fixed-term contract taken as a whole are at least as favourable as those of the comparable permanent employee[65].

## 14-35  Remedy

Both part-time and fixed-term employees can present a complaint of less favourable treatment to the Employment Tribunal within three months of the date of the less favourable treatment. This period can be extended if the tribunal thinks it just and equitable to do so. The tribunal may make a declaration as to the parties' rights; make an order for compensation; or make recommendations to reduce or obviate the effect of the less favourable treatment[66].

## 13.  HEALTH AND SAFETY AT WORK

**14-36**  An employer is under a common law duty to have regard to the safety of his employees. Statutory obligations have also been imposed on the employer, mainly by the Health and Safety at Work etc Act 1974 and the regulations published under it. Breach of the provisions of the Act of 1974 gives rise to criminal liability only[67] whereas breach of the regulations published under the Act of 1974 which causes injury or damage gives rise to civil liability[68]. Any provision in the contract of employment excluding liability for breaches of the said regulations is void[69].

**14-37**  Broadly speaking the Act of 1974 contains provisions which correspond to the general common law duty imposed on an employer to take reasonable care of the safety of its employee. In addition the Act imposes more specific duties. For example, where an employer employs five or more employees[70], the employer must prepare (and

---

[65]     See the Fixed-term Employees (Prevention of Less Favourable Treatment) Regulations 2002 (SI 2002/2034).
[66]     Health and Safety at Work etc Act 1974, s. 47(1).
[67]     Ibid. s. 47(2).
[68]     Ibid. s. 47(2).
[69]     Ibid. s. 47(5).
[70]     See the Employers' Health and Safety Policy Statements (Exception) Regulations 1975 (SI 1975/1584).

revise, if necessary) a written statement of its general policy with respect to the health and safety of its employees, which is to be displayed on an easily accessible notice board[71]. In addition, information as to health, safety and welfare must be given to employees by means of posters and leaflets approved and published by the Health and Safety Executive[72].

**14-38**    In many respects the employer's common law duties have been rendered obsolete by regulations published over the last 15 years to implement the  various EU Directives relating to health and safety at work. These common law and statutory duties may be summarised as follows[73]:

*(1)  Safe place of work*
   The employer is under a common law duty to provide a reasonably safe place of work and means of access to work. The Workplace (Health, Safety and Welfare) Regulations 1992 now impose a statutory duty to ensure that workplaces are made and kept in an efficient state, efficient working order and good repair[74]. The regulations also include a range of specific requirements relating to lighting, cleanliness, room dimensions, arrangement of workstations, spillages and obstructions on floors etc[75].

*(2)  Safe system of work*
   At common law the employer's duty is to take reasonable steps to provide a system which will be reasonably safe, having regard to the nature of the work being carried out. Long established practice is usually regarded as strong evidence that the system being operated is a reasonable one[76]. Providing a safe system of work by itself is not sufficient. The employer must take such steps as are reasonably practicable to *implement* the system. The system must also now comply with such regulations as relate to the work being undertaken. There are a myriad of regulations covering such topics as noise at work, handling dangerous substances, construction work and asbestos[77]. The following regulations are likely to have most practical significance for clubs:

---

71       Health and Safety at Work etc Act 1974, s. 2(3).
72       See the Health and Safety Information for Employees Regulations 1989 (SI 1989/ 682).
73       See *Munkman of Employers' Liability* (13th edn, 2001) for more detailed guidance.
74       See reg. 5 of these regulations (SI 1992/3004).
75       Ibid. regs. 8 to 12.
76       *General Cleaning Contractors Ltd v Christmas* [1953] AC 180 at 195.
77       The complete and annotated health and safety regulations are to be found in *Redgrave's Health and Safety* (4th edn, 2000).

    (a)  the Management of Health and Safety at Work Regulations 1999[78]. These regulations require employers to put in place a proper health and safety procedure. In particular regulation 3 requires employers to carry out risk assessments of the work to be undertaken by their employees;

    (b)  the Manual Handling Operations Regulations 1992[79]. These regulations require employers inter alia to take steps to reduce the risk of injury from manual handling operations to the lowest level reasonably practicable. Manual handling operations are widely defined to include most manual tasks but the regulations particularly apply to lifting;

    (c)  the Health and Safety (Display Screen Equipment) Regulations 1992[80]. These regulations require employers to ensure that the workstations of employees who use computers are properly set up so as to reduce the risk of their developing conditions such as repetitive strain injuries.

*(3)   Safe equipment and materials*

At common law an employer's duty is to take reasonable steps to provide equipment, materials and clothing which allow the employee to carry out his work in safety. The Provision and Use of Work Equipment Regulations 1998 now impose on employers a statutory duty to ensure that work equipment is suitable for the purposes for which it was provided and that the equipment is maintained in an efficient state, in efficient working order and in good repair[81]. The regulations also include a range of specific requirements relating to such matters as training, lighting, dangerous parts etc[82]. The Personal Protective Equipment at Work Regulations 1992[83] impose similar obligations in relation to protective equipment e.g. gloves, hats, goggles etc.

*(4)   Competent fellow employees*

The employer's duty is to provide competent fellow employees. So the known inadequacy of a particular employee should not be tolerated. In addition, under the doctrine of vicarious liability[84] the employer is liable for the acts of his employee if they are committed in the course of his employment, so that the negligent

---

[78]    SI 1999/3242.
[79]    SI 1992/2793 especially reg. 4.
[80]    SI 1992/2792.
[81]    See regs. 4 and 5 of these regulations (SI 1998/2306).
[82]    Ibid. regs. 9, 11 and 21.
[83]    SI 1992/2966.
[84]    See **12-20** above.

act of one employee towards another employee causing injury will render the employer liable to the injured employee. Any term in the contract of employment excluding this liability is void[85].

**14-39**   If an employee establishes a breach of his employer's common law or statutory duties then the employee is entitled to damages for his injury and for the past and future losses consequent upon the injury. These damages will be reduced by the extent to which the employee's negligence (if any) contributed to his injury[86].

## 14.   COMPULSORY INSURANCE

**14-40**   Every employer carrying on a business[87] must maintain insurance, under one or more approved policies with an authorised insurer, against liability for bodily injury or diseases sustained by employees arising out of and in the course of their employment in Great Britain[88]. The sum insured must not be less than £5 million in respect of any one occurrence[89]. The insurer's annual certificate must be displayed at every place where the employer carries on business and be easily seen and read by every person employed there.

## 15.   TERMINATION OF THE CONTRACT OF EMPLOYMENT

**14-41**   The contract may be terminated in various ways:

(1) *by mutual agreement*;

(2) *by expiry of the fixed term of employment*:
    In certain circumstances this expiry may qualify for compensation for unfair dismissal or a redundancy payment;

(3) *by frustration of the contract*:
    (a) frustration occurs where the performance of the contract becomes impossible or substantially different from the contract contemplated at the outset by the parties through some unforeseen event and through no fault of the parties[90];

---

85      Law Reform (Personal Injuries) Act 1948, s. 1(3) (which Act abolished the doctrine of common employment).

86      See generally *Munkman on Employers' Liability* (13th edn, 2001).

87      This would almost invariably include a club employing staff.

88      Employers' Liability (Compulsory Insurance) Act 1969.

89      Employers' Liability (Compulsory Insurance) Regulations 1998 (SI 1998/2573).

90      *Williams v Watsons Luxury Coaches Ltd* [1990] ICR 536 (illness); *FC Shepherd & Co Ltd v Jerrom* [1986] ICR 802 (custodial prison sentence).

(b) termination of the contract is automatic, so there can be no claim for unfair or wrongful dismissal or for a redundancy payment;

(4) *by notice of dismissal given by the employer*:

The contract of employment should always contain the length of notice the employee is entitled to receive when his employment is being terminated. If the contract is silent, the employee is entitled to reasonable notice[91]. The length of notice, however, must not be less than the statutory minimum[92], namely:

(a) one week for an employee who has been continuously employed for one month or more but less than two years,

(b) one week for every year of employment for an employee who has been continuously employed for two years or more but less than 12 years,

(c) not less than 12 weeks for an employee who has been continuously employed for 12 years or more;

(5) *by notice of resignation given by the employee*:

(a) an employee may resign with or without notice. The statutory minimum period of notice is one week where the employee has been employed for one month or more[93] but the contractual period of notice is frequently longer than this. Failure to give proper notice is a breach of contract on the employee's part;

(b) if an employee resigns on notice, it is often over some disagreement with his employer; hence it is wise to let the period of notice be worked with the employee at home rather at work;

(6) *summary dismissal by the employer*:

Most contracts of employment give the employer an express right to dismiss an employee without notice for gross misconduct. Such contracts usually contain a list of examples of gross misconduct such as violent or abusive behaviour, dishonesty, wilful disobedience of a lawful order or persistent misconduct.

(7) *by the other party's acceptance of a serious repudiatory breach of the contract of employment on the part of the employer or employee*:

(a) it is essential that the breach is accepted by the innocent party as determining the contract. Acceptance of the breach, however, will be readily inferred. Acceptance by the employee

---

[91] *Reda v Flag Ltd* [2002] 1 IRLR 747.
[92] Employment Rights Act 1996, s. 12.
[93] Ibid. s. 86(2).

will mean in many cases that the employee can assert that he was constructively dismissed by the employer;

(b) this mode of termination includes summary dismissal of the employee without notice or wages in lieu of notice, for example, serious misconduct involving wilful disobedience to a lawful order or theft of the employer's property or drunkenness whilst on duty;

(c) when an employee is sacked for whatever reason, on notice or summarily, it is always a wise practice to insist that the employee forthwith leaves the employer's premises as the employer does not want disgruntled employees to upset the rest of the workforce. If the dismissal is on notice, it is worth paying wages in lieu of notice.

## 16.  WRONGFUL DISMISSAL

**14-42**   An employee who is dismissed by his employer in breach of the contractual terms agreed between them is entitled to bring a claim for damages in the courts where the limitation period for bringing a claim is six years from the date of dismissal[94] or in the employment tribunal where the claim must be brought within three months (and where the tribunal does not have jurisdiction to award damages in excess of £25,000)[95]. This claim is quite distinct from the statutory remedy of compensation for unfair dismissal.  The measure of damages for wrongful dismissal is the amount which the employee would have received had the employer complied with his contractual and statutory obligations[96]. This will include loss of pay and related benefits such as the provision of a motor car. No damages will be awarded for injured feelings or distress caused by the dismissal[97].

## 17.  UNFAIR DISMISSAL

**14-43**   Compensation for unfair dismissal was first introduced in 1971 and is now governed by the Employment Rights Act 1996. Under this Act the employee has the right not to be unfairly dismissed. In a nutshell, the club employer who dismisses an employee without good reason or without following a fair procedure is vulnerable to a claim

---

[94]     Limitation Act 1980, s. 6.

[95]     See the Employment Tribunals' Extension of Jurisdiction (England and Wales) Order 1994 (SI 1994/1623).

[96]     *Laverack v Woods of Colchester* [1967] 1 QB 278, cf *Clark v BET plc* [1997] IRLR 348.

[97]     *Bliss v South East Thames Regional Health Authority* [1987] ICR 700 CA.

for unfair dismissal being bought against it in the employment tribunal[98]. Generally speaking, any term in the contract of employment restricting the right to bring an unfair dismissal claim is void[99].

**14-44** In order to bring a claim the employee must satisfy the following pre-conditions:
(1) that he was employed under a contract of employment[100];
(2) that he was dismissed as defined by the Act[101];
(3) that his period of continuous employment was of sufficient length for him to bring a claim[102].

As to *dismissal*, this means:
(a) the contract of employment was terminated by the employer with or without notice; or
(b) where the contract was for a fixed term, that term had expired without the contract of employment being renewed[103]; or
(c) the contract was terminated by the employee with or without notice because of the employer's conduct (i.e. a case of constructive dismissal).

As to the *qualifying period*, this is now one year[104] but subject to certain exceptions. No qualifying period is necessary, for example, where the reason or principal reason for the dismissal was a maternity-related reason[105]; or was a health-and-safety reason[106]; or was because of the employee's assertion of a statutory right[107]; or was a reason connected with the assertion of rights under the minimum wage legislation[108]. In order to calculate the qualifying period one needs to know the effective date of termination of the employment: in most cases this will be the date when the employee ceases work, but where the employment is terminated by notice the effective date will be the date on which the notice expires, and where the employee is engaged

---

[98]     See, for example, *Warnes v Cheriton Oddfellows Social Club* [1993] IRLR 58.
[99]     Employment Rights Act 1996, s. 203(1).
[100]    Ibid. ss. 94(1) and 230(1).
[101]    Ibid. s. 95(1).
[102]    Ibid. s. 108(1).
[103]    The Employment Relations Act 1999, s. 18(1) repealed the provisions of the Employment Rights Act 1996 which had permitted agreements to exclude unfair dismissal provisions in fixed-term contracts.
[104]    The Unfair Dismissal and Statement of Reasons for Dismissal (Variation of Qualifying Period) Order 1999 (SI 1999/1436).
[105]    Employment Rights Act 1996, s. 108(3)(b).
[106]    Ibid. s. 108(3)(c).
[107]    Ibid. s. 108(3)(g).
[108]    Ibid. s. 108(3)(gg).

under a contract for a fixed term the effective date will be the date on which the term expires[109].

**14-45** It should be noted that as an exception an employee cannot bring a claim if on or before the effective date of termination he has attained the age which, in the undertaking in which he was employed, is the normal retiring age for an employee holding the position he held and the retiring age is the same for both men and women[110]. Where there is no normal retiring age, no claim will lie for an employee aged 65 years or more[111]. As an exception to the exception, an employee who is over the normal retiring age or over 65 *can* bring a claim if the reason for the dismissal was an unacceptable one, ie one of the reasons for disapplying the qualifying period.

## 14-46  Reasons for dismissal

Once the dismissal has been established it is for the employer to show what was the reason or principal reason for the dismissal. If there is a dispute as to the reason, the employer has the onus of proving the reason[112]. It is important to note that the employer cannot at the employment tribunal rely on facts which he discovered *after* the dismissal to justify it, although this may affect the level of compensation[113].

Acceptable reasons for the dismissal are[114]:
(1) reasons relating to the capability or qualifications of the employee for performing work of the kind which he was employed to do. As to capability, it is essential for the employer to show what was required of the employee and that the employee was informed accordingly;
(2) reasons relating to the conduct of the employee. The misconduct relied on must be sufficiently serious to warrant dismissal or, if of less serious kind, there must be repetitive misbehaviour[115];
(3) that the employee was redundant[116];

---

109    Ibid. s. 97(1).
110    Employment Rights Act 1996, s. 109(1).
111    Ibid. s. 109(1).
112    *Maund v Penwith District Council* [1984] ICR 143.
113    *W. Devis & Sons Ltd v Atkins* [1977] ICR 662. This is contrary to the common law where in an action for wrongful dismissal the employer can justify the dismissal by facts subsequently discovered: *Bell v Lever Bros* [1932] AC 161. If an *internal* appeal is heard in respect of the dismissal, the employer *may* rely on facts subsequently discovered at the appeal hearing: *West Midlands Co-operative Society Ltd v Tipton* [1986] ICR 192 HL.
114    Employment Rights Act 1996, s. 98(1), (2).
115    *Auguste Noel Ltd v Curtis* [1990] ICR 604 EAT.
116    For the topic of redundancy see **14-54** below.

(4) that the employee could not continue to work in the position which he held without contravention (on his part or the employer's part) of a duty or restriction imposed by or under an enactment;

(5) that there was 'some other substantial reason'. For example, a 'substantial reason' could be the necessary reorganisation of the business of the club,[117] or the imposition of necessary economies in running the club,[118] in circumstances which do not quite satisfy the statutory definition of redundancy. In practice employment tribunals uphold dismissals for 'some other substantial reason' only in rare cases.

## 14-47 Fairness of the dismissal

Some reasons for dismissal are automatically deemed unfair. Generally speaking, these deeming provisions apply to employees who have been dismissed for exercising any of the primary employment rights or for carrying out any of the protected activities referred to in **14-29** above. For example, in *Maziak v. City Restaurants* [1999] IRLR 780 EAT, which concerned a health-and-safety dismissal, it was held that Mr Maziak's dismissal was automatically unfair where he refused to cook food which he considered to be a hazard to public health. This was because under section 100(1)(e) of the Employment Rights Act 1996 he had been dismissed for 'taking steps to protect other persons from danger'. It did not matter that the 'other persons' were his co-employees.

**14-48**   If the reason for dismissal was an acceptable one, it is then for the employment tribunal to decide whether it was fair or unfair in all the circumstances (including the size and administrative resources of the employer's undertaking)[119]. Neither side has any evidentiary burden in this enquiry[120]. In making this decision the tribunal must consider whether the dismissal fell within 'the range of reasonable responses'[121]. So, for example, in a capability dismissal the tribunal is likely to enquire whether the employer had available other, more suitable work for the employee or whether the employer had considered an offer to train the employee up to the required standard. The tribunal will also take into account whether the employer had adopted a fair procedure in dismissing the employee[122]. This will be

---

[117]   See *Hollister v National Farmers' Union* [1979] ICR 542.

[118]   See *Durrant and Cheshire v Clariston Clothing Co Ltd* [1974] IRLR 360.

[119]   Employment Rights Act 1996, s. 98(4).

[120]   *Foley v Post Office* and *HSBC Bank* (formerly Midland Bank) *v Madden* [2000] IRLR 827.

[121]   See *Foley's* case.

[122]   *Lock v Connell Estate Agents* [1998] IRLR 358. A common failure is the omission to give any warnings about poor performance before the dismissal.

important in misconduct dismissals. The rules of natural justice operate here: the employee must be told of the alleged misconduct and given a proper opportunity to defend the allegation or explain his behaviour. and the employer must act in good faith in dealing with the matter. Furthermore the employer should be satisfied that during the course of the process he has carried out a reasonable investigation of the issues raised[123].

**14-49** Recent legislation has emphasised the importance of procedural fairness[124]. As from 1 October 2004 employers and employees must follow dismissal and disciplinary procedures and grievance procedures which satisfy the minimum requirements of the statutory procedures[125]. The statutory dismissal and disciplinary procedure applies (with some limited exceptions) to all dismissals i.e. not just to dismissals for misconduct but also to dismissals (e.g. for redundancy) which have no disciplinary flavour to them at all. The statutory dismissals and disciplinary procedure requires the following steps to be taken without unreasonable delay:

(1) Step 1: the employer must give the employee a written statement of the grounds for the proposed action and invite the employee to a meeting;

(2) Step 2: the meeting (which must not take place unless and until the employer has informed the employee what the basis was for including in the Step 1 statement the grounds given in it, and the employee has had a reasonable opportunity of considering that information). The meeting must be conducted in a manner that enables both employer and employee to explain their cases. After the meeting the employer must inform the employee of his decision and notify him of his right of appeal;

(3) Step 3: the appeal. If the employee informs the employer of his wish to appeal the employer must invite him to attend an appeal meeting. After this appeal meeting the employer must inform the employee of his final decision[126].

The legislation also provides for a modified procedure which does away with the requirement for an initial meeting in those rare cases

---

[123]     Employment Act 2002, ss. 29, 31, 32; and the Employment Act (Dispute Resolution) Regulations 2004 (SI 2004/752).

[124]     Ibid. s. 29 introduces the statutory procedures; regs. 3 to 11 set out the circumstances in which the procedures apply.

[125]     E.g. redundancy.

[126]     Employment Act 2002, Sch. 2 , Part 1, Chapter 1.

of obviously gross misconduct which justify immediate summary dismissal[127]. If the employer fails to follow any dismissal procedure or follows a procedure which does not satisfy the minimum requirements of the statutory procedure, then the dismissal is deemed to be automatically unfair[128].

**14-50**  It should be noted that the right to be accompanied to any disciplinary meeting by either a work colleague or union representative[129] is a free standing statutory right and not a requirement of the statutory dismissal and disciplinary procedure. A breach of this right does not mean that the dismissal is deemed to be automatically unfair.

## 14-51  Remedies

This in itself is a complex area where commonly changes take place, such as the raising of the ceiling of compensation, so that the club would be well advised to take professional advice on this topic. An employee who has been unfairly dismissed can present a complaint to the Employment Tribunal within three months beginning with the effective date of termination or within such further period as the tribunal considers reasonable if it was not reasonably practicable to present the complaint within the three-month period[130]. An employee whose complaint is based on a constructive dismissal must (subject to limited exceptions) first raise his complaint as a formal grievance with his employer before presenting his complaint to the tribunal[131].

**14-52**  Where the employment tribunal upholds the complaint of unfair dismissal, it may make any of the following orders:

(1) *an order for reinstatement*[132]:
   This is defined as an order that the employer shall treat the complainant in all respects as if he had not been dismissed. This order is rarely made;

---

[127]   Ibid. Chapter 2.
[128]   Employment Rights Act 1996, s. 98(1).
[129]   Employment Relations Act 1999, s. 10.
[130]   Employment Rights Act 1996, s. 111(2). See also the Employment Act 2002 (Dispute Resolution) Regulations 2004, reg. 15 which extends the time limit for a further threee months if there is an ongoing appeal or if the case involves constructive dismissal, so that the claimant can first raise his complaints as a grievance with his employer.
[131]   At least 28 days must have elapsed since the employee raised his grievance before he can present his claim to the Tribunal: Employment Act 2002, s. 32, Sch. 2, Pt. 2 and regs. 6 to 11 of the regulations referred to in footnote 131.
[132]   Employment Rights Act 1996, ss. 114, 116(1).

(2) *an order for re-engagement*[133]:

This is defined as an order that the complainant be engaged by the employer in employment comparable to that from which he was dismissed or other suitable employment. This means the employee will not get his old job back. This order is rarely made;

(3) *a basic award*[134]:

Where the tribunal makes an award of compensation it must consist of a basic award and a compensatory award[135]. These two awards are the ones most commonly made. The maximum amount is presently (2004) the sum of £8,100. The amount of the award depends on basic weekly pay (subject to a maximum of, presently, £270 per week) length of service, and age. The award is essentially calculated in the same way as a redundancy payment;

(4) *a compensatory award*[136]:

The maximum amount is presently (2004) the sum of £55,000[137]. The amount of the award may take into account past and future loss of earnings, loss of benefits, loss of pension rights, and loss of statutory rights[138].The employee's duty to take reasonable steps to mitigate his loss generally determines the period for which he is awarded compensation. Thus a tribunal is unlikely to compensate the employee for any period beyond the date by which he should have found alternative employment. Furthermore, if the tribunal finds that the employee had been unfairly dismissed merely because the employer had failed to follow the proper procedure then the tribunal may discount any compensatory award to reflect the chance that the employee would still have been dismissed even if the proper procedure had been followed[139].

(5) *an additional award*[140].

An additional award of compensation is made where the order for reinstatement or re-engagement has not been complied with.

---

133    Employment Rights Act 1996, ss. 115 and 116(2).
134    Ibid. s. 119.
135    Ibid. s. 118(1).
136    Ibid. s. 123 (1).
137    There are limited exceptions where no maxima apply, e.g. the Employment Rights Act 1996, ss. 103A, 106(6A).
138    A conventional figure of £200 is often awarded under this head.
139    See *Polkey v AE Dayton Services* [1988] AC 344 (this decision has been partially reversed by the Employment Rights Act 1996, s. 98A but the principle stated above is unaffected); cf. *O'Donoughue v Redcar and Cleveland Borough Council* [2001] IRLR 615.
140    Employment Rights Act 1996, s. 117.

**14-53** When a tribunal makes no order for reinstatement or re-engagement but instead awards compensation:

(1) if the tribunal finds that the dismissal was caused or contributed to by any blameworthy conduct on the part of the employee then the tribunal will reduce the award by such proportion as it considers just and equitable having regard to that finding[141];

(2) if either the statutory dismissal and disciplinary procedure or the statutory grievance procedure applied to the subject matter of the complaint and the appropriate procedure was not completed before the complaint was presented to the tribunal then the tribunal must increase any award by such percentage as it thinks just and equitable ( but not less than 10% and not more than 50%) if the non-completion was attributable to a failure by the employer; alternatively the tribunal must reduce the award if the non-completion was attributable to a failure by the employee[142].

## 18.   REDUNDANCY

**14-54** Redundancy payments were first introduced in 1965 and are now governed by the Employment Rights Act 1996. Subject to limited exceptions, any provision in the contract of employment excluding or limiting the right to a redundancy payment is void[143]. These payments are made in certain circumstances where the employee has lost his job. The employer also has a duty to consult the employees' representatives where it is proposing to dismiss as redundant at least 20 employees within a period of 90 days or less[144]. A person is made redundant if the dismissal was wholly or mainly attributable to[145]:

(1) the fact that the employer has ceased, or intends to cease, to carry on the business for the purposes of which the employee was employed, alternatively to carry on such business in the place where the employee was employed; or

---

[141]     Employment Rights Act 1996,. s. 123(6).

[142]     See the Employment Act 2002, s. 31, Sch. 2 and the Employment Act 2002 (Dispute Resolutions) Regulations 2004. The statutory dismissal and disciplinary procedures are summarised in **14-49** above. The statutory grievance procedures follow a similar form, save that they are initiated by a written statement from the employee, not the employer.

[143]     Employment Rights Act 1996, s. 203(1).

[144]     Trade Union and Labour Relations (Consolidation) Act 1992 as amended by the Collective Redundancies and Transfer of Undertakings (Protection of Employment) (Amendment) Regulations 1999 (SI 1999/1925).

[145]     Ibid. s.139(1).

[146]     Employment Rights Act 1996, s. 155.

(2) the fact that the requirements of that business for employees to carry out work of a particular kind have ceased or diminished, or are expected to cease or diminish; alternatively have so ceased or diminished in the place where the employee was employed by the employer.

**14-55**  The employee must satisfy the same pre-conditions as set out in paragraph **14-44** above in relation to claims for unfair dismissal, save that the reason for dismissal must of course be redundancy and save that the qualifying period of continuous employment is two years ending with the relevant date[146]. The 'relevant date' corresponds to the 'effective date of termination' in claims for unfair dismissal[147]. An employee who commences employment before his eighteenth birthday is treated as if his employment had commenced on that date[148]. The amount of the redundancy payment is based on the employee's age, length of continuous employment and gross average wage. The maximum amount of a week's pay which is allowed in computing a statutory redundancy payment is presently (2004) the sum of £270[149]. This means that the maximum redundancy payment is £8,100.

**14-56**  Certain employees are not entitled to a redundancy payment. They include:
(1) an employee who has attained the age which, in the undertaking in which he was employed, was the normal retiring age for an employee holding the position he held and the retiring age was the same for both men and women[150]. Where there is no such normal retiring age, no claim will lie for an employee aged 65 years or more[151];
(2) an employee who has been offered suitable alternative employment and has unreasonably refused the offer[152];
(3) an employee who is dismissed for misconduct[153].

**14-57**  An employee is not entitled to a redundancy payment unless within six months of the 'relevant date' he has made a written claim to his employer for such a payment or he has presented a claim for unfair dismissal to the employment tribunal[154]. It is important to note that where the reason for dismissal is redundancy, the employer may

---

[147]   Employment Rights Act 1996, s. 145.
[148]   Ibid. s. 211(2).
[149]   Ibid. s. 227 and the Employment Rights (Increase of Limits) Order 2002 (SI 2002/10).
[150]   Employment Rights Act 1996, s. 156(1)(a).
[151]   Ibid. s. 156(1)(b).
[152]   Ibid. s. 141.
[153]   Ibid. s. 140.
[154]   Ibid. s. 164(1).

be liable for a claim for unfair dismissal *in addition* to the redundancy payment if the employer has acted unfairly towards him in dismissing him for redundancy[155].

## 19.  DISCRIMINATION IN EMPLOYMENT

### 14-58   Disability discrimination

The Disability Discrimination Act 1995 makes it unlawful to discriminate against disabled persons in employment (and other areas)[156]. Under the Act a disabled person is one who has a physical or mental impairment which has a substantial and long-term adverse effect on his ability to carry out normal day-to-day activities[157]. 'Long-term' here means if the effect has lasted at least 12 months; or if it is likely to last that long; or if it is likely to last for the rest of the affected person's life; or if it is likely to recur although in remission[158]. A substantial effect is one which is more than 'minor' or 'trivial'[159]. Pursuant to section 3 of the Act the Secretary of State has issued guidance[160] about matters to be taken into account in determining what counts as day-to-day activities; whether an impairment has a substantial adverse effect on a person's ability to carry out these day-to-day activities; and whether such an impairment has a long-term effect. By section 3(3) an employment tribunal must take into account this guidance. There is also a Code of Practice published by the Secretary of State which contains practical advice with numerous examples of how the Act should work in practice[161].

**14-59**   It is unlawful for an employer to discriminate against a disabled employee by dismissing him, harassing him or subjecting him to any other detriment[162]. Discrimination may take place in one of three ways: direct discrimination[163]; discrimination by way of the

---

[155]    Employment Rights Act 1996, s. 105 [C] [T 49.11].
[156]    See also Disability Discrimination (Meaning of Discrimination) Regulations 1996 (SI 1996/1455) and Disability Discrimination (Employment) Regulations 1996 (SI 1996/1456).
[157]    Disability Discrimination Act 1995, s. 1(1), Sch. 1, para 4(1). See also *Vicary v. British Telecommunications plc* [1999] IRLR 680, EAT.
[158]    Ibid. Sch. 1 paras 2(1) and 2(2) of the Act.
[159]    See the guidance published by the Secretary of State referred to in the next footnote.
[160]    Guidance on Matters to be Taken into Account in Determining Matters relating to Disability (1996).
[161]    Code of Practice for the Elimination of Discrimination in the Field of Employment against Disabled Persons or Persons who have a Disability.
[162]    Disability Discrimination Act 1995, s. 4.
[163]    Ibid. s. 5(1).

employer's failure to comply with the duty to make adjustments[164]; and discrimination by way of victimisation[165]. In relation to a particular category of direct discrimination and to any failures to make reasonable adjustments, the employer is entitled to show that the discrimination was justified[166]. A difficulty may arise where the club is occupying its premises under a lease in that the club may not be entitled under the terms of the lease to make the necessary alterations to the premises in order to comply with its statutory obligations. Section 16 of the Act provides that the lease shall have the effect as if it provided for the occupier to be entitled to make the necessary alterations with the consent of the lessor, such consent not to be withheld unreasonably[167].

**14-60** *Remedy*   An employee who has been discriminated against must present his complaint to the employment tribunal within 3 months from the date the act complained of was done or within such further time as the tribunal considers just and equitable[168]. An employee who complains of matters other than dismissal must (subject to limited exceptions) first raise his complaint as a grievance with his employer before presenting it to the tribunal[169]. The sanction for committing an unlawful act of disability discrimination is an award of compensation comprising an award for injury to feelings in addition to compensation for past and future financial losses.

## 14-61   Sex Discrimination

The Sex Discrimination Act 1975 makes it unlawful to discriminate against men or women in the field of employment; there must be equal treatment between the sexes[170]. This Act applies to all club employees. Discrimination may occur in one of three ways: direct discrimination[171]; indirect discrimination[172] and victimisation[173]. As

---

[164]   Disability Discrimination Act 1995, s. 6(1).

[165]   Ibid. s. 55 (1).

[166]   Ibid. ss. 5(2) and 5(3). See *HJ Heinz Co Ltd v Kendrick* [2000] IRLR 144 EAT (concerning direct discrimination) and *Morse v Wiltshire County Council* [1998] IRLR 352 [EAT] (concerning the duty to make adjustments).

[167]   See also reg. 14 of the Disability Regulations 1996 (SI 1996/1456) (concerning the lessor's ability to impose reasonable conditions, and reinstatement at the end of the lease, etc); and s.16A of the Act which deals with sub-leases.

[168]   Disability Discrimination Act 1995, Sch. 3 para 3; and see reg.15 referred to in footnote 131 above.

[169]   See footnote 132 above.

[170]   Sex Discrimination Act 1975, s. 6.

[171]   Ibid. s. 1(1)(a).

[172]   Ibid. s. 1(1)(b) as substituted by the Sex Discrimination (Indirect Discrimination and Burden of Proof) Regulations 2001 (SI 2001/2660).

regards direct discrimination, the question to ask is, has the complainant been less favourably treated than his or her opposite-sex counterpart? Thus, for example, it was direct discrimination to make free entry to a swimming pool dependent upon state pensionable age because men and women in the UK become pensionable at different ages: *James v Eastleigh Borough Council* [1990] ICR 554. In carrying out the comparison like must be compared with like. It is not sufficient for, say, a woman to show that she has been treated unfavourably; she must show that the unfavourable treatment is because of her sex. So if the alleged discriminator treats men in the same unfavourable or unreasonable manner in comparable circumstances, there is no discrimination[174]. Nor will it suffice for a woman-complainant to demonstrate that men are or would be treated differently; the treatment must be less favourable. Thus, in *Smith v Safeway plc* [1996] ICR 868, CA, where male and female employees were made subject to different but comparably restrictive dress requirements, there was no discrimination.

**14-62** There are a number of other areas of direct discrimination of which clubs should be aware. First, there is the discrimination on the grounds of pregnancy. This can be a difficult area. Take the case of *O'Neill v Governors of St Thomas More RCVA Upper School* [1997] ICR 33 EAT where a Roman Catholic school dismissed a religious education teacher who was made pregnant by a priest. The school contended that it was not the pregnancy itself but the circumstances of the pregnancy which caused the dismissal, but the appeal tribunal held that if one asked the simple question, 'On an objective basis was the dismissal on the ground of pregnancy?' the answer was in the affirmative, and it upheld the complaint of sex discrimination. Or take the case of *Rees v Apollo Watch Repairs plc* [1996] ICR 466 EAT where the employer refused to allow the complainant to resume her employment after maternity leave because he thought her temporary replacement was better at the job. The appeal tribunal held that the employer's dismissal was discriminatory because the effective cause had been the pregnancy; without this the replacement would never have been employed.

**14-63** As regards indirect discrimination, the matter was simplified by the introduction in 1991 of a new section 1(1)(b) of the Act whereby an employer discriminates against a woman if he applies to her a provision, criterion or practice which he applies or would apply

---

[173] Sex Discrimination Act 1975, s. 4(1).
[174] *Glasgow City Council v Zafar* [1998] ICR 120, HL.

equally to a man but which is such that it would be to the detriment of a considerably larger proportion of women than men, and which the employer cannot show to be justifiable irrespective of the sex of the person to whom it applies. As regards victimisation, this occurs where an employer treats any person less favourably than others because that person threatens to bring proceedings; or to give evidence or information; or to take any action or make any allegation concerning the employer with reference to the Act; or that person has done any of those things[175].

**14-64**   The employer is vicariously liable for discriminatory acts committed by his employee except where the employer can show that he took such steps as were reasonably practicable to prevent the employee from committing those acts[176].

**14-65**   *Remedy*   No legal action may be taken against an employer for a breach of any provision of the Act except as expressly provided for in the Act[177]. The only means of direct enforcement available to an individual for sex discrimination in employment is by application to an Employment Tribunal[178]. The tribunal has power to make declarations as to the rights of the complainant; to order the employer to make compensation; and to order the employer to take action for the purpose of obviating or reducing the act of discrimination complained of[179]. As to compensation, any pecuniary loss is measured in the same way as in tort, namely, the complainant is to be put back as far as possible into the position he or she would have been in, had the act of discrimination not occurred[180]. The tribunal may award compensation for injury to feelings[181] and for personal injury[182]; and may award aggravated damages[183] and interest on any sums awarded[184].

---

[175]    Sex Discrimination Act 1975, s. 4(1).
[176]    Ibid. s. 41.
[177]    Ibid. s. 76; and Reg. 15 referred to in footnote 131 above.
[178]    See footnote 132 above.
[179]    Ibid. s. 65 (1).
[180]    *Ministry of Defence v Cannock* [1994] ICR 918 EAT. The statutory cap on the limit of compensation was removed by the Sex Discrimination and Equal Pay (Remedies) Regulations 1993 (SI 1993/2798). The present regulations are the Sex Discrimination and Equal Pay (Miscellaneous Amendment) Regulations 1996 (SI 1996/438).
[181]    Sex Discrimination Act 1975, s. 66(4); and see *HM Prison Service v Johnson* [1997] ICR 275.
[182]    *HM Prison Service v Salmon* [2001] IRLR 412 EAT
[183]    *Zaiwalla & Co. v Walia* [2002] IRLR 697 EAT; *ICTS (UK) Ltd v Tchoula* [2000] IRLR 643 EAT.
[184]    Employment Tribunals (Interest on Awards in Discrimination Cases) Regulations 1996 (SI 1996/2803).

## 14-66 Racial discrimination

Discrimination on racial grounds is governed by the Race Relations Act 1976. Its provisions are similar those under the Sex Discrimination Act 1975. An employer is prohibited from discrimination on grounds of race at all stages of employment 'at an establishment in Great Britain'[185]. It is considered that an establishment would include a members' club. The Act applies to all the club's employees, whether full-time or part-time. As with sex discrimination it is important to distinguish between *unfavourable* treatment, where the complainant is treated badly, and *less favourable* treatment, where other employees receive better treatment even though their circumstances are not materially different. It is only the latter which is relevant. Thus an employer who treats all his employees equally badly regardless of race is not normally guilty of racial discrimination. It is not possible to exclude the operation of the Act by a term of the employment contract[186].

**14-67** As with sex discrimination, there may be direct discrimination[187], indirect discrimination[188] and victimisation[189]. As regards direct discrimination, this occurs where the employer treats an employee less favourably on racial grounds. 'Racial grounds' is defined in the Act as grounds based on colour, race, nationality, or ethnic or national origins[190]. In this connection it is to be noted that 'travellers' are a racial group[191]. The test for racial discrimination is a comparative one; there must be either an actual comparator or a hypothetical one. One must compare like with like[192]. Thus in *Wakeman v Quick Corporation* [1999] IRLR 424, CA the UK employees of a Japanese company could not complain about higher rates of pay enjoyed by colleagues seconded from Japan. The secondment meant that their circumstances were materially different. The less favourable treatment too must be directly related to the act complained of. Thus in *Sidhu v Aerospace Composite Technology Ltd* [2001] ICR 167 the employee was dismissed for fighting at work. The employer had adopted a policy of dismissing any employee for fighting. This policy ignored any acts of provocation. The complainant had in fact been provoked by acts of racial abuse and violence. The court held that the

---

[185]   Race Relations Act 1976, s. 8(1).
[186]   Ibid. s. 72(3).
[187]   Ibid. s. 1(1)(a) of the Act.
[188]   Ibid. ss. 1(1)(b) and 1 (1A).
[189]   Ibid. s. 2.
[190]   Ibid. s. 3(1).
[191]   *Commission for Racial Equality v Dutton* [1989] IRLR 8.
[192]   Race Relations Act 1976, s. 3(4) of the Act.

complainant had not been treated less favourably on the grounds of race.

**14-68**   As regards indirect discrimination, it is defined as occurring where a provision, criterion or practice puts persons of the same racial or ethnic or national origins at a particular disadvantage compared with others, and which cannot be shown to be proportionate means of achieving a legitimate aim[193].

**14-69**   As regards victimisation, this occurs where an employer treats any person less favourably than others because that person threatens to bring proceedings, or to give evidence or information, or to take any action or make any allegation concerning the employer with reference to the Act, or that person has done any of those things. It is necessary for the complainant to show that the less favourable treatment was meted out on the grounds of race.  Thus in the case of *Aziz v Trinity Street Taxis* Ltd [1988] ICR 534 CA the complainant covertly recorded conversations at work to support an allegation of racial discrimination.  For this conduct he was dismissed.  The employer's case was that it would have dismissed any employee who covertly recorded conversations at work, and the applicant lost his claim for victimisation.

**14-70**   There are some limited exceptions to the Act. An employer may lawfully discriminate in selecting employees for a job where a member of a particular racial group is a genuine occupational qualification for the job[195]. It would therefore be lawful, for example, for a drama club to employ a professional black actor to play the part of Othello in order to give authenticity to its production of the play, or for an art club or camera club to employ a Chinese model for the purpose of learning painting or photography.

**14-71**   *Vicarious liability*   An unlawful act of racial discrimination (other than a criminal offence) committed by an employee in the course of his employment is treated as also having been committed by his employer, whether or not the employer knew or approved of the act[196]. The words, 'in the course of employment', are in this context to be construed as meaning committed '*at* work' rather than the narrower meaning of committed '*as* work' (i.e. a mode, albeit

---

193     *Harvey on Industrial Relations and Employment Law* (2001).
195     Race Relations Act 1976, s. 5.
196     Ibid. s. 32(1).

improper one, of carrying out his work)[197]. The employer will have a defence if he can prove that he took such steps as were reasonably practicable to prevent his employee from doing the unlawful act in question or from doing that kind of act during the course of his employment[198].

**14-72** *Remedy*  As with sex discrimination the employee must apply to the employment tribunal within three months or such further time as the tribunal considers just and equitable[199]. An employee who complains about matters other than dismissal must (subject to limited exceptions) first raise his complaint as a grievance with his employer[200]. The same remedies are available as in cases of sex discrimination.

## 14-73 Equal pay

Unequal pay between men and women is another form of discrimination. This discrimination is covered by the Equal Pay Act 1970 as amended[201]. In addition, the subject is governed by Article 141 of the Treaty of Rome which states:

> Each Member State shall ensure that the principle of equal pay for male and female workers for equal work or work of equal worth is applied.

This article and the Equal Pay Directive (75/117) issued by the European Council underpin the domestic legislation[202] and have also led to free-standing Article 141 claims[203]. The Act covers both men and women although most complainants are women. The Act applies to all club employees whether full-time or part-time nor is there any qualifying period of employment before the Act applies.

---

[197]     *Jones v Tower Boot Co Ltd* [1997] ICR 254 CA; and see *Lister v Hesley Hall Ltd* [2002] 1 AC 215 at **12-19** above.

[198]     Race Relations Act 1976, s. 33 (2).

[199]     Ibid. s. 68; and see reg. 15 referred to in footnote 131 above.

[200]     See footnote 132 above.

[201]     Amended *inter alia* by the Sex Discrimination Act 1975, the Equal Pay (Amendment) Regulations 1983 (SI 1983/1794), the Sex Discrimination Act 1986 and the Pensions Act 1995.

[202]     *Scullard v Knowles* [1996] IRLR 344 EAT (where the statutory definition of a comparator under the Equal Pay Act 1970, s. 1(6)(c) of the Act required one of two employers to be a company whereas the European law had no such restriction, and the appeal tribunal disapplied the restriction by relying on Art.141).

[203]     *Biggs v Somerset County Council* [1996] IRLR 203 CA.

**14-74**  Unlike the Sex Discrimination Act 1975 and the Race Relations
Act 1976, this Act does not prohibit direct or indirect discrimination
but instead it implies into every contract of employment an 'equality
clause'[204]. That equality clause operates as follows:
(1) if any term of a woman's contract is, or becomes, less favourable
    to the woman than a term of a similar kind in a contract under
    which a man is employed, that term in the woman's contract is
    modified to become as favourable as the corresponding term on
    the man's contract, or
(2) if at any time a woman's contract does not include a beneficial
    term which is in a man's contract, the woman's contract will be
    modified so as to include that term[205].

The equality clause only applies where the woman is engaged on like
work to a man, on work rated equivalent to work done by a man or
on work of equal value to that done by a man[206].

**14-75**  In deciding whether the work done by the man and the
woman is 'like work', a broad approach should be adopted.  Thus in
*Capper Pass Ltd v Lawton* [1977] ICR 83 EAT a cook in a directors'
dining room was held to be engaged on like work as the assistant chefs
in the company's factory canteen.  There needs to be a specific
comparator, not merely a hypothetical one[207]. The comparator does
not have to be contemporaneously employed with the applicant[208].
A woman can only claim that her work is 'rated equivalent' to that
done by a man if there has been a completed job evaluation study
which has concluded so.  A claim based on work of 'equal value' is
likely to require the support of complex expert evidence to prove
the necessary equivalence.

**14-76**  If the employer can show that the variation between the
woman's contract and the man's contract is genuinely due to a
material factor which is not a difference of sex, the claim for equal
pay will fail[209]. 'Material' here means 'significant and relevant'[210].
Thus in *Benveniste v University of Southampton* [1989] ICR 617 a woman
employee was on a lower rate of pay than existing male colleagues

---

[204]  Equal Pay Act, 1970, s. 1(1).
[205]  Ibid. s. 1(2).
[206]  Ibid. s. 1(2).
[207]  See *Alabaster v Woolwich plc and Secretary of State for Social Security* [2000] IRLR 754 EAT.
[208]  *Kells v Pilkingtion plc* [2002] IRLR 693 EAT; *Diocese of Hallam Trustees v Connaughton* [1996] IRLR 505 EAT.
[209]  Equal Pay Act 1970, s. 1(3)(a) and (b). Note the slightly wider defence under (b).
[210]  *Rainey v Greater Glasgow Health Board* [1987] ICR 129 HL per Lord Keith at 140.

owing to financial constraints imposed on the university. This amounted to a material factor. But once these constraints had been removed the employer had no defence to her claim for equal pay.

**14-77** *Remedy* Proceedings must be brought in the employment tribunal. The procedure is complicated. In broad terms, the proceedings must be brought within six months after the last day of the claimant's employment. If the tribunal finds the case proved then it may award the claimant up to six years arrears in pay.

## 14-78 Other discrimination

It is now unlawful to discriminate against employees or potential employees either on grounds of their religion or belief (see the Employment Equality (Religion or Belief) Regulations 2003[211]) or on grounds of their sexual orientation (see the Employment Equality (Sexual Orientation Regulations 2003[212]). In essence the protection provided by these regulations is similar to that provided by the sex and racial discrimination legislation.

## 20. REFERENCES

**14-79** Generally speaking, the employer has no obligation to give a reference to a departing employee[213], but usually does so. It is essential that the reference is honestly and accurately given[214], because the old employer may lay itself open to a tortious claim for negligent misstatement at the suit of the new employer if in its desire to see the back of a troublesome employee it paints too rosy a picture of the employee's character and capabilities. On the other hand, if a reference is given, the employer owes a contractual duty of care to the employee to see that the reference is not misleading or negligently inaccurate because, if it is, it may be liable to the employee if he thereby suffers damage[215]. If a reference turns out to be inaccurate, the employer will not liable to the employee for defamation of character

---

[211]   SI 2003/1660.

[212]   SI 2003/1661.

[213]   The failure to give a reference may amount to victimisation: *Coote v Granada Hospitality* [1999] ICR 100 ECJ and *Coote v Granada Hospitality (No.2)* [1999] IRLR 452 EAT.

[214]   *Bartholomew v London Borough of Hackney* [1999] IRLR 246 CA.

[215]   *Spring v Guardian Assurance plc* [1994] ICR 596 HL; *Cox v Sun Alliance Life Ltd* [2001] IRLR 458 CA.

if it was given honestly and in the belief that the information was correct[216]. It is good practice to mark the letter and the envelope in which it is sent 'Private and confidential'.

**14-80**   The old employer may be asked specific questions about the employee but if a general reference is required, it should normally deal with the positions held by the employee and his competence and length of service; his honesty; his reasons for leaving; and other personal characteristics such as his good/poor time-keeping or his few/many days of absence from work through sickness.

---

[216]      The employer will be protected by the defence of qualified privilege: *Hodgson v Scarlett* [1818] 1 B & Ald 239. For the topic of defamation see **12-42** and **12-56** above.

# Chapter 15

## RESPONSIBILITY FOR CRIME

## 1.   INTRODUCTION

**15-01**   Managing committees need to be generally aware that, although clubs in the ordinary course of their activities manage to steer clear of brushes with the criminal law, we live in a complex society which, for better for worse, is much regulated and therefore some understanding of the criminal law insofar as it affects clubs is a desirable attribute. Many of the 'crimes' capable of being committed these days have no immorality about them but are simply enacted by statute for the general well-being of society. A good example is the health and safety legislation. Another example which will shortly arise is on the implementation of the Licensing Act 2003 where there are numerous new offences to be considered. Some modern offences too are properly described as offences of strict liability, that is to say, they do not depend on the prosecution proving the fault of the accused, but only the fact of the criminal activity. If the club or its members have the misfortune to be involved in any accusations of criminal activity, the first thing to do is to contact a local solicitor for help and advice.

## 2.   UNINCORPORATED BODIES

**15-02**   Unincorporated members' clubs are not legal persons in the eyes of the common law of England and it is self-evident that an entity which is not a legal person cannot be guilty of a crime under such law[1]. (It

---

[1]    *Attorney General v Able* [1984] QB 795 (concerning the Voluntary Euthanasia Society where Woolf J at 810D said, 'It must be remembered that [the society] is an unincorporated body and there can be no question of the society committing an offence').

should be added that it is equally self-evident that a member of a club as an individual is subject to the criminal law in the same way as every other citizen). But Parliament, which is sovereign, has intervened and, strange though it may seem, has given unincorporated bodies a criminal personality. By sections 2 and 19 of the Interpretation Act 1889 the word 'person' in any enactment creating an offence passed after that Act 'includes a body of persons corporate or un incorporate', and this definition of a person has been carried through to the Interpretation Act 1978[2]. In addition, some statutes specifically provide that offences created by them can be committed by unincorporated associations. The Licensing Act 2003, probably the most significant piece of legislation to affect clubs for a long time, makes specific provision as how to deal with unincorporated clubs:

(1) proceedings for an offence alleged to have been committed by an unincorporated club must be brought in the name of the club, and not in that of any of its members[3];

(2) a fine imposed on an unincorporated club on its conviction for an offence is to be paid out of the funds of the club[4].

## 15-03   Vicarious liability

The real problem arises when a person, who may or may not be a member of the club, commits an offence in the course of his activities on behalf of the club. Who in the club, apart from the wrongdoer himself, can be held responsible? The answer lies in the doctrine of vicarious liability[5]. The club will not be liable for a criminal offence simply because it has been committed by a member. Liability for a crime can only arise on the part of the club if it is committed by someone identifiable as part of the management of the club. Thus in many instances the persons or persons who will be criminally liable are the persons in control of the club, that is, the managing committee and the officers of the club. Vicarious liability covers both the club's members and its employees.

## 15-04   Knowledge

No hard and fast rule can be laid down as to when the committee or officers might be held liable. At common law a person can be held

---

[2]       Interpretation Act 1978, s. 5 and Sch. 1.

[3]       Licensing Act 2003, s. 188(2).

[4]       Ibid. s. 188(1). Similar provisions are contained in the Financial Services and Markets Act 2000, s. 403(2) and in the Companies Act 1985, s. 734 (offences in relation to failure to provide information to auditors). Common sense dictates that the only penalty which can be imposed upon a club is financial.

[5]       See Archbold, *Criminal Pleadings, Evidence and Practice* (2005 edn) para 17-25.

liable for 'aiding and abetting' a crime where he or she is not the principal offender. It is normally the case that offences are committed only when the accused *knowingly* does something which the criminal law forbids him to do. The lack of knowledge does not always allow the principal to escape liability where an employee or subordinate has committed the offence without the knowledge or connivance of the principal. This is because of the operation of the doctrine of vicarious liability[6]. Consider the following trilogy of unlawful drinking cases. In *Vane v Yiannopoullos* [1965] AC 486 the licensee of a restaurant was physically present in the premises and actively in control when, unbeknown to him, an employee committed the offence of serving intoxicating liquor to customers who had not ordered a meal. The House of Lords upheld his acquittal of knowingly selling to persons to whom he was not permitted by the conditions of his licence to sell[7], on the basis that he had no knowledge of the commission of the offence. Lord Reid said that there was a long-standing distinction between, on the one hand, the vicarious liability of a licensee for the acts done without his knowledge by an employee to whom he has delegated the entire management of the premises and, on the other hand, his non-liability for such acts done while he himself retains the general supervision of the premises. In *R v Winson* [1969] 1 QB 371 CCA the licensee of a licensed club took no active part in the running of the club and delegated this task to a manager who unlawfully permitted alcohol to be sold to persons who had not been members for 48 hours[8]. The licensee was convicted of knowingly selling alcohol unlawfully. And in *Anderton v Rogers* [1981] Crim LR 404 alcohol was unlawfully sold to a non-member of an unincorporated club[9]. The members of the committee were unaware of this fact yet were convicted of knowingly selling alcohol unlawfully.

**15-05** Part of the reason why the accused were found guilty in the two last-mentioned cases was because knowledge does not only include actual knowledge but also includes deliberately shutting one's eyes or mind to an obvious means of knowledge[10]. Thus simply appointing a manager of a club and leaving him to get on with the job will not normally exonerate the committee from criminal liability, as Lord Reid stated in the case of *Vane* above. The committee will be expected to

6 *Mousell Bros Ltd v London and North Western Railway Co.* [1917] 2 KB 836 at 844 (Viscount Reading CJ).
7 Contrary to the Licensing Act 1961, s. 22(1).
8 Contrary to the Licensing Act 1964, s. 161(1).
9 Contrary to the Licensing Act 1964, s. 160(1).
10 *Goodwin v Baldwin* (1974) *The Times*, 2 February; *Buxton v Chief Constable of Northumbria* [1983] 148 JP Jo 9; *Oxford v Lincoln* (1982) *The Times* 1 March.

put in place proper procedures for managing and supervising the activities being carried on at the club[11]. In *Linnett v Metropolitan Police Commissioner* [1946] KB 290 an absentee licensee of a public house was convicted of 'knowingly permitting disorderly conduct' where he had left control of the premises to another, who had in fact knowingly permitted the conduct complained of. Lord Goddard CJ said[12]:

> [I]f the manager chooses to delegate the carrying on of the business to another, whether or not that other is his servant, then what that other does or what he knows must be imputed to the person who put the other into that position.

The committee would not, however, be responsible for the criminal acts of a stranger or third party who committed an offence on club premises without its knowledge, or in its absence[13]. For offences under the Licensing Act 2003 the position is now largely covered by the provisions of section 187[14].

## 15-06   Strict liability and 'due diligence'

These days a committee will have to take cognisance of many statutory obligations set out in various Acts of Parliament which regulate club activity, for example, the Licensing Acts, the Gaming Act 1968, the Lotteries and Amusements Act 1976, the Weights and Measures Act 1985, and the Health and Safety legislation. The obligations are often offences of strict liability, that is to say, the offence can be committed without any fault of the part of the committee. In some statutes Parliament has permitted a defence of 'due diligence' whereby the accused can escape liability if he can prove that he took all reasonable steps to ensure compliance with his statutory obligation; for example, Parts II and III of the Gaming Act 1968 permit a 'due diligence' defence in relation to offences committed contrary to the provisions of Parts II and III. It would appear, somewhat surprisingly, that if the committee as principal is acquitted under the 'due diligence' defence in relation to a *non*-strict-liability offence, the employee or club member of an unincorporated members' club[15], who will have been the perpetrator of the offence, will likewise be acquitted[16].

---

11      *R. v Souter* [1971] 1 WLR 1187.

12      At p 295.

13      *Taylor v Speed* [1979] Crim LR 114.

14      See Appendix 8 and **15-09** below.

15      Different considerations would apply if the club was incorporated: *Coupe v Govett* [1973] 1 WLR 669 CA at 675B.

16      *Coupe v Guyett* [1973] 1 WLR 669 CA.

## 3.    CORPORATE BODIES

**15-07**   Incorporated clubs, such as incorporated members' clubs and IPSA clubs, are legal persons and so can be prosecuted and fined, or committed for sentence to the Crown Court[17]. Here again, whether the act of an agent or employee is to be attributed to the company is to be decided on the issue of the closeness of the relationship between the agent and the company. The guilty mind of a workman who is not closely identified with the management of the company will not render it liable, whereas the guilty mind of a director, or a manager, will do so[18]. On the other hand, where a company caused the pollution of a controlled water supply it was held liable for the criminal consequences of the acts and omissions of its employees who were acting within the course of their employment[19].

## 4.    SPECIFIC STATUTES

### 15-08   Health and safety legislation[20]

Not only are unincorporated clubs liable to be convicted as 'persons'[21], they may also be employers, and as such would be liable for offences that use the definition 'employer'. A small business must carry out a risk assessment[22] which, if the business employs five or more people, must be recorded in writing[23]. The Health and Safety at Work etc Act 1974 provides that it is an offence for a person to contravene[24] specified provisions of the Act, in particular it is an offence:

(1) for an employer to fail to discharge a general duty imposed on him[25];

(2) for any person to contravene the duty not to interfere with or

---

[17]    *R v Tyler and the International Commercial Co Ltd* [1891] 2 QB 588, Magistrates' Court Act 1980 s. 38.

[18]    *H L Bolton (Engineering) Co Ltd v T J Graham and Sons Ltd.* [1957] 1 QB159; *John Henshall Quarries Ltd. v Harvey* [1965] 1 All ER 725.

[19]    *National Rivers Authority v Alfred McAlpine Homes (East) Ltd.* [1994] 4 All ER 286.

[20]    For a full discussion of this subject see *Halsbury's Laws of England* (4th edn, 2004) vols 20(1) and 20(2).

[21]    See **15-02** above.

[22]    For a convenient self-assessment form, see the Health and Safety Executive web-site at *www.hse.gov.uk/smallbusinesses*.

[23]    And see **14-37**, above.

[24]    Which includes failure to comply; Health and Safey at Work etc Act 1974, s. 82(1)(b).

[25]    Ibid. ss. 2–6, and 33(1)(a).

misuse anything provided in the interests of health, safety or welfare[26];

(3) for an employer to contravene the duty not to charge employees for anything done or provided in pursuance of his duties under the Act[27];

(4) for any person to contravene health and safety regulations[28];

(5) for any person to contravene any requirements imposed by an inspector under sections 20 to 25[29].

There is no six-month time limit on the bringing of a summary prosecution under the Act, where the offence is triable summarily or on indictment[30].

## 15-09   Licensing Act 2003

There are numerous offences which can be committed under the new régime. Most are contained in Part 7 of the Act of 2003, under the heading of 'Unauthorised licensable activities': see Appendix 8. It is essential that the members of the committee of any club selling or supplying alcohol[31] familiarise themselves with this formidable list of offences, which fall into three categories:

(1) offences relating to the management of the licensable activity (sections 136 to 138);

(2) offences relating to the premises where the licensable activities are being carried on (sections 140 to 153);

(3) a range of offences arising from the various duties connected with the application process.

Examples of the third category are the offence under section 96 of obstructing an 'authorised person'[32] in the exercise of the power to enter and inspect club premises on an application for a premises certificate; and the offence under section 108 of obstructing an 'authorised officer'[33] (rather than an authorised person) in the execution of his right to enter premises to which a temporary event

---

[26]    Health and Safety at Work etc Act 1974, ss. 8 and 33(1)(b).

[27]    Ibid. s. 9 and 33(1)(b).

[28]    Ibid. s. 33(1)(c).

[29]    Ibid. s. 33(1)(d).

[30]    *Kemp v Liebherr GB Ltd.* [1987] 1 All ER 885.

[31]    See **9-01** above for the definition of alcohol.

[32]    Licensing Act 2003, s. 69(2): that is, an officer of the licensing authority, an inspector appointed under the Fire Precautions Act 1971 or the Health and Safety at Work etc. Act 1974, and an environmental health inspector.

[33]    Licensing Act 2003, s. 108(5): that is, an officer of the licensing authority.

notice relates in order 'to assess the likely effect of the notice on the promotion of the crime prevention objective'[34]. Indeed, it can be said that, wherever there is a right is conferred on the licensing authority or a duty imposed on the person carrying on the licensable activity, obstruction of the licensing authority in the exercise of its rights or failure to fulfil the duty, will render that person liable to prosecution for a summary offence.

**15-10** *The defence of 'due diligence'* This is provided by section 139: where a person is charged with carrying on an unauthorised licensable activity[35]; or exposing alcohol for unauthorised sale[36]; or keeping alcohol on premises for unauthorised sale[37], it is a defence if (1) his act was due to mistake; or to reliance on information given to him; or to an act or omission by another person; or to some other cause beyond his control[38], and if (2) he took all reasonable precautions and exercised all due diligence to avoid committing the offence[39]. This defence is also available to a charge of selling alcohol to a child[40] (i.e. a person under the age of eighteen years). Where a person (and this includes a club[41]) is charged with this offence by reason of the act or default of another person, it is a defence that all due diligence was exercised to avoid the commission of the offence[42]. It is also a defence to this offence that the person charged had a reasonable belief that the individual concerned was over eighteen[43]. Similar provisions apply to the offence of supplying liqueur confectionery to a person under the age of sixteen[44].

**15-11** *Personal liability of club member* An important point to note is that in the case of the offences of allowing disorderly conduct on premises covered by a club premises certificate[45]; selling alcohol to a person who is drunk[46]; keeping smuggled goods[47]; breach of the prohibition of unaccompanied children in certain premises[48]; allowing

---

[34]    Licensing Act 2003, s. 108(3).
[35]    Ibid s. 136.
[36]    Ibid s. 137.
[37]    Ibid s. 138.
[38]    Ibid s. 139(1)(a).
[39]    Ibid s. 139(1)(b).
[40]    Ibid s. 146.
[41]    Ibid s. 146(2).
[42]    Ibid s. 146(6).
[43]    Ibid s. 146(4).
[44]    Ibid s. 148.
[45]    Ibid s. 140(2)(c).
[46]    Ibid s. 141(2)(c).
[47]    Ibid s. 144(2)(c).
[48]    Ibid s. 145(3)(c).

the sale of alcohol to children[49]; consumption of alcohol by children[50]; delivering alcohol to children[51]; and the prohibition of unsupervised sales by children[52], an offence is committed by *any member or officer of the club who is present at the premises at the time of the offence in question in a capacity which enables him to prevent it.* This provision is contained in each of the sections creating these offences, and means that any club member present at the time when the prohibited conduct is taking place, and *knowing* it is taking place, will potentially be guilty of an offence. The courts, however, will find themselves with the task of deciding in individual cases whether the person charged was present in a 'capacity' which enabled him to prevent the conduct in question. Does this imply an element of control over the club activities at the relevant time? On the face of it, it does not. Theoretically any adult club member could be said to have some responsibility for ensuring the proper running of his own club, and consequently to be present in such a capacity. What, then, of the club member who is quietly minding his own business in a corner of the bar when he notices someone who plainly looks under the age of 18 going up to the bar and ordering an alcoholic drink which is supplied to him, and then he sees this person consuming the drink at the bar? Assume the supply and consumption of alcohol constitute offences under the Act[53]. His natural instinct might be to shrug his shoulders and to continue to mind his own business, but under the new legislation he could well be held to be present in a capacity which enabled him to prevent the unlawful conduct. By his inaction he might find himself guilty of a criminal offence.

**15-12** *Miscellaneous points*   Club rules are commonly altered, often for minor corrections, improvements or additions. Every alteration, however small, must be notified by the club secretary to the licensing authority within 28 days following the day on which the alteration was made[54], in default of which the secretary commits an offence[55].

**15-13**   A person who is drunk or disorderly commits an offence[56] if he fails without reasonable excuse to leave relevant premises when asked to do so by a constable; or by a person working at the premises

---

[49]   Licensing Act 2003, s. 147(4)(b).
[50]   Ibid. s. 150(3)(b).
[51]   Ibid. s. 151(5)(b).
[52]   Ibid. s. 153(4)(b).
[53]   See ibid. ss. 147 and 150.
[54]   Ibid. s. 82(4).
[55]   Ibid. s. 82(6).
[56]   Ibid. s. 143(1)(a).

in a capacity which authorises him to make such a request[57]; or by a similarly authorised member or officer of the club present on the premises[58].

**15-14** Note should also be made of the offences of the purchase of alcohol by or on behalf of children[59]; delivering alcohol to children[60] and sending a child to obtain alcohol[61].

**15-15** If an offence under the Licensing Act 2003 has been committed by a club (whether incorporated or unincorporated) and it is shown to have been committed with the consent or connivance[62] of an officer of the club or a member of its governing body, or to be attributable to his neglect[63], that officer or member is also guilty of the offence[64].

## 15-16 Road Traffic Offenders Act 1988

An unincorporated club will be liable as a 'person' for a fixed penalty road traffic offence[65].

## 15-17 Theft Act 1968

It is an offence for the officers of an incorporated or unincorporated club to publish a written statement about the club's financial affairs with intent to deceive either the club members or its creditors[66].

---

[57] Licensing Act 2003, s. 143(2)(a).
[58] Ibid. s. 143(2)(c).
[59] Ibid. s. 149.
[60] Ibid. s. 151.
[61] Ibid. s. 152.
[62] See *A-G's Reference (No 1 of 1995)* [1996] 1 WLR 970.
[63] See *Huckerby v Elliott* [1970] 1 All ER 189 DC (which concerned the New Embassy Club owned by a limited company and where the defendant's conviction was quashed because the prosecution had not proved that the offence of using the premises without a gaming licence was attributable to her neglect, she having properly relied on another director).
[64] Licensing Act 2003, s. 187. There are similar provisions in s. 400 of the Financial Services and Markets Act 2000 in relation to offences under that Act.
[65] *R v Clerk to Croydon Justices ex p. Chief Constable of Kent* [1995] RTR 257.
[66] By Theft Act 1968, s. 19(1).

**15-18   Trade Descriptions Acts 1968–1972**

It is worth noting that the 'due diligence' defence is provided[67] even though strict liability is imposed[68].

## 5.   DISQUALIFICATION OF DIRECTOR-MEMBER

**15-19**   If a director-member of an incorporated members' club was convicted of an indictable offence, whether on indictment or summarily, for example, the offence under the Theft Act 1968 referred to in **15-17** above, then he would become vulnerable to being disqualified as a company director under the Directors' Disqualification Act 1996[69]. This could have serious repercussions in the member's private life and is another good reason for responsibly discharging one's duties as a director of an incorporated members' club.

**15-10**  *Insurance*   The club cannot insure the director against the consequences of criminal liability on his part for obvious public policy reasons, but it would not be improper for the club to consider taking out some insurance for legal expenses in the event that the director-members are accused of criminal conduct.

---

[67]   By the Trade Descriptions Act 1968, s. 24.

[68]   See *John v Matthews* [1970] 2 WLR 1246 DC (concerning the Gorse Hill Working Men's Club where the court held that the object of the Act was to protect the public, not a club from one of its members).

[69]   Directors' Disqualification Act 1996, s. 2.

# Chapter 16

## CHALLENGING A CLUB'S DECISION

## 1.  INTRODUCTION

**16-01**   There are many occasions when a third party who is not a member of the club is affected by a decision taken by the club. The decision may adversely affect his standing in the community or his lifestyle or his means of livelihood, and he may therefore wish to challenge the club's decision. This is therefore an important topic which contains a number of complexities when trying to find the right answer to any given problem. This chapter applies to all clubs, no matter into what category they fall.

**16-02**   The Jockey Club, which was an unincorporated members' club until its incorporation by royal charter in 1970, controls both flat and steeplechasing horseracing throughout Great Britain. The club makes the rules of horse racing; sanctions the holding of race meetings; issues trainer's licences; and has disciplinary powers as the governing body of horse racing. The club provides useful examples of the various challenges made to its decisions:

(a) In *Russell v Duke of Norfolk* [1949] 1 All ER 109 the plaintiff was a trainer whose licence was withdrawn by the club's stewards 'in their absolute discretion' and then published the fact of withdrawal in its Racing Calendar. Mr Russell unsuccessfully sued for damages for breach of contract and libel.

(b) In *Nagle v Fielden* [1966] 2 QB 633 CA the plaintiff was a very experienced woman trainer who was refused a trainer's licence based on the grounds of the stewards' unfettered discretion but in reality because she was a woman. The court allowed her case to go trial on the basis that the unwritten rule of no women trainers was contrary to public policy[1].

(c) In *R. v Disciplinary Committee of the Jockey Club, ex p. Massingberd-Mundy* [1993] 2 All ER 207 CA[2] the applicant challenged the club's disciplinary committee's decision to remove his name from the list of those eligible to sit as chairmen of local panels of stewards. The court held that Mr Massingberd-Mundy enjoyed a non-renewable privilege which was a domestic decision not capable of judicial review, although Mr Justice Roch at 224 did consider that if the Jockey Club's disputed decision did not arise, or not wholly arise, from contract, then judicial review might lie.

(d) In *R. v The Jockey Club, ex p. RAM Racecourses Ltd* [1993] 2 All ER 225 CA[3] the club accepted publicly a report it had commissioned that 60 additional fixtures should be made available in 1990 and 1991, including allocations to new racecourses. The applicant established a new racecourse and sought an allocation of 15 fixtures which the club declined to make. On an application for judicial review the court held that the applicant had no legitimate expectation of any allocation and dismissed the application, although Lord Justice Stuart-Smith at 243 said he did not rule out such an application in appropriate circumstances eg where the club had made an unambiguous statement to anyone seeking to open a new racecourse that they *would* be allocated a certain number of fixtures.

(e) In *R. v Disciplinary Committee of the Jockey Club, ex p. The Aga Khan* [1993] 1 WLR 909 CA the Aga Khan's winning filly was disqualified by the club's disciplinary committee and his trainer fined. The court held that the Aga Khan's legal position was governed by his contract with the Jockey Club and was a matter of private law not involving any public law principles, and so they dismissed his application for judicial review. Lord Justice Hoffman at 933 commented, 'I do not think one should try to patch up the remedies available against domestic bodies by pretending that they are organs of government'.

---

[1]     There is force in Simon Brown J's comment in *R v Jockey Club ex p RAM Racecourses* [1993] 2 All ER 225 at 248 that since Mrs Nagle had no contract with the Jockey Club, it was not a case of an improper contract in restraint of trade but instead involved considerations of public law.

[2]     A case decided in December 1989.

[3]     A case decided in March 1990.

## 2.   GENERAL PROPOSITIONS

**16-03**   As regards each challenge the claimant and the club should
be clear as to what remedy the claimant is seeking and whether the
claimant has sufficient standing or interest in seeking his remedy. In
considering the challenge, the following nine propositions should be
borne in mind:

(1) One first has to distinguish between private law rights and public
    law rights. Public law rights are where the body is performing
    public law duties or exercising public law powers. The essential
    elements which comprise a public law body are:
    (a) a 'public element' (which may take many forms[4]), and
    (b) the exclusion of bodies whose sole source of power is
        consensual submission to their jurisdiction[5].

(2) The private law remedies are declaration, injunction and damages.
    The public law remedies are quashing orders, prohibiting orders
    and mandatory orders[6], although in appropriate cases the public
    law remedies will encompass the private law remedies[7].

(3) Private law rights are enforced in all the courts by way of the claim
    form procedure whereas public law rights are enforced in the High
    Court of Justice by way of judicial review. Judicial review is the
    means by which the courts control administrative action by public
    bodies.

(4) If the dispute is governed by a contract between the claimant and
    the club, it will in most cases be governed by private law rights[8].

(5) If there is no contractual relationship between the claimant and
    the club, the claimant may be able to have the club's decision
    judicially reviewed[9]. But judicial review should be considered the
    remedy of last resort[10]. Insofar as the claimant has to apply for

---

[4]    See *R (Beer trading as Hammer Trout Farm) v Hampshire Farmers' Markets Ltd* [2004] 1
WLR 233 CA.
[5]    *R. v Panel on Take-overs and Mergers, ex p. Datafin plc* [1987] QB 815
[6]    Replacing the former prerogative writs of certiorari, prohibition and mandamus.
[7]    See ss. 31(2) and 31(4)of the Supreme Court Act 1981; *R v Secretary of State for
Transport, ex p. Factortame Ltd (No.2)* [1991] 1 AC 603 (injunction); *Roy v Kensington and
Chelsea and Westminster Family Practitioner Committee* [1992] 1 AC 624 (declaration); *R v
Secretary of State for Transport, ex p Factortame Ltd (No. 5)* [2000] 1 AC 524 (damages).
[8]    *Law v National Greyhound Racing Club Ltd* [1983] 1 WLR 1302; *R v Disciplinary
Committee of the Jockey Club, ex p. the Aga Khan* [1993] 1 WLR 909 CA; *R v Football
Association Ltd, ex p. Football League* [1993] 2 All ER 833.
[9]    *Page v Hull University Visitor* [1993] AC 682; *R v Visitor to the Inns of Court, ex p.
Calder* [1994] QB 1.
[10]    *R v Law Society, ex p. Kingsley* [1996] COD 59.

permission to proceed with a claim for judicial review[11], this acts as a filter to weed out hopeless cases[12].

(6) Some cases may fall into both private law and public law categories[13]. If so, the claimant should look to the practical consequences of his choice of remedies rather than deciding on technical grounds whether his case falls on one side of the line or the other[14].

(7) If the case is suitable for judicial review, the claimant will still have to satisfy the court that he has sufficient standing or interest to justify his application for judicial review[15]. Historically the courts have always been reluctant to interfere with domestic decisions made by clubs[16], but this reluctance is on the wane[17].

(8) A judicial review is not an appeal but, as its name indicates, is a review of the decision complained of [18]. The public law remedies which the courts give on judicial review are discretionary, even where the grounds for review have been made out. The court has withheld remedies on a number of grounds but usually for some good reason such as the claimant failing to pursue a suitable and available alternative remedy[19] or where the remedy will serve no practical purpose[20].

(9) The grounds for holding the reviewed decision as invalid are normally illegality[21], irrationality[22] and procedural impropriety[23].

---

[11]     Supreme Court Act 1981, s. 31(3).
[12]     *R v Inland Revenue Commissioners, ex p. National Federation of Self-Employed and Small Businesses* [1982] AC 617; *R v General Council of the Bar, ex p. Percival* [1990] 3 All ER 137 at 153.
[13]     *Andreou v Institute of Chartered Accountants for England & Wales* [1998] 1 All ER 114.
[14]     *Trustees of the Dennis Rye Pension Fund v Sheffield City Council* [1998] 1 WLR 840.
[15]     Supreme Court Act 1981, s. 31(3). Representative groups may have sufficient standing to warrant an application for judicial review: *R v Secretary of State for Social Services, ex p. Child Poverty Action Group* [1990] 2 QB 540.
[16]     See **5-20** above; and see *Hole v Garney* [1930] AC 471 at 491 (Lord Sumner).
[17]     See, e.g., Simon Brown J's comment in *R. v Jockey Club, ex p. RAM Racecourses Ltd* [1993] 2 All ER 225 at 247j to 248b.
[18]     *R v Richmond upon Thames Borough Council, ex p. C* [2001] LGR 146 CA.
[19]     *R v Secretary of State for the Home Department, ex p. Swati* [1986] 1 WLR 477.
[20]     *R v Gloucestershire County Council, ex p. P* [1994] ELR 334.
[21]     *Council of Civil Service Unions v Minister for the Civil Service* [1985] AC 374. Breach of convention rights under the Human Rights Act 1998 comes under this heading.
[22]     This includes *Wednesbury* unreasonableness (i.e. the decision being so unreasonable that no reasonable person could have come to it): *Associated Picture Houses Ltd v.Wednesbury Corporation* [1948] 1 KB 223 CA.
[23]     This includes bias on the part of the decision maker (*R v Gough* [1993] AC 646) and breach of the rules of natural justice (see **16-05** below).

## 3. DECISIONS MADE UNDER A CONTRACT

**16-04** These present no difficulty from a legal point of view. If the decision which is being challenged arises in the course of a contract between the club and the third party, the normal rules of the law of contract will apply. In certain circumstances there may be no contract between the club and the third party but nevertheless the third party has consensually submitted to the club's jurisdiction[24]. Here we are in the realm of private law rights. The courts do not exist as a 'court of appeal' at the behest of a third party in relation to unpalatable decisions made by the club[25]. The court will only intervene where the decision has involved some dishonesty, bias or caprice on the part of the club[26] or where the decision was plainly beyond the powers of the club[27].

### 16-05 Rules of natural justice

In this context the rules of natural justice contain two main elements: (1) the right to know the opposing case and (2) a fair opportunity to answer that case. Whether the court will intervene in a domestic dispute between the club and a third party if the latter complains of a breach of the rules of natural justice[28] or unfair treatment at the hands of the club is still an uncertain area of the law. The formal introduction into English law of the convention rights under the Human Rights Act 1998 is part of a process which by and large has made the courts more willing to entertain claims by third parties that the club has acted unfairly towards him. Various questions arise under this heading: in contesting the club's decision is the third party entitled to an oral hearing? Is the third party allowed legal representation? Is the club as decision maker obliged to give reasons for its decision? Has the decision maker departed from its usual practice or policy? How inflexible is that policy? Has the claimant a legitimate expectation that he will be consulted before the decision is made? And so on. In *Ridge v Baldwin* [1964] AC 40 the House of Lords said that the overall test was: What would a reasonable man consider to be fair in the

---

[24] See *R v Association of British Travel Agents, ex p. Sunspell Ltd* (2000) *The Independent*, November 27.

[25] *Currie v Barton* (1988) *The Times*, February 12, CA (no breach of rules of natural justice where county tennis association banned a player from the amateur county team without first hearing the player because ban did not affect his earning ability).

[26] *McInnes v Onslow-Fane* [1978] 1 WLR 1520 at 1535.

[27] *Davis v Carew-Pole* [1956] 2 All ER 524 at 527.

[28] Different considerations apply as between the club and its members: see **7-15** above.

particular circumstances? But this begs the question: What is fair? The answer would appear to be that if the liberty of the claimant or his livelihood or his property is at stake, the court is likely to require the rules of natural justice or, perhaps better expressed, the rules of fair play, to be properly observed so that there is even-handedness between the parties[29]; otherwise the court is unlikely to intervene in disputes between the club and a third party even if the rules of natural justice have not been strictly observed[30].

# 4.  SUFFICIENT STANDING FOR JUDICIAL REVIEW

**16-06**  The courts will always check that the claimant has sufficient standing or interest in making his claim. The test for deciding whether a claimant has sufficient interest in making his claim is a 'threshold' test only when making the application for permission to bring judicial review proceedings but at the substantive hearing a more rigorous test is applied. Has the claimant a direct legal or financial interest which needs protecting? [31]. It is fair to say, however, that the greater the factual merits the more likely the court will be satisfied as to the claimant's standing[32].

## 16-07  Livelihood claims

These claims will much more readily be entertained by the court. Restraint of trade, and its corollary the right to work[32a], have been the subject of much litigation. Suffice it to say, that the courts will always look askance at a club rule which restricts the manner in which or the area in which a non-member may work. Prima facie such a restriction is void on grounds of public policy and a rule which is unreasonable or goes beyond what is necessary to protect the

---

[29]	*Lau Liat Meng* [1968] AC 391; *Gaiman v National Association for Mental Health* [1971] 1 Ch 317 at 336; *R. v Army Board of the Defence Council, ex p. Anderson* [1992] QB 169; *R. v. Ministry of Defence, ex p. Cunningham* [1998] COD 134 DC.

[30]	*Currie v Barton* [1988] cited in footnote 25 above.

[31]	*R v Inland Revenue Commissioners, ex p. National Federation of Self-Employed and Small Businesses Ltd* [1982] AC 617.

[32]	*R v Secretary of State for Foreign and Commonwealth Affairs, ex p. World Development Movement Ltd* [1995] 1 WLR 386 DC; *R v Inspectorate of Pollution, ex p. Greenpeace Ltd* [1994] 1 WLR 570.

[32a]	There is no right to work as such under the European Convention on Human Rights, but its provisions do protect workplace activities and the European Court has emphasised the right to earn a livelihood; see Articles 4, 6, 8, 9, 10 and 11 of the Convention and see *Starmer on Human Rights Law* (1999) para 28.1.

legitimate interests of the club will be struck down[33].

(a) In *Breen v Amalgamated Engineering Union* [1971] 2 QB 175 Lord Denning MR at 200 laid down the modern approach to this issue. Having referred to the need for statutory bodies to act fairly, he continued:

> Does all this apply to a domestic body? I think it does, at any rate when it is a body set up by one of the powerful associations which we see nowadays. Instances are readily to be found in the books, notably the Stock Exchange, the Jockey Club, the Football Association and innumerable trade unions. All these delegate power to committees. These committees are domestic bodies which control the destiny of thousands. They have quite as much power as the statutory bodies of which I have been speaking. They can make or mar a man by their decisions. Not only by expelling him from membership, but also by refusing to admit him as a member: or, it may be, by a refusal to [give him a] licence or to give their approval. Often their rules are framed so as to give them a discretion. They claim that it is an 'unfettered discretion' with which the courts have no right to interfere. They go too far.

(b) In *Nagle v Fielden* [1966] 2 QB 633 (the woman trainer refused a licence by the Jockey Club) Lord Denning MR stated:

> When an association, who have the governance of a trade, take it upon themselves to license persons to take part in it, then it is at least arguable that they are not at liberty to withdraw a man's licence – and thus put him out of business – in their uncontrolled discretion. If they reject him arbitrarily or capriciously, there is ground for thinking that the court can interfere.

(c) In *Greig v Insole* [1978] 1 WLR 302 the International Cricket Conference and the Test and County Cricket Board, both unincorporated associations, proposed new rules which would have disqualified professional cricketers from playing international test cricket indefinitely if they played in matches organised by the World Series Cricket, a rival organisation set up by Kerry Packer. The player-plaintiff obtained a declaration that these rules were *ultra vires* the Conference and the Board and were void as being in unreasonable restraint of trade.

## 5.   DISCRIMINATION CLAIMS

16-08   Modern legislation in the shape of sex discrimination[34] and race discrimination[35] impinges on a club's decisions where the club or other body confers authorisation or qualifications which are needed

---

[33]    *Nordenfelt v Maxim Nordenfelt Guns and Ammunition Co. Ltd* [1894] AC 535; compare *Eastham v Newcastle United Football Club Ltd* [1964] Ch 413 at 437.
[34]    Sex Discrimination Act 1975, s. 13.
[35]    Race Discrimination Act 1976, s. 12.

for or facilitates, engagement in any particular profession or trade[36]. Such decisions are open to challenge on the grounds of sex or race discrimination.

- In *British Judo Association v Petty* [1981] ICR 660 the Association refused to allow a woman referee to act as a referee in men's international competitions. This decision was held to amount to unlawful sex discrimination.

---

[35] Article 14 of the European Convention on Human Rights deals with discrimination. It is not a free-standing right but has to invoked in conjunction with one of the other Convention rights.

# Chapter 17

## TAXATION AND NON-DOMESTIC RATES

## 1.  TAXATION

### 17.01  Introduction

Depending on its nature, it is quite likely that some part of the activities of a members' club will result in a taxable gain or profit which will necessitate the submission of an annual return to the Inland Revenue. The form of taxation will be corporation tax which is a direct tax. If goods or services are supplied to its members, the club will have to add value added tax to the price of the goods or services where the club is registrable for taxable supplies. This is a form of indirect taxation. The law relating to taxation is complex and constantly changing. The Inland Revenue and Customs and Excise publish helpful pamphlets on the subject of taxation but there is no substitute for retaining the services of a qualified accountant in relation the taxation affairs of a members' club, if they are at all complicated. Proprietary clubs are in a different category since they are established for commercial reasons and will be subject to taxation, both direct and indirect, in the ordinary course of events.

## 2.  DIRECT TAXATION

### 17-02  Corporation tax

An unincorporated members' club comes within the definition of 'company' for the purposes of the Income and Corporation Taxes Act

1988[1]. Notwithstanding the fact that such a club has no legal personality[2], the liability to tax is that of the club itself rather than the individual members who comprise the club[3]; in other words, strange though it may seem, as a matter of law the club has a *fiscal* personality. Prior to 1970, if tax was payable by an unincorporated members' club, it would have been income tax and capital gains tax; since 1970 taxable profits on business transactions and chargeable capital gains are all now computed as corporation tax[3a].

## 17-03   Mutual trading

This is the guiding principle in considering whether a members' club is liable to tax and it is helpful to a club if it is applicable. Mutual trading occurs where several persons combine together and contribute to a common fund for the financing of their venture or object and where they have no dealings or relations with an outside body; in these circumstances any surplus which is returned to these persons (or to which they become entitled) is not profit which is chargeable to tax[4]. The reasoning behind the principle is simple: you don't tax a group of people who are trading with themselves. A members' club is an example of a mutual undertaking[5]. The necessary quality of mutuality which removes a club from the category of trader must be genuine, and there must be a reasonable relationship between what the member contributes and what he may expect to withdraw from the common fund, that is to say, a reasonable relationship between his liabilities and his rights[6]. There can still be mutuality where the members' club carries on its business through the structure of a company provided that the identity of the club members is the same as the company membership[7].

---

[1]      Income and Corporation Taxes Act 1988, s. 832(1); and see *Conservative and Unionist Central Office v Burrell* [1982] 1 WLR 522 CA (where the Conservative Party was held to be a political movement rather than an unincorporated association).

[2]      See **1-08** above.

[3]      *Worthing Rugby Football Club Trustees v IRC* [1985] 1 WLR 409 (liability of unincorporated members' club for corporation tax and development land tax).

[3a]      Income and Corporation Taxes Act 1970, s. 238, now Income and Corporation Taxes Act 1998, s. 6.

[4]      *New York Life Insurance Co. v Styles* [1889] 14 App Cas 381.

[5]      *IRC v Eccentric Club Ltd* [1924] 1 KB 390 CA.

[6]      *Fletcher v Income Tax Commissioner* [1972] AC 414 PC (where a members' club called The Doctor's Cave Bathing Club owned a beach in Jamaica and changed its rules to permit 'hotel members' to join the club; held that the relationship between the ordinary members and the hotel members was in reality a trading relationship giving rise to a tax liability).

[7]      *IRC v Eccentric Club Ltd* [1924] 1 KB 390 CA.

**17-04** Subject to the protection of a minimum threshold of £10,000 gross profits[8], the moment the club steps outside the circle of self-trading it will become liable to tax[9]. Therefore, broadly speaking, members' clubs will be liable to tax on trading activities with non-members, on interest received from investments or deposits of money, on dividends and rents, on gains from the disposal of assets and on capital sums derived from an asset. Income from sponsorship is also liable to tax. In December 1997 the Inland Revenue published a booklet entitled 'Clubs, Societies and Voluntary Associations' in which it stated:

> If members use the club's premises or facilities for personal events, such as a private party, and a separate charge is made, the money the club receives will be classed as income which is liable to corporation tax. However, a proportion of any running costs incurred may be allowed against it.

It might be asked why such a party is not mutual trading. Let us assume that we are talking about the Basset Rugby Football Club and it is one member's party to celebrate his Silver Wedding to which he and his wife invite both members and non-members alike. The club charges the member a fee for the hire of the room and for its facilities. The answer to the question is that the income is being derived from the member in his *personal* capacity rather then his capacity as member of the club, and this is partly evidenced by the nature of the function and partly by the fact that some guests may be present not as guests of the club member but as guests of the member's wife who is not a club member. Therefore the income has to be declared for tax purposes. However, it all depends on the factual circumstances. Suppose another member held a private party (for which the club charged him a fee) at the club to celebrate his selection for England at an international match at Twickenham and invited only members of the club to the function. We would regard this function as a species of mutual trading. Would it make any difference if this member said that that each invited member could bring one guest with him to join in the celebration? We consider that the party would still remain as an item of mutual trading because the presence of the guests would make no difference to the fact that the member was acting in his capacity of club member in holding the party[10].

---

[8]    See **17-07** below.
[9]    *Carlisle and Silloth Golf Club v Smith* [1913] 3 KB 75 CA (where the club was assessable for income tax in respect of visitors' green fees).
[10]   It is assumed that the club rules permit guests in the circumstances outlined.

## 17-05   The club's accounts

Under Companies Act 1985 there are prescribed various detailed requirements as to the form and contents of accounts. This is not the case with clubs registered under the Friendly Societies Act or the Industrial and Provident Societies Act. However, the Financial Services Authority issues guidance on what type of information it considers should be included in the accounts of a registered club. We consider that this guidance should be followed by unincorporated members' clubs too. The overriding consideration is that the accounts must give a true and fair view of the financial and trading position of the club[11]. This last consideration means that the club should comply with all major Statements of Standard Accounting Practice (SSAPs) and Financial Reporting Standards (FRSs) issued by the Institute of Chartered Accountants. The principles set out in the SSAPs and FRSs are considered in the guidance notes issued by the Financial Services Authority and are too detailed to be set out here. If the club qualifies on account of its small size, it may be able to prepare its accounts under the Financial Reporting Standard for Smaller Entities (FRSSE). The main advantage of applying this standard is the exemption from complying with FRS 3 (Reporting Financial Performance).

- In the ordinary course of events all the provisions of FRS 3 will be applicable to clubs. Therefore, at a minimum, there should be a statement regarding the recognised gains and losses at the bottom of the profit and loss account; a statement on continuing activities; and a reconciliation of members' funds in the balance sheet notes. A more detailed account will be necessary in certain circumstances, for example, if there has been a revaluation of the club's property in the financial year.

## 17-06   Returns to Inland Revenue

Members' clubs, whether incorporated or unincorporated, come within the corporation tax self-assessment scheme known as 'Pay and File'[12] and Form CT 600 has to be submitted to the Inland Revenue within 12 months of the end of each 12-month accounting period[12a]. The booklet IR46 contains an example how a club should complete this form. Where an unincorporated club is permitted to file a set of accounts for a period in excess of 18 months, for example, on its

---

[11]      FRS 18 Accounting Policies.
[12]      Finance Act 1998, s. 117(1) and Sch. 18. This system came into effect on 1 July 1999.
[12a]     Ibid. Sch. 18, para 14(1)(a).

formation, it must file its Pay and File return within 30 months from the date of commencement of the period for which the accounts are made up[13]. Thus if a club was formed on 1 January 2000 and prepared its first set of accounts for a period of 24 months up to 31 December 2001, it would be required to complete its first Pay and File return by 30 June 2002. There are substancial penalties for failure to comply with the obligation of making a return[13a].

## 17-07  Payment, rates and bands of corporation tax

Corporation tax on taxable income, such as investment income and profits from trading with non-members, has to be paid within nine months of the end of each accounting period or, later, within 30 days after the assessment is issued[14]. The following are applicable for the financial year to 31 March 2005, there being no change from the financial year to 31 March 2004. It goes without saying, however, that there is always a likelihood that, come the following year, the rates and bands will be altered. The figures quoted are intended to give some indication of the present level of taxation:

Nil band rate: £0 – £10,000 gross profits
Main rate: 30%
Small companies rate: 19%
Small companies limit: £300,000[15]
Small companies marginal band: £300,000 – £1,500,000
Marginal rate: 32.75%
Starting rate: 0%[16]
Upper profit limit: £10,000[17]
Marginal relief upper profit limit: £50,000[18]
Effective marginal rate: 23.75%.

## 17-08  Liability of treasurer in members' club

The treasurer of a members' club is personally liable for ensuring compliance with the club's obligations under the tax régime relating to the assessment of the club's liability to tax and the payment of

---

[13]     Ibid. Sch. 18, para 14(1)(c).
[13a]   Ibid. Sch. 18 paras 17 and 18.
[14]     Taxes Management Act 1970, s. 59E (as inserted by s. 30 of the Finance Act 1998) and the Corporation Tax (Instalment Payments) Regulations 1998 (SI 1998/3175) as amended.
[15]     To be shared among active associated companies.
[16]     Unless distributed, when it is 19%.
[17]     To be shared among active associated companies.
[18]     Ditto.

corporation tax, but he is entitled to retain sufficient club monies coming into his hands to satisfy the tax and, if this is insufficient, he is entitled to be indemnified out of club funds in respect of all tax payments made by him[18a].

## 17-09   Auditor

Clubs which are registered under the Friendly Societies Act and the Industrial and Provident Societies Act are required to have audited accounts[19], as are members' clubs incorporated under the Companies Act[20]. If an unincorporated members' club is of any substance, we strongly recommend that an auditor or honorary auditor is appointed.

## 17-10   Registered clubs

Working men's clubs are treated in the same way as other members' clubs when it comes to the question of taxation but because of their structure can automatically claim the benefit of mutual trading. Although they are registered under the Friendly Societies Act they are not friendly societies as such[21] and therefore they are not entitled to the tax exemptions granted to those societies[22]. Clubs registered under the Industrial and Provident Societies Act are usually eligible to claim the benefit of mutual trading and, in some respects, are more favourably treated than unincorporated members' clubs. These registered clubs are treated as companies for the purposes of the tax régime[23] but from 1973/74 onwards they have been able to claim the benefit of a special rate of tax[24]. The current rate (2004) is 27 per cent. It should be added that any share interest or loan interest paid by an IPSA club to a member is subject to income tax on the member's part[25]. The payment, however, is to be made without deduction of tax, save where the recipient's usual abode is not within the United Kingdom, in which case the club must deduct tax at the standard rate and account to the Crown[26].

---

[18a]     See **5-11** above.
[19]      See **5-14** above.
[20]      See **5-14** above.
[21]      See Friendly Societies Act 1974, s. 7(1)(a).
[22]      Income and Corporation Taxes Act 1970, ss. 331, 332 as amended by the Finance Act 1980, s. 57.
[23]      Income and Corporation Taxes Act 1970, s. 526(5); Taxes Management Act 1970, s. 118(1). IPSA clubs are not 'close' companies: s. 82(1)(b) of the former Act.
[24]      Finance Act 1972, s. 96 (as amended).
[25]      Income and Corporation Taxes Act 1970, s. 340(2),  (3).
[26]      Ibid. s. 340(2) and s. 54.

## 17-11   Charitable bodies

Charities do not enjoy general exemption from income or corporation tax[27] but instead have the benefit of particular exemptions. They are, for example, exempt under Schedule A and D in respect of rents and profits of land vested in trustees for charitable purposes and applied solely for charitable purposes; or under Schedule D in respect of distribution made insofar as such distribution is solely applied to charitable purposes; or under Schedule F if the profits from trading are applied solely for purposes of charity and either the trade is exercised in the course of the actual carrying out of a primary purpose of the charity or the work in connection with the charity is mainly carried on by the beneficiaries of the charity[28]. Any club which is a charity should seek professional advice in relation to its tax affairs.

## 17-12   Community amateur sports clubs

The tax position of these clubs is set out in Appendix 16 under the column heading of 'CASC'. See also the comments made in **1-50** and **1-51** above.

## 17-13   Proprietary clubs

Proprietary clubs are invariably runs on commercial lines and the proprietor of the club, whether a company or an individual, will be subject to the usual incidence of taxation in respect of net profits made in running the club.

## 17-14   Tax implications of incorporating an unincorporated club

It has been said that the incorporation of an unincorporated members' club provides a good example of a common theme in fiscal law, namely, what should be a straightforward exercise turns out to have complex tax implications[29]. The difficulties and factors to take into consideration in making the decision whether to incorporate arise over the transfer of property; the question of whether the incorporation involves a taxable distribution by either the old club or the new club;

---

[27]   *Brighton College v Marriott* [1925] 1 KB 312 at 317 (Pollock MR).
[28]   Income and Corporation Taxes Act 1988, s. 505 (as amended).
[29]   See Francis Fitzpatrick in his article *Incorporating an Unincorporated Association* in the Tax Journal 30 September 1993.

the application of roll-over relief; the imposition of stamp duty; and the incidence of taxation on a solvent winding up of the club. The fuller discussion of this topic is beyond the scope of this book.

## 3.    CLUB SUBSCRIPTION AS A DEDUCTIBLE ITEM

**17-15**    It is sometimes asked whether a member's subscription is deductible in computing his liability to income tax.  For an item of expense to be deductible it must have been incurred exclusively in the course of business. Thus in *Brown v Bullock* [1961] 1 WLR 1095 CA the plaintiff-taxpayer was appointed the bank manager of the Pall Mall branch of the Midland Bank. Like his predecessors for the past 40 years he joined the Devonshire Club in St James at the *insistence* of his employers, in order to foster local contacts and his business relationship with the bank's customers. The Court of Appeal held that in order to be deductible the test was whether the duties of the office or employment necessitated the incurring of the particular outlay, irrespective of what the employer had prescribed, and on this test the club subscription was not deductible. A hard but probably correct decision[30]. However, in the Irish case of *Elwood v Utitz* [1966] 42 TC 482 the managing director of a Northern Ireland company was required to go to London from time to time and he joined two London clubs solely for the purpose of overnight accommodation and using their business facilities instead of staying at a suitable hotel which was the more expensive option. The Northern Ireland Court of Appeal distinguished the *Brown v Bullock* case and allowed the club subscriptions as a necessary expense and therefore was a deductible item.

## 4.    INDIRECT TAXATION

### 17-16    Value added tax

The main type of indirect taxation which a club will encounter is value added tax (VAT). First introduced in 1973, this form of taxation is simple in concept but complex in its practical application. The principal Act is now the Value Added Tax Act 1994. Value added tax causes a lot more problems for clubs than does direct taxation because no allowance is made for the concept of mutual trading[31].

---

[30]    Harman LJ found some of the arguments [of the Crown] so distasteful that he declined to give a judgment but agreed in dismissing the taxpayer's appeal.
[31]    *Carlton Lodge Club v Custom and Excise Commissioners* [1975] 1 WLR 66.

## 17-17   Basic principle

The basic principle is that each supplier, whether wholesaler or retailer, must add VAT to the price of goods or services supplied by way of business[32]. This VAT charge is called an 'output'. The supplier must give a VAT receipt and must account to the Commissioners of Customs and Excise, usually on a quarterly basis, for the amount collected. In making his return to the Commissioners the supplier is entitled to set off (or, more accurately, to reclaim) the VAT charges which he has paid in his capacity of recipient of taxable goods and services. The items of set-off (or reclamation) are called 'inputs'. At present (2004) the standard rate of tax is 17.5 per cent. Some items are zero-rated and other items are exempt[33].

- *Zero-rated*   Schedule 8 of the Act of 1994 sets out the zero-rated supplies of goods and services. The schedule is divided into groups. The groups that are likely to be of interest to clubs are: books; caravans and houseboats; charities; clothing and footwear; construction of buildings; drugs, medicines and aids for the handicapped; food (which includes drink but excludes snack foods e.g. potato crisps, and excludes drink charged with excise duty); protected buildings; sewerage services and water; talking books for the blind and handicapped and wireless sets for the blind; and transport.

- *Exempt supplies*   Schedule 9 of the Act of 1994 sets out the exempt supplies of goods and services. The schedule is divided into groups. The groups that are likely to be of interest to clubs are: betting, gaming and lotteries; education; fund-raising events by charities and other qualifying bodies; health and welfare; insurance; the grant of any interest or right over land (there are many exceptions in this group); postal services; and sports, sports competitions and physical education.

## 17-18   Need for registration

Under section 94(2)(a) of the Value Added Tax Act 1994 the definition of 'business' includes the provision by a club, association or organisation (for a subscription or other consideration) of the facilities

---

[32]   Value Added Tax Act 1994, s. 4(1).
[33]   There is a reduced rate of 5% on certain items: ibid. sch. 7A.

or advantages available to members[34]. A club has to register with HM Customs and Excise for VAT purposes once it supplies taxable goods or services to its members in excess of £55,000 per year. Thus the supply of goods or services by a members' club to its own members can be subject to VAT even if the profits generated by this supply are not subject to corporation tax by reason of the mutual trading principle[35].

**17-19**  *Registration by choice*   A club may choose to register below the threshold of £55,000 limit and might consider doing so if its inputs equal or exceed its outputs, that is to say, the club supplies taxable goods or services of a relatively small value but needs to buy taxable goods or services of an equal or greater value. The Commissioners of Customs and Excise have a duty to register a person under the Act if he makes a request to be registered and he satisfies certain conditions[36]. Once registered, it may prove difficult to de-register.

## 17-20  Club subscription

This provides a good example of how the simple concept has got mired in technicalities. The following propositions should be borne in mind:

(1) If the subscription covers nothing more than the bare membership of the club, the subscription will be subject to VAT. This is because the subscription is the consideration for the privileges of membership, and such privileges would fall to be treated as 'a supply of services'[37];
  - in this situation the club will no doubt be charging its members an economic rate for its facilities and the provision of food and drink and relying of the mutual trading principle to avoid corporation tax on its profits.

(2) If (which is a common occurrence) the subscription covers to a greater or lesser extent the provision of facilities to its members,

---

[34]    A purely voluntarily body is not carrying on business for VAT purposes: *Greater London Red Cross Blood Transfusion Services v Customs and Excise Commissioners* [1983] VATTR 241. This still applies if the voluntary body requires reimbursement of expenses, as did the blood donor service.  Schedule 9 to the Value Added Tax Act 1994 sets out the list of exempt supplies and of goods and services.

[35]    *Carlton Lodge Club v Customs and Excise Commissioners* [1975] 1 WLR 66. But see *Customs & Excise Commissioners v Professional Footballers' Association (Enterprises) Ltd* [1993] 1 WLR 153 HL (where it was held that no separate output tax was payable on the cost of trophies presented at a dinner where the dinner tickets included VAT, since the price of the ticket included the provision of trophies).

[36]    Value Added Tax Act 1994, Sch. 1, para 9.

[37]    Ibid. ss. 4(1), 5(2)(b) and sch. 4.

the subscription has to be analysed to ascertain what proportion of the subscription covers the supply of taxable goods and services (other than zero-rated or exempt supplies) and VAT will be need to be added to that proportion of the subscription:

- in *Commissioners of Customs and Excise v The Automobile Association* [1974] 1 WLR 1477 CA the member's annual subscription to the AA contained a package of benefits, such a free handbook, a free magazine and free legal advice, and the VAT Tribunal, upheld by the Divisional Court, held that the subscription had to be 'dissected' to see which elements in it attracted VAT[38]. The court held that it was irrelevant that the package might vary from time to time;

- in *Trewby v Commissioners of Customs and Excise* [1976] 1 WLR 932 CA the court held that the subscription to a country club did not include any share of an interest in the club's land, which would have been an exempt supply.

(3) If the subscription contains an element of donation, as it might well do in the case of a subscription to a charitable organisation such as the Variety Club of Great Britain, the donation element will not attract VAT[39].

## 17-21 Exemption for sports services

Article 13(A)(1)(m) of the Sixth Council Directive (77/388/EEC) stipulated that sports services provided by a non-profit making organisation were to be the subject of a compulsory exemption. This took effect on 1 January 1990[40]. This exemption will apply even where the club makes a 'profit' on the services. In *Kennemer Golf and Country Club v Staatssecretaris van Financiën* [2003] 3 WLR 829 a substantial proportion of the income of the golf club in the Netherlands was derived from day membership fees paid by non-members for the use of the course and associated facilities. The club regularly made an operating surplus which was paid into a reserve fund for non-annually-recurring expenditure. The European Court of Justice held that VAT was not payable on the fees provided that the surplus was not distributed to the club members as profits.

---

[38] The handbook and magazine would be zero-rated and the legal advice would be a taxable service.

[39] Customs and Excise Note No 701.

[40] And is now enacted into domestic law: see Group 10 of sch. 9 to the Value Added Tax Act 1994.

**17-22**   The English tax authority, Customs and Excise, complied with
the Sixth Directive by issuing VAT Notice 701/45/94 on 1 April 1994.
This gave rise to refunds of VAT which had been levied since 1
January 1990, and caused an ancillary problem as to whom the
refunds belonged. Although it may seem unjust to the member who
had provided the money for the tax, the answer is that the refunds
belonged to the club because it was the club which had actually paid
the tax with its own monies. It therefore lay with the club to decide
what to do with the refund, whether to reimburse the member or to
put the monies into its general funds.

## 17-23   Exemption for cultural services

Another compulsory exemption is in relation to the supply of cultural
services[41]. In *Zoological Society of London v Customs and Excise
Commissioners* [2002] 3 WLR 829 the society, a non-profit-making
body, operated the London Zoo and Whipsnade Wild Animal Park.
The society was governed by a council, management boards and
committees, none of whose members received any remuneration, but
it also had paid employees including directors who attended meetings
of the governing bodies. The society claimed exemption from VAT in
respect of non-members' day subscriptions and the admission charges
to the zoos on the ground that it was supplying cultural services. The
European Court of Justice upheld this claim, despite the fact that the
society had paid employees; this was because the society was being
'managed and administered on an essentially voluntary basis'[42].

## 17-24   Exemption for fund-raising events

This is covered by Group 12 of Schedule 9 to the Act of 1994. The
exemption applies to the supply of goods and services by a charity in
connection with a fund-raising event organised for charitable
purposes[43], or the supply of goods and services by a qualifying body
in connection with a fund-raising event organised exclusively for its
own benefit[44]. A 'qualifying body' includes any non-profit-making
body established for the principal purpose of providing facilities for
participating in sport or physical education[45]. A fund-raising event
means a fête, ball, bazaar, gala show, performance or similar event,

---

[41]   Sixth Council Directive (77/388/EEC) art. 13(A)(1)(n).
[42]   Ibid. art. 13(A)(2)(a).
[43]   Item 1 of Group 12.
[44]   Item 2 of Group 12.
[45]   Note (3) to Group 12.

which is separate from and does not form part of a series or a regular run of like or similar events[46]. This is not a happy definition in that it could in theory it could apply to fund raising at the club's annual dinner, since this is a regular feature of such dinners. The case of *Reading Cricket and Hockey Club* (VAT Tribunal ref:13656) is instructive in that the club organised a three-day real ale and jazz festival. Customs and Excise disputed the exemption on the ground that the festival was part of a series of similar events, not a single event[47]. The tribunal, however, found that the festival could be properly considered as a single event. On the other hand, the exemption only applies where the supply is made 'in connection with' a fund-raising event. The club therefore has to be careful that Customs and Excise do not have grounds for saying that the event is a social occasion where the fund-raising is of marginal significance[47a].

## 17-25  Input recovery

The implementation of exemptions to cover the income sources of a non-profit-making club can have an adverse impact on input recovery, so the club needs to consider whether it is acting prudently in claiming exemptions. This is particularly so where the club is embarking on a large capital project, such as an extension to the clubhouse, where input tax will be payable on many goods and services in connection with the project.

## 17-26  Taxable supplies

The following points need to be borne in mind by committees to ensure compliance with VAT obligations. Customs and Excise publish guidance notices in respect of all the following topics.

*Bar sales and catering charges*  Food and drink is standard-rated where it is supplied in the course of catering; this includes food and drink supplied for consumption on the premises and hot take-away food. Premises means the whole clubhouse or its grounds.

*Admission charges*  These are normally standard-rated.

---

[46]  Note (1) to Group 12.
[47]  A theatre club which put on fund-raising performances of a play for three consecutive nights would, we surmise, have to levy VAT as this would be a series of separate performances. However, it is a moot point whether the *first* performance would be an eligible exemption.
[47a]  As was held in the case of the *Blaydon Rugby Football Club* (VAT Tribuanl ref: 13901).

*Bingo*  The payment of VAT depends on whether cash bingo or prize bingo is played. It also depends on whether the club premises are licensed or registered under Part II of the Gaming Act 1968. Admission charges are standard-rated save for certain one-off fund-raising events.

*Discos, dances, socials and similar events*  Admission charges are standard-rated save for certain one-off fund-raising events. The club is accountable on the gross amount of taxable supplies, not simply on the net amount, that is to say, the club cannot offset the expenses of the event when calculating the amount of taxable supplies.

*Gaming and amusement machines*  All receipts from gaming and amusement machines are standard-rated[48].

*Lotteries, raffles, etc.*  Income from lotteries, raffles, totes, instant bingo tickets and the like is exempt.

*Letting room on hire*  Income from letting a room or hall on hire is exempt provided that:
(1) the hirer has exclusive use of the room and hall during the period of hire;
(2) the room is not designed or equipped for sport or physical recreation;
(3) the club has not 'opted to tax' the building in which the room or hall is situated. This exemption covers facilities within or next to the room or hall, such as a kitchen or bar, and covers those fixtures and fittings which form part of the hire, such as the lighting and sound equipment[49].

## 17-27  The administration of VAT

If the club has a turnover in taxable supplies exceeding £55,000 per year or chooses to register for VAT it needs to understand its obligations which are set out in summary form below:

(1) *Registered name*  The registration may be in the name of the club, association or organisation and no account shall be taken of any change in its members.

---

[48]    See the case of *Moorthorpe Empire Working Men's Club* (VAT Tribunal ref 1127) where the club kept no proper records of its receipts from gaming machines and the Tribunal upheld an estimated assessment by Customs and Excise in the sum of £24,405 in respect of the undeclared receipts.

[49]    Notice 700 (the Vat Guide) and Notice 742 (Land and Property).

(2) *Identification*   Every person registered for VAT will receive a VAT number. Constitutional arrangements may be important here. Suppose that the Basset Sports Club operates three separate sections, say cricket, hockey and tennis. Are these all separate 'taxable persons'? The answer is that they probably will be counted as separate if each section is managed with its own committee and operates its own bank account, so that the sections are financially independent of one another.

(3) *Responsible persons*   Regulation 10 the VAT (General) Regulations 1985[50] governs the position. Anything required to be done for VAT purposes is the joint and several liability of every member holding office as president, chairman, treasurer, secretary or any similar officer of the club. In default, the persons liable will be every member holding office as a member of a committee[51]. In default of this last provision, every member of the club will be liable[52].

(4) *Records*   Every taxable person must keep such records as the Commissioners by regulations require[53]. These records must be kept for six years[54].

(5) *VAT returns*   The standard accounting period is three months. In order to stagger the quarter days the Commissioners divided occupations into groups. Clubs will in general fall within Group 2 under Classification 28 (Miscellaneous Services) and under Trade Codes 8822, 8829 and 8870 or, the case of gaming clubs, Trade Code 8830. The quarter days for clubs are the last days of January, April, July and October. Not later than the end of the month following the quarter day (e.g. by 28 February for the quarter day of 31 January) the taxable person must make a return on a prescribed form, showing the amount of tax due from or to him. At the same time he must pay any tax which is due to Customs and Excise.

(6) *Appeals*   There is an appeal procedure to a VAT tribunal in respect of the numerous matters set out in section 83 of the Value Added Tax Act 1994. It is worth noting that an appeal will not be entertained unless the appellant has made all the returns which

---

[50]   SI 1985/886.

[51]   Note that this says *a* committee, not *the* committee.

[52]   This is an astonishingly draconian default measure, bearing in mind that the member's liability is normally limited to his entrance fee and his subscriptions (*Wise v Perpetual Trustee Co* [1903] AC 139), but, we surmise, it is unlikely to be invoked in practice.

[53]   Value Added Tax Act 1994, Sch. 11, para 6(1).

[54]   Ibid. Sch. 11, para 6(3).

he was required to make and has paid all the tax shown as due on the returns[55].

## 17-28   Charitable bodies

Value added tax is only chargeable on the supply of goods and services when the supply is in the course of a business carried on by the charity, as opposed to the supply of good or services to objects of the charity when it is exempt[56]. The supply of certain goods or services to a charity are zero-rated, such as the supply by a charity of goods donated to it for sale or the sale of donated goods by a taxable person who has agreed in writing to give all the profits of the sale to such a charity[57].

## 17-29   Proprietary clubs

The general principles relating to value added tax, as set out above, will apply to the proprietor of a proprietary club.

# 5.   NON-DOMESTIC RATES

## 17-30   Introduction

Every club, however small, which occupies premises will need to understand the legal position concerning its liability for non-domestic rates. Rates are levied by the rating authority in which the club property is situated. The basis of liability for rates is occupation and the quantum of rates is based on the rateable value of the property.

# 6.   OCCUPATION

**17-31**   The basis of liability for rates is well settled. There are four necessary ingredients in rateable occupation. They are[58]:
(1) there must be actual occupation of the hereditament; ('hereditament' is the technical term for a unit of occupation);

---

[55]    Value Added Tax Act 1994, s. 84(2).
[56]    See *Yoga for Health Foundation v Customs and Excise* [1984] STC 360.
[57]    See s. 30 of the Value Added Tax Act 1994 (as amended).
[58]    *Laing v Kingswood Assessment Committee* [1949] 1 KB 344 CA approved by the House of Lords in *London County Council v Wilkins (VO)* [1957] AC 362.

(2) there must be exclusive occupation for the particular purposes of the possessor occupier;

(3) the occupation must be of some value or benefit to the possessor;

(4) the occupation must not be for too transient a period.

**17-32**   In every case the necessary degree of occupation is a question of fact, not a question of legal title to the property[59]. As is common with legal concepts there is a grey area which can give rise to difficulty. It is plain that, at one end of the scale, a club which uses a club room or hall belonging to someone else say once a week or once a month is not liable for rates. It is equally plain that, at the other end, a club which is the freeholder or leaseholder of club premises that are regularly used week in and week out is liable for rates. It is the cases which fall in the middle which need to be more carefully analysed. An instructive comparison can be made between the cases of *Peak (VO) v Burley Golf Club* [1960] 1 WLR 568 and *Pennard Golf Club v Richards (VO)* [1976] RA 203. In the former case the club was held not liable for rates on its golf course where non-members were entitled as of right to play there without paying green fees to the club. On the other hand, in the latter case the club was held liable to pay rates on its golf course even though non-members had access over it by means of rights of way. The distinction between the two cases depends on the *exclusivity* of the occupation: in the former case the club members were sharing their occupation of the golf course with outsiders whereas in the latter case the club members' occupation was not diminished by the fact that outsiders had the ability to walk across their land.

**17-33**   The fact that the club holds the club premises on a licence or a tenancy at will not exempt the club from paying rates[60]. If a club has exclusive use of part of premises it will be liable for rates on that part[61]. A club can still be the occupier of premises even though the licensor has occasional use of them as of right and has possession of a key to the premises[62].

---

[59]    *Holywell Union v Halkyn District Mines Drainage Co* [1895] AC 117.

[60]    *R v Green* [1829] 9 B & C 203 (occupants of almshouses); *Case (VO) v British Railways Board* [1972] 16 RRC 127 CA at 147 (where a staff association was held liable for rates in respect of premises held on a licence, terminable on short notice, from the employer).

[61]    *O'Reilly v Cock* [1981] 260 EG 293.

[62]    *Squibb (VO) v Vale of White Horse District Council and Central Electricity Generating Board* [1982] RA 271.

## 17-34  Who is liable

With regard to unincorporated members' clubs it is the actual occupiers who are liable to pay the rates, that is to say, the trustees of the club if the property is vested in them or the managing committee if there are no trustees[63]. It can never be the club itself which is in occupation[64]. Individual members of an unincorporated members' club are not in the ordinary course of events liable for rates[65], but if the club were of a sufficiently small size the members might collectively be held liable for rates as *joint* occupiers of the premises[66]. This liability might arise even though the assessment is on one occupier only[67]. Working men's clubs registered under the Friendly Societies Act and all clubs registered under Industrial and Provident Societies Act will automatically have trustees of the club's property who are responsible for the payment of rates. With regard to an incorporated members' club, the club itself will be liable for rates unless the property is vested in trustees when it is they who are liable. The proprietor of a proprietary club is the person liable for rates. In default of payment the rating authority will take proceedings in the magistrates' court seeking a liability order against the ratepayer[68].

# 7.   VALUATION

**17-35**   The rateable value of a property is the amount which it might reasonably be expected to let from year to year, if the tenant undertook to pay all usual tenant's rates and taxes and to bear the cost of repairs and insurance and other expenses necessary to maintain the property in a state to command that rent[69], and making the assumption that

---

[63]     *Verrall v Hackney London Borough Council* [1983] QB 445 CA at 461H (May LJ).

[64]     Ibid. at 416G.

[65]     Ibid. at 462 (where Mr Verrall, a prominent member and officer of the National Front, an unincorporated members' club, was held not liable for rates because he was not in actual occupation of the hereditament).

[66]     *Westminster City Council v Tomlin* [1990] 1 All ER 920 CA (where Mr Tomlin and seven others formed an unincorporated association called the Guild of Transcultural Studies and occupied the former Cambodian Embassy as trespassers. The rating assessment was on Mr Tomlin alone but it was held on the facts that all eight were liable for rates as joint occupiers).

[67]     See the *Tomlin* case cited in the last footnote.

[68]     Non-Domestic Rating (Collection and Enforcement) (Local Lists) Regulations 1989 (SI 1989/1058), reg. 12(5).

[69]     Local Government Act 1988, Sch. 6, para 2(1) as amended by of the Local Government and Housing Act 1989, s. 139, Sch. 5, paras 38, 79(3).

the property was vacant and to let[70]. In his assessment of the value the valuation officer should consider the property as it stands and account should be taken of all the intrinsic circumstances which could affect its value[71]. There is no uniform method of valuation[72]. Generally speaking, the rent for rating purposes is based on a hypothetical tenancy[73]. This means that the rateable value of the occupation is not necessarily measured by the actual rent which is being paid, although the actual rent and comparable assessments are relevant[74]. In the absence of rental evidence of value, the accounts, receipts or profits of the occupier of the property may be relevant[75]. Where there is a strong demand for the same kind of use of similar property the rateable value will be same, whether the club in question is making full or scant use of the premises and irrespective of whether the club is rich or poor. On the other hand, if the occupier is the only possible tenant of the property, his ability to pay is a relevant consideration. On this basis a club's ability to pay has been considered as relevant in a number of cases before the Lands Tribunal and the valuation adjusted accordingly[76]. Once the valuation has taken place the resulting rateable value is entered in a valuation list.

## 17-36   Challenging the valuation

It is a sensible practice for the club to try to agree the valuation with the valuation officer. Both the club and the rating authority may initiate proposals as to the valuation figure and either has the right

---

[70]   *London County Council v Churchwardens etc of Erith Parish and Dartford Union Assessment Committee* [1893] AC 562 at 588 (case decided under previous rating legislation).
[71]   39(1) *Halsbury's Laws of England* (4th edn, 1998) vol 39(1) para 687.
[72]   Ibid. para 695; and see *Avondale Lawn Tennis Club v Murton (VO)* [1976] 20 RRC 308 at 312. This case contains a discussion of the basis on which clubs should be valued.
[73]   See *R v West Middlesex Waterworks* [1859] 28 LJMC 135 at 137 (case decided under previous rating legislation). And see *Tomlinson (VO) v Plymouth Argyle Football Club Ltd* [1960] 6 RRC 173 CA at 179 (Lord Evershed MR): 'The question is not what would be a fair rent for the landlord, real or hypothetical, to ask but what would be a reasonable rent for a hypothetical tenant and a hypothetical landlord to agree between them'. This inevitably means a compromise of some sort.
[74]   *Halsbury's Laws of England* op. cit. paras 683 and 696.
[75]   *March (VO) v Gravesend and Northfleet Football Club Ltd* [1959] 4 RRC 299 (Lands Tribunal); *Tomlinson (VO) v Plymouth Argyle Football Club Co Ltd* (cited above) (valuation by reference to gate receipts was rejected).
[76]   See *Tomlinson (VO) v Plymouth Argyle Football Club Co Ltd* (cited above); *Hitchin Town Football Club v Wallace (VO)* [1961] RVR 462; *Sussex Motor Yacht Club Ltd v Gilmore (VO)* [1966] RA 43; *Heaton Cricket Club v Westwood (VO)* [1959] 5 RRC 98; *Addington Community Association v Croydon Corporation and Gudgion (VO)* [1967] 13 RRC 126 (community hall) and *Downe Village Residents' Association v Valentine (VO)* [1976] RA 117 (village hall).

to object to a proposal. If it considers that its property has been assessed at too high a figure, a club may as a person aggrieved[77] make a proposal for alteration of the list by serving such proposal in writing on the valuation officer[78]. If agreement cannot be reached, the club can take the matter to a Valuation and Community Charge Tribunal[79], where no costs are awarded for or against any party. An appeal from this tribunal lies to the Lands Tribunal and from there, on a point of law only, to the Court of Appeal (where costs are normally awarded against the losing party).

## 8.   RELIEF FROM RATES

**17-37**   The position is now governed by the Local Government Finance Act 1988 and the Non-Domestic Rating (Discretionary Relief) Regulations 1989 (SI 1989/1059). Some relief is mandatory, other relief is discretionary and as a general proposition any form of non-profit-making club, whether it be a members' club or (which is unlikely) a proprietary club, may qualify for mandatory or discretionary relief from rates under the Act

### 17-38   Mandatory relief

If the premises are occupied by a club (or its trustees) which is a charity or if the premises are used wholly or mainly for charitable purposes, there is a mandatory relief of 80 per cent of the rate levied[80]. Registration under the Charities Act 1993 is conclusive proof that a club is charitable[81]. If not so registered, the club will have to satisfy the rating authority that it is established for charitable purposes. The right to charity relief may be established by proceedings in the High Court for a declaration[82] or by resisting proceedings in the magistrates' court brought by the rating authority for non-payment of rates[83].

---

[77]     As to the meaning of 'a person aggrieved' see *Arsenal Football Club v Smith* [1977] AC 1. An unincorporated members' club is, as a matter of practice, regarded as a person aggrieved (see *Warburton on Unincorporated Associations* (2nd edn, 1992) p 57).
[78]     Non-Domestic Rating (Alteration of Lists and Appeals) Regulations 199 (SI 1990/582), reg. 10.
[79]     Ibid. reg. 22.
[80]     Local Government Finance Act 1988, ss. 43(6), 45(6).
[81]     *Wynn v Skegness UDC* [1967] 1 WLR 52 (case decided under the former Rating and Valuation Act 1961).
[82]     *Oxfam v Birmingham City District Council* [1976] AC 126.
[83]     *Royal Society for the Protection of Birds v Hornsea UDC* [1975] RA 26 DC. It is considered that both procedures (viz. declaration and resisting proceedings) are still available under the Act of 1988: see Halsbury's Laws of England (4th edn, 1998) vol 39(1), para 671.

**17-39** *Facilities for the disabled* A club property is exempt from non-domestic rates to the extent that it consists of property used wholly for providing facilities for disabled persons or persons suffering from illness[84].

**17-40** *Application* Since 1 April 1990 the application for relief need not be in writing and since 1 April 1997 the relief will commence when the club meets the necessary requirements. There is no need for further application and the relief will stay in force until the circumstances change[85].

## 17-41 Discretionary relief

The rating authority has a discretion whether to grant rating relief to three types of organisation[86]:
(1) charities;
(2) institutions and other organisations not established or conducted for profit and whose main objects are charitable or otherwise philanthropic or religious or concerned with education, social welfare, science, literature or the fine arts;
(3) clubs, societies or other organisations not established or conducted for profit and whose premises are wholly or mainly used for the purposes of recreation.

**17-42** *Charities* Here the rating authority can grant discretionary relief over and above the 80 per cent mandatory relief.

**17-43** *Institutions with eligible main objects and not for profit* A club is not to be taken as established or conducted for profit merely because it makes a financial surplus from investments or activities[87]. 'Education' in this context includes dramatic societies[88]. 'Social welfare' means the needs of the community which, as a matter of social ethics, ought to be met in the attainment of some acceptable standard[89]. 'Fine art'

---

[84]    Local Government Finance Act 1988, s. 51, Sch. 5 paras 16, 20, 21. Para 16 defines what is meant by 'facilities', 'disabled' and 'illness'.
[85]    Ibid. s. 47.
[86]    Ibid. s. 47(2).
[87]    *National Deposit Friendly Society Trustees v Skegness UDC* [1958] AC 293 (surplus from investments); *North of England Zoological Society v Chester RDC* [1959] 1 WLR 773 CA (surplus from operations); *Ladbroke Park Golf Club Ltd v Stratford-on-Avon RDC* [1957] 1 RRC 202 (bar 'profits' in a members' club).
[88]    *Newport Playgoers' Society v Newport County Borough Council* [1957] 1 RRC 279; *Trustees of Stoke-on-Trent Repertory Players v Stoke-on-Trent Corporation* [1957] 1 RRC 279.
[89]    *National Deposit Friendly Society Trustees v Skegness UDC* [1959] AC 293 at 314. It has been suggested that a club concerned with social welfare is probably a charitable organisation within the meaning of the Recreational Charities Act 1958: see Warburton in [1980] Conv. 173.

has been held not to include commercial photography[90] or folk dancing[91].

**17-44** *Recreational clubs not for profit*   This appears to be a very wide category in respect of which there is no case law. The Oxford Shorter English Dictionary defines recreation as 'the action of recreating (oneself or another), or fact of being recreated, by some pleasant occupation, pastime or amusement'. There is no requirement that the recreation must be open-air recreation nor is it confined to games of physical sport[92]. It would seem that the making of a charge for admission to the recreation does not disqualify the hereditament from this relief[93].

**17-45** *Application*   Since 1 April 1990 the application for relief need not be in writing and since 1 April 1997 a determination will only be invalid if made more than six months after the end of the financial year in which the chargeable day falls[94].

---

[90]      *Royal Photographic Society of Great Britain v City of Westminster and Cane (VO)* [1957] 2 RRC 169. This decision may be right on its facts but we consider that the stance adopted by the tribunal may be somewhat out of date: the famous Getty Museum in Los Angeles exhibits not only paintings but photographs as part of its collection. Many people think that black-and-white photography is an art form in itself.

[91]      *O'Sullivan v English Folk Dance and Song Society* [1955] 1 WLR 907.

[92]      Ryde on Rating and Council Tax, loose-leaf (November 2004) para D369.

[93]      Ibid. para D369.

[94]      Local Government Finance Act 1988, s. 47(7) as amended by the Local Government and Rating Act 1997, s. 23.

# Part 4

# Clubs as parties in civil proceedings

# Chapter 18

## INVOLVEMENT IN CIVIL PROCEEDINGS

## 1.  INTRODUCTION

**18-01**  It will be a very fortunate club that can avoid disputes altogether either as claimant or as defendant. It is therefore necessary for every club to know how to bring and defend court proceedings in respect of any claim made by or against it[1]. With effect from 26 April 1999 there came into force a new, unified set of rules called the Civil Procedure Rules (CPR)[2] which now govern the practice and procedure in the county courts, the High Court of Justice and the civil division of the Court of Appeal. These rules embody the most radical reform of civil procedure since the Judicature Acts 1873–75. One of the important innovations was to introduce an overriding objective[3] by which the court is enabled to deal with cases justly, expeditiously and fairly. 'Justly' means ensuring that the parties are on an equal footing; saving expense; and applying the concept of proportionality. The parties themselves have a duty to help the court to further the overriding objective[4].

**18-02**  If the club is involved in any litigation of any substance, whether as claimant or defendant, it is a wise move to call a special meeting of the members to obtain their express sanction for the litigation and to confirm that the costs of the litigation shall be borne out of club funds. It is recommended that this procedure should be followed even if the committee or the club or the trustees, as the case

---

[1]  Criminal responsibility is the subject matter of CHAPTER 15.
[2]  SI 1998/3123. As at 31 December 2004 some small parts of the Rules of the Supreme Court (RSC) and of the County Court Rules (CCR) still remain in force but these will eventually be phased out by new CPR rules.
[3]  CPR rule 1.1(1) and (2).
[4]  CPR rule 1.3.

may be, are empowered under the rules, either generally or specifically, to conduct litigation on behalf of the club.

## 2. PURSUING CLAIMS

### 18-03 Unincorporated members' clubs

Proceedings cannot be brought in the name of the club because it is not a legal person[5]. The action must therefore be brought either in the names of the individual members, on the basis of their personal rights (where they exist) or in the name of one or more members as representing all or some relevant part of the membership such as the managing committee.

### 18-04 Representative action

This is governed by CPR rule 19.6. Where more than one person has the same interest in a claim the claim may be begun, or the court may order its continuance, by one or more of the persons who have the same interest as representatives of any other persons having the same interest. In club cases it is usual for the one of more of the important officers to perform the representative role. The words, 'the same interest in a claim', appearing in rule 19.6 are to be construed so as to give effect to the overriding objective. In *National Bank of Greece SA v Outhwaite 317 Syndicate at Lloyd's* [2001] Lloyd's Rep 652 it was held that it was proper to bring proceedings against one individual as representative of all members of the 39 Lloyd's syndicates which had subscribed to a particular insurance policy, even though the selected individual was only a member of one of the syndicates, there being no leading underwriter clause in the policy. Had the situation been reversed, namely, had the Outhwaite 317 Syndicate been suing the National Bank of Greece, the same principle would have applied. Further, it is no bar to a representative action that the exact natures of the interest represented differ somewhat; the procedural rule is not to be treated as a rigid matter of principle but as a flexible tool of convenience in the administration of justice[6].

---

[5] *London Association for Protection of Trade v Greenlands Ltd* [1916] 2 AC 15.
[6] *John v Rees* [1970] Ch 345 at 370 (Megarry J) (where there was a clear common interest between all the club members in having the issue resolved, but the members themselves were far from united in the way they wished it to be resolved).

**18-05** The representative capacity of the claimant and the class of persons represented must be made clear in the claim form. For example, it should state 'Peter Davy, Daniel Whiddon and Harry Hawk as representing themselves and all other members of the Basset Pony Club' (on the basis that Mr Davy was the chairman of the club, Mr Whiddon was its secretary and Mr Hawk was its treasurer). Any exception must be explicitly spelt out. So that if the committee on behalf of the club was bringing an action against Tom Pearce, who was a club member, for defective saddlery supplied to the Club the claim form should read, 'Peter Davy, Daniel Whiddon and Harry Hawk as representing themselves and all other members of the Basset Pony Club except the Defendant herein [Tom Pearce]'[7]. The claimant does not need to obtain the court's permission to issue a claim form as a representative of other claimants, but the court retains a power to order that a particular person may not act as a representative[8]. It has also been stated[9] that a person suing in a representative capacity does not need to obtain the consent of those he represents, even though they will be bound by the result of the case. As far as unincorporated clubs are concerned, this statement needs qualification, bearing in mind the contractual basis of membership. If, as would be the norm, the members have put the control of the club's affairs into the hands of a managing committee and the committee resolve to bring a claim by way of representative action, it would seem perfectly in order for the committee to nominate, say, the chairman and the secretary of the club to represent all the club members in the action, even if one of the members was adamant in his opposition in bringing the claim. This is because the opposing member would have *impliedly consented* to the intended course of action by his agreement pursuant to the rules that the committee should have control of the club's affairs.

**18-06** The representative claimant has full control as to how to run the litigation on behalf of the class[10]. The represented persons are not parties to the litigation so that, for example, disclosure of documents can only be ordered against them as non-parties under CPR rule 31.17[11] and the represented parties are not liable for costs[12]. Unless the court otherwise directs, any judgment or order given in the claim in which a party is acting as a representative claimant is binding on

---

7      *Harrison v Abergavenny* [1887] 3 TLR 324; *Woodford v Smith* [1971] 1 WLR 806 (Megarry J) at 810G to 811D.

8      CPR rule 19.6(2).

9      See *Atkin's Court Forms* (1997 edn), vol 36, para 40.

10     See para 15/12/26 in vol 1 of the *Supreme Court Practice* 1999.

11     *Ventouris v Mountain* [1990] 1 WLR 1370.

12     *Markt & Co Ltd v Knight Steamship Co Ltd* [1910] 2 KB 1021 at 1039.

all those persons represented in the claim but may only be enforced by a non-party with the permission of the court[13].

**18-07** *Trustees*  If the property of the club is vested in trustees, and the claim touches or concerns this property, the proper claimants in any action will be the trustees acting on behalf of all the members of the club. Under CPR rule 19.7A(1) where proceedings are brought by trustees, it is not necessary to join the club members as persons having a beneficial interest; the trustees automatically represent this class of person, and the beneficiaries will be bound by any judgment or order given or made in the claim, unless the court order otherwise in the same or some other proceedings[14].

## 18-08	Literary and scientific institutions

If unincorporated, the position is governed section 21 of the Literary and Scientific Institutions Act 1854[15]. The institution can sue in the name of the president, chairman, principal secretary or clerk, as determined by the institute's rules and regulations.  In default of such determination the governing body shall appoint an appropriate person to sue on behalf of the institution. If incorporated, the position will be the same as for an incorporated members' club (see **18-12** below)[16].

## 18-09	Working men's clubs

The club cannot bring a claim in its own name because it is an unincorporated members' club. However, under the Friendly Societies Acts the appointment of officers and trustees of the club is a mandatory provision of the rules[17]. By section 103(1) of the Act of 1974 the trustees of the club, or any officers authorised by the rules, may bring, or may cause to be brought, any action or other legal proceedings in any court 'touching or concerning any property, right or claim' belonging to the club. They may sue in their proper names without any other description than the title of their office[18]. Legal proceedings shall not abate or be discontinued by the death,

---

13	CPR rule 19.6 (4).
14	CPR rule 19.7A(2).
15	See APPENDIX 1.
16	The opening words of section 21 concerning those incorporated institutions not entitled to sue can now be disregarded in the light of the Interpretation Act 1978, s. 5 and sch. 1.
17	See s. 7(2) of the Friendly Societies Act 1974 and Part I (5) of Sch. 2 thereof.
18	Ibid. s. 103(1).

resignation or removal from office of any officer[19]. Where proceedings are to be taken against a trustee of the club, the other trustees of the club may bring the requisite proceedings in their name[20].

## 18-10   IPSA clubs

The club is a body corporate and may sue in its own name in respect of any claim it may wish to bring[21].

## 18-11   Shop clubs

The club is an unincorporated members' club and the same considerations apply as set out in **18-03** to **18-06** above.

## 18-12   Incorporated members' clubs

The club is a legal person[22] and may sue in its own name in respect of any claim it may wish to bring.

## 18-13   Proprietary clubs

Any claim against a third party concerning the club's affairs will be brought by the proprietor and will be of no concern to the members.

## 3.   DEFENDING CLAIMS

### 18-14   Unincorporated members' clubs

The club itself cannot be sued because it is not a legal person[24]. It is essential for the club to ensure that, when sued, the right persons have been joined as defendants to any action either personally or in a representative capacity. CPR rule 19.6 applies equally to proceedings brought *against* the club as proceedings brought *by* the club. Suppose the claim against the club is for damages for noise nuisance caused by the club members on six consecutive Saturday nights. It will be no good describing the defendants as 'all the members of the Basset Social

---

[19]   Friendly Societies Act 1974, s. 103(3).
[20]   Ibid. s. 103(7).
[21]   Industrial and Provident Societies Act 1965, s. 3.
[22]   Interpretation Act 1978, s. 5 and Sch. 1.
[24]   *John v Rees* [1970] Ch 345 at 398D (Megarry J).

Club' since this is too vague and, anyway, some of the members may have joined the club after the six Saturdays in question. Nor is it good enough to describe the defendants as 'Some of the members of the Basset Social Club' because, once again, this is too vague a description[25]. The solution is for the class of defendants to be defined by reference to the date (or dates) on which the cause of action arose, as happened in the case of *Campbell v Thompson* [1953] 1 WLR 656 where the court ordered the writ to be amended so that the defendants were described as 'H R Thompson and C G Surtees Shill on their own behalf and on behalf of all the other members of the City Livery Club on June 29, 1949' (the date of the alleged accident)[26].

**18-15** Or take another example. Suppose a claim against the Basset Social club is made by the local wine merchant for the price of goods sold and delivered pursuant to an order given by the club secretary, Daniel Whiddon. The claim might be framed against the secretary that he was personally liable. His defence might be that he was simply acting as the disclosed agent of the committee and therefore was not personally liable. So it is likely that the claim form would cite the defendant as being 'Daniel Whiddon on his own behalf and on behalf of all the committee members of the Basset Social Club'. But this description might be inaccurate if the goods had been sold before some of the members had joined the committee[27]. So it might be necessary to describe the defendant with reference to the date of the order, namely, 'Daniel Whiddon on his own behalf and behalf of all the committee members of the Basset Social Club as at 15 March 2004'.

**18-16** *Acknowledgment of service* Despite the radical overhaul of the procedural rules in 1998, the present position as far as unincorporated members' clubs are concerned, is far from satisfactory. CPR Part 6 deals with the service of the claim form and CPR Part 10 deals with the acknowledgment of service of that form. The acknowledgment is a very important document because the failure to file it may result in a default judgment against the person being sued[28]. What the current rules omit is any provision dealing with service on unincorporated associations (except partnerships) and what to do if the claim form is

---

[25]    *Markt & Co Ltd v Knight SS Co Ltd* [1910] 2 KB 1021 CA.

[26]    This was, unusually, an action against all the members of an unincorporated club. See also *Irish Shipping Ltd v Commercial Assurance plc* [1991] 2 QB 206 CA (plaintiff permitted to sue two insurers as representing 77 insurers involving 77 separate but identical contracts of marine insurance but with differing proportions of liability for each insurer).

[27]    See *Roche v Sherrington* [1982] 1 WLR 599.

[28]    CPR rule 10.2.

not capable of being responded to. In the 1999 edition of the Supreme Court Practice appeared the following helpful note[29]: 'Unincorporated club. If sued in the name of the club, acknowledgment of service may be given for the members of the committee as such, but a members' club cannot acknowledge service in the club's name, and should not be so sued'. What happens, however, if the local wine merchant does issue a claim form against 'the Basset Social Club', an unincorporated members' club, for goods sold and delivered? As a matter of law the claim form is without legal effect as the claimant has sued a non-existent person and the form could be ignored. But in most cases this would not be a wise move, unless the limitation period was about to expire. The better way forward is to serve, using Form N9, an acknowledgment of service saying, 'The Basset Social Club is an unincorporated members' club and should not have been sued. This acknowledgment of service is filed by Peter Davy, Daniel Whiddon and Harry Hawk for and on behalf of the committee of the Basset Social Club. We do not propose to take any further step in this action until the defendant has been properly identified.'

**18-17**   If the defects in the claim form are less serious, say the claimant had misspelt Mr Davy's name and/or Mr Whiddon was no longer a member of the club, but otherwise the claim form was correctly suing the committee of the club, the club should deal with the problem under CPR PD 10 paragraph 5.2 by stating in the acknowledgment of service the correct name of the defendant followed by the incorrect name: 'Peter Davy, Bill Brewer and Harry Hawk for and on behalf of the committee of the Basset Social Club, described in the claim form as Peter Davey, Daniel Whiddon and Harry Hawk for and on behalf of the Basset Social Club'. Then it will be up to the claimant to amend his claim form (normally at his expense) so that the proper defendants are before the court.

**18-18**   It is not possible for the sake of convenience for a club to name any individual or individuals it chooses as representing the club in an action which the club intends to defend. The persons acting on behalf of the club in a representative capacity must be properly named and properly described in the claim form[30]. Thus in our example Mr Davy was the chairman of the club, Mr Whiddon had been the secretary of the club whose office had been taken over by Mr Brewer, and Mr Hawk was the treasurer of the club, all of whom were on the

---

[29]   Vol. 1, para 12/L/2 p 135.
[30]   *Adams v Naylor* [1946] AC 543.

committee at the date of the acknowledgment of service. Any person wrongly sued in a representative capacity may apply to the court for a direction that he is not to act as a representative[31]. On the other hand, the claimant does not need the permission of the court to bring an action against named defendants as representatives[32] and, indeed, people can be appointed against their own will to defend on behalf of others[33]. Unless the court otherwise directs, any judgment or order given in the action in which a party is acting as a representative defendant is binding on all those persons represented in the action but may only be enforced against a person who is not a party with the permission of the court[34].

**18-19**  *Enforcement of judgment*   The enforcement provisions in a representative action are set out in CPR rule 19.6(4) which states:

> Unless the court otherwise directs any judgment or order given in a claim in which a party is acting as a representative under this rule:
> (a)   is binding on all persons represented in the claim; but
> (b)   may only be enforced by or against a person who is not a party to the claim with the permission of the court.

The rule it replaced, namely, RSC Order 15, rule 12(5) was stated in different terms:

> Notwithstanding that a judgment or order to which any application [for leave to enforce against a represented non-party] is binding on the person against whom the application is made, that person may dispute liability to have the judgment or order enforced against him on the ground that by reason of the facts and matters particular to his case he is entitled to be exempted from such liability.

Suppose the goods were ordered by the secretary on behalf of the managing committee of the Basset Social Club, and the claimant has obtained a regular judgment against Peter Davy, Bill Brewer and Harry Hawk representing the committee of the club. The claimant now applies for enforcement of the judgment against Jan Stewer, another member of the committee. Under the former rule, if the member was a non-party but represented in the action, he was entitled *as of right* to dispute his liability when it came to enforcement against

---

[31]     CPR rule 19.6(2) and (3).
[32]     *Andrews v Salmon* [1888] WN 102 (Kay J) (where the plaintiff had been expelled from the Randolph Churchill Conservative Club in Wanstead and without their consent brought an action against the chairman of the committee and the hon. secretary as representing all the members of the club; and this procedure was upheld by the court).
[33]     *Wood v McCarthy* [1893] 1 QB 775.
[34]     CPR rule 19.6(4).

himself. The equivalent rule in the CPR, namely, rule 19.6, contains no such provision. The member can still argue that no enforcement should be made against him because, for example, he had expressly dissented from authorising the contract sued on (see **12-04(2)(a)** above), but he now has to rely on the *discretion* of the court in opposing enforcement. This means that the club should take especial care in ensuring that in defending representative proceedings the defendants in the action are precisely and accurately defined as to whom is being represented.

## 18-20   Literary and scientific institutions

If unincorporated, the position is governed by section 21 of the Literary and Scientific Institutions Act 1854[35]. The same provisions which apply for suing apply equally where the institution is being sued: see **18-08** above. In addition, if the claimant applies to the institution for a person to be nominated as defendant to his claim and the institution fails to make any such nomination, the claimant will be entitled to sue the president or the chairman as representing the institution. If a claimant obtains judgment against the person named as the defendant on behalf of the institution, its enforcement shall not be made against that person but only against the property of the institution. If incorporated, the position will be the same as for an incorporated members' club (see **18-24** below)[36].

## 18-21   Working men's clubs

The position is governed by section 103(1) of the Friendly Societies Act 1974. The same provisions which apply for suing apply equally where the club is being sued: see **18-09** above.

## 18-22   IPSA clubs

The club is a body corporate and may be sued in its own name[37].

---

[35]   See APPENDIX 1.

[36]   The opening words of section 21 concerning incorporated institutions not entitled to be sued can now be disregarded in the light of the Interpretation Act 1978, s. 5, Sch.1.

[37]   Industrial and Provident Societies Act 1965, s. 3.

### 18-23  Shop clubs

The club is an unincorporated member's club and the same considerations apply in respect of defending claims as set out in **18-14** to **18-19** above.

### 18-24  Incorporated members' clubs

The club is a legal person[38] and may be sued in its own name.

### 18-25  Proprietary clubs

In any matter concerning the club's affairs, the claimant will proceed against the proprietor, whether he is an individual or it is a company, and it is the proprietor who has the burden of defending the claim and meeting any liability as a result of such claim.

## 4.  LIMITATION

**18-26**  At common law there was no time limit on bringing a claim against another person, and for public policy reasons the ability to bring an action has for several centuries been regulated by statute. The principal Act now in force is the Limitation Act 1980[39]. Deciding on a period of limitation is by definition an arbitrary process, so what counts is not the spirit of the law but the letter of the law. This topic is therefore replete with legal learning and decided cases on the various issues which have arisen over the years. What follows is necessarily a very brief outline of the law relating to limitation.

**18-27**  As with its predecessors, the Act of 1980 mostly bars the remedy, not the substantive right[40], so that any limitation defence must be expressly pleaded. Most of the ordinary periods of limitation are calculated from the date on which the cause of action accrued:

- *One year limit*    Actions for libel, slander and malicious falsehood[41].

---

[38]      Interpretation Act 1978, s. 5, Sch. 1.
[39]      The Act of 1980 consolidated the Acts of 1939, 1963, 1975 and the Amendment Act of 1980.
[40]      See 28 *Halsbury's Laws* (4th edn, reissue) para 856. In civil law jurisdictions it is normally the right which is extinguished.
[41]      Limitation Act 1980, s. 4A.

- *Three year limit*    Actions for negligence, nuisance and breach of duty (whether arising in tort or in contract or by statute) where the damages claimed by the claimant consist of or include damages in respect of personal injuries[42].
- *Six year limit*    Most actions founded on tort[43] and contract[44] and actions to recover arrears of rent[45].
- *Twelve year limit*    Actions upon specialties[46] and actions to recover land[47].

## 18-28    Extension of time limits

The Act of 1980 also provides for the extension and exclusion of certain periods of limitation. Where the claimant was under a disability at the time when the cause of action accrued, i.e. was a minor or of unsound mind, the action may be brought at any time before the expiration of six years from the date when he ceased to be under a disability or died (whichever first occurred), notwithstanding that the ordinary period of limitation has expired[48]. Where the action is based on the fraud of the defendant[49] or where any fact relevant to the claimant's right of action has been deliberately concealed by the defendant[50], the period of limitation does not begin to run until the claimant has discovered the fraud or concealment or could have done so with reasonable diligence[51]. The court also has the discretion to exclude the time limit for libel, slander and malicious falsehood[52] and the time limit for actions in respect of personal injuries and death[53]. The Latent Damage Act 1996 inserted new sections 14A and 14B into the Limitation Act 1980 under which special time limits were introduced for actions for damages in the tort of negligence (other than actions for personal injuries) where the facts relevant to the cause

---

[42]    Limitation Act 1980, ss. 11 and 11A(4)–(7).

[43]    Ibid. s. 2, but note the special time limit in the case of theft (s. 4).

[44]    Ibid. s. 5, but note the special time limit for actions in respect of certain loans (s. 6). In particular, where money is repayable on demand, the limitation period will not begin to run in favour of the borrower until the lender has made a written demand for repayment.

[45]    Ibid. s. 19.

[46]    Ibid. s. 8. A specialty is a contract under seal contained in a deed.

[47]    Ibid. s. 15.

[48]    Ibid. ss. 28 and 28A. See, e.g., *Headford v Bristol and District Health Authority* [1995] 6 Med LR 1 CA  (where the action was brought 28 years after the events complained of).

[49]    Ibid. s. 32(1)(a).

[50]    Ibid. s. 32(1)(b).

[51]    Ibid. s. 32(1). The case of *Sheldon v RHM Outhwaite (Underwriting Agencies) Ltd* [1996] AC 102 is a classic example of the difficulties in interpreting correctly the provisions of the Act of 1980: see the speech of Lord Nicholls of Birkenhead at 52.

[52]    Ibid. s. 32A.

[53]    Ibid. s. 33.

of action were not known at the date when the cause of action accrued, subject to an overriding time limit of 15 years[54].

# 5.   ALTERNATIVE DISPUTE RESOLUTION

## 18-29   Introduction

Civil litigation is expensive. It is time-consuming for lawyers to investigate a dispute before proceedings are issued and thereafter to prepare for the trial once they are issued. And time costs money. On the other hand, we live in a complex society and acting as one's own lawyer is an unwise activity. Despite the advent of the Civil Procedure Rules and better case management of litigation by the courts, high costs are endemic in properly conducted litigation. Furthermore, litigation takes place in the public domain and for members' clubs it is often apposite that clubs should consider ways of resolving disputes privately rather than by litigation[54a]. Indeed, in *Halsey v Milton Keynes General NHS Trust* [2004] 1 WLR 302 CA the Court of Appeal emphasised that those members of the legal profession who conduct litigation should routinely consider with their clients whether their disputes were suitable for alternative dispute resolution (or ADR as it is commonly called)[55]. The Court of Appeal did add, however, that the court's role was to encourage but not to compel the parties to go to ADR[56]. What follows is an outline of alternative dispute resolution which is available. It must be remembered, however, that there is no one-size-fits-all solution to the problem of resolving disputes if an alternative is sought to litigation. Every dispute needs to be assessed individually to ascertain the best way forward.

## 18-30   Arbitration

Almost any dispute that can be resolved by litigation can be settled by arbitration. Arbitration was practised in classical times[57]. Domestic

---

[54]     Limitation Act 1980 s. 14A only applies to claims in negligence in the tort of negligence, not to claims in negligence framed in contract: *Société Commerciale de Réassurance v ERAS (International) Ltd* [1992] 2 All ER 82 CA. This is a curious distinction, which turned on the words, 'an action for damages in negligence', and which demonstrates the legalistic approach of the courts in this branch of the law.

[54a]    See **5-48** above.

[55]     At para 11 of the judgment of the court.

[56]     Ibid. para 11. A party's unreasonable refusal to go to ADR carries the risk of an adverse order for costs at the costs stage of the litigation: ibid. para 13.

[57]     See e.g. 'Ancient Greek Arbitration' by Prof. Derek Roebuck published by Holo Books (2001) describing arbitration and mediation from the time of Homer to Cleopatra.

arbitration is now governed by the Arbitration Act 1996. The arbitrator's decision is final and legally binding. There is very little scope for appealing to the court. The process is confidential, and is generally more flexible and simpler than litigation and contains a power to cap costs[58]. It can in suitable cases be conducted on documents only. One downside is that no third party procedure is available so that, for example, if pursuant to an arbitration clause a builder in an arbitration was claiming monies from a club in respect of building work, the club would not be entitled to bring into the arbitration its surveyor or architect as a third party on the ground that it was their fault the building costs were so high. This is because arbitration is a consensual procedure, and the surveyor or architect might not consent to being joined in the arbitration and the builder himself might object to the presence of an additional party. As to costs generally, they are in the discretion of the arbitrator, subject to any agreement between the parties[59], and as a matter of general principle they should follow the event[60]. The parties are, however, jointly and severally liable to pay the arbitrator's reasonable fees and expenses[61].

**18-31** An agreement to arbitrate under the provisions of the Arbitration Act 1996 must be in writing[62]. Although arbitration is a consensual process in that parties cannot be compelled to go to arbitration unless they have agreed to resolve their dispute by this means, the process may become compulsory where a valid agreement to arbitrate is in existence. Accordingly, if one party to an arbitration agreement brings legal proceedings against another party, that other party can obtain from the court a mandatory stay of the legal proceedings to allow the arbitration to take place[63]. An exception to the mandatory stay is where the court is satisfied that the arbitration agreement is 'null and void, inoperative or incapable of being performed'[64]. If the club is incorporated, a conflict can arise between the right to go to arbitration and the right to go to court. In *Exeter Football Club Ltd v Football Conference Ltd* [2004] 1 WLR 2910 the former

---

[58] Arbitration Act 1996, s. 65.
[59] Ibid. s. 61(1).
[60] Ibid. s. 61(2).
[61] Ibid. s. 28(1).
[62] Ibid. s. 5. It is possible to have a valid oral arbitration agreement at common law (see Bernstein's *Handbook of Arbitration and Dispute Resolution Practice* (4th edn, 2003) para 2–113) but it is not governed by the Act of 1996 and may lead to difficulties of procedure and enforcement; and the answer is to convert the oral agreement into a written one.
[63] Ibid. s. 9. The procedure for making the application for a stay is set out in CPR Part 62 and the application should be made to the court dealing with the legal proceedings.
[64] Ibid. s. 9(4).

was a member of the latter, a company limited by guarantee, and the court held that the statutory rights conferred on members of a company to apply to the court for relief was inalienable and could not be diminished or removed by a contract to resolve the dispute by arbitration, so that the court had a discretion whether or not to stay the court proceedings despite the mandatory nature of section 9(4) of the Arbitration Act 1996.

## 18-32   Mediation

Mediation (and conciliation) shares many of the characteristics of arbitration and take place where the parties agree to use a neutral person to help solve the dispute. Mediation is a confidential process. The mediator, however, is not a judge or arbitrator but a 'facilitator' who helps the parties to reach their own solution. One of mediation's crucial ingredients is the mediator's ability to talk to each side privately (on a strictly confidential basis). Another advantage of mediation is that the parties are looking for a commercial solution rather than deciding precise legal rights and obligations which litigation and arbitration are required to do. A successful facilitative mediation will therefore invariably involve the disputants in a compromise. A mediation involving a complex set of facts can often be dealt with in one full day's mediation, and so this procedure has the potential to save great expense in appropriate cases. Mediation can accommodate third party participation if the parties are agreeable to this course. Mediation is not legally binding or enforceable through the courts unless the parties agree to be bound by the decision reached with the mediator. Sometimes mediation and arbitration are combined; mediation is attempted first and, if no agreement results, the dispute will go to arbitration where a binding decision will be issued (this process is known as med-arb); in this event the mediator and the arbitrator should be different persons because the mediator may well be informed of confidential matters by the parties which should not be within the knowledge of the arbitrator. As to costs, if the mediation is successful they will be absorbed into the settlement agreement. If unsuccessful, it is common for each side to agree to bear their own costs and to share the payment of the mediator's fees and expenses. In med-arb, if the mediation is unsuccessful, it is sometimes agreed that each side will bear their own costs in any event and at other times that they will be costs in the arbitration, to be dealt with by the arbitrator, subject in either event to the parties sharing, or sharing initially, the payment of the mediator's fees and expenses.

## 18-33   Early neutral evaluation

This is where an independent neutral appraises the case and gives an assessment of the parties' chances of success if litigation were to be pursued. It has the advantage of giving both parties a realistic assessment of the costs and potential gains from litigation. This evaluation is a confidential process. As to costs, this is a matter for agreement between the parties, but the neutral will no doubt seek a prior agreement with the parties that they will be jointly and severally liable for his reasonable fees and expenses.

## 18-34   Adjudication

Adjudicators too have been around for a long time. They are persons appointed to resolve a dispute but in a less formal manner than an arbitrator. For example, complaints by members of friendly societies may be referred to an adjudicator under section 81(1)(b) of the Friendly Societies Act 1992. Recently in the UK adjudication is a process which has been introduced into the construction industry to expedite resolution of disputes where litigation or arbitration might otherwise cause expensive contractual delays. There is a statutory right to have a dispute under a construction contract resolved by adjudication[65] and this process is governed by Part II of the Housing Grants, Construction and Regeneration Act 1996. It is intended to provide a swift, summary, interim means of resolving disputes as to payments which is binding on the parties until the dispute is finally resolved by litigation or arbitration[66]. The parties may, however, agree that the adjudication will be the final process. To keep the process short and simple no reasons need be given for the adjudication, unless the parties agree (which they often do) that reasons should be given[67]. Each party is jointly and severally liable to the adjudicator for the payment of such reasonable amount as he may determine by way of fees and expenses, and the adjudicator has power to apportion this payment as between the parties[68]. Otherwise the adjudicator has no power to order costs against any party. The information and documents provided to the adjudicator are to be treated as confidential if the party supplying the same has indicated their confidentiality to him, except to the extent

---

[65]     Arbitration Act 1996, s. 108(1).

[66]     *RJT Consulting Engineers Ltd v DM Engineering (Northern Ireland) Ltd* [2002] 1 WLR 2344 CA; see also The Scheme for Construction Contracts (England and Wales) Regulations 1998 (SI 1988/649).

[67]     Ibid. reg 22

[68]     Ibid. reg 11.

it is necessary for the purposes of, or in connection with, the adjudication[69].

## 18-35   Expert determination

Here the parties agree as a matter of contract that the dispute shall be resolved by an expert, who will almost invariably be an expert in the subject matter of the dispute, and that his decision will be legally binding on both parties. Once again no reasons are normally given for the determination unless the parties agree that they should be given. This process can in appropriate cases provide a quick and efficacious resolution to the dispute. As to costs, this is a matter for agreement between the parties, but the expert will no doubt seek a prior agreement with the parties that they will be jointly and severally liable for his reasonable fees and expenses.

---

[69]    SI 1998/649, reg 18.

# Appendix 1

## LITERARY AND SCIENTIFIC INSTITUTIONS ACT 1854 (AS AMENDED)

*18.    Trustees may sell or exchange lands or buildings; or may let*

If it shall be deemed advisable to sell any land or building not previously part of the possessions of the Duchy of Lancaster or Cornwall held in trust for any institution, or to exchange the same for any other site, the trustees in whom the legal estate in the said land or building shall be vested may, by the direction or with the consent of the governing body of the said institution, if any such there be, sell the said land or building, or part thereof, or exchange the same for other land or building suitable to the purposes of their trust, and receive on any exchange any sum of money by way of effecting an equality, and apply the money arising from such sale or given on such exchange in the purchase of another site, or in the improvement of other premises used or to be used for the purposes of such trust; and such trustees may, with like direction to consent, let portions of the premises belonging to the institution not required for the purposes thereof, for such term, and under such covenants or agreements, as shall be deemed by such governing body to be expedient, and apply the rents thereof to the benefit of the institution.

*19.    Trustees to be indemnified from charges; in default thereof empowered   to mortgage or sell the premises*

The trustees of such institution who, by reason of their being the legal owner of the building premises, shall become liable to the payment of any rate, tax, charge, costs, or expenses, shall be indemnified and kept harmless by the governing body thereof from the same, and in default of such indemnity shall be entitled to hold the said building or premises and other property vested in them as a security for their reimbursement and indemnification and, if necessity shall arise, may mortgage or sell the same, or part thereof, free from the trust of the institution, and apply the amount obtained by such mortgage or sale to their reimbursement, and the balance (if any) to the benefit of the institution, subject to the restrictions hereinbefore contained with regard to lands given and lands belonging to the Duchies aforesaid.

### 20.    *Property of institution, how to be vested*

Where any institution shall be incorporated, and have no provision applicable to the personal property of such institution, and in all cases where the institution shall not be incorporated, the money, securities for money, goods, chattels, and personal effects belonging to the said institution, and not vested in trustees, shall be deemed to be vested for the time being in the governing body of such institution, and in all proceedings, civil and criminal, may be described as the monies, securities, goods, chattels, and effects of the governing body of such institution, by their proper title.

### 21.    *How suits by and against institutions to be brought*

Any institution incorporated which shall not be entitled to sue and be sued by any corporate name, and every institution not incorporated, may sue or be sued in the name of the president, chairman, principal secretary, or clerk, as shall be determined by the rules and regulations of the institution, and, in default of such determination, in the name of such person as shall be appointed by the governing body for the occasion: Provided, that it shall be competent for any person having a claim or demand against the institution to sue the president or chairman thereof, if, on application to the governing body, some other officer or person be not nominated to be the defendant.

### 22.    *[Repealed]*

### 23.    *How judgment to be enforced against [institutions]*

If a judgment shall be recovered against the person or officer named on behalf of the institution, such judgment shall not be put in force against the goods, chattels, or lands, or against the body of such persons or officer, but against the property of the institution;

## 24.   Institution may make byelaws to be enforced

In any institution the governing body, if not otherwise legally empowered to do so, may, at any meeting specially convened according to its regulations, make any byelaw for the better governance of the institution, its members or officer, and for the furtherance of its purpose and object, and may impose a reasonable pecuniary penalty for the breach thereof, which penalty, when accrued, may be recovered in any local court of the district wherein the defendant shall inhabit or the institution shall be situated, as the governing body thereof shall deem expedient: Provided always, that no pecuniary penalty imposed by any byelaw for the breach thereof shall be recoverable unless the byelaw shall have been confirmed by the votes of three fifths of the members present at a meeting specially convened for the purpose.

## 25.   Members liable to be sued as strangers

Any member who may be in arrear of his subscription according to the rules of the institution, or may be or shall possess himself to detain any property of the institution in a manner or for a time contrary to such rules, or shall injure or destroy the property of the institution, may be sued in the manner hereinbefore provided: but if the defendant shall be successful in any action or other proceeding at the instance of the institution, and shall be adjudged to recover his costs, he may elect to proceed to recover the same from the officer in whose name the suit shall be brought, or from the institution, and in the latter case shall have process against the property of the said institution in the manner above described.

## 26.   Members guilty of offences punishable as strangers

Any member of the institution who shall wilfully and maliciously, or wilfully and unlawfully, destroy or injure the property of such institution, whereby the funds of the institution may be exposed to loss, shall be subject to the same prosecution, and if convicted shall be liable to be punished in like manner, as any person not a member would be subject and liable to in respect of the like offence.

## 27. *Institution enabled to alter, extend, or abridge their purposes*

Whenever it shall appear to the governing body of any institution (not having a Royal Charter, nor established nor acting under any Act of Parliament,) which has been established for any particular purpose or purposes that it is advisable to alter, extend, or abridge such purpose, or to amalgamate such institution, either wholly or partially, with any such institution or institutions, such governing body may submit the proposition to their members in a written or printed report, and may convene a special meeting for the consideration thereof according to the regulations of the institution; but no such proposition shall be carried into effect unless such report shall have been delivered or sent by post to every member ten days previous to the special meeting convened by the governing body for the consideration thereof, nor unless such proposition shall have been agreed to by the votes of three-fifths of the members present at such meeting, and confirmed by the votes of three-fifths of the members present at a second special meeting convened by the governing body at an interval of one month after the former meeting.

## 28. *Power to Board of Trade to suspend such alteration, if applied to by two-fifths dissentients*

If any members of the institution, being not less than two-fifths in number, consider that the proposition so carried is calculated to prove injurious to the institution, they may, within three months after the confirmation thereof, make application in writing to the Lords Committee of her Majesty's Privy Council for Trade and Foreign Plantations, who, at their discretion, shall entertain the application, and if, after due inquiry, they shall decide that the proposition is then calculated to prove injurious to the institution, the same shall not be then carried into effect; but such decision shall not prevent the members of such institution from reconsidering the same proposition on a future occasion.

## 29. *Provision for the dissolution of institutions and adjustment of their affairs*

Any number not less than three-fifths of the members of any institution may determine that it shall be dissolved, and thereupon it shall be dissolved forthwith, or at the time then agreed upon, and all necessary steps shall be taken for the disposal and settlement of the property of the institution, its claims and liabilities, according to the rules of the said institution, applicable thereto, if any, and if not, then as the governing body shall find expedient: Provided, that in the event of any dispute arising among the said governing body, or the members of the institution, the adjustment of its affairs shall be referred to the judge of the county court of the district in which the principal building of the institution shall be situated, and he shall make such order or orders in the matter as he shall deem requisite, or if he find it necessary, shall direct that proceedings shall be taken in the Court of Chancery for the adjustment of the affairs of the institution.

### 30. Upon a dissolution, no member to receive profit – Proviso for joint-stock companies

If upon the dissolution of any institution there shall remain, after the satisfaction of all its debts and liabilities, and property whatsoever, the same shall not be paid to or distributed among the members of the said institution or any of them, but shall be given to some other institution, to be determined by the members at the time of the dissolution, or in default thereof by the judge of the county court aforesaid: Provided, however, that this clause shall not apply to any institution which shall have been founded or established by the contributions of shareholders in the nature of a joint stock company.

### 31. Who is a member

For the purposes of this Act, a member of an institution shall be a person who, having been admitted therein according to the riles and regulations thereof, shall have paid a subscription, or shall have signed the roll or list of members thereof: but in all proceedings under this Act no person shall be entitled to vote or be counted as a member whose current subscription shall be in arrear at the time.

### 32. The governing body defined

The governing body of the institution shall be the council, directors, committee, or other body to whom, by Act of Parliament, charter, or the rules and regulations or the institution, the management of its affairs is entrusted; and if no such body shall have been constituted on the establishment of the institution, it shall be competent for the members thereof, upon due notice, to create for itself a governing body to act for the institution thenceforth.

## 33.   *To what institutions the Act shall apply*

The Act shall apply to every institution for the time being established for the promotion of science, literature, for fine arts, for adult instruction, the diffusion of useful knowledge, the foundation or maintenance of libraries or reading rooms for general use among the members or open to the public, or public museums and galleries of paintings and other works of art, collections of natural history, mechanical and philosophical inventions, instruments, or designs: Provided, the Royal Institution shall be exempt from the operation of this Act.

# Appendix 2

## SHOP CLUBS ACT 1902

Section 3

### SCHEDULE

### REGULATIONS AS TO CERTIFICATION UNDER THIS ACT

The rules of a shop club or thrift fund (herein-after termed "the society") shall provide for the following matters:–

i.    The name and place of office of the society.
ii.   The whole of the objects for which the society is to be established, the purposes for which the finds thereof shall be applicable, the terms of admission of members the conditions under which any member may become entitled to any benefit assured thereby, and the fines and forfeitures to be imposed on any member and the consequences of non-payment of any subscription or fine.
iii.  The mode of holding meetings and right of voting, and the manner of making, altering and rescinding rules.
iv.   The appointment and removal of a committee of management (by whatever name), of a treasurer and other officers, and of trustees.
v.    The investment of the funds, the keeping of the accounts, and the audit of the same once a year at least.
vi.   Annual returns to the registrar of the receipts, funds, effects and expenditure and numbers of members of the society.
vii.  The inspection of the books of the society by every person having an interest in the funds of the society.
viii. The manner in which disputes shall be settled.
ix.   The keeping separate accounts of all moneys received or paid on account of every particular fund or benefit assured for which a

separate table of contributions payable shall have been adopted, and the keeping separate account of the expenses of management and of all contributions on account thereof.

x.   A valuation once at least in every five years of the assets and liabilities of the society, including the estimated risks and contributions.

xi.  The voluntary dissolution of the society by consent of not less than five-sixths in value of the persons contributing to the funds of the society, and of every person for the time being entitled to any benefit from the funds of the society, unless his claim be first satisfied or adequately provided for.

xii. The right of one-fifth of the total number of members, or of one hundred members in the case of a society of one thousand members and not exceeding ten thousand, or of five hundred members in the case of a society of more than ten thousand members, to apply to the chief registrar, or, in any case of societies registered and doing business exclusively in Scotland or Ireland, to the assistant registrar for Scotland or Ireland, for an investigation of the affairs of the society or for winding up the same.

# Appendix 3

---

## LICENSING ACT 1964

Sections 41 and 42 of the Act

### SCHEDULE 7

### PROVISIONS AS TO CLUB RULES

*Management of club*
1. The affairs of the club, in matters not reserved for the club in general meeting or otherwise for the decision of the general body of members, must, under the rules, be managed by one or more elective committees; and one committee must be a general committee, charged with the general management of those affairs in matters not assigned to special committees.

*General meetings*
2. (1)     There must, under the rules, be a general meeting of the club at least once in every year, and fifteen months must not elapse without a general meeting.
(2) The general committee must be capable of summoning a general meeting at any time on reasonable notice.
(3) Any members entitled to attend and vote at a general meeting must be capable of summoning one or requiring one to be summoned at any time on reasonable notice, if a specified number of them join to do so, and the number required must not be more than thirty nor more than one-fifth of the total number of the members so entitled.
(4) At a general meeting the voting must be confined to members, and all members entitled to use the club premises must be entitled to

vote, and must have equal voting rights, except that –

(a)  the rules may exclude from voting, either generally or on particular matters, members below a specified age (not greater than twenty-one), women if the club is primarily a men's club, and men if the club is primarily a women's club, and

(b)  if the club is primarily a club for persons qualified by service or past service, or by any particular service or past service, in Her Majesty's forces, the rules may exclude persons not qualified from voting, either generally or on particular matters; and

(c)  if the rules make special provision for family membership or family subscriptions or any similar provision, the rules may exclude from voting, either generally or on particular matters, all or any of the persons taking the benefit of that provision as being members of a person's family, other than that person.

*Membership*

3.  (1)    Ordinary members must, under the rules, be elected either by the club in general meeting or by an elective committee, or by an elective committee with other members of the club added to it for the purpose; and the names and address of any person proposed for election must, for not less than two days before the election, be prominently displayed in the club premises or principal club premises in a part frequented by the members.

(2)    The rules must not make any such provision for the admission of persons to membership otherwise than as ordinary members (or in accordance with the rules required for ordinary members by sub-paragraph (1) of this paragraph) is likely to result in the number of members so admitted being significant in proportion to the total membership.

*Meaning of "elective committee"*

4.  (1)    In this Schedule "elective committee" means, subject to the following provisions of this paragraph, a committee consisting of members of the club who are elected to the committee by the club in accordance with sub-paragraph (8) of this paragraph for a period of not less than one year nor more than five years, and paragraph 2(4) of this Schedule shall apply to voting at the election as it applies to voting at general meetings.

(2)    Elections to the committee must be held annually, and if all the elected members do not go out of office in every year, there must be fixed rules for determining, those that are to; and all members of the club entitled to vote at the election and of not less

than two years' standing, must be equally capable of being elected (subject only to any provision made for nomination by members of the club and to any provision prohibiting or restricting re-election) and, if nomination is required, must have equal rights to nominate persons for election.

(3)     Except in the case of a committee with less than four members, or of a committee concerned with the purchase for the club or with the supply by the club of intoxicating liquor, a committee of which not less than two-thirds of the members are members of the club elected to the committee in accordance with sub-paragraphs (1) and (2) of this paragraph shall be treated as an elective committee.

(4)     A sub-committee of an elective committee shall also be treated as an elective committee if its members are appointed by the committee and not less than two-thirds of them (or, in the case of a sub-committee having less than four members, or concerned with the purchase for the club or with the supply by the club of intoxicating liquor, all of them) are members of the committee elected to the committee in accordance with sub-paragraphs (1) and (2) of this paragraph who go out of office in the sub-committee on ceasing to be members of the committee.

(5)     For the purposes of this paragraph a person who on a casual vacancy is appointed to fill the place of a member of an elective committee for the remainder of his term and no longer shall, however appointed, be treated as elected in accordance with sub-paragraphs (1) and (2) of this paragraph if the person whose place he fills was so elected or is to be treated as having been so elected.

# Appendix 4

## INDUSTRIAL AND PROVIDENT SOCIETIES ACT 1965

Section 1 of the Act

### SCHEDULE 1

### MATTERS TO BE PROVIDED FOR IN SOCIETY'S RULES

1. The name of the society, which shall comply with the requirements of section 5 of this Act.
2. The objects of the society.
3. The place which is to be the registered office of the society to which all communications and notices to the society may be addressed.
4. The terms of admission of the members, including any society or company investing funds in the society under the provisions of this Act.
5. The mode of holding meetings, the scale and right of voting, and the mode of making, altering or rescinding rules.
6. The appointment and removal of a committee, by whatever name, and of managers or other officers and their respective powers and remuneration.
7. Determination in accordance with section 6 of this Act of the maximum amount of the interest in the shares of the society which may be held by any member otherwise than by virtue of section 6(1)(a), (b) or (c) of this Act.
8. Determination whether the society may contract loans or receive moneys on deposit subject to the provisions of this Act from members or others; and, if so, under what conditions, under what security, and to what limits of amount.
9. Determination whether the shares or any of them shall be transferable, and provision for the form of transfer and registration

of the shares, and for the consent of the committee thereto; determination whether the shares or any of them shall be withdrawable, and provision for the mode of withdrawal and for payment of the balance due thereon on withdrawing from the society.

10. Provision for the audit of accounts by one or more approved auditors.
11. Determination whether and, if so, how members may withdraw from the society, and provision for the claims of the representatives of deceased members, or the trustees of the property of bankrupt members or, in Scotland, members whose estate has been sequestrated, and for the payment of nominees.
12. The mode of application of profits of the society.
13. Provision for the custody and use of the society's seal.
14. Determination whether and, if so, by what authority, and in what manner, any part of the society's funds may be invested.

# Appendix 5

## GAMING ACT 1968
## (AS AMENDED)

**1.    Gaming to which Part 1 applies**
(1) Except as provided by the next following subsection, this Part of this Act applies to all   gaming which takes place elsewhere than on premises in respect of which either–
  (a)  a licence under this Act is for the time being in force, or
  (b)  a club or a miners' welfare institute is for the time being registered under Part II of this Act.
(2) This part of this Act does not apply to–
  (a)  gaming by means of any machine to which Part III of this Act applies, or
  (b)  gaming to which sections 41 of this Act applies, or
  (c)  gaming which constitutes the provision of amusements with prizes as mentioned in section 15(1) or 16(1) of the Lotteries and Amusements Act 1976.

**2.    Nature of game**
(1) Subject to the following provisions of this section, no gaming to which this Part of the Act applies shall take place where any one or more of the following conditions are fulfilled, that is to say–
  (a)  the game involves playing or staking against a bank, whether the bank is held by one of the players or not;
  (b)  the nature of the game is such that the chances in the game are not equally favourable to all the players;
  (c)  the nature of the game is such that the chances in it lie between the player and some other person, or (if there are two or more players) lie wholly or partly between the players and some other person, and those chances are not as favourable to the player or players as they are to that other person.

(2) The preceding subsection shall not have effect in relation to gaming which takes place on a domestic occasion in a private dwelling, and shall not have effect in relation to any gaming where the gaming takes place in a hostel, hall of residence or similar establishment which is not carried on by way of a trade or business and the players consist exclusively or mainly of persons who are residents or inmates in the establishment.

### 3.    No charge for taking part in gaming

(1) Subject to the following provisions of this section, no gaming to which this Part of this Act applies shall take place in circumstances where (apart from any stakes hazarded) a charge, in money or money's worth, is made in respect of that gaming.

(2) Subject to the next following subsection, any admission charge shall, unless the contrary is proved, be taken to be a charge made as mentioned in subsection (1) of this subsection.

(3) For the purposes of this section a payment which constitutes payment of, or of a quarterly or half-yearly instalment of, an annual subscription to a club, or which constitutes payment of an entrance subscription for membership of a club, shall not be taken to be a charge made as mentioned in subsection (1) of this section:

Provided that this subsection shall not apply to a club unless it is shown that the club is so constituted and conducted, in respect of membership and otherwise, as not to be of a temporary character, and, in relation to an entrance subscription, shall not apply unless it is shown that the payment is not made in respect of temporary membership of the club.

(4) The preceding provisions of this section shall have effect subject to section 40 this Act.

### 4.    No levy on stakes or winnings

Without prejudice to the generality of section 3 of this Act, no gaming to which this Part of the Act applies shall take place where a levy is charged on any of the stakes or on the winnings of any of the players, whether by way of direct payment or deduction, or by the exchange of tokens at a lower rate than the rate at which they were issued, or by any other means.

*o0o*

### 9.    Gaming to which Part II applies
This part of this Act applies to all gaming which takes place on premises in respect of which either–
(a) a licence under this Act is for the time being in force, or
(b) a club or a miners' welfare institute is for the time being registered under this Part of this Act, and which is not gaming by means of any machine to which Part III of this Act applies.

*o0o*

### 12.    Who may participate in gaming to which Part II applies
(1) Where gaming to which this Part of the Act applies takes place on any premises, then, subject to the following provisions of this section, no person shall participate in the gaming–
  (a) if he is not present on the premises at the time when the gaming takes place there, or
  (b) on behalf of another person who is not present on the premises at the time.

(2) Where gaming to which this Part of this Act applies takes place on the premises in respect of which a licence under this Act is for the time being in force, then, subject to the following provisions of this section, no person shall participate in the gaming unless either–
  (a) he is a member of the club specified in the licence who, at the time when he begins to take part in the gaming, is eligible to take part in it, or
  (b) he is a bona fine guest of the person who is a member of that club and who, at the time when the guest begins to take part in the gaming, is eligible to take part in it,
and neither the holder of the licence nor any person acting on his behalf or employed on the premises in question shall participate in the gaming.
(3) For the purposes of subsection (2) of this section a member of the club specified in the licence is eligible to take part in the gaming at any particular time if either–
  (a) he was admitted to membership of the club in pursuance of an application in writing made by him in person on the premises in question, and at that time at least twenty-four hours have elapsed since he applied for membership of the club, or
  (b) since becoming a member of the club he has given notice in writing in person on those premises to the holder of the

licence, or to a person acting on behalf of the holder of the licence, of his intention to take part in gaming on those premises, and at that time at least twenty-four hours have elapsed since he gave that notice.

(4) Where gaming takes place on premises in respect of which a licence under this Act for the time being in force, and consists of a game which involves playing or staking against a bank, nothing in subsection (1) or subsection (2) of this section shall prevent the holder of the licence or a person acting on his behalf from holding the bank or having a share or interest in it.

(5) For the purposes of subsection (2) of this section a person shall not be precluded from being a bona fide guest as mentioned in paragraph (b) of that subsection by reason only that he makes a payment which is lawfully required in accordance with section 14 of this Act.

(6) Where gaming to which this part of this Act applies takes place on premises in respect of which a club or miners' welfare institute and the time being registered under this Part of this Act, no person shall participate in the gaming unless either–

   (a) he is a member of the club or institute and there has been an interval of at least forty-eight hours between the time when he applied or was nominated for membership of the club or institute and the time when he begins to take part in the gaming, or

   (b) he is a bona fide guest of a person who is a member of the club or institute and there has been an interval of at least forty-eight hours between the time when that person applied or was nominated for membership of the club or institute and the time when the guest begins to take part in the gaming;

and for the purposes of paragraph (b) of this subsection a person shall be taken not to be a bona fide guest if he himself makes any payment required for enabling him to obtain access to the premises, or to a part of them which is a part in which the gaming takes place, or if (apart from any stakes hazarded and the payment of any losses incurred by him in the gaming) he makes any payment in money or money's worth in respect of the gaming.

(7) For the purposes of this section a person participates in the gaming if–

   (a) he takes part in the gaming as a player, or

   (b) where the game involves playing or staking against a bank, he holds the bank or has a share or interest in it.

(8) The preceding provisions of this section shall have effect subject to section 20 of this Act.

*oOo*

### 26. Scope of Part III

(1) This Part of this Act applies to any machine which–
   (a) is constructed or adapted for playing a game of chance by means of the machine, and
   (b) has a slot or other aperture for the insertion of money or money's worth in the form of cash or tokens.
(2) In the preceding subsection the reference to playing a game of chance by means of a machine includes playing a game of chance partly by means of the machine and partly by other means if (but only if) the element of chance in the game is provided by means of the machine.
(3) In this Part of this Act "charge for play" means an amount paid in money or money's worth by or on behalf of the player in order to play one or more games by means of a machine to which this Part of this Act applies.

*oOo*

### 30. Registration under Part III

The provisions of Schedule 7 to this Act shall have effect with respect to the registration of clubs and miners' welfare institutes under this Part of this Act in England and Wales, and the provisions of Schedule 8 to this Act shall have effect with respect to the registration of clubs and miners' welfare institutes under this Part of this Act in Scotland.

*oOo*

### 33. Use of machines at non-commercial entertainments

(1) This section applies to any entertainment which takes place elsewhere than on the premises in respect which–
   (a) a licence under this Act is for the time being in force, or
   (b) a club or miners' welfare institute is for the time being registered under Part II or under this Part of this Act,
   and which is an entertainment of any of the following kinds, that is to say, bazaars, sales of work, fêtes, dinners, dances, sporting or athletic events and other entertainments of a similar character, whether limited to one day or extending over two or more days.
(2) Where a machine to which this Part of this Act applies is used for gaming as an incident of an entertainment, the whole proceeds of the entertainment, after deducting the expenses of the

entertainment, shall be devoted to purposes other than private gain.

(2A) Where a machine to which this Part of this Act applies is used for gaming as an incident of an entertainment to which this section applies, the opportunity to win prizes by means of the machine, or that opportunity together with any other facilities for participating in lotteries or gaming shall not be the only, or the only substantial, inducement to persons to attend the entertainment.

(3) [*repealed*]

(4) [*repealed*]

(5) The Secretary of State may be regulations impose such restrictions (in addition to those specified in subsections (2) and (2A) of this section) as he may consider necessary or expedient with respect to the use of any machine to which this Part of this Act applies for gaming as an incident of an entertainment to which this section applies.

*o0o*

## 36 Removal of money from machines

(1) Where a machine to which this Part of this Act applied is installed on premises in respect of which–

(a) a licence under this Act is for the time being in force, or

(b) a club or miners' welfare institute is for the time being registered under Part II or under this Part of this Act,

no person who is not an authorised person for the purposes of this section shall remove from the machine any money, other than any money delivered by the machine as, or as part of, a prize in respect of a game played by means of the machine.

(2) For the purposes of this section the following are authorised persons to relation to a machine according to the premises on which it is installed, that is to say–

(a) in the case of premises in respect of which a licence under this Act is for the time being in force, the holder of the licence and any person employed by him in connection with the premises;

(b) in the case of premises in respect of which a club is for the time being registered under Part II or under this Part of this Act, any officer or ember of the club in connection with the premises;

(c) in the case of premises in respect of which a miner's welfare institute is for the time being so registered, any officer of the institute, any person for the time being enrolled as a members

of the institute, and any person employed in connection with
the premises by or on behalf of the persons so enrolled.

*oOo*

**40.   Special charges for play at certain clubs and institutes**
(1) This section applies to gaming which–
   (a)  is carried on as one of the activities of a club or a miners'
        welfare institutes, whether the club or institute is registered
        under Part II or Part III of this Act or not, and
   (b)  is gaming in respect of which none of the conditions specified
        in section 2(1) of this Act is fulfilled.
(2) Subject to the following provisions of this section, nothing in
    section 3 or section 14 of  this Act shall have effect so as to prevent
    a charge from being made in respect of any person for the right
    to take part in gaming to which this section applies, if the charge
    or (if  more than one) the aggregate amount of the charges, made
    in respect of that person for the tight to take part in such gaming
    on any one day does not exceed sixpence or such other sum as
    may be specified in an order made by the Secretary of State for
    the purposes of this subsection.
    The power of the Secretary of State under this subsection includes
    power to specify–
   (a)  in the case of gaming carried on as an activity of a members'
        club or a miners' welfare institute, a sum different from that
        applicable in the case of gaming carried on as an activity of
        any other club; and
   (b)  in the case of gaming which consists exclusively of playing
        bridge or whist, to bridge and whist, and takes place on a day
        on which the premises therefor are not used for any other
        gaming, or for any other gaming except by means of a
        machine to which Part III of this Act applies, a sum greater
        than that applicable in all other cases.
(3) Any such charge as is mentioned in subsection (2) of this section
    may be made in addition to–
   (a)  any stakes hazarded in the gaming; and
   (b)  in the case of a club or institute registered under Part II of this
        Act, any charge authorised by regulations under section
        14(2)(b) of this Act.
(4) The preceding provisions of this section shall not have effect in
    relation to a club unless it is shown–
   (a)  [*repealed*]
   (b)  that it has not less than twenty-five members; and

(c) that it is so constituted and conducted, in respect of membership and otherwise, as not to be of a temporary character.

## 41.   Gaming at entertainments not held for private gain

(1) The Provisions of this section shall have effect in relation to gaming which–

(a) consists of games played at an entertainment promoted otherwise than for purposes of private gain, and

(b) is not gaming to which Part II of this Act applies or gaming by means of a machine to which Part III of this Act applied, and

(c) does not constitute the provision of amusements with prizes as mentioned in section 15(1) or 16(1) of the Lotteries and Amusements Act 1976;

and any reference in this Act to gaming to which this section applies is a reference to gaming in respect of which the conditions specified in paragraphs (a) to (c) of this subsection are fulfilled.

(2) Section 2 of this Act shall have effect in relation to gaming to which this section applies as it has effect in relation to gaming to which Part I of this Act applies.

(3) In respect of all games played at the entertainment which constitute gaming to which this section applies, not more than one payment (whether by way of entrance fee or stake or otherwise) shall be made by each player, and no such payment shall exceed £3.00.

(4) Subject to subsections (7) and (8) of this section, the total value of all prizes and award distributed in respect of those games shall not exceed £300.

(5) The whole of the proceeds of such payments as are mentioned in subsection (3) of this section, after deducting sums lawfully appropriated on account of expenses or for the provision of prizes or awards in respect of the games, shall be applied for purposes other than private gain.

(6) The sum appropriated out of those proceeds in respect of expenses shall not exceed the reasonable cost of the facilities provided for the purposes of the games.

(7) Where two or more entertainments are promoted on the same premises by the same persons on the same days, subsections (3) to (6) of this sections shall have effect in relation to those entertainments collectively as if there were a single entertainment.

(8) Where a series of entertainments is held otherwise than as mentioned in subsection (7) of this section–

(a) subsections (3) to (6) of this section shall have effect separately in relation to each entertainment in the series, whether some or all of the persons taking part in any one of those entertainments are thereby qualified to take part in any other of them or not, and

(b) If each of the persons taking part in the games played at the final entertainment of the series is qualified to do so by reason of having taken part in the games played ay another entertainment of the series held on a previous day, subsection (4) of this section shall have effect in relation to that final entertainment as if for the words "fifty pounds" there were substituted the words "[£600]".

(9) The Secretary of State may by order provide that, in relation to entertainments held on or after the day on which the order comes into operation this section shall have effect as if, for such one or more of the following sums as may be specified in the order, that is to say–

(a) the sum of £3,000 specified in subsection (3) of this section;

(b) the sum of £300 specified in subsections (4) and (8)(b) of this section; and

(c) the sum of £6,000 specifies in subsection (8)(b) of this section, there were substituted such larger sum as is specified in the order.

(10) Subsections (1) to (4) of section 8 of this Act shall have effect as if in those subsections  any reference to sections 2 to 4 or to Part I of this Act included a reference to this section.

# Appendix 6

## FRIENDLY SOCIETIES ACT 1974

Section 7(2) of the Act

### SCHEDULE 2

### MATTERS TO BE PROVIDED FOR BY THE RULES OF SOCIE-TIES REGISTERED UNDER THIS ACT

*PART I   PROVISIONS APPLICABLE TO ALL SOCIETIES*
1. The name of the society.
2. The place which is to be the registered office of the society, to which all communications and notices may be addressed.
3. (1) Subject to sub-paragraph (2) below, the whole of the objects for which the society is to be established, the purposes for which the funds thereof shall be applicable, the terms of admission of members the conditions under which any member may become entitled to any benefit assured by the society, and the fines and forfeitures to be imposed on any member and the consequences of non-payment of any subscription or fine.
   (2) Nothing in sub-paragraph (1) above shall require the inclusion in the rules of a registered society of tables relating to the benefits payable to or in respect of any members of the society in pursuance of approved group insurance business as defined in section 65 of this Act.
4. The mode of holding meetings and right of voting, and the manner of making, altering or rescinding rules.
5. The appointment and removal of a committee of management (by whatever name), of a treasurer and other officers and of trustees and, in the case of a society with branches, the composition and

powers of the central body and the conditions under which a branch may secede from the society.

6. The investment of the funds, the keeping of the accounts and the audit of the accounts at least once a year.
7. Annual returns to the registrar relating to the affairs and numbers of members of the society.
8. The inspection of the books of the society by every person having an interest in the funds of the society.
9. The manner in which disputes shall be settled.
10. In the case of dividing societies, a provision for meeting all claims upon the society existing at the time of division before any such division takes place.
11. (1) For the avoidance of doubt it is hereby declared that nothing in paragraph 3 above requires the rules of a society to contain tables in accordance with which obligations to provide benefits to members have been undertaken or policies of assurance have been issued by the society, if the rules of the society provide that no further obligations may be undertaken or (as the case may be) no further policies may be issued in accordance with any such tables.

(2) Subject to sub-paragraph (1) above and sub-paragraph (3) below, the tables which the rules of a registered society are required to contain by virtue of paragraph 3 above and any tables contained in the rules of a branch shall, in the case of a society or branch which proposes to carry on long term business within the meaning of the Insurance Companies Act 1974, be tables which, in so far as they relate to that business, have been certified by a qualified actuary.

(3) Sub-paragraph (2) above does not apply:
   (a) to a society first registered before 26th July 1968, nor
   (b) to a branch of such a society, nor
   (c) to a society formed by the amalgamation of two or more such societies.

# Appendix 7

## LOTTERIES AND AMUSEMENTS ACT 1976
## (AS AMENDED)

### 1.    Illegality of lotteries

All lotteries which do not constitute gaming are unlawful, except as provided by this Act and section 2(1) of the National Lottery etc Act 1993.

### 2.    General lottery offences

(1) Subject to the provisions of this section, every person who in connection with any lottery promoted or proposed to be promoted either in Great Britain or elsewhere–

(a)  prints any tickets for use in the lottery; or

(b)  sells or distributes, or offers or advertises for sale or distribution, or has in his possession for the purpose of sale or distribution, any tickets or chances in the lottery; or

(c)  prints, publishes or distributes, or has in his possession for the purpose of publication or distribution–

    (i)   any advertisement of the lottery; or

    (ii)  any list, whether complete or not, of prize winners or winning tickets in the lottery; or

    (iii) any such matter descriptive of the drawing or intended drawing of the lottery, or otherwise relating to the lottery, as is calculated to act as an inducement to persons to participate in that lottery or in other lotteries; or

(d)  brings, or invites any person to send, into Great Britain from a place outside the British Islands and the member States for the purpose of sale or distribution any ticket in, or advertisement of, the lottery; or

(e)  sends or attempts to send out of Great Britain to a place outside the British Islands and the member States any money or valuable thing received in respect of the sale or distribution, or any document recording the sale or distribution, or the identity of the holder, of any ticket or chance in the lottery; or

(f) uses any premises, or causes or knowingly permits any premises to be used, for purposes connected with the promotion or conduct of the lottery; or

(g) causes, procures or attempts to procure any person to do any of the above-mentioned acts, shall be guilty of an offence.

(2) In any proceedings instituted under subsection (1) above, it shall be a defence to prove either–

(a) that the lottery to which the proceedings relate was a lottery declared not to be unlawful by sections 3, 4 or 25(6) below, and that at the date of the alleged offence the person charged believed, and had reasonable ground for believing, that none of the conditions required by the relevant enactment to be observed in connection with the promotion and conduct of the lottery had been broken; or

(b) that the lottery to which the proceedings relate was a society's lottery or a local lottery, and that at the date of the alleged offence the person charged believed, and had reasonable ground for believing, that it was being conducted in accordance with the requirements of this Act; or

(c) that the lottery to which the proceedings relate was not promoted wholly or partly outside Great Britain and constituted gaming as well as a lottery; or

(d) that the lottery to which the proceedings relate was a lottery forming part of the National Lottery for the purposes of Part 1 of the National Lottery etc Act 1993 or that at the date of the alleged offence the person charged believed, and had reasonable ground for believing, it to be such a lottery.

(2A) In any proceedings instituted under subsection (1) above in respect of the printing, sale or possession of any tickets, advertisements or other documents or in respect of anything done with a view to or in connection with the printing, sale or export from Great Britain of any tickets, advertisements or other documents, it shall be a defence to prove that at the date of the alleged offence the person charged believed, and had reasonable ground for believing–

(a) that the lottery to which the proceedings relate was not being, and would not be, promoted or conducted wholly or partly in Great Britain; and

(b) that the tickets, advertisements or other documents were not being, and would not be, used in Great Britain in or in connection with that or any other lottery.

(3) In England and Wales, proceedings under subsection (1)(c)(iii) above in respect of any matter published in a newspaper shall not be instituted except by, or by direction of, the Director of Public Prosecutions.

## 3. Small lotteries incidental to exempt entertainments

(1) In this Act "exempt entertainment" means a bazaar, sale of work, fete, dinner, dance, sporting or athletic event or other entertainment of a similar character, whether limited to one day or extending over two or more days.

(2) Where a lottery is promoted as an incident of an exempt entertainment, that lottery is not unlawful, but the conditions set out in subsection (3) below shall be observed in connection with its promotion and conduct and, if any of those conditions is contravened, every person concerned in the promotion or conduct of the lottery shall be guilty of an offence unless he proves that the contravention occurred without his consent or connivance and that he exercised all due diligence to prevent it.

(3) The conditions referred to in subsection (2) above are that—
    (a) the whole proceeds of the entertainment (including the proceeds of the lottery) after deducting—
        (i) the expenses of the entertainment, excluding expenses incurred in connection with the lottery; and
        (ii) the expenses incurred in printing tickets in the lottery; and
        (iii) such sum, if any, not exceeding £50 or such other sum as may be specified in an order made by the Secretary of State, as the promoters of the lottery think fit to appropriate on account of any expenses incurred by them in purchasing prizes in the lottery,
    shall be devoted to purposes other than private gain;
    (b) none of the prizes in the lottery shall be money prizes;
    (c) tickets or chances in the lottery shall not be sold or issues, nor shall the result of the lottery be declared, except on the premises on which the entertainment takes place and during the progress of the entertainment; and
    (d) the facilities for participating in lotteries under this section, or those facilities together with any other facilities for participating in lotteries or gaming, shall not be the only, or the only substantial, inducement to persons to attend the entertainment.

## 4. Private lotteries

(1) In this Act "private lottery" means a lottery in Great Britain which is promoted–

    (a) for members of one society established and conducted for purposes not connected with gaming, betting or lotteries;

    (b) for persons all of whom work on the same premises; or

    (c) for persons all of whom reside on the same premises,

and which satisfies the conditions in subsections (1A) and (1B) below.

(1A) The lottery must be promoted by persons each of whom–

    (a) is one of the persons for whom the lottery is promoted; and

    (b) in the case of a lottery promoted for the members of a society, is authorised in writing by the governing body of the society to promote the lottery.

(1B) The sale of tickets or chances in the lottery must be confined–

    (a) to the persons for whom the lottery is promoted; and

    (b) in the case of a lottery promoted for the members of a society, to any other persons on the society's premises.

(2) For the purposes of this section, each local or affiliated branch or section of a society shall be regarded as a separate and distinct society.

(3) A private lottery is not unlawful, but the following conditions shall be observed in connection with its promotion and conduct, that is to say–

    (a) the whole proceeds, after deducting only expenses incurred for printing and stationery, shall be devoted to the provision of prizes for purchasers of tickets or chances, or, in the case of a lottery promoted for the members of a society, shall be devoted either–

        (i) to the provision of prizes as aforesaid; or

        (ii) to purposes which are purposes of the society; or

        (iii) as to part to the provision of prizes as aforesaid and as to the remainder to such purposes as aforesaid;

    (b) there shall not be exhibited, published or distributed any written notice or advertisement of the lottery other than–

        (i) a notice of it exhibited on the premises of the society for whose members it is promoted or, as the case may be, on the premises on which the persons for whom it is promoted work or reside; and

        (ii) such announcement or advertisement of it as is contained in the tickets, if any;

    (c) the price of every ticket or chance shall be the same, and the price of any ticket shall be stated on the ticket;

    (d) every ticket shall bear upon the face of it the name and address of each of the promoters and a statement of the persons to whom the sale of tickets or chances by the promoters is restricted, and a statement that no prize won in the lottery shall be paid or delivered by the promoters to any person other than the person to whom the winning ticket or chance was sold by them, and no prize shall be paid or delivered except in accordance with that statement;

(e) no ticket or chance shall be issued or allotted by the promoters except by way of sale and upon receipt of its full price, and no money or valuable thing so received by a promoter shall in any circumstances be returned; and

(f) no tickets in the lottery shall be sent through the post.

(4) Subject to subsection (5) below, if any of the conditions set out in subsection (3) above is contravened, each of the promoters of the lottery, and, where the person by whom the condition is broken is not one of the promoters, that person also, shall be guilty of an offence.

(5) It shall be a defence for a person charged with an offence under subsection (4) above only by reason of his being a promoter of the lottery to prove that the contravention occurred without his consent or connivance and that he exercised all due diligence to prevent it.

## 5. Societies' lotteries

(1) In this Act "society's lottery" means a lottery promoted on behalf of a society which is established and conducted wholly or mainly for one or more of the following purposes, that is to say–

(a) charitable purposes;

(b) participation in or support of athletic sports or games or cultural activities;

(c) purposes which are not described in paragraph (a) or (b) above but are neither purposes of private gain nor purposes of any commercial undertaking.

(2) Any purpose for which a society is established and conducted and which is calculated to benefit the society as a whole shall not be held to be a purpose of private gain by reason only that action in its fulfilment would result in benefit to any person as an individual.

(3) Subject to the provisions of this Act, a society's lottery is not unlawful if–

(a) it is promoted in Great Britain; and

(b) the society is for the time being registered under the appropriate Schedule; and

(c) it is promoted in accordance with a scheme approved by the society;

(3A)  The appropriate Schedule for the purposes of subsection (3)(b) above–

  (a)  is Schedule 1 to this Act if none of subsections (3B) to (3D) below applies to the lottery;

  (b)  is Schedule 1A to this Act if any of those subsections applies to the lottery.

(3B)  This subsection applies to a lottery if the total value of the tickets or chances sold or to be sold in the lottery is more than £20,000.

(3C)  This subsection applies to a lottery if the total value of–

  (a)  the tickets or chances sold or to be sold in the lottery; and

  (b)  the tickets or chances sold or to be sold in all earlier lotteries held by the same society in the same year,

is more than £250,000.

(3D)  This subsection applies to a lottery if subsection (3B) or (3C) above applied to any earlier lottery held by the same society in the same year or any of the three preceding years.

(3E)  For the purposes of this section–

  (a)  a lottery is earlier than another lottery if any tickets or chances in it are sold, distributed or offered for sale before any tickets or chances in the other lottery are sold, distributed or offered for sale, and

  (b)  a lottery is held in the year in which the date of the lottery falls.

(3F)  In this section "year" means a period of twelve months beginning with 1st January.]

(4)  The whole proceeds of a society's lottery, after deducting sums lawfully appropriated on account of expenses or for the provision of prizes, shall be applied to purposes of the society such as are described in subsection (1) above.

(5)  Schedules 1 and 1A to this Act shall have effect.

*oOo*

## 15.   Provision of amusements with prizes at exempt entertainments

(1)  This section applies to the provision at any exempt entertainment of any amusement with prizes which constitutes a lottery or gaming or both but does not constitute–

  (a)  gaming to which Part II of the Gaming Act 1968 applies, or

  (b)  gaming by means of a machine to which Part III of that Act applies.

(2)  Where any such amusement constitutes a lottery, nothing in section 1 or 2 above shall apply to it.

(3) In relation to any such amusement (whether it constitutes a lottery or not) the conditions set out in subsection (4) below shall be observed, and if either of those conditions is contravened every person concerning in the provision or conduct of that amusement shall be guilty of an offence unless he proves that the contravention occurred without his consent or connivance and that he exercised all due diligence to prevent it.

(4) The conditions referred to in subsection (3) above are–

    (a) that the whole proceeds of the entertainment, after deducting the expenses of the entertainment, shall be devoted to purposes other than private gain;

    (b) that the facilities for winning prizes at amusements to which this section applies, or those facilities together with any other facilities for participating in lotteries or gaming, shall not be the only, or the only substantial, inducement to persons to attend the entertainment.

(5) Where any payment falls to be made–

    (a) by way of a hiring, maintenance or other charge in respect of a machine to which Part III of the Gaming Act 1968 applies, or

    (b) in respect of any requirement for holding a lottery or gaming at any entertainment,

then if, but only if, the amount of that charge falls to be determined wholly or partly by reference to the extent to which that or some other such machine or equipment is used for the purposes of lotteries or gaming, that payment shall be held to be an application of the proceeds of the entertainment for the purposes of private gain.

(6) The reference to expenses in subsection (4)(a) above shall accordingly not include a reference to any charge mentioned in subsection (5) above and falling to be determined as there mentioned.

*oOo*

## 22. Meaning of "private gain" in relation to proceeds of entertainments, lotteries and gaming promoted on behalf of certain societies

(1) For the purposes of this Act proceeds of any entertainment, lottery or gaming promoted on behalf of a society to which this subsection extends which are applied for any purpose calculated to benefit the society as a whole shall not be held to be applied for purposes of private gain by reason only that their application for that

purpose results in benefit to any person as an individual.

(2) Subsection (1) above extends to any society which is established and conducted either–

  (a) wholly for purposes other than purposes of any commercial undertaking; or

  (b) wholly or mainly for the purpose of participation in or support of athletic sports or athletic games.

# Appendix 8

## LICENSING ACT 2003

PART 1

LICENSABLE ACTIVITIES

**1.    Licensable activities and qualifying club activities**

(1) For the purposes of this Act the following are licensable activities–
   (a) the sale by retail of alcohol,
   (b) the supply of alcohol by or on behalf of a club to, or to the order of, a member of the club,
   (c) the provision of regulated entertainment, and
   (d) the provision of late night refreshment.

(2) For those purposes the following licensable activities are also qualifying club activities–
   (a) the supply of alcohol by or on behalf of a club to, or to the order of, a member of the club,
   (b) the sale by retail of alcohol by or on behalf of a club to a guest of a member of the club for consumption on the premises where the sale takes place, and
   (c) the provision of regulated entertainment where that provision is by or on behalf of a club for members of the club or members of the club and their guests.

(3) In this Act references to the supply of alcohol by or on behalf of a club to, or to the order of, a member of the club do not include a reference to any supply which is a sale by retail of alcohol.

(4) Schedule 1 makes provision about what constitutes the provision of regulated entertainment for the purposes of this Act.

(5) Schedule 2 makes provision about what constitutes the provision of late night refreshment for those purposes (including provision that certain activities carried on in relation to certain clubs or hotels

etc, or certain employees, do not constitute provision of late night refreshment and are, accordingly, not licensable activities).

(6) For the purposes of this Act premises are "used" for a licensable activity if that activity is carried on or from the premises.

(7) This section is subject to sections 173 to 175 (which exclude activities from the definition of licensable activity in certain circumstances).

## 2.    Authorisation for licensable activities and qualifying club activities

(1) A licensable activity may be carried on–
  (a)  under and in accordance with a premises licence (see Part 3), or
  (b)  in circumstances where the activity is a permitted temporary activity by virtue of Part 5.

(2) A qualifying club activity may be carried on under and in accordance with a club premises certificate (see Part 4).

(3) Nothing in this Act prevents two or more authorisations having effect concurrently in

(4) For the purposes of subsection (3) "authorisation" means–
  (a)  a premises licence;
  (b)  a club premises certificate;
  (c)  a temporary event notice.

*o0o*

## PART 4

## CLUBS

### Introductory

## 60.    Club premises certificate

(1) In this Act "club premises certificate" means a certificate granted under this Part–
  (a)  in respect of premises occupied by, and habitually used for the purposes of, a club,
  (b)  by the relevant licensing authority, and
  (c)  certifying the matters specified in subsection (2).

(2) Those matters are–
  (a)  that the premises may be used by the club for one or more qualifying club activities specified in the certificate, and
  (b)  that the club is a qualifying club in relation to each of those activities (see section 61).

**61.  Qualifying clubs**

(1) This section applies for determining for the purposes of this Part whether a club is a qualifying club in relation to a qualifying club activity.

(2) A club is a qualifying club in relation to the supply of alcohol to members or guests if it satisfies both–

    (a)  the general conditions in section 62, and

    (b)  the additional conditions in section 64.

(3) A club is a qualifying club in relation to the provision of regulated entertainment if it satisfies the general conditions in section 62.

**62.  The general conditions**

(1) The general conditions which a club must satisfy if it is to be a qualifying club in relation to a qualifying club activity are the following.

(2) Condition 1 is that under the rules of the club persons may not–

    (a)  be admitted to membership, or

    (b)  be admitted, as candidates for membership, to any of the privileges of membership,

without an interval of at least two days between their nomination or application for membership and their admission.

(3) Condition 2 is that under the rules of the club persons becoming members without prior nomination or application may not be admitted to the privileges of membership without an interval of at least two days between their becoming members and their admission.

(4) Condition 3 is that the club is established and conducted in good faith as a club (see section 63).

(5) Condition 4 is that the club has at least 25 members.

(6) Condition 5 is that alcohol is not supplied, or intended to be supplied, to members on the premises otherwise than by or on behalf of the club.

**63.  Determining whether a club is established and conducted in good faith**

(1) In determining for the purposes of condition 3 in subsection (4) of section 62 whether a club is established and conducted in good faith as a club, the matters to be taken into account are those specified in subsection (2).

(2) Those matters are–

(a) any arrangements restricting the club's freedom of purchase of alcohol;

(b) any provision in the rules, or arrangements, under which–
   (i) money or property of the club, or
   (ii) any gain arising from the carrying on of the club, is or may be applied otherwise than for the benefit of the club as a whole or for charitable, benevolent or political purposes;

(c) the arrangements for giving members information about the finances of the club;

(d) the books of account and other records kept to ensure the accuracy of that information;

(e) the nature of the premises occupied by the club.

(3) If a licensing authority decides for any purpose of this Act that a club does not satisfy condition 3 in subsection (4) of section 62, the authority must give the club notice of the decision and of the reasons for it.

**64    The additional conditions for the supply of alcohol**

(1) The additional conditions which a club must satisfy if it is to be a qualifying club in relation to the supply of alcohol to members or guests are the following.

(2) Additional condition 1 is that (so far as not managed by the club in general meeting or otherwise by the general body of members) the purchase of alcohol for the club, and the supply of alcohol by the club, are managed by a committee whose members

(a) are members of the club;

(b) have attained the age of 18 years; and

(c) are elected by the members of the club.

This subsection is subject to section 65 (which makes special provision for industrial and provident societies, friendly societies etc.).

(3) Additional condition 2 is that no arrangements are, or are intended to be made for any person to receive at the expense of the club any commission, percentage or similar payment on, or with reference to, purchases of alcohol by the club.

(4) Additional condition 3 is that no arrangements are, or are intended to be, made for any person directly or indirectly to derive any pecuniary benefit from the supply of alcohol by or on behalf of the club to members or guests, apart from–

(a) any benefit accruing to the club as a whole, or

(b) any benefit which a person derives indirectly by reason of the supply giving rise or contributing to a general gain from the carrying on of the club.

**65 Industrial and provident societies, friendly societies etc.**

(1) Subsection (2) applies in relation to any club which is–
  (a) a registered society, within the meaning of the Industrial and Provident Societies Act 1965 (see section 74(1) of that Act),
  (b) a registered society, within the meaning of the Friendly Societies Act 1974 (see section 111(1) of that Act), or
  (c) a registered friendly society, within the meaning of the Friendly Societies Act 1992 (see section 116 of that Act).

(2) Any such club is to be taken for the purposes of this Act to satisfy additional condition 1 in subsection (2) of section 64 if and to the extent that–
  (a) the purchase of alcohol for the club, and
  (b) the supply of alcohol by the club,
are under the control of the members or of a committee appointed by the members.

(3) References in this Act, other than this section, to–
  (a) subsection (2) of section 64, or
  (b) additional condition 1 in that subsection,
are references to it as read with subsection (1) of this section.

(4) Subject to subsection (5), this Act applies in relation to an incorporated friendly society as it applies in relation to a club, and accordingly–
  (a) the premises of the society are to be treated as the premises of a club,
  (b) the members of the society are to be treated as the members of the club, and
  (c) anything done by or on behalf of the society is to be treated as done by or on behalf of the club.

(5) In determining for the purposes of section 61 whether an incorporated friendly society is a qualifying club in relation to a qualifying club activity, the society is to be taken to satisfy the following conditions–
  (a) condition 3 in subsection (4) of section 62,
  (b) condition 5 in subsection (6) of that section,
  (c) the additional conditions in section 64.

(6) In this section "incorporated friendly society" has the same meaning as in the Friendly Societies Act 1992 (see section 116 of that Act).

**66 Miners' welfare institutes**

(1) Subject to subsection (2), this Act applies to a relevant miners' welfare institute as it applies to a club, and accordingly–
  (a) the premises of the institute are to be treated as the premises

of a club,

(b) the persons enrolled as members of the institute are to be treated as the members of the club, and

(c) anything done by or on behalf of the trustees or managers in carrying on the institute is to be treated as done by or on behalf of the club.

(2) In determining for the purposes of section 61 whether a relevant miners' welfare institute is a qualifying club in relation to a qualifying club activity, the institute is to be taken to satisfy the following conditions–

(a) condition 3 in subsection (4) of section 62,

(b) condition 4 in subsection (5) of that section,

(c) condition 5 in subsection (6) of that section,

(d) the additional conditions in section 64.

(3) For the purposes of this section–

(a) "miners' welfare institute" means an association organised for the social well-being and recreation of persons employed in or about coal mines (or of such persons in particular), and

(b) a miners' welfare institute is "relevant" if it satisfies one of the following conditions.

(4) The first condition is that–

(a) the institute is managed by a committee or board, and

(b) at least two thirds of the committee or board consists–

(i) partly of persons appointed or nominated, or appointed or elected from among persons nominated, by one or more licensed operators within the meaning of the Coal Industry Act 1994, and

(ii) partly of persons appointed or nominated, or appointed or elected from among persons nominated, by one or more organisations representing persons employed in or about coal mines.

(5) The second condition is that–

(a) the institute is managed by a committee or board, but

(b) the making of–

(i) an appointment or nomination falling within subsection (4)(b)(i), or

(ii) an appointment or nomination falling within subsection (4)(b)(ii),

is not practicable or would not be appropriate, and

(c) at least two thirds of the committee or board consists–

(i) partly of persons employed, or formerly employed, in or about coal mines, and

(ii) partly of persons appointed by the Coal Industry Social Welfare Organisation or a body or person to which the functions of that Organisation have been transferred under section 12(3) of the Miners' Welfare Act 1952

(6) The third condition is that the premises of the institute are held on trusts to which section 2 of the Recreational Charities Act 1958 applies.

INTERPRETATION

## 67 Associate members and their guests

(1) Any reference in this Act (other than this section) to a guest of a member of a club includes a reference to–

  (a) an associate member of the club, and

  (b) a guest of an associate member of the club.

(2) For the purposes of this Act a person is an "associate member" of a club if–

  (a) in accordance with the rules of the club, he is admitted to its premises as being a member of another club, and

  (b) that other club is a recognised club (see section 193).

## 68 The relevant licensing authority

(1) For the purposes of this Part the "relevant licensing authority" in relation to any premises is determined in accordance with this section.

(2) Subject to subsection (3), the relevant licensing authority is the authority in whose area the premises are situated.

(3) Where the premises are situated in the areas of two or more licensing authorities, the relevant licensing authority is–

  (a) the licensing authority in whose area the greater or greatest part of the premises is situated, or

  (b) if there is no authority to which paragraph (a) applies, such one of those authorities as is nominated in accordance with subsection (4).

(4) In a case within subsection (3)(b), an applicant for a club premises certificate must nominate one of the licensing authorities as the relevant licensing authority in relation to the application and any certificate granted as a result of it.

## 69 Authorised persons, interested parties and responsible authorities

(1) In this Part in relation to any premises each of the following expressions has the meaning given to it by this section–

  "authorised person",

  "interested party",

"responsible authority".

(2) "Authorised person" means any of the following–

    (a) an officer of a licensing authority in whose are the premises are situated who is authorised by that authority for the purposes of this Act,

    (b) an inspector appointed under section 18 of the Fire Precautions Act 1971,

    (c) an inspector appointed under section 19 of the Health and Safety at Work etc. Act 1974,

    (d) an officer of a local authority, in whose area the premises are situated, who is authorised by that authority for the purposes of exercising one or more of its statutory functions in relation to minimising or preventing the risk of pollution of the environment or of harm to human health,

    (e) in relation to a vessel, an inspector, or a surveyor of ships, appointed under section 256 of the Merchant Shipping Act 1995 ,

    (f) a person prescribed for the purposes of this subsection.

(3) "Interested party" means any of the following–

    (a) a person living in the vicinity of the premises,

    (b) a body representing persons who live in that vicinity,

    (c) a person involved in a business in that vicinity,

    (d) a body representing persons involved in such businesses.

(4) "Responsible authority" means any of the following–

    (a) the chief officer of police for any police area in which the premises are situated,

    (b) the fire authority for any area in which the premises are situated,

    (c) the enforcing authority within the meaning given by section 18 of the Health and Safety at Work etc. Act 1974 for any area in which the premises are situated,

    (d) the local planning authority within the meaning given by the Town and Country Planning Act 1990 for any area in which the premises are situated,

    (e) the local authority by which statutory functions are exercisable in any area in which the premises are situated in relation to minimising or preventing the risk of pollution of the environment or of harm to human health,

    (f) a body which–

        (i) represents those who, in relation to any such area, are responsible for, or interested in, matters relating to the protection of children from harm, and

        (ii) is recognised by the licensing authority for that area for the purposes of this section as being competent to advise it on such matters,

(g) any licensing authority (other than the relevant licensing authority) in whose area part of the premises is situated,

(h) in relation to a vessel–

   (i) a navigation authority (within the meaning of section 221(1) of the Water Resources Act 1991) having functions in relation to the waters where the vessel is usually moored or berthed or any waters where it is, or is proposed to be, navigated at a time when it is used for qualifying club activities,

   (ii) the Environment Agency,

   (iii) the British Waterways Board, or

   (iv) the Secretary of State,

(i) a person prescribed for the purposes of this subsection.

(5) For the purposes of this section, "statutory function" means a function conferred by or under any enactment.

## 70    Other definitions relating to clubs

In this Part–

"secretary", in relation to a club, includes any person (whether or not an officer of the club) performing the duties of a secretary;

"supply of alcohol to members or guests" means, in the case of any club:

(a) the supply of alcohol by or on behalf of the club to, or to the order of a member of the club, or

(b) the sale by retail of alcohol by or on behalf of the club to a guest of a member of the club for consumption on the premises where the sale takes place,

and related expressions are to be construed accordingly.

GRANT OF CLUB PREMISES CERTIFICATE

## 71    Application for club premises certificate

(1) A club may apply for a club premises certificate in respect of any premises which are occupied by, and habitually used for the purposes of, the club.

(2) Any application for a club premises certificate must be made to the relevant licensing authority.

(3) Subsection (2) is subject to regulations under–

   (a) section 91 (form etc. of applications and notices under this Part);

   (b) (b) section 92 (fees to accompany applications and notices).

(4) An application under this section must also be accompanied by–
   (a) a club operating schedule,
   (b) a plan of the premises to which the application relates, in the prescribed form, and
   (c) a copy of the rules of the club.
(5) A "club operating schedule" is a document which is in the prescribed form, and includes a statement of the following matters–
   (a) the qualifying club activities to which the application relates ("the relevant qualifying club activities"),
   (b) the times during which it is proposed that the relevant qualifying club activities are to take place,
   (c) any other times during which it is proposed that the premises are to be open to members and their guests,
   (d) where the relevant qualifying club activities include the supply of alcohol, whether the supplies are proposed to be for consumption on the premises or both on and off the premises,
   (e) the steps which it is proposed to take to promote the licensing objectives, and
   (f) such other matters as may be prescribed.
(6) The Secretary of State must by regulations–
   (a) require an applicant to advertise the application within the prescribed period–
     (i) in the prescribed form, and
     (ii) in a manner which is prescribed and is likely to bring the application to the attention of the interested parties likely to be affected by it;
   (b) require an applicant to give notice of the application to each responsible authority, and such other persons as may be prescribed within the prescribed period;
   (c) prescribe the period during which interested parties and responsible authorities may make representations to the relevant licensing authority about the application.

**72   Determination of application for club premises certificate**
(1) This section applies where the relevant licensing authority–
   (a) receives an application for a club premises certificate made in accordance with section 71, and
   (b) is satisfied that the applicant has complied with any requirement imposed on the applicant under subsection (6) of that section.
(2) Subject to subsection (3), the authority must grant the certificate in accordance with the application subject only to–

    (a)  such conditions as are consistent with the club operating schedule accompanying the application, and

    (b)  any conditions which must under section 73(2) to (5) or 74 be included in the certificate.

(3)  Where relevant representations are made, the authority must–

    (a)  hold a hearing to consider them, unless the authority, the applicant and each person who has made such representations agree that a hearing is unnecessary, and

    (b)  having regard to the representations, take such of the steps mentioned in subsection (4) (if any) as it considers necessary for the promotion of the licensing objectives.

(4)  The steps are–

    (a)  to grant the certificate subject to–

        (i)  the conditions mentioned in subsection (2)(a) modified to such extent as the authority considers necessary for the promotion of the licensing objectives, and

        (ii)  any conditions which must under section 73(2) to (5) or 74 be included in the certificate;

    (b)  to exclude from the scope of the certificate any of the qualifying club activities to which the application relates;

    (c)  to reject the application.

(5)  Subsections (2) and (3)(b) are subject to section 73(1) (certificate may authorise off-supplies only if it authorises on-supplies).

(6)  For the purposes of subsection (4)(a) the conditions mentioned in subsection (2)(a) are modified if any of them is altered or omitted or any new condition is added.

(7)  For the purposes of this section, "relevant representations" means representations which–

    (a)  are about the likely effect of the grant of the certificate on the promotion of the licensing objectives, and

    (b)  meet the requirements of subsection (8).

(8)  The requirements are–

    (a)  that the representations were made by an interested party or responsible authority within the period prescribed under section 71(6)(c),

    (b)  that they have not been withdrawn, and

    (c)  in the case of representations made by an interested party (who is not also a responsible authority), that they are not, in the opinion of the relevant licensing authority, frivolous or vexatious.

(9)  Where the authority determines for the purposes of subsection (8)(c) that any representations are frivolous or vexatious, it must notify the person who made them of the reasons for its determination.

(10)  In discharging its duty under subsection (2) or (3)(b) a licensing authority may grant a club premises certificate subject to different conditions in respect of–
   (a)  different parts of the premises concerned;
   (b)  different qualifying club activities.

## 73   Certificate authorising supply of alcohol for consumption off the premises

(1)  A club premises certificate may not authorise the supply of alcohol for consumption off the premises unless it also authorises the supply of alcohol to a member of the club for consumption on those premises.
(2)  A club premises certificate which authorises the supply of alcohol for consumption off the premises must include the following conditions.
(3)  The first condition is that the supply must be made at a time when the premises are open for the purposes of supplying alcohol, in accordance with the club premises certificate, to members of the club for consumption on the premises.
(4)  The second condition is that any alcohol supplied for consumption off the premises must be in a sealed container.
(5)  The third condition is that any supply of alcohol for consumption off the premises must be made to a member of the club in person.

## 74   Mandatory condition: exhibition of films

(1)  Where a club premises certificate authorises the exhibition of films, the certificate must include a condition requiring the admission of children to the exhibition of any film to be restricted in accordance with this section.
(2)  Where the film classification body is specified in the certificate, unless subsection (3)(b) applies, admission of children must be restricted in accordance with any recommendation made by that body.
(3)  Where–
   (a)  the film classification body is not specified in the certificate, or
   (b)  the relevant licensing authority has notified the club which holds the certificate that this subsection applies to the film in question,
   admission of children must be restricted in accordance with any recommendation made by that licensing authority.
(4)  In this section–
   "children" means persons aged under 18; and

"film classification body" means the person or persons designated as the authority under section 4 of the Video Recordings Act 1984 (authority to determine suitability of video works for classification).

## 75 Prohibited conditions: associate members and their guests

(1) Where the rules of a club provide for the sale by retail of alcohol on any premises by or on behalf of the club to, or to a guest of, an associate member of the club, no condition may be attached to a club premises certificate in respect of the sale by retail of alcohol on those premises by or on behalf of the club so as to prevent the sale by retail of alcohol to any such associate member or guest.

(2) Where the rules of a club provide for the provision of any regulated entertainment on any premises by or on behalf of the club to, or to a guest of, an associate member of the club, no condition may be attached to a club premises certificate in respect of the provision of any such regulated entertainment on those premises by or on behalf of the club so as to prevent its provision to any such associate member or guest.

## 76 Prohibited conditions: plays

(1) In relation to a club premises certificate which authorises the performance of plays, no condition may be attached to the certificate as to the nature of the plays which may be performed, or the manner of performing plays, under the certificate.

(2) But subsection (1) does not prevent a licensing authority imposing, in accordance with section 72(2) or (3)(b), 85(3)(b) or 88(3), any condition which it considers necessary on the grounds of public safety.

## 77 Grant or rejection of application for club premises certificate

(1) Where an application is granted under section 72, the relevant licensing authority must forthwith–
   (a) give a notice to that effect to–
      (i) the applicant,
      (ii) any person who made relevant representations in respect of the application, and
      (iii) the chief officer of police for the police area (or each police area) in which the premises are situated, and
   (b) issue the club with the club premises certificate and a summary of it.

(2) Where relevant representations were made in respect of the

application, the notice under subsection (1)(a) must specify the authority's reasons for its decision as to the steps (if any) to take under section 72(3)(b).

(3) Where an application is rejected under section 72, the relevant licensing authority must forthwith give a notice to that effect, stating its reasons for that decision, to–

    (a) the applicant,

    (b) any person who made relevant representations in respect of the application, and

    (c) the chief officer of police for the police area (or each police area) in which the premises are situated.

(4) In this section "relevant representations" has the meaning given in section 72(6).

## 78    Form of certificate and summary

(1) A club premises certificate and the summary of such a certificate must be in the prescribed form.

(2) Regulations under subsection (1) must, in particular, provide for the certificate to–

    (a) specify the name of the club and the address which is to be its relevant registered address, as defined in section 184(7);

    (b) specify the address of the premises to which the certificate relates;

    (c) include a plan of those premises;

    (d) specify the qualifying club activities for which the premises may be used;

    (e) specify the conditions subject to which the certificate has effect.

## 79    Theft, loss, etc. of certificate or summary

(1) Where a club premises certificate or summary is lost, stolen, damaged or destroyed, the club may apply to the relevant licensing authority for a copy of the certificate or summary.

(2) Subsection (1) is subject to regulations under section 92(1) (power to prescribe fee to accompany application).

(3) Where an application is made in accordance with this section, the relevant licensing authority must issue the club with a copy of the certificate or summary (certified by the authority to be a true copy) if it is satisfied that–

    (a) the certificate or summary has been lost, stolen, damaged or destroyed, and

    (b) where it has been lost or stolen, the club has reported the loss or theft to the police.

(4) The copy issued under this section must be a copy of the club premises certificate or summary in the form in which it existed immediately before it was lost, stolen, damaged or destroyed.

(5) This Act applies in relation to a copy issued under this section as it applies in relation to an original club premises certificate or summary.

DURATION OF CERTIFICATE

## 80   Period of validity of club premises certificate

(1) A club premises certificate has effect until such time as–
    (a) it is withdrawn under section 88 or 90, or
    (b) it lapses by virtue of section 81(3) (surrender).

(2) But a club premises certificate does not have effect during any period when it is suspended under section 88.

## 81   Surrender of club premises certificate

(1) Where a club which holds a club premises certificate decides to surrender it, the club may give the relevant licensing authority a notice to that effect.

(2) The notice must be accompanied by the club premises certificate or, if that is not practicable, by a statement of the reasons for the failure to produce the certificate.

(3) Where a notice is given in accordance with this section, the certificate lapses on receipt of the notice by the authority.

DUTY TO NOTIFY CERTAIN CHANGES

## 82   Notification of change of name or alteration of rules of club

(1) Where a club–
    (a) holds a club premises certificate, or
    (b) has made an application for a club premises certificate which has not been determined by the relevant licensing authority,
the secretary of the club must give the relevant licensing authority notice of any change in the name, or alteration made to the rules, of the club.

(2) Subsection (1) is subject to regulations under section 92(1) (power to prescribe fee to accompany application).

(3) A notice under subsection (1) by a club which holds a club premises certificate must be accompanied by the certificate or, if that is not

practicable, by a statement of the reasons for the failure to produce the certificate.

(4) An authority notified under this section of a change in the name, or alteration to the rules, of a club must amend the club premises certificate accordingly.

(5) But nothing in subsection (4) requires or authorises the making of any amendment to a club premises certificate so as to change the premises to which the certificate relates (and no amendment made under that subsection to a club premises certificate has effect so as to change those premises).

(6) If a notice required by this section is not given within the 28 days following the day on which the change of name or alteration to the rules is made, the secretary of the club commits an offence.

(7) A person guilty of an offence under subsection (6) is liable on summary conviction to a fine not exceeding level 2 on the standard scale.

**83    Change of relevant registered address of club**

(1) A club which holds a club premises certificate may give the relevant licensing authority notice of any change desired to be made in the address which is to be the club's relevant registered address.

(2) If a club which holds a club premises certificate ceases to have any authority to make use of the address which is its relevant registered address, it must as soon as reasonably practicable give to the relevant licensing authority notice of the change to be made in the address which is to be the club's relevant registered address.

(3) Subsections (1) and (2) are subject to regulations under section 92(1) (power to prescribe fee to accompany application).

(4) A notice under subsection (1) or (2) must also be accompanied by the club premises certificate or, if that is not practicable, by a statement of the reasons for the failure to produce the certificate.

(5) An authority notified under subsection (1) or (2) of a change to be made in the relevant registered address of a club must amend the club premises certificate accordingly.

(6) If a club fails, without reasonable excuse, to comply with subsection (2) the secretary commits an offence.

(7) A person guilty of an offence under subsection (6) is liable on summary conviction to a fine not exceeding level 2 on the standard scale.

(8) In this section "relevant registered address" has the meaning given in section 184(7).

VARIATION OF CERTIFICATES

## 84 Application to vary club premises certificate

(1) A club which holds a club premises certificate may apply to the relevant licensing authority for variation of the certificate.

(2) Subsection (1) is subject to regulations under–
- (a) section 91 (form etc. of applications);
- (b) section 92 (fees to accompany applications).

(3) An application under this section must also be accompanied by the club premises certificate or, if that is not practicable, by a statement of the reasons for the failure to provide the certificate.

(4) The duty to make regulations imposed on the Secretary of State by subsection (6) of section 71 (advertisement etc. of application) applies in relation to applications under this section as it applies in relation to applications under that section.

## 85 Determination of application under section 84

(1) This section applies where the relevant licensing authority–
- (a) receives an application, made in accordance with section 84, to vary a club premises certificate, and
- (b) is satisfied that the applicant has complied with any requirement imposed by virtue of subsection (4) of that section.

(2) Subject to subsection (3) and section 86(6), the authority must grant the application.

(3) Where relevant representations are made, the authority must–
- (a) hold a hearing to consider them, unless the authority, the applicant and each person who has made such representations agree that a hearing is unnecessary, and
- (b) having regard to the representations, take such of the steps mentioned in subsection (4) (if any) as it considers necessary for the promotion of the licensing objectives.

(4) The steps are–
- (a) to modify the conditions of the certificate;
- (b) to reject the whole or part of the application;

and for this purpose the conditions of the certificate are modified if any of them is altered or omitted or any new condition is added.

(5) In this section "relevant representations" means representations which–
- (a) are about the likely effect of the grant of the application on the promotion of the licensing objectives, and
- (b) meet the requirements of subsection (6).

(6) The requirements are–

(a) that the representations are made by an interested party or responsible authority within the period prescribed under section 71(6)(c) by virtue of section 84(4),

(b) that they have not been withdrawn, and

(c) in the case of representations made by an interested party (who is not also a responsible authority), that they are not, in the opinion of the relevant licensing authority, frivolous or vexatious.

(7) Subsections (2) and (3) are subject to sections 73 and 74 (mandatory conditions relating to supply of alcohol for consumption off the premises and to exhibition of films).

**86    Supplementary provision about applications under section 84**

(1) Where an application (or any part of an application) is granted under section 85, the relevant licensing authority must forthwith give a notice to that effect to–

(a) the applicant,

(b) any person who made relevant representations in respect of the application, and

(c) the chief officer of police for the police area (or each police each) in which the premises are situated.

(2) Where relevant representations were made in respect of the application, the notice under subsection (1) must specify the authority's reasons for its decision as to the steps (if any) to take under section 85(3)(b).

(3) The notice under subsection (1) must specify the time when the variation in question takes effect.

That time is the time specified in the application or, if that time is before the applicant is given the notice, such later time as the relevant licensing authority specifies in the notice.

(4) Where an application (or any part of an application) is rejected under section 85, the relevant licensing authority must forthwith give a notice to that effect stating its reasons for rejecting the application to–

(a) the applicant,

(b) any person who made relevant representations, and

(c) the chief officer of police for the police area (or each police area) in which the premises are situated.

(5) Where the relevant licensing authority determines for the purposes of section 85(6)(c) that any representations are frivolous or vexatious, it must give the person who made them its reasons for that determination.

(6) A club premises certificate may not be varied under section 85 so

as to vary substantially the premises to which it relates.

(7) In discharging its duty under subsection (2) or (3)(b) of that section, a licensing authority may vary a club premises certificate so that it has effect subject to different conditions in respect of–
    (a) different parts of the premises concerned;
    (b) different qualifying club activities.

(8) In this section "relevant representations" has the meaning given in section 85(5).

REVIEW OF CERTIFICATES

## 87    Application for review of club premises certificate

(1) Where a club holds a club premises certificate–
    (a) an interested party,
    (b) a responsible authority, or
    (c) a member of the club,
may apply to the relevant licensing authority for a review of the certificate.

(2) Subsection (1) is subject to regulations under section 91 (form etc. of applications).

(3) The Secretary of State must by regulations under this section–
    (a) require the applicant to give a notice containing details of the application to the club and each responsible authority within such period as may be prescribed;
    (b) require the authority to advertise the application and invite representations relating to it to be made to the authority;
    (c) prescribe the period during which representations may be made by the club, any responsible authority and any interested party;
    (d) require any notice under paragraph (a) or advertisement under paragraph (b) to specify that period.

(4) The relevant licensing authority may, at any time, reject any ground for review specified in an application under this section if it is satisfied–
    (a) that the ground is not relevant to one or more of the licensing objectives, or
    (b) in the case of an application made by a person other than a responsible authority, that–
        (i)    the ground is frivolous or vexatious, or
        (ii)    the ground is a repetition.

(5) For this purpose a ground for review is a repetition if–
    (a) it is identical or substantially similar to–
        (i)   a ground for review specified in an earlier application for

review made in respect of the same club premises certificate and determined under section 88, or

    (ii) representations considered by the relevant licensing authority in accordance with section 72, before it determined the application for the club premises certificate under that section, and

  (b) a reasonable interval has not elapsed since that earlier application or that grant.

(6) Where the authority rejects a ground for review under subsection (4)(b), it must notify the applicant of its decision and, if the ground was rejected because it was frivolous or vexatious, the authority must notify him of its reasons for making that decision.

(7) The application is to be treated as rejected to the extent that any of the grounds for review are rejected under subsection (4).

Accordingly, the requirements imposed under subsection (3)(a) and (b) and by section 88 (so far as not already met) apply only to so much (if any) of the application as has not been rejected.

## 88   Determination of application for review

(1) This section applies where–

  (a) the relevant licensing authority receives an application made in accordance with section 87,

  (b) the applicant has complied with any requirement imposed by virtue of subsection (3)(a) or (d) of that section, and

  (c) the authority has complied with any requirement imposed on it under subsection (3)(b) or (d) of that section.

(2) Before determining the application, the authority must hold a hearing to consider it and any relevant representations.

(3) The authority must, having regard to the application and any relevant representations, take such of the steps mentioned in subsection (4) (if any) as it considers necessary for the promotion of the licensing objectives.

(4) The steps are–

  (a) to modify the conditions of the certificate;

  (b) to exclude a qualifying club activity from the scope of the certificate;

  (c) to suspend the certificate for a period not exceeding three months;

  (d) to withdraw the certificate;

and for this purpose the conditions of the certificate are modified if any of them is altered or omitted or any new condition is added.

(5) Subsection (3) is subject to sections 73 and 74 (mandatory

conditions relating to supply of alcohol for consumption off the premises and to exhibition of films).

(6) Where the authority takes a step within subsection (4)(a) or (b), it may provide that the modification or exclusion is to have effect for only such period (not exceeding three months) as it may specify.

(7) In this section "relevant representations" means representations which–

    (a) are relevant to one or more of the licensing objectives, and

    (b) meet the requirements of subsection (8).

(8) The requirements are–

    (a) that the representations are made by the club, a responsible authority or an interested party within the period prescribed under section 87(3)(c),

    (b) that they have not been withdrawn, and

    (c) if they are made by an interested party (who is not also a responsible authority), that they are not, in the opinion of the relevant licensing authority, frivolous or vexatious.

(9) Where the relevant licensing authority determines that any representations are frivolous or vexatious, it must give the person who made them its reasons for that determination.

(10) Where a licensing authority determines an application for review under this section it must notify the determination and its reasons for making it to–

    (a) the club,

    (b) the applicant,

    (c) any person who made relevant representations, and

    (d) the chief officer of police for the police area (or each police area) in which the premises are situated.

(11) A determination under this section does not have effect–

    (a) until the end of the period given for appealing against the decision, or

    (b) if the decision is appealed against, until the appeal is disposed of.

**89 Supplementary provision about review–**

(1) This section applies where a local authority is both–

    (a) the relevant licensing authority, and

    (b) a responsible authority,

in respect of any premises.

(2) The authority may, in its capacity as responsible authority, apply under section 87 for a review of any club premises certificate in respect of the premises.

(3) The authority may in its capacity as licensing authority determine that application.

WITHDRAWAL OF CERTIFICATES

## 90  Club ceasing to be a qualifying club

(1) Where–
  - (a)  a club holds a club premises certificate, and
  - (b)  it appears to the relevant licensing authority that the club does not satisfy the conditions for being a qualifying club in relation to a qualifying club activity to which the certificate relates (see section 61),

  the authority must give a notice to the club withdrawing the certificate, so far as relating to that activity.

(2) Where the only reason that the club does not satisfy the conditions for being a qualifying club in relation to the activity in question is that the club has fewer than the required number of members, the notice withdrawing the certificate must state that the withdrawal–
  - (a)  does not take effect until immediately after the end of the period of three months following the date of the notice, and
  - (b)  will not take effect if, at the end of that period, the club again has at least the required number of members.

(3) The references in subsection (2) to the required number of members are references to the minimum number of members required by condition 4 in section 62(5) (25 at the passing of this Act).

(4) Nothing in subsection (2) prevents the giving of a further notice of withdrawal under this section at any time.

(5) Where a justice of the peace is satisfied, on information on oath, that there are reasonable grounds for believing–
  - (a)  that a club which holds a club premises certificate does not satisfy the conditions for being a qualifying club in relation to a qualifying club activity to which the certificate relates, and
  - (b)  that evidence of that fact is to be obtained at the premises to which the certificate relates, he may issue a warrant authorising a constable to enter the premises, if necessary by force, at any time within one month from the time of the issue of the warrant, and search them.

(6) A person who enters premises under the authority of a warrant under subsection (5) may seize and remove any documents relating to the business of the club in question.

GENERAL PROVISIONS

**91    Form etc. of applications and notices under Part 4**

In relation to any application or notice under this Part, regulations may prescribe–

(a) its form;

(b) the manner in which it is to be made or given;

(c) information and documents that must accompany it.

**92    Fees**

(1) Regulations may–

    (a)  require applications under any provision of this Part (other than section 87) to be accompanied by a fee, and

    (b)  prescribe the amount of the fee.

(2) Regulations may also require the payment of an annual fee to the relevant licensing authority by or on behalf of a club which holds a club premises certificate.

(3) Regulations under subsection (2) may include provision–

    (a)  imposing liability for the making of the payment on the secretary or such other officers or members of the club as may be prescribed,

    (b)  prescribing the amount of any such fee, and

    (c)  prescribing the time at which any such fee is due.

(4) Any fee which is owed to a licensing authority under subsection (2) may be recovered as a debt due to the authority from any person liable to make the payment by virtue of subsection (3)(a).

PRODUCTION OF CERTIFICATE, RIGHTS OF ENTRY, ETC.

**93    Licensing authority's duty to update club premises certificate**

(1) Where–

    (a)  the relevant licensing authority, in relation to a club premises certificate, makes a determination or receives a notice under this Part, or

    (b)  an appeal against a decision under this Part is disposed of,

the relevant licensing authority must make the appropriate amendments (if any) to the certificate and, if necessary, issue a new summary of the certificate.

(2) Where a licensing authority is not in possession of the club premises certificate, it may, for the purpose of discharging its obligations under subsection (1), require the secretary of the club to produce the certificate to the authority within 14 days from the

date on which the club is notified of the requirement.

(3) A person commits an offence if he fails, without reasonable excuse, to comply with a requirement under subsection (2).

(4) A person guilty of an offence under subsection (3) is liable on summary conviction to a fine not exceeding level 2 on the standard scale.

## 94 Duty to keep and produce certificate

(1) This section applies whenever premises in respect of which a club premises certificate has effect are being used for one or more qualifying club activities authorised by the certificate.

(2) The secretary of the club must secure that the certificate, or a certified copy of it, is kept at the premises in the custody or under the control of a person (the "nominated person") who–
  (a) falls within subsection (3),
  (b) has been nominated for the purpose by the secretary in writing, and
  (c) has been identified to the relevant licensing authority in a notice given by the secretary.

(3) The persons who fall within this subsection are–
  (a) the secretary of the club,
  (b) any member of the club,
  (c) any person who works at the premises for the purposes of the club.

(4) The nominated person must secure that–
  (a) the summary of the certificate or a certified copy of that summary, and
  (b) a notice specifying the position which he holds at the premises,
  are prominently displayed at the premises.

(5) The secretary commits an offence if he fails, without reasonable excuse, to comply with subsection (2).

(6) The nominated person commits an offence if he fails, without reasonable excuse, to comply with subsection (4).

(7) A constable or an authorised person may require the nominated person to produce the club premises certificate (or certified copy) for examination.

(8) An authorised person exercising the power conferred by subsection (7) must, if so requested, produce evidence of his authority to exercise the power.

(9) A person commits an offence if he fails, without reasonable excuse, to produce a club premises certificate or certified copy of a club premises certificate in accordance with a requirement under subsection (7).

(10)  A person guilty of an offence under this section is liable on summary conviction to a fine not exceeding level 2 on the standard scale.

(11)  In subsection (4) the reference to the summary of the certificate is a reference to the summary issued under section 77 or, where one or more summaries have subsequently been issued under section 93, the most recent summary to be so issued.

(12)  Section 95 makes provision about certified copies of club premises certificates and of summaries of club premises certificates for the purposes of this section.

## 95   Provision supplementary to section 94

(1)  Any reference in section 94 to a certified copy of a document is a reference to a copy of the document which is certified to be a true copy by–
   (a)  the relevant licensing authority,
   (b)  a solicitor or notary, or
   (c)  a person of a prescribed description.

(2)  Any certified copy produced in accordance with a requirement under subsection 94(7) must be a copy of the document in the form in which it exists at the time.

(3)  A document which purports to be a certified copy of a document is to be taken to be such a copy, and to comply with the requirements of subsection (2), unless the contrary is shown.

## 96   Inspection of premises before grant of certificate etc.

(1) Subsection (2) applies where–
   (a)  a club applies for a club premises certificate in respect of any premises,
   (b)  a club applies under section 84 for the variation of a club premises certificate held by it, or
   (c)  an application is made under section 87 for review of a club premises certificate.

(2)    On production of his authority–
   (a)  an authorised person, or
   (b)  a constable authorised by the chief officer of police,
may enter and inspect the premises.

(3) Any entry and inspection under this section must take place at a reasonable time on a day–
   (a)  which is not more than 14 days after the making of the application in question, and
   (b)  which is specified in the notice required by subsection (4).

(4) Before an authorised person or constable enters and inspects any

premises under this section, at least 48 hours' notice must be given to the club.

(5) Any person obstructing an authorised person in the exercise of the power conferred by this section commits an offence.

(6) A person guilty of an offence under subsection (5) is liable on summary conviction to a fine not exceeding level 2 on the standard scale.

(7) The relevant licensing authority may, on the application of a responsible authority, extend by not more than 7 days the time allowed for carrying out an entry and inspection under this section.

(8) The relevant licensing authority may allow such an extension of time only if it appears to the authority that–

    (a) reasonable steps had been taken for an authorised person or constable authorised by the applicant to inspect the premises in good time, but

    (b) it was not possible for the inspection to take place within the time allowed.

## 97  Other powers of entry and search

(1) Where a club premises certificate has effect in respect of any premises, a constable may enter and search the premises if he has reasonable cause to believe–

    (a) that an offence under section 4(3)(a), (b) or (c) of the Misuse of Drugs Act 1971 (supplying or offering to supply, or being concerned in supplying or making an offer to supply, a controlled drug) has been, is being, or is about to be, committed there, or

    (b) that there is likely to be a breach of the peace there.

(2) A constable exercising any power conferred by this section may, if necessary, use reasonable force.

## PART 5

## PERMITTED TEMPORARY ACTIVITIES

### INTRODUCTORY

## 98  Meaning of "permitted temporary activity"

(1) A licensable activity is a permitted temporary activity by virtue of this Part if–

    (a) it is carried on in accordance with a notice given in accordance with section 100, and

   (b)  the following conditions are satisfied.

(2) The first condition is that the requirements of sections 102 (acknowledgement of notice) and 104(1) (notification of police) are met in relation to the notice.

(3) The second condition is that the notice has not been withdrawn under this Part.

(4) The third condition is that no counter notice has been given under this Part in respect of the notice.

## 99   The relevant licensing authority

In this Part references to the "relevant licensing authority", in relation to any premises, are references to–

   (a)  the licensing authority in whose area the premises are situated, or

   (b)  where the premises are situated in the areas of two or more licensing authorities, each of those authorities.

TEMPORARY EVENT NOTICES

## 100   Temporary event notice

(1) Where it is proposed to use premises for one or more licensable activities during a period not exceeding 96 hours, an individual may give to the relevant licensing authority notice of that proposal (a "temporary event notice").

(2) In this Act, the "premises user", in relation to a temporary event notice, is the individual who gave the notice.

(3) An individual may not give a temporary event notice unless he is aged 18 or over.

(4) A temporary event notice must be in the prescribed form and contain–

   (a)  a statement of the matters mentioned in subsection (5),

   (b)  where subsection (6) applies, a statement of the condition mentioned in that subsection, and

   (c)  such other information as may be prescribed.

(5) Those matters are–

   (a)  the licensable activities to which the proposal mentioned in subsection (1) relates ("the relevant licensable activities"),

   (b)  the period (not exceeding 96 hours) during which it is proposed to use the premises for those activities ("the event period"),

   (c)  the times during the event period when the premises user

    proposes that those licensable activities shall take place,
- (d) the maximum number of persons (being a number less than 500) which the premises user proposes should, during those times, be allowed on the premises at the same time,
- (e) where the relevant licensable activities include the supply of alcohol, whether supplies are proposed to be for consumption on the premises or off the premises, or both, and
- (f) such other matters as may be prescribed.

(6) Where the relevant licensable activities include the supply of alcohol, the notice must make it a condition of using the premises for such supplies that all such supplies are made by or under the authority of the premises user.

(7) The temporary event notice–
- (a) must be given to the relevant licensing authority (in duplicate) no later than ten working days before the day on which the event period begins, and
- (b) must be accompanied by the prescribed fee.

(8) The Secretary of State may, by order–
- (a) amend subsections (1) and (5)(b) so as to substitute any period for the period for the time being specified there;
- (b) amend subsection (5)(d) so as to substitute any number for the number for the time being specified there.

(9) In this section "supply of alcohol" means–
- (a) the sale by retail of alcohol, or
- (b) the supply of alcohol by or on behalf of a club to, or to the order of, a member of the club.

## 101  Minimum of 24 hours between event periods

(1) A temporary event notice ("notice A") given by an individual ("the relevant premises user") is void if the event period specified in it does not–
- (a) end at least 24 hours before the event period specified in any other temporary event notice given by the relevant premises user in respect of the same premises before or at the same time as notice A, or
- (b) begin at least 24 hours after the event period specified in any other such notice.

(2) For the purposes of subsection (1)–
- (a) any temporary event notice in respect of which a counter notice has been given under this Part or which has been withdrawn under section 103 is to be disregarded;
- (b) a temporary event notice given by an individual who is an associate of the relevant premises user is to be treated as a

notice given by the relevant premises user;

   (c) a temporary event notice ("notice B") given by an individual who is in business with the relevant premises user is to be treated as a notice given by the relevant premises user if–

     (i) that business relates to one or more licensable activities, and

     (ii) notice A and notice B relate to one or more licensable activities to which the business relates (although not necessarily the same activity or activities);

   (d) two temporary event notices are in respect of the same premises if the whole or any part of the premises in respect of which one of the notices is given includes or forms part of the premises in respect of which the other notice is given.

(3) For the purposes of this section an individual is an associate of another person if that individual is–

   (a) the spouse of that person,

   (b a child, parent, grandchild, grandparent, brother or sister of that person,

   (c) an agent or employee of that person, or

   (d) the spouse of a person within paragraph (b) or (c).

(4) For the purposes of subsection (3) a person living with another as that person's husband or wife is to be treated as that person's spouse.

## 102 Acknowledgment of notice

(1) Where a licensing authority receives a temporary event notice (in duplicate) in accordance with this Part, it must acknowledge receipt of the notice by sending or delivering one notice to the premises user–

   (a) before the end of the first working day following the day on which it was received, or

   (b) if the day on which it was received was not a working day, before the end of the second working day following that day.

(2) The authority must mark on the notice to be returned under subsection (1) an acknowledgement of the receipt in the prescribed form.

(3) Subsection (1) does not apply where, before the time by which the notice must be returned in accordance with that subsection, a counter notice has been sent or delivered to the premises user under section 107 in relation to the temporary event notice.

## 103 Withdrawal of notice

(1) A temporary event notice may be withdrawn by the premises user giving the relevant licensing authority a notice to that effect no

later than 24 hours before the beginning of the event period specified in the temporary event notice.

(2) Nothing in section 102 or sections 104 to 107 applies in relation to a notice withdrawn in accordance with this section.

## 104 Objection to notice by the police

(1) The premises user must give a copy of any temporary event notice to the relevant chief officer of police no later than ten working days before the day on which the event period specified in the notice begins.

(2) Where a chief officer of police who receives a copy notice under subsection (1) is satisfied that allowing the premises to be used in accordance with the notice would undermine the crime prevention objective, he must give a notice stating the reasons why he is so satisfied (an "objection notice")–

   (a) to the relevant licensing authority, and

   (b) to the premises user.

(3) The objection notice must be given no later than 48 hours after the chief officer of police is given a copy of the temporary event notice under subsection (1).

(4) Subsection (2) does not apply at any time after the relevant chief officer of police has received a copy of a counter notice under section 107 in respect of the temporary event notice.

(5) In this section "relevant chief officer of police" means–

   (a) where the premises are situated in one police area, the chief officer of police for that area, and

   (b) where the premises are situated in two or more police areas, the chief officer of police for each of those areas.

## 105 Counter notice following police objection

(1) This section applies where an objection notice is given in respect of a temporary event notice.

(2) The relevant licensing authority must–

   (a) hold a hearing to consider the objection notice, unless the premises user, the chief officer of police who gave the objection notice and the authority agree that a hearing is unnecessary, and

   (b) having regard to the objection notice, give the premises user a counter notice under this section if it considers it necessary for the promotion of the crime prevention objective to do so.

(3) The relevant licensing authority must–

    (a) in a case where it decides not to give a counter notice under this section, give the premises user and the relevant chief officer of police notice of the decision, and

    (b) in any other case–

        (i) give the premises user the counter notice and a notice stating the reasons for its decision, and

        (ii) give the relevant chief officer of police a copy of both of those notices.

(4) A decision must be made under subsection (2)(b), and the requirements of subsection (3) must be met, at least 24 hours before the beginning of the event period specified in the temporary event notice.

(5) Where the premises are situated in the area of more than one licensing authority, the functions conferred on the relevant licensing authority by this section must be exercised by those authorities jointly.

(6) This section does not apply–

    (a) if the objection notice has been withdrawn (whether by virtue of section 106 or otherwise), or

    (b) if the premises user has been given a counter notice under section 107.

(7) In this section "objection notice" and "relevant chief officer of police" have the same meaning as in section 104.

## 106 Modification of notice following police objection

(1) This section applies where a chief officer of police has given an objection notice in respect of a temporary event notice (and the objection notice has not been withdrawn).

(2) At any time before a hearing is held or dispensed with under section 105(2), the chief officer of police may, with the agreement of the premises user, modify the temporary event notice by making changes to the notice returned to the premises user under section 102.

(3) Where a temporary event notice is modified under subsection (2)–

    (a) the objection notice is to be treated for the purposes of this Act as having been withdrawn from the time the temporary event notice is modified, and

    (b) from that time–

        (i) this Act has effect as if the temporary event notice given under section 100 had been the notice as modified under that subsection, and

      (ii)  to the extent that the conditions of section 98 are satisfied in relation to the unmodified notice they are to be treated as satisfied in relation to the notice as modified under that subsection.

(4) A copy of the temporary event notice as modified under subsection (2) must be sent or delivered by the chief officer of police to the relevant licensing authority before a hearing is held or dispensed with under section 105(2).

(5) Where the premises are situated in more than one police area, the chief officer of police may modify the temporary event notice under this section only with the consent of the chief officer of police for the other police area or each of the other police areas in which the premises are situated.

(6) This section does not apply if a counter notice has been given under section 107.

(7) In this section "objection notice" has the same meaning as in section 104(2).

LIMITS ON TEMPORARY EVENT NOTICES

## 107  Counter notice where permitted limits exceeded

(1) Where a licensing authority–
    (a)  receives a temporary event notice ("notice A") in respect of any premises ("the relevant premises"), and
    (b)  is satisfied that subsection (2), (3), (4) or (5) applies,
the authority must give the premises user ("the relevant premises user") a counter notice under this section.

(2) This subsection applies if the relevant premises user–
    (a)  holds a personal licence, and
    (b)  has already given at least 50 temporary event notices in respect of event periods wholly or partly within the same year as the event period specified in notice A.

(3) This subsection applies if the relevant premises user–
    (a)  does not hold a personal licence, and
    (b)  has already given at least five temporary event notices in respect of such event periods.

(4) This subsection applies if at least 12 temporary event notices have already been given which–
    (a)  are in respect of the same premises as notice A, and
    (b)  specify as the event period wholly or partly within the same year as the event period specified in notice A.

(5) This subsection applies if, in any year in which the event period specified in notice A (or any part of it) falls, more than 15 days

are days on which one or more of the following fall–
(a) that event period or any part of it,
(b) an event period specified in a temporary event notice already given in respect of the same premises as notice A or any part of such a period.
(6) If the event period in notice A straddles two years, subsections (2), (3) and (4) apply separately in relation to each of those years.
(7) A counter notice under this section must be in the prescribed form and given to the premises user in the prescribed manner.
(8) No such counter notice may be given later than 24 hours before the beginning of the event period specified in notice A.
(9) In determining whether subsection (2), (3), (4) or (5) applies, any temporary event notice in respect of which a counter notice has been given under this section or section 105 is to be disregarded.
(10) In determining for the purposes of subsection (2) or (3) the number of temporary event notices given by the relevant premises user–
(a) a temporary event notice given by an individual who is an associate of the relevant premises user is to be treated as a notice given by the relevant premises user;
(b) a temporary event notice ("notice B") given by an individual who is in business with the relevant premises user is to be treated as a notice given by the relevant premises user if-
(i) that business relates to one or more licensable activities, and
(ii) notice A and notice B relate to one or more licensable activities to which the business relates (but not necessarily the same activity or activities).
(11) Where a licensing authority gives a counter notice under this section it must, forthwith, send a copy of that notice to the chief officer of police for the police area (or each of the police areas) in which the relevant premises are situated.
(12) The Secretary of State may, by order, amend subsection (2)(b), (3)(b), (4) or (5) so as to substitute any number for the number for the time being specified there.
(13) For the purposes of this section–
(a) a temporary event notice is in respect of the same premises as notice A if it is in respect of the whole or any part of the relevant premises or premises which include the whole or any part of those premises,
(b) "year" means calendar year,
(c) "day" means a period of 24 hours beginning at midnight, and
(d) subsections (3) and (4) of section 101 (meaning of "associate") apply as they apply for the purposes of that section.

RIGHTS OF ENTRY, PRODUCTION OF NOTICE, ETC.

## 108   Right of entry where temporary event notice given

(1) A constable or an authorised officer may, at any reasonable time, enter the premises to which a temporary event notice relates to assess the likely effect of the notice on the promotion of the crime prevention objective.

(2) An authorised officer exercising the power conferred by this section must, if so requested, produce evidence of his authority to exercise the power.

(3) A person commits an offence if he intentionally obstructs an authorised officer exercising a power conferred by this section.

(4) A person guilty of an offence under this section is liable on summary conviction to a fine not exceeding level 2 on the standard scale.

(5) In this section "authorised officer" means–
    (a) an officer of the licensing authority in whose area the premises are situated, or
    (b) if the premises are situated in the area of more than one licensing authority, an officer of any of those authorities,
authorised for the purposes of this Act.

## 109   Duty to keep and produce temporary event notice

(1) This section applies whenever premises are being used for one or more licensable activities which are or are purported to be permitted temporary activities by virtue of this Part.

(2) The premises user must either–
    (a) secure that a copy of the temporary event notice is prominently displayed at the premises, or
    (b) meet the requirements of subsection (3).

(3) The requirements of this subsection are that the premises user must–
    (a) secure that the temporary event notice is kept at the premises in–
    (i) his custody, or
    (ii) in the custody of a person who is present and working at the premises and whom he has nominated for the purposes of this section, and
    (b) where the temporary event notice is in the custody of a person so nominated, secure that a notice specifying that fact and the position held at the premises by that person is prominently displayed at the premises.

(4) The premises user commits an offence if he fails, without

reasonable excuse, to comply with subsection (2).

(5) Where–

    (a)  the temporary event notice is not displayed as mentioned in subsection (2)(a), and

    (b)  no notice is displayed as mentioned in subsection (3)(b), a constable or authorised officer may require the premises user to produce the temporary event notice for examination.

(6) Where a notice is displayed as mentioned in subsection (3)(b), a constable or authorised officer may require the person specified in that notice to produce the temporary event notice for examination.

(7) An authorised officer exercising the power conferred by subsection (5) or (6) must, if so requested, produce evidence of his authority to exercise the power.

(8  A person commits an offence if he fails, without reasonable excuse, to produce a temporary event notice in accordance with a requirement under subsection (5) or (6).

(9) A person guilty of an offence under this section is liable on summary conviction to a fine not exceeding level 2 on the standard scale.

(10)  In this section "authorised officer" has the meaning given in section 108(5).

MISCELLANEOUS

## 110  Theft, loss, etc. of temporary event notice

(1) Where a temporary event notice acknowledged under section 102 is lost, stolen, damaged or destroyed, the premises user may apply to the licensing authority which acknowledged the notice (or, if there is more than one such authority, any of them) for a copy of the notice.

(2) No application may be made under this section more than one month after the end of the event period specified in the notice.

(3) The application must be accompanied by the prescribed fee.

(4) Where a licensing authority receives an application under this section, it must issue the premises user with a copy of the notice (certified by the authority to be a true copy) if it is satisfied that–

    (a)  the notice has been lost, stolen, damaged or destroyed, and

    (b)  where it has been lost or stolen, the premises user has reported that loss or theft to the police.

(5) The copy issued under this section must be a copy of the notice in the form it existed immediately before it was lost, stolen, damaged or destroyed.

(6) This Act applies in relation to a copy issued under this section as it applies in relation to an original notice.

*oOo*

## PART 7

## OFFENCES

### UNAUTHORISED LICENSABLE ACTIVITIES

### 136 Unauthorised licensable activities

(1) A person commits an offence if–
- (a) he carries on or attempts to carry on a licensable activity on or from any premises otherwise than under and in accordance with an authorisation, or
- (b) he knowingly allows a licensable activity to be so carried on.

(2) Where the licensable activity in question is the provision of regulated entertainment, a person does not commit an offence under this section if his only involvement in the provision of the entertainment is that he–
- (a) performs in a play,
- (b) participates as a sportsman in an indoor sporting event,
- (c) boxes or wrestles in a boxing or wrestling entertainment,
- (d) performs live music,
- (e) plays recorded music,
- (f) performs dance, or
- (g) does something coming within paragraph 2(1)(h) of Schedule 1 (entertainment similar to music, dance, etc).

(3) Subsection (2) is to be construed in accordance with Part 3 of Schedule 1.

(4) A person guilty of an offence under this section is liable on summary conviction to imprisonment for a term not exceeding six months or to a fine not exceeding £20,000, or to both.

(5) In this Part "authorisation" means–
- (a) a premises licence,
- (b) a club premises certificate, or
- (c) a temporary event notice in respect of which the conditions of section 98(2) to (4) are satisfied.

## 137 Exposing alcohol for unauthorised sale

(1) A person commits an offence if, on any premises, he exposes for sale by retail any alcohol in circumstances where the sale by retail of that alcohol on those premises would be an unauthorised licensable activity.

(2) For that purpose a licensable activity is unauthorised unless it is under and in accordance with an authorisation.

(3) A person guilty of an offence under this section is liable on summary conviction to imprisonment for a term not exceeding six months or to a fine not exceeding £20,000, or to both.

(4) The court by which a person is convicted of an offence under this section may order the alcohol in question, and any container for it, to be forfeited and either destroyed or dealt with in such other manner as the court may order.

## 138 Keeping alcohol on premises for unauthorised sale etc.

(1) A person commits an offence if he has in his possession or under his control alcohol which he intends to sell by retail or supply in circumstances where that activity would be an unauthorised licensable activity.

(2) For that purpose a licensable activity is unauthorised unless it is under and in accordance with an authorisation.

(3) In subsection (1) the reference to the supply of alcohol is a reference to the supply of alcohol by or on behalf of a club to, or to the order of, a member of the club.

(4) A person guilty of an offence under this section is liable on summary conviction to a fine not exceeding level 2 on the standard scale.

(5) The court by which a person is convicted of an offence under this section may order the alcohol in question, and any container for it, to be forfeited and either destroyed or dealt with in such other manner as the court may order.

## 139 Defence of due diligence

(1) In proceedings against a person for an offence to which subsection (2) applies, it is a defence that–
   (a) his act was due to a mistake, or to reliance on information given to him, or to an act or omission by another person, or to some other cause beyond his control, and
   (b) he took all reasonable precautions and exercised all due diligence to avoid committing the offence.

(2) This subsection applies to an offence under–
   (a) section 136(1)(a) (carrying on unauthorised licensable activity),

   (b)  section 137 (exposing alcohol for unauthorised sale), or

   (c)  section 138 (keeping alcohol on premises for unauthorised sale).

DRUNKENNESS AND DISORDERLY CONDUCT

### 140  Allowing disorderly conduct on licensed premises etc.

(1) A person to whom subsection (2) applies commits an offence if he knowingly allows disorderly conduct on relevant premises.

(2) This subsection applies–

   (a)  to any person who works at the premises in a capacity, whether paid or unpaid, which authorises him to prevent the conduct,

   (b)  in the case of licensed premises, to-

      (i)  the holder of a premises licence in respect of the premises, and

      (ii)  the designated premises supervisor (if any) under such a licence,

   (c)  in the case of premises in respect of which a club premises certificate has effect, to any member or officer of the club which holds the certificate who at the time the conduct takes place is present on the premises in a capacity which enables him to prevent it, and

   (d)  in the case of premises which may be used for a permitted temporary activity by virtue of Part 5, to the premises user in relation to the temporary event notice in question.

(3) A person guilty of an offence under this section is liable on summary conviction to a fine not exceeding level 3 on the standard scale.

### 141  Sale of alcohol to a person who is drunk

(1) A person to whom subsection (2) applies commits an offence if, on relevant premises, he knowingly–

   (a)  sells or attempts to sell alcohol to a person who is drunk, or

   (b)  allows alcohol to be sold to such a person.

(2) This subsection applies–

   (a)  to any person who works at the premises in a capacity, whether paid or unpaid, which gives him authority to sell the alcohol concerned,

   (b)  in the case of licensed premises, to–

      (i)  the holder of a premises licence in respect of the premises, and

(ii) the designated premises supervisor (if any) under such a licence,

(c) in the case of premises in respect of which a club premises certificate has effect, to any member or officer of the club which holds the certificate who at the time the sale (or attempted sale) takes place is present on the premises in a capacity which enables him to prevent it, and

(d) in the case of premises which may be used for a permitted temporary activity by virtue of Part 5, to the premises user in relation to the temporary event notice in question.

(3) This section applies in relation to the supply of alcohol by or on behalf of a club or to the order of a member of the club as it applies in relation to the sale of alcohol.

(4) A person guilty of an offence under this section is liable on summary conviction to a fine not exceeding level 3 on the standard scale.

## 142 Obtaining alcohol for a person who is drunk

(1) A person commits an offence if, on relevant premises, he knowingly obtains or attempts to obtain alcohol for consumption on those premises by a person who is drunk.

(2) A person guilty of an offence under this section is liable on summary conviction to a fine not exceeding level 3 on the standard scale.

## 143 Failure to leave licensed premises etc.

(1) A person who is drunk or disorderly commits an offence if, without reasonable excuse–

(a) he fails to leave relevant premises when requested to do so by a constable or by a person to whom subsection (2) applies, or

(b) he enters or attempts to enter relevant premises after a constable or a person to whom subsection (2) applies has requested him not to enter.

(2) This subsection applies–

(a) to any person who works at the premises in a capacity, whether paid or unpaid, which authorises him to make such a request,

(b) in the case of licensed premises, to–

(i) the holder of a premises licence in respect of the premises, or

(ii) the designated premises supervisor (if any) under such a licence,

(c)   in the case of premises in respect of which a club premises certificate has effect, to any member or officer of the club which holds the certificate who is present on the premises in a capacity which enables him to make such a request, and

(d)   in the case of premises which may be used for a permitted temporary activity by virtue of Part 5, to the premises user in relation to the temporary event notice in question.

(3)   A person guilty of an offence under subsection (1) is liable on summary conviction to a fine not exceeding level 1 on the standard scale.

(4)   On being requested to do so by a person to whom subsection (2) applies, a constable must–

(a)   help to expel from relevant premises a person who is drunk or disorderly;

(b)   help to prevent such a person from entering relevant premises.

SMUGGLED GOODS

## 144   Keeping of smuggled goods

(1)   A person to whom subsection (2) applies commits an offence if he knowingly keeps or allows to be kept, on any relevant premises, any goods which have been imported without payment of duty or which have otherwise been unlawfully imported.

(2)   This subsection applies–

(a)   to any person who works at the premises in a capacity, whether paid or unpaid, which gives him authority to prevent the keeping of the goods on the premises,

(b)   in the case of licensed premises, to–

(i)   the holder of a premises licence in respect of the premises, and

(ii)   the designated premises supervisor (if any) under such a licence,

(c)   in the case of premises in respect of which a club premises certificate has effect, to any member or officer of the club which holds the certificate who is present on the premises at any time when the goods are kept on the premises in a capacity which enables him to prevent them being so kept, and

(d)   in the case of premises which may be used for a permitted temporary activity by virtue of Part 5, to the premises user in relation to the temporary event notice in question.

(3)   A person guilty of an offence under this section is liable on summary conviction to a fine not exceeding level 3 on the standard scale.

(4) The court by which a person is convicted of an offence under this section may order the goods in question, and any container for them, to be forfeited and either destroyed or dealt with in such other manner as the court may order.

CHILDREN AND ALCOHOL

**145 Unaccompanied children prohibited from certain premises**

(1) A person to whom subsection (3) applies commits an offence if-
  (a) knowing that relevant premises are within subsection (4), he allows an unaccompanied child to be on the premises at a time when they are open for the purposes of being used for the supply of alcohol for consumption there, or
  (b) he allows an unaccompanied child to be on relevant premises at a time between the hours of midnight and 5 a.m. when the premises are open for the purposes of being used for the supply of alcohol for consumption there.

(2) For the purposes of this section–
  (a) "child" means an individual aged under 16,
  (b) a child is unaccompanied if he is not in the company of an individual aged 18 or over.

(3) This subsection applies–
  (a) to any person who works at the premises in a capacity, whether paid or unpaid, which authorises him to request the unaccompanied child to leave the premises,
  (b) in the case of licensed premises, to–
    (i) the holder of a premises licence in respect of the premises, and
    (ii) the designated premises supervisor (if any) under such a licence,
  (c) in the case of premises in respect of which a club premises certificate has effect, to any member or officer of the club which holds the certificate who is present on the premises in a capacity which enables him to make such a request, and
  (d) in the case of premises which may be used for a permitted temporary activity by virtue of Part 5, to the premises user in relation to the temporary event notice in question.

(4) Relevant premises are within this subsection if–
  (a) they are exclusively or primarily used for the supply of alcohol for consumption on the premises, or
  (b) they are open for the purposes of being used for the supply of alcohol for consumption on the premises by virtue of Part 5 (permitted temporary activities) and, at the time the

temporary event notice in question has effect, they are exclusively or primarily used for such supplies.

(5) No offence is committed under this section if the unaccompanied child is on the premises solely for the purpose of passing to or from some other place to or from which there is no other convenient means of access or egress.

(6) Where a person is charged with an offence under this section by reason of his own conduct it is a defence that–

    (a) he believed that the unaccompanied child was aged 16 or over or that an individual accompanying him was aged 18 or over, and

    (b) either–

       (i) he had taken all reasonable steps to establish the individual's age, or

       (ii) nobody could reasonably have suspected from the individual's appearance that he was aged under 16 or, as the case may be, under 18.

(7) For the purposes of subsection (6), a person is treated as having taken all reasonable steps to establish an individual's age if–

    (a) he asked the individual for evidence of his age, and

    (b) the evidence would have convinced a reasonable person.

(8) Where a person ("the accused") is charged with an offence under this section by reason of the act or default of some other person, it is a defence that the accused exercised all due diligence to avoid committing it.

(9) A person guilty of an offence under this section is liable on summary conviction to a fine not exceeding level 3 on the standard scale.

(10) In this section "supply of alcohol" means–

    (a) the sale by retail of alcohol, or

    (b) the supply of alcohol by or on behalf of a club to, or to the order of, a member of the club.

### 146 Sale of alcohol to children

(1) A person commits an offence if he sells alcohol to an individual aged under 18.

(2) A club commits an offence if alcohol is supplied by it or on its behalf–

    (a) to, or to the order of, a member of the club who is aged under 18, or

    (b) to the order of a member of the club, to an individual who is aged under 18.

(3) A person commits an offence if he supplies alcohol on behalf of a

club–
  (a) to, or to the order of, a member of the club who is aged under 18, or
  (b) to the order of a member of the club, to an individual who is aged under 18.
(4) Where a person is charged with an offence under this section by reason of his own conduct it is a defence that–
  (a) he believes that the individual was aged 18 or over, and
  (b) either–
    (i) he had taken all reasonable steps to establish the individual's age, or
    (ii) nobody could reasonably have suspected from the individual's appearance that he was aged under 18.
(5) For the purposes of subsection (4), a person is treated as having taken all reasonable steps to establish an individual's age if–
  (a) he asked the individual for evidence of his age, and
  (b) the evidence would have convinced a reasonable person.
(6) Where a person ("the accused") is charged with an offence under this section by reason of the act or default of some other person, it is a defence that the accused exercised all due diligence to avoid committing it.
(7) A person guilty of an offence under this section is liable on summary conviction to a fine not exceeding level 5 on the standard scale.

**147   Allowing the sale of alcohol to children**
(1) A person to whom subsection (2) applies commits an offence if he knowingly allows the sale of alcohol on relevant premises to an individual aged under 18.
(2) This subsection applies to a person who works at the premises in a capacity, whether paid or unpaid, which authorises him to prevent the sale.
(3) A person to whom subsection (4) applies commits an offence if he knowingly allows alcohol to be supplied on relevant premises by or on behalf of a club–
  (a) to or to the order of a member of the club who is aged under 18, or
  (b) to the order of a member of the club, to an individual who is aged under 18.
(4) This subsection applies to–
  (a) a person who works on the premises in a capacity, whether paid or unpaid, which authorises him to prevent the supply, and

    (b)  any member or officer of the club who at the time of the supply is present on the relevant premises in a capacity which enables him to prevent it.

(5)  A person guilty of an offence under this section is liable on summary conviction to a fine not exceeding level 5 on the standard scale.

### 148   Sale of liqueur confectionery to children under 16

(1)  A person commits an offence if he–
    (a)  sells liqueur confectionery to an individual aged under 16, or
    (b)  supplies such confectionery, on behalf of a club-
        (i)  to or to the order of a member of the club who is aged under 16, or
        (ii)  to the order of a member of the club, to an individual who is aged under 16.

(2)  A club commits an offence if liqueur confectionery is supplied by it or on its behalf–
    (a)  to or to the order of a member of the club who is aged under 16, or
    (b)  to the order of a member of the club, to an individual who is aged under 16.

(3)  Where a person is charged with an offence under this section by reason of his own conduct it is a defence that–
    (a)  he believed that the individual was aged 16 or over, and
    (b)  either–
        (i)  he had taken all reasonable steps to establish the individual's age, or
        (ii)  nobody could reasonably have suspected from the individual's appearance that he was aged under 16.

(4)  For the purposes of subsection (3), a person is treated as having taken all reasonable steps to establish an individual's age if–
    (a)  he asked the individual for evidence of his age, and
    (b)  the evidence would have convinced a reasonable person.

(5)  Where a person ("the accused") is charged with an offence under this section by reason of the act or default of some other person, it is a defence that the accused exercised all due diligence to avoid committing it.

(6)  A person guilty of an offence under this section is liable on summary conviction to a fine not exceeding level 2 on the standard scale.

(7)  In this section "liqueur confectionery" has the meaning given in section 191(2).

**149 Purchase of alcohol by or on behalf of children**

(1) An individual aged under 18 commits an offence if–
    (a)  he buys or attempts to buy alcohol, or
    (b)  where he is a member of a club–
        (i)   alcohol is supplied to him or to his order by or on behalf of the club, as a result of some act or default of his, or
        (ii)  he attempts to have alcohol supplied to him or to his order by or on behalf of the club.

(2) But subsection (1) does not apply where the individual buys or attempts to buy the alcohol at the request of–
    (a)  a constable, or
    (b)  a weights and measures inspector,
who is acting in the course of his duty.

(3) A person commits an offence if–
    (a)  he buys or attempts to buy alcohol on behalf of an individual aged under 18, or
    (b)  where he is a member of a club, on behalf of an individual aged under 18 he–
        (i)   makes arrangements whereby alcohol is supplied to him or to his order by or on behalf of the club, or
        (ii)  attempts to make such arrangements.

(4) A person ("the relevant person") commits an offence if–
    (a)  he buys or attempts to buy alcohol for consumption on relevant premises by an individual aged under 18, or
    (b)  where he is a member of a club–
        (i)   by some act or default of his, alcohol is supplied to him, or to his order, by or on behalf of the club for consumption on relevant premises by an individual aged under 18, or
        (ii)  he attempts to have alcohol so supplied for such consumption.

(5) But subsection (4) does not apply where–
    (a)  the relevant person is aged 18 or over,
    (b)  the individual is aged 16 or 17,
    (c)  the alcohol is beer, wine or cider,
    (d)  its purchase or supply is for consumption at a table meal on relevant premises, and
    (e)  the individual is accompanied at the meal by an individual aged 18 or over.

(6) Where a person is charged with an offence under subsection (3) or (4) it is a defence that he had no reason to suspect that the individual was aged under 18.

(7) A person guilty of an offence under this section is liable on summary conviction–
    (a)  in the case of an offence under subsection (1), to a fine not

exceeding level 3 on the standard scale, and
  (b) in the case of an offence under subsection (3) or (4), to a fine not exceeding level 5 on the standard scale.

## 150  Consumption of alcohol by children

(1) An individual aged under 18 commits an offence if he knowingly consumes alcohol on relevant premises.

(2) A person to whom subsection (3) applies commits an offence if he knowingly allows the consumption of alcohol on relevant premises by an individual aged under 18.

(3) This subsection applies–
  (a) to a person who works at the premises in a capacity, whether paid or unpaid, which authorises him to prevent the consumption, and
  (b) where the alcohol was supplied by a club to or to the order of a member of the club, to any member or officer of the club who is member of the club, to any member or officer of the club who is present at the premises at the time of the consumption in a capacity which enables him to prevent it.

(4) Subsections (1) and (2) do not apply where–
  (a) the individual is aged 16 or 17,
  (b) the alcohol is beer, wine or cider,
  (c) its consumption is at a table meal on relevant premises, and
  (d) the individual is accompanied at the meal by an individual aged 18 or over.

(5) A person guilty of an offence under this section is liable on summary conviction–
  (a) in the case of an offence under subsection (1), to a fine not exceeding level 3 on the standard scale, and
  (b) in the case of an offence under subsection (2), to a fine not exceeding level 5 on the standard scale.

## 151  Delivering alcohol to children

(1) A person who works on relevant premises in any capacity, whether paid or unpaid, commits an offence if he knowingly delivers to an individual aged under 18–
  (a) alcohol sold on the premises, or
  (b) alcohol supplied on the premises by or on behalf of a club to or to the order of a member of the club.

(2) A person to whom subsection (3) applies commits an offence if he knowingly allows anybody else to deliver to an individual aged under 18 alcohol sold on relevant premises.

(3) This subsection applies to a person who works on the premises in

a capacity, whether paid or unpaid, which authorises him to prevent the delivery of the alcohol.

(4) A person to whom subsection (5) applies commits an offence if he knowingly allows anybody else to deliver to an individual aged under 18 alcohol supplied on relevant premises by or on behalf of a club to or to the order of a member of the club.

(5) This subsection applies–
  (a) to a person who works on the premises in a capacity, whether paid or unpaid, which authorises him to prevent the supply, and
  (b) to any member or officer of the club who at the time of the supply in question is present on the premises in a capacity which enables him to prevent the supply.

(6) Subsections (1), (2) and (4) do not apply where–
  (a) the alcohol is delivered at a place where the buyer or, as the case may be, person supplied lives or works, or
  (b) the individual aged under 18 works on the relevant premises in a capacity, whether paid or unpaid, which involves the delivery of alcohol, or
  (c) the alcohol is sold or supplied for consumption on the relevant premises.

(7) A person guilty of an offence under this section is liable on summary conviction to a fine not exceeding level 5 on the standard scale.

## 152  Sending a child to obtain alcohol

(1) A person commits an offence if he knowingly sends an individual aged under 18 to obtain–
  (a) alcohol sold or to be sold on relevant premises for consumption off the premises, or
  (b) alcohol supplied or to be supplied by or on behalf of a club to or to the order of a member of the club for such consumption.

(2) For the purposes of this section, it is immaterial whether the individual aged under 18 is sent to obtain the alcohol from the relevant premises or from other premises from which it is delivered in pursuance of the sale or supply.

(3) Subsection (1) does not apply where the individual aged under 18 works on the relevant premises in a capacity, whether paid or unpaid, which involves the delivery of alcohol.

(4) Subsection (1) also does not apply where the individual aged under 18 is sent by–
  (a) a constable, or
  (b) a weights and measures inspector,

who is acting in the course of his duty.

(5) A person guilty of an offence under this section is liable on summary conviction to a fine not exceeding level 5 on the standard scale.

### 153  Provision of unsupervised sales by children

(1) A responsible person commits an offence if on any relevant premises he knowingly allows an individual aged under 18 to make on the premises–

   (a)  any sale of alcohol, or

   (b)  any supply of alcohol by or on behalf of a club to or to the order of a member of the club,

unless the sale or supply has been specifically approved by that or another responsible person.

(2) But subsection (1) does not apply where–

   (a)  the alcohol is sold or supplied for consumption with a table meal,

   (b)  it is sold or supplied in premises which are being used for the service of table meals (or in a part of any premises which is being so used), and

   (c)  the premises are (or the part is) not used for the sale or supply of alcohol otherwise than to persons having table meals there and for consumption by such a person as an ancillary to his meal.

(3) A person guilty of an offence under this section is liable on summary conviction to a fine not exceeding level 1 on the standard scale.

(4) In this section "responsible person" means–

   (a)  in relation to licensed premises–

      (i)   the holder of a premises licence in respect of the premises,

      (ii)  the designated premises supervisor (if any) under such a licence, or

      (iii) any individual aged 18 or over who is authorised for the purposes of this section by such a holder or supervisor,

   (b)  in relation to premises in respect of which there is in force a club premises certificate, any member or officer of the club present on the premises in a capacity which enables him to prevent the supply in question, and

   (c)  in relation to premises which may be used for a permitted temporary activity by virtue of Part 5–

      (i)   the premises user, or

      (ii)  any individual aged 18 or over who is authorised for the purposes of this section by the premises user.

**154 Enforcement role for weights and measures authorities**

(1) It is the duty of every local weights and measures authority in England and Wales to enforce within its area the provisions of sections 146 and 147, so far as they apply to sales of alcohol made on or from premises to which the public have access.

(2) A weights and measures inspector may make, or authorise any person to make on his behalf, such purchases of goods as appear expedient for the purpose of determining whether those provisions are being complied with.

CONFISCATION OF ALCOHOL

**155 Confiscation of sealed containers of alcohol**

(1) In section 1 of the Confiscation of Alcohol (Young Persons) Act 1997 (right to require surrender of alcohol)–

(a) in subsection (1), omit "(other than a sealed container)",

(b) after that subsection insert–

"(1A) But a constable may not under subsection (1) require a person to surrender any sealed container unless the constable reasonable believes that the person is, or has been, consuming, or intends to consume, alcohol in any relevant place", and

(c) in subsection (6), after "subsection (1)" insert "and (1A)".

(2) In section 12(2)(b) of the Criminal Justice and Police Act 2001 (right to require surrender of alcohol, omit "(other than a sealed container)".

VEHICLES AND TRAINS

**156 Prohibition on sale of alcohol on moving vehicles**
[*omitted*]

**157 Power to prohibit sale of alcohol on trains**
[*omitted*]

FALSE STATEMENT RELATING TO LICENSING ETC

**158 False statements made for the purposes of this Act**

(1) A person commits an offence if he knowingly or recklessly makes a false statement in or in connection with–

    (a)  an application for the grant, variation, transfer or review of a premises licence or club premises certificate,

    (b)  an application for a provisional statement,

    (c)  a temporary event notice, an interim authority notice or any other notice under this Act,

    (d)  an application for the grant or renewal of a personal licence, or

    (e)  a notice within section 178(1) (notice by freeholder etc conferring right to be notified of changes to licensing register).

(2) For the purposes of subsection (1) a person is to be treated as making a false statement if he produces, finishes, signs or otherwise makes use of a document that contains a false statement.

(3) A person guilty of an offence under this section is liable on summary conviction to a fine not exceeding level 5 on the standard scale.

INTERPRETATION

## 159  Interpretation of Part 7

In this Part–

    "authorisation" has the meaning given in section 136(5);

    "relevant premises" means–

    (a)  licensed premises, or

    (b)  premises in respect of which there is in force a club premises certificate, or

    (c)  premises which may be used for a permitted temporary activity by virtue of Part 5;

    "table meal" means a meal eaten by a person seated at a table, or at a counter or other structure which serves the purpose of a table and is not used for the service of refreshment for consumption by persons not seated at a table or structure serving the purpose of a table; and

    "weights and measures inspector" means an inspector of weights and measures appointed under section 72(1) of the Weights and Measures Act 1985 (c 72).

*o0o*

## 175  Exemption for raffle, tombola, etc.

(1) The conduct of a lottery which, but for this subsection, would to any extent constitute a licensable activity by reason of one or more of the prizes in the lottery consisting of alcohol, is not (for that reason alone) to be treated as constituting a licensable activity if–

(a) the lottery is promoted as an incident of an exempt entertainment,

(b) after the deduction of all relevant expenses, the whole proceeds of the entertainment (including those of the lottery) are applied for purposes other than private gain, and

(c) subsection (2) does not apply.

(2) This subsection applies if–

(a) the alcohol consists of or includes alcohol not in a sealed container,

(b) any prize in the lottery is a money prize,

(c) a ticket or chance in the lottery is sold or issued, or the result of the lottery is declared, other than at the premises where the entertainment takes place and during the entertainment, or

(d) the opportunity to participate in a lottery or in gaming is the only or main inducement to attend the entertainment.

(3) For the purposes of subsection (1)(b), the following are relevant expenses–

(a) the expenses of the entertainment, excluding expenses incurred in connection with the lottery,

(4) In this section–

"exempt entertainment" has the same meaning as in section 3(1) of the Lotteries and Amusements Act 1976;

"gaming" has the meaning given by section 52 of the Gaming Act 1968;

"money" and "ticket" have the meaning given by section 23 of the Lotteries and Amusements Act 1976; and

"private gain", in relation to the proceeds of an entertainment, is to be construed in accordance with section 22 of that Act.

oOo

## 177 Dancing and live music in certain small premises

(1) Subsection (2) applies where–

(a) a premises licence authorises–

   (i) the supply of alcohol for consumption on the premises, and

   (ii) the provision of music entertainment, and

(b) the premises–

   (i) are used primarily for the supply of alcohol for consumption on the premises, and

   (ii) have a permitted capacity of not more than 200 persons.

(2) At any time when–

(a) the premises–

    (i)   are open for the purposes of being used for the supply of
        alcohol for consumption on the premises, and

    (ii)  are being used for the provision of music entertainment,
        and

  (b)  subsection (4) does not apply,

any licensing authority imposed condition of the premises licence
which relates to the provision of music entertainment does not
have effect, in relation to the provision of that entertainment,
unless it falls within subsection (5) or (6).

(3) Subsection (4) applies where–

  (a)  a premises licence authorises the provision of music
      entertainment, and

  (b)  the premises have a permitted capacity of not more than 200
      persons.

(4) At any time between the hours of 8 a.m. and midnight when the
premises–

  (a)  are being used for the provision of music entertainment which
      consists of–

    (i)   the performance of unamplified, live music, or

    (ii)  facilities for enabling persons to take part in entertainment
        within sub-paragraph (i), but

  (b)  are not being used for the provision of any other description
      of regulated entertainment,

any licensing authority imposed condition of the premises licence
which relates to the provision of the music entertainment does not
have effect, in relation to the provision of that entertainment,
unless it falls within subsection (6).

(5) A condition falls within this subsection if the premises licence
specifies that the licensing authority which granted the licence
considers the imposition of the condition necessary on one or both
of the following grounds–

  (a)  the prevention of crime and disorder,

  (b)  public safety.

(6) A condition falls within this subsection if, on a review of the
premises licence–

  (a)  it is altered so as to include a statement that this section does
      not apply to it, or

  (b)  it is added to the licence and includes such a statement.

(7) This section applies in relation to a club premises certificate as it
applies in relation to a premises licence except that, in the
application of this section in relation to such a certificate, the
definition of "licensing authority imposed condition" in subsection
(8) has effect as if for "section 18(3)(b)" to the end there were
substituted "section 72(3)(b) (but is not referred to in section 72(2))

or which is imposed by virtue of section 85(3)(b) or 88(3)".

(8) In this section–

"licensing authority imposed condition" means a condition which is imposed by virtue of section 18(3)(b) (but is not referred to in section 18(2)(a)) or which is imposed by virtue of 35(3)(b), 52(3) or 167(5)(b) or in accordance with section 21;

"music entertainment" means–

(a) entertainment of a description falling within, or of a similar description to that falling within, paragraph 2(1)(e) or (g) of Schedule 1, or

(b) facilities enabling persons to take part in entertainment within paragraph (a);

"permitted capacity", in relation to any premises, means–

(a) where a fire certificate issued under the Fire Precautions Act 1971 (c.40) is in force in respect of the premises and that certificate imposes a requirement under section 6(2)(d) of that Act, the limit on the number of persons who, in accordance with that requirement, may be on the premises at any one time, and

(b) in any other case, the limit on the number of persons who may be on the premises at any one time in accordance with a recommendation made by, or on behalf of, the fire authority for the area in which the premises are situated (or, if the premises are situated in the area of more than one fire authority, those authorities); and

"supply of alcohol" means–

(a) the sale by retail of alcohol, or

(b) the supply of alcohol by or on behalf of a club to, or to the order of, a member of the club.

*o0o*

## 179 Rights of entry to investigate licensable activities

(1) Where a constable or an authorised person has reason to believe that any premises are being, or are about to be, used for a licensable activity, he may enter the premises with a view to seeing whether the activity is being, or is to be, carried on under and in accordance with an authorisation.

(2) An authorised person exercising the power conferred by this section must, if so requested, produce evidence of his authority to exercise the power.

(3) A person exercising the power conferred by this section may, if necessary, use reasonable force.

(4) A person commits an offence if he intentionally obstructs an authorised person exercising a power conferred by this section.

(5) A person guilty of an offence under subsection (4) is liable on summary conviction to a fine not exceeding level 3 on the standard scale.

(6) In this section-

"authorisation" means–

(a) a premises licence,

(b) a club premises certificate, or

(c) a temporary event notice in respect of which the conditions of section 98(2) to (4) are satisfied; and

"authorised person" means an authorised person within the meaning of Part 3 or 4 or an authorised officer within the meaning of section 108(5).

(7) Nothing in this section applies in relation to premises in respect of which there is a club premises certificate but no other authorisation.

## 180 Right of entry to investigate offences

(1) A constable may enter and search any premises in respect of which he has reason to believe that an offence under this Act has been, is being or is about to be committed.

(2) A constable exercising a power conferred by this section may, if necessary, use reasonable force.

*oOo*

## 187 Offences by bodies corporate etc.

(1) If an offence committed by a body corporate is shown–

(a) to have been committed with the consent or connivance of an officer, or

(b) to be attributable to any neglect on his part,

the officer as well as the body corporate is guilty of the offence and liable to be proceeded against and punished accordingly.

(2) If the affairs of a body corporate are managed by its members, subsection (1) applies in relation to the acts and defaults of a member in connection with his functions of management as if he were a director of the body.

(3) In subsection (1) "officer", in relation to a body corporate, means–

(a) a director, member of the committee of management, chief executive, manager, secretary or other similar officer of the body, or a person purporting to act in any such capacity, or

(b) an individual who is a controller of the body.

(4) If an offence committed by a partnership is shown–
    (a)  to have been committed with the consent or connivance of a partner, or
    (b)  to be attributable to any neglect on his part,
the partner as well as the partnership is guilty of the offence and liable to be proceeded against and punished accordingly.

(5) In subsection (4) "partner" includes a person purporting to act as a partner.

(6) If an offence committed by an unincorporated association (other than a partnership) is shown–
    (a)  to have been committed with the consent or connivance of an officer of the association or a member of its governing body, or
    (b)  to be attributable to any neglect on the part of such an officer or member,
that officer or member as well as the association is guilty of the offence and liable to be proceeded against and punished accordingly.

(7) Regulations may provide for the application of any provision of this section, with such modifications as the Secretary of State considers appropriate, to a body corporate or unincorporated association formed or recognised under the law of a territory outside the United Kingdom.

(8) In this section "offence" means an offence under this Act.

*oOo*

## 193  Other definitions

In this Act–
    "recognised club" means a club which satisfies conditions 1 to 3 of the general conditions of section 62.

*oOo*

# SCHEDULE 8

## PART 2

### CLUB PREMISES CERTIFICATES

**Introductory**

13.
(1) In this Part–
"existing club certificate" means a certificate held by a club under Part 2 of the 1964 Act for any premises;
"existing qualifying club activities" means the qualifying club activities authorised by the relevant existing club certificate in respect of those premises;
"first appointed day" means such day as may be specified as the first appointed day for the purposes of this Part;
"relevant existing club certificate", in relation to an application under paragraph 14, means the existing club certificate to which the application relates;
"relevant licensing authority" has the same meaning as in Part 4 of this Act (club premises certificates); and
"second appointed day" means such day as may be specified as the second appointed day for the purposes of this Part.
(2) In the application of section 68 (relevant licensing authority in Part 4 of this Act) for the purposes of this Part, the reference in subsection (4) of that section to an applicant for a club premises certificate is to be read as a reference to an applicant under paragraph 14 for the grant of a certificate under paragraph 16.

**Application for conversation of existing club certificate**

14.
(1) This paragraph applies where, in respect of any premises, a club holds an existing club certificate on the first appointed day.
(2) The club may, within the period of six months beginning with the first appointed day, apply to the relevant licensing authority for the grant of a certificate under paragraph 16 to succeed the existing club certificate so far as it relates to those premises.
(3) An application under this Part must specify the existing qualifying club activities and such other information as may be specified.
(4) The application must also be in the specified form and accompanied by–

    (a)  the relevant documents, and

    (b)  the specified fee.

(5) The relevant documents are–

    (a)  the relevant existing club certificate (or a certified copy of it),

    (b)  a plan in the specified form of the premises to which that certificate relates, and

    (c)  such other documents as may be specified.

(6) In this paragraph any reference to a certified copy of a document is a reference to a copy of that document certified to be a true copy–

    (a)  by the chief executive of the licensing justices for the licensing district in which the premises are situated,

    (b)  by a solicitor or notary, or

    (c)  by a person of a specified description.

(7) A document which purports to be a certified copy of an existing club certificate is to be taken to be such a copy unless the contrary is shown.


## Police consultation

15.

(1) Where a person makes an application under paragraph 14, he must give a copy of the application (and any documents which accompany it) to the chief officer of police for the police area (or each police area) in which the premises are situated no later than 48 hours after the application is made.

(2) Where–

    (a)  an appeal is pending against a decision to revoke, or to reject an application for the renewal of, the relevant existing club certificate, and

    (b)  a chief officer of police who has received a copy of the application under sub-paragraph (1) is satisfied that converting that existing club certificate in accordance with this Part would undermine the crime prevention objective,

he must give the relevant licensing authority and the applicant a notice to that effect.

(3) Where a chief officer of police who has received a copy of the application under sub-paragraph (1) is satisfied that, because of a material change in circumstances since the relevant time, converting the relevant existing club certificate in accordance with this Part would undermine the crime prevention objective, he must give the relevant licensing authority and the applicant a notice to that effect.

(4) For this purpose "the relevant time" means the time when the relevant existing club certificate was granted or, if it has been renewed, the last time it was renewed.

(5) The chief officer of police may not give a notice under sub-paragraph (2) or (3) after the end of the period of 28 days beginning with the day on which he received a copy of the application under sub-paragraph (1).

**Determination of application**

16.

(1) This paragraph applies where an application is made in accordance with paragraph 14 and the applicant complies with paragraph 15(1).

(2) Subject to sub-paragraphs (3) and (5), the licensing authority must grant the application.

(3) Where a notice is given under paragraph 15(2) or (3) (and not withdrawn), the authority must–
   (a) hold a hearing to consider it, unless the authority, the applicant and the chief officer of police who gave the notice agree that a hearing is unnecessary, and
   (b) having regard to the notice, reject the application if it considers it necessary for the promotion of the crime prevention objective to do so.

(4) If the relevant licensing authority fails to determine the application within the period of two months beginning with the day on which it received it, then, subject to sub-paragraph (5), the application is to be treated as granted by the authority under this paragraph.

(5) An application must not be granted (and is not to be treated as granted under sub-paragraph (4)) if the existing club certificate has ceased to have effect at–
   (a) the time of the determination of the application, or
   (b) in a case within sub-paragraph (4), the end of the period mentioned in that sub-paragraph.

(6) Section 10 applies as if the relevant licensing authority's functions under sub-paragraph (3) were included in the list of functions in subsection (4) of that section (functions which cannot be delegated to an officer of the licensing authority).

**Notification of determination and issue of new certificate**

17.
(1) Where an application is granted under paragraph 16, the relevant licensing authority must forthwith–
  (a)  give the applicant a notice to that effect, and
  (b)  issue the applicant with–
    (i)  a certificate in respect of the premises ("the new certificate") in accordance with paragraph 18, and
    (ii)  a summary of the new certificate.
(2) Where an application is rejected under paragraph 16, the relevant licensing authority must forthwith give the applicant a notice to that effect containing a statement of the authority's reasons for its decision to reject the application.
(3) The relevant licensing authority must give a copy of any notice it gives under sub-paragraph (1) or (2) to the chief officer of police for the police area (or each police area) in which the premises to which the notice relates are situated.

**The new certificate**

18.
(1) The new certificate is to be treated as if it were a club premises certificate (see section 60), and sections 73, 74 and 75 apply in relation to it accordingly.
(2) The new certificate takes effect on the second appointed day.
(3) The new certificate must authorise the premises to be used for the existing qualifying club activities.
(4) Subject to sections 73, 74 and 75, the new certificate must be granted subject to such conditions as reproduce the effect of the conditions subject to which the relevant existing club certificate has effect at the time the application is granted.
(5) The new certificate must also be granted subject to conditions which reproduce the effect of any restriction imposed on the use of the premises for the existing qualifying club activities by any enactment specified for the purposes of this Part.
(6) Nothing in sub-paragraph (4) or (5) requires the new certificate to be granted for a limited period.

**Variation of new certificate**

19.

(1) A person who makes an application under paragraph 14 may (notwithstanding that no certificate has yet been granted in consequence of that application) at the same time apply under section 84 for a variation of the certificate, and, for the purposes of such an application, the applicant is to be treated as the holder of that certificate.

(2) In relation to an application within sub-paragraph (1), the relevant licensing authority may discharge its functions under section 85 only if, and when, the application under this Part has been granted.

(3) Where an application within sub-paragraph (1) is not determined by the relevant licensing authority within the period of two months beginning with the day the application was received by the authority, it is to be treated as having been rejected by the authority under section 85 at the end of that period.

**Existing club certificate revoked after grant of new certificate**

20.

Where the relevant licensing authority grants a new certificate under this Part, that certificate lapses if and when–

(a) the existing club certificate is revoked before the second appointed day, or

(b) where an appeal against a decision to revoke it is pending immediately before that day, the appeal is dismissed or abandoned.

**Appeals**

21.

(1) Where an application under paragraph 14 is rejected by the relevant licensing authority, the applicant may appeal against that decision.

(2) Where a licensing authority grants such an application, any chief officer of police who gave a notice under paragraph 15(2) or (3) (that was not withdrawn) may appeal against that decision.

(3) Section 181 and paragraph 15(1) and (2) of Schedule 5 (general provision about appeals against decisions under Part 4 of this Act) apply in relation to appeals under this paragraph as they apply in relation to appeals under Part 2 of that Schedule.

(4) Paragraph 15(3) of that Schedule applies in relation to an appeal under sub-paragraph (2).

**False statements**

22.
(1) A person commits an offence if he knowingly or recklessly makes a false statement in or in connection with an application under paragraph 14.
(2) For the purposes of sub-paragraph (1) a person is to be treated as making a false statement if he produces, furnishes, signs or otherwise makes use of a document that contains a false statement.
(3) A person guilty of an offence under this section is liable on summary conviction to a fine not exceeding level 5 on the standard scale.

# Appendix 9

## 1985 TABLE A: ARTICLES OF ASSOCIATION

*Companies (Tables A to F) Regulations 1985 (SI 1985/805) as amended by the Companies (Tables A to F) (Amendment) Regulations 1985 (SI 1985/1052)*

### GENERAL MEETINGS

36.   All general meetings other than annual general meetings shall be called extraordinary meetings.

37.   The directors may call general meetings and, on the requisition of members pursuant to the provisions of the [Companies] Act [1985], shall forthwith proceed to convene an extraordinary general meeting for a date not later than eight weeks after receipt of the requisition. If there are not within the United Kingdom sufficient directors to call a general meeting, any director or member of the company may call a general meeting.

*Notice of General Meetings*

38.   An annual general meeting and an extraordinary general meeting called for the passing of a special resolution appointing a person as a director shall be called by at least twenty-one clear days' notice. All other extraordinary general meetings shall be called by at least fourteen clear days' notice but a general meeting may be called by shorter notice if it is so agreed–
(a) in the case of an annual general meeting, by all the members entitled to attend and vote thereat; and
(b) in the case of any other meeting by a majority in number of the members having a right to attend and vote being a majority together holding not less than ninety-five per cent in nominal value of the shares giving that right.

The notice shall specify the time and place of the meetings and the general nature of the business to be transacted and, in the case of an annual general meeting, shall specify the meeting as such.

Subject to the provisions of the articles and to any restrictions imposed on any shares, the notice shall be given to all the members, to all persons entitled to a share in consequence of the death or bankruptcy of a members and to the directors and auditors.

39.   The accidental omission to give notice of a meeting to, or the non-receipt of notice of a meeting by, an person entitled to receive notice shall not invalidate the proceedings at that meeting.

*Proceedings at General Meetings*

40.   No business shall be transacted at any meetings unless a quorum is present.  Two persons entitled to vote upon the business to be transacted, each being a member or a proxy for a member or a duty authorised representative of a corporation, shall be a quorum.

41.   If such a quorum is not present within half an hour from the time appointed for the meetings, or if during a meeting such a quorum ceases to be present, the meeting shall stand adjourned to the same day in the next week at the same time and place or [to] such time and place as the directors may determine.

42.   The chairman, if any, of the board of directors or in his absence some other director nominated by the director shall preside as chairman of the meeting, but if neither the chairman nor such other director (if any) be present within fifteen minutes after the time appointed for holding the meeting and willing to act, the directors present shall elect one of their number to be chairman and, if there is only one director present and wiling to act, he shall be chairman.

43.   If no director is willing to act as chairman, or if no director is present within fifteen minutes after the time appointed for holding the meeting, the members present and entitled to vote shall choose one of their number to be chairman.

44.   A director shall, notwithstanding that he is not a member, be entitled to attend and speak at any general meeting and at any separate meeting of the holders of any class of shares in the company.

45.   The chairman may, with the consent of a meeting at which a quorum is present (and shall if so directed by the meeting), adjourn

the meeting from time to time and from place to place, but no business shall be transacted at an adjourned meeting had the adjournment not taken place. When a meeting is adjourned for fourteen days or more, at least seven clear days' notice shall be given specifying the time and place of the adjourned meeting and the general nature of then business to be transacted. Otherwise it shall not be necessary to give any such notice.

46.    A resolution put to the vote of a meeting shall be decided on a show of hands unless before or on the declaration of the result of the show of hands a poll is duly demanded. Subject to the provisions of the Act, a poll may be demanded–
(a) by the chairman; or
(b) by at least two members having the right to vote at the meeting; or
(c) by a member or members representing not less than one-tenth of the total voting rights of all the members having the right to vote at the meeting; or
(d) by a member or members holding shares conferring a right to vote at the meeting being shares on which an aggregate sum has been paid up equal to not less than one-tenth of the total sum paid up on all the shares conferring that right;
and a demand by a person as proxy for a member shall be the same as a demand by the member.

47.    Unless a poll is duly demanded a declaration by the chairman that a resolution has been carried or carried unanimously, or by a particular majority, or lost, or not carried by a particular majority and an entry to that effect in the minutes of the meeting shall be conclusive evidence of the fact without proof of the number of proportion of the votes recorded in favour of or against the resolution.

48.    The demand for a poll may, before the poll is taken, be withdrawn but only with the consent of the chairman and a demand so withdrawn shall not be taken to have invalidated the result of a show of hands declared before the demand was made.

49.    A poll shall be taken as the chairman directs and he may appoint scrutineers (who need not be members) and fix a time and place for declaring the result of the poll. The result of the poll shall be deemed to be the resolution of the meeting at which the poll was demanded.

50.    In the case of an equality of votes, whether on a show of hands

or on a poll, the chairman shall be entitled to a casting vote in addition to any other vote he may have.

51.  A poll demanded on the election of a chairman or on a question of adjournment shall be taken forthwith. A poll demanded on any other question shall be taken either forthwith or at such time and place as the chairman directs not being more than thirty days after the poll is demanded. The demand for a poll shall not prevent the continuance of a meeting for the transaction of any business other than the question on which the poll was demanded. If a poll is demanded before the declaration of the result of a show of hands and the demand is duly withdrawn, the meeting shall continue as if the demand had not been made.

52.  No notice need be given of a poll not taken forthwith if the time and place at which it is to be taken are announced at the meeting at which it is demanded. In any other case at least seven clear days' notice shall be given specifying the time and place at which the poll is to be taken.

53.  A resolution in writing executed by or on behalf of each member who would have been entitled to vote upon it if it had been proposed at a general meeting at which he was present shall be as effectual as if it had been passed at a general meeting duly convened and held and may consist of several instruments in the like form each executed by or on behalf of one or more members.

*Votes of Members*

54.  Subject to any rights or restrictions attached to any shares, on a show of hands every member who (being an individual) is present in person or (being a corporation) is present by a duly authorised representative, not being himself entitled to vote, shall have one vote and on a poll every members shall have one vote for every share of which he is the holder.

55.  In the case of joint holders the vote of the senior who tenders a vote, whether in person or by proxy, shall be accepted to the exclusion of the votes of the other joint holders, and seniority shall be determined by the order in which the names of the holders stand in the register of members.

56.  A member in respect of whom an order has been made by any court having jurisdiction (whether in the United Kingdom or

elsewhere) in matters concerning mental disorder may vote, whether on a show of hands or on a poll, by his receiver, curator bonis or other person authorised in that behalf appointed by that court, and any such receiver, curator bonis or other person may, on a poll, vote by proxy. Evidence to the satisfaction of the directors of the authority of the person claiming to exercise the right to vote shall be deposited at the office, or at such other place as is specified in accordance with the articles for the deposit of instruments of proxy, not less than 48 hours before the time appointed for holding the meeting or adjourned meeting at which the right to vote is to be exercised and in default the right to vote shall not be exercisable.

57.   No member shall vote at any general meeting or at any separate meeting of the holders of any class of shares in the company, either in person or by proxy, in respect of any share held by him unless all moneys presently payable by him in respect of that share have been paid.

58.   No objection shall be raised to the qualification of any voter except at the meeting or adjourned meeting at which the vote objected to is tendered, and every vote not disallowed at the meeting shall be valid.   Any objection made in due time shall be referred to the chairman whose decision shall be final and conclusive.

59.   On a poll vote may be given either personally or by proxy. A member may appoint more than one proxy to attend on the same occasion.

60.   The appointment of a proxy shall be executed or on behalf of the appointer and shall be in the following form (or in a form as near thereto as circumstances allow or in any other form which is usual or which the directors may approve)–

### [Royal Basset Golf Club Limited]

I/We, [Peter Davy], of [Tor View, Nether Basset], being a member/members of the above named company, hereby appoint [Daniel Whiddon] of [The Gables, Nether Basset], or failing him, [Harry Hawk] of [10 The Avenue, Basset] as my/our proxy to vote in my/our name[s] and on my/our behalf at the annual/extraordinary general meeting of the company to be held on [15 March 2005], and at any adjournment thereof.

Signed on [15 February 2005].

61. Where it is desired to afford members on opportunity of instructing the proxy how he shall act the appointment of a proxy shall be in the following form (or in a form as near thereto as circumstances allow or in any other form which is usual or which the directors may approve)–

### [Royal Basset Golf Club Limited]

I/We, [Peter Davy], of [Tor View, Nether Basset], being a member/members of the above named company, hereby appoint [Daniel Whiddon] of [The Gables, Nether Basset], or failing him, [Harry Hawk] of [10 The Avenue, Basset] as my/our proxy to vote in my/our name[s] and on my/our behalf at the annual /extraordinary general meeting of the company to be held on [15 March 2005], and at any adjournment thereof.

This form is to be used in respect of the resolutions mentioned below as follows:
Resolution No. 1 *for *~~against~~
Resolution No. 2 *~~for~~ *against
*Strike out whichever is not desired.
Unless otherwise instructed, the proxy may vote as he thinks fit or abstain from voting.

Signed this [15th] day of [February 2005]

62. The appointment of a proxy and any authority under which it is executed or a copy of such authority certified notarially or in some other way approved by the directors may–
(a) [in the case of an instrument in writing] be deposited at the office or at such other places within the United Kingdom as is specified in the notice convening the meetings or in any instrument of proxy sent out by the company in relation to the meeting not less than 48 hours before the time for holding the meeting or adjourned meeting at which the person named in the instrument proposes to vote; or
(aa) in the case of an appointment contained in an electronic communication, where an address has been specified for the purpose of receiving electronic communications–
  (i) in the notice convening the meeting, or
  (ii) in any instrument of proxy sent out by the company in relation to the meeting, or
  (iii) in any invitation contained in an electronic communication to appoint a proxy issued by the company in relation to the meeting, to be received at such address not less than 48 hours before the time for holding the meeting or adjourned meeting at which the person named in the appointment proposes to vote;

(b) in the case of a poll taken more than 48 hours after it is demanded, be deposited received as aforesaid after the poll has been demanded and not less than 24 hours before the time appointed for the taking of the poll; or

(c) where the poll is not taken not more than 48 hours after it was demanded, but delivered at the meeting at which the poll was demanded to the chairman or to the secretary or to any director,

and an appointment of proxy which is not deposited; delivered or received in a manner so permitted shall be invalid.

In this regulation and the next "address", in relation to electronic communications includes any number or address used for the purposed of such communications.

63.    A vote given or poll demanded by proxy or by the duly authorised representative of a corporation shall be valid notwithstanding the previous determination of the authority of the person voting or demanding a poll unless notice of the determination was received by the company at the office or at such other place at which the instrument of proxy was duly deposited or, where the appointment of the proxy was contained in an electronic communication, at the address at which such appointment was duly received before the commencement of the meeting or adjourned meeting at which the vote is given or the poll demanded or (in the case of a poll taken otherwise than on the same day as the meeting or adjourned meeting) the time appointed for taking the poll.

# Appendix 10

## 1985 TABLE C: ARTICLES OF ASSOCIATION

*Companies (Tables A to F) Regulations 1985 (SI 1985/805) as amended by the Companies (Tables A to F) (Amendment) Regulations 1985 (SI 1985/1052)*

### ARTICLES OF ASSOCIATION

*Preliminary*

1.    Regulations 2 to 35 inclusive, 54, 55, 57, 59, 102 to 108 inclusive, 110, 114, 116 and 117 of Table A, shall not apply to the company but the articles hereinafter contained and, subject to the modifications hereinafter expressed, the remaining regulations of Table A shall constitute the articles of association of the company.

*Interpretation*

2.    In regulation 1 of Table A, the definition of "the holder" shall be omitted.

*Members*

3.    The subscribers to the memorandum of association of the company and such other persons as are admitted to membership in accordance with the articles shall be members of the company. No person shall be admitted a member of the company unless he is approved by the directors. Every person who wishes to become a member shall deliver to the company an application for membership in such form as the directors require executed by him.

4.    A member may at any time withdraw from the company by giving at least seven clear days' notice to the company. Membership shall not be transferable and shall cease on death.

*Notice of General Meetings*

5.    In regulation 38 of Table A–
    (a)  in paragraph (b) the words "of the total voting rights at the meeting of all the members" shall be substituted for "in nominal value of the shares giving that right" and
    (b)  the words "The notice shall be given to all the members and to the directors and auditors" shall be substituted for the last sentence.

*Proceedings at General Meetings*

6.    The words "and at any separate meeting of the holders of any class of shares in the company" shall be omitted from regulation 46 of table A shall be omitted.

7.    Paragraph (d) of regulation 46 of Table A shall be omitted.

*Votes of Members*

8.    On a show of hands every member present in person shall have one vote. On a poll every member present in person or by proxy shall have one vote.

*Directors' Expenses*

9.    The words "of any class of shares or "shall be omitted from regulation 83 of Table A.

*Proceedings of Directors*

10.    In paragraph (c) of regulation 94 of Table A the word "debentures" shall be substituted for the words "shares, debentures or other securities" in both places where they occur.

*Minutes*

11.    The words "of the holders of any class of shares in the company" shall be omitted from regulation 100 of Table A.

# Appendix 11

## STATUTES AFFECTING CLUB ACTIVITIES

[*Note: The under-mentioned list is not intended to comprise an exhaustive list of relevant statutes. In many cases only part of the statute is relevant to the club activity in question. Those with a double asterisk are due to be repealed when the Licensing Act 2003 comes fully into force*].

### (1) Agricultural societies

*E.g. farmers' clubs; landowners' associations; growers' associations*

Agriculture Acts 1947–1993
Agricultural Marketing Act 1983
Cereals Marketing Act 1965
Deer Act 1991
Dogs (Protection of Livestock Act) 1953
Food Act 1984
Food and Environment Protection Act 1985
Forestry Acts 1967–1991
Highways Act 1980
Highways (Amendment) Act 1986
Hill Farming Acts 1946, 1954 and 1985
Livestock Rearing Act 1951
Protection of Badgers Act 1992
Transport Act 1968
Weeds Act 1959
Wildlife and Countryside Act 1981

### (2) Allotment societies

Agriculture Act 1947 and 1970
Allotments Acts 1922-1950
Land Settlement (Facilities) Act 1919
Small Holdings and Allotment Acts 1908 and 1926

### (3) Angling and fishing clubs

Conservation of Seals Act 1970

Countryside Act 1968
Diseases of Fish Acts 1937 and 1983
Fisheries Act 1891–1981
Fishery Limits Act 1964 and 1976
Import of Live Fish (England and Wales) Act 1980
Rivers (Prevention of Pollution) Acts 1951 and 1961
Salmon Act 1986
Salmon and Freshwater Fisheries Act 1975
Sea Fish (Conservation) Acts 1967 and 1992
Sea Fisheries (Wildife Conservation) Act 1992
Theft Act 1968
Water Act 1973
Water Acts 1945–1989
Water Resources Acts 1963–1991

## (4)  Animal- or bird-related clubs

*E.g. canine societies, pigeon fanciers' clubs, poultry clubs*
Animal Boarding Establishment Act 1963
Animal Health Acts 1981 and 2002
Animal Health and Welfare Act 1984
Animals Act 1971
Animals (Cruel Poisons) Act 1962
Animals (Scientific Procedures) Act 1986
Birds (Registration Charges) Act 1997
Breeding of Dogs Acts 1973 and 1991
Dangerous Dogs Acts 1989 and 1991
Destructive Imported Animals Act 1932
Docking and Nicking of Horses Act 1949 Dogs Acts 1871–1906
Dogs (Amendment) Act 1928
Dogs (Fouling of Land) Act 1996
Endangered Species (Import and Export) Act 1976
Highways Acts 1980
Metropolitan Police Act 1839
Pet Animals Acts 1951
Pet Animals Act 1951 (Amendment) Act 1983
Prevention of Damage by Rabbits Act 1939
Protection of Animals Acts 1911
Protection of Animals (Amendment) Act 2000
Protection of Animals (Anaesthetics) Acts 1954 and 1964
Protection of Animals (Penalties) Act 1987
Wildlife and Countryside Act 1981

## (5) Archaeological societies
*E.g. treasure-hunters' clubs[1]*
    Coroners Act 1988
    National Heritage Acts 1980–2002.
    Protection of Military Remains Act 1986
    Protection of Wrecks Act 1973
    Treasure Act 1996


## (6) Camping & caravan clubs
    Caravan Sites Act 1968
    Caravan Sites and Control of Development 1960
    Countryside and Rights of Way Act 2000
    National Parks and Access to the Countryside Act 1949 (as amended)


## (7) Cycling clubs
    Cycle Tracks Act 1984
    Road Traffic Act 1988


## (8) Drama clubs
*E.g. theatre clubs, dramatic and operatic societies*
    Copyright, Designs and Patents Act 1988
    Fire Precautions Act 1971
    Licensing Act 2003
    Occupiers' Liability Acts 1957 & 1984
    Private Places of Entertainment (Licensing) Act 1967**
    Restriction of Offensive Weapons Acts 1959 and 1961
    Sunday Entertainment Act 1932**
    Theatres Act 1968 **
    Theatres Trust Act 1976


## (9) Film clubs
    Cinemas Act 1985**
    Cinematograph Films (Animals) Act 1937
    Films Act 1985
    Licensing Act 2003
    Video Recordings Acts 1984 and 1993

---

[1] An example of this type of club was referred to in the Times 26 July 1973 at p.18.

**(10)  Flying clubs**
Aviation and Maritime Security Act 1990
Aviation (Offences) Act 2003
Civil Aviation Act 1982
Civil Aviation (Amendment) Act 1996
Customs and Excise Management Act 1979
Railways and Transport Safety Act 2003
Transport Act 2000

**(11)  Golf clubs**
Occupiers' Liability Acts 1957 and 1984
Trees Act 1970
Water Acts 1945–1989
Water Resources Acts 1963–1991

**(12)  Holiday clubs**
*E.g. time-sharing clubs*
Financial Services Act 1986
Timeshare Act 1992
Trade Descriptions Act 1968

**(13)  Horticultural societies**
*E.g. garden clubs, flower-arranging societies*
Farm and Garden Chemicals Act 1967
Horticulture Act 1960
Horticulture Produce Act 1986
Horticulture Produce (Sales on Commission) Act 1926
Horticulture (Special Payments) Act 1974
Plant Health Act 1967
Plant Varieties Act 1997
Plant Varieties and Seeds Act 1964

**(14)  Hunting clubs**
*E.g. fox-hunting clubs, staghounds clubs*
Deer Act 1991
Hares Preservation Act 1892
Hunting Act 2004[2]
Wild Creatures and Forest Laws Act 1971
Welfare of Animals at Slaughter Act 1991
Wildlife and Countryside Act 1981

---

[2]     The hunting of wild animals with dogs was abolished with effect from 18 February 2005, with certain exemptions such as the hunting of rats and rabbits.

**(15) Motor racing and motor cycling clubs**
Motor Cycle Noise Act 1987
Noise Act 1996
Noise and Statutory Nuisance Act 1993
Road Traffic Act 1988
Road Traffic (Temporary Restrictions) Act 1991
Road Traffic Regulation (Special Events) Act 1994
Transport Acts 1962–2000

**(16) Musical societies**
*E.g. concert clubs, discotheque clubs, ballroom-dancing clubs*
Copyright Designs and Patents Act 1988
Fire Precautions Act 1971
Licensing Act 2003
Occupiers' Liability Acts 1957 and 1984
Private Places of Entertainment (Licensing) Act 1967**
Sunday Entertainment Act 1932**

**(17) Nature clubs**
*E.g. birdwatching clubs, field societies, conservation societies*
Nature Conservancy Council Act 1973
Wild Creatures and Forest Laws Act 1971
Wild Mammals (Protection) Act 1996
Wildlife and Countryside Acts 1981
Wildlife and Countryside (Amendment) Act 1991
Wildlife and Countryside (Service of Notices) Act 1985

**(18) Political clubs**
*E.g. national party associations, (non-party) ratepayers' associations, (non-party) residents' associations*
Finance (No.2) Act 1983
Political Parties, Elections and Referendums Act 2000
Representation of the People Acts 1983–2000

**(19) Preservation societies**
*E.g. railway and canal preservation societies[3]*
Ancient Monuments and Archaeological Areas Act 1979
British Waterways Act 1995
Canals Protection (London) Act 1898

---

[3]    There are many private and local Acts of Parliament governing railways and canals
which may be relevant in any given case.

Historic Buildings and Ancient Monuments Act 1953
National Heritage Acts 1980–2002
Railway Heritage Act 1996

## (20) Radio clubs

Wireless Telegraphy Acts 1949–1998

## (21) Rambling associations

Commons Acts 1876–1908
Commons Registration Act 1965
Countryside Act 1968
Countryside and Rights of Way Act 2000
Dogs (Protection of Livestock) Act 1953
Forestry Act 1967
Highways Acts 1980 and 1986
National Parks and Access to Countryside Act 1949
Open Spaces Act 1906

## (22) Riding clubs

*E.g. pony clubs*

Animal Health Acts 1981 and 2002
Docking and Nicking of Horses Act 1949
Farriers Registration Acts 1975 and 1977
Horses (Protective Headgear for Young Riders) Act 1990
Protection against Cruel Tethering Act 1988
Riding Establishments Acts 1964 and 1970

## (23) Sailing clubs

*E.g. yacht clubs*

Coast Protection Act 1949
Countryside Act 1968
Customs and Excise Management Act 1979
Docks and Harbours Act 1966
Harbours Act 1964
Marine Insurance Act 1906
Marine Safety Act 2003
Merchant Shipping Acts 1988 and 1995
Merchant Shipping and Maritime Security Act 1997
Pilotage Act 1987
Railways and Transport Safety Act 2003

**(24) Shooting clubs**

*E.g. rifle clubs, clay pigeon shooting clubs, shooting syndicates*
Firearms Act 1968
Firearms (Amendment) Act 1997
Firearms (Amendment) (No.2) Act 1997
Game Acts 1831 and 1970
Game Laws (Amendment) Act 1960
Game Licences Act 1860
Ground Game Acts 1880
Ground Game (Amendment) Act 1906
Gun Barrel Proof Acts 1868–1978
Hares Act 1848
Hares Preservation Act 1892
Theft Act 1968
Wild Creatures and Forest Laws Act 1971
Wildlife and Countryside Act 1981

**(25) Sports clubs (other than golf clubs)**

Activity Centres (Young Persons Safety) Act 1995
Fire Safety and Safety of Places of Sport Act 1987
Football (Offences and Disorder) Act 1999
Football (Disorder) (Amendment) Act 2002
Football Spectators Act 1989
Safety of Sports Grounds Act 1975
Sporting Events (Control of Alcohol etc) Amendment Act 1992**
Water Resources Act 1991

**(26) Tenants' associations**

Housing Acts 1988–1996
Housing Associations Act 1985
Housing Grants, Construction and Regeneration Act 1996
Protection from Eviction Act 1977
Rent Act 1977
Rent (Amendment) Act 1985

**(27) Welfare associations**

*E.g. clubs for the disabled, Darby and Joan clubs, over-sixties clubs, youth clubs, leagues of friends of hospitals*
Chronically Sick and Disabled Persons Acts 1970
Chronically Sick and Disabled Persons (Amendment) Act 1976
Disabled Persons Act 1981
Disabled Persons (Employment) Acts 1944 and 1958

Disabled Persons (Services, Consultation and Representation) Act
   1986
Registered Homes Acts 1984
Registered Homes (Amendment) Act 1991

**(28) Wine-and beer-making clubs**
Licensing Act 1964**
Licensing Act 2003

# Appendix 12

## SYNOPSIS OF THE OLD RÉGIME UNDER THE LICENSING ACT 1964

**A12-1** *Registration certificate* In order to qualify for a registration certificate under the Act of 1964 a members' club must comply with the provisions of section 41, or section 42 if registered under the provisions of the Industrial and Provident Societies Act 1965 or the Friendly Societies Act 1974, and its rules must comply with Schedule 7 the Act.

**A12-2** Originally granted for one year, on the second or subsequent renewal the registration certificate can be renewed for up to 10 years[1]. Application for a certificate is lodged with the clerk to the justices and must contain prescribed particulars relating to the premises and to the constitution of the club[2], with sufficient copies for the clerk to send to the police, fire authority and local authority[3]. Notice must be given to the public in a manner similar to that prescribed in relation to an on-licence. The local authority, the fire authority, and the police have rights of inspection on an application for a certificate[4] or renewal. If there is no objection to the grant or renewal of a certificate the court cannot refuse, save on the limited grounds set out in section 44 of the Act[5], and it has to state those grounds in writing. Appeal against

---

[1] S. 40(2) and (3).
[2] Sch. 5.
[3] Sch. 6.
[4] Ss. 45, 46.
[5] The grounds are (1) that the application did not fully set out all the information required by the Act or was otherwise not in conformity with the Act; (2) that the club premises were not suitable for their purpose given the size and nature of the club; (3) that the conditions in section 41 (1) and (2) were not satisfied or that the application should be refused under section 43 (premises disqualified under section 47, or person involved in management of club not a fit person in view of his known character, etc.); (4) that the club is conducted in a disorderly manner or for an unlawful purpose or that the rules are habitually disregarded; (5) that the premises are habitually used for unlawful purposes.

refusal of a registration certificate lies to the Crown Court[6]. If a club does not qualify for a registration certificate, it can apply for a justices' licence which is sometimes called a "club licence"[7]. The application procedure is as for other justices' on-licences. The justices will probably impose conditions, such as restrictions on sales to non-members. This provision was originally specifically devised for proprietary clubs.

**A12-3** *Qualifications for registration* The Act of 1964 stipulates a number of conditions which must be fulfilled for the club to be eligible for a registration certificate. It establishes the "two day rule" whereby no person may be to membership or is admitted as a candidate for membership without an interval of at least two days between their nomination or application for membership and their election, or, where there is no procedure for nomination or application, between becoming a member and admission to the club[8]. Since the requirement is for two clear days, the effect is that membership cannot be acquired for three days after application. The main criteria for the grant are that the club must be conducted in good faith as a club and have not less than twenty-five members[9]; that intoxicating liquor is not sold on the premises other than by or on behalf of the club[10]; that the purchase and supply of intoxicating liquor is managed either by the club in general meeting or by an "elective committee"[11]; and that no person receives at the expense of the club any commission on purchases by the club of intoxicating liquor or derives any profit from sales to members or guests[12].

**A12-4** In determining whether the club is established and conducted in good faith the magistrates may have regard to any restrictions on the club's freedom of purchase of intoxicating liquor[13], the provisions in the rules for the sale of intoxicating liquor[14], the club's financial structure and provisions for informing the membership thereof[15] and the nature of the club's premises[16]. Where the rules of the club conform with Schedule 7 to the Act the magistrates' court is in effect to assume that the club is essentially being run in good faith[17] and that the

---

[6]      S. 50(1).
[7]      S. 55.
[8]      S. 41(1); para 3(1) of schedule 7.
[9]      S. 41(2)(a).
[10]     S. 41(2)(b).
[11]     S. 41(2)(c) para 4(3) of schedule 7.
[12]     S. 41(2)(d).
[13]     S. 41(3)(a).
[14]     S. 49(2).
[15]     S. 41(3)(b) and (c).
[16]     S. 41(3)(d).
[17]     S. 41(4).

provisions for the purchase and sale of intoxicating liquor are appropriate.

**A12-5** *Schedule 7 rules*[18] Schedule 7 of the Act of 1964 contains general directions as to the rules relating to the constitution of the club, general meetings, voting rights and election of members. It is worth summarising the provisions of this important piece of legislation, which, surprisingly, has not been repeated in any form in the Act of 2003:

(1) If the club is not managed by the members in general meeting, it must be managed by an "elective committee", (or committees), one of which must be a general committee charged with the general management of those matters which are not assigned to special committees[19].

(2) An elective committee is one in which the members are elected by the membership for a period of not less than one year nor for more than five years; elections must be held annually and there must be fixed rules as to the procedure for retirement from the committee of those members who have served the maximum period; all members of the club of not less than two years' standing and entitled to vote must equally be entitled to stand for election or nominate persons for election, subject to restrictions in the rules. The rules may also provide for the period which must elapse before a retiring committee member is allowed to stand again for election.

(3) If the committee comprises four or more members it will be treated as an elective committee if not less than two-thirds of its members are duly elected (unless it is concerned with the purchase or supply by the club of intoxicating liquor, in which case all the members must be elected)[20].

(4) The committee is allowed to co-opt members. If a co-opted member of a committee fills the place of an elected member he shall serve the remainder of the term which would have been filled by the elected member, and shall be treated as having been elected[21].

(5) There must be a general meeting of members at least once in every year and there must be not more than 15 months between each meeting[22].

(6) The committee must be able to call a general meeting[23] and every member entitled to vote must be able to call a meeting, although rules may require a specific minimum number of members to do

---

[18] See **APPENDIX 3** for the full text of this schedule.
[19] Sch. 7 paras 1 and 4.
[20] Sch. 7 para 4(3).
[21] Sch. 7 para 4(5).
[22] Sch. 7 para 2(1).
[23] Sch. 7 para 2(2).

this. This number must be not more than thirty, nor more than one-fifth of the members entitled to do so (whichever is the less)[24].

(7) All members must be entitled to vote at a general meeting, unless excluded from voting on the grounds of age (not greater than twenty-one) and must have equal voting rights unless the club is "primarily a men's club"[25], when women can be excluded from the vote, (or primarily a women's club, when men can be excluded). The word "primarily" may cause difficulty, because of the lack of definition in the Act. In order to answer this question one needs to look at (a) the objects clause in the rules, (b) the membership rule and (c) the actual proportion of one sex in relation to the other sex. On this last point, a rough guide is that the proportion of the other sex must be very small to allow a club to maintain that it is primarily a men's club, it is considered that a female membership of upwards of about ten to fifteen per cent of the total would render the club no longer able to discriminate in this fashion[26].

**A12-6**  Therefore, to comply with Schedule 7, voting rights should be given to all club members, male and female, including five-day members, elderly members receiving a discount and student members over the age of twenty-one.

**A12-7**  *Supply to non-members*  Under the Act of 1964 a registered club is permitted to supply alcohol to its members and their guests on club premises[27], and to members only for consumption off club premises[28]. Further, a registered club is allowed to sell alcohol to non-members of the club[29] for consumption on the premises, provided the rules authorise such sale, and the relevant rule does not offend against the general requirement that the club was established and is conducted in good faith as a club[30]. The magistrates can impose conditions on such sale[31]. Subject to certain exceptions[32], the supply of alcohol in

---

[24]     Sch. 7 para 2(3).
[25]     Sch. 7 para 2(4)(a).
[26]     Such discrimination was particularly common in golf clubs, with consequent considerable and unwelcome publicity. In recent years the position has changed, a result partly of advice and partly of increased attention from magistrates' clerks who have been keener to look at clubs' rules when dealing with an application to renew a registration certificate.
[27]     S. 39(1).
[28]     S. 39(2).
[29]     S. 49(1).
[30]     S. 49 (2).
[31]     S. 49(3).
[32]     Such as a special hours certificate (s.78) or an occasional licence (s.80).

clubs is restricted to the permitted hours generally applicable[33]. In addition, a registered club can sell alcohol to a person admitted to the club premises as a member of another club where (1) the other club has a registration certificate but is temporarily closed, (2) both clubs exist for learned, educational or political objects of a similar nature, (3) both clubs are primarily for service personnel and are members of an organisation established by Royal Charter and consisting wholly or mainly of such personnel, and (4) both clubs are working men's clubs[34].

**A12-8** *Permitted hours*   The Licensing Act has remained largely unchanged since 1964; however, the permitted hours have been amended on two occasions:
(1) In 1988 section 62 of the 1964 Act was amended by the Licensing Act 1998 to read:

> The permitted hours in premises in respect of which a club is registered shall be –

> (a) on weekdays other than Christmas Day or Good Friday, the general licensing hours.

This amendment removed the need for clubs to fix the hours 'by or under the rules of the club'. The general licensing hours were amended at the same time to become:
For weekdays other than Christmas Day or Good Friday 11 a.m. to 11 p.m. Christmas Day and Good Friday hours were amended to become:

> 12 midday to 10.30 p.m., with a break of four hours beginning at 3 p.m.

Section 63(1)(a) of the 1964 Act was also amended to allow an extension of 'drinking up' time from 10 minutes to 20 minutes.
(2) In 1995 the Sunday restrictions still in force were amended by the Licensing (Sunday Hours) Act 1995. Section 62 of the Act of 1964 was amended so that the permitted hours on Sundays (except when Christmas Day falls on a Sunday) and Good Friday would be the same as general licensing hours. Permitted hours for clubs on these days are now 12 midday through to 10.30 p.m. without a break. As a consequence of this change, the need for clubs to notify the Clerk to the Justices of the hours chosen by the club to supply intoxicating liquor on Sundays and Good Fridays was

---

[33]   S. 62 (as amended by s. 1(5) of the Licensing Act 1988).
[34]   S. 49.

removed. However, clubs must continue to fix hours for Christmas Day and notify the Clerk to the Justices[35].

## Special provisions

**A12-9**  *Restaurant certificate*[36]  The secretary (or holder of the licence) may apply to the chief officer of police on notice served not less than fourteen days from the desired commencement day for an extension to the permitted hours for the period on Christmas Day between the two parts of the general licensing hours, or for the hour following the general licensing hours. The extension must be for the purposes of the sale or supply of intoxicating liquor to persons taking table meals in the premises in a part of the premises usually set aside for the service of such persons[37], and for its consumption as an ancillary to a meal[38]. There is an overriding requirement that the premises are structurally adapted and bona fide used for the purpose of supplying "substantial refreshment", to which the sale and supply of intoxicating liquor is ancillary, to persons frequenting the premises[39].

**A12-10**  *Extended hours order*[40]  This provides for the extension of the hours where the premises are bona fide used for the purposes of habitually providing live entertainment as well as substantial refreshment, and for the ancillary sale or supply of intoxicating liquor. Under these provisions the magistrates may grant an extension until one a.m., or half past midnight on a Sunday. No person may be supplied who has been admitted to the premises after midnight (11.30 p.m. on Sunday), or less than half an hour before the entertainment is due to end, unless he is to have a meal.

**A12-11**  1 *Exemption orders*[41]  A registered private members' club can apply to the magistrates for an order for its permitted hours to be extended for such period as is specified in the order for a special function to be held on the premises. This order is known as a special order of exemption[42]. The order may only be made when the magistrates are satisfied that the occasion in question is 'special': whether the occasion qualifies or not is a matter for the court, but

---

| | |
|---|---|
| 35 | S. 62(3). |
| 36 | Ss. 68, 69. |
| 37 | S. 68(2)(a). |
| 38 | S. 68(2)(b). |
| 39 | S. 68(3). |
| 40 | S. 70. |
| 41 | S. 74. |
| 42 | S. 74(4). |

landmark birthdays (18th, 50th, 60th etc) wedding receptions and silver wedding anniversaries are generally accepted as being 'special'. A charge is made for each grant made on a particular date so if a club is able to group several applications together and make them on the same date, there will only be one fee payable.

**A12-12** *Special hours certificate*[43]   A club may apply for a special hours certificate extending the permitted hours to two o'clock in the morning, where music and dancing extends until that time, or until such earlier time that that activity ceases[44]. Application is made to the magistrates' court which will grant the application if it is satisfied that the premises have been certified by the local authority as suitable for music and dancing under the provisions of section 79 and that the premises are structurally adapted, and bona fide used, or intended to be used, for the purpose of providing for club members music and dancing and the supply of substantial refreshment to which the supply of intoxicating liquor will be ancillary[45]. If the club has a section 79 certificate and is in the process of being structurally adapted in accordance with plans which are deposited with the court a provisional grant may be made, which the court can make final upon being satisfied that the work has been carried out. Again, if the court refuses the application in these circumstances it must state its reasons in writing[46].

**A12-13** *Sporting Events (Control of Alcohol etc.) Act 1985*   This makes provisions regulating the supply of intoxicating liquor at 'designated sporting events' which are defined in the Act[47] so as to exclude events to which competitors are to take part otherwise than for reward, and to which spectators are to be admitted free of charge. We are talking here of major sporting events with paying spectators, not with ordinary club activities.

**A12-14** *Justices' on-licence*   Where a members' club is for any reason ineligible for a registration certificate, it can sell alcohol if it obtains a justices' on-licence. Application is made on notice to the licensing justices, the notice being addressed to the justices, the police, the fire service and the local authority. Notice to the general public is given by a notice displayed at the premises for at least seven of the twenty-eight days preceding the hearing, and by advertisement in a local

---

[43]   S. 76.
[44]   S. 76(2). And note that the extension is until half past midnight on a Sunday.
[45]   S. 78(a) and (b).
[46]   S. 78A.
[47]   S. 9.

newspaper in the period between twenty-eight and fourteen days preceding the hearing. The application must inform the public of how they may object to the application, and all parties must be provided with plans of the premises to be covered by the licence[48]. The licence must be taken out in the name of an officer of the club nominated for the purpose[49]. In the case of a limited company it is usual for the licence to be held by a director, the secretary or some other officer of the company.

**A12-15** *Objectors* They need not give notice of their objections until the hearing. The licensing justices have discretion as to the grant of new licences, which they must exercise judicially. Using their local knowledge they are entitled to refuse an application despite a lack of objections, but detailed reasons for the refusal have to be given. Appeal lies to the Crown Court. If the justices have a particular policy as regards applications, this must be published so as to allow applicants to be able properly to prepare their case.

**A12-16** *Conditions* Conditions can be attached to the licence; for example, limiting the sale or consumption to specified parts of the premises, or a requirement for the maintenance of fire-fighting equipment, secondary lighting etc. or an emergency exit. The licence holder need not reside on the premises.

**A12-17** *Disqualification* Disqualification arises under the provisions of the Act following conviction for one of a number of specific offences. The justices may grant a licence to any person, not disqualified from holding a licence, as they think fit and proper[50]. As to whether the applicant is a "fit and proper person", such determination is within the discretion of the justices, again to be exercised judicially

**A12-18** *Duration of licence* A justices' on-licence lasts for three years[51]. The licensing period for all licences was fixed by section 26 (1) of the Act to run until 4th April 1989 and thereafter until each third anniversary of that date. Present licences in consequence will run until 4 April 2007[52]. Application for renewal must be made to the general licensing committee at the appropriate licensing sessions. An on-licence authorises the sale of intoxicating liquor for consumption both on and off the premises.

---

[48]    Sch. 2.
[49]    S. 55(2).
[50]    S. 3(1).
[51]    S. 26(5)
[52]    Until overtaken by the implementation of the Licensing Act 2003..

**A12-19** *Children*   No person under the age of fourteen years may be in the bar of licensed premises unless there is in force a children's certificate, when the person may be in the bar to which the certificate relates if he is in the company of adults.

# Appendix 13

## SIMPLE SET OF RULES FOR A
## MEMBERS' CLUB

## BASSETSHIRE HOCKEY UMPIRES ASSOCIATION[1]

### RULES

1. **Name**   The Association shall be called the Bassetshire Hockey Umpires Association ("the Association").
2. **Affiliation**   The Association shall be affiliated to the Bassetshire Hockey Association and the Mid-Counties Hockey Umpires Association.
3. **Object**   The object of the Association is to provide and promote quality hockey umpiring through development, training, grading, support, and opportunity for all the members and the teams which it serves.
4. **Membership**   Membership shall be open to men and women over the age of 18 years who are interested in the object of the Association, and the Association shall consist of Ordinary Members, Appointed Members, and Honorary Members.
5. **Election of members**   The election of each category of member shall be vested in the Committee. A person who wishes to be elected as an Ordinary Member shall fill in an application form provided by the Honorary Secretary. A person who wishes to be elected as an Appointed Member, if he is not already an Ordinary

---

[1]     Based on the actual rules of an umpiring association. The association will have no clubhouse or premises, so the rules do not have to cater for such topics as alcohol licensing or trusteeship of property, nor is there any call for bye-laws. Their form and contents can be expressed in a straightforward manner, yet tailored to suit the needs of the association. These rules take into account all the basic rules set out in **2-03** above.

Member, shall fill in an application form; if he is already an Ordinary Member he should informally approach the Honorary Secretary to make known his wish, who will pass on this information to the Committee.

The Committee may accept as a probationer any person requesting election as an Appointed Member. The Committee will not elect any person as an Appointed Member unless it is satisfied that the candidate has the knowledge and ability to apply the rules of hockey and is suitable to be elected an Appointed Member of the Association. Active members of other hockey umpires associations may be elected Appointed Members of the Association.

Appointed Members will be placed on either the Active List or the Non-Active List.

The Committee may elect as Honorary Members those persons, not exceeding five in number, who in its opinion have rendered such service to the Association as to merit this status. Honorary Members shall be exempt from paying subscriptions and shall enjoy all the privileges of membership, save that they shall have no voting rights nor may they be elected to any office of the club.

6. **Subscriptions**   A member's annual subscription shall be such sum as the members determine at the AGM. All subscriptions shall become due on the 1 October in each year. Any member not paying his subscription by the due date may, at the Committee's discretion, be disqualified from umpiring any match where the appointment is made by the Association.

7. **Resignation of members**   A member may resign from the association by informing the Honorary Secretary in writing of his intention to do so. A member remains liable for his subscription for the year in which he resigned (a year for this purpose shall run from 1 October to the following 30 September).

8. **Suspension and expulsion of members**   The Committee shall have the power to suspend for a period not exceeding 12 months or to expel a member who infringes any of these rules or whose conduct, whether on or off the field, is in the opinion of the Committee injurious to the good name of the Association or renders him unfit for membership. No person shall be suspended or expelled without first being summoned before the Committee and full opportunity afforded to him to advance a defence nor unless three-quarters of the Committee then present shall vote for his suspension or expulsion. No suspended member may be elected as an officer of the Association.

The Committee shall have the power to stand down any member from umpiring pending the hearing of the case against him (including umpiring at non-appointed matches).

Complaints received by the Association concerning an umpiring member should be recorded in writing by the Honorary Secretary and then referred to the Committee for its consideration.

9. **Officers of the association**  The Association shall have the following officers, all of whom shall be elected at the AGM: a Chair, a Vice-Chair, an Honorary Secretary, an Honorary Treasurer, two Appointment Secretaries (men/women); a Development Officer, two Regional Representatives (men/women) and a Publicity Officer. Upon election all officers shall hold office until the next AGM when their term of office shall expire but they may offer themselves for re-election.

10. **Management of the association**  The management and control of all the affairs of the Association shall be vested in a committee of members ("the Committee"). The Committee shall consist of the Chair, the Vice-Chair, the Honorary Secretary, the Honorary Treasurer, and two other officers who shall be chosen from their own number.  The Committee shall meet as and when appropriate. A quorum for meetings of the Committee shall be three members. The chair of any committee meeting shall have a casting vote in addition to his ordinary vote.

11. **Powers of the committee**  For the avoidance of doubt the Committee shall have the following specific powers:
    (1)  to fill any vacancy amongst the officers until the next AGM;
    (2)  to appoint such sub-committees as it deems necessary. A sub-committee shall conduct its business in accordance with the directions of the Committee and shall periodically report its proceedings to the Committee for approval and ratification;
    (3)  to retain and hold as property of the Association all sums of money coming into the Association and to bank the funds of the Association. All cheques drawn by the Association shall be signed by the Chair and the Honorary Treasurer, or by such other officers of the Association as may be duly authorised by the Committee, provided that all cheques are signed by two officers;
    (4)  to invest sums of money in any prudent manner which the Committee thinks will benefit the Association;
    (5)  to permit, unless a contrary direction is given, all officers to pay out-of-pocket expenses or fees authorised by the Committee;
    (6)  to arrange insurance cover for members in respect of all their umpiring activities, whether or not they are acting as appointed umpires;
    (7)  to assess on an on-going basis the performance of the

Appointed Members and to re-grade them, higher or lower, as and when necessary;

(8) to appoint, at the request of any club or school affiliated to the Bassetshire Hockey Association, one or two Appointed Members as the umpires for any match, provided that the club or school shall pay (if so requested by the Association) the notified appointment fees and expenses, and provided that they agree to be bound by the rules of the Association as may be made from time to time.

12. **Annual General Meeting** The Annual General Meeting ("AGM") of the Association shall be held in June of each year for the purpose of receiving the reports of the Committee, any sub-committee and the Honorary Treasurer in respect of the Association's activities since the previous AGM (including the election of any Honorary Member); receiving and, if thought fit, approving the accounts in respect of the preceding financial year; electing the officers of the Association (including the appointment of any Honorary Auditor); fixing the subscriptions; and for the transaction of the general business of the Association. All categories of members shall receive 14 days' notice in writing of the date of such meeting.

No member, save with the permission of the chair of the meeting, may bring any matter before the meeting unless, before 10 May in that year, he has given notice in writing to the Honorary Secretary of the substance of the matter which he wishes to raise at the meeting.

13. **Special meetings** An Extraordinary General Meeting ("EGM") shall be convened by the Honorary Secretary within 28 days of receipt by him of a direction by the Committee or of a requisition signed by not fewer than one-fifth of the total membership. All categories of members shall receive 14 days' notice in writing of such meeting. The notice will specify the purpose of the meeting and no other matter may be brought before such meeting.

14. **Quorum and voting at meetings** A general meeting (that is, an AGM or an EGM) may proceed to business if 25 members are present within half an hour after the time fixed for the meeting; otherwise the meeting, if convened on the requisition of the members, shall be dissolved but, if convened by direction of the Committee, shall stand adjourned to the same time in the following week, save that the adjourned meeting may proceed to business whatever the number of members present.

Only fully paid up members shall be allowed to vote at a general meeting. The chair of the meeting shall have a casting vote in addition to his ordinary vote. Any motion to be carried shall require a simple majority of those entitled to vote and present at the meeting, save for any amendment of the rules or the dissolution of the Association which shall require a two-thirds majority of those entitled to vote and present at the meeting.

15. **Amendment of the rules**   These rules may be added to, altered or revoked by members at an EGM or, if the amendment is proposed by the Committee, at an AGM.  Any amendment to be proposed at the AGM must be contained in the notice of the AGM sent under Rule 12.

16. **Interpretation**   The reference in these rules to the masculine gender shall in all cases apply equally to the feminine gender.

17. **Dissolution of the association**   In the event that the members pass a resolution to dissolve the Association, any property belonging to the Association shall not be distributed to the members if there is a surplus of assets over liabilities, but will be given or transferred to the Bassetshire Hockey Association or to such other association having similar objects to the Association as the members may decide upon.

# Appendix 14

## COMPLEX SET OF RULES WITH BYE-LAWS AND ANNEXE FOR A MEMBERS' CLUB[1]

## SOUTH BASSETSHIRE GOLF CLUB

### RULES

1. **Name**   The club shall be called the South Bassetshire Golf Club ("the Club").
2. **Objects**   The objects of the Club are:
   (1)   to promote and provide for the benefit of members of the Club amenities for the pursuit of the game of golf and for social and recreational activities in relation thereto;
   (2)   to foster links with, support and co-operate with other persons or organisations with similar objects as set out in this rule;
   (3)   to do all things incidental to or conducive to the attainment of the above-mentioned objects.
3. **Rules of golf**   The rules of the game of golf played by the Club shall be those adopted from time to time by the Royal and Ancient Golf Club of St Andrews, subject to any modification set out in the Club's bye-laws.
4. **Trustees**
   (1)   All property and assets of the Club shall be vested in not less than two nor more than four trustees appointed from time to time by the Committee from membership of the Club. The trustees shall hold the same for and on behalf of the members of the Club. No member shall be appointed over the age of 75. Any trustee must have been a member of the Club for at least five years before the date of appointment.

---

[1]   Based on the rules, by-laws and annexe of an actual golf club.

(2) Trustees shall be appointed for a term of five years but at the expiry of this period shall be eligible for re-appointment. The trustee's tenure of office will terminate on the resignation, retirement or death of the trustee. In addition, a trustee may be removed by a vote of three-quarters of the members present and entitled to vote at a special meeting.

(3) The Committee shall have power to nominate a new trustee if a vacancy occurs by reason of one of the grounds set out in (2) above. For the purpose of giving effect to such nomination the Committee is hereby nominated as the person to appoint a new trustee of the Club within the meaning of section 36 of the Trustee Act 1925. The Committee shall by deed duly appoint the person or persons nominated by the Committee, and the provisions of the Trustee Act 1925 shall apply to such appointment. Every statement of fact in the deed of appointment shall be conclusive evidence of this fact in favour of the person dealing in good faith and for value with the Club or its trustees.

(4) The trustees shall deal with the Club's property and assets as directed by the Committee from time to time. Without derogation from this obligation, the trustees shall have power to sell the property of the Club; borrow money; or give security for borrowed money by mortgage or charge on the Club's property, provided that the transaction in question does not involve a greater sum than £15,000. Any transaction involving a greater sum than £15,000 shall require the consent of two-thirds of the members present and entitled to vote at a general meeting of the Club.

(5) The trustees shall be indemnified against risk and expense out of the Club's funds.

6. **Membership**   The membership shall consist of:
   (1) Ordinary members;
   (2) Honorary life members;
   (3) Restricted members;
   (4) Honorary members;
   (5) Temporary members;
   (6) Associate members.

7. **Ordinary Members**   There shall not be more than 800 Ordinary Members. This number shall be split equally between men and women, save that if the membership falls below 700 the Committee shall have the power to elect a greater percentage of men or a greater percentage of women, as the case may be, in order bring the membership nearer to 800. These members shall have the full privileges of membership and full voting rights.

8. **Honorary Life Members**   A member may be elected an Honorary Life Member at a general meeting of the Club on the recommendation of the Committee. A member who has paid his annual subscription for 40 years of more may be proposed as an honorary life member by an Ordinary Member of at least five years' standing. Notice of a proposal to elect an Honorary Life Member must appear on the agenda of a general meeting. Honorary Life Members shall have the full privileges of membership and full voting rights, but shall not be liable to pay any further subscription.

8. **Restricted Members**   The categories of Restricted Members shall be set out in the Club's bye-laws. These members shall have such privileges and voting rights as are set out in the bye-laws.

9. **Honorary Members**   The Committee may elect as Honorary Members those persons, not exceeding 10 in number, who in the opinion of the Committee have for good or sufficient reason merited this status. Honorary Members shall be exempt from paying any entrance fee or subscription and shall be entitled to all the privileges of membership, save that they shall have no voting rights nor may they be appointed to any office or committee of the Club.

10. **Temporary Members**   Competitors in the South Bassetshire Annual Open Competition may apply to the Committee for temporary membership for the duration of the tournament. [OR Holiday residents staying at the South Bassetshire Camping and Caravan Park may apply to the Committee for temporary membership for the duration of their stay at the Park for a period not exceeding 14 days in any one year.] Temporary members may introduce their caddies and guests into the club. Temporary members shall be entitled to all the privileges of membership, save that they shall have no voting rights nor may they be appointed to any office or committee of the club.

11. **Associate Members**
    (1)  The Committee shall be entitled to offer associate membership to members of the Royal Basset Golf Club when the playing of golf at that club is reserved for the qualifying rounds of the Open Tournament.

    [(2) A member of another club which is a recognised club within the meaning of section 193 of the Licensing Act 2003 may be admitted into the club as an associate member provided that he or she first pays the stipulated green fees. Associate members may introduce their guests into the club][2].

---

[2]     This is a new rule necessary to permit associate members into the club under the Licensing Act 2003 (see **9-36** above).

(3) Associate members shall be entitled to all the privileges of membership, save that they shall have no voting rights nor may they be appointed to any office or committee of the club.

12. **Election and admission of members**

   (1) The election of all categories of member shall be vested in the Committee.

   (2) A candidate for Ordinary Membership or Restricted Membership must be proposed and seconded by at least two Ordinary Members of at least five years' standing at the date of the proposal. The application must be made on an application form provided by the Secretary. The candidate's name and address must be prominently displayed in the clubhouse for at least two clear days before his name is submitted for election.

   (3) An application for Temporary Membership may be authorised, and only authorised, by two members of the Committee nominated by the Committee to carry out this task. Save as aforesaid, the provisions of (2), (4), (6) and (7) of this rule shall apply to this category of member, except that (a) the first sentence of (2) shall be disregarded and (b) a Temporary Member shall be exempt from paying any entrance fee.

   (4) The candidate or applicant may be asked to demonstrate his playing ability at golf before his application is considered by the Committee.

   (5) The election may be made by ballot if requested by a member of the Committee. A candidate receiving two adverse votes shall not be elected a member.

   (6) Upon election or admission the member will be notified accordingly and will be provided with a copy of these rules, together with a copy of the bye-laws, all of which shall be binding on him.

   (7) The elected or admitted member shall not be entitled to any privileges of membership until he has paid the entrance fee and his first subscription.

   (8) The admission of an Associate Member is conditional upon his first signing the Visitors' Book. By signing this book the Associate Member agrees to be bound by the rules and bye-laws of the Club. This book shall be open to inspection by the Ordinary Members of the Club on reasonable notice being given to the Secretary.

13. **Notice**   Every member shall be under a continuing duty to notify the Secretary of his up-to-date address and, where applicable, the details of his telephone and fax numbers, and also his e-mail

address. All notices in writing required to be given by the Club to the members under these rules may be sent by post or by electronic means. All notices sent to the member at his notified address, whichever means of communication is used, shall be deemed to have arrived three days after despatch by the Club. The non-arrival of any notice sent by the Club shall not invalidate any meeting convened by the Club nor any other Club activity which requires notice to be sent to the member.

14. **Entrance fee** Entrance fees for Ordinary Members and Restricted Members shall be such sum as the Committee may decide from time to time. On transfer from one category to another the member shall pay the entrance fee applicable to the new category, credit being given for any entrance fee already paid.

15. **Subscriptions**
    (1) A member's subscription shall be such sum as the members shall determine at the annual general meeting. All subscriptions shall become due and payable on 1st April in each year.
    (2) If a member is elected after the 1st October, his first subscription shall be reduced by one-half.
    (3) The Committee may authorise members to pay their subscriptions by two equal instalments, the first instalment becoming due on 1st April and the second instalment becoming due on 1st October, provided that both instalments are paid by standing order.
    (4) If the whole subscription or the first instalment or the second instalment, as the case may be, is not paid within one calendar month of its due date, the member shall cease to enjoy the privileges of membership until payment is made. If the subscription or any part thereof remains unpaid after two months of its due date, the Secretary will send to the member a written reminder of his arrears, and after three months of its due date the member shall automatically cease to be a member of the Club, unless by that date the full amount of the arrears has been paid.
    (5) In special cases the Committee shall have the power to remit the whole or any part of a member's subscription.
    (6) Fees and subscriptions payable by Temporary Members and Associate Members shall be at the discretion of the Committee.
    (7) If the members in general meeting approve that monies should be raised by a levy on the members, the obligation to pay the same or any part thereof shall be decided at the meeting. Honorary Life Members and suspended members shall be subject to this levy. Honorary Members, Temporary Members

and Associate Members shall be exempt from this levy.

16. **Resignation**  A member may resign from the Club by informing the Secretary in writing of his intention to do so. If a resignation is received after 1st March in any year, the member shall be liable to pay his subscription for the following year.

17. **Suspension and expulsion**

(1)  The Committee shall have the power to suspend for a period not exceeding 12 months or to expel any member whose conduct, whether within the club premises or elsewhere, is in opinion of the Committee injurious to the good name of the Club or renders him unfit for membership of the Club.

(2)  No member shall be suspended or expelled without first being summoned before the Committee and full opportunity given to him to advance an explanation or defence, nor unless three-quarters of the Committee then present shall vote for his suspension or expulsion. The Chair of the Committee who hears the case shall not have a casting vote on this occasion.

(3)  The Committee shall have the power to exclude the member from the clubhouse pending the hearing of the case against him.

(4)  A suspended member shall cease to have any of the privileges of membership, nor may he be nominated for or hold office whilst suspended, but he shall remain liable to pay his subscription.

(5)  A member who is suspended shall have the right to seek a review of his suspension by the Committee if he so requests in writing to the Secretary within 7 days of his suspension. The review shall take place within 14 days of the request. The composition of the review body shall, if possible, comprise different members from the Committee which imposed the suspension. If this is not possible, the review body shall be chaired by an independent, senior Ordinary Member of at least 10 years' standing, who shall be entitled to vote on the review.

(6)  A member who is expelled shall have the right of appeal to the members at a special meeting if he so requests in writing to the Secretary within 7 days of his expulsion. The meeting shall be convened by the Secretary within 21 days of the expulsion. If at least two-thirds of the members present and entitled to vote at the meeting are in favour of allowing the appeal, the member shall be automatically reinstated.

(7)  If the member so requests, he may have legal representation at any hearing before the Committee or the members in general meeting.

## 18. Disciplinary proceedings

(1) The Committee shall have the power to establish a system of disciplinary proceedings for dealing with complaints made in respect of any act or omission which in the opinion of the Committee is discreditable or prejudicial to the interests of the golfing world and which relates to or is connected with the member's conduct whilst participating in the game of golf.

(2) The hearing of the disciplinary proceedings shall be vested in the Committee who shall have power to delegate the hearing to a Disciplinary Sub-Committee if it thinks fit;

(3) The procedures which shall apply to disciplinary proceedings shall be the same as those applying to cases of suspension, including a right of review as set out in Rule 17(5) above;

(4) If the complaint is upheld, the Committee (or the Disciplinary Sub-Committee on behalf of the Committee) shall have the power to impose one or more of the following sanctions:

   (a) to warn the member about his future conduct;
   (b) to censure him;
   (c) to fine him in a sum not exceeding £500;
   (d) to disqualify him from taking part in any match play or competitions;
   (e) to deprive him for a specified period of his privileges of membership as set out in Rule 17(4) above;
   (f) to impose on him an order for costs;

## 19. Officers

(1) The officers of the Club shall consist of a President; such Vice-Presidents as are elected in accordance with sub-rule (3) below; a Chair of the Club; two Captains (Men/Ladies); two Vice-Captains (Men/Ladies); an Honorary Secretary, unless there is a paid secretary (either being referred to in these rules as "the Secretary"); and an Honorary Treasurer, unless there is a paid treasurer (either being referred to in these rules as "the Treasurer").

(2) Nominations for the office of President shall be presented by the Committee to the members at a general meeting, and upon election by the members the President shall serve for a term of three years, but shall be eligible for re-election at the end of each term.

(3) There shall from time to time be Vice-Presidents not exceeding three in number. Nominations for the office of Vice-President shall be presented by the Committee to the members at a general meeting, and upon election by the members the Vice-Presidents shall serve for a term of three years, renewable once only. After six years in office a Vice-President must stand

down for a year before being eligible to be nominated as a Vice-President for a further term.

(4) The other officers of the Club shall be elected by ballot annually by the members at the annual general meeting if the election is contested. Nominations signed by not less than two Ordinary Members of at least three year's standing or Honorary Life Members must be received by the Secretary at least 14 days before the meeting. All these officers shall be eligible for re-election.

(5) The duties of the Secretary shall include: keeping an up-to-date list of the names and addresses of the members and their contact numbers; collecting subscriptions; dealing with correspondence of the Club; organising and attending general meetings of the Club and preparing minutes thereof; and liaising between the Committee and the sub-committees; and to prepare a report on the club's activities since the last annual general meeting and to circulate the same amongst the membership.

(6) The duties of the Treasurer shall include: keeping the accounts of the Club in good order; banking without delay in the Club's name all monies received from the Secretary; preparing an audited statement of account (including a balance sheet and a profit and loss account) for the members at the annual general meeting and circulating the same amongst the membership; and being answerable to the Committee as to the state of the Club's finances during the year leading up the annual general meeting.

20. **Auditor**   There shall be an independent auditor appointed on an annual basis.

21. **Management of the Club**

(1) The management and control of all the affairs of the Club shall be vested in an elective committee (referred to in these rules as "the Committee"), including the supply or sale of intoxicating liquor on the Club's premises[3].

(2) The Committee shall have the power to make, alter or revoke such bye-laws as it considers necessary for the good governance and well-being of the Club. All such bye-laws shall be published annually and a copy displayed in the clubhouse. The Committee shall have the power to fine any

---

[3]     This is a requirement of the Licensing Act 1964 which is to be repealed by the Licensing Act 2003. 'Intoxicating liquor' under the 1964 Act will become 'alcohol' under the 2003 Act. Apart from this one change, it is recommended that this form of words still be used once the Act of 2003 has come into force. Although brief it is one of the most important rules in the rule book.

member up to a maximum of £200 for any substantial breach or repeated breaches of any bye-law.

## 22. The Committee

(1)   The Committee shall consist of the officers set out in Rule 19 except the President, plus seven Ordinary Members of the Club. If the Secretary is a paid official, the number of Ordinary Members shall be increased to eight. If both the Secretary and the Treasurer are paid officials, the number of Ordinary Members shall be increased to nine.

(2)   Those Ordinary Members forming part of the Committee shall be elected by ballot annually by the members at the annual general meeting. Nominations signed by not less than two Ordinary Members of at least three years' standing or by Honorary Life Members must be received by the Secretary at least 14 days before the annual general meeting.

(3)   All the Committee members may offer themselves for re-election, save for Vice-Presidents whose second three-year term will expire at the next annual general meeting.

(4)   The Committee shall be chaired by the elected Chair of the Club. At its first meeting after the annual general meeting the Committee shall choose a Vice-Chair from one of its own number who will undertake the duties of the Chair in his or her absence.

(5)   The Committee shall meet on a regular basis, and sufficiently often to carry out its duties efficiently. The quorum for a meeting of the Committee shall be six persons. The Chair of the Committee, whether it be the formally chosen person or an ad hoc choice, shall have an additional casting vote at any meeting. All resolutions or decisions taken by the Committee shall require a simple majority of those present at the meeting.

(6)   If for any reason a vacancy occurs during its term of office, the Committee shall have power to appoint another Ordinary Member to fill that vacancy for the remainder of the term.

## 23. Sub-committees

(1)   The Committee may from time to time appoint from the Ordinary Members such sub-committees as it shall deem necessary or expedient to assist it in managing the affairs of the Club. All sub-committees shall conduct their business in accordance with directions from the Committee and shall periodically report their proceedings to the Committee for approval or ratification.

(2)   The President and the Vice-Presidents shall be ex-officio members of all the sub-committees, save that they shall have no voting rights at any meetings of sub-committees.

(3)  Subject to sub-rule (2) above, all members of sub-committees shall automatically retire on the date on which the annual general meeting is held but shall be eligible for re-appointment by the incoming Committee immediately following the annual general meeting.

(4)  A sub-committee at its first meeting after the annual general meeting shall choose a Chair from one of its own number and shall decide on the quorum for any meeting of the sub-committee, and notify the Secretary accordingly. The Chair of a sub-committee, whether it be the formally chosen person or an ad hoc choice, shall have an additional casting vote at any meeting. All resolutions or decisions taken by a sub-committee shall require a simple majority of those present at the meeting.

(5)  If for any reason a vacancy occurs during its period of appointment, the sub-committee shall so notify the Committee, who shall have power to appoint another Ordinary Member to fill that vacancy for the remainder of the period.

(6)  A list of sub-committees their composition and function shall appear as an annexe to these rules. The Annexe shall also contain the composition and function of other groups of members which have a recognised and distinct existence within the membership of the Club.

24. **Declaration of interest**   A member must disclose to the Chair of the Committee or any sub-committee on which he sits any interest which may conflict with the proper consideration of a matter under discussion. If the disclosing member is the Chair of the Committee or of the sub-committee, he shall disclose his interest to the next most senior person. A member disclosing an interest shall not be entitled to vote on the matter under discussion and the other members at the meeting shall decide whether the disclosing member may participate in discussion thereof.

25. **Annual General Meeting**

(1)  There shall be an annual general meeting of the Club held on a date fixed by the Committee not later than 30 June in each year, provided that not more than 15 months shall elapse between each meeting.

(2)  The purposes for which the meeting is convened shall be:

 (a)  to receive a report from the Secretary in respect of the Club's activities since the previous annual general meeting;

 (b)  to receive and , if thought fit, to approve the Club's audited accounts in respect of the preceding financial year;

 (c)  to elect the President (if the office be vacant), the Vice-

Presidents (if there be any vacancy), the officers of the Club and the members of the Committee;

(d) to appoint an auditor for the ensuing year;

(e) to discuss or decide any matter of general business of the Club duly submitted to the meeting.

(3) All members shall receive 28 days' notice in writing of the meeting, together with the agenda of the meeting. No member, save with the consent of the Chair of the meeting, shall bring any matter before the meeting unless he has given notice of motion in writing to the Secretary not less than 14 days before the meeting (although points for discussion only may be received up to 48 hours before the meeting). A notice of agenda shall be posted in the clubhouse for at least 14 days prior to the meeting.

26. **Special meetings**

(1) A special general meeting shall be convened by the Secretary within 28 days of receipt by him of a direction of the Committee or of a requisition signed by not less than 30 members entitled to attend and vote at a general meeting or by one-fifth of such members (whichever is the smaller number)[4]. All members will receive not less than 14 days' notice in writing of the meeting. The notice shall specify the purpose of the meeting and no other business may be brought before the meeting.

(2) If the Secretary fails to convene the meeting within the 28 day period, the requisitionists themselves may convene a special meeting to be held not later than 56 days after the deposit of the requisition with the Secretary.

27. **Procedure at general meetings**

(1) A general meeting may proceed to business if 30 Ordinary Members are present within half an hour after the time fixed for the meeting. If no quorum is then present, the meeting if convened by requisition of the members shall be dissolved; and if convened by direction of the Committee it shall stand adjourned to the week following on the same day and at the same time. If at the adjourned meeting there is still no quorum the meeting shall be dissolved.

(2) If a general meeting is adjourned for want of time, the members present at the meeting will be notified there and then of the adjourned date, if this is practicable. If not, and the matter is adjourned for more than 14 days, all the members

---

[4]     A requirement of the Licensing Act 1964 which is to be repealed by the Licensing Act 2003. It is recommended, however, that this or a similar rule be retained under the new régime.

shall receive notice in writing of the adjourned hearing; otherwise only those who attended the original meeting will be notified of the adjourned date.

(3)  Unless otherwise stipulated in these rules, any motion to be carried shall require the votes of a simple majority of the members present and voting at the meeting.

(4)  No member who is in arrear with the payment of his subscription shall be entitled to exercise his vote at a general meeting.

(5)  The Chair of any meeting shall be entitled to a casting vote only[5].

## 28. Financial powers

(1)  The Committee shall have power to borrow money, whether on a secured or unsecured basis. No borrowing shall take place which exceeds the sum of £10,000 save with the prior consent of the members given at a general meeting.

(2)  The Committee may in its discretion establish and maintain a sinking fund or a reserve fund for such purposes as it shall think fit.

(3)  The Committee shall have power to invest the Club's funds in any prudent manner which in the reasonable opinion of the Committee will benefit the Club.

(4)  The Committee shall have power to spend the Club's funds in furtherance of the objects set out in Rule 2 above, as well as in compliance with its duties of management under Rule 21 above.

(5)  The Club shall have power to defray out of the Club's funds expenses wholly and necessarily incurred by members of the Committee or any sub-committee, or incurred by any member acting on the authority of the Committee, which relates to or is connected with carrying out their duties or responsibilities on behalf of the Club. For the avoidance of doubt, this shall include legal expenses incurred in connection with any litigation or alternative dispute resolution involving the Club.

(6)  All cheques drawn by the Club shall be signed by the Chair of the Club and the Treasurer or by such other officers as may be authorised by the Committee, provided that all cheques are signed by two officers.

---

[5]    The Licensing Act 1964, if it is applicable, lays down that all members must have equal voting rights at a general meeting of the members, hence the reason for giving the chairman a casting vote only. This Act is being repealed by the Licensing Act 2003 without carrying forward this rule into the new Act, so in future the chairman may be given a casting vote in addition to his ordinary vote if the rules so provide.

## 29. Visitors and guests

   (1)  The Committee shall have power by way of bye-law to regulate the introduction of visitors to the privileges of the golf course and the clubhouse and the payment of green fees and, in particular, to regulate the sale of intoxicating liquor to such visitors pursuant to the Licensing Act 1964[6].

   (2)  Members may personally introduce guests into the Club's premises, but must accompany such guests during their stay at the Club, and no guest so introduced shall be permitted to make any payment for intoxicating liquor directly or indirectly[7]. The Committee shall have absolute discretion to exclude any visitor or guest so introduced.

## 30. Interpretation of the rules

The reference in these rules to the masculine gender shall in all cases apply equally to the feminine gender. If any question or dispute arises as to the meaning or interpretation of these rules or of the bye-laws made thereunder, the matter must be referred to the Committee for a ruling thereon.

## 31. Amendment of the rules

   (1)  These rules may be added to, altered or revoked by the members at a special meeting or at the annual general meeting. Any amendment to be proposed at the annual general meeting must be sent out as part of the agenda referred to in Rule 25(3) above.

   (2)  To be carried, any motion to amend the rules shall require the votes of two-thirds of the members present and voting at the meeting.

   (3)  In the discussion of a motion to amend the rules, any proposed amendment to the motion may be carried by a simple majority of the members present and voting at the meeting.

## 32. Arbitration

Any dispute between the Club and its members or between the members themselves which arises out of or is in connection with these rules (or the bye-laws) or which concerns the affairs of the Club shall be referred to the arbitration of a sole arbitrator to be appointed in accordance with section 16(3) of the Arbitration Act 1996, the seat of such arbitration being hereby designated as London, England. In the event of failure of the

---

[6]    When the Licensing 2003 comes fully into force the words, 'to regulate the sale of intoxicating liquor to such visitors pursuant to the Licensing Act 1964' should be replaced by the words, 'to regulate the sale of alcohol to associate members and their guests pursuant to the Licensing Act 2003'.

[7]    This involves s. 49 of the Act of 1964. This is not repeated in the Act of 2003, but it is important for the committee to retain its discretion as to whom should be admitted as guests of the club.

parties to make the appointment pursuant to section 16(3), the appointment shall be made by the President of the Chartered Institute of Arbitrators. The arbitrator shall decide the dispute according to the laws of England and Wales.

33. **Dissolution of the Club**
    (1) Any motion to dissolve the Club must be the subject matter of a special meeting.
    (2) To be carried, any motion to dissolve the Club shall require the votes of three-quarters of the members present at the meeting and entitled to vote thereat.
    (3) In the event that the members pass a resolution to dissolve the Club, any property or assets belonging to the Club shall not be distributed to the members if there is a surplus of assets over liabilities, but will be given or transferred to [name of organisation] or to such other club or entity having similar objects to the Club, as the members may decide upon.

Date of Rules:  [say 15 March 1999]

Date of [first] amendment of Rules:  [say 30 June 2003]

# BYE-LAWS

*Issued pursuant to Rule 21(2) of the Rules of
the South Bassetshire Golf club*

[**Note**: these bye-laws are not intended to be comprehensive but instead to show the reader the sort of subject matter which may be put into bye-laws rather than in the main club rules because they contain matters of detail as opposed to matters of principle. Many other topics such as the use of mobile phones in the clubhouse; the playing of certain permitted card games; the regulation of gaming machines; the prohibition or restriction on smoking in the clubhouse; the regulation of golf playing times for men and women; etc. are all suitable material for bye-laws. Bye-laws have the advantage that they are more easily altered than the club rules because this alteration will be done by the Committee rather than by the members in general meeting]

1. **Restricted membership**
    A. There shall be the following categories of restricted membership:
       (1) *Time-restricted member*  Play prohibited after 4 pm on Monday to Friday inclusive and on Bank Holidays, and before 4pm on Saturday and Sunday.
       (2) *Five-day member*  Play restricted to Monday to Friday inclusive. No play allowed at the weekend.

(3) *Country member*   Must be a full member of another private golf club and live outside a radius of 50 miles from the clubhouse. [No restriction on the time of play.]

(4) *Student member*   Full-time student aged between 18 and 22 years (both ages inclusive). [Play restricted to ...]

(5) *Junior member*   One who is aged between 15 and 17 years (both ages inclusive). [Play restricted to ...]

(6) *Social member*   Must be aged 18 years or over. Entitled to use all the facilities of the clubhouse and attend social functions. Also entitled [occasionally] to play golf on payment of the full green fee. [Play restricted to ...]

B.   *Privileges of Restricted Members*

(1)   All Restricted Members are entitled to use the facilities of the clubhouse, save that Junior Members under 18 are not allowed to purchase any alcoholic drink and are not allowed in the main bar except when accompanied by an adult. Unaccompanied Junior Members may use the Course Bar up to 8.30 pm to buy soft drinks.

(2)   Restricted Members may play golf as indicated in Bye-law 1A.

(3)   No Restricted Member shall have any voting rights save as indicated in Bye-law 1C. All Restricted Members may attend general meetings of the members, save Junior Members, and Social Members who may only attend at the invitation of the Committee.

C.   *Voting at general meetings*

Time-restricted members, five-day members, country members and student members over the age of 21 years shall be entitled to vote at general meetings[8] unless the Chair of the meeting considers that any particular motion may be prejudicial to the Ordinary Members, in which case he may rule that Ordinary Members only shall be entitled to vote thereon. The presence of non-voting members at a meeting shall not count towards any necessary quorum.

2. **Use of the clubhouse**

The following bye-laws shall apply:

(1)   The locker rooms shall be opened at 8 am and closed when the Club closes.

(2)   The remainder of the clubhouse shall be opened daily at 9 am and closed one hour after the expiration of the time fixed for the supply or sale of intoxicating liquor, provided that this time is not later than midnight, except on such

---

[8]   See para 2(4) of Sch. 7 to the Licensing Act 1964

special occasions as the Committee may decide from time
to time.

(3) The times for the supply or sale and consumption of
intoxicating liquor shall be:

Monday to Saturday: 11 am to 11 pm

Sunday: noon to 3 pm and from 7 pm to 10.30 pm.

Christmas Day, Boxing Day and New Year's Day: as
decided by the Committee.

## 3. Dress code

The following will apply:

(1) *Lounge and dining room*   Members should dress tidily at
all times. Casual dress is allowed from Monday to Friday
and at the weekend until 7 pm. At other times men must
wear appropriate jackets with collared shirt and tie.
Tailored shorts may be worn by ladies only whilst
registering for open competitions. The wearing of golf shoes
is prohibited at all times in the Club except in the locker
room and the adjacent corridor leading to the
Professional's Shop.

(2) *Course and Course Bar*   Casual dress is allowed at all times
but members are requested to dress tidily. The wearing of
T-shirts, jeans, training shoes and clothes with prominent
logos is prohibited. All shirts must have a visible collar or
roll neck. Ladies are permitted to wear tailored shorts. Men
are only allowed to wear tailored shorts whilst purchasing
drinks, after which they must vacate the room.

## 4. Use of trolleys

During the winter months (the beginning of October to the
end of March) members aged 60 or over may use wide-wheel
pull trolleys (non-motorised) on the course. Members with a
letter of dispensation from the Secretary may use such a
trolley at all times, unless a Captain is of the opinion that
damage may be caused by the use of the trolley

## 5. Bye-laws relating to competitions

(These bye-laws have been prepared by the Competitions
Committee and approved by the Committee. They may be
printed as a separate document as well as appearing in the
main body of the Club's bye-laws).

# BYE-LAWS OF THE COMPETITION COMMITTEE OF THE SOUTH BASSETSHIRE GOLF CLUB

1. **Categories of handicaps**
   Division 1: scratch to 12 inclusive
   Division 2: 13 to 18 inclusive
   Division 3: 19 to 28 inclusive
   Junior division: all junior [male] players up to but excluding 18 years of age.

2. **General rules**
   (a) All competitions must start from the 1st tee in accordance with starting board times unless otherwise authorised by the Competitions Committee.
   (b) At all times the starting board times must be adhered to unless notified to the contrary by the Competitions committee.
   (c) Entrance fees must be paid before playing in any competition.
   (d) In fourball alliance competitions the gross score being recorded must be entered in the correct 'players column' on the score card.
   (e) All cards must be signed by the player and marker.
   (f) Entrance fees, prizes, vouchers and sweeps for all competitions shall be decided by the Competitions Committee.
   (g) Handicap limits for all competitions, both club and open, shall be decided by the Competitions Committee.

3. **Junior playing members**
   (a) Junior members may only compete in Junior Division Medal Competition, Junior Division Bogey and Stableford Competitions, Junior Division Running Competitions and any other competition as may be decided by the Competitions Committee.
   (b) Junior Medal, Bogey, Stableford and Running Competitions shall take place on the same days as the Senior Competitions, or as agreed with the Competition Committee.
   (c) Junior members may play only from the yellow tees unless otherwise authorised by the Competitions Committee.

Etc.

Date of issue of the Bye-laws: [say 30 April 2003]

# ANNEXE

*Published pursuant to Rule 23(6) of the Rules of
the South Bassetshire Golf Club*

[**Note**: This annexe will contain the constitution and functions of various sub-committees and other distinct entities within the golf club. It is common for sub-committees to be called committees rather than sub-committees. Below is set out a list of likely sub-committees or other entities in a golf club, but the only sub-committee set out in detail here is that relating to the Competitions Committee:
The Finance Committee
The House Committee
The Greens Committee
The Competitions Committee
The Forward Planning Committee
The Rules Committee
The Disciplinary Sub-Committee
The Captains' Society [in effect, a club within a club]
The Senior Members' Section].

## THE COMPETITIONS COMMITTEE

*Constitution*
1. The committee shall consist of the following persons:
    (1) the Chair of the committee
    (2) the Competitions Secretary
    (3) the Match Secretary
    (4) the Treasurer
    (5) the Junior Section Organiser
    (6) the Scratch League Organiser
    (7) the Mid-Counties League Organiser.
2. The Chair of this committee shall be appointed by the Committee as soon as reasonably practicable after the annual general meeting.
3. The appointments to the committee (save for the Treasurer) will be made by the Chair of the committee after discussion with the Captains.
4. A quorum for committee meetings shall be three members.
5. The committee shall have power to co-opt members of the Club to assist it in its business, but such co-opted members shall have no voting rights at committee meetings.

*Functions*
6. To co-ordinate the fixture list of competitions [for adults] of the Club and to  present such list to the Secretary. To this end, after

the annual general meeting, a meeting will be held between the Men's Captain, the Ladies Captain and the Chair of the Competitions Committee to prepare a proposed calendar of events for the following year. This will then be checked by them, together with the members of the Competitions Committee, at a separate meeting arranged by the incoming Captains. The final draft will then be submitted to the [managing] Committee for approval.

7. To organise competitions and matches for junior members.
8. To determine the playing handicaps of playing members; to revise, as and when necessary, such handicaps within the rules of the English Golf Union; and to keep a proper record of such revisions.
9. To produce and to revise, as and when necessary, the stroke index and card of the course for all sections of the Club.
10. To monitor and maintain an adequate stock of score cards for use by all sections of the Club.
11. To arrange with the Club Professional the control of starting times for the Club's Open Competition and other major competitions.
12. To ensure that the conduct of all playing members and visitors on the course satisfies the requirements of the [managing] Committee.
13. To liaise with the Secretary for the allocation of dates for all golfing societies and inter-club fixtures.

Date of Annexe: [say 30 July 2004]

# Appendix 15

## NOTICE AND AGENDA FOR AGM

### BASSETSHIRE HISTORICAL SOCIETY

Notice is hereby given that the seventy-fifth Annual General Meeting of the Society will be held at the Constitutional Club, Basset, BA1 3XA on Thursday 27 May 2004 at 7.30pm.

(Signed)
Daniel Whiddon
Honorary Secretary

27 April 2004

### AGENDA

1. To receive apologies for absence.
2. To approve the minutes of the previous Annual General Meeting.
3. To receive a report from the Honorary Secretary on the Society's activities since the previous Annual General Meeting.
4. To receive and, if thought fit, to approve the Society's audited accounts for the preceding financial year ended 31 December 2003.
5. To elect for the forthcoming year the President, the Vice-President and the other officers of the Society and the members of the Committee, and also to appoint the Honorary Auditor.
6. To fix the subscriptions of the various categories of member.
7. To present Professor Tom Cobleigh FBA with an inscribed and illustrated Special Edition of the History of Basset in Roman Times in recognition of his exemplary work on behalf of the Society.

8. **Special Business** To consider the recommendation of the Committee that a junior section of the Society be established in accordance with the motion referred to below.

MOTION

(1) That this meeting resolves that membership of the Society be open to children between the ages of 10 and 18 years.
(2) That pursuant to the said resolution a new Rule 6A be added to the Rules of the Society as follows:

6A **Junior Membership** Membership shall be open to boys and girls over the age of 10 years and under the age of 18 years. A parent or sponsor must countersign the application form of a junior member. No junior member shall be entitled to attend general meetings of the Society but may do so at the discretion of the Committee. If he or she does so attend, the junior member may not vote thereat nor shall his or her presence count towards any requisite quorum. A junior member wishing to be elected an adult member must follow the procedure laid down in Rule 8.

Note: as item (2) of the motion will entail amendment of the rules of the Society, a two-thirds majority of those present and entitled to vote will be required, in accordance with Rule 20, if this item is to be passed at the Annual General Meeting.

9. Any other business.

Note: A member who wishes to bring any other matter of general business before the Annual General Meeting must give notice in writing to the Hon Secretary of such matter by 6 May 2004 pursuant to Rule 15.

# Appendix 16

## TABLE OF COMPARISON OF SPORTS CLUBS TAX REGIMES[1]

| No special status | Charitable status | CASC[2] status |
|---|---|---|
| **Regulation** | | |
| 1 Little financial regulation other than to meet members'requirements | Charity Commission regulation and audit | Inland Revenue regulation; generally a "lighter" touch |
| 2 No definitions to meet | Sports clubs need to meet Charity Commission's definition of promoting healthy recreation | CASCs need to meet Inland Revenue's definition of sport |
| 3 Can have restricted membership | Community participation (membership open to all members of the public) | Membership open to all members of the public |
| 4 No restrictions on sports pursued | Healthy sports including elements of strength/stamina/suppleness[3] | Sports drawn from Sports Council's lists |
| 5 No restrictions on activities | Significant social activity and trading e.g. a bar, to be kept separate from charitable activities | Social membership and trading e.g. a bar, generally permitted |
| 6 *Prima facie* no restrictions on distribution of profits and assets to members | Cannot distribute profits or assets to members | Cannot distribute profits or assets to members |

---

[1]      Based on Appendix 1 of *Community Amateur Sports Clubs – The Tax Options*, published by Deloitte & Touche Sports, 2003, and printed here with their consent.
[2]      Community Amateur Sports Clubs.
[3]      This may therefore exclude such sports as angling, ballooning, crossbow, darts, flying, gliding, motor sports, parachuting, rifle and pistol shooting, and snooker.

| No special status | Charitable status | CASC status |
|---|---|---|
| **Regulation** — *contd* | | |
| 7  No need change to club rules | Club will have to change its rules since its objects must be exclusively charitable, i.e. to promote community participation in healthy recreation/sport | Club may need to change its rules e.g. if it does not have a dissolution rule providing for its net assets to go to community sport or charitable purposes rather than to its members |
| 8  Players can be paid | Players cannot be paid unless they also coach; they can receive reimbursement of expenses | Players cannot be paid unless they also coach; they can receive reimbursement of expenses |
| **Incentives to give** | | |
| 9  No tax relief | Gift Aid on individual and company donations | Gift Aid on individual donations (no relief on company donations) |
| 10  No Payroll Giving | Payroll Giving allowed | No Payroll Giving |
| 11  No tax relief | Income and corporation tax relief for gifts of shares and properties | No income or corporation relief for  gifts of shares and property |
| 12  No tax relief | Inheritance tax relief on gifts | Inheritance tax relief on gifts |
| 13  No tax relief | Gifts of assets on 'no-gain no-loss' basis for capital gains | Gifts of assets on 'no-gain no-loss' basis for capital gains |
| **Fund raising** | | |
| 14  Relief if gift constitutes business sponsorship | Business: relief on gifts or trading stock | Business: relief on gifts or trading stock |
| 15  Reliance on existing sources of funding | Grants may be available from other charities e.g. community foundations and other bodies supporting charities | No new sources of funding envisaged |
| **Direct taxes** | | |
| 16  Income from non-members taxable | Primary purpose trading income exempt from tax | Income from non-members taxable |
| 17  Fund-raising income taxable | Other fund raising income exempt from tax either by concession or by using a 'trading subsidiary' | Fund raising income exempt from tax where turnover less than £15,000 (if more, it is all taxable without marginal relief) |
| 18  Rental income taxable | All rental income exempt from tax | First £10,000 pa of rental income exempt from tax (if more, it is all taxable without marginal relief) |

| No special status | Charitable status | CASC status |
|---|---|---|
| **Direct taxes** — *contd* | | |
| 19  Capital gains and interest taxable (subject to re-investment relief) | Capital gains and interest exempt from tax | Capital gains and interest exempt from tax |
| 20  No corporation tax on taxable profits of less than £10,000 pa | No corporation tax on taxable profits of less than £10,000 pa | No corporation tax on taxable profits of less than £10,000 pa |
| 21  Discretionary rate relief (up to 100%) | 80% mandatory rate relief; discretionary relief as to the remaining 20% | No additional business rate relief other than discretionary (up to 100%) |
| 22  Funds can be applied generally for any purpose within the rules | Corporate tax liabilities can arise if funds applied for non-qualifying purposes | Corporate tax liabilities can arise if funds applied for non-qualifying purposes |

# INDEX

References are to paragraph numbers.